Building with Light

CW01651530

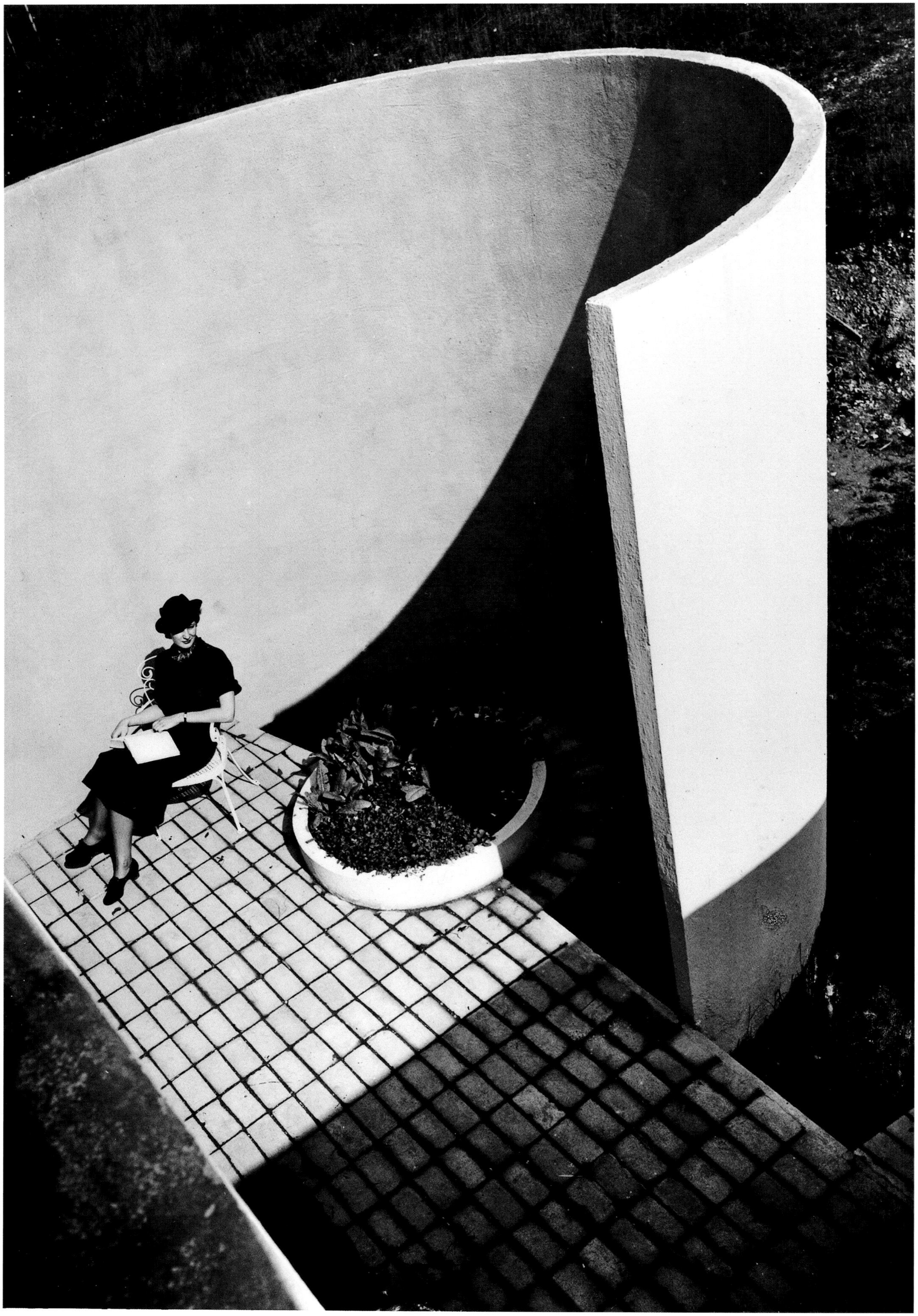

Building with Light

The International History of Architectural Photography

Robert Elwall

RIBA

MERRELL
LONDON • NEW YORK

First published by Merrell Publishers Limited

Head office
42 Southwark Street
London SE1 1UN

New York office
49 West 24th Street
New York, NY 10010

www.merrellpublishers.com

in association with
The Royal Institute of British Architects
66 Portland Place
London W1B 1AD

RIBA

This publication has been made possible by generous grants from the Marc Fitch Fund; the Scouloudi Foundation in association with the Institute of Historical Research, University of London; the Kraszna-Krausz Foundation; and the RIBA's Gordon Ricketts Memorial Fund.

Text copyright © 2004 Royal Institute of British Architects
Design and layout copyright © 2004 Merrell Publishers Limited
Photographs copyright © the copyright holders; see page 235
The right of Robert Elwall to be indentified as the author of this work has been asserted by him in accordance with the Copyright, Design and Patents Act of 1988.

All rights reserved. No part of this publication may be reproduced, stored in any retrieval system or transmitted, in any form or by any means, electronic, mechanical, photocopying, recording or otherwise, without the prior permission in writing from the publishers.

Publisher: Hugh Merrell
Editorial Director: Julian Honer
US Director: Joan Brookbank
Sales and Marketing Director: Emilie Amos
Sales and Marketing Executive: Emily Sanders
Managing Editor: Anthea Snow
Editor: Sam Wythe
Design Manager: Nicola Bailey
Production Manager: Michelle Draycott
Editorial and Production Assistant: Matt Packer

British Library Cataloguing-in-Publication Data:
Elwall, Robert
Building with light : the international history of architectural photography
1.Architectural photography – History
I.Title II.Royal Institute of British Architects
778.9'4'09

ISBN 1 85894 215 2

Produced by Merrell Publishers
Designed by SMITH
Copy-edited by Michael Bird
Indexed by Hilary Bird
Printed and bound in Italy

Jacket front: Henk Snoek (1915–1980), Cathedral of Christ the King, Liverpool, 1967. Gelatine silver print. Architects: Frederick Gibberd & Partners
Jacket back: Bisson Frères (Auguste-Rosalie Bisson [1826–1900] and Louis-Auguste Bisson [1814–1876]), Münster, Basel, 1860. Albumen print.
Page 2: Dell & Wainwright (Mark Oliver Dell [1883–1959] and H.L. Wainwright), Sun-catch, House B, Whipsnade, Bedfordshire, 1936. Gelatine silver print. Architects: Lubetkin & Tecton

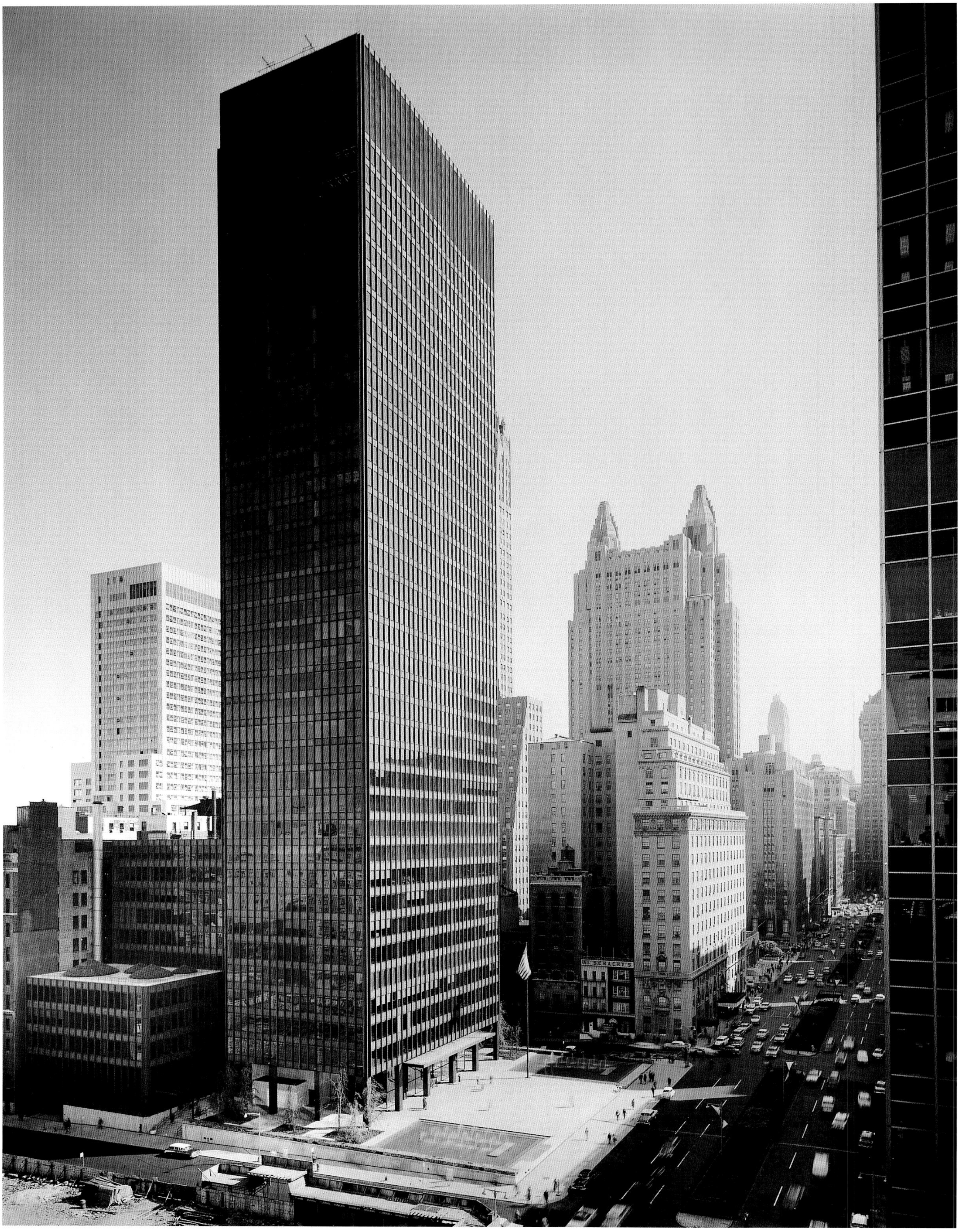
AL SCHACHT'S

Introduction

page 6

EZRA STOLLER
(born 1915)

Seagram Building, New York, 1958
Gelatine silver print
Architects: Ludwig Mies van der Rohe and Philip Johnson

Echoing Le Corbusier's famous dictum that "architecture is the masterly, correct, and magnificent play of masses brought together in light",[1] the influential architectural photographer Eric de Maré described photography as "building with light",[2] thus underlining the close and symbiotic relationship that has existed between the two disciplines ever since the invention of photography. In addition to their visual kinship, photography has exerted a profound influence on both the study and the practice of architecture. Our first, sometimes only, impression of a building is often formed by a photograph, and the skilled photographer can help us to see even the most seemingly familiar structures with a fresh eye. The persuasive images of past photographers have not only shaped the way their contemporaries viewed the architecture of their period, but also continue to influence the way we perceive it today. At Wells Cathedral in south-west England, tripod marks eat away the stone as amateurs jostle to stand where Frederick Evans stood to photograph *A Sea of Steps*; the refulgent new automobile remains parked in front of the gleamingly immaculate, eternally sunlit Modernist villa (opposite); devotees of Frank Lloyd Wright perch precariously in the waters of Bear Run, Pennsylvania, seeking to match the acrobatics of Bill Hedrich's shot of Fallingwater; and the crepuscular Californian light forever bathes Richard Neutra's (or is it Julius Shulman's?) Kaufmann House in Palm Springs. For good or ill, photographs have become the indispensable "currency of architectural exchange".[3]

Despite this undeniable influence, however, the literature devoted to architectural photography is paltry, particularly when compared to the extensive bibliography commanded by architectural drawing. The reasons for this reveal much about the current state of both architectural and photographic history and the attitudes underlying their practice. The fact that photography does not even merit a walk-on part in David Watkin's otherwise authoritative *The Rise of Architectural History* (1980) is symptomatic of a world in which the continuing obsession of curators and architectural historians with architects' original intentions (as revealed in drawings) has led to a neglect of the way in which executed buildings are most commonly encountered. Eschewing the usual evaluative skills they bring to bear on other documentary sources, architectural historians too often treat photographs as if they were the buildings themselves and not particular interpretations of them made at particular moments. For their part, photographic historians, taking their cue from the self-consciously 'artistic' photographers of the nineteenth century, continue to view architectural photography as an arcane technical subject, a murky cul-de-sac deviating from photography's true path towards the status of art.

This situation has been compounded by the way in which, despite the increasing professionalization of photographic history, few photographic writings have managed to chart the narrow strait between the Scylla of curators anxious to bolster the status of their collections and the Charybdis of dealers eager to boost the market value of their holdings. The result has been a distortion of photographic history in which, too often, the medium is held to have been advanced by the heroic exploits of a few photographic masters and, perversely for a mass medium, print rarity is prized above all else. Seen in this light, the history of architectural photography enjoys an initial golden age until about 1860, by which date its revered pioneers have been engulfed by the rising tide of thoughtless commercialization, a fall from artistic grace redeemed only at the turn of the century by the sensitivity of such photographers as Alfred Stieglitz and Frederick Evans. While some architectural photographs may now be regarded as art, the primary purpose of most was utilitarian. If, therefore, we look at the development of architectural photography less from the perspective of art appreciation and more from a viewpoint that seeks to explain how and why particular photographs were made, what audience they were intended to serve, and, crucially but often forgotten, how they reached that audience, then a different story emerges. Far from dealing with the photograph as a 'unique' work of art or with those self-consciously artistic photographers who turned only occasionally to the subject, we need to explore the oeuvre of lesser-known professional photographers whose images often made the more telling contribution to architectural discourse precisely because of their ubiquity – a ubiquity that owed much to the fact that these images were more likely to be seen in reproduction than in their original form. Our experience of a building has thus often been through a complex process of filtering involving the vision of the photographer and the design skills of the art editor. It is this process we need to analyse.

Architectural photography today stands at a critical juncture. On the one hand it is undergoing a revival of popularity with many young photographers, as well as established photographers hitherto noted for their expertise in other areas, increasingly eager to explore architectural subjects. On the other hand, although there is nothing new in such criticisms, the architectural photograph has come under increasingly intense attack for forcing "architecture into a straitjacket, the straitjacket of being photogenic, or at least comprehensible through photographs",[4] and for appearing as nothing more than a product of today's media-dominated consumer market, commissioned by architects for its promotional power, laid out by art editors for its dramatic visual impact, and selling to an unwary public a glossy dream of perfection attained that leaves the audience unprepared for 'the shock of the real'. Paradoxically, it could also be argued that, despite the constant outpouring of images, our vision of architecture and, more crucially, our expectations of it have been diminished by the desensitizing repetition of the same views and the degree of control exercised by commissioning agents striving ever more strenuously to ensure that the photographs of their buildings project the appropriate public-relations message. All these issues have been given greater urgency by the advent of digital technology and the Internet, which are beginning to reshape fundamentally the way photographs are produced, disseminated and received. A new look at the history of architectural photography is therefore timely, as H.S. Goodhart-Rendel's ironically perceptive observation made in the 1930s about the power of images as substitutes for reality has even greater relevance today: "The modern architectural drawing is interesting, the photograph is magnificent, the building is an unfortunate but necessary stage between the two."[5]

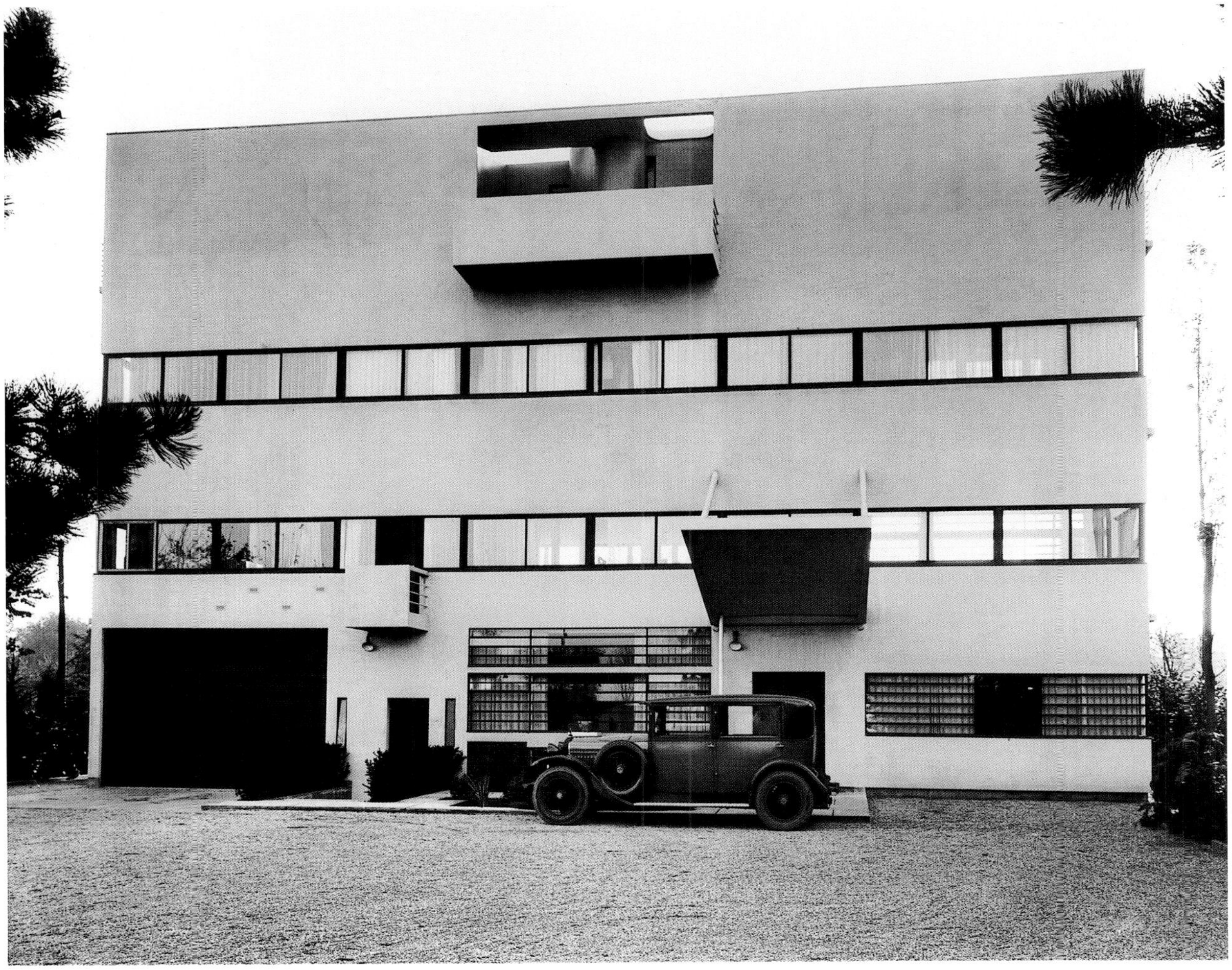

FRANCIS ROWLAND YERBURY (1885–1970)

Villa Stein-de Monzie, Garches, 1927

Gelatine silver print

Architects: Le Corbusier and Pierre Jeanneret

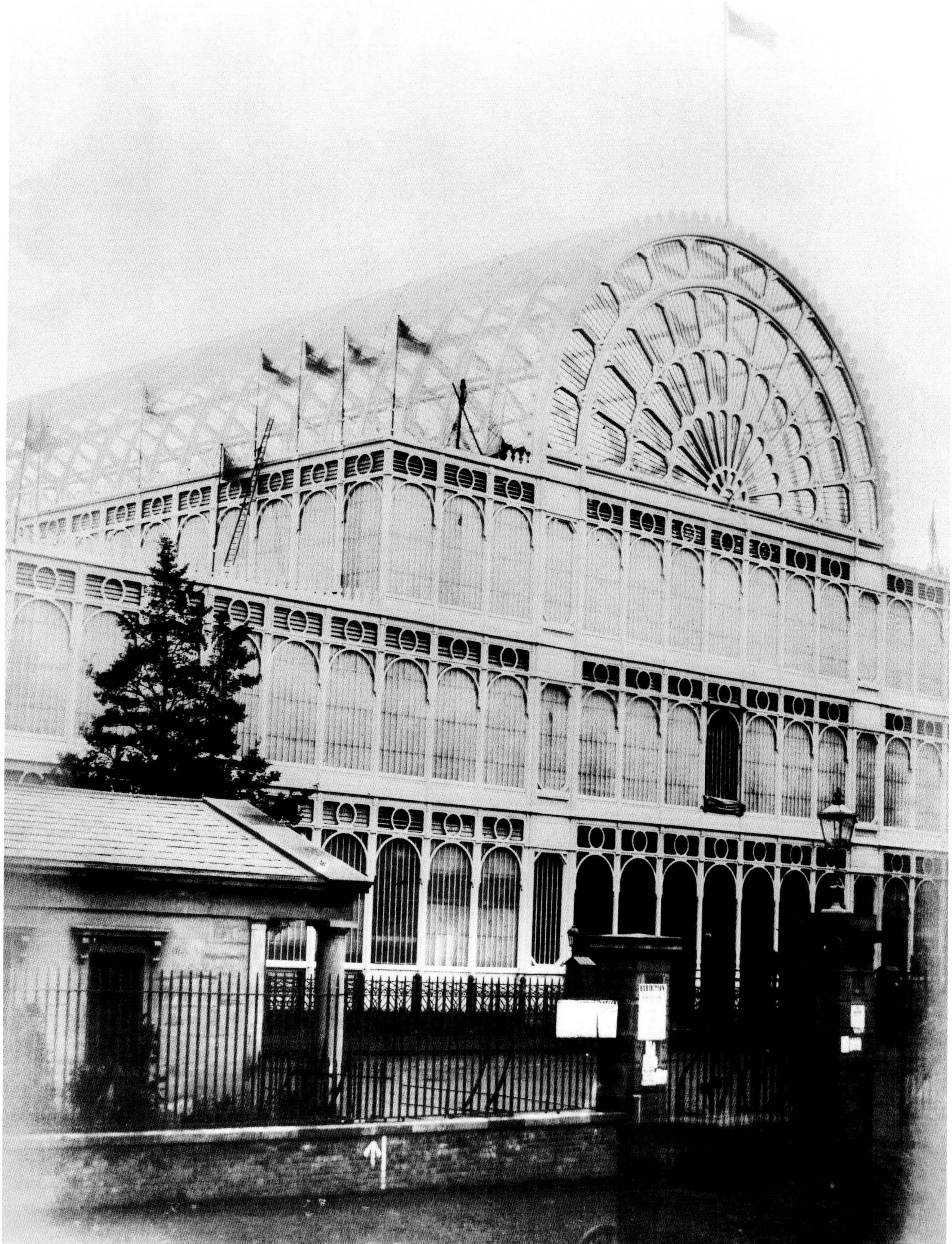

Chapter 1 The Triumph of the Apparatus 1839–1860

page 10

HUGH OWEN (1804–1881) and **CLAUDE-MARIE FERRIER** (1811–1889)

Crystal Palace, Hyde Park, London, 1851
Salt print from the *Industry of All Nations Exhibition, London, 1851, Reports by the Juries* (London: Spicer Brothers and W. Clowes & Son, 1852), vol. II
Architect: Sir Joseph Paxton

When details of the first viable photographic process, the daguerreotype, were revealed in Paris in January 1839, to be hastily followed four months later by the announcement of William Henry Fox Talbot's rival calotype process, the new medium's potential for architectural recording was quickly recognized. The British scientist Sir John Robison declared "accurate views of architecture"[1] to be one of photography's chief merits, while the *Gazette de France* boldly asserted that "Inanimate nature, and architecture, are the triumph of the apparatus."[2] For its first two decades architectural subjects were to be in the forefront of experiments with the fledgeling medium and at the heart of the debate about its aesthetics. Similarly, they had played a crucial role in its invention. Louis-Jacques-Mandé Daguerre had trained as an architect, and the depiction of architecture had been central to his attempts to find a more realistic way of presenting the subjects featured in his illusionistic spectacles, the dioramas.

For its part, photography fell on fertile architectural soil, reflecting not only the trend towards archaeological exactitude in building but also a more scientific attitude to architectural study revealed in the increased precision of drawings by such architects as Louis Duc and Léon Vaudoyer and the new emphasis on pictorial truth that underlay the work of topographical artists such as John Britton. In addition, a vastly expanded market had been created for architectural illustrations through the broadening of patronage and the evolution of architectural practice from a gentlemanly pursuit into an organized profession. In catering to this market, photography was perceived to have three main advantages: it could delineate details not easily seen with the naked eye; it was much faster than sketching; and, above all, it was 'truthful', thus freeing architects from the draughtsman's "blundering of the eye and hand".[3] For Eugène-Emmanuel Viollet-le-Duc photographs supplied "indisputable reports",[4] and the *Building News* hailed photography's "veraciousness of representation … like Caesar's wife, it cannot ever be suspected"[5] – an illusion eagerly fostered by photographers, even as they doctored their negatives to achieve the desired results. Despite this close relationship with the camera, however, a specific genre of architectural photography took time to emerge, and its development was not geographically uniform. Not only were there considerable technical difficulties to be overcome, but photography also had to compete with a highly organized and sophisticated engraving industry. Above all, however, the development of architectural photography was shaped by differing patterns of patronage and by contrasting notions of the medium's role – artistic, commercial, utilitarian – that helped to determine not only what was photographed but also how it was photographed.

Apart from such major projects as the Crystal Palace in London or the New Louvre in Paris, it is immediately striking how few contemporary buildings were photographed during the medium's initial decades. The reasons for this lay variously in the historicist nature of the period's architecture, which led architects to look to the past for inspiration; the early use of photography in building restoration; the concern that there was a fast disappearing world that should be recorded; the popularity of photographs of historic monuments as tourist souvenirs; and, above all, the continuing lure of the picturesque. If early architectural photography was temporally circumscribed, it was geographically diverse. As early as 1839 the optician Noël-Marie Paymal Lerebours dispatched daguerreotypists to Europe and the Middle East – the painter Horace Vernet reported from Alexandria that he and his companion Frédéric Goupil-Fesquet, one of Lerebours's photographers, were "daguerreotyping like lions".[6] Aquatint copies of the views obtained were reproduced in Lerebours's *Excursions daguerriennes*, published in Paris in parts from 1841 to 1844. Similarly, the daguerreotypes taken in Egypt by the Canadian Pierre-Gustave Joly de Lotbinière served as the basis of coloured aquatints in the architect Hector Horeau's *Panorama d'Egypte et Nubie* (1842). Beyond the established tourist itineraries, early photographers accompanied pioneering settlers; diplomatic missions (Linnaeus Tripe, for example, was official photographer to the British Mission to the Court of Ava, Burma, in 1855); archaeological expeditions (Corporals Spackman and McCartney of the Royal Engineers photographed Charles Newton's and Richard Popplewell Pullan's excavations at the ancient Greek sites of Halicarnassus, Cnidus and Branchidae, in what is now western Turkey, between 1856 and 1861); and military surveys. By 1861, thanks to the efforts of these photographers, it could be justly claimed that the Architectural Photographic Association had offered architects "a choice of photographs which may be useful to those practising in almost every style under the sun".[7]

If the past supplied the subject-matter, early photographers were equally reliant on traditional methods of architectural representation, particularly the elevation and the perspective drawing. The latter had been introduced in the late eighteenth century as a means of rendering buildings more pictorially intelligible to a wider audience, a role that photographers were keen to usurp. This dependence on an existing visual syntax is hardly surprising, since many photographers emerged from backgrounds in painting or the graphic arts – Leopoldo Alinari was an engraver; Edouard Baldus a painter; and Charles Marville a painter, engraver and lithographer, for example – and photographs were routinely discussed as if they were paintings or engravings. Talbot himself regarded the calotype, which contemporaries compared to the mezzotint, merely as an improved means of, or "royal road to", drawing.[8] In France photographs were often referred to as *dessins photographiques*; and even the daguerreotype, which could not be easily assimilated into any existing artistic category, was dubbed 'the silver canvas'. Nor was mimetic photography necessarily considered superior to the established diagrammatic modes of architectural illustration – plan, section, elevation – possessing as it did major disadvantages. The low sensitivity of early emulsions, which resulted in long exposure times, not only banished people from the frame altogether or rendered them ghostly apparitions, but it also meant that few interior views were attempted. Early emulsions were also oversensitive to blue, making skies appear lifeless patches of dull white; and, at a time when polychromy was of increasing importance in architecture, the medium was colourless. Above all, however, photographs could not be reproduced directly on the printed page, thus significantly undermining their influence on architectural discourse. William Burges's advice to his fellow architects in 1861 to "Measure much, sketch little, and, above all, keep your fingers out of chemicals" was not without justification.[9]

The daguerreotype was a direct positive image formed on a silver-coated copper plate that was marked by its ability to render fine detail. Although used mainly for portraiture, it enjoyed some architectural successes, chiefly in France, where in 1839 one eyewitness reported that there was no square in Paris without "three-legged dark-boxes planted in front of churches and palaces",[10] and in America. While

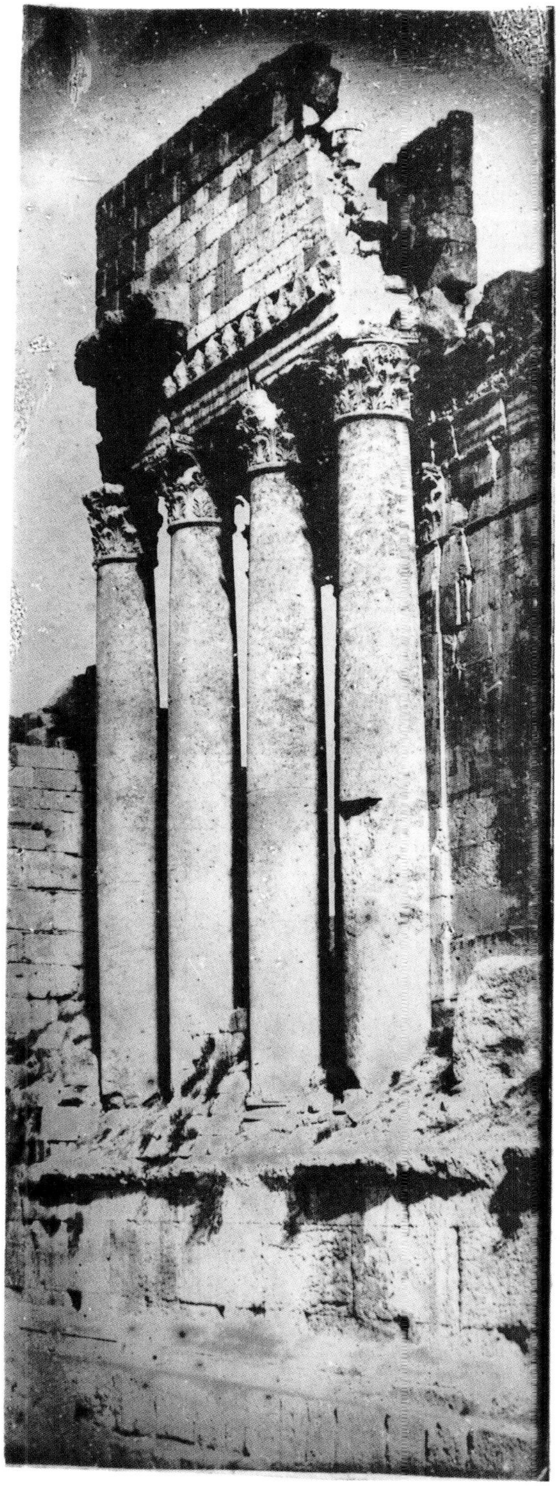

JOSEPH-PHILIBERT GIRAULT DE PRANGEY
(1804–1893)

Temple of Jupiter, Baalbec, c. 1842–45
Daguerreotype

Friedrich von Martens produced some astonishing panoramas of Paris (see page 23), many of the most impressive French daguerreotypes were made on foreign soil, including those by Joseph-Philibert Girault de Prangey (see pages 13, 24), an authority on Islamic architecture. At the Great Exhibition in London (1851) it was American daguerreotypes, however, that earned the plaudits of the jury on account of their "beauty of execution, the broad and well-toned masses of light and shade, and the total absence of glare".[11] In America early photographers captured a newly emergent nation with a refreshing directness, turning their cameras not only on examples of civic grandeur, but also on humble buildings, such as grist mills and log cabins, that would have been deemed unworthy of regard by their European counterparts (see page 25). Again in contrast to European practice, American photographers had perforce to concentrate on the new buildings that were transforming the urban landscape. While the daguerreotype flourished in America, it made little impact in England, where it was hamstrung by patents. A notable exception was its employment from 1845 to 1852 by John Ruskin to capture the microscopic details of Venetian architecture (see page 27).

Despite Daguerre's contention that one of its chief applications would be to document every man's castle and country estate, the daguerreotype had major drawbacks for architectural use. The equipment was bulky and difficult to use in the field, and it produced not only a mirror image but also one too small to permit ready interpretation of a building's minute details in context, for which purpose measured drawings continued to afford a more informative alternative. The daguerreotype was also attacked by writers and artists, such as Gustave Flaubert and Eugène Delacroix, for its promiscuity, which seemed to give equal weight to everything on the plate no matter how trivial. Indeed, architectural engravings copied from daguerreotypes can often be identified by the presence of scaffolding and other signs of building activity that the engraver, seeking a more artistic impression, would usually have excluded. For Prosper Merimée, Director of France's Commission des Monuments Historiques, this 'warts and all' effect vitiated the daguerreotype's architectural usefulness: "Yesterday I was shown views of Damascus and Saint-Jean d'Acre that were so ugly they looked just like the suburbs." He added in further condemnation, "Until a means is found of substituting paper for metal plaques, there will always be a cold tinge I don't like the looks of."[12] Despite these disadvantages, the daguerreotype played an important part in the development of architectural photography, providing a training ground for several of its most successful later exponents, such as Charles Nègre and Bisson Frères, and helping to acquaint architects with the new medium. In France, Félix Duban, Viollet-le-Duc and Jean-Baptiste Lassus all used daguerreotypes as aids in their restoration projects (see page 26); in Britain, Charles Barry Jr experimented with the medium; and Frederick Catherwood daguerreotyped Mayan remains in Central America, some of the images being engraved and published in John Stephens's *Incidents of Travel in Yucatan* (1843).

Whereas the daguerreotype was constrained by the fact that it was a single, non-reproducible image, Talbot's process was the first by which multiple images (salt prints) could be pulled from a single negative (calotype). Its coarse paper fibres sacrificed the daguerreotype's rendition of fine detail for broader, softer-toned effects that, in architectural terms, emphasized mass at the expense of line. These attributes rendered the calotype and its various improvements the chosen medium of the army of amateur photographers whose romantic vision dominated British architectural photography for its first two decades. Underlying this vision was an unquenchable belief that the true aim of photography was to imitate paintings and engravings – a belief that not only led them to prefer paper negatives and prints to glass and albumen equivalents, but also dictated that their subject-matter be chosen strictly in accordance with picturesque conventions as articulated by such theorists as William Gilpin: "the elegant relics of ancient architecture, the ruined tower, the Gothic arch, the remains of castles and abbeys".[13] As the influential photographer and critic Thomas Sutton argued, "It must be admitted on all hands that the true poetry of photography lies not in portraits ... but in views, by which, I mean, of course, not garden-gates, stiff houses, or spick and span modern buildings, but such grand scenes or artistic sites as a painter would select."[14] The photography of contemporary buildings undermined photography's claim to be art and was therefore to be avoided (see page 30, top). For these amateurs the concern was less to analyse architectural forms than to use buildings as starting-points

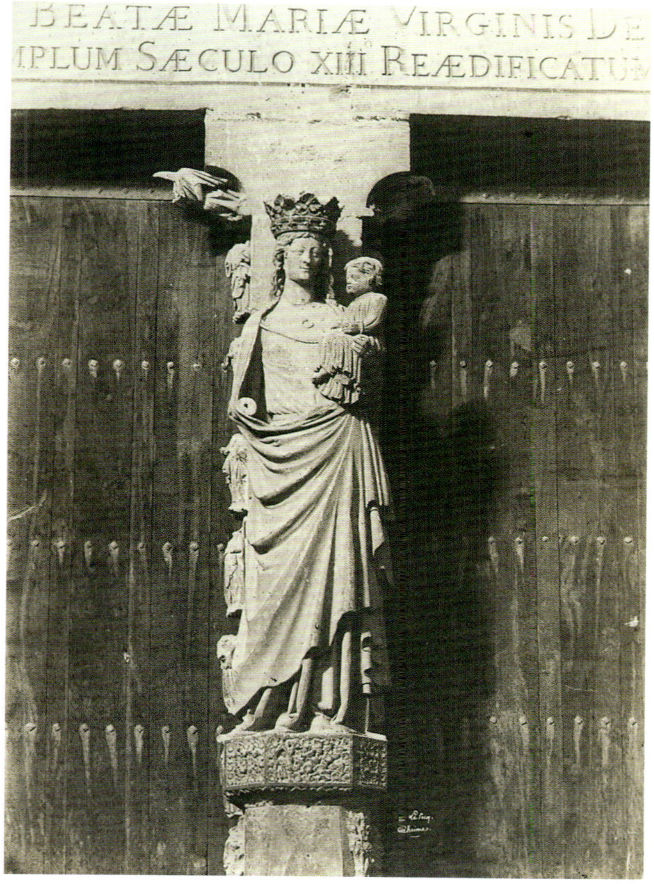

JEAN-LOUIS-HENRI LE SECQ DES TOURNELLES
(1818–1882)

Virgin and Child, Central Portal, West Front, Rheims Cathedral, *c.* 1850
Salt print

for musings on the ravages of time or the inevitability of transience – themes that photographers such as Eugène Atget would revisit at the turn of the century. As photography demanded leisure and money, many such amateurs came from the ranks of the aristocracy, and this accounts for the preponderance of country house views as the camera and photo album supplanted the paintbox and sketchbook. Whereas in France and America early architectural photography was largely an urban phenomenon, in Britain, where patent restrictions hindered professionalization, it was a product of the landed estates.[15]

Apart from the views of New York buildings made by the expatriate Frenchman Victor Prevost, paper photography made little headway in America. In France, however, it enjoyed a brief but brilliant flowering ushered in by the publication of amendments to the calotype by Louis-Désiré Blanquart-Evrard in 1847 and further improvements made by Gustave Le Gray in 1850. Le Gray, who, like so many other photographers of the period including Nègre, Prevost and Roger Fenton, had trained in the studio of the artist Paul Delaroche, waxed his negatives, thereby shortening exposure times and rendering them better able to retain detail. Unlike their calotype and collodion equivalents, these negatives could be used dry, thus allowing them to be sensitized in advance of any photographic expedition and so lessening the amount of equipment the photographer needed to carry. Le Gray's process was exploited to magisterial effect by another former pupil of Delaroche, Henri Le Secq, in his documentation of Rheims Cathedral (*c.* 1850; right).

The refinement of paper photography into a subtle means of architectural exploration was undoubtedly one of the factors that led the Commission des Monuments Historiques to establish its pioneering Mission Héliographique in 1851. As the first instance of the state patronage of photography, the Mission gave an important boost to the youthful medium in general and to architectural photography in particular. In addition, it helped to bring architects and photographers closer together and to stimulate debate about the best means of photographing buildings. The Mission's aim was to make a photographic inventory of France's architectural heritage as a prelude to the historically accurate repair of any endangered monuments – an idea first proposed by Baron Isidore Taylor in 1839 but rejected, partly because of Merimée's hostility to the daguerreotype. Taylor himself, with Charles Nodier, had been instrumental in establishing the *Voyages pittoresques et romantiques dans l'ancienne France* (1820–78), an immensely ambitious undertaking to document France's ancient monuments by the then new medium of lithography, which included among its artists Daguerre and Viollet-le-Duc and which clearly served as the model for the Mission. Five photographers were awarded 'missions', each being assigned to a specific region. Edouard Baldus was sent mainly to Burgundy and Provence; Hippolyte Bayard to Normandy; and Le Secq to Champagne, Alsace and Lorraine. These initial three were followed by Le Gray and Mestral, who seemed to have combined their missions and worked together in an area that included Orléans, Poitou, the Charente and the Auvergne.

A subcommittee of the Commission, including Merimée and the architect Léon Vaudoyer, drew up a list of the

DELAMOTTE & CUNDALL
(Philip Henry Delamotte [1820–1899] and Joseph Cundall [1818–1895])

Fountains Abbey, Yorkshire
Albumen print from *A Photographic Tour Among the Abbeys of Yorkshire*, London (Bell & Daldy) 1856

monuments to be photographed and the kind of views required, but the instructions regarding the latter were cursory and in practice allowed the photographers a wide degree of latitude. With the exception of Bayard, who used glass, all made paper negatives. By 1852 over three hundred negatives and some prints had been deposited with the Commission, where, surprisingly, they were to languish largely unused and unpublished. One possible reason for this is that the Mission proved not to be the exercise in objective recording that the Commission had expected but instead revealed significant differences in style and emphasis between photographers. As Le Gray maintained, "by varying the focus and exposure times, the artist can emphasize or sacrifice any part he wants, and depending on how he feels, go from extremes of powerful shadow and light to effects of softness and suavity in the same site and subject".[16] This approach, eloquently realized by Le Gray himself in his painterly images of the fortress at Carcassonne (see page 31), echoed the 'theory of sacrifices' prevalent among contemporary artists by which selection was held to lie at the heart of artistic endeavour. Le Secq's work was characterized by a fascination with chiaroscuro, shown in the way he controlled the evanescent effects of light and shadow to illumine the richly complex forms of Gothic sculptural decoration (see page 32). His photographs have an almost hallucinatory quality. If Le Secq's photography was one of halting suggestion, Baldus's was one of clinical statement, in which atmosphere was less important than the conveyance of information (see page 33). In their very different ways, both photographers anticipated the strategy of Modernist photographers – Le Secq in his concentration on details that let the telling part speak for the whole, and Baldus in the way he isolated the building from its surrounding landscape.

The Mission clearly demonstrated that, even with given subjects such as buildings, photography was not a mechanical act but one in which the photographer could exercise interpretative choices. This was a point underlined by Nègre when recalling the photographs he had taken in the Midi (southern France) in 1852:

> In the reproduction of these monuments of the middle ages and ancient times that I am offering to the public, I have attempted to join the picturesque aspect to the serious study of details so sought after by artists, architects, sculptors and painters. ... Thus, I have produced a general view of each monument for the architect. In placing the horizon line at the mid-point of the building's height and the point of view at the centre, I have tried to avoid perspective distortions and have attempted to give to the drawings the aspect and the precision of a geometric elevation ... . Wherever I could dispense with architectural precision I have indulged in the picturesque; in which case I have sacrificed a few details, when necessary, in favour of an imposing effect that would give to a monument its real character and would also preserve the poetic charm that surrounded it.[17]

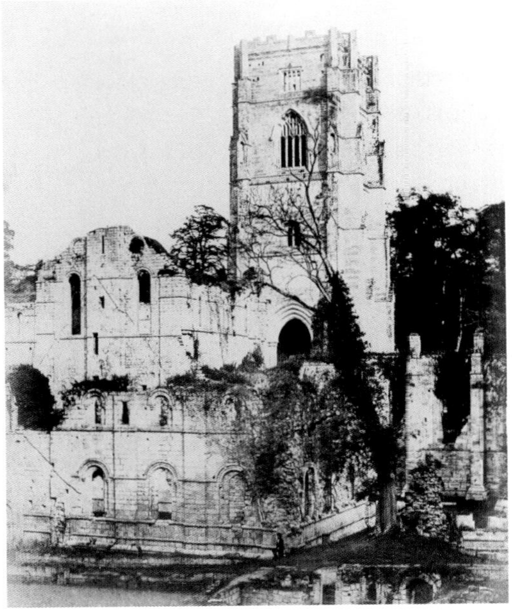

Nègre's distinction between architectural accuracy and picturesque views echoed similar sentiments expressed a year earlier by the English artist and amateur photographer Sir William Newton, and could serve as a description of the polarity that became increasingly evident between British and French architectural photographers in the 1850s.

As in France, in Britain the 1850s was a formative decade when photography, in the words of the *Building News*, "advanced from recreation to trade"[18] and began to be professionally organized. A significant boost was given to the medium by the Great Exhibition of 1851, both through its display of over seven hundred photographs from six countries and through the decision to illustrate the accompanying *Reports by the Juries* (1852) with pasted-in photographs (see page 10). In the same year Frederick Scott Archer introduced his wet collodion on glass process, which combined the acuity of the daguerreotype with the calotype's facility for making multiple prints. Even though the plates had to be sensitized, exposed and developed before the collodion dried, forcing the itinerant photographer to take an entire darkroom with him on his travels, the collodion negative together with the albumen print soon became the standard process for architectural photography (see page 38, bottom).[19]

This development was abhorred by many amateurs as signalling a shift away from photography as art towards photography as information – a split that continued to resonate throughout the history of architectural photography with important consequences. It did not, however, kill off the vogue for the picturesque, which remained strong in the work of such newly emergent professionals as Roger Fenton and Francis Bedford, who, though not concentrating on the subject to the extent that Baldus did, were the leading British photographers of architecture during the 1850s. Bedford was reckoned by the architect T.L. Donaldson to be "particularly successful in his combinations of building and landscape scenery" (see page 34).[20] Not surprisingly, the treatment of their conservative subject-matter was determined by pre-photographic modes of representation, in particular the topographical watercolour and the perspective drawing, in which the building was characteristically depicted in its landscape setting. Even P.H. Delamotte, whose celebrated views of the Crystal Palace at Sydenham (1855; see page 35) were among the most innovative architectural images of the period, worked predominantly within the picturesque tradition. His *A Photographic Tour Among the Abbeys of Yorkshire* (1856; opposite), jointly published with Joseph Cundall, used the sharp detail of collodion to unashamedly romantic ends. Significantly, both Bedford and Delamotte had been schooled in the graphic media of lithography and engraving.

In France a very different approach was adopted by Baldus, especially in his documentation of the New Louvre, and by Bisson Frères (right). Their work became increasingly analytical, demonstrating a mature understanding of how architects studied and interpreted buildings. Baldus received his official commission to photograph the New Louvre, the centrepiece of Napoleon III's campaign to transform Paris, at the instigation of its architect, Hector Lefuel, in 1855. The sheer scale of the commission was unprecedented, and Baldus made more than five thousand views, charting not only the progress of the construction (see page 34) and the completed works but also their copious amount of statuary and ornament. It was his images of the richly decorated pavilions, however, that revealed Baldus to be the supreme architectural photographer of the period (see page 36). The large glass plates he employed resulted in pin-sharp clarity of detail and, together with his tightly framed compositions focusing on the building to the exclusion of all else, imparted a commanding presence to the photographs that perfectly complemented and celebrated the monumentality of the Second Empire style. Many of these views were photographed head-on, being deliberately composed to simulate elevational drawings and at the same time to suggest that they were anonymous, dispassionate records. The same compositional strategy was frequently used by Bisson Frères, whose work is often overlooked today but

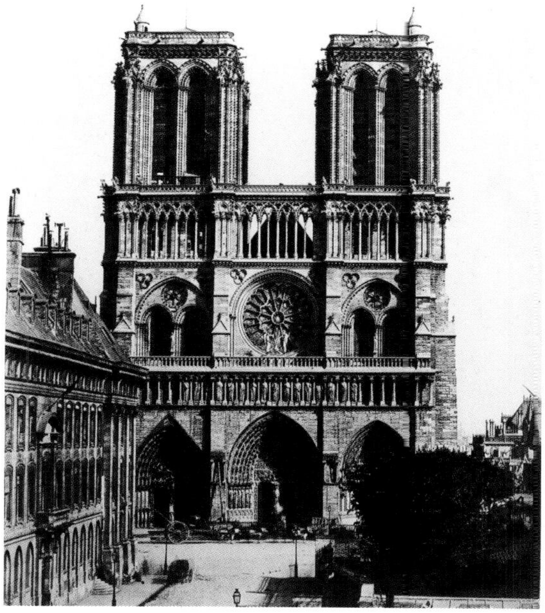

BISSON FRÈRES
(Auguste-Rosalie Bisson [1826–1900] and Louis-Auguste Bisson [1814–1876])
Notre-Dame, Paris, late 1850s
Albumen print

who at the time enjoyed a critical reputation second to none, particularly for their large-scale portrayals – up to 100 x 80 cm (40 x 32 in.) – of Gothic details (see page 37). The adjectives most frequently applied to their images by contemporary critics – clear, sharp, rigorous – emphasized that, while they had little of the mystery or emotive power of similar works by Le Secq and Bedford, they were in tune with the prevailing style of French architectural drawing that was based on orthogonal modes of representation – plan, section and elevation – rather than on the more picturesque perspective. Indeed, the hard linear quality of the steel engravings that dominated the *Revue générale de l'architecture* is not dissimilar to that displayed in the Bissons' photographs. Significantly, the elder brother, Louis-Auguste, had trained as an architect.

In Britain the Bissons' photographs played an important role in undermining the dominance of the picturesque through their display by the Architectural Photographic Association. Founded in 1857 by a group of architects headed by Robert Hesketh and including Sir Charles Barry and Anthony Salvin, the Association aimed to supply its members with "photographs of architectural works of various countries, by means of a moderate subscription".[21] Its creation was prompted by both a recognition of the importance of photography in architecture and a realization that British architects had yet to exploit the medium successfully. Although its existence was short-lived, the four exhibitions the Association held between 1858 and 1861 were among the most remarkable of the period, attracting contributions from many of the most prominent photographers of the day, including Robertson and Beato, Charles Clifford, and Robert MacPherson (see page 37), and acting as a forum for debate about the nature of architectural photography. The contributions of the home photographers, Bedford and Fenton pre-eminent among them, came under sustained attack from critics and architects such as G.E. Street for their trite subject-matter and method of representing it. As the *Photographic News* maintained:

> In most of their productions, the English photographers appear to have aimed chiefly at the picturesque. To render architectural photographs valuable as studies to the architect, the picturesque must frequently give way to the exhibition of form and detail. It is necessary for the photographer to know what the architect requires in representation of edifices. It is but too evident that the majority of the photographers whose works are exhibited are entirely ignorant of what the architect requires.[22]

In stark contrast, the photographs submitted by Bisson Frères, such as the principal doorway of Rheims Cathedral and the staircase at the château of Blois, were praised for their usefulness to the architect on account of their large scale (their prints were twice as large as Bedford's), their crisp precision, and their portrayal of details often ignored by British photographers. The *Building News* justly concluded:

> We have wrought well in landscape and in stereoscopic scenes; but architectural photography has not here met with that special attention it has on the continent. … It is natural that landscape should here attract attention, because it is a great school with us, and it is natural that the Parisian or Italian photographer should first resort to the great monuments of art which decorate his cities.[23]

In showcasing such foreign examples, the Association was instrumental in creating a new climate in which British architectural photography would flourish in the ensuing decades.

The superiority of French architectural photography during this initial period can be explained, in part, by the positivist philosophy that encouraged the use of photography as a means of disseminating information and by the early forging of close links between architects and photographers, but the crucial factor was state patronage. The Mission Héliographique and Baldus's recording of the New Louvre were but two high-profile instances of a widespread pattern of governmental commissioning of photography, during the 1850s and beyond, which largely insulated photographers from the fickle demands of the commercial market. Both Maxime du Camp's *Egypte, Nubie, Palestine et Syrie* (1852; see page 39) and Baldus's *Villes de France photographiées* (1852–53) were subsidized by the state's agreement to purchase copies of the images, and Nègre's photographs of the Imperial Asylum at Vincennes (1859; opposite) were also made at official behest. By 1855 Bisson Frères had already received a stream of commissions from different government

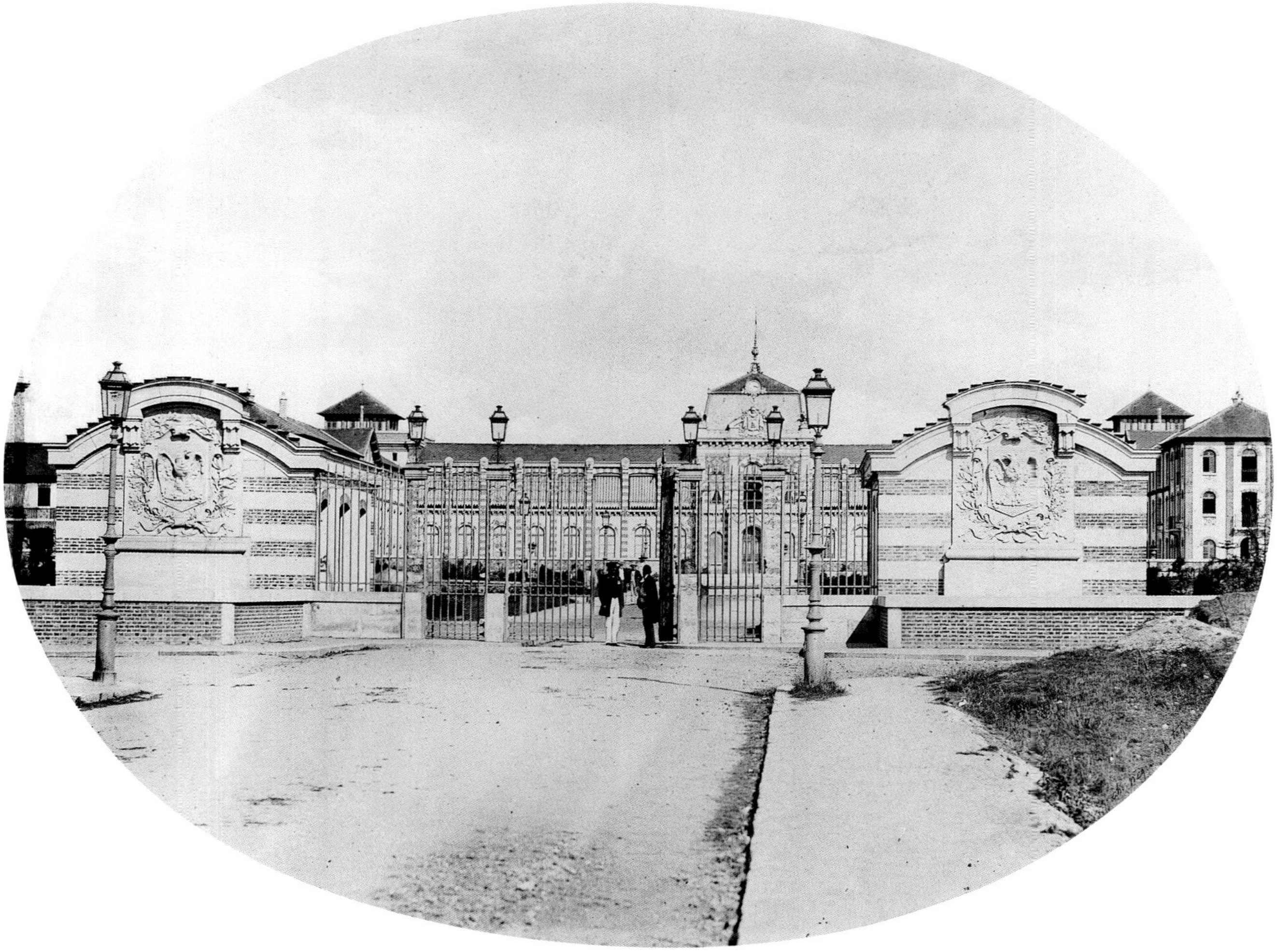

CHARLES NÈGRE
(1820–1880)

Imperial Asylum for Disabled Workmen, Vincennes, 1859
Albumen print

ministries that amply justified their sobriquet *photographes des ministères*. The scope of this state patronage was unparalleled and eloquent testimony to the importance attached by Napoleon III's régime to the part played by photography in celebrating its achievements.

Photographers' reliance on official commissions was underlined once they became fewer and the competition more intense. By 1860 Le Gray had been forced to close his business and seek sanctuary abroad; Bisson Frères were declared bankrupt in 1863; and Baldus, despite strenuous efforts to market his photographs, died in penury in 1889. The attempt by Blanquart-Evrard to distribute photographic prints, including many architectural views, in large numbers at reasonable prices ended in failure with the closure of his printing establishment at Lille in 1855. Whereas in 1853 architectural views had accounted for 37% of the French market, by 1860 this had shrunk to a miserly 5%.[24] Writing from Ravenna, the British photographer Stephen Thompson lamented:

> Picturesque views are few indeed; of architectural studies the number is endless. But the sale of such works, notwithstanding all that may be said to the contrary, is not remunerative generally. Men like Mr Street, Mr Ruskin, and some others, will admire them greatly, and what is more to the purpose, buy them; but there it ends. ... The fact is, it requires not only a special taste

CHARLES CLIFFORD
(died 1863)
Main Portal, New Cathedral, Salamanca, late 1850s
Albumen print

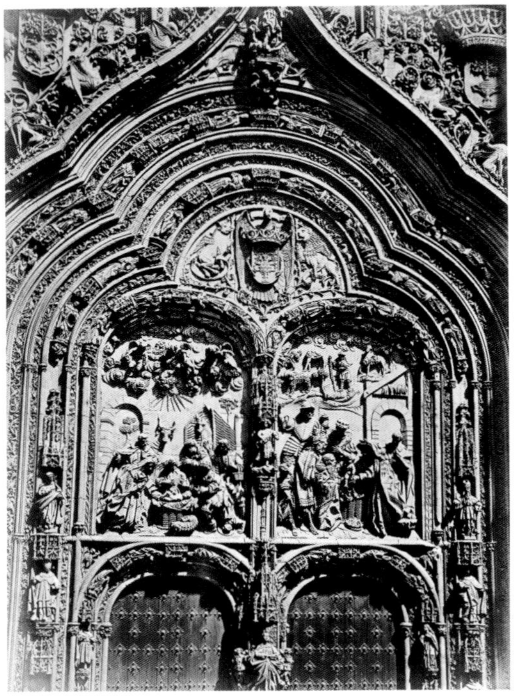

and aptitude, but also a special education ... before such things can be appreciated and enjoyed. Thus the stimulus which brings people to the purchasing point of admiration is wanting.[25]

The truth was that picturesque views sold, and while his French confrères slipped into obscurity, Bedford went on to become one of the nineteenth century's most successful topographical photographers.

Although not as extensive as in France, official patronage played a significant role in the development of architectural photography elsewhere. In Belgium it was behind Guillaume Claine's tentative attempts to photograph significant Belgian monuments at the beginning of the 1850s, as it was again in the early 1860s, when several city councils commissioned architectural photographs from Edmond Fierlants (see page 41). Although this latter venture was more successful, Fierlants died in debt, leaving the photography of Belgian buildings as a sideline for photographers engaged in the more profitable business of portraiture. In Spain one of the most accomplished architectural photographers of the 1850s, Charles Clifford, enjoyed the patronage of Queen Isabella II, which enabled him to photograph widely throughout the country, depicting both Christian and Moorish monuments (left; page 41). Over four hundred of these photographs, made from a mixture of paper and glass negatives, were published in Paris in 1856 under the title *Voyages en Espagne* and were warmly received by critics such as Ernest Lacan, who generously declared Clifford to be of the French photographic school. Certainly, in their large-scale delineation of details, Clifford's views bear comparison to those of Bisson Frères. It was in India, however, that, next to France, official patronage had the biggest impact.

Although news of photography's invention reached India with remarkable speed, it was not until the 1850s that it emerged as a significant force. This was largely due to the active support of the East India Company and various government agencies, which saw photography as the key means of recording and assimilating the vast and heterogeneous array of monuments under their control. In 1855 the East India Company announced:

> We have recently desired the Government of Bombay to discontinue the employment of draughtsmen in the delineation of antiquities of Western India, and to employ photography instead, and it is our desire that this method be generally substituted throughout India, in cases where it may be considered desirable by the Government to obtain representation of objects of interest.[26]

Most of the photography was undertaken by officially trained and equipped army officers, such as John Murray, Medical Officer in charge of the Medical School at Agra from 1849 (see page 43); Colonel Thomas Biggs of the Bombay Artillery, who was appointed official photographer to the Bombay Presidency in 1855 (a post he was forced to relinquish within a year, owing to other army duties, and to which he was succeeded by William Henry Pigou of the Bombay Medical Service); and Captain Linnaeus Tripe, appointed official photographer to the Madras Presidency in 1856 (see page 43). The photographs of Murray and Tripe are among the finest examples of paper photography of the period. Reminiscent in their soft romanticism of the work of Le Secq, they provide a marked contrast to the more straightforward record imagery of Biggs and Pigou. An added impetus was given to this official photography not only by the sad state of disrepair into which many of the monuments had fallen (Tripe wrote that he aimed "to secure *before they disappear* the objects of the Presidency that are interesting to the Antiquary, Architect, Sculptor, Mythologist and Historian")[27] but also by a political agenda that saw the photographs used to emphasize the economic and social benefits of British colonial rule. During the next decade they would also provide valuable source material to historians such as James Fergusson. Despite the varied purposes these photographs served, government officials soon became concerned that photography had not met their high expectations. Not only had it proved considerably slower and more expensive than anticipated, but the images were seen to be highly subjective, thus devaluing their usefulness as official records – a sentiment with which the Commission des Monuments Historiques would have sympathized. As a result, official commissioning of photography was greatly reduced and proceeded on a more piecemeal basis. The photographic establishments of Bombay and Madras were effectively closed in 1857 and 1859 respectively, with Sir Charles Trevelyan, the Governor of Madras, declaring Tripe's post "an article of high luxury ... unsuited to the present state of our finances".[28]

In Italy a different situation pertained. There a thriving commercial market for photographs of buildings was created by the boundless appetite of Grand Tourists for pictorial mementos. Initially, Italian architectural photography was dominated by foreign amateurs – the French in the persons of Frédéric Flacheron, Eugène Constant and the 1846 Prix de Rome architect, Alfred-Nicolas Normand, with the British represented by daguerreotypists such as Dr Alexander Ellis (whose meticulously recorded exposure times varied between six to ten minutes at midday and twenty-five to thirty minutes in the evening), and calotypists such as Calvert Jones and the Revd George Bridges. By the mid-1850s, however, commercial firms, both indigenous and foreign, had sprung up, primarily to cater to the needs of the tourist market. These included: in Florence, Fratelli Alinari, founded in 1854; in Venice, Giuseppe Cimetta, Carlo Naya and Carlo Ponti; and in Rome, James Anderson (see page 44), Robert MacPherson and Pietro Dovizielli. These photographers were the direct heirs to the tradition of the *vedutisti*, those frequently anonymous viewmakers whose compositions, often produced with the help of mechanical aids such as the *camera ottica*, were so highly prized by their tourist customers for providing a seemingly impartial, eyewitness record of the sites they had visited. Some of these firms, such as the Alinari, Naya, Ponti and Anderson, were to become large photographic enterprises dominating Italian output in the ensuing decades with a popular mixture of landscapes, views of important historical monuments and reproductions of works of art.

Although his output was small in comparison, during the 1850s it was the work of the expatriate Scot and former landscape painter Robert MacPherson that was held in most regard (see page 46). MacPherson was not a great technician, but his prints, which were usually large in scale and expensive, commanded extensive sales and won him international recognition through exhibitions such as that at the Architectural Union Company's premises in London in 1862, where more than four hundred were displayed. A master of composition and massing, MacPherson was particularly fond of high tonal contrasts, which he exploited to create frames full of tension between the competing elements of black and white. Though admired by staunch classical architects such as Donaldson and Sir William Tite, MacPherson's photographs were intended predominantly for tourists and from a purely architectural standpoint were strongly criticized for "a great want of that which we are always led to expect in architectural drawings – mathematical precision".[29] Thus, while sharing some of Baldus's monumentality, MacPherson's images were far less useful to an architectural audience. In this respect, the photographs bought in 1859 by Sir Henry Cole, director of the South Kensington Museum, from Dovizielli as possible exemplars for the buildings (especially the Horticultural Society) to be erected in that part of London, were of far greater architectural import (see page 47). It was, however, this constant tension between photography of buildings conceived as topographical records, architectural documentation or works of art that was at the heart of the genre's creativity.

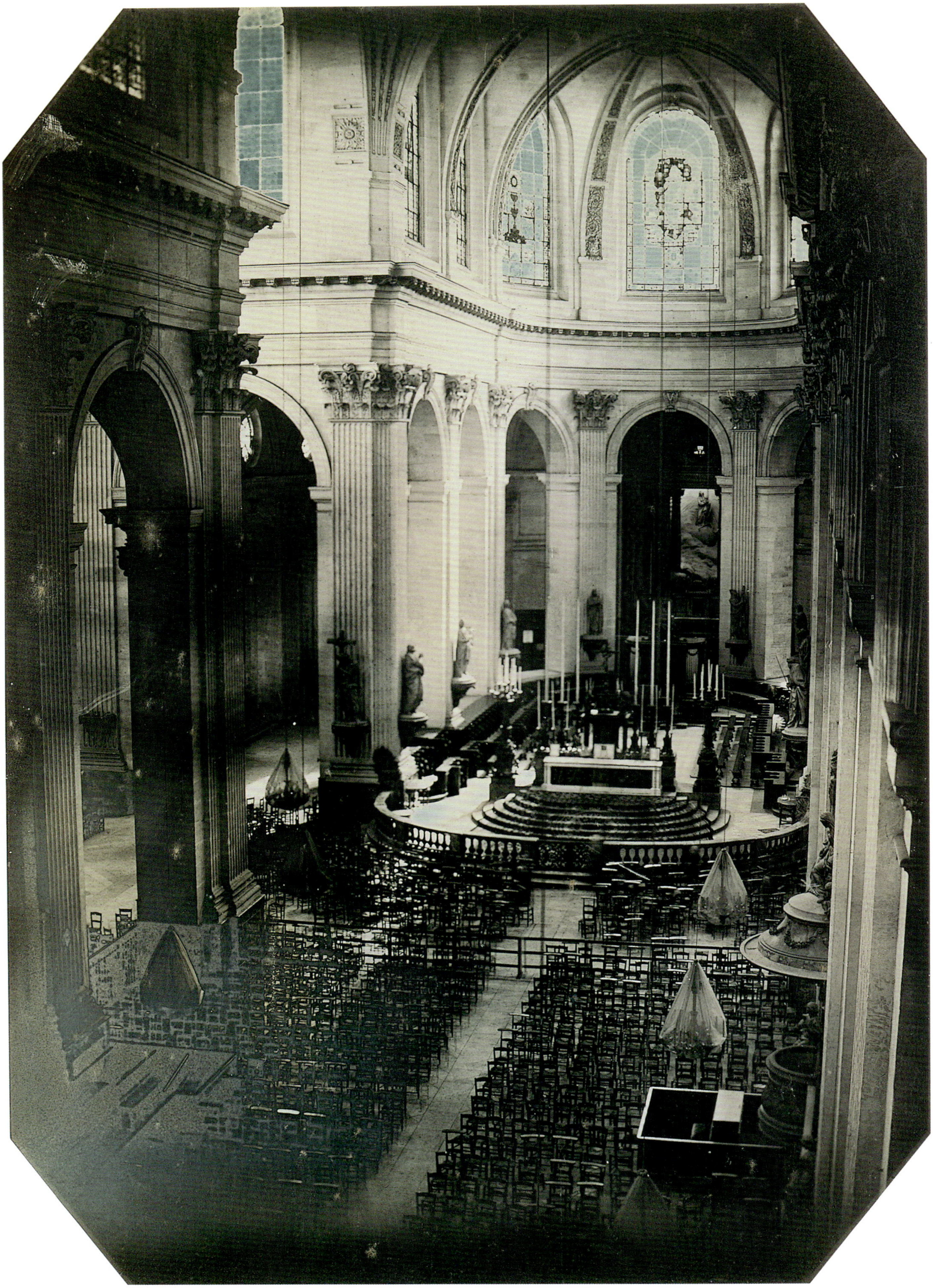

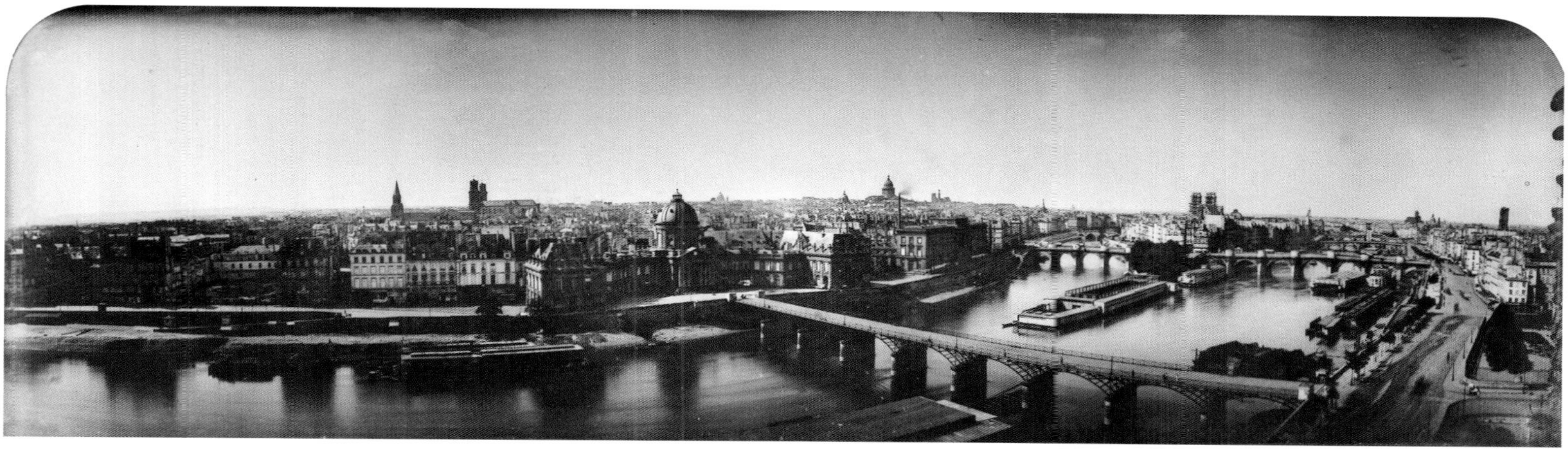

opposite

MARIE-CHARLES-ISIDORE CHOISELAT (1815–1858) and **STANISLAS RATEL** (1824–1904) (attrib.)

Church of Saint-Sulpice, Paris, c. 1845–50

Daguerreotype

Interior views are rare during this early period and daguerreotypes of interiors rarer still. The photographer's skills were fully tested by the low and varying light levels inside buildings since there was no adequate means of artificial lighting and plates were not backed against halation (blurring caused by reflection and dispersion of light). In addition, early emulsions were particularly sensitive to blue light, which was most evident in the shadow areas of gloomy interiors. Exposures in such conditions could last hours or even, as MacPherson revealed in 1862, days. As late as 1874 Naya took five days to obtain a single view of a church interior.

above

FRIEDRICH VON MARTENS (1809–1875) (attrib.)

The Seine, the Left Bank and the Ile de la Cité, Paris, c. 1845–50

Daguerreotype

Of German stock, Martens was born in Venice but settled in Paris c. 1840. In 1845 he patented a panoramic camera with a 150° arc, allowing him to replicate photographically the city views he had made previously as an engraver. Although specialized and expensive, panoramas were an important feature of architectural photography, their inclusivity at once revealing the sweep of the city and suggesting that it was amenable to human control. Other noteworthy panoramas during this period were produced by Claudet in London and Lorenzo Suscipj in Rome. The form culminated in Eadweard Muybridge's huge panorama of San Francisco (1878).

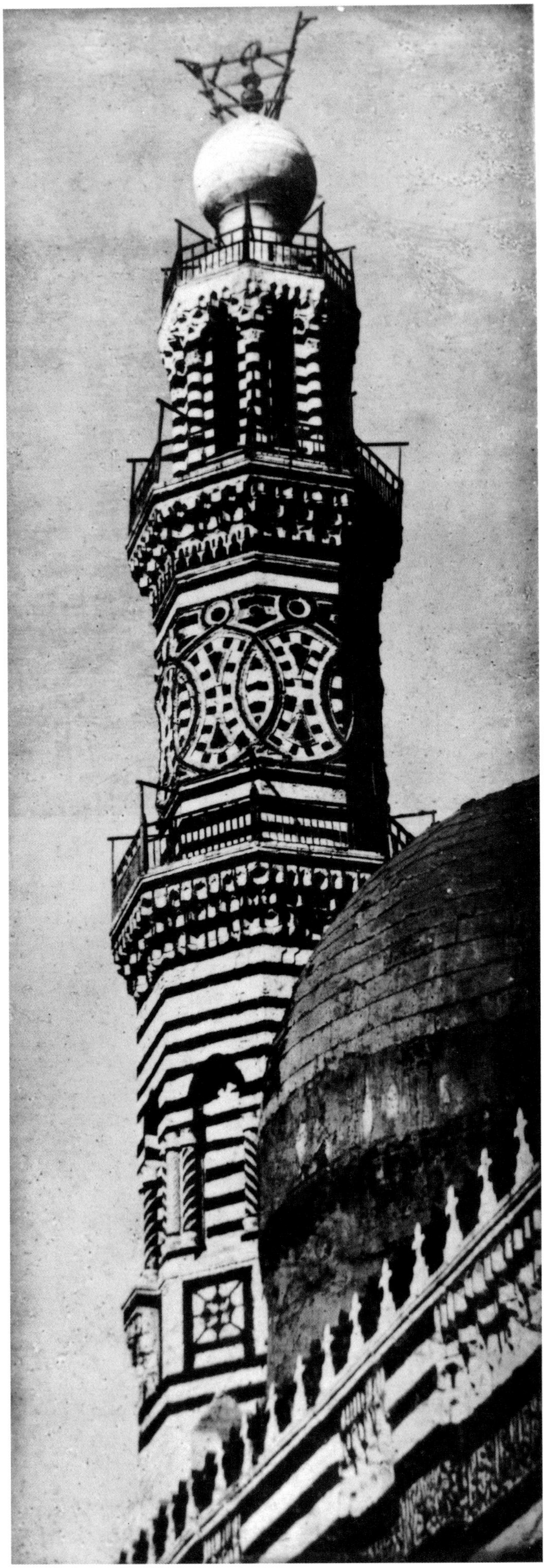

left

JOSEPH-PHILIBERT GIRAULT DE PRANGEY
(1804–1893)

Minaret of Mosque Kalaun, Cairo, 1842

Daguerreotype

Archaeologist and draughtsman Girault de Prangey, who had trained at the Académie des Beaux-Arts in Paris, travelled in Italy, Egypt, Syria, Palestine and Greece for two years before returning in 1844 with more than a thousand daguerreotypes. Some of these were used as the basis of the lithographs in Girault's *Monuments arabes d'Egypte, de Syrie et d'Asie Mineure dessinés et mésurés de 1842 à 1845* (Paris, 1846). While Girault used the daguerreotype to ensure the accuracy of his Islamic details, a decade earlier the British architect Owen Jones had had no choice but to take casts to achieve the same end in his publication on the Alhambra, Granada.

opposite top

JOHN PLUMBE JR (1809–1857)

The United States Capitol, Washington, D.C., c. 1846

Daguerreotype

Architects: Benjamin Henry Latrobe and Charles Bulfinch

Like many early photographers, Plumbe was a fortune-seeking entrepreneur. From 1841 he established galleries in several American cities including Washington, from where the *United States Journal* reported in 1846 that he was "engaged in taking views of all the public buildings which are executed in a style of elegance, that far surpasses any we have seen".[10] Plumbe's photographs of the Capitol are the earliest known; this luminous composition, looking from an oblique, slightly elevated viewpoint, wonderfully conveys America's burgeoning sense of national pride. After abandoning photography in 1849, participating in the California gold rush and going bankrupt, Plumbe committed suicide.

opposite bottom

ROBERT H. VANCE (1825–1876)

Rix Family and Residence, Oakland, California, 1855

Daguerreotype

Encouraged by the sunny climate, a population proud of its fledgeling culture that was willing to absorb new inventions and eager to memorialize its successes, and little competition from other visual media, outdoor daguerreotypy flourished in San Francisco, and Robert Vance was one of its leading exponents. The family proudly lined up in front of its town house or business establishment – an egalitarian, urbanized version of the English vogue for country house portraiture – consequently became for a short period a significant subgenre of American photography.

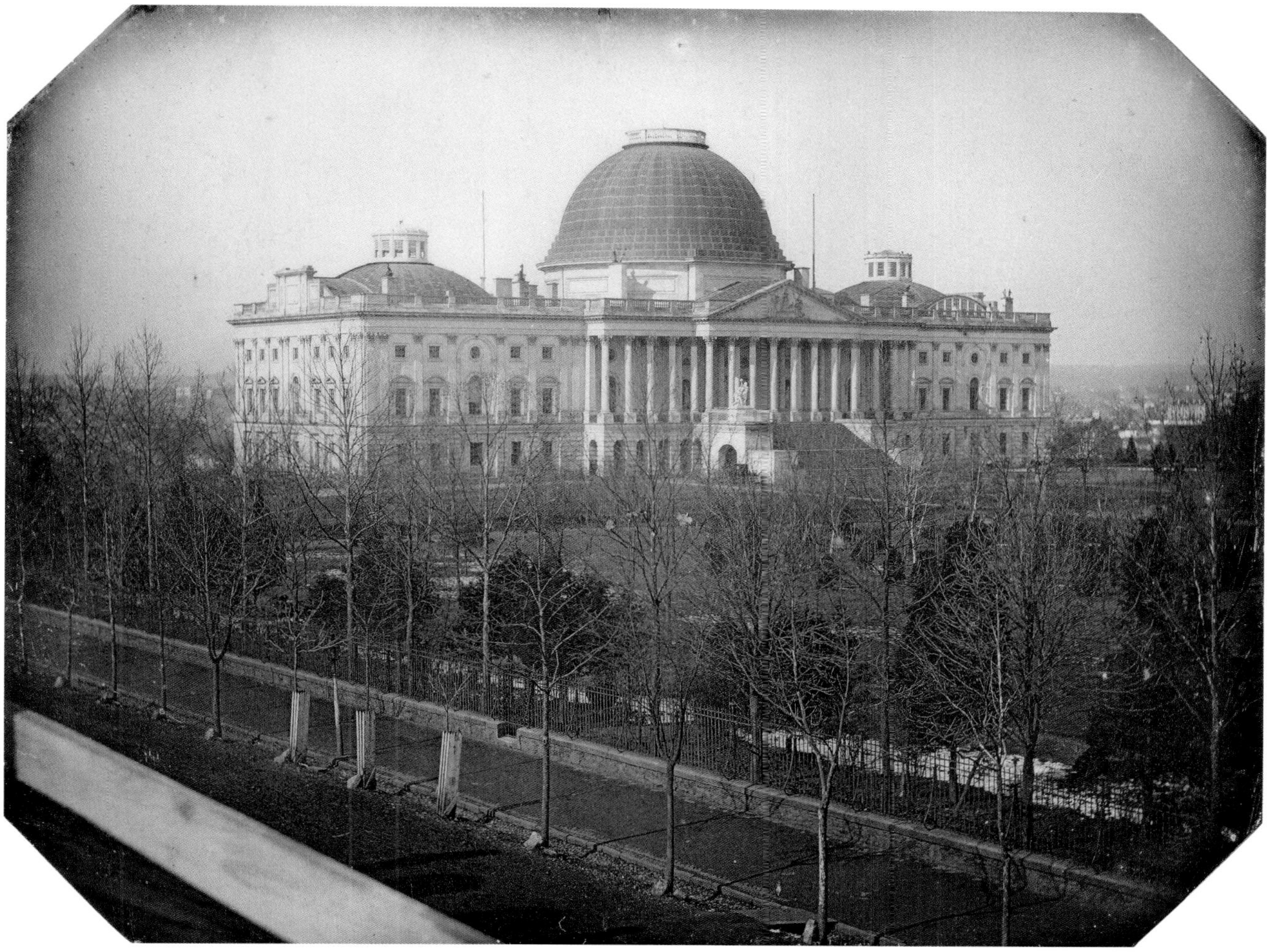

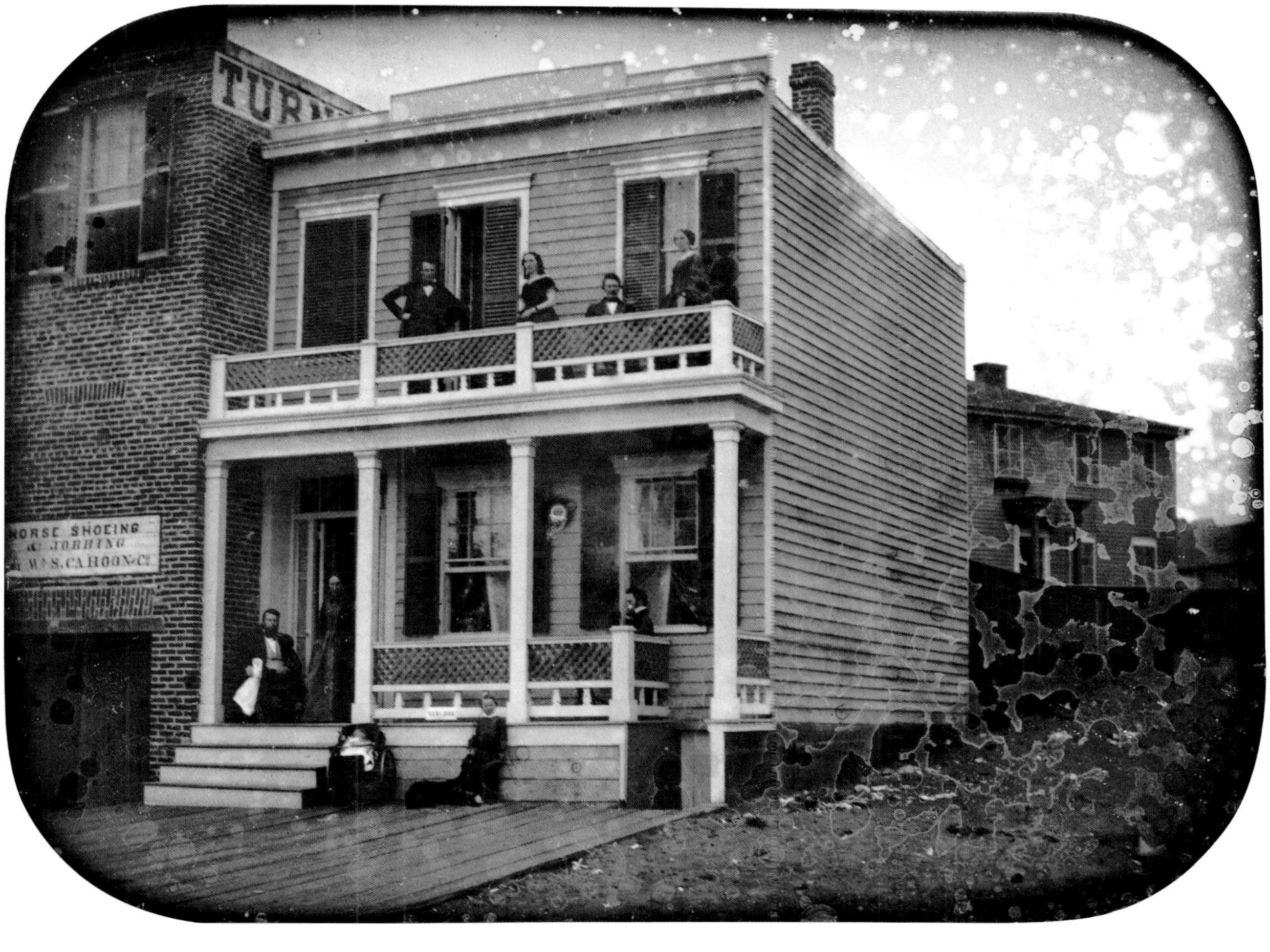
TUR
ORSE SHOEING
& JOBBING
Wm S. CAHOON & Co

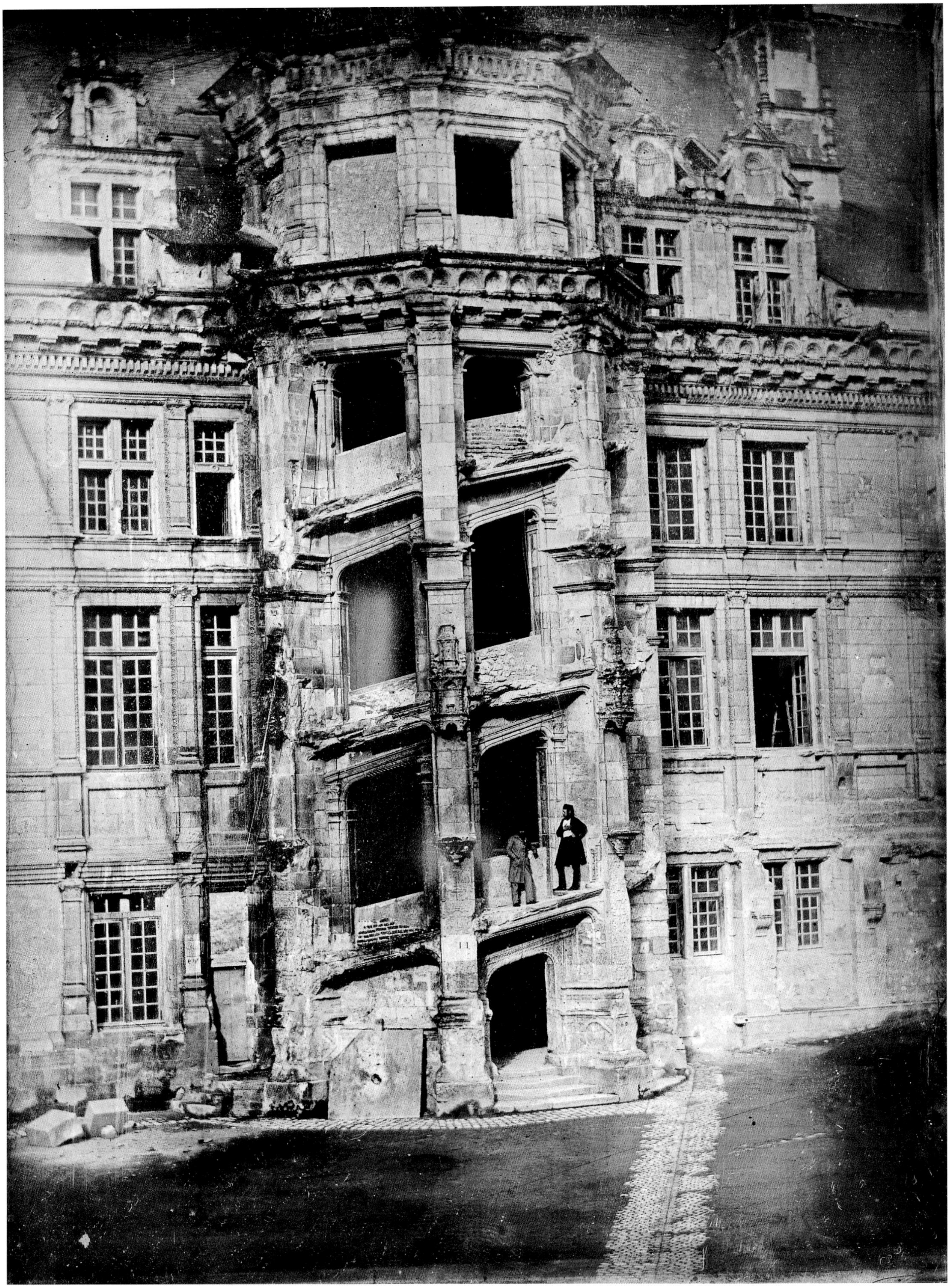

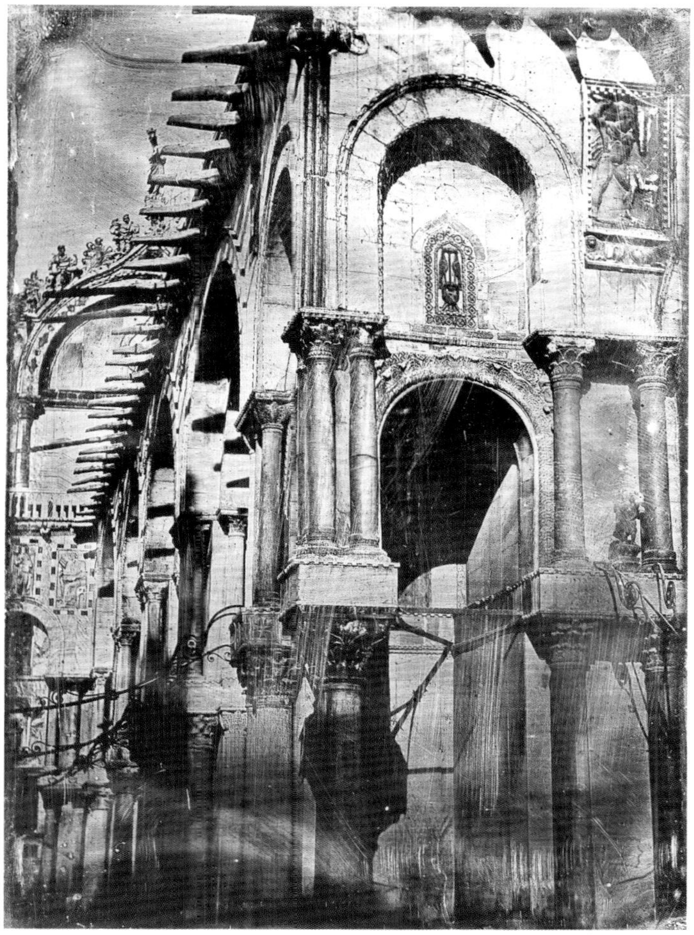

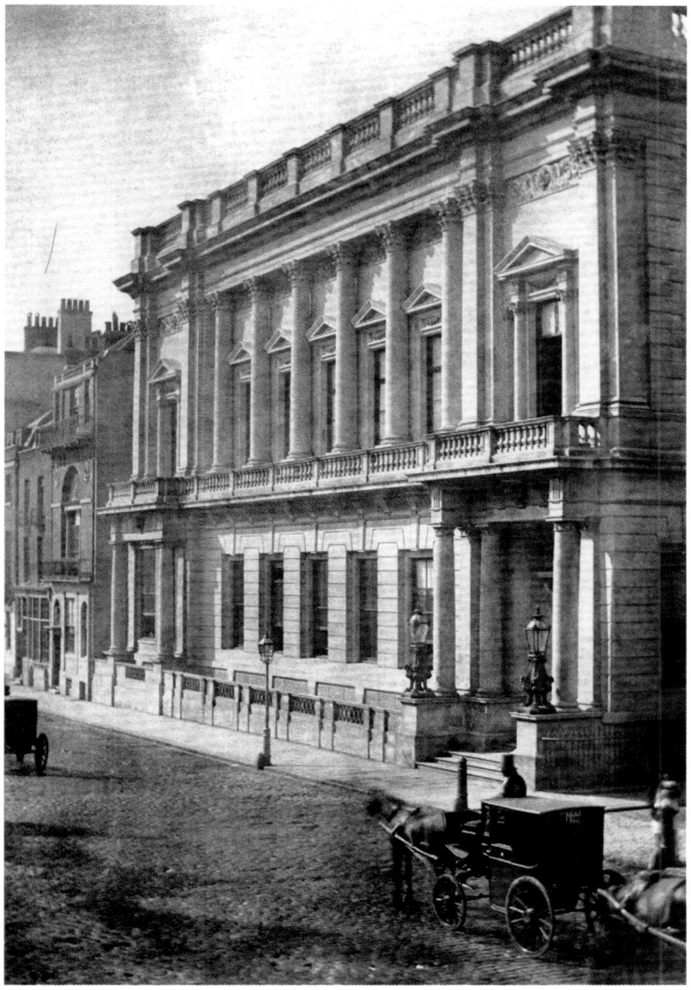

opposite

HIPPOLYTE BAYARD (1801–1887)

View of the Staircase of the François I Wing of the Château, Blois, 1843

Daguerreotype

Architect for restoration: Félix Duban

In France photography was soon used as an aid to restoration, being employed on both major projects of the 1850s – the château at Blois and Notre-Dame, Paris. At Blois its restorer, Duban, commissioned fifty daguerreotypes from Bayard, hitherto known for his paper photography, which were used to ascertain the type and amount of work required and later to justify Duban's intervention. Duban, who significantly used the camera lucida to achieve precision in his drawings, commissioned further photographs to chart the restoration's progress, and the restored staircase became a favourite subject of later photographers.

top left

JOHN RUSKIN (1819–1900)

North-West Porch, Basilica of St Mark's, Venice, *c.* 1850–51

Daguerreotype

Ruskin was one of the earliest and most enthusiastic proponents of photography as an aid to architectural study. He first purchased daguerreotypes in Venice in 1845 and then acquired his own camera, operated by his valet, John Hobbs. For Ruskin the daguerreotype was "a most blessed invention",[31] which perfectly complemented his two-dimensional vision of architecture, with its emphasis on surface articulation and the identification of architecture with sculpture and ornament. Above all, it allowed him to experience buildings at close quarters, satisfying his desire to investigate minute details: "Every chip of stone and stain is there", he wrote excitedly.[32]

bottom left

WILLIAM HENRY FOX TALBOT (1800–1877)

The Conservative Club-House, St James's Street, London, *c.* 1845

Modern print from original calotype negative

Architects: George Basevi and Sydney Smirke

Although Talbot was concerned to demonstrate the versatility of the calotype and photographed a wide variety of subjects, architecture figured prominently, with Talbot claiming his family seat at Lacock Abbey to be "the first [building] to have drawn its own picture".[33] His finest architectural images are his series of London buildings (*c.* 1845), which were in the tradition of the engraved views illustrating such publications as Thomas Shepherd's and James Elmes's *Metropolitan Improvements* (1827) and that similarly bore eloquent witness to the architectural transformation that had grandiosely reshaped London in the wake of Napoleon's defeat at Waterloo.

ANTOINE CLAUDET (1797–1867)

Palm House, Kew, London, 1847

Daguerreotype

Architect: Decimus Burton with Richard Turner, engineer

This image – one of a pair – is a rare example of a British architectural daguerreotype, the interior shot being facilitated by the building's transparency. It lies at the beginning of a rich tradition of photographs of engineers' architecture, such as the Crystal Palace and the Galerie des Machines, Paris (1889), which resulted in some of the nineteenth century's most powerful images. Claudet, a noted London photographer, concentrated mainly on portraiture after failing to sell architectural views imported from Lerebours, the Parisian publisher of *Excursions daguerriennes*, claiming that London's "misty vapours" prevented "the formation of clear images".[34]

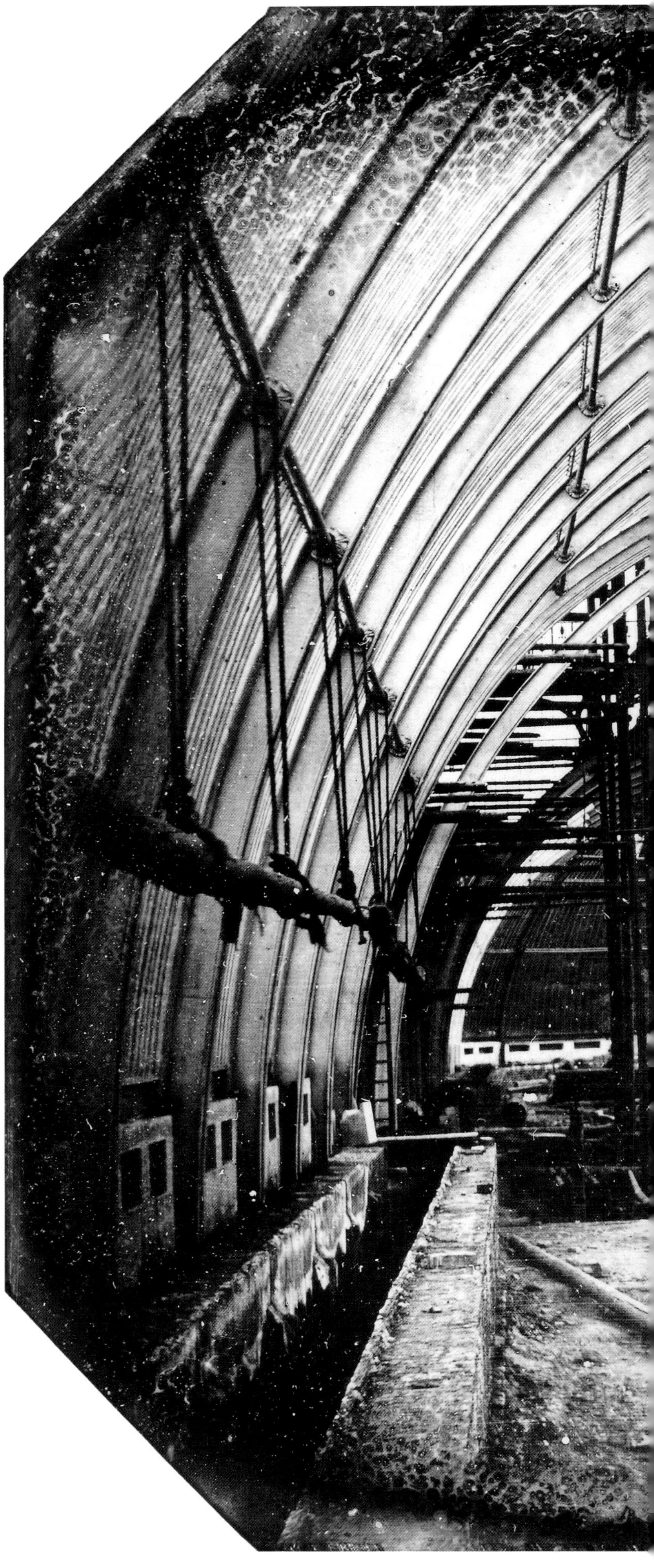

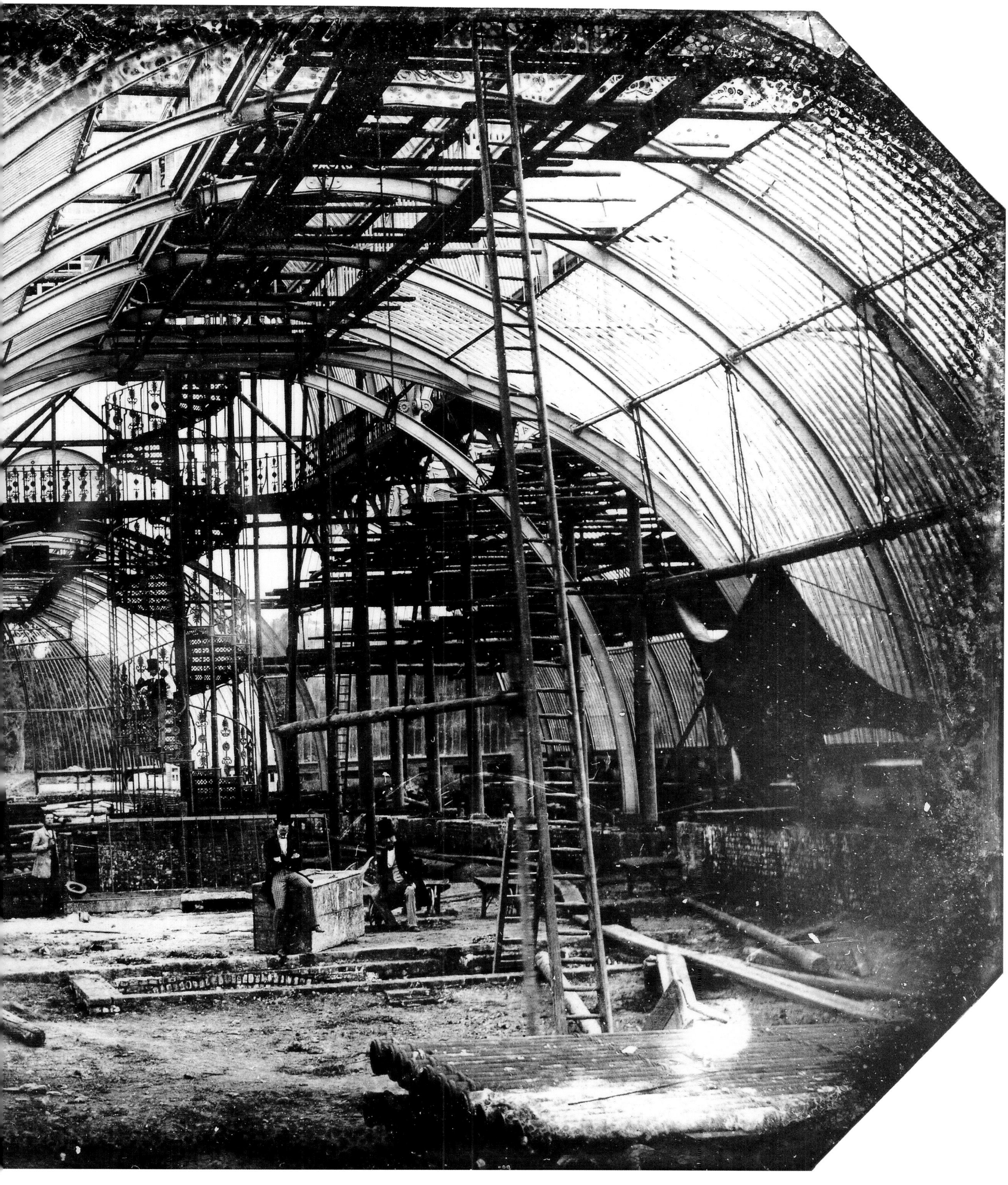

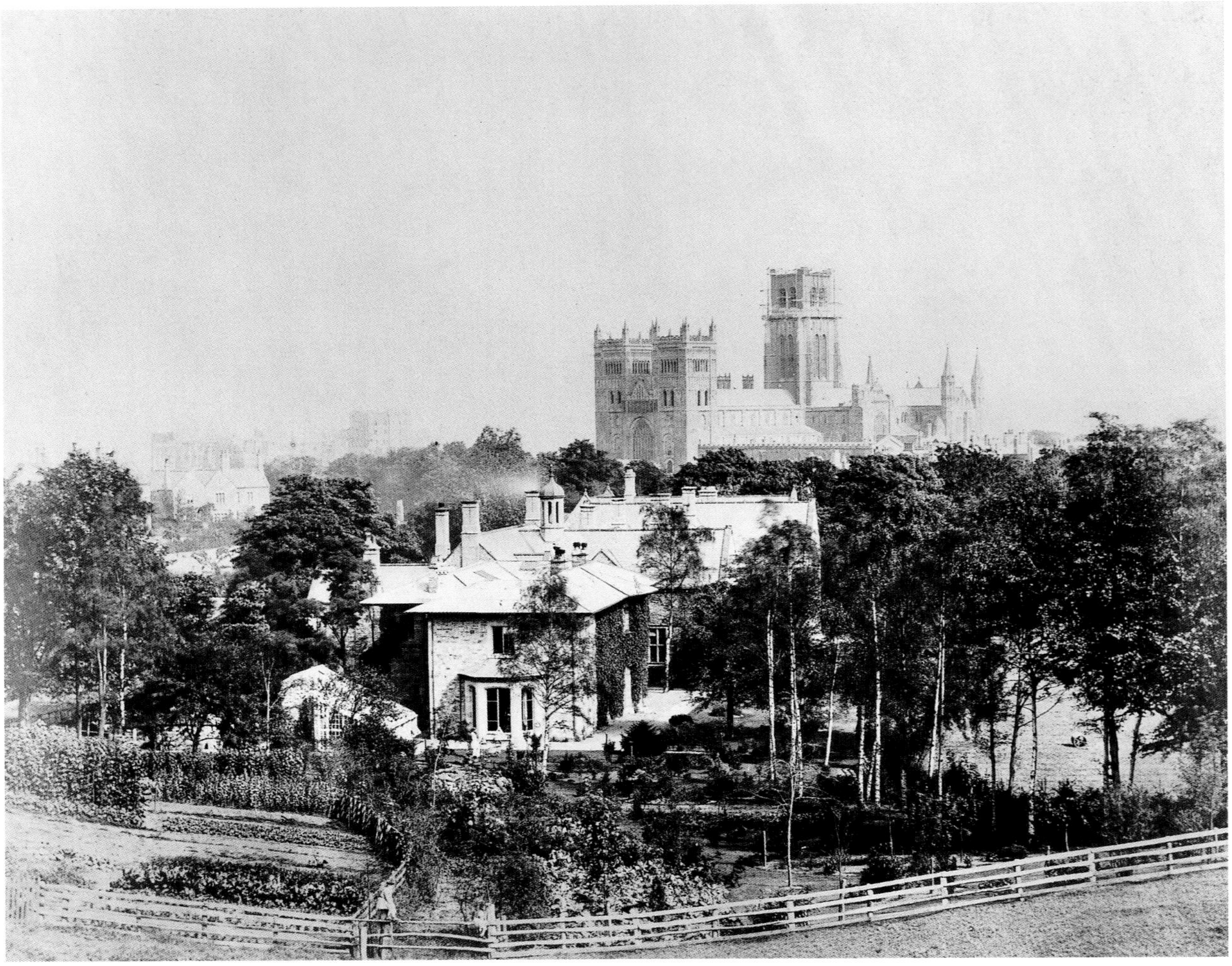

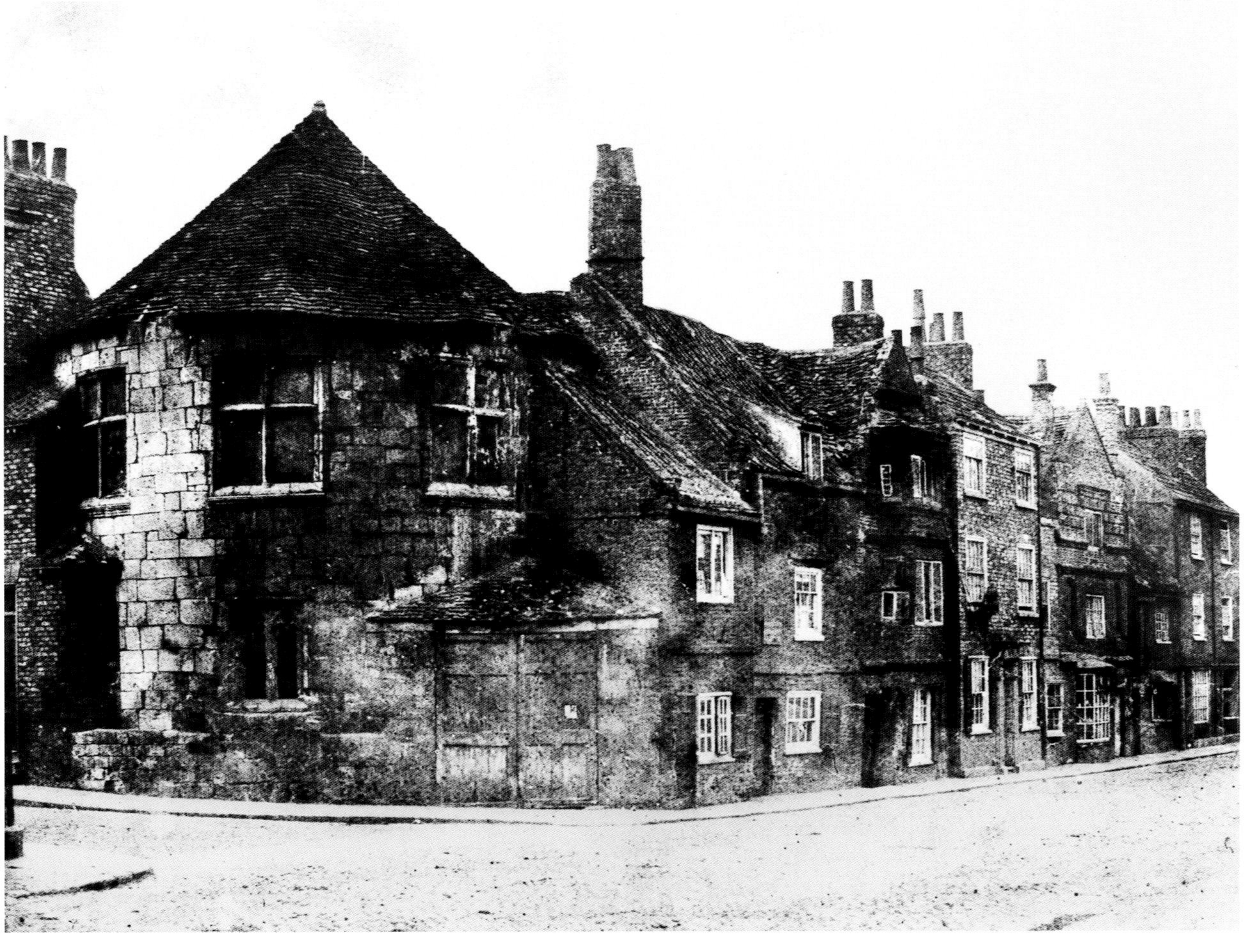

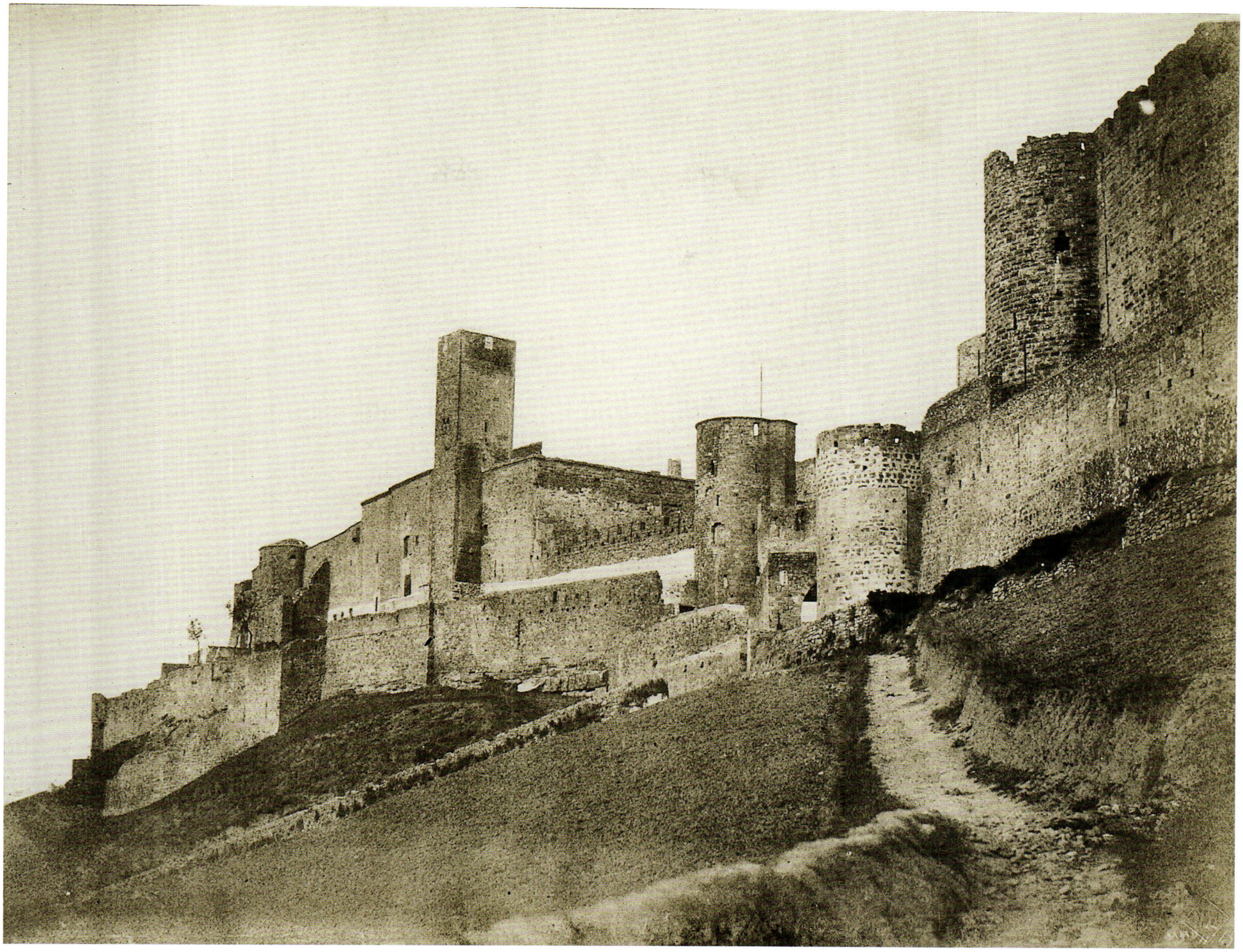

opposite top

DR HENRY HOLDEN (1814–1909)

Durham Cathedral, c. 1852

Albumen print

Dr Henry Holden was a prominent amateur photographer and member of both the Photographic Exchange Club and the Photographic Club, which were important forums for disseminating information about the medium and allowing photographers to exchange and compare their work. Exhibited at the Society of Arts' pioneering photographic exhibition in London in 1852, this view was significantly entitled *Durham Cathedral*, even though its outline could be only dimly discerned in the distance. The 'modern' Georgian house dominating the foreground was conveniently ignored, emphasizing the amateur taboo on the photography of such buildings.

opposite bottom

GEORGE FOWLER JONES (1818–1905)

Coney Street, York, c. 1853

Modern print from original calotype negative

Jones was one of the first architects to practise photography. He recorded both his own buildings – mostly in and around York, where his office was based – and historic architecture at home and abroad from 1846 until his death. Such architect-photographers were to make an influential contribution to the genre in the forthcoming years. Their ranks boasted among their early members the French Prix de Rome scholar Alfred-Nicolas Normand (1822–1909), who photographed Roman remains during his sojourn there between 1847 and 1851, and the American Richard Morris Hunt (1827–1895).

above

GUSTAVE LE GRAY (1820–1882) and **MESTRAL**

Ramparts of Carcassonne, 1851

Salt print

Le Gray's Mission Héliographique photographs, unlike those of Baldus, which stressed architectural legibility, were romantic in spirit. Areas of strongly illuminated detail contrasted with dense shadows, suggesting only the merest hint of what lay within, produced images of brooding intensity. Nature and landscape were treated as essential architectural features. His Mission images of the decaying but imposing Visigothic fortifications at Carcassonne in southern France, taken with Mestral, well illustrate the critic Francis Wey's observation that his photographs encapsulated "the strange vigour, powerful relief, and almost fantastic impression of the engravings of Piranesi".[35]

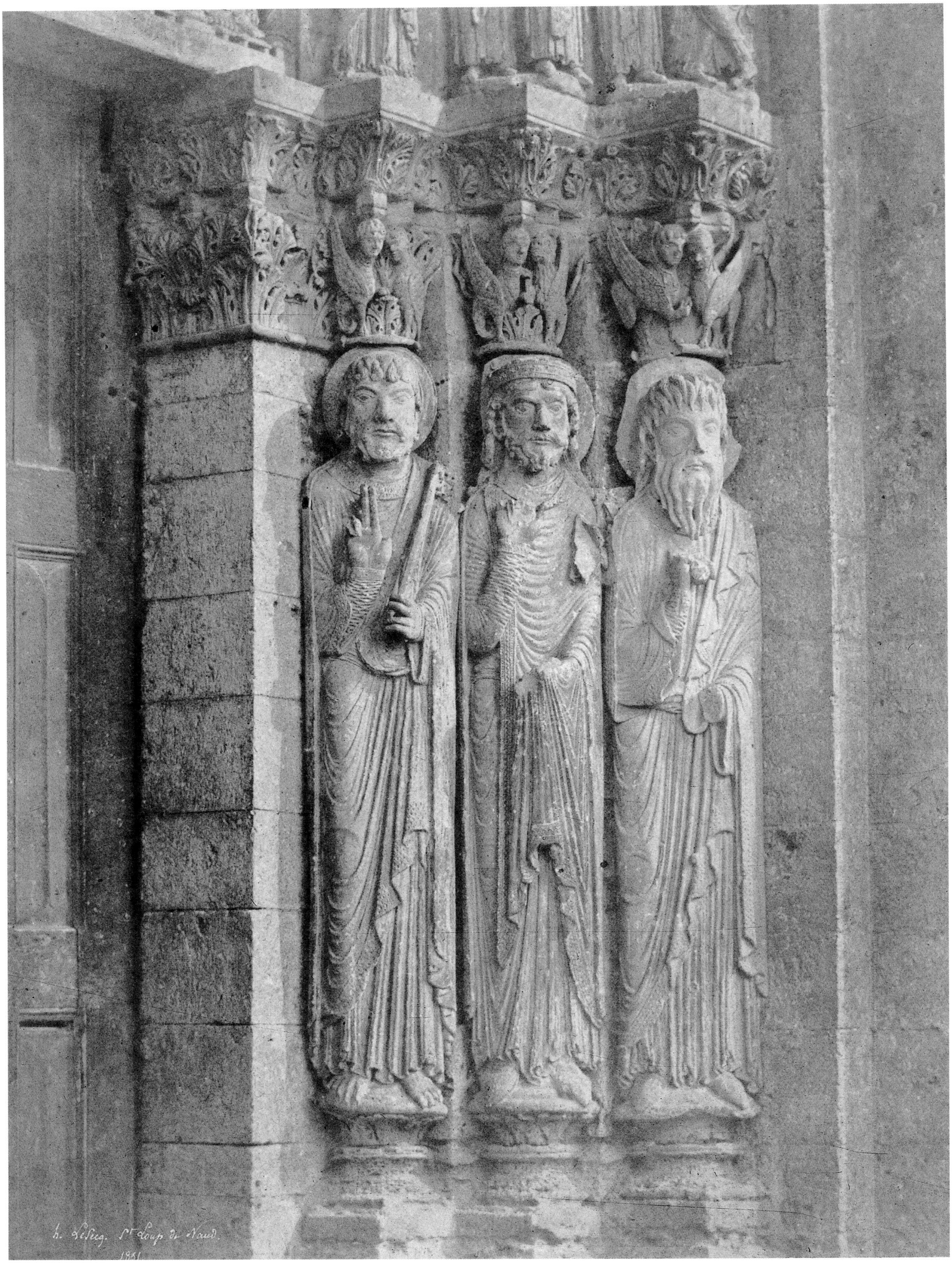
h. LeSecq. St Loup de Naud.
1851

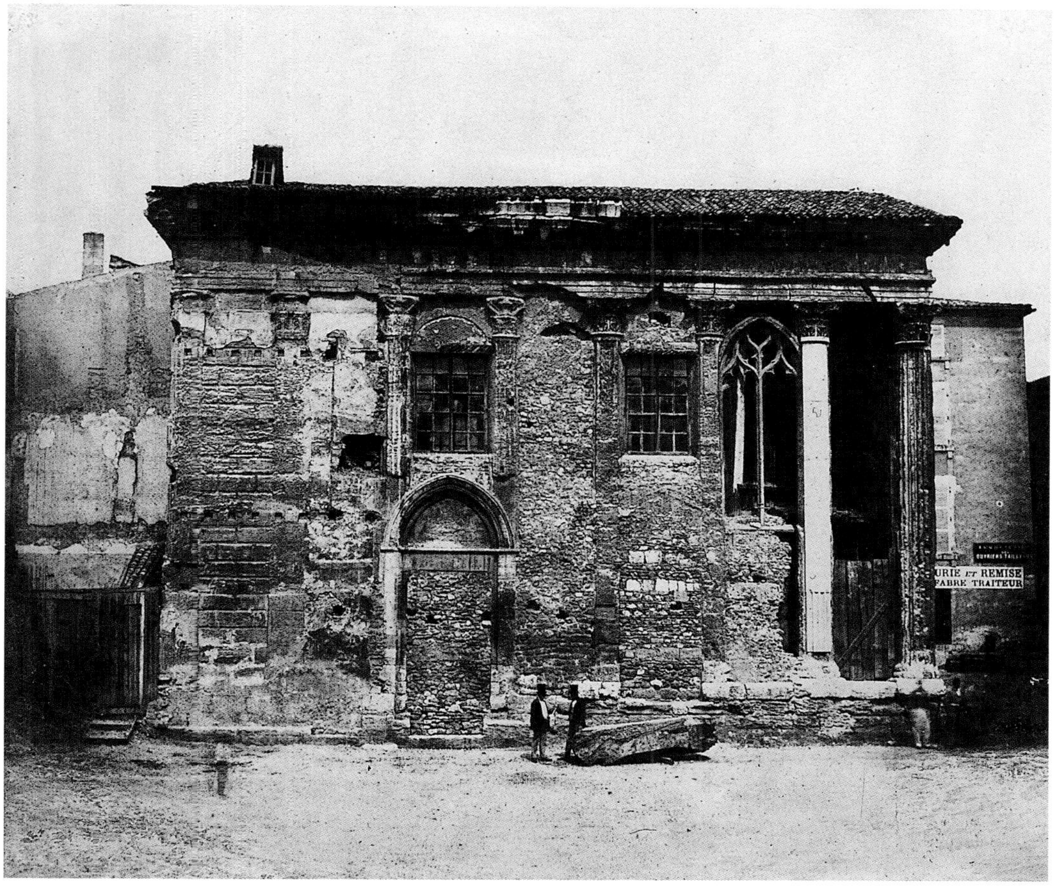

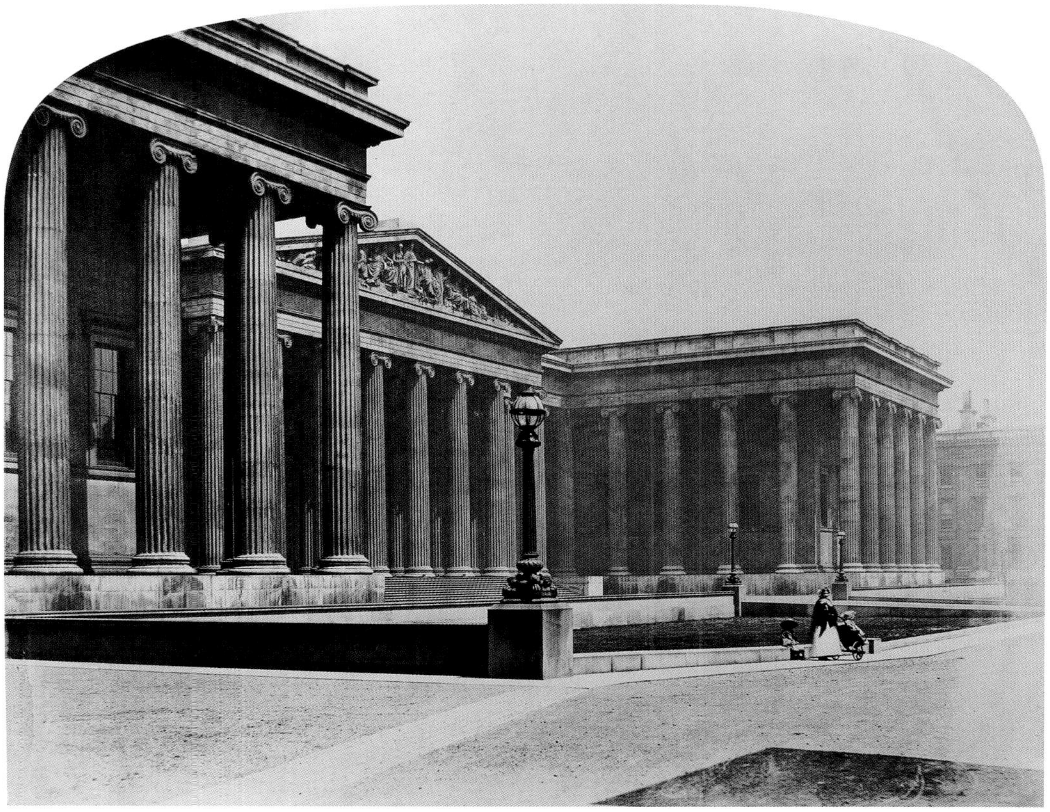

opposite

JEAN-LOUIS-HENRI LE SECQ DES TOURNELLES
(1818–1882)

Statuary Group, West Door, Church of Saint-Loup, Saint-Loup-de-Naud, 1851
Salt print

A minor painter, Le Secq turned to photography in about 1848, encouraged by his friend Le Gray, and soon established a reputation as one of France's greatest architectural photographers. In addition to his Mission work, he photographed the cathedrals of Amiens, Chartres and Rheims, and the demolition of Paris's medieval buildings ordered by Baron Haussmann's predecessor as Prefect of the Seine, Jean-Jacques Berger. Le Secq's approach was highly individual. Working exclusively on paper, he produced prints of melancholic beauty in which tectonic elements were frequently depicted as a series of isolated fragments. He abandoned photography in the late 1850s.

top left

EDOUARD BALDUS (1813–1889)

Temple of Augustus and Livia, Vienne, 1851
Salt print

Born in Grunebach, Prussia, Baldus took up photography in about 1848 after an undistinguished career as a painter. The mission he was awarded in 1851 detailed fifty-one buildings and three paintings to be photographed. His surviving negatives show Baldus moving away from a reliance on the romantic compositions of the *Voyages pittoresques* towards the formulation of his own photographic style, marked by its solemnity and sense of the monumental. The two figures – perhaps his assistants, as they recur in several photographs – are posed not as mere romantic scene dressing but to give scale to the elevational composition.

bottom left

ROGER FENTON (1819–1869)

British Museum, London, 1857
Albumen print
Architect: Sir Robert Smirke

Although he is now best known for his Crimean War photographs, Fenton's architectural work was more highly regarded at the time. It embraced both conventional picturesque views and more classical compositions, which reflected his training as a Neo-classical painter and were heavily influenced by his close ties with French photographers. In these latter views, Fenton displayed a keen eye for the abstract and symmetrical. This image of the British Museum, where he was official photographer, is typical in its tight composition and complex geometrical patterning.

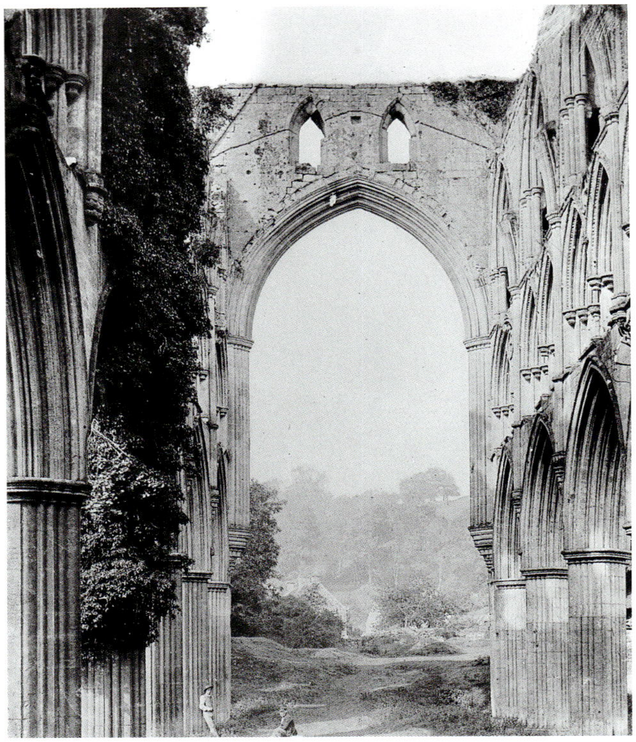

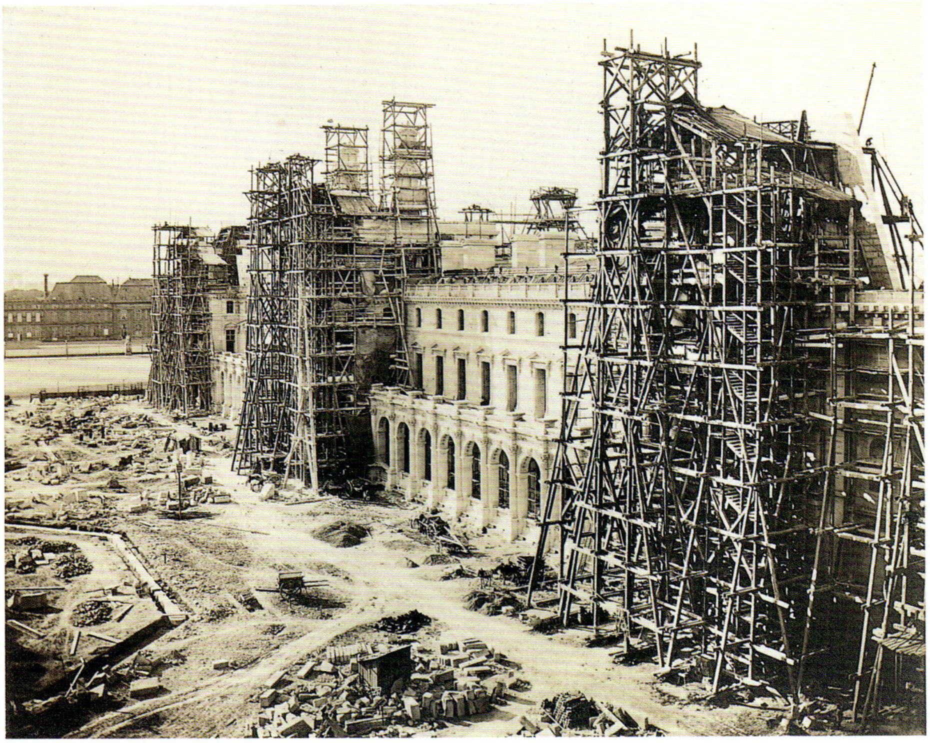

above left

FRANCIS BEDFORD (1816–1894)

Rievaulx Abbey, Yorkshire, late 1850s

Albumen print

Son of a noted Greek Revival architect, Bedford was the chief exponent of the picturesque approach to architectural photography, as shown in his depiction of such subjects as the cathedrals of Canterbury and York and the ruined abbeys of Tintern and Rievaulx. Praised by photographic critics for their radiant, luminous beauty, Bedford's compositions were heavily influenced by his experience from the late 1830s onwards as a lithographer and by his admiration for the work of Samuel Prout, a close study of whose romantic lithographs Bedford recommended to all architectural photographers.

above right

EDOUARD BALDUS (1813–1889)

New Louvre Under Construction, Paris, c. 1855

Albumen print

Architects: Louis-Tullius-Joachim Visconti and Hector-Martin Lefuel

Baldus's 'stone by stone' documentation of the Louvre was practical and propagandist.[36] Small paper photographs of plaster casts of the Old Louvre's decoration served as exemplars, while others of the new wing's sculptural models and completed ornament helped to record progress. Beyond the limited issue in 1857–58 of presentation sets, each of over two thousand photographs, Baldus's images were widely distributed to schools of drawing and libraries, especially through the photogravure reproductions in *Palais du Louvre et des Tuileries* (1869–71),[37] thereby helping to promulgate the Second Empire style. This print was used to illustrate a paper read at the Royal Institute of British Architects.

opposite

PHILIP HENRY DELAMOTTE (1820–1899)

The Upper Gallery, Crystal Palace, Sydenham, London

Albumen print from *Photographic Views of the Progress of the Crystal Palace, Sydenham*, London (Joseph Cundall) 1855

Architect: Sir Joseph Paxton

Delamotte, who had already made several calotypes of the disassembly of the Crystal Palace in Hyde Park (its original location for the Great Exhibition of 1851), was commissioned by its directors to photograph its re-erection at Sydenham. His two-volume luxury edition of 160 albumen prints from wet collodion negatives represented the first attempt to record a building systematically by photography from the levelling of the site to the opening ceremony. Delamotte's fascination with the abstract patterns of the building's ironwork anticipated the concern for form of Modernist photographers such as László Moholy-Nagy, while his juxtapositions of exhibits and structure now seem almost Surrealist in nature.

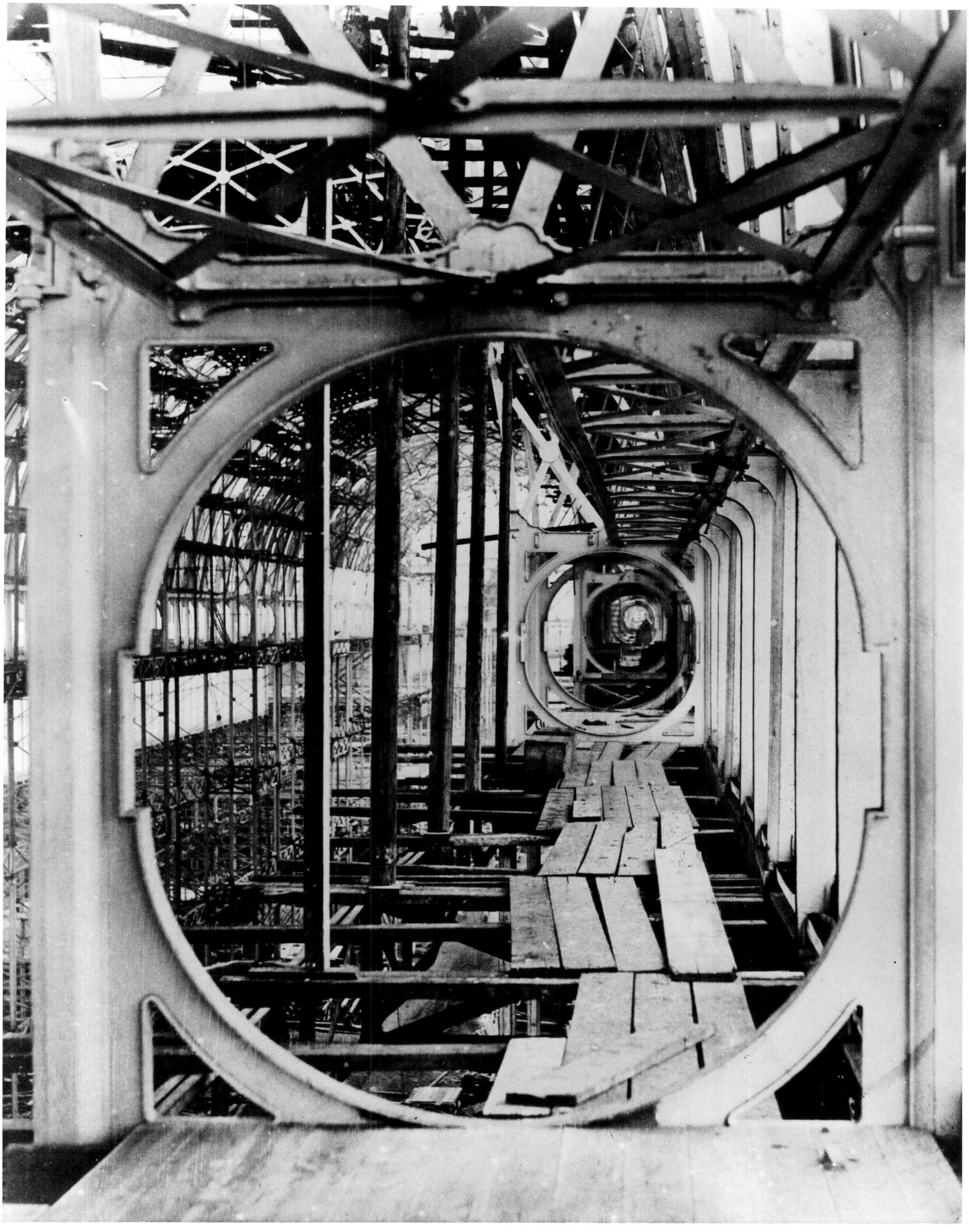

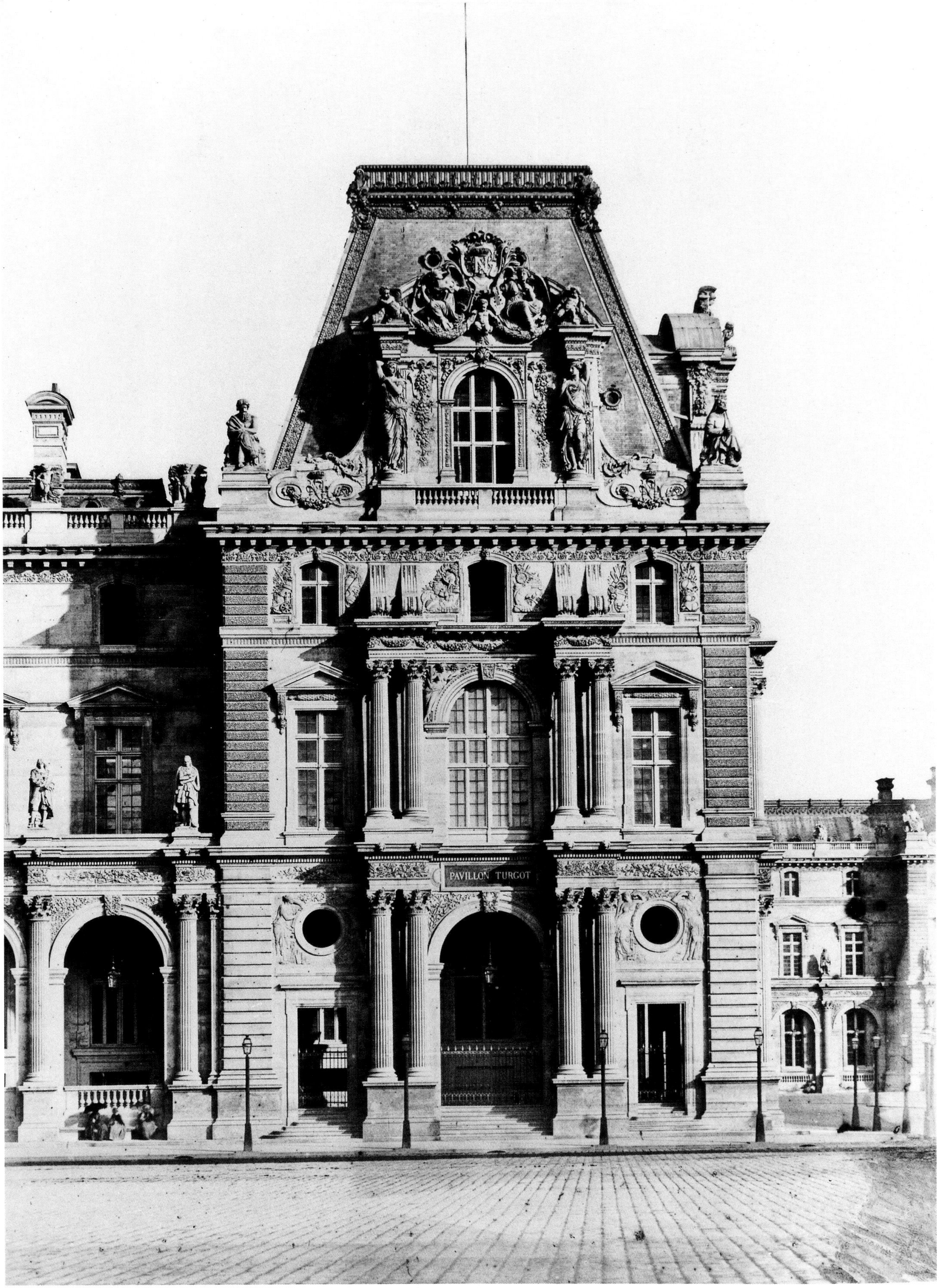
PAVILLON TURGOT

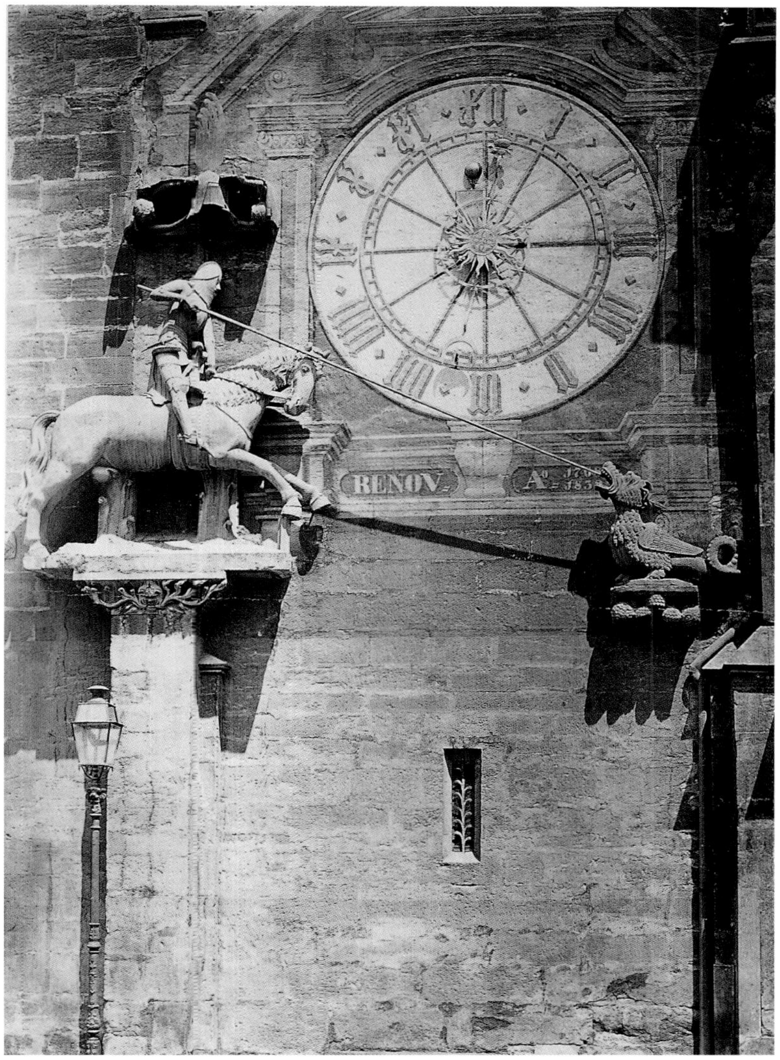

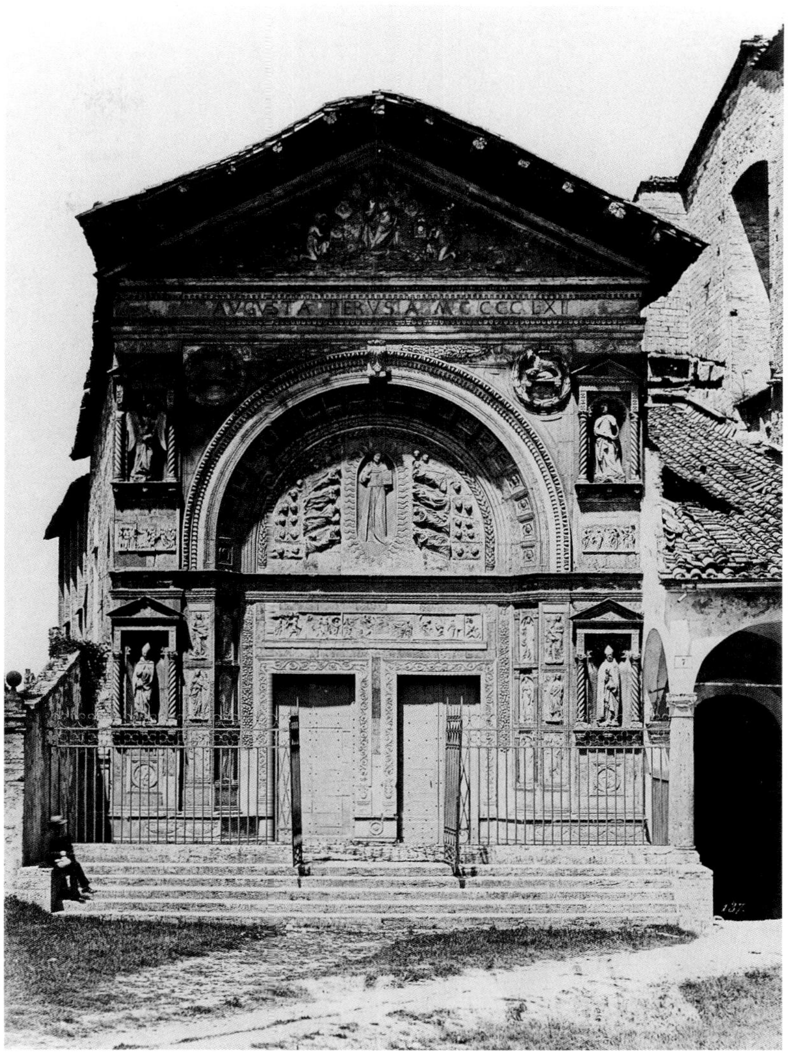

opposite

EDOUARD BALDUS (1813–1889)

Pavillon Turgot, New Louvre, Paris, c. 1856

Albumen print

Architects: Louis-Tullius-Joachim Visconti and Hector-Martin Lefuel

Baldus's documentation of the New Louvre pavilions represents the apogee of his architectural photography and its espousal of an elevational manner of composition. This severe, monumental style, decontextualizing the buildings he photographed, was reinforced on occasion by the combination printing of several negatives to achieve larger prints and by liberal retouching to remove unwanted contiguous features. The inventor of his own paper process, which he preferred for its portability, Baldus was able to use glass negatives in photographing the Louvre's pavilions, as he enjoyed the luxury of a darkroom on site and the help of twelve assistants.

above left

BISSON FRÈRES (Auguste-Rosalie Bisson [1826–1900] and Louis-Auguste Bisson [1814–1876])

Münster, Basel, 1860

Albumen print

At a time when enlarging was impossible and all printing was by contact, the large size of the Bissons' prints rendered them outstanding technical accomplishments. The great portraitist Nadar, their neighbour on the fashionable Boulevard des Capucines, related how the Bissons employed a former policeman who could coat a 100 x 80 cm (40 x 32 in.) glass plate with collodion in one arm movement without a run, bubble or speck of dust. In England the Bissons' prints were considered "rank sorcery" and sold for twenty-two shillings each. This view was probably taken when they accompanied Napoleon III on his official tour of Switzerland.

above right

ROBERT MACPHERSON (1811–1872)

Oratory of San Bernardino, Perugia

Shown at the second exhibition of the Architectural Photographic Association, 1858

Albumen print

The Architectural Photographic Association not only acted as a showcase for the period's finest architectural photographers, supplying their work to subscribers who, at the Association's peak in 1859, numbered twelve hundred and were to be found as far afield as Australia, but also organized lectures on the exhibited photographs by such luminaries as Ruskin and James Fergusson. Its hopes to lessen the cost of photographs and encourage work that, G.E. Street argued, was "not of sufficient popular interest to be done by private speculators"[18] went unrealized. Beset by financial troubles, the Association abandoned its exhibitions but continued to issue photographs intermittently until 1867.

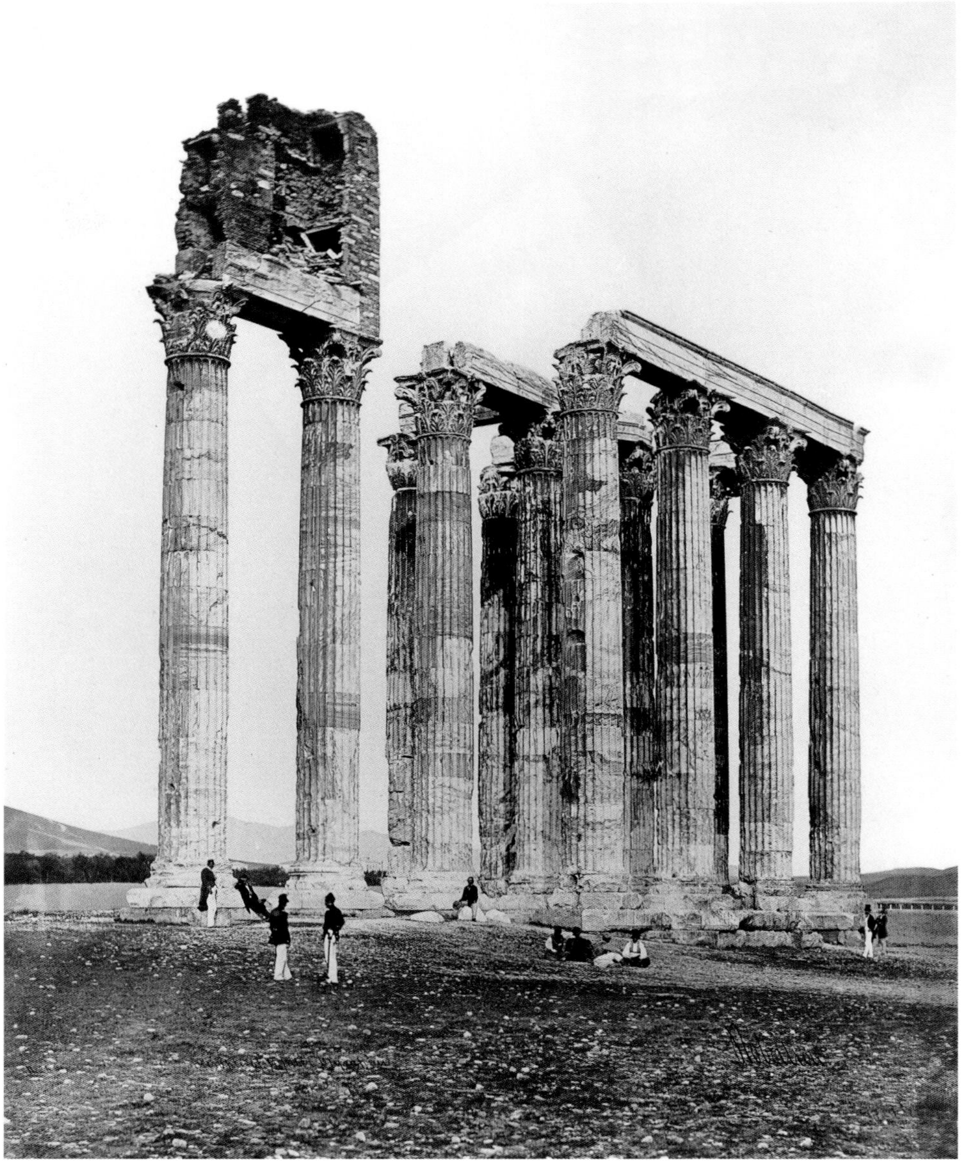

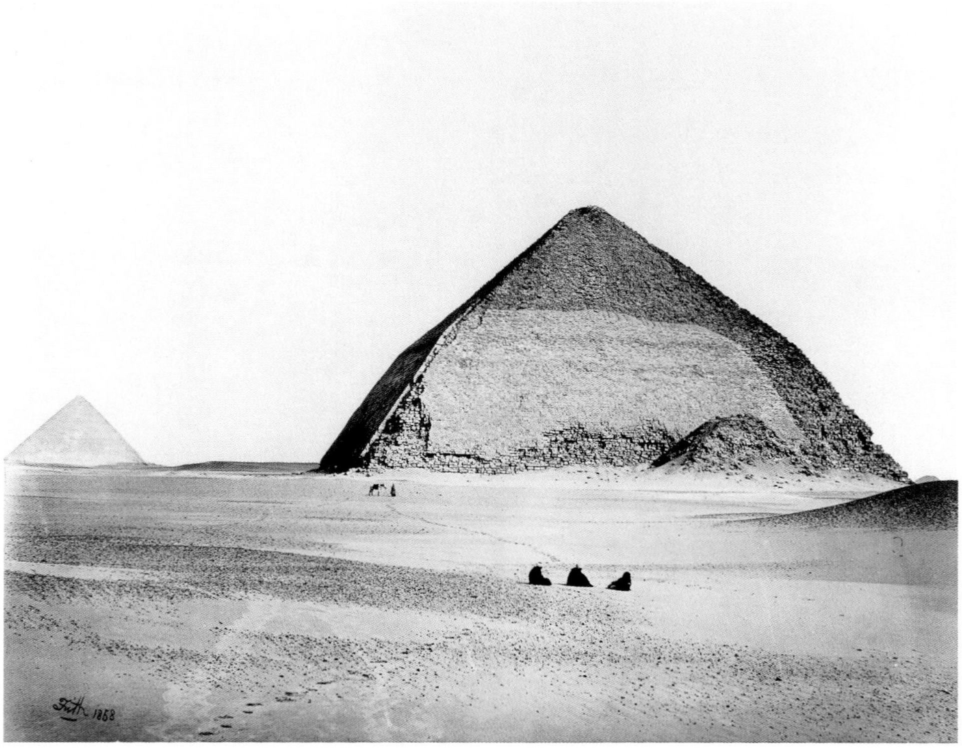

top left

JAMES ROBERTSON (1813–1888)

The Temple of Olympian Zeus, Athens, c. 1853–54

Albumenized salt print

Robertson settled in Constantinople in 1841, becoming chief engraver to the Imperial Mint. In the early 1850s he opened a photographic studio, hoping to exploit renewed interest in the eastern Mediterranean region. He photographed Greek Classical remains in 1853–54 and made subsequent photographic forays to Malta, Jerusalem and Cairo. Some of the resultant images were displayed at the Architectural Photographic Association's first three exhibitions. An album of his Greek photographs entitled *Photographic Views of the Antiquities of Athens, Corinth, Aegina etc.* was published in London in 1854 by Joseph Cundall. As here, Robertson's photographs often included carefully posed figures.

bottom left

FRANCIS FRITH (1822–1898)

Pyramids of Dashoor from the South-West, 1858

Albumen print

Between 1857 and 1860 Frith undertook three arduous expeditions to photograph ancient Egyptian monuments, travelling as far as the Nile's sixth cataract with his portable darkroom and glass plates as large as 16 x 20 inches (40.6 x 50.8 cm). He wrote: "Nothing can be more satisfactory than the performance of the collodion. I still get landscapes with the smallest aperture of the view-lens in four seconds, and have taken capital pictures in the heat of the day. I should imagine the temperature in my little tent could not be less than 130°F; the developing solution was quite hot."[39]

opposite

MAXIME DU CAMP (1822–1894)

Palais du Karnak, 1852

Salt print from Louis-Désiré Blanquart-Evrard, *Egypte, Nubie, Palestine et Syrie*, Paris (Gide et J. Baudry) 1852

Accompanied by Gustave Flaubert and backed by the French Ministry of Public Instruction, Du Camp took about two hundred paper negatives of Egyptian monuments between 1849 and 1851, of which 125 were printed by Blanquart-Evrard and published in 1852. Unlike other photographers of Egypt, such as his fellow countryman Félix Teynard, who concentrated on the emotionally charged interplay of light and shadow, Du Camp looked to photography to provide the accuracy his previous drawings lacked. Despite this tendency towards literal transcription, the hazy nature of Blanquart-Evrard's paper process employed by Du Camp lent his prints a dreamlike, timeless quality.

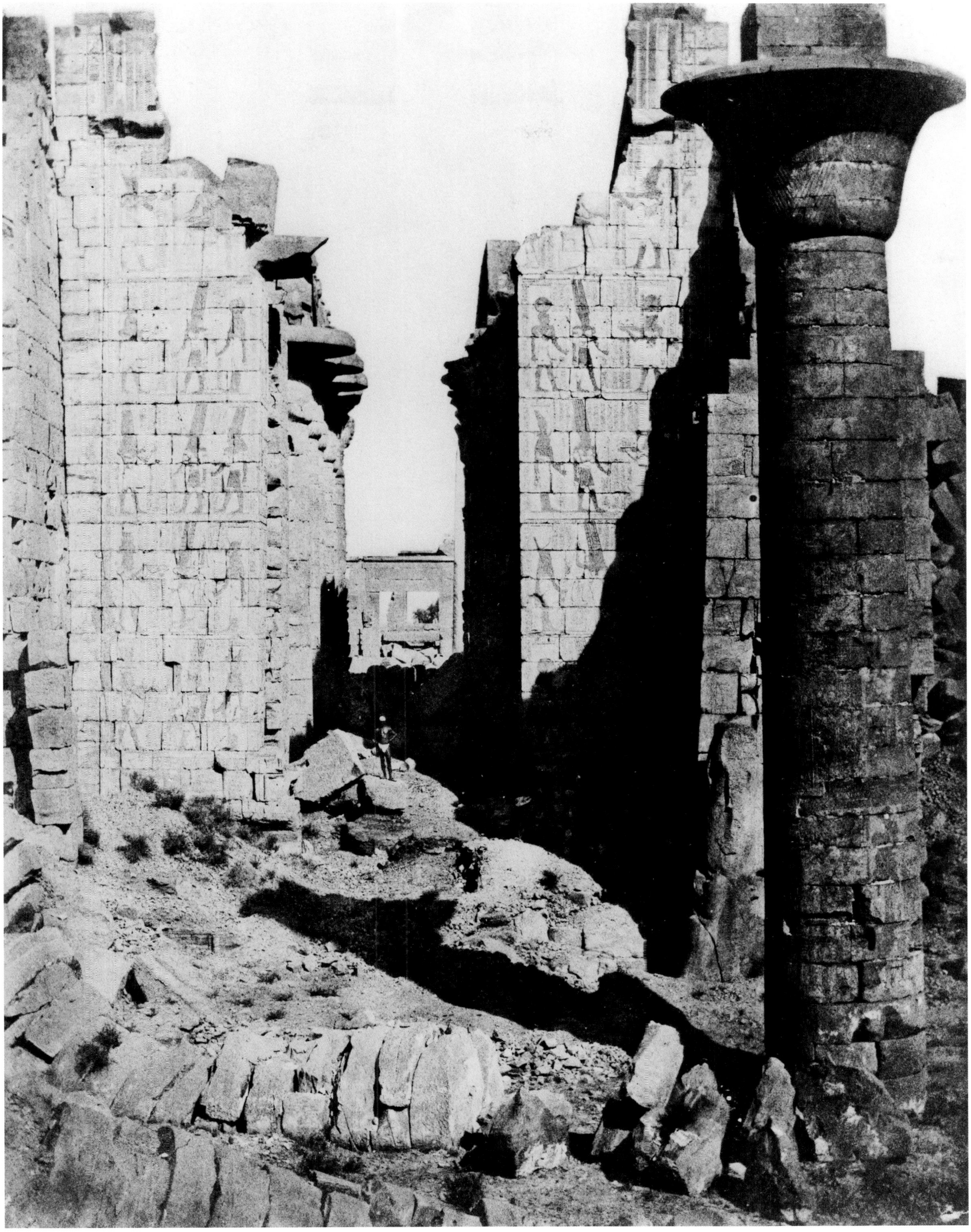

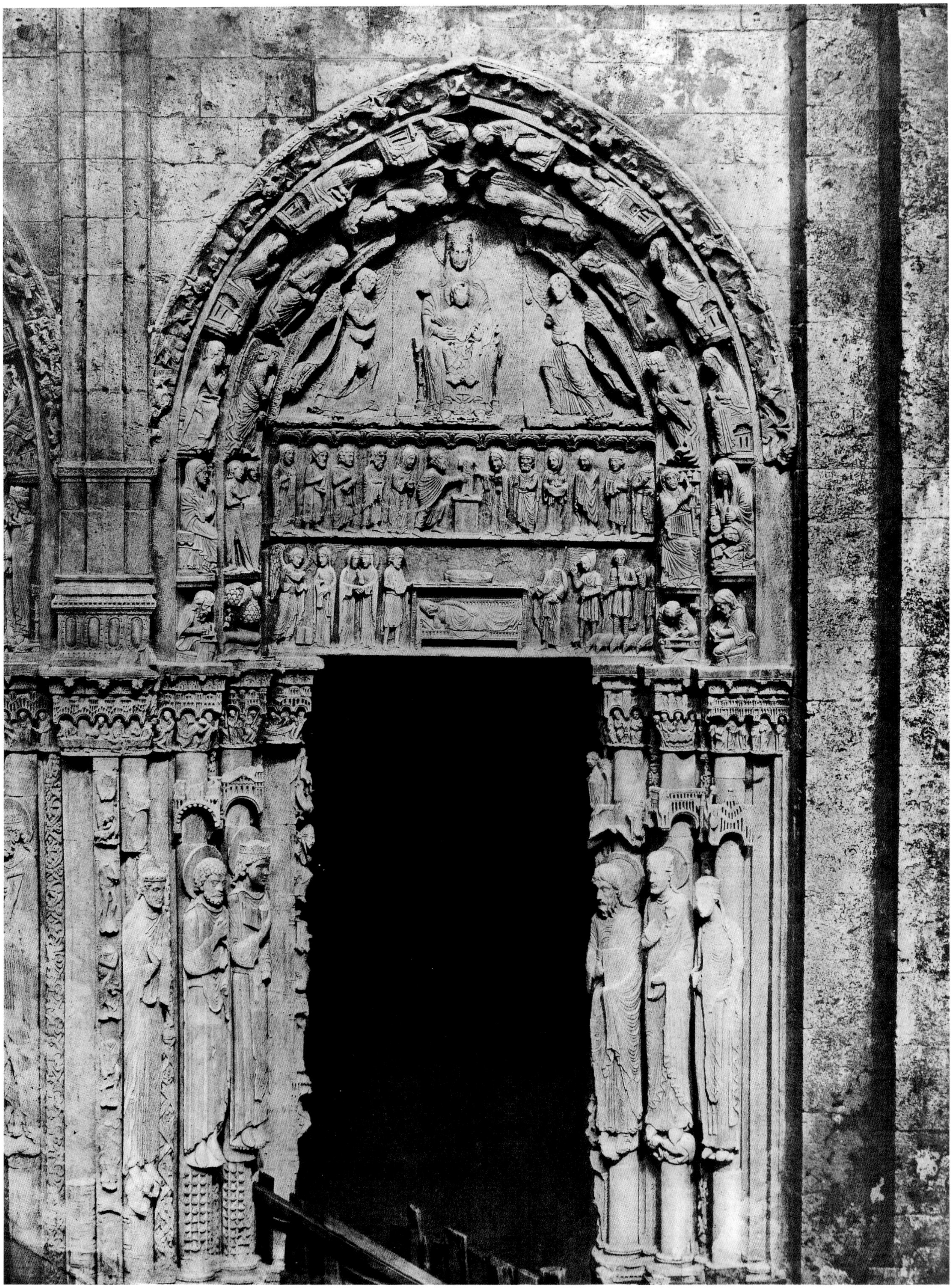

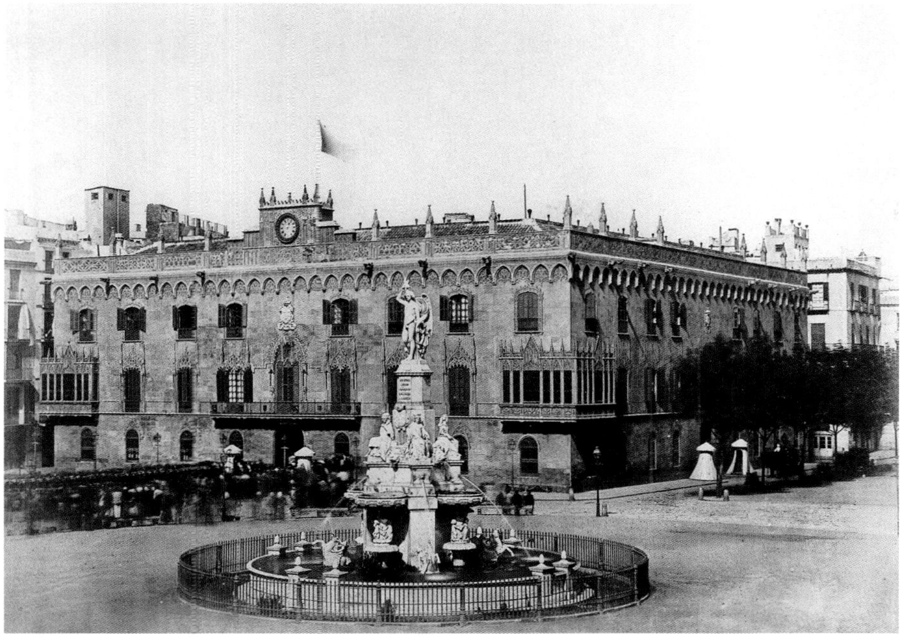

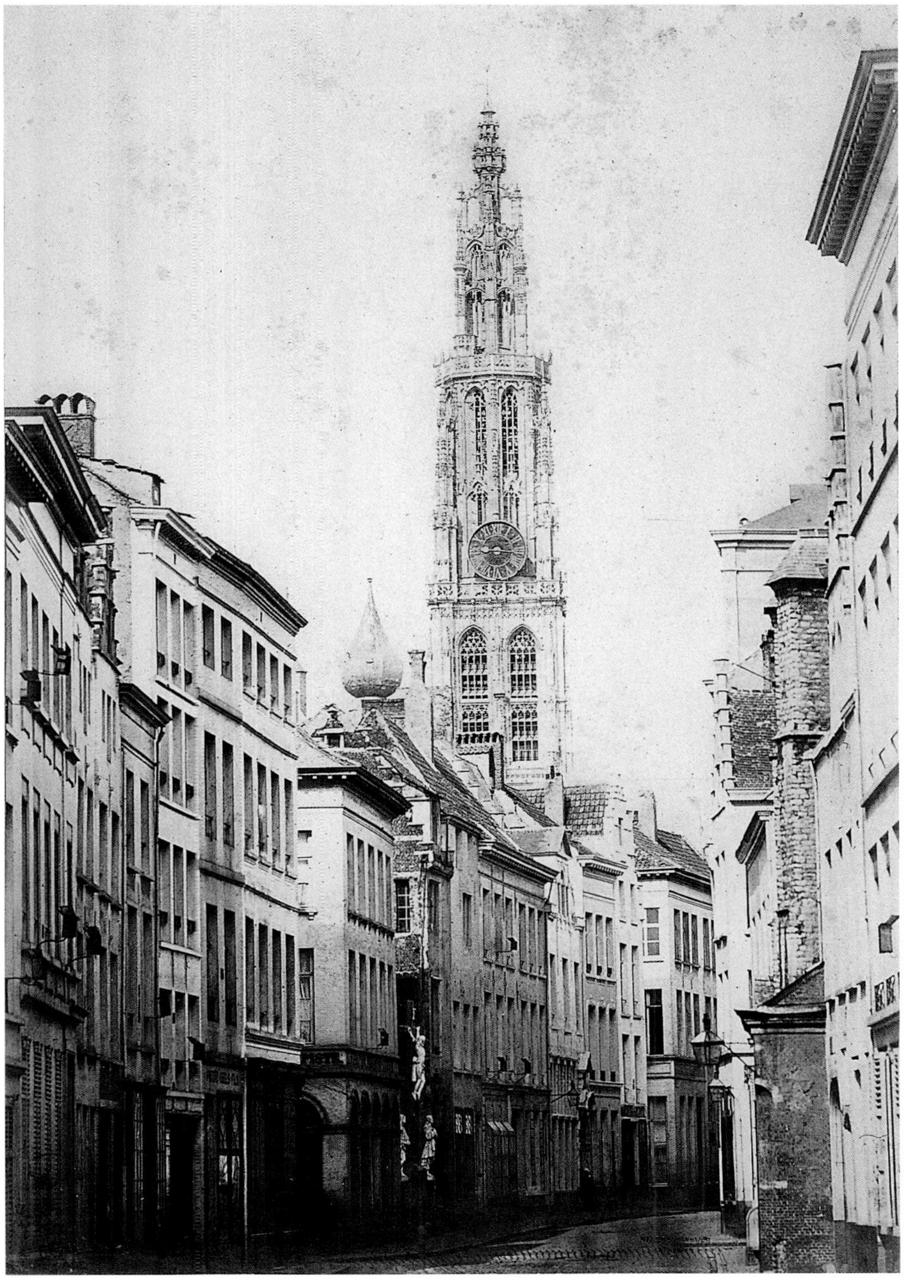

opposite

CHARLES NÈGRE (1820–1880)

Right Door, Western Front, Chartres Cathedral, 1855

Photogravure from J.B. Lassus *et al.*, *Monographie de la cathédrale de Chartres*, Paris (Imprimerie Impériale) 1867

In 1852 Nègre undertook his own 'mission' to his home territory of the Midi, where he photographed its landscape and people and proved himself a discerning renderer of architecture. Concerned about the impermanence of photographic prints, he experimented with the permanent ink reproductive process of photogravure. Thanks to the advocacy of its architect-restorer, J.B. Lassus, he won a government commission to make two photogravure plates of Chartres Cathedral in 1855, which supplemented the photographs he had already taken there. These were subsequently published in Lassus's monumental monograph, their large size conveying a wealth of detail delicately depicted.

top left

CHARLES CLIFFORD (died 1863)

Pla de Palau, Barcelona, late 1850s

Albumen print

Although Spain was not part of the Grand Tour, interest in its architecture, particularly its Moorish remains, had grown steadily during the first half of the nineteenth century. Its most important early photographers were the shadowy Lousada and the Welsh-born Charles Clifford, who settled in Madrid in 1850. Hailed as "perfectly marvelous for their intricacy of detail" and marked by subtle handling of light and shade,[40] Clifford's compositions usually placed their subjects off-centre, with important subsidiary elements filling the picture frames to their very edges. They thus differ markedly from the more classical compositions of Fenton or Baldus.

bottom left

EDMOND FIERLANTS (1819–1869)

Antwerp Cathedral from the Nieuwstraat, 1860

Albumen print

Fierlants was Belgium's most accomplished nineteenth-century architectural photographer. He worked both in his native Brussels and in Paris, where he became a founding member of the Société Française de Photographie before settling in Brussels in 1857. Specializing also in highly regarded reproductions of works of art, Fierlants was commissioned by the city councils of Antwerp (1860), Brussels (1862) and Louvain (1864) to photograph those cities' historic buildings, which, as Fierlants pointed out, were threatened by redevelopment. Influenced by Bayard and the example of the Mission Héliographique, Fierlants advocated photography as a means of creating "un inventaire vivant" or "living inventory" of Belgium's endangered monuments.[41]

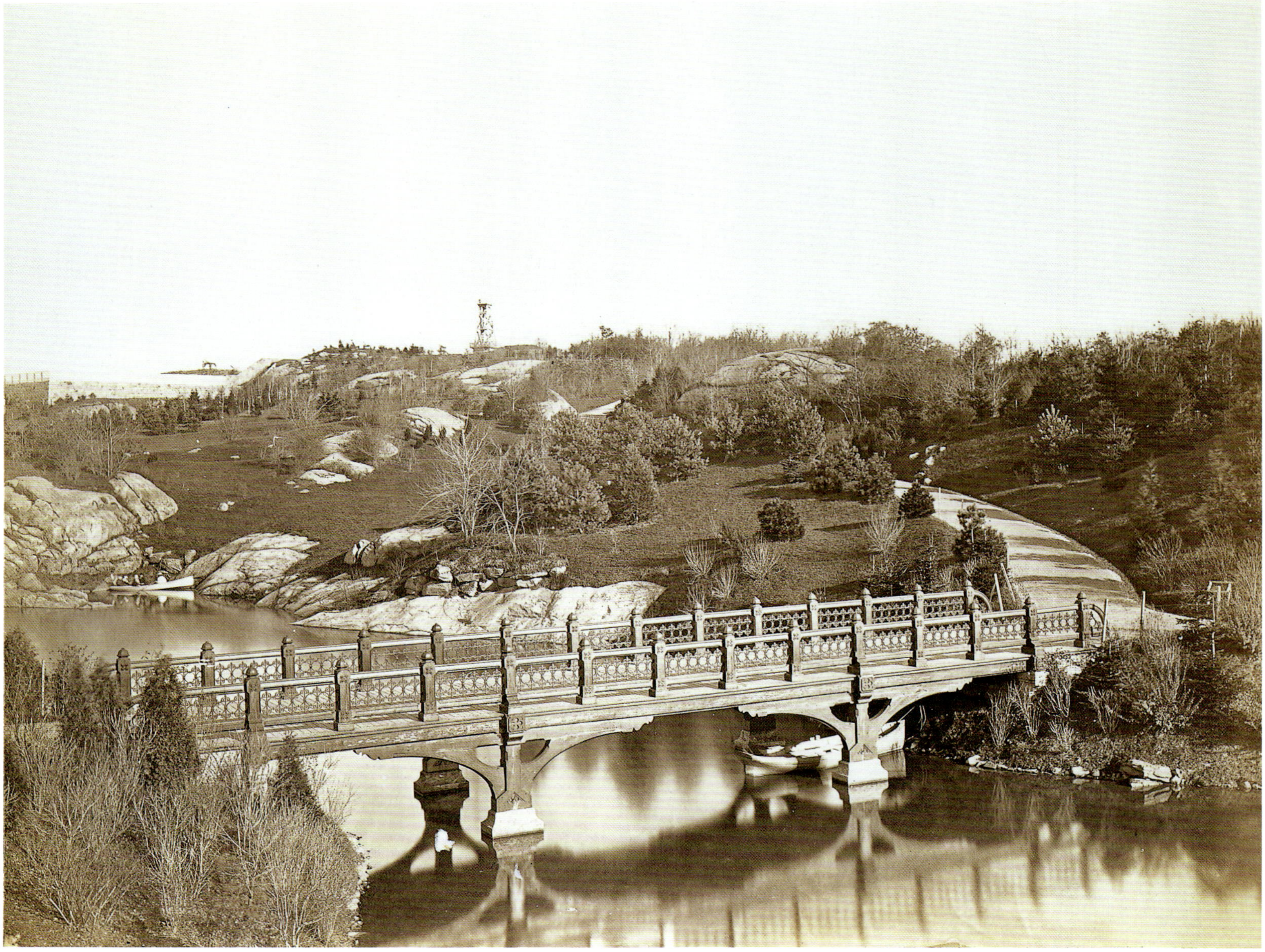

above

PHOTOGRAPHER UNKNOWN

Central Park, New York, *c.* 1860

Albumen print

Architects: Frederick Law Olmsted and Calvert Vaux

During the second half of the nineteenth century the appearance of American cities was transformed by its city parks movement. The prototype was Central Park, New York, a seemingly naturalistic but artfully designed *rus in urbe*. Although Mathew Brady photographed the site in 1857, this photograph, one of several documenting Vaux's different modes of bridge construction, is among the earliest to show the park's structures. It predates the photographs published by Prevost in *Central Park in 1862*, E. & H.T. Anthony's 1863 stereographs, and the images by W.H. Guild published in Frederic Beecher Perkin's *The Central Park* (1864).

opposite top

DR JOHN MURRAY (1809–1898)

Aurangzeb's Mosque, Muttra, 1857

Salt print

Like other British photographers in India, such as Tripe and Bourne, Murray brought a Western picturesque sensibility to bear on the monuments and landscapes he photographed – principally the Mughal architecture of north-west India. Distinguished by their delicate chiaroscuro, Murray's prints adroitly overcame the difficulties posed by the subcontinent's harsh sunlight and deep shadows. A selection of Murray's photographs was published in *Agra and its Vicinity* (London: Hogarth, 1858) and also in J.T. Boileau's *Picturesque Views in the North West Province of India* (1859). In 1861 Murray exhibited twenty views at the Architectural Photographic Association's fourth exhibition.

opposite bottom

LINNAEUS TRIPE (1822–1902)

Side Entrance to the Temple of the Great Bull, Tanjore

Salt print from *Photographic Views in Tanjore and Trivady*, 1858

Tripe's self-declared aim was "to practise Photography for some really useful purpose",[42] particularly the recording of buildings under threat. He thus photographed the intricately carved details of temples, such as that of the Great Bull at Tanjore, achieving an astonishing degree of clarity with the waxed paper process (his version differed from Le Gray's in that the negatives were waxed after, not before, processing). In addition to these close views Tripe also took photographs illustrating the building's relation to the landscape. "The Picturesque", he maintained, "may be allowed, perhaps, supplementally".[43]

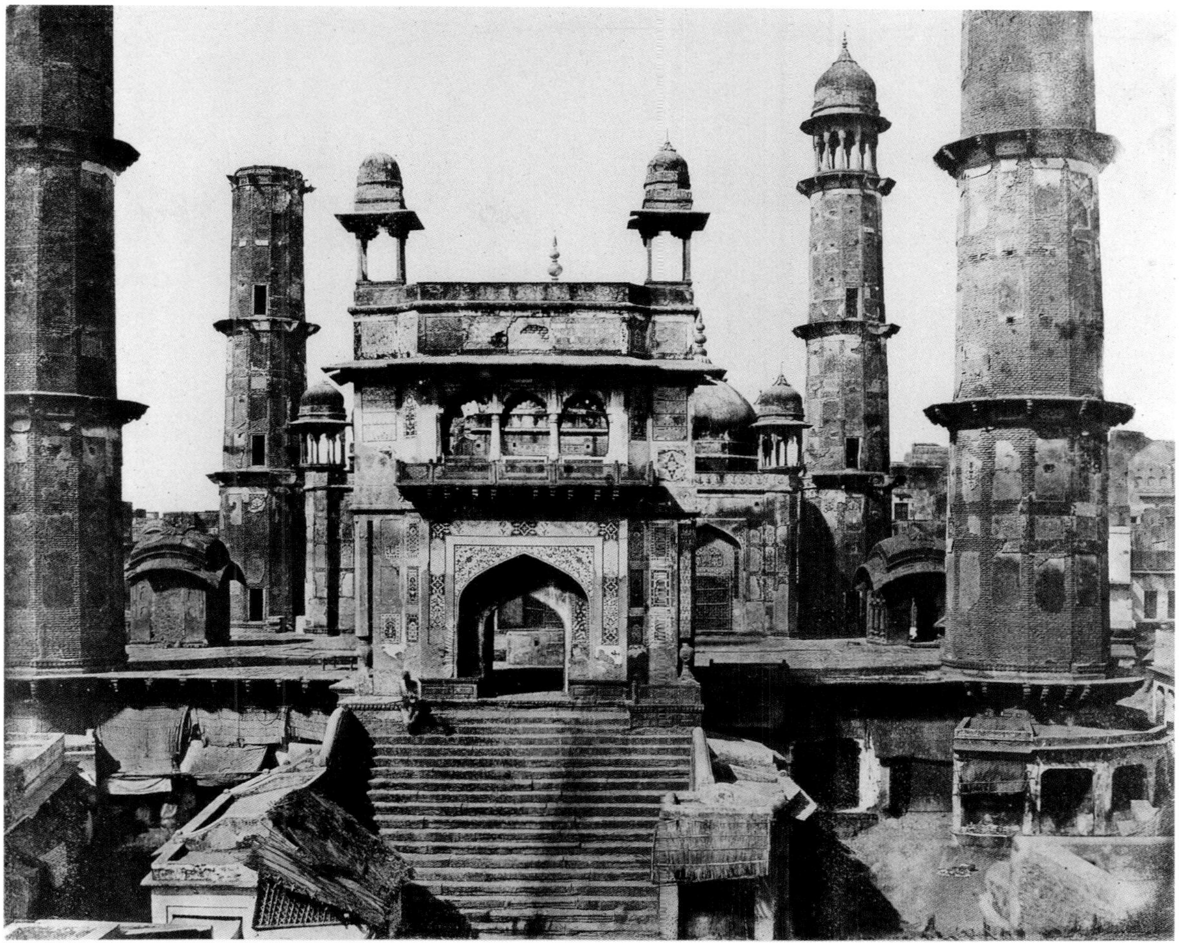

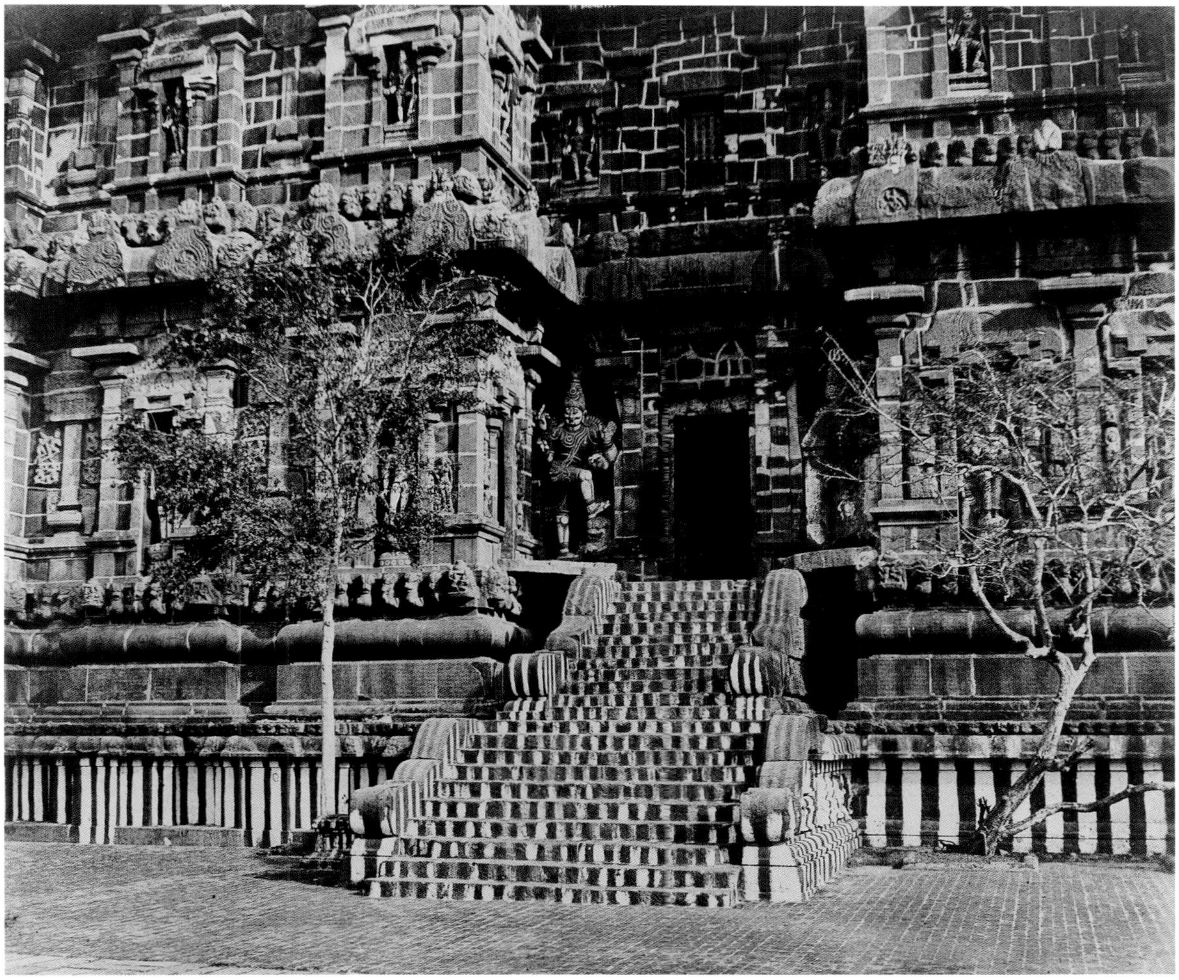

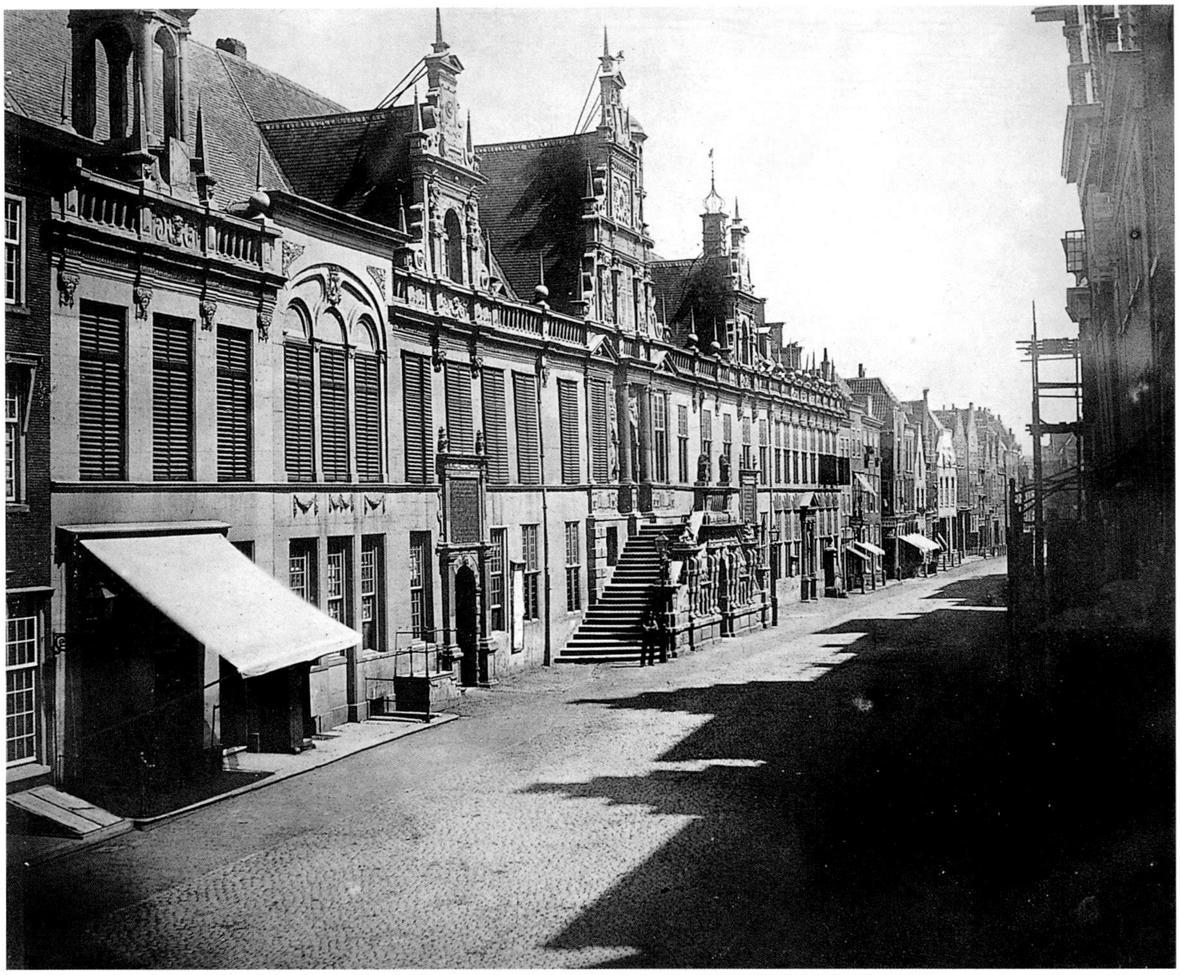

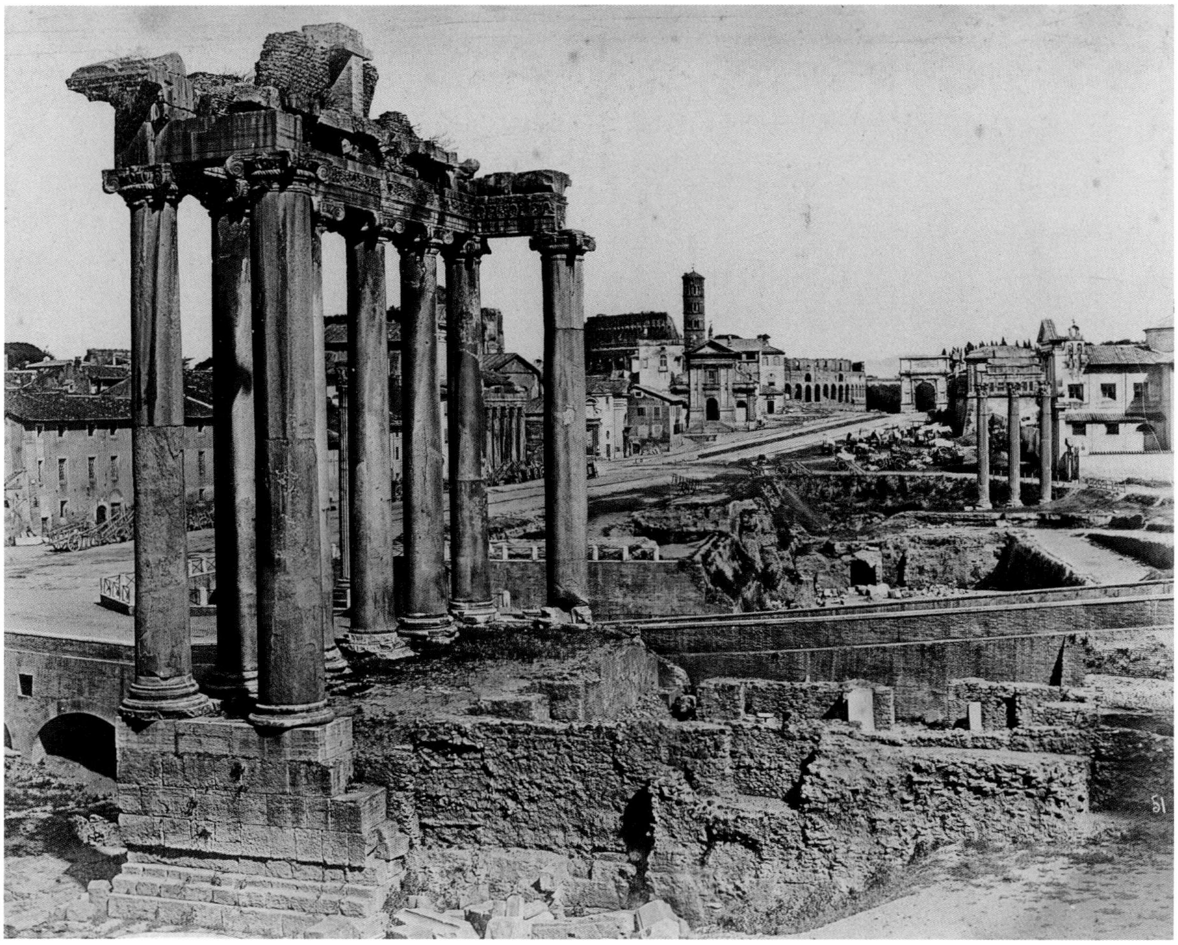
51

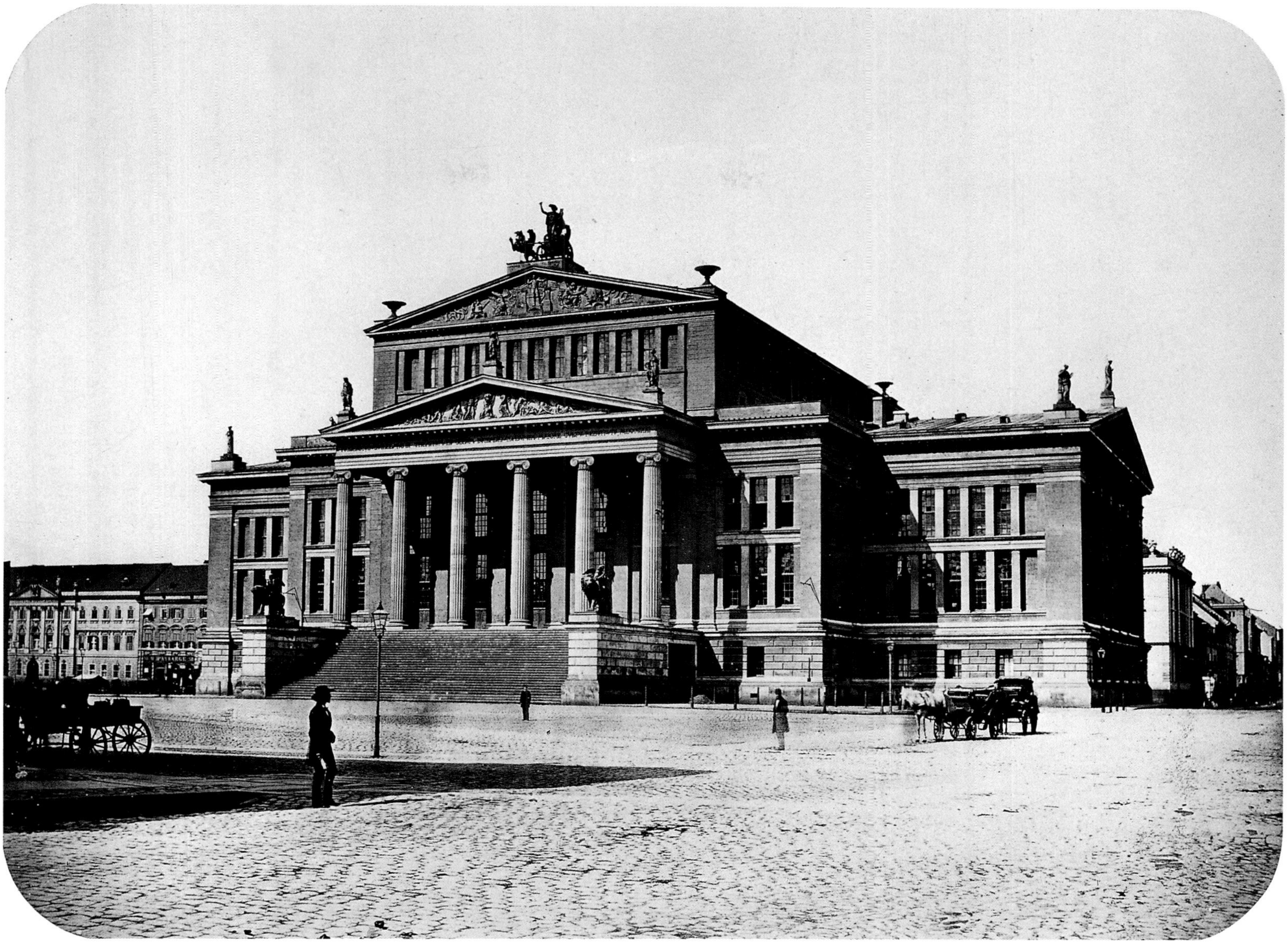

opposite top

MARIA HILLE (born 1827)

Breestraat with the Town Hall, Leiden, 1858

Albumen print

Most early Dutch architectural views were executed by foreign photographers, especially Germans such as Maria Hille, who has a claim to be the first woman architectural photographer. She photographed principally in The Hague but was also commissioned in 1859 by the Society for the Advancement of Architecture to photograph Middleburg's town hall. A single image was subsequently published in the Society's loose-leaf periodical *Illustrations of Old Existent Buildings*, the print run of which required the production of no fewer than eight hundred prints from Hille's negative.

opposite bottom

JAMES ANDERSON (1813–1877)

The Forum, Rome, late 1850s

Albumen print

A former painter and maker of miniature bronzes of sculptures, Anderson (né Isaac Atkinson in Cumberland) established in Rome in 1853 what proved one of the most successful family photographic firms (it closed only in 1960, when it was acquired by Alinari). Although Anderson specialized in artwork reproductions, architecture formed a major part of his portfolio, and his production outstripped and undercut in price that of his main rival, Robert MacPherson. Murray's *Handbook of Rome and Its Environs* (1864) hailed his images as "the best we have seen ... and of different sizes to suit all purses and purchasers".[44]

above

LEOPOLD AHRENDTS (1825–1870)

Das Schauspielhaus, Berlin, c. 1856

Albumen print

Architect: Karl-Friedrich Schinkel

The extant city views of Berlin by Ahrendts demonstrate a high level of sophistication unusual in German architectural photography of the 1850s. A former draughtsman, painter and lithographer, Ahrendts photographed the city at the height of its transformation by Schinkel in images that, though smaller than those of French photographers, were, with some degree of nationalistic hyperbole, hailed by the magazine *Deutsches Kunstblatt* as their equal "in their refinement and the clarity with which they reproduce forms, in the hazy quality of their shadows, the delicacy of toning and care in production".[45]

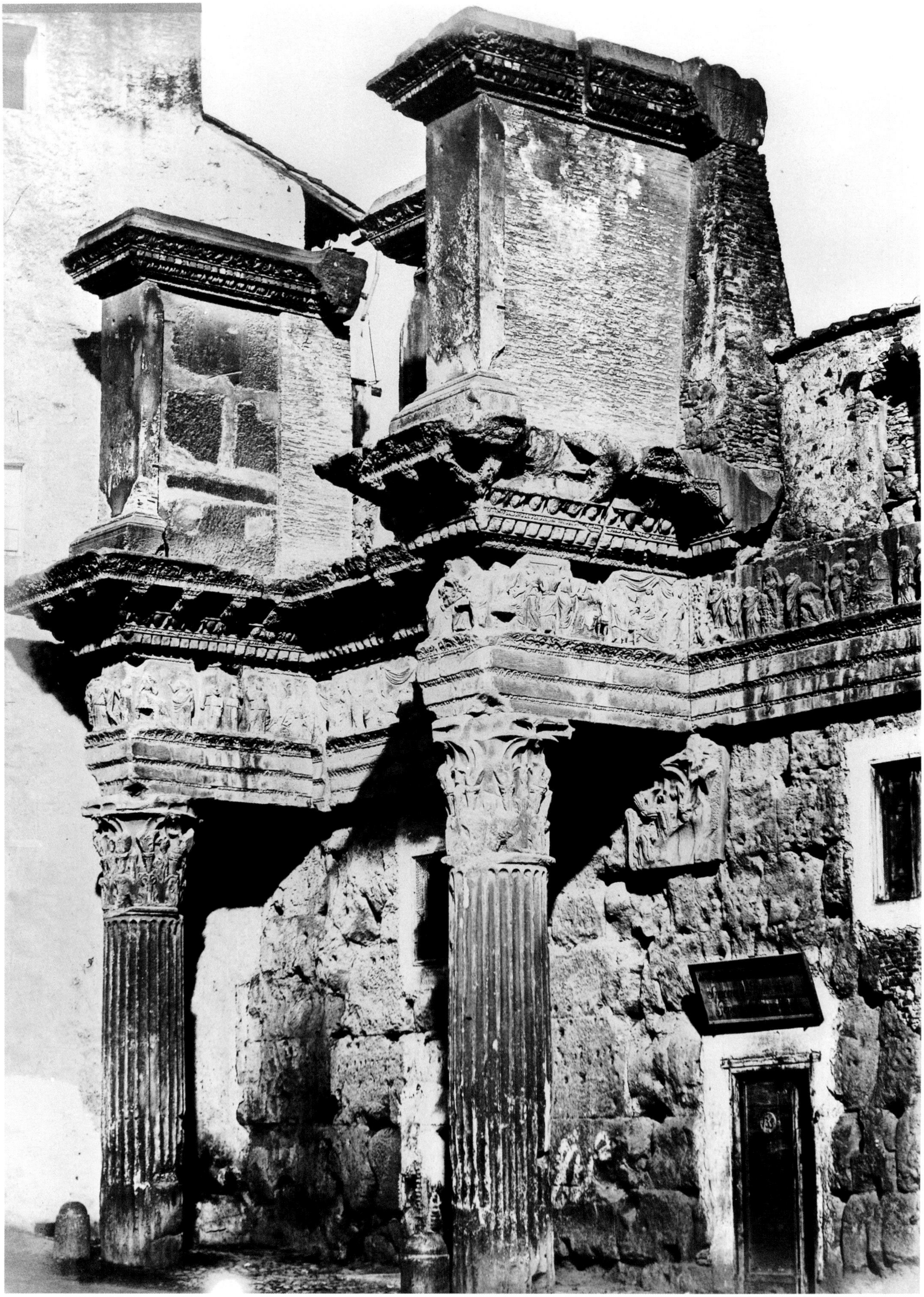

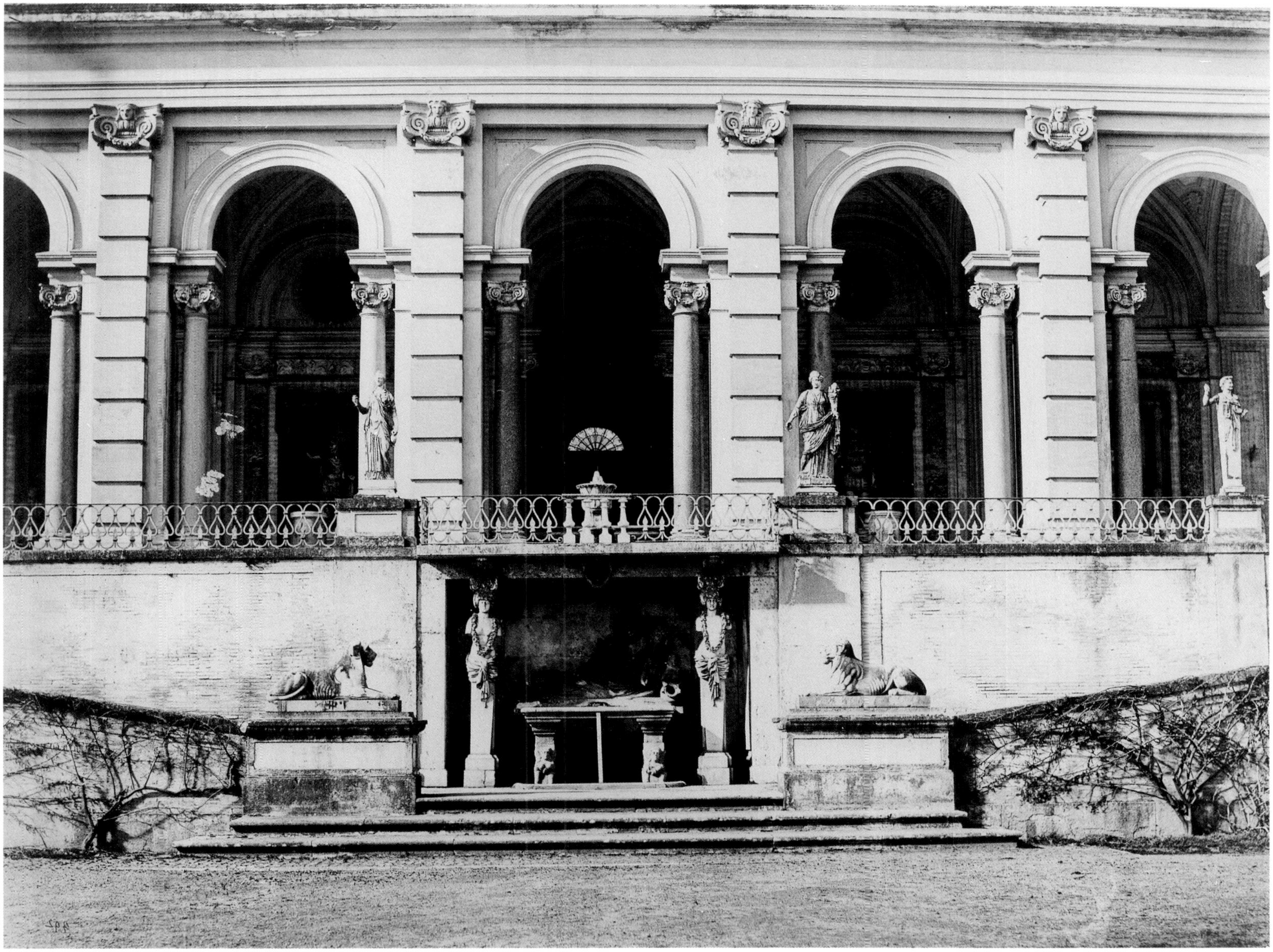

opposite

ROBERT MACPHERSON (1811–1872)

Forum of Nerva, Rome, c. 1858

Albumen print

Like his fellow Scottish photographer Thomas Keith, MacPherson trained in medicine before turning to painting and then photography. Whenever necessary, he readily sacrificed architectural details and the principles of perspective in order to conjure up the *genius loci* and a sense of the magnificence of the past. This he did admirably in his photographs of Roman antiquities, many made from viewpoints similar to those of topographical engravers, which well conveyed not only the grandeur and nobility of the remains but also that "perfection of decay" necessary to engender the appropriate emotional frisson in his Grand Tourist clients.

above

PIETRO DOVIZIELLI (1804–1885)

Villa Albani, Rome, 1859

Albumen print

This is one of forty-four photographs bought by Sir Henry Cole for five *scudi* each from Dovizielli, one of the most accomplished photographers of Rome's architectural heritage. The overtly utilitarian nature of the photographs, evident from their concentration on non-picturesque tectonic elements and the discreet inclusion of a three-foot scale, sets them apart from Dovizielli's customary tourist views.

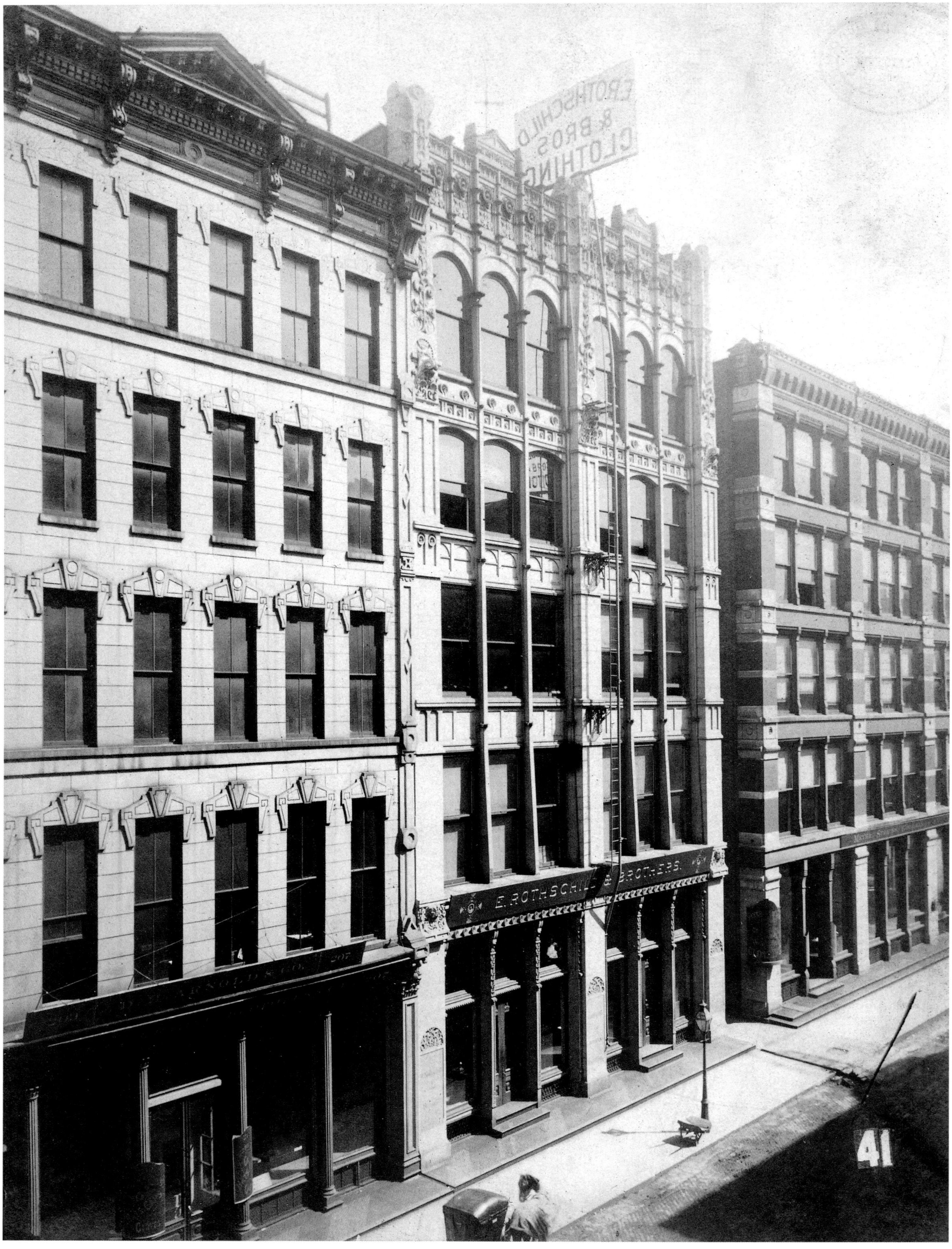
E. ROTHSCHILD & BROTHERS.
41

Chapter 2 **Volumes of Hints, Suggestions and Realities 1860–1895**

page 48

JOHN WILSON TAYLOR
(1846–1918)

Rothschild Building, 210 West Monroe Street, Chicago, 1881
Albumen print
Architects: Adler & Sullivan

In 1858 the architect Charles Robert Cockerell "looked forward to the time when, as a pictorial art, [photography] would sink in their estimation, but never as delivering to them the truth of effects, which were, above many things, essential to an architect".[1] Cockerell's wish was granted in the years after 1860 when architectural photography was dominated by large studios of topographical viewmakers and a growing number of specialist firms, whom the critic and photographer Jabez Hughes labelled "mechanical" photographers by dint of their concern to provide a literal transcription of a given scene. These practitioners were to be distinguished from those pursuing photography for nobler, more artistic ends – a division that profoundly affected the status of architectural photography. Whereas this had previously been a testing ground for improvements in the medium and had attracted the leading photographers of the day, by the early 1860s many of these, such as Fenton and Le Secq, had abandoned photography and were being replaced by a new breed of commercial entrepreneurs. As photography divided along traditional artistic lines, architectural photography was relegated to its technical or commercial sphere – a black art in which no aspiring artistic photographer should dabble. Despite this pariah status, however, it was precisely during this period that photography began markedly to influence architectural practice and study, a process aided by technological advances. Chief among these were faster films, which allowed interiors to be more readily photographed; increased camera flexibility, with features such as rising and sliding fronts; sharper lenses with a greater variety of focal lengths; and, above all, the introduction in the 1880s of commercially available gelatine dry plates, which finally freed the photographer from the burden of the portable darkroom, thereby facilitating a significant increase in the number of exposures that could be made each day.

Topographical viewmakers, such as Pascal Sébah of Constantinople and Carlo Ponti of Venice, supplied the growing middle-class tourist market created by the advent of the railway and steamship. Now it was possible to experience the Grand Tour simply by turning the pages of a photograph album filled, perhaps, with views of Egypt by Félix Bonfils, of Spain by Juan Laurent, or of India by Samuel Bourne (see pages 58–59). Using factory methods of production and a sophisticated distributive network, such topographical firms produced millions of views. By the 1880s the annual output of George Washington Wilson & Co. was around a million prints (below), and his printing works at Aberdeen stretched over half an acre. His Dundee rival, James Valentine, employed forty assistants and was producing 18,000 albumen prints each day. Bonfils had studios in Alexandria, Cairo and Alais (France), agents in New York, London and other European cities, and a well-organized mail order service. Although the images produced by these firms were not aimed primarily at architects, the regularity with which they are found in the extant collections of such figures as George Devey and Henry Hobson Richardson pays testimony not only to their sheer ubiquity but also to their architectural suggestiveness. Architecture was indeed a major component in the carefully calculated commercial strategy of topographical firms, and, even though their subject-matter was conservative and restricted to the well-trodden tourist routes (Egypt being especially popular), their images familiarized architects with a wider variety of architectural styles and building methods. In addition, through their exploitation of cheap mass-market formats, such as the stereograph (see page 61) and later the postcard, these photographers made architecture accessible for the first time to a popular audience, while their issuing of images in the form of lantern slides (see page 60) helped to transform architectural education.

Despite views by Francis Frith or George Washington Wilson of gleaming new seats of local government, or by Giorgio Sommer of the Neo-classical buildings that were beginning to adorn the streets and squares of Naples, the topographers largely ignored contemporary architecture.

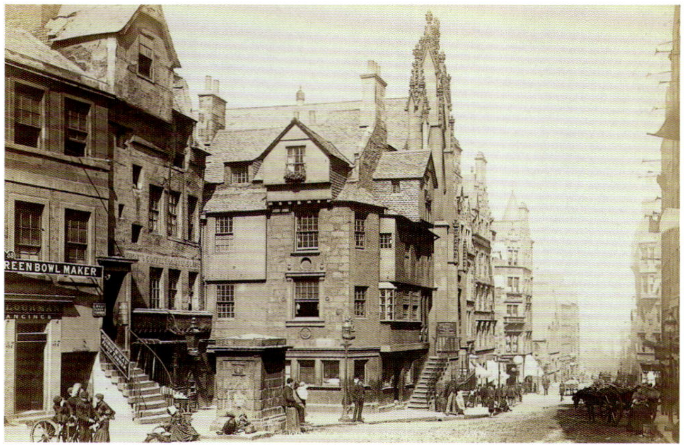

GEORGE WASHINGTON WILSON (1823–1893)

View of John Knox House and Royal Mile, Edinburgh, 1880s
Albumen print

In Greece images of the Acropolis were framed to exclude all traces of the modern city and to concentrate on the monuments of the fifth century BC in an act of editing that paralleled the earlier removal by archaeologists and architect-restorers of all vestiges of the post-Classical period (right). The 'reality' revealed by the camera had to be made to match as closely as possible the nineteenth century's visual idealization of the Athenian Golden Age as well as satisfying the cultural aspirations of Greek nationalism. In Britain the topographers extended and commercialized the amateur vision of architecture that had dominated the 1850s. Bedford's picture of an unchanging world of sleepy villages, half-timbered houses and delightful parish churches provided a photographic equivalent to the revival of vernacular architecture pioneered by Devey, Richard Norman Shaw and George Bodley, and drew its inspiration from the same sources – a continued attachment to the values and idioms expressed in topographical watercolour paintings and foreboding about the onward march of industrialization.

If the subject-matter of the topographers was strictly controlled, so too were their methods of depicting buildings, which aimed above all at what Wilson termed "the genuine presentment of the object under consideration".[2] Despite the large number of competing companies and the fact that, even though they might bear a single maker's stamp, most topographical photographs were taken by a variety of employees or represented stock purchased from conveniently placed local photographers, stylistic homogeneity prevailed. Both Frith and Fratelli Alinari (see page 63), for example, issued strict guidelines to their assistants to ensure a unified vision. In addition, the practice of companies swapping images and marketing them as their own served to underline further those images' interchange-ability, even though some studios – Sébah, Bonfils, Alinari for instance – maintained high standards and a certain distinctiveness. In their treatment of architecture, it was general views, not details, that were the norm. The creative use of light and shadow that had characterized the best architectural photography of the 1840s and 1850s was eschewed for pictures taken in even light, allowing "all the parts ... to be equally sharp and perfect".[3] The personal view of the photographer was suppressed in favour of sober, matter-of-fact presentation. The topographers not only determined what their audience saw and how they saw it, but also implied that theirs was the only way it could be seen. Far from decrying photography's status as a mechanical craft, these photographers took advantage of it to validate the authenticity of their views. For their audience, the photograph became invisible – an open window on to a scene to be studied or enjoyed. As Cockerell implied, the anonymous nature of this viewmaking struck a chord with architects seeking to fill their exemplar albums with bald presentations of the tectonic facts.

Beyond the tourist-orientated world of the topographical photographer the photography of contemporary buildings, which had been at a premium during the 1840s and 1850s, during the next decades became a matter of routine (see pages 64–65). Architects wanted photographs to keep track of their works in progress and to impress prospective clients, fellow architects or the public at large. Clients were similarly anxious to have their creations commemorated. These developments, combined with the unprecedented building boom throughout Europe and America in the latter part of the century, created a new demand for architectural imagery. Even so, many of these images were made not by specialists but by generalist photographers, such as E. & H.T. Anthony & Co. of New York, for whom architecture was but one small part of a much wider portfolio, or by obscure jobbing professionals to whom the only references today are to be found in the yellowed pages of nineteenth-century street directories.

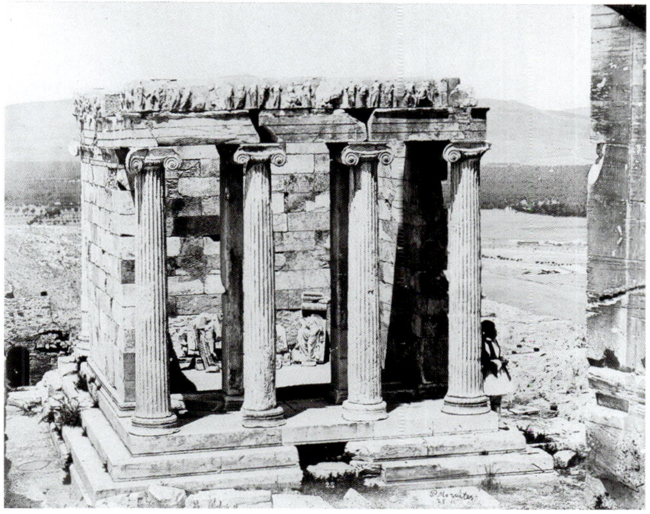

P. MORAITES

Temple of Athena Nike, Acropolis, Athens, 1875

Albumen print

The market for architectural photography remained uncertain, and diversification was seen as the key to economic success. Even those firms for whom architectural views constituted a significant proportion of their work found it commercially imperative to include other subjects in their repertoire, most often the reproduction of artworks or industrial photography. Fratelli Alinari and Thomas Annan of Glasgow were key instances of the former, the Parisian firm of Delmaet & Durandelle a good example of the latter. It was this firm in its various manifestations that was responsible for documenting several of France's most prestigious building projects, including Charles Garnier's Paris Opéra (1875; see page 68), Paul Abadie's Sacré-Coeur (begun 1875) and Contamin & Dutert's Galerie des Machines at the Paris International Exposition of 1889. In so doing, it produced some of the period's most iconic images, which not only matched Delamotte's appreciation of modern constructional methods but also foreshadowed the work of Constructivist photographers of the 1920s. Although such companies as Delmaet & Durandelle were successful in attracting private clients, many firms continued to be heavily reliant on patronage by central or local government. Thus Auguste Hippolyte Collard was commissioned by the French Ministry of Agriculture, Commerce and Public Works to record bridges, railways and aqueducts, and Médéric Mieusement, best known for his photographs of the château at Blois, worked for more than twenty years from 1876 for the Commission des Monuments Historiques.

Given the vast amount of building activity and the repeated assertions by architects that architectural photography required specialist expertise, it is surprising how few firms made it their sole or even prime concern. The most prominent company in this respect, far outstripping such American rivals as John Wilson Taylor of Chicago (see page 48), for example, was Bedford Lemere & Co., whose photographs have done most to fix our image of late Victorian and Edwardian British architecture (see page 70). Although it photographed buildings from the start, its concentration on architecture gained added momentum when, in 1881, Harry Bedford Lemere joined the firm that had been established twenty years before by his father. Counting among its clients architects, builders, decorators and owners, the company was the first to exploit successfully the growing market for architectural photography. By 1895 it was advertising 50,000 views for sale, either singly or in sets, all taken on 12 x 10 inch (30.5 x 25.4 cm) glass dry plates, used mostly with a mahogany Meagher bellows camera. The sets, usually in the form of gold-toned albumen prints or more occasionally carbon or platinum prints, covered a wide range of topics – Classical, Romanesque and Renaissance details; town and country houses and mercantile buildings; and decorative and antique furniture. They were also distributed internationally through such agents as Albert Levy of Paris and New York (one of the period's most influential publishers and distributors), to whose *Albert Levy's Architectural Photographic Series* Bedford Lemere & Co. contributed. The company's stock thus formed one of the richest sources then available for the study of British architecture. Furthermore, in terms of both subject-matter and technique, the firm's output marked a new era in British architectural photography rejecting the picturesque conventions that up to then had governed its practice.

In sharp contrast to the photographers of the 1850s, Bedford Lemere & Co. concentrated almost wholly on new buildings and the urban environment. Meticulously crafted, the photographs, either by Lemere himself or one of the three to four other photographers the company employed, were usually taken in dull, diffuse light using very small lens apertures. This technique required long exposures and hence excluded people, but it did facilitate the overall sharp definition insisted upon by the company's clients, to whose wishes the photographers were obliged to defer. Similarly, the views were framed not for pictorial effect but to convey the maximum amount of information on a single plate. Unlike topographical photographers working in Britain, for whom the building was generally part of a larger scene, for Bedford Lemere & Co. it was the essence of the composition and, in defiance of picturesque orthodoxy, its surroundings were largely ignored. This isolation of the building from its context, together with a conception of the photographer as self-effacing recordist, rendered the firm's photographic aesthetic similar to that of Italian topographical viewmakers, especially Fratelli Alinari who knew and admired the British company's work.

One of the most important aspects of late nineteenth-century architectural photography was the way in which photographers responded to rapid urbanization. While some, such as Anthony, Wilson and Valentine Blanchard, issued 'instantaneous' views, which from the late 1850s attempted to capture the city in all its dynamic energy, Lemere's treatment of the urban milieu as static, the aggregate of an orderly procession of individual, monumentalized buildings, was the more characteristic. Here the photographer was cast in the role of apologist for the new civic order, helping to promulgate the message of civilization and progress that civic leaders declaimed from their platforms and to which architects sought to give reality on the streets. Typical are the photographs of Corporation Street and other Birmingham civic landmarks taken by Thomas Lewis in the 1870s, which proved him to be he most effective visual propagandist for Joseph Chamberlain's ambitious programme of urban reform, and the 1878 publication by Alfred Brothers, *Manchester As It Is*, whose forty autotype plates[4] and eulogistic text presented the 'real' Manchester as a city of wide streets and handsome buildings, unrecognizable as the sink of urban squalor denounced in the writings of Friedrich Engels and Elizabeth Gaskell.

It was in America, however, where the use of photography as a form of urban boosterism reached its apogee. There, in photography's early decades, the panorama and the image made from an elevated viewpoint looking down the street to emphasize the effect of spatial recession had been favoured compositional devices. Both, however, made it difficult to suppress unsightly elements before the introduction of a greater range of camera movements allowed photographers to work increasingly at street level and to achieve tighter, more controlled framing. The result was a heavier emphasis on individual buildings at the expense of urban context and streetscapes. This is shown clearly in the plates in *L'Architecture américaine*, a three-volume photographic anthology published in Paris in 1886 by André, Daly fils et Cie, in which the focus is entirely on decontextualized single buildings, and elevated viewpoints are chosen only when it would otherwise have been impossible to encompass the whole building within the frame. Canonized by the photographer, the architectural set piece became the prime indicator of urban refinement (see page 75). Like those of Victorian architecture by Lemere & Co., these views by American photographers underlined the ruggedly individualistic and eclectic nature of American architecture of the Gilded Age and the way in which buildings derived their rationale from within, from a reading of their richly allusive decoration, rather than from any sense of compatibility with their neighbours. A markedly different ideal was propounded by the World's Columbian Exposition of 1893 in Chicago, where Beaux-Arts classicism and axial planning were presented as the harmonious antidote to the stylistic promiscuity of the preceding decades. Consequently, it was photographed in an entirely different manner. Charles Arnold, the official photographer to the exposition, expressed its values through sweeping vistas and high-angle views, which pictured the individual buildings as integral parts of the grander unified whole of what was dubbed the White City (see page 76).[5]

Photography was used not only to celebrate the 'improved' city but also, as the scale of rebuilding intensified concern for the past, to document buildings being swept away. Both aspects can be seen in the work of Charles Marville, who from the late 1850s was commissioned by Haussmann's Préfecture of the Seine to record areas earmarked for demolition, together with the demolition works themselves and the resultant new streets and buildings (see page 77). Working under the auspices of the Service des Travaux Historiques, and officially named Photographe de la Ville de Paris in 1862, Marville was one of the first photographers to engage fully with urban planning. His survey was both comprehensive and systematic, with each street being photographed twice from reverse angles together with its destruction and subsequent transformation. These photographs were meant to be read not individually but as part of an unfolding sequence that gave a unique insight into the process of urban renewal.

Similar in intent, though compositionally very different, were the 10,000 photographs taken by Georg Koppmann & Co. from 1872 onwards for Hamburg's building authorities. These images documented both the city's condemned old quarters and their replacements, such as the new Free Port that opened in 1888 (see page 76). By contrast, the photographs made by Thomas Annan for the Trustees of the Glasgow Improvement Scheme from 1868 onwards of the wynds (narrow streets), closes and tenements scheduled for demolition were more limited in extent but informed by the same concern to preserve a record of the city's disappearing urban fabric (see page 79). This concern was a key theme of Annan's architectural photography, as revealed in two

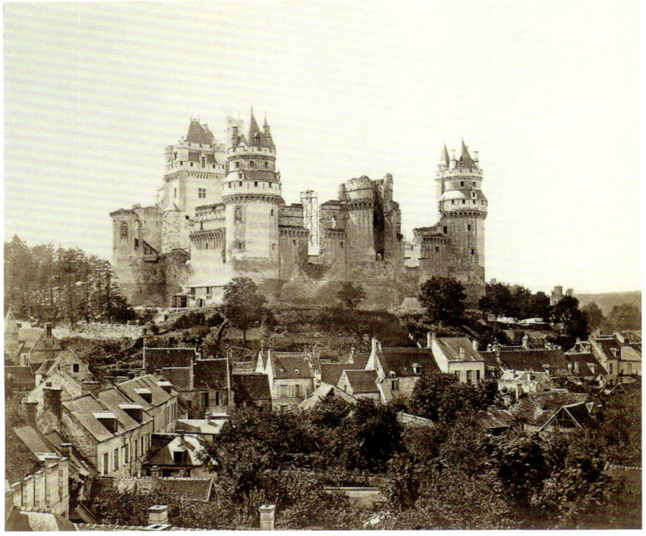

CUNDALL DOWNES & CO.

Château, Pierrefonds,
early 1860s
Albumen print
Architect for restoration: Eugène-Emmanuel Viollet-le-Duc

publications contemporaneous with his work for the Trust, *The Old Country Houses of the Old Glasgow Gentry* (1870) and *Memorials of the Old College of Glasgow* (1871), and in his fear that Glasgow would come to look "almost as new as Chicago".[6] Annan's Trust photographs, which were small in number – only thirty-one were taken between 1868 and 1871 – and had a limited but extremely complex distribution, were therefore not conceived as part of a campaign for social reform, as were the views published in Jacob Riis's celebrated *How the Other Half Lives: Studies Among the Tenements of New York* (1890), with which Annan's are often compared. Unlike Riis, Annan was uninterested in the city's inhabitants and took no interior views. Nevertheless, his photographs represent an early attempt to use the camera to record some of the sordid realities of slum housing, a venture completely subverted by the two posthumous 1900 editions of his images, in which liberal retouching and the mellowness of the photogravure reproductions effectively distanced the spectator from the subject in a way very much in keeping with the softer pictorial vision then in vogue.

Although infused with an element of nostalgia, especially in Annan's case, all these officially commissioned photographs implicitly endorsed the improvements made. The photographs of threatened buildings issued by the Society for Photographing Relics of Old London (SPROL) were, however, a testament to the period's increasing cultural pessimism (see page 79). The Society was established in 1875 by a group of friends anxious to record the doomed Oxford Arms, one of London's oldest inns, and was wound up in 1886. Although the views themselves, taken initially by A. & J. Bool and then from 1877 by Henry Dixon and his son, T.J. Dixon, were largely unremarkable, the Society was an important force in drawing attention to lesser-known buildings and in reinforcing the increasingly common argument that historic structures of whatever period or style could be significant, not just on account of any architectural merit they might possess but also as a living testament to a past way of life. This notion of the building as a record or piece of evidence, which informs SPROL's photographs, similarly underlay the subsequent formation of a plethora of local amateur photographic preservation groups in Britain as well as bodies elsewhere, such as the Deutsche Heimatschutzbund, which emphasized the role of photography in helping to preserve German traditional architecture and culture. The result was a significant enlargement of the range and scope of buildings that came before the camera's lens.

Besides recording endangered buildings, photography was increasingly used as an aid to restoration (left). After his initial experiments with the daguerreotype, Viollet-le-Duc continued to make heavy use of the medium to the extent that Merimée caustically remarked, "Viollet no longer carries pencils."[7] In his *Dictionnaire raisonné de l'architecture française* (1866), Viollet argued that

> Photography has naturally led architects to be still more scrupulous than before in their respect for the slightest vestiges of an ancient arrangement, and to take more accurate observations of the construction; while it provides them with the permanent means of justifying their operations. Photography cannot be too sedulously used in restorations; for very frequently a photograph discovers what had not been perceived in the building itself.[8]

Viollet's championing of photography in restoration was echoed in England by Ruskin and that other great nineteenth-century restorer, Sir George Gilbert Scott, who recommended its use in *Conservation of Ancient Monuments and Remains: General Advice to Promoters of the Restoration of Ancient Buildings* (1865) and recounted its valuable role in recording the carved and moulded stones lying among the debris after the collapse of the tower of Chichester Cathedral in 1861 so that "we were not left to conjecture for any detail of the tower, and much was refixed in the new work."[9] Scott also utilized Victor Prout's photographs in his position of Surveyor to the Fabric of Westminster Abbey, as did George Austin with his own photographs at Canterbury Cathedral. In The Netherlands photography's importance in restoration and conservation was given official sanction by the establishment in 1874 and 1875 respectively of the Board of National Advisers for the Monuments of the History of Art and the Department of Arts and Sciences within the Ministry of Internal Affairs, while in Italy the architectural theorist Camillo Boito was a key figure in advocating photography before, during and after restoration.

The use of photographs in restoration and to record architects' works saw them firmly established as essential tools in the architect's office, where they were also used to copy drawings and even occasionally in photomontages, a technique employed, for example, by the Florentine architect Giuseppe Poggi. Of even greater importance was the role of photographs as exemplars or what one critic termed "volumes of hints, suggestions, and indeed realities, ready for transplanting into new work".[10] The search for precedents underlay the architectural creativity of the late nineteenth century and photography, prized for its fidelity and rapidity, greatly expanded their supply. One of the most impressive collections of photographic exemplars was assembled by the American architect Henry Hobson Richardson. Including French, Spanish, Italian and English examples, Richardson's photographs were carefully arranged for ease of consultation, either topographically or by building feature, and formed a key part of his outstanding library. As one student reported, "Inspiration is the key-note of Mr. Richardson's idea in the student's training ... your eyes are arrested by the choice selection of photographs of mediaeval and other architecture which cover every available wall-space, so that the student when wearied with his pencil may refresh his vision and mind by a study of what is around him."[11] Richardson fed these exemplars into his own highly successful work, although the historian Henry-Russell Hitchcock contended that photography had a debilitating effect on his use of ornament: "As he grew ever busier he became more satisfied with detail best described as bad photo-sculpture of old work."[12]

The British architect John B. Gass, who visited America as a Royal Institute of British Architects Godwin Bursary holder in 1885, observed that, whereas British students at the Royal Academy were busy sketching and making measured drawings of parts of buildings, their American counterparts were "getting the whole impression, sketching little, but buying photographs to which they could refer for details".[13] Richardson's compatriot, the architect and writer Russell Sturgis, assembled an even larger collection of more than 15,000 photographs, which included works by Baldus, Clifford and Bonfils. McKim Mead & White also avidly collected photographs, chiefly of the buildings of antiquity and the Renaissance, which they bound into more than one hundred scrapbooks and quarried as sources for their Classical Revival architecture. In Spain in the early 1870s the young Antoni Gaudí's imagination was fired by his close study of heliotype reproductions of photographs acquired by the Escuela de Arquitectura de Barcelona, which included images of Spanish buildings by Juan Laurent, Frith's Indian series, and others of Egypt and Palestine. These were to be important sources for the oriental strain in Gaudí's architecture. In England, John Loughborough Pearson began collecting photographs in the mid-1850s, which helped to crystallize his design ideas: his best-known church, St Augustine, Kilburn, north London (1870), owes an obvious debt to the cathedral at Albi, of which he possessed photographs. Mieusement's photographs of the château at Blois (see page 56), owned by Aston Webb, were the inspiration for Webb's Victoria Law Courts, Birmingham (1886–91), designed with his partner, E. Ingress Bell. Similarly, Samuel Bourne's photographs informed John Norton's Indian interiors of Elveden Hall (1871) – a compliment returned by William Emerson, who took with him to Calcutta "many scores of photographs of the most beautiful or famous classical buildings in the world" in an attempt to persuade his clients to build in the Classical style.[14]

Although photography was employed to advocate or justify particular styles, its overall effect was to exacerbate the period's rampant eclecticism. As T.R. Smith, Professor of Architecture at University College, London, lamented, "foreign travel, photography and the multiplication of all kinds of pictorial illustrations, have made all the art of the past the

SÉRAPHIN-MÉDÉRIC MIEUSEMENT (1840–1905)

Château, Blois, 1860s

Albumen print

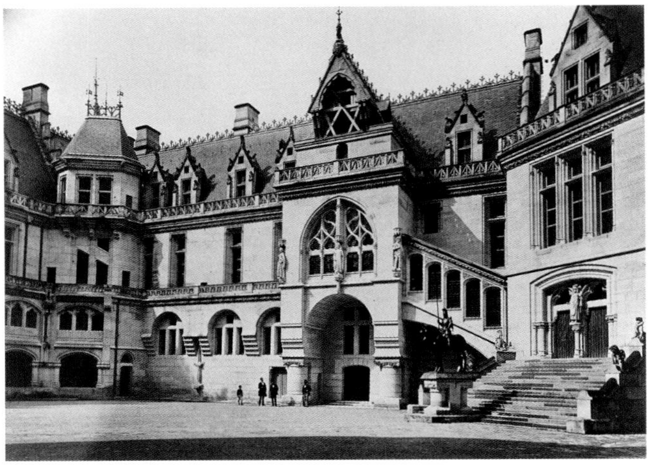

property of the present ... our very wealth of knowledge is always likely to prevent our universal adherence to any one style or manner in art."[15] If James Hay's design for the Anglican cathedral at Liverpool (1886; below right), a photographically inspired melange of architectural styles, seemed to confirm Smith's worst fears, contemporaries were divided as to whether the ready availability of architectural photographs constituted a boon or a millstone. William Burges feared that it would lead to servile copyism; Scott, like Smith, that it would inevitably doom attempts to create a style that would reflect the spirit of the age. The American critic Montgomery Schuyler opined that it placed an added responsibility on the architect to "admire rightly" and "with discrimination".[16] The Scottish architect Hippolyte Blanc, himself a keen photographer, took a more positive view:

> By the camera the best examples of old and modern work are weekly circulated among the architectural profession, so unknown gems of architectural art are distributed, and an increasing supply of new materials disseminated. As water poured into the pump of a dry well will start anew a water supply, so shall the supply of a knowledge of old forms inspire new.[17]

In addition to its use by practising architects, photography was critical to the methodology of a growing number of architectural historians and critics. For Cockerell the camera had placed "the perfect history of architecture" before the nineteenth century.[18] Not only did photography furnish historians with more, and more reliable, evidence of the past, it also fitted well with the new scientific-empirical approach to history, with its fetishistic insistence on garnering the facts. Above all it facilitated comparison, allowing geographically widespread buildings to be compared with one another and the creations of the present to be measured against the products of the past. One of the historians who took advantage of these attributes was Viollet-le-Duc, who, besides using photography in his restoration work, employed photographs extensively in his voluminous historical writings, often basing his research and drawings on them. As he had never visited the country, his observations on Russian architecture, for example, in *L'Art russe* (1877) were largely founded on the photographs and other source material sent to him by the Director of Moscow's Museum of Art and Industry, Viktor Butovsky.[19] Viollet did not, however, use photographs indiscriminately but argued that the purely mechanical act of photography imparted only a superficial knowledge of buildings and that true understanding could be attained only through the more analytical process of drawing.

The same point was made by Ruskin, whose initial enthusiasm for photography soon waned to such an extent that he claimed "a square inch of man's engraving is worth all the photographs that ever were dipped in acid".[20] Even while growing increasingly hostile to photography in his public pronouncements, however, Ruskin continued to use photographs for didactic purposes, especially as visual aids for educating artisans at his Guild of St George and its museum, established in Sheffield in 1878, and in his

JAMES HAY (1823/24–1915)

Unexecuted Design for the Anglican Cathedral, Liverpool, 1886

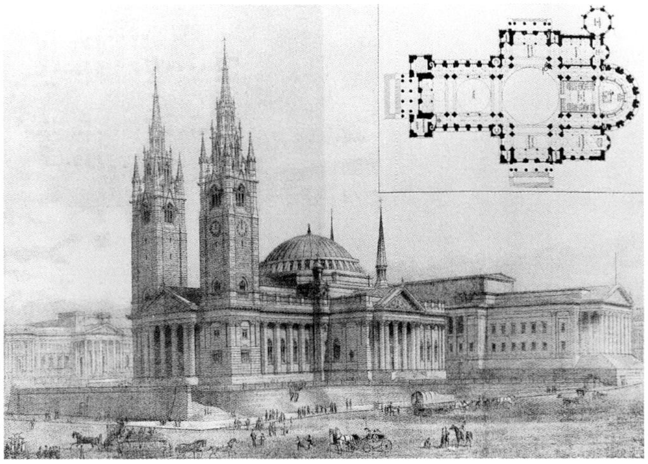

publications, such as *The Bible of Amiens* (1880–85). This was illustrated by twenty-six original photographs that Ruskin considered afforded a unique insight into the cathedral's sculptural decoration. For Ruskin, as for Viollet, photography was a working tool. Unlike Viollet, however, who used photography to buttress the vast synoptic sweep of his writings, for Ruskin, who concentrated on the small scale, photographs were a supplement to, not a substitute for, the personal experience that remained at the heart of his architectural exploration.

Ruskin's friend and fellow Gothic enthusiast John Henry Parker, whose reissue of Robert Willis's classic *Architectural History of Canterbury Cathedral* (1867) included tipped-in photographs, pioneered photography's use in the study of Roman remains. *The Archaeology of Rome*, published in thirteen parts between 1865 and 1877, contained an impressive 3391 photographs but was not a success, mainly due to the disparity between the attempted scientific objectivity of the images and Parker's text, which was marred by his tendency to treat legend as history. Parker's work, too, found little favour with an architectural profession determined to forge its own identity separate from the archaeologists. One of its most important historians, James Fergusson, demanded that the Royal Institute of British Architects "write over its doors, 'Archaeology is not architecture'".[21] Indeed, it was Fergusson himself who proved to be one of photography's most committed and influential advocates. His copious writings were marked not just by the extent to which he employed photographs but also by the careful and systematic manner in which he deployed them. This was shown above all in his publications on Indian architecture, which were illustrated either by pasted-in original photographs or by wood engravings that had mostly been copied from photographs in his own large collection.

Chief among these were the three ambitious photographically illustrated works produced under the auspices of the Committee of Architectural Antiquities of Western India in 1866, to which Fergusson contributed architectural commentaries – *Architecture at Ahmedabad*, *Architecture at Beejapoor* (above right) and *Architecture in Dharwar and Mysore* (see page 82) – all of which vividly illustrated the role of army photographers in documenting India's sadly neglected architecture. For Fergusson, the chief merit of photography, besides its accuracy, was that it made buildings legible – they could be 'read' and hence classified and compared. This quality was put to good effect in his *History of Architecture in All Countries from the Earliest Times to the Present Day* (1865–67), which was the first comprehensive history of world architecture to be written in the English language. Illustrated with wood engravings largely redrawn from photographs by, for example, John Thomson of Cambodia, Felice Beato of China and Ephraim Squier of Peru, the history was praised for the accuracy of its illustrations and for being full of "suggestive comparisons between types of buildings usually regarded as far remote from one another, architecturally as well as topographically".[22] Fergusson's example was followed by Banister Fletcher, whose long-lasting textbook first appeared in 1896 under the title *A History of Architecture for the Student, Craftsman, and Amateur being a Comparative View of the Historical Styles from the Earliest Period*. This novel form of comparative history owed much to photography; the hope expressed by *The Builder* in 1858 that photography would introduce a new age of more extensive 'parallels' appeared to have been amply fulfilled.[23]

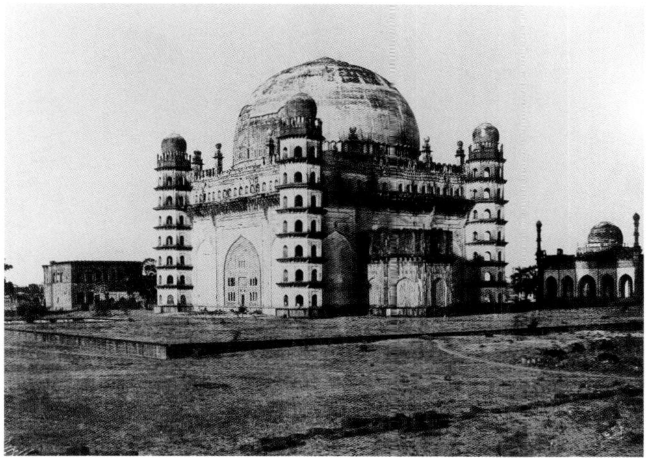

COLONEL THOMAS BIGGS (1822–1905)

The Gol Goomuz. General View, 1856

Albumen print from Philip Meadows Taylor and James Fergusson, *Architecture at Beejapoor*, London (John Murray) 1866

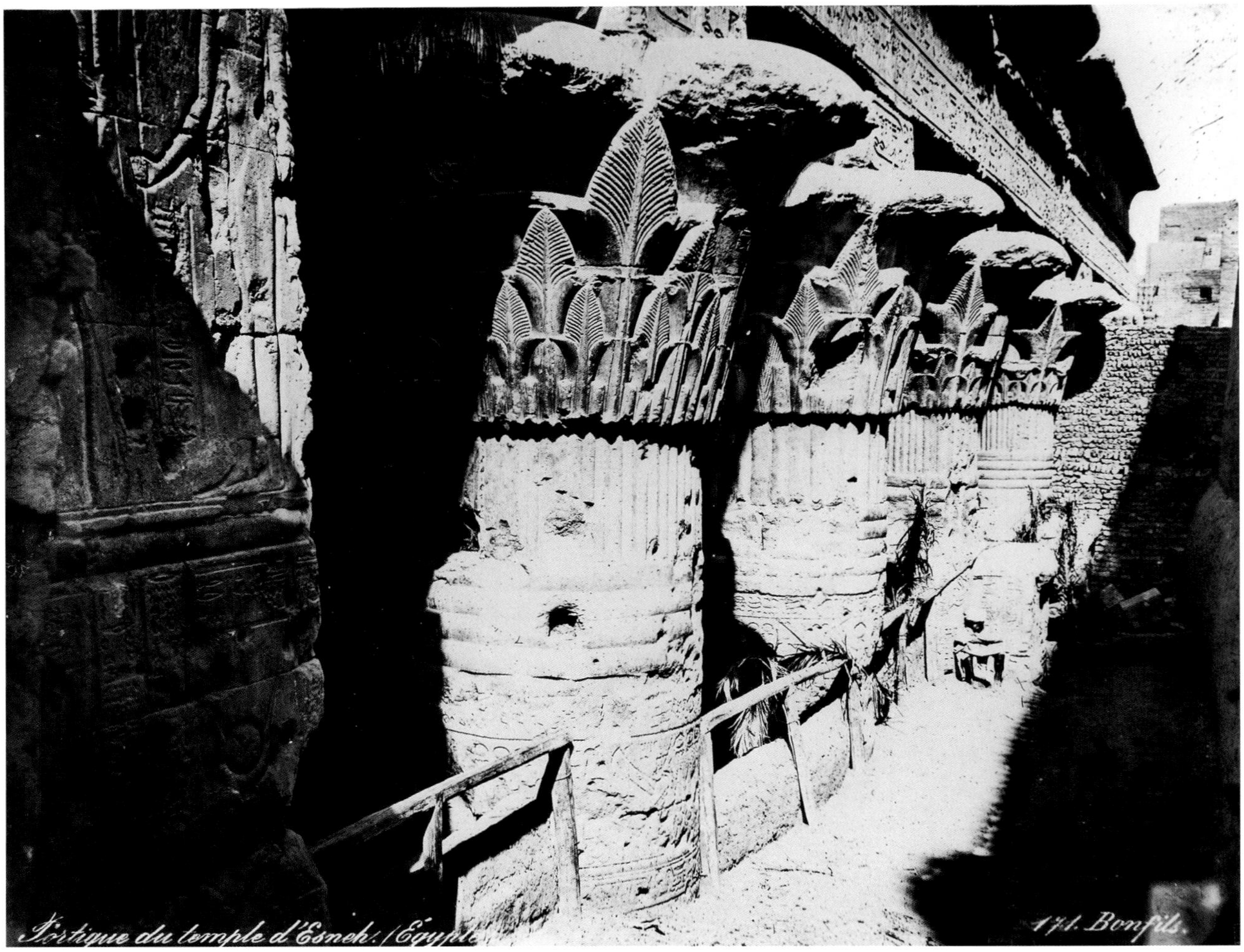
Portique du temple d'Esneh. (Egypte
171. Bonfils.

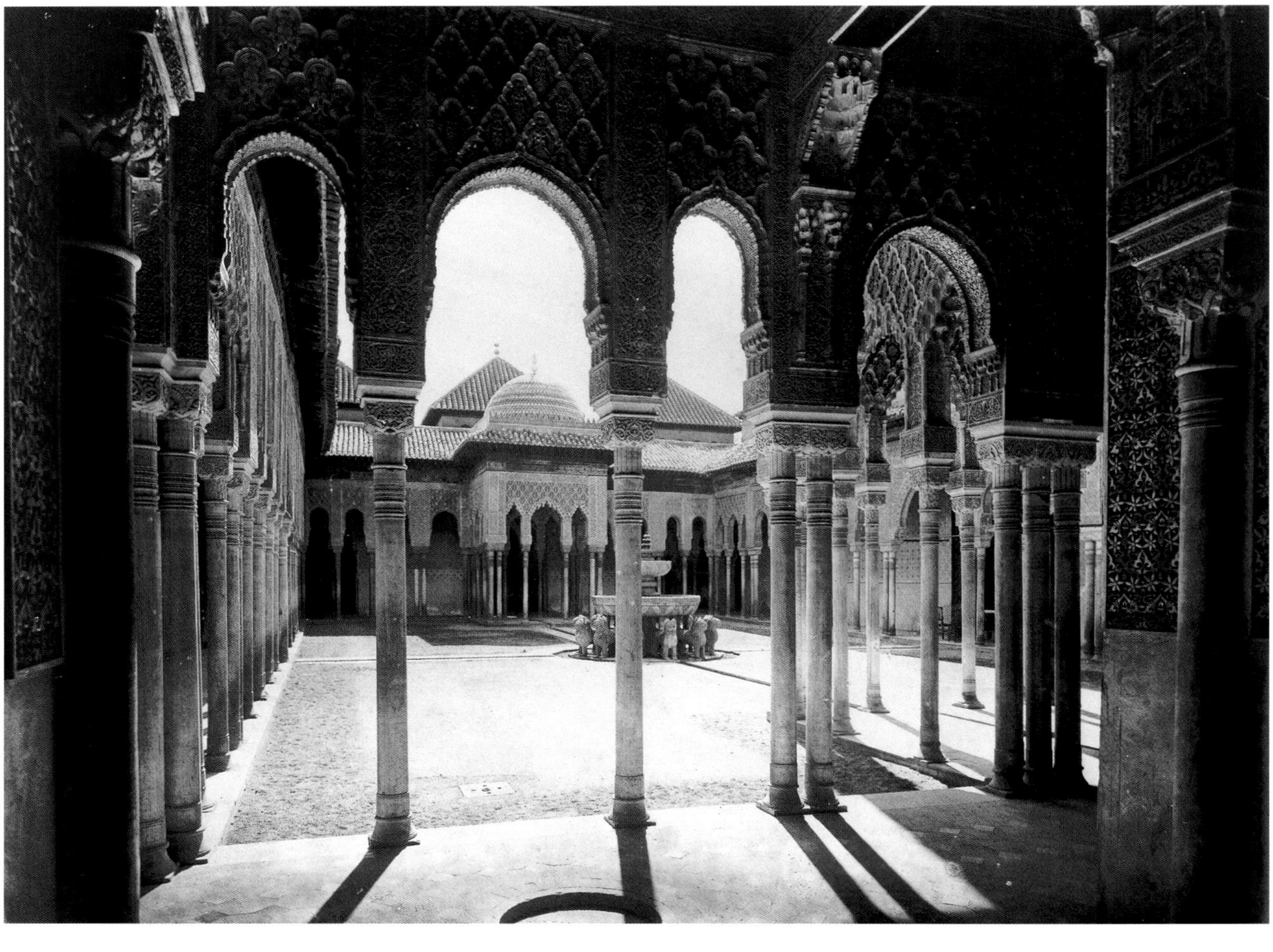

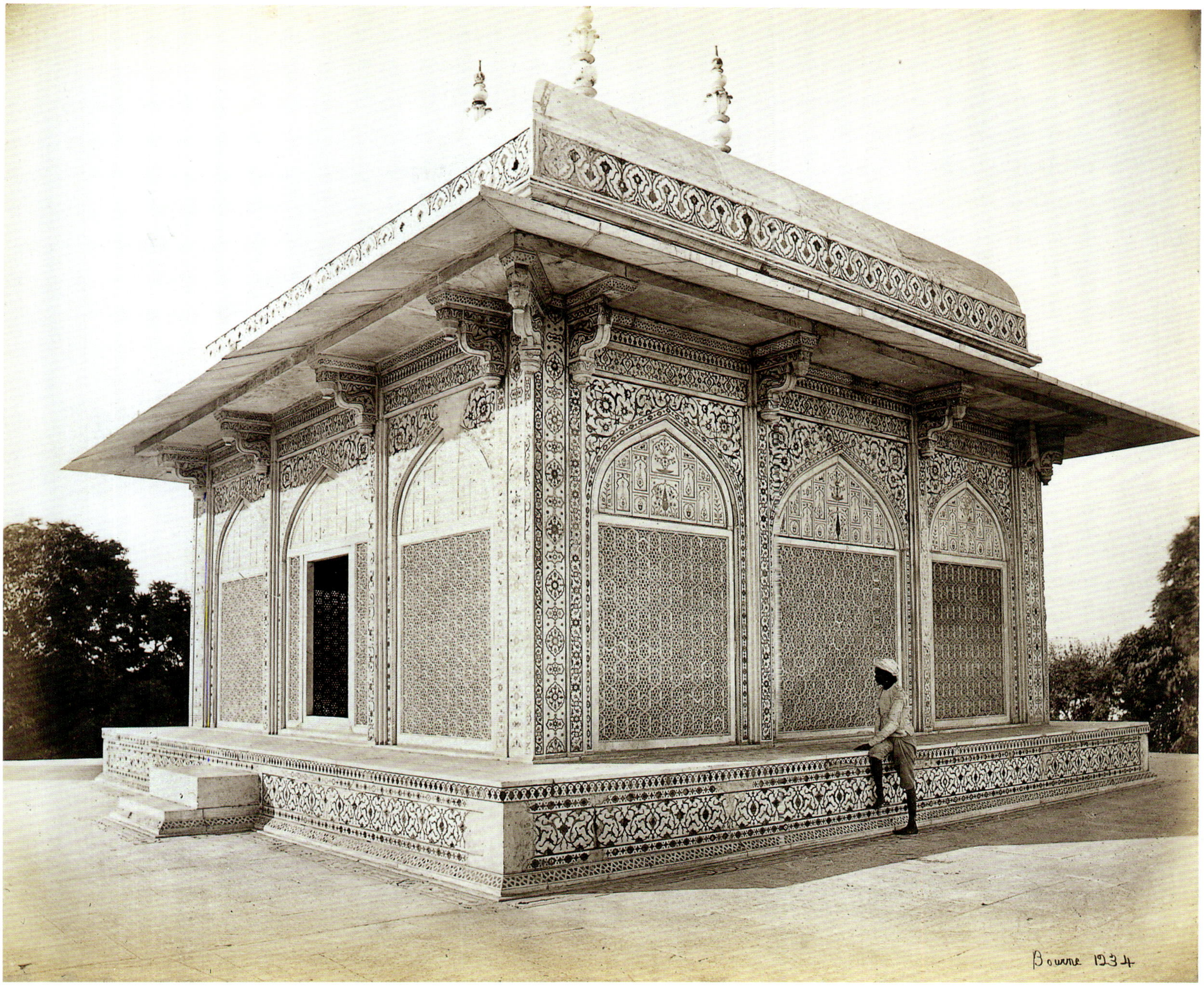

opposite top

FÉLIX BONFILS (1831–1885)

Portico of the Temple of Esna, 1870s

Albumen print

Born in Alais, France, Bonfils set up his studio in 1867 in Beirut, where he had been on military service during the 1850s. He quickly became one of the most prolific purveyors of eastern Mediterranean scenes, with 15,000 prints and 4000 stereo views in stock by 1871. His wife, Lydie, and son, Adrien, were also photographers and continued the business after Félix's death. In their lighting and composition, his architectural views frequently show a sensitivity to the subject unmatched by his competitors.

opposite bottom

JUAN LAURENT (1816–1892)

The Court of the Lions, the Alhambra, Granada, 1870s

Albumen print

Photography was an important tool in helping to forge a sense of national identity and in determining how the image of nationhood was presented abroad. In Spain this role was played by the French-born Juan Laurent, who opened his Madrid studio in 1856 followed by a retail outlet in Paris. Laurent not only made the monuments of Spain's past better known, he also photographed contemporary achievements, such as the country's public works projects – after 1880 in association with Martinez Sanchez.

above

SAMUEL BOURNE (1834–1912)

Tomb of Itmad-ud-Daula, Agra, 1860s

Albumen print

Although in India only from 1863 to 1870, the Nottingham-bred Bourne, in partnership with Charles Shepherd, became the subcontinent's most successful commercial photographer, setting up studios in Simla (1863), Calcutta (1867) and Bombay (1870). His photographs combined voyeuristic peeps into the exotic with images designed to reassure that British rule, through its social customs and architecture, was imposing order on this disquietingly alien world. Although aimed primarily at the expatriate community, Bourne's superb images were architecturally informative. They were, for example, heavily used by Fergusson, who displayed them at London's South Kensington Museum in 1866 and at the 1867 Exposition Universelle in Paris.

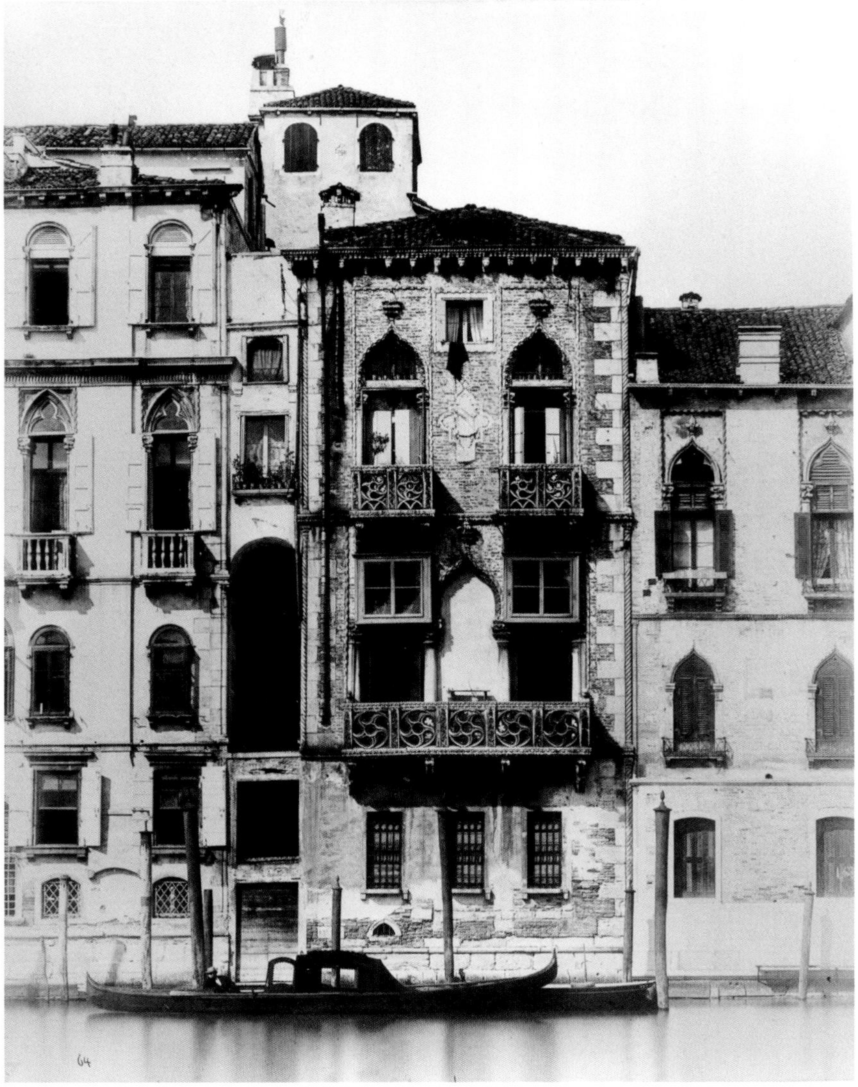

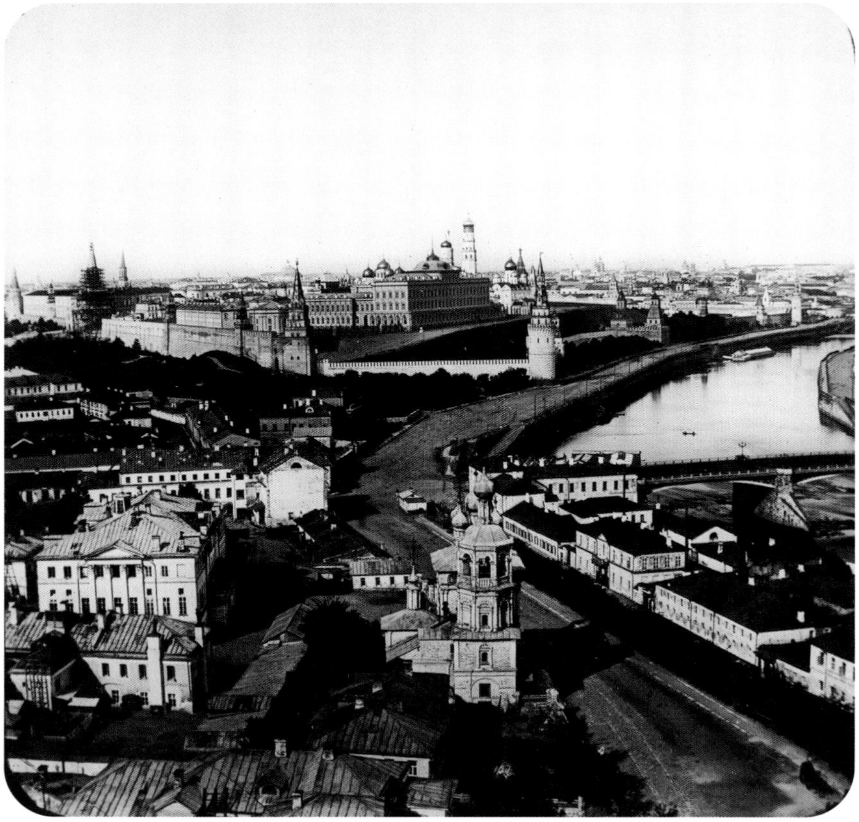

top left

CARLO NAYA (1816–1882)

Palazzo Contarini Fasan, Venice, 1860s

Albumen print

Among the wealth of photographic talent in Venice, which included Carlo Ponti and Domenico Bresolin, Naya was one of the leading lights. After studying law at Pisa University and travelling widely with his brother, during which time he learnt the daguerreotype process, he commenced professional practice in Venice at the ripe age of forty-one. His prints were initially distributed by Ponti, but this arrangement ended in acrimony and litigation. Like other topographical photographers, Naya issued the same views in different formats, the souvenir album being especially popular.

bottom left

PHOTOGRAPHER UNKNOWN

Moscow, 1880s

Lantern slide

During the nineteenth century lectures on architecture were often illustrated by an accompanying display of photographic prints, but this cumbersome method was supplanted once images became more readily available in the form of lantern slides. This format was introduced by the Philadelphia photographers William and Frederick Langenheim in 1849 and adopted by many topographical firms, who issued views of cities and monuments in large numbers. The lantern slide both revolutionized architectural education and brought architecture to a wider public through the perennially popular magic lantern show.

opposite

FRANCIS BEDFORD (1816–1894)

Stereograph of St Augustine's Gate, College Green, Bristol, 1860s

Albumen print

With its seductive combination of amusement and instruction, the stereograph was the most common means by which architecture found its way into the parlour until the advent of photographically illustrated magazines at the turn of the century. When viewed through a stereoscope that merged and magnified them, the small, paired images taken with a twin-lens camera produced an astonishingly three-dimensional illusion of reality. The use of lenses of a shorter focal length also facilitated 'instantaneous' views of the kind issued by E. & H.T. Anthony of New York. These proved exceedingly popular in the early 1860s, when the mania for collecting stereos peaked.

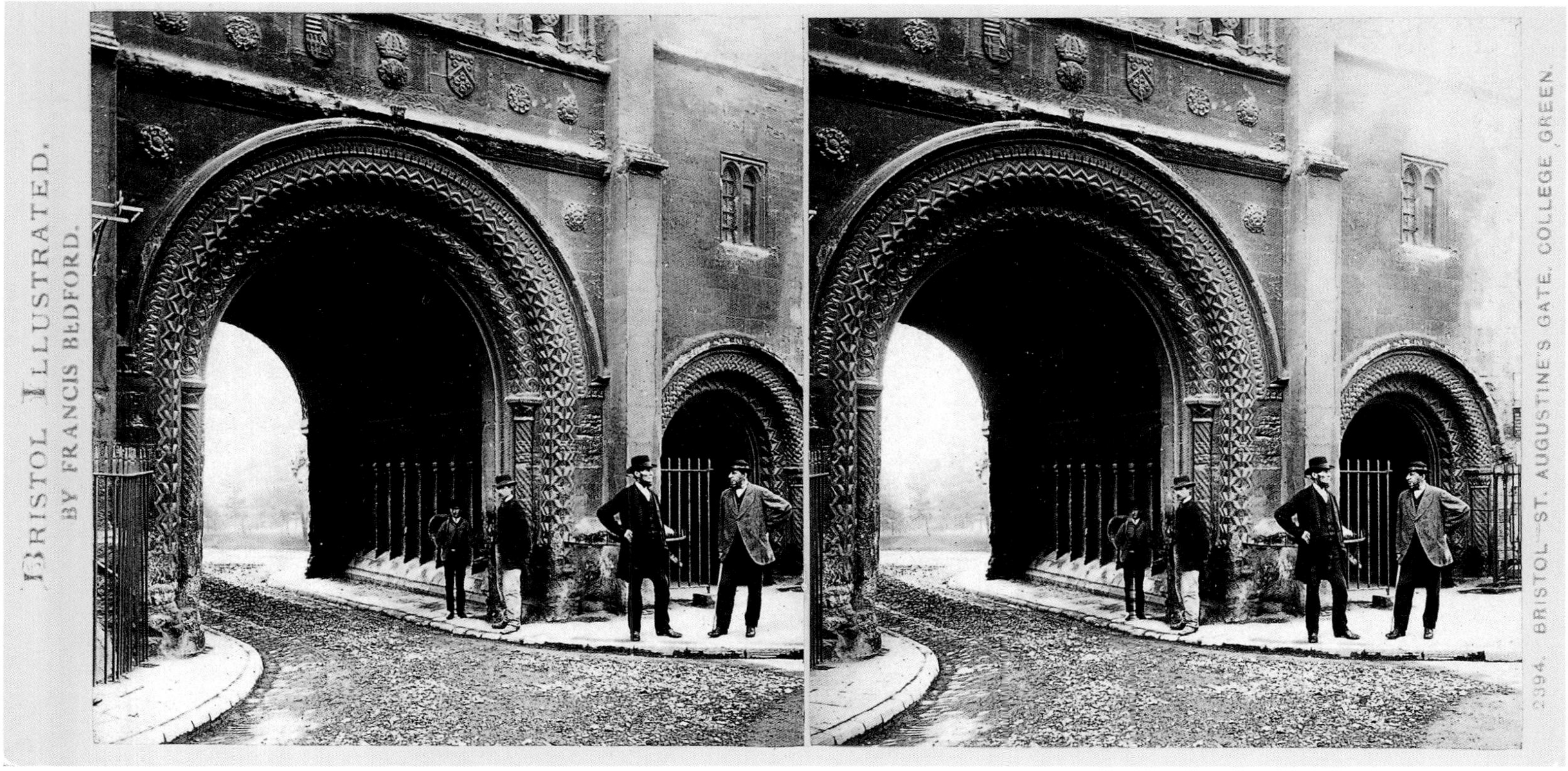
BRISTOL ILLUSTRATED.
BY FRANCIS BEDFORD.
2394. BRISTOL—ST. AUGUSTINE'S GATE, COLLEGE GREEN.

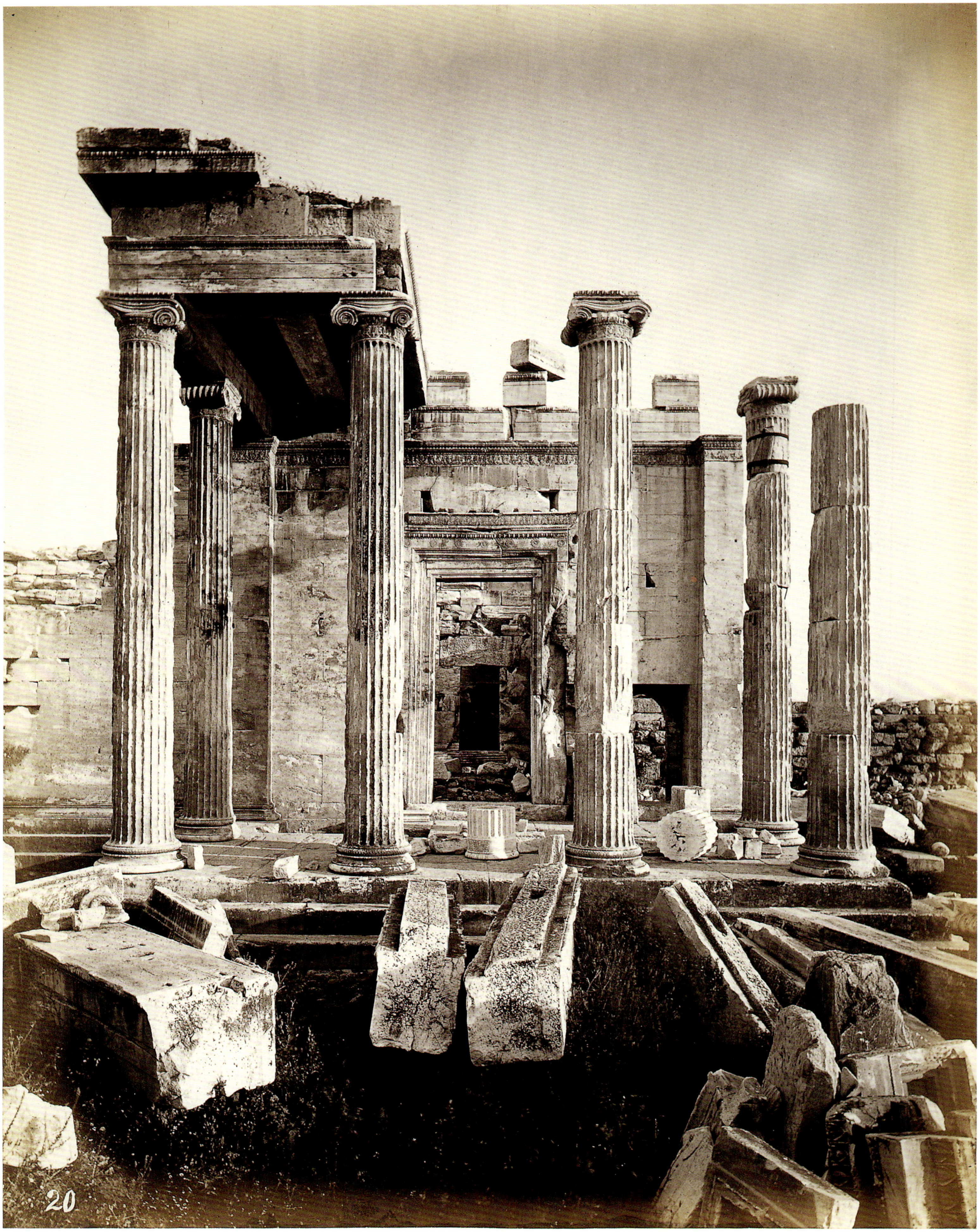
20

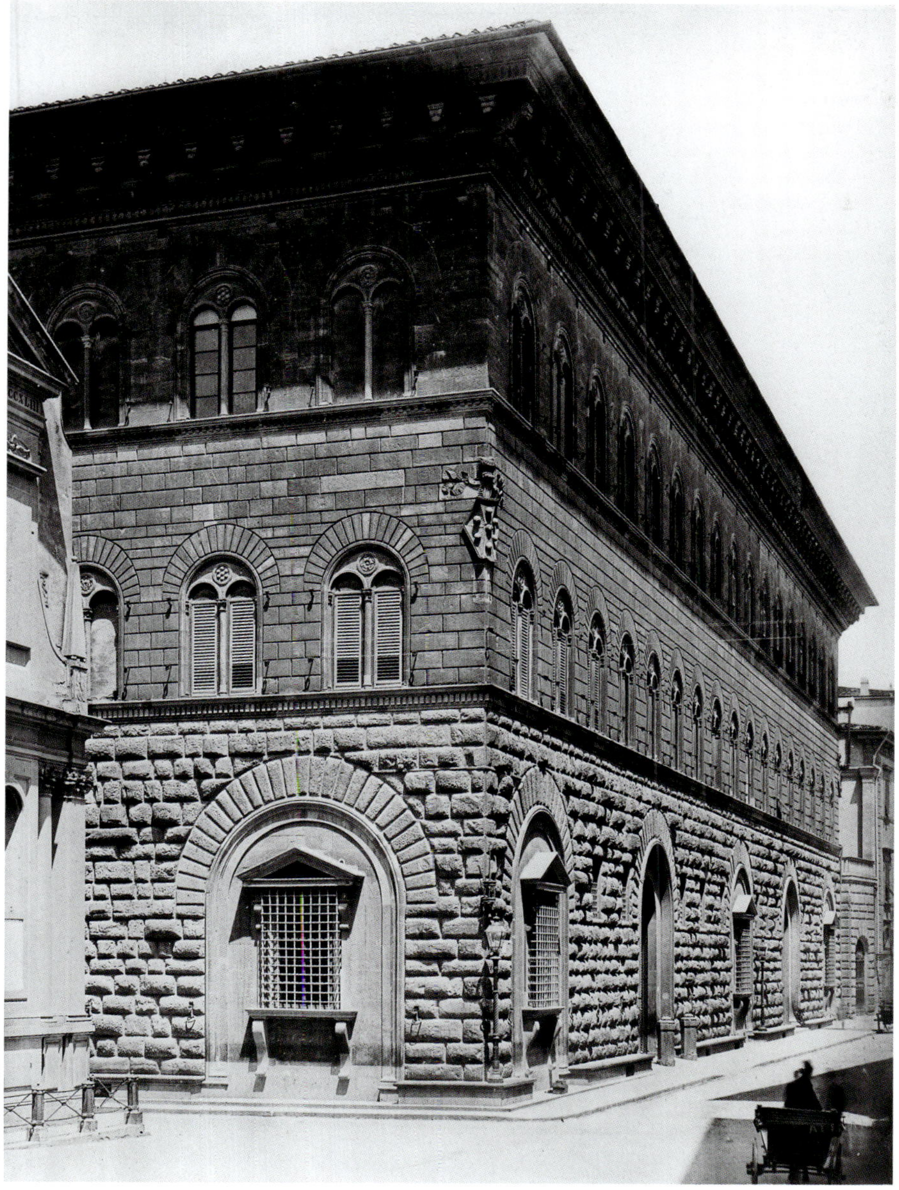

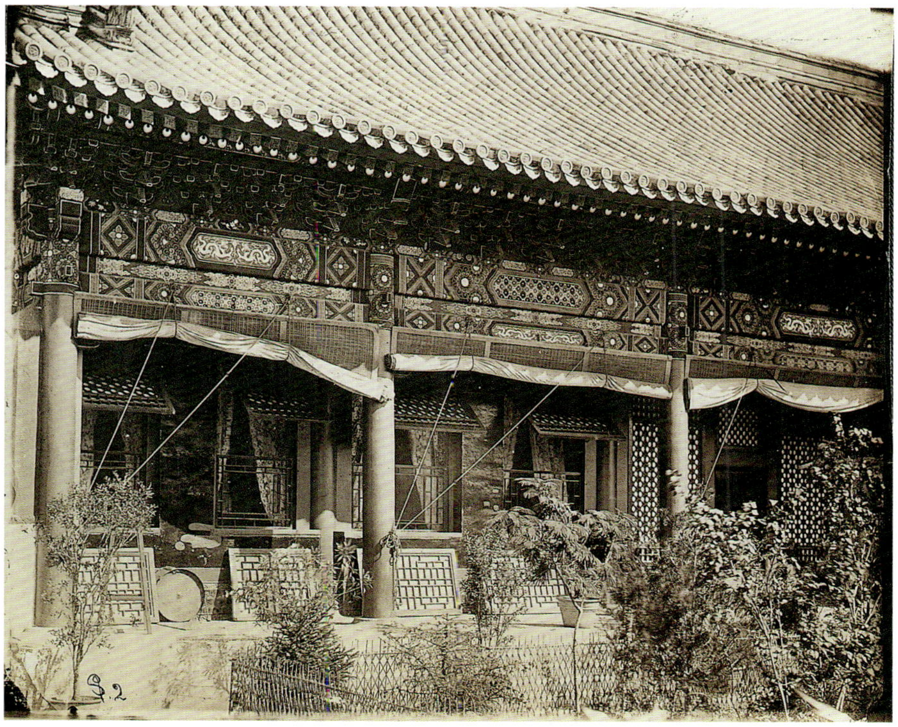

opposite

WILLIAM JAMES STILLMAN (1828–1901)

North Porch, Erechtheion, Acropolis, Athens, 1868–69

Albumen print

Stillman used photography to supplement his income, and his output was small. An eventful life saw him abandon painting after criticism by Ruskin and serve as American consul in Rome and Crete. Scornful of the inadequacies of existing views, he published twenty-five carbon prints in *The Acropolis of Athens Illustrated Picturesquely and Architecturally in Photography* (1870), which exhibited a lingering romanticism, though he was concerned they should be architecturally accurate: "The negatives are produced with Dallmeyer's rectilinear lenses, and the façades, as far as practicable, photographed from points exactly equidistant from the extremities."[24]

top left

FRATELLI ALINARI

Palazzo Medici-Riccardi, Florence, 1870s

Albumen print

Architect: Michelozzo di Bartolommeo

Of all the topographical viewmaking firms, Fratelli Alinari, founded in 1854 by the brothers Leopoldo and Giuseppe, was the most architecturally significant, with an audience of art historians and architects as well as tourists. The Alinari developed a standardized approach to architecture, in parallel to their photography of paintings and sculpture, whereby the architectural monument was revered as an artwork to be viewed separately from its surroundings. Adhering to the Renaissance perspectival tradition, the pictures were usually composed in a classical manner that, when combined with precisely detailed caption information, gave the impression of documentary objectivity.

bottom left

PHOTOGRAPHER UNKNOWN

British Legation Building, Beijing, 1860s

Albumen print

Photography of buildings by both indigenous and foreign practitioners flourished in China after 1860, with the opening up of the country following the Opium Wars. One of the first to practise there was Felice Beato (1830–1906), Robertson's former assistant. He was followed by the Edinburgh-born John Thomson (1837–1921), one of the nineteenth century's most remarkable photographers, who established a studio in Hong Kong in 1868 and visited Beijing in 1871. Also active was the Hong Kong business simply called The Firm, which acquired and printed negatives abandoned by itinerant photographers.

right

PHOTOGRAPHER UNKNOWN

Chafyn-Grove Almshouses, Zeals, Wiltshire, c. 1865

Albumen print

Architect: George Devey

Devey was one of the first British architects to commission photography of his own work on a regular basis and to collect photographs as exemplars. These focused on the best examples of English architecture of the sixteenth and seventeenth centuries – Hardwick Hall, Longleat and, on a more modest scale, Parham, Brereton Hall and Speke Hall – which Devey ingeniously adapted in his own country houses. Ironically, he did this so skilfully that his houses were frequently photographed by topographical photographers such as Frith and Wilson in the mistaken belief that they were genuine relics of the nation's past.

page 66

PHOTOGRAPHER UNKNOWN

Wholesale Store, New York, c. 1860

Albumen print

Architect: Samuel Adams Warner

This is one of 102 photographs presented to the Royal Institute of British Architects in 1867–68 by William Ware, a Boston member of the recently formed American Institute of Architects, in an attempt to convince his ill-informed British colleagues that American architecture was worthy of critical regard. Including works by a clutch of East Coast architects, among them Samuel Warner and Richard Morris Hunt, Ware's donation demonstrated the increasing importance of photography in the communication of architectural ideas. Fuelled by further photographic deposits, British interest in American architecture culminated in 1893, when Hunt became the first American to receive the Royal Institute of British Architects' Royal Gold Medal.

page 67

EXCELSIOR PHOTO CO.

Royal Arcade, Sydney, c. 1882

Albumen print

Architect: Thomas Rowe

Although little is known about nineteenth-century Australian architectural photography, the evidence of surviving photographs of work by both indigenous architects and foreigners, such as William Butterfield, indicates a flourishing trade. In addition, Melbourne Public Library was among the subscribers to the Architectural Photographic Association. Photographs presented to the Royal Institute of British Architects by Australian members during the 1870s and 1880s suggest a high level of technical accomplishment.

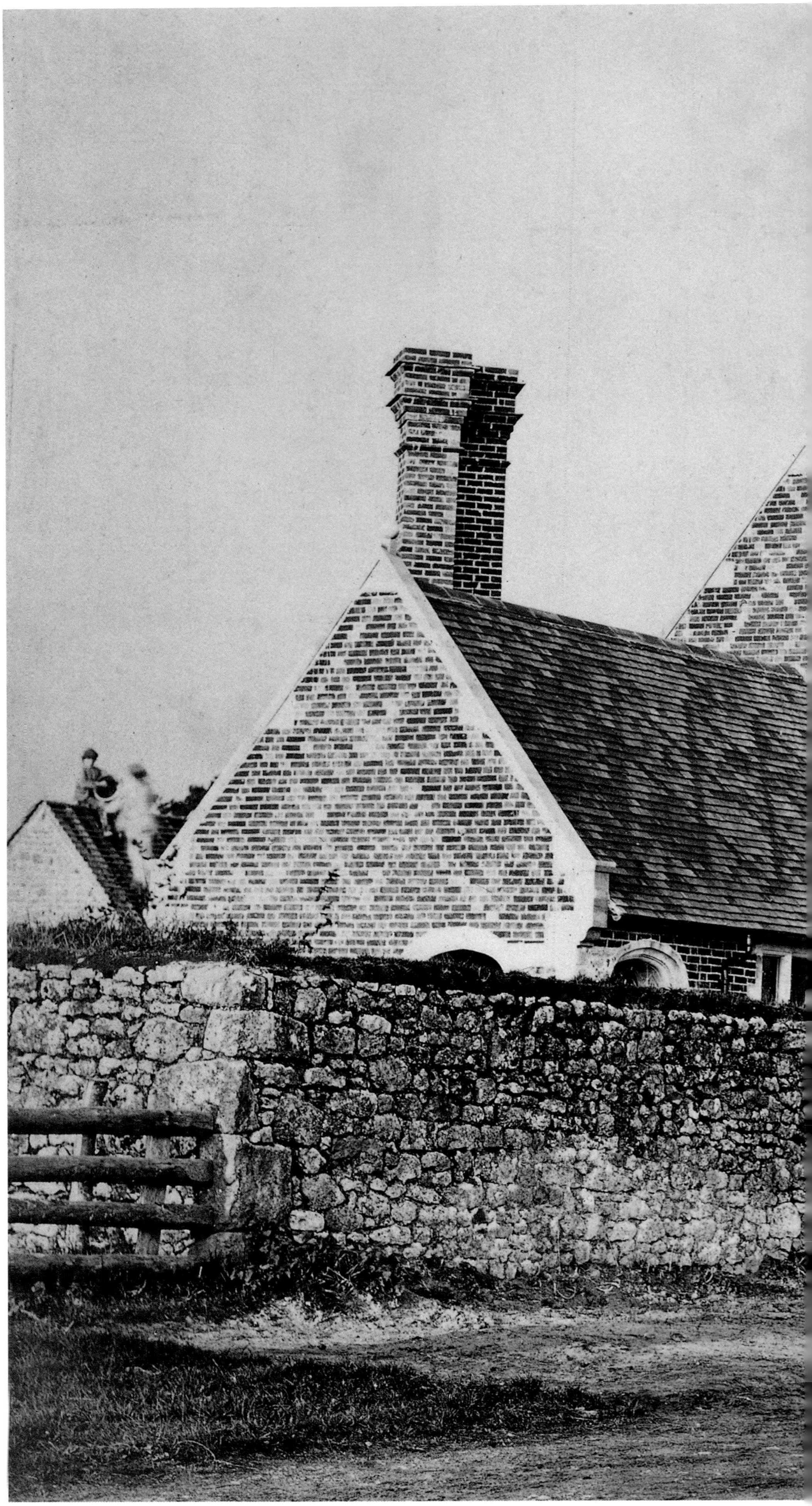

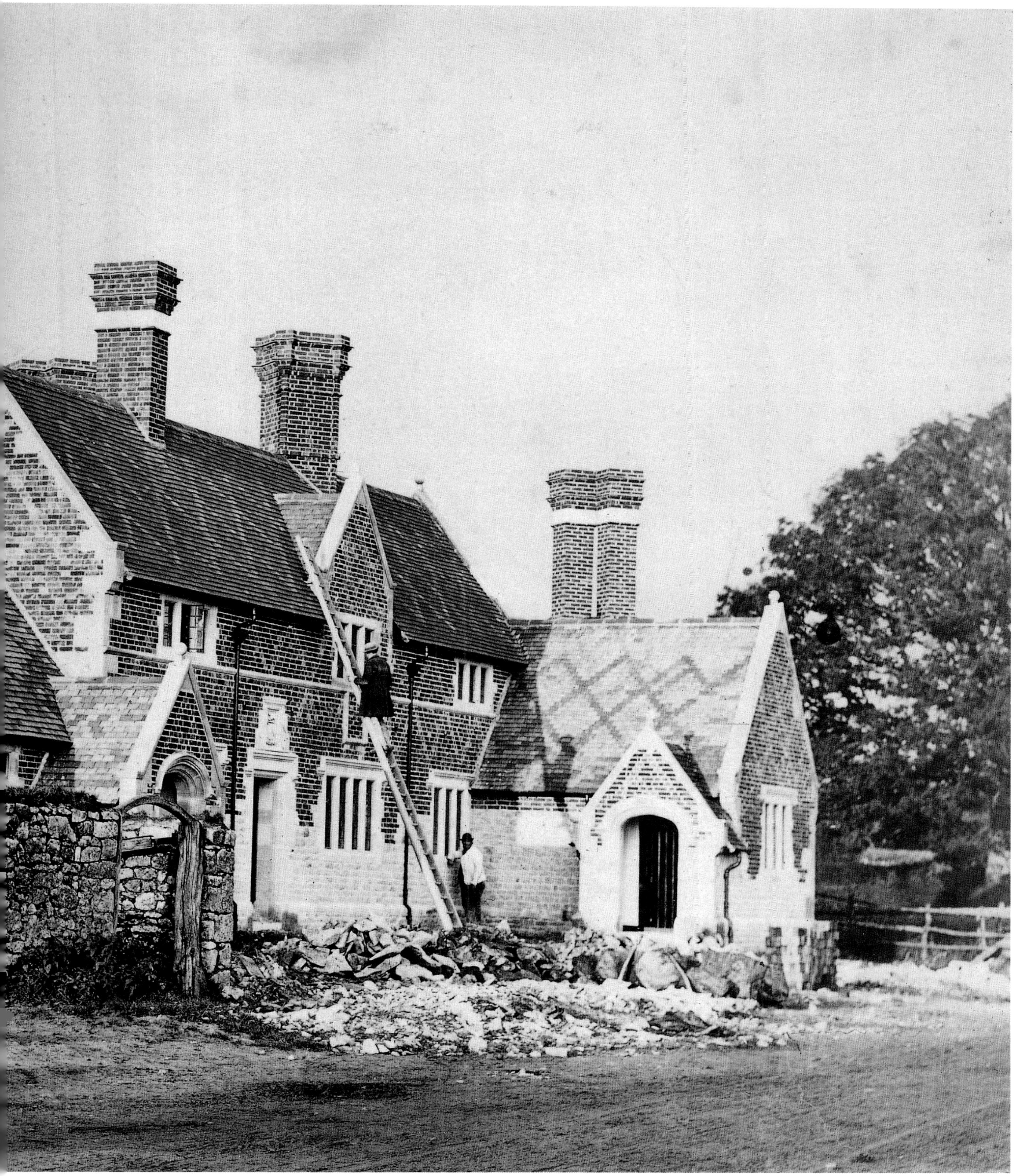

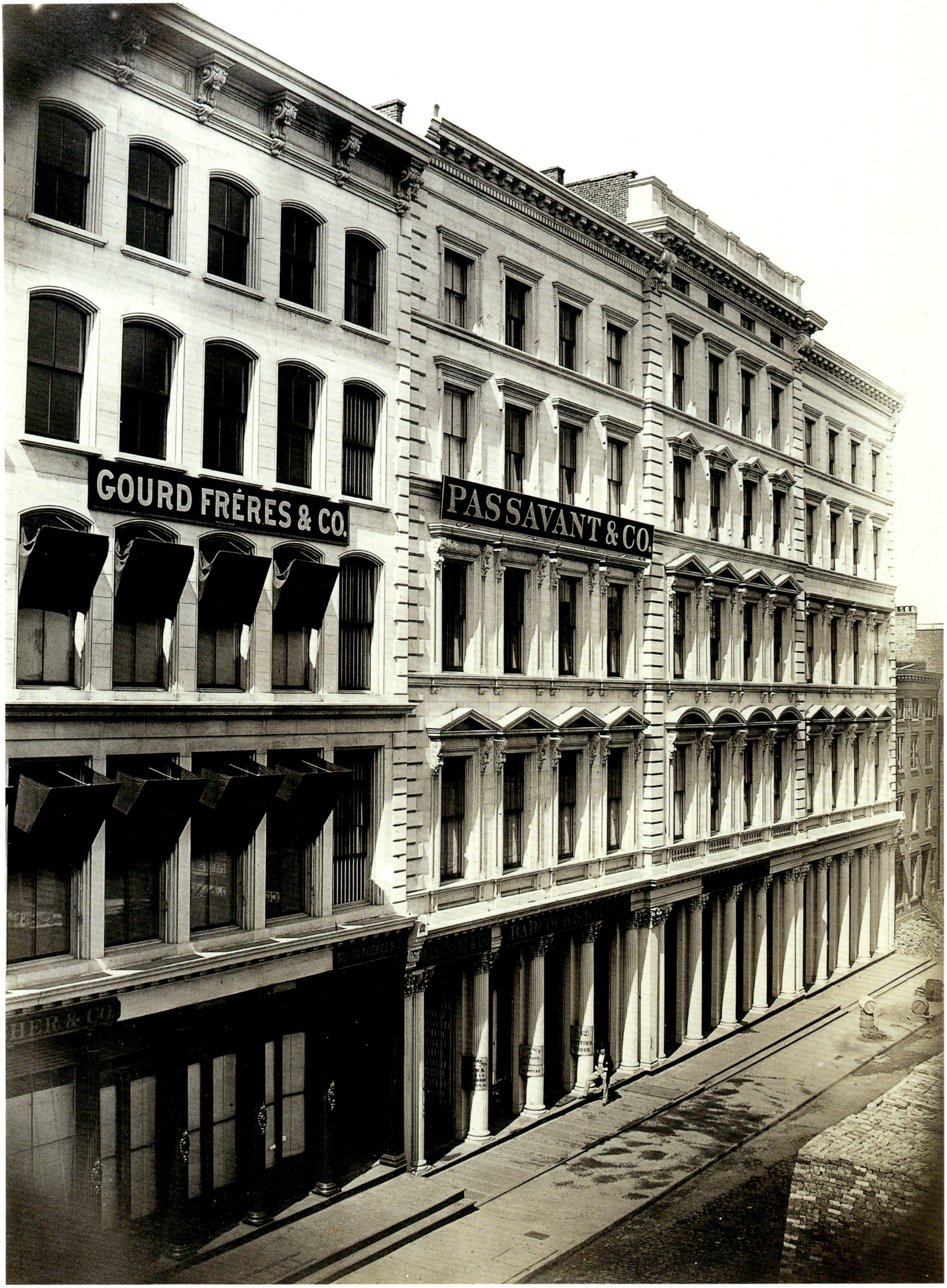
GOURD FRÉRES & CO.
PASSAVANT & CO.

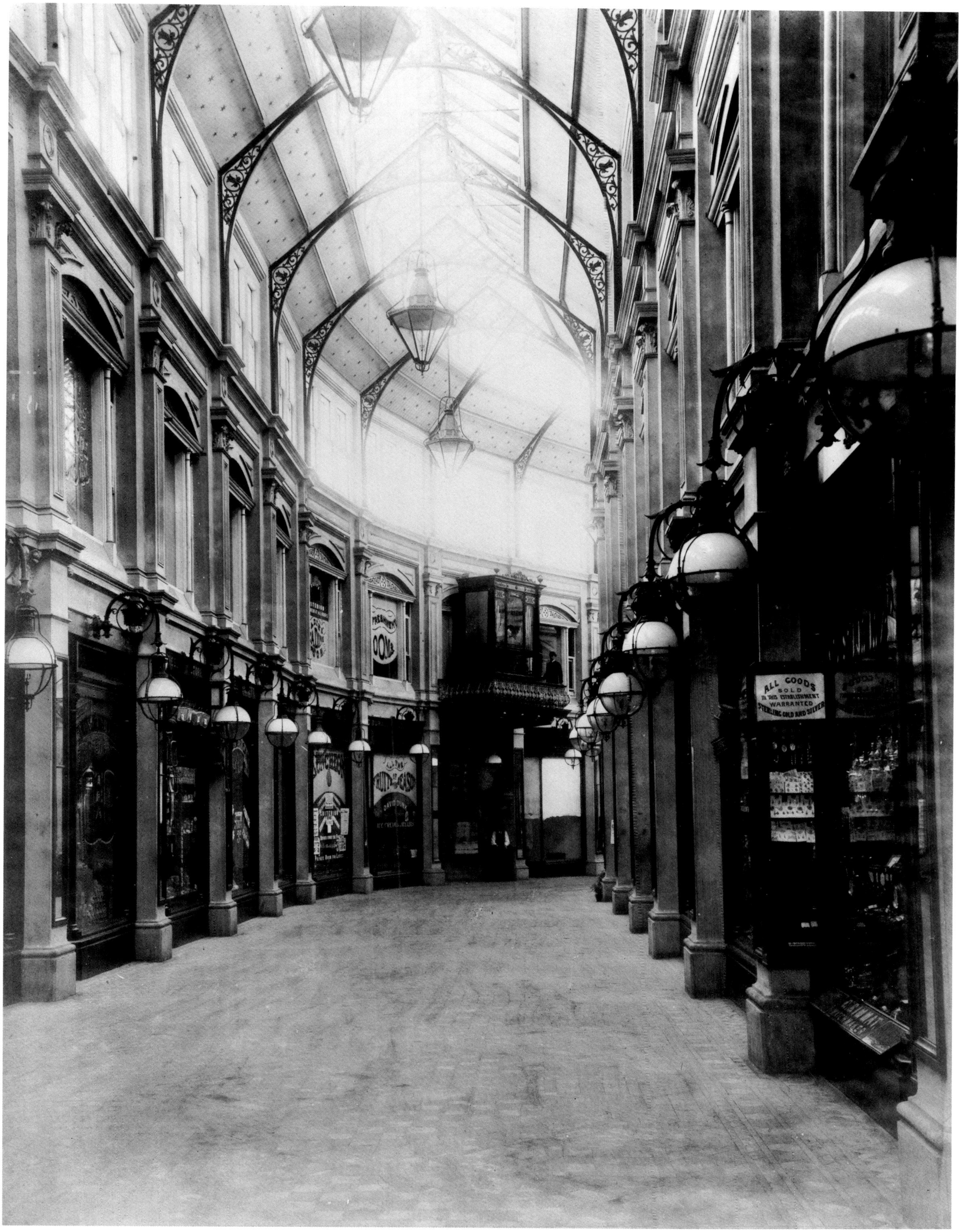
ALL GOODS
SOLD
IN THIS ESTABLISHMENT
WARRANTED
STERLING GOLD AND SILVER

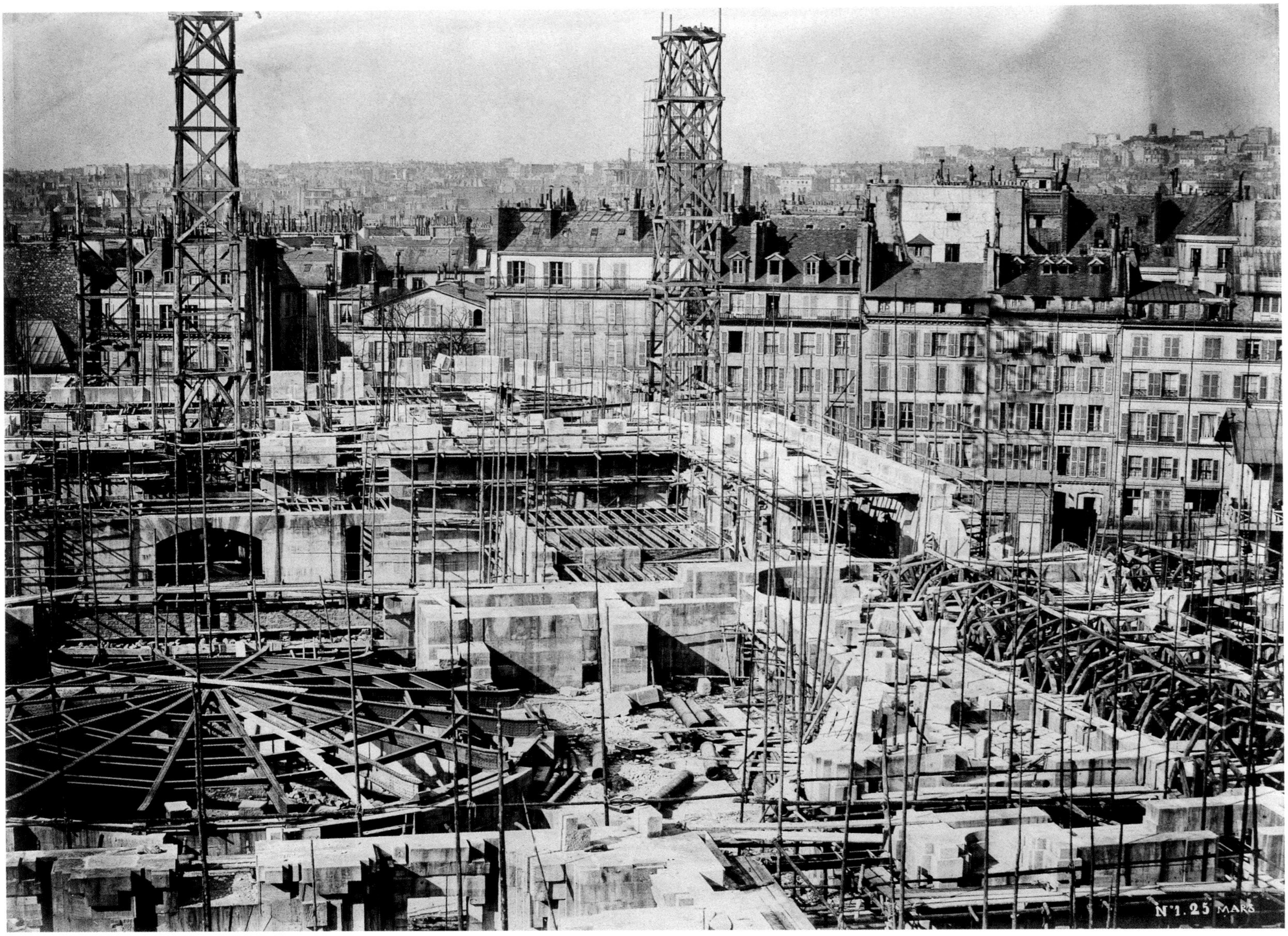
N°1. 25 MARS

opposite

DELMAET & DURANDELLE

(Hyacinthe César Delmaet [1828–1862] and Louis-Emile Durandelle [1839–1917])

Opéra, Paris, 1865

Albumen print

Architect: Charles Garnier

Following the example of Baldus at the New Louvre, the firm of Delmaet & Durandelle, founded in 1861, documented the construction of the Opéra, taking photographs, according to Garnier, "every time important changes occurred in the building works",[25] and of the ornamental details, both in plaster model form and as completed. For Garnier, the firm's two hundred photographs were both working tools and the raw material that could later facilitate the production of a monograph on the building – a hope that was realized with the production of *Le Nouvel Opéra de Paris* (1876–80).

top right

NEURDEIN FRÈRES

(Etienne Neurdein [*fl.* 1860–1912] and Antoine Neurdein [*c.* 1840–*c.* 1912])

Library Staircase. Cathedral, Rouen, 1870s

Albumen print

From the 1860s until about 1900, when they appear to have gravitated towards printing and publishing, Neurdein Frères – Etienne and Antoine – built up under their ND stamp an impressive archive of photographs, chiefly of France's medieval and Renaissance architecture. While their predecessors, such as Bisson Frères, went bankrupt, the Neurdeins survived in a competitive climate by issuing straightforward documentary albumen prints – many 18 x 24 cm (7 x 9½ in.) in size and therefore significantly smaller than those of the Bissons – artfully calculated to appeal to both tourists and those with a professional interest in architecture.

bottom right

LOUIS-EMILE DURANDELLE (1839–1917)

Maison de Repression de Nanterre, *c.* 1885

Albumen print

Architect: Achille Hermant

After Delmaet's death in 1862, Durandelle continued the business with Delmaet's widow, whom he later married. He was especially adept at conveying structural complexity and geometrical form in compositions of great power and rigour that appealed to such architects as Hermant. This image forms part of an album of thirty views that documented the building and its drawings. The firm also issued a series of folio albums of details to architects under such titles as *Sculpture ornamentale* and *Statues décoratives* before, in 1886, Durandelle was bought out by an employee, Albert Chevojon. The firm subsequently became Chevojon Frères.

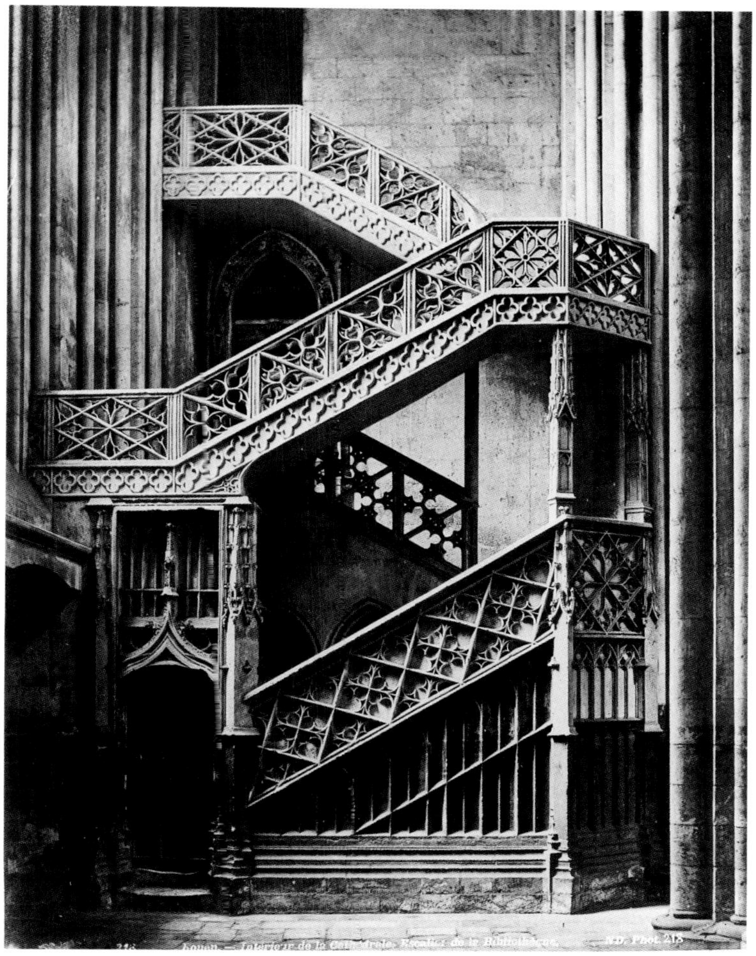

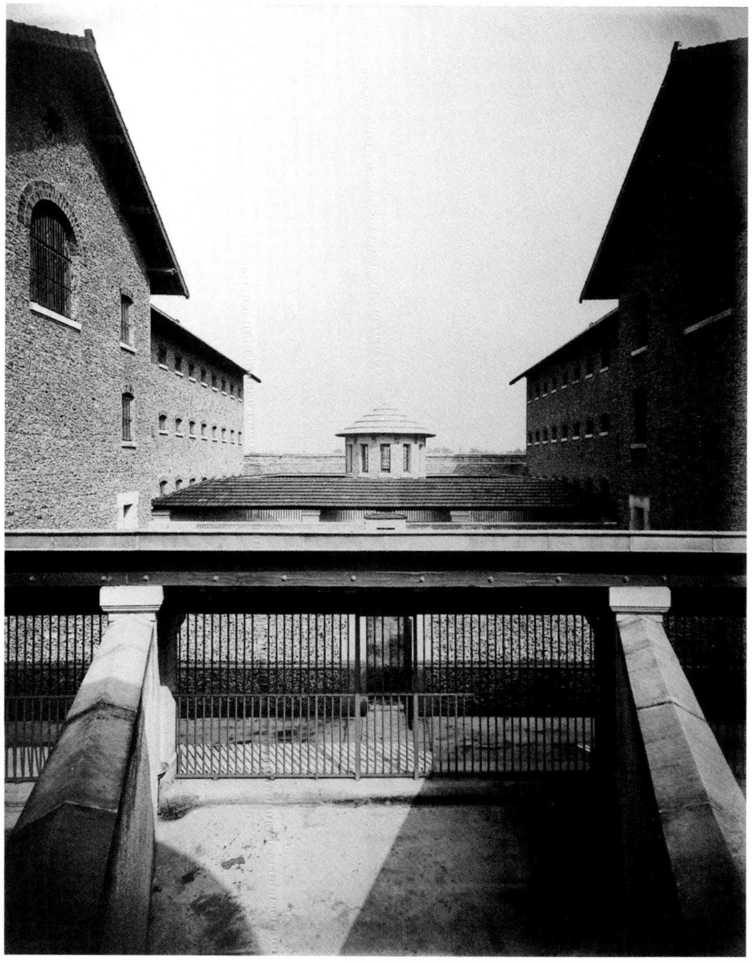

top right

BEDFORD LEMERE & CO.

Victoria Assize Courts, Birmingham, 1891

Albumen print

Architects: Sir Aston Webb & E. Ingress Bell

This image contains all the typical ingredients of a Lemere photograph – a contemporary subject; flat light; an absence of people; the building fully fitting the frame to the exclusion of its urban context; and exceptional detail made possible by the use of a 12 x 10 inch (30.5 x 25.4 cm) glass plate. With photographs such as these, Lemere's career highlights the way in which architectural photography increasingly became the preserve of specialist professionals, communicating to a specialist audience through specialist outlets.

bottom right

BEDFORD LEMERE & CO.

Saloon, Eaton Hall, Cheshire, 1887

Albumen print

Architect: Alfred Waterhouse

Founded in 1861, Bedford Lemere & Co. was active until the death of Harry Bedford Lemere (1865–1944), although after the First World War its leading position was assumed by several younger firms. During its early years, country house photography formed an important part of its business. Interior views such as this, however, are an unreliable guide to period room settings, for, as Harry's assistant, Louis de Baudot, recalled, "He would, if necessary, move every ornament in the place, shift every piece of furniture. ... Often he would turn a place 'upside down' to get it to what he felt right."[26]

opposite

JACOB OLIE (1834–1905)

Oude Schans seen from the Montelbaanstoren, Amsterdam, c. 1865

Modern print from original glass negative

In the latter decades of the nineteenth century in The Netherlands, in response to urban expansion, the number of photographers documenting architecture grew steadily. Among the most important were Pieter Oosterhuis, the firms of Wegner & Mottu and Emrik & Binger, and Jacob Olie. Although he was trained as an architect, Olie's photographs – primarily townscapes – were distinguished more by their feeling for place and atmosphere than by concern for purely architectural documentation.

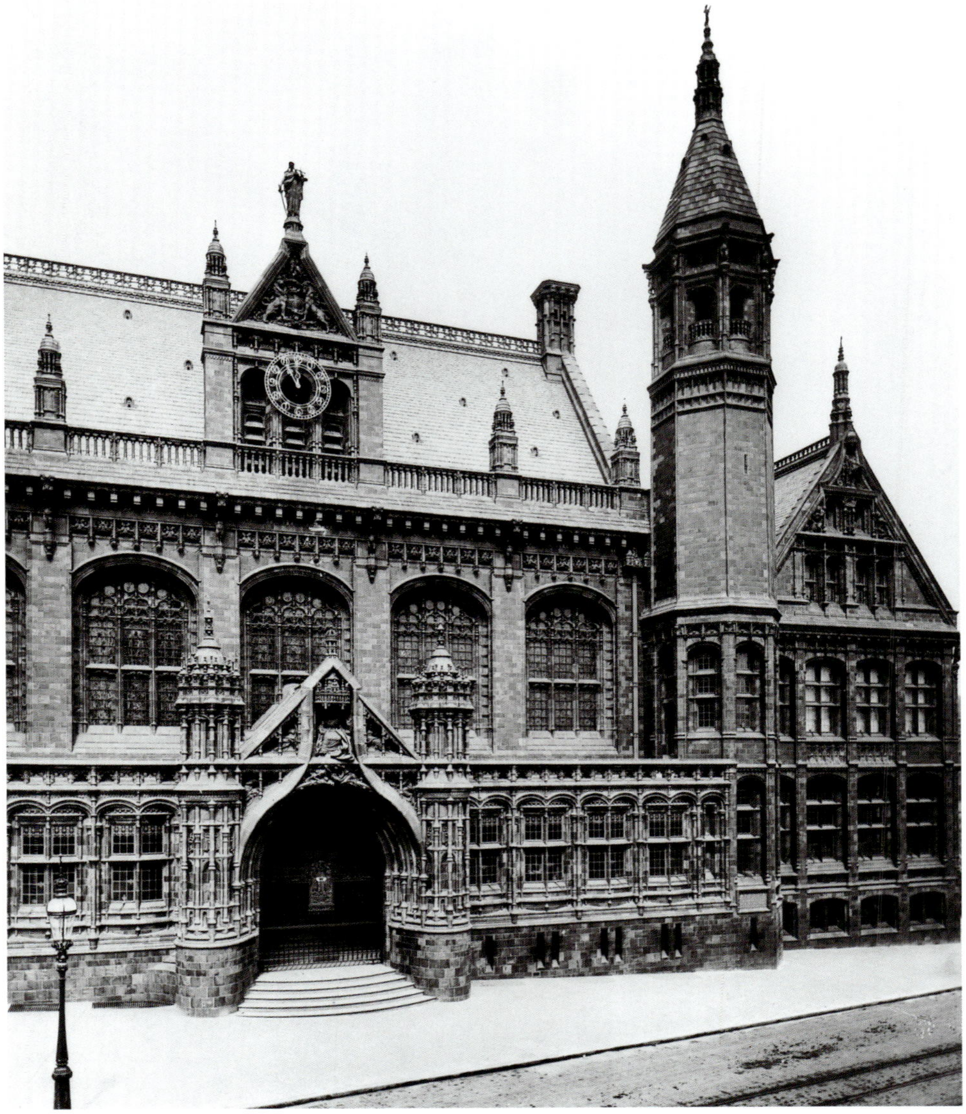

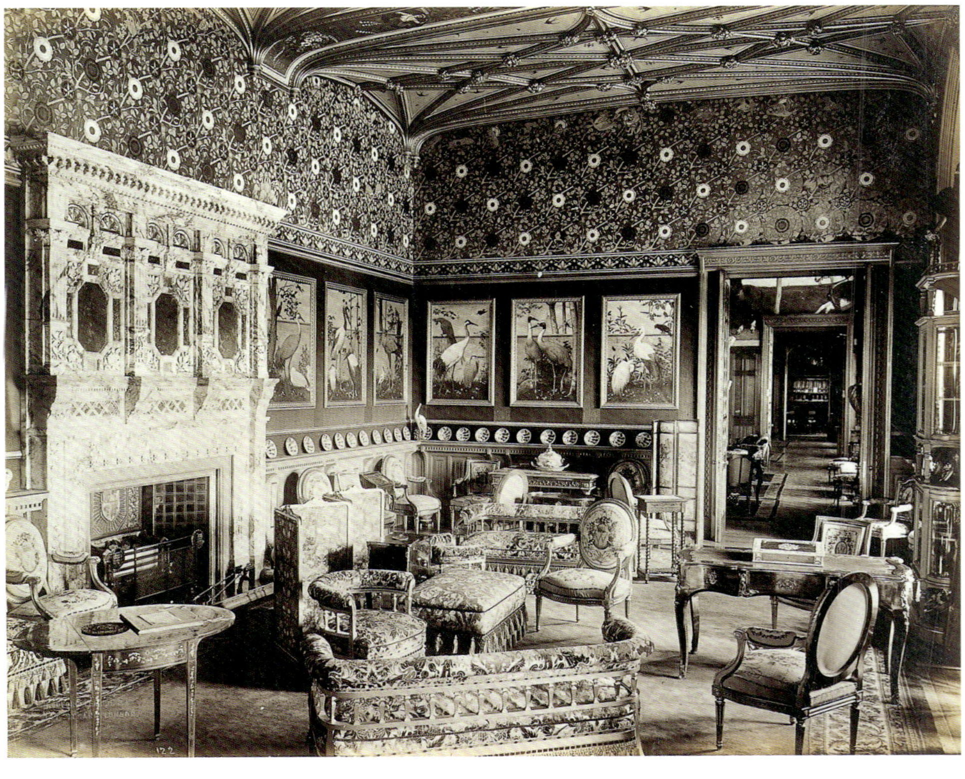

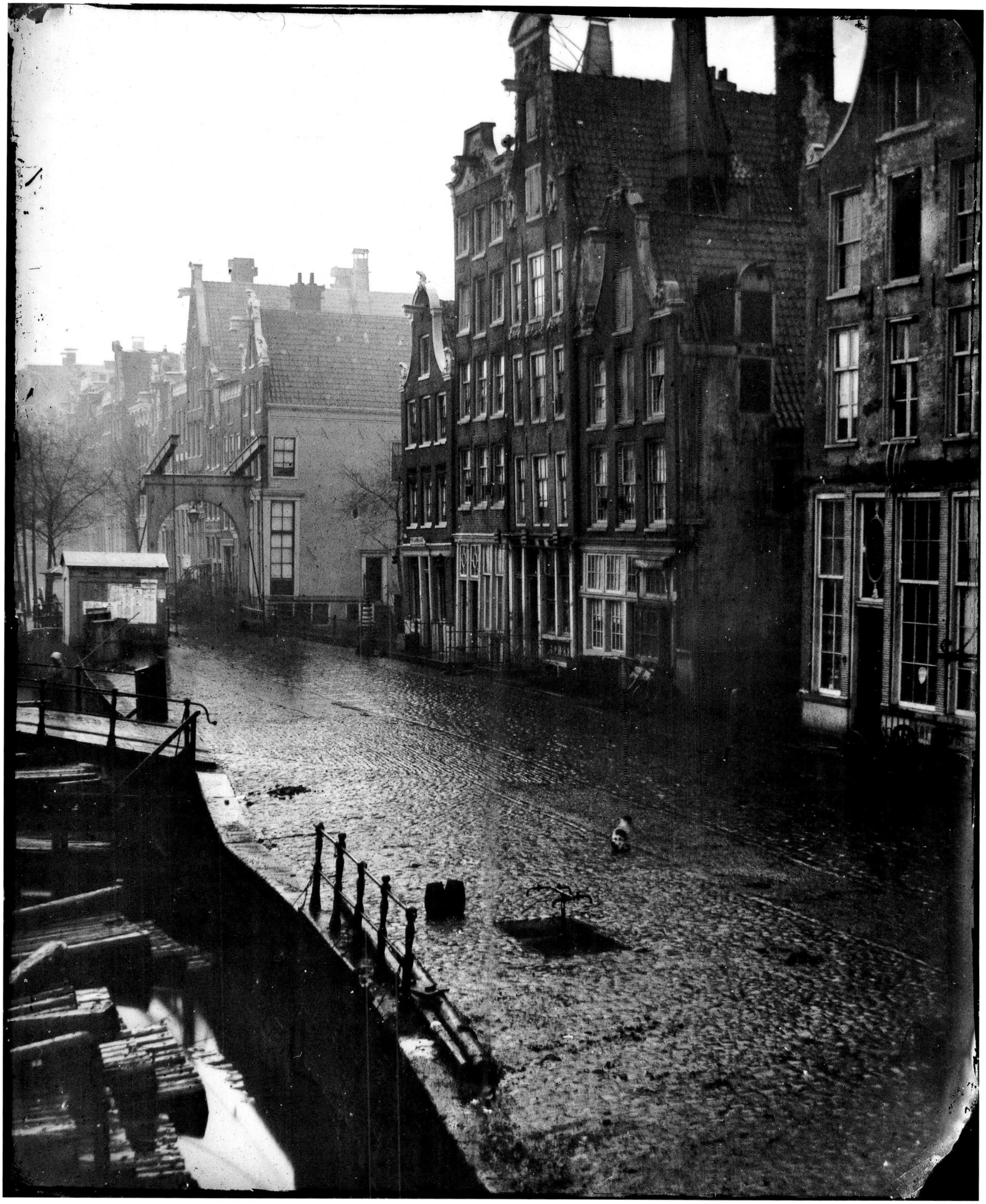

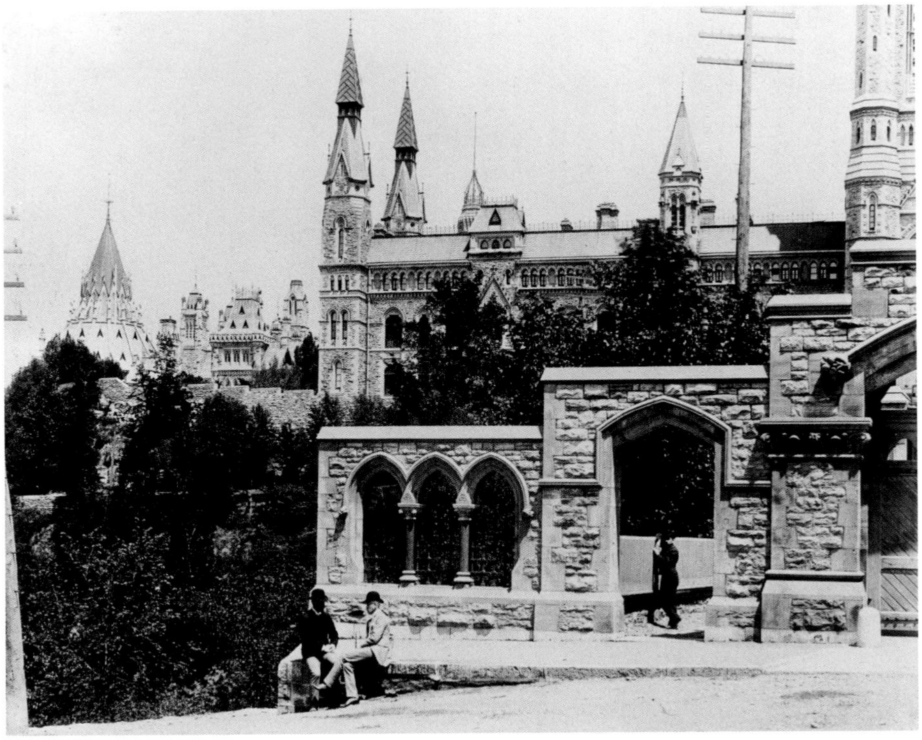

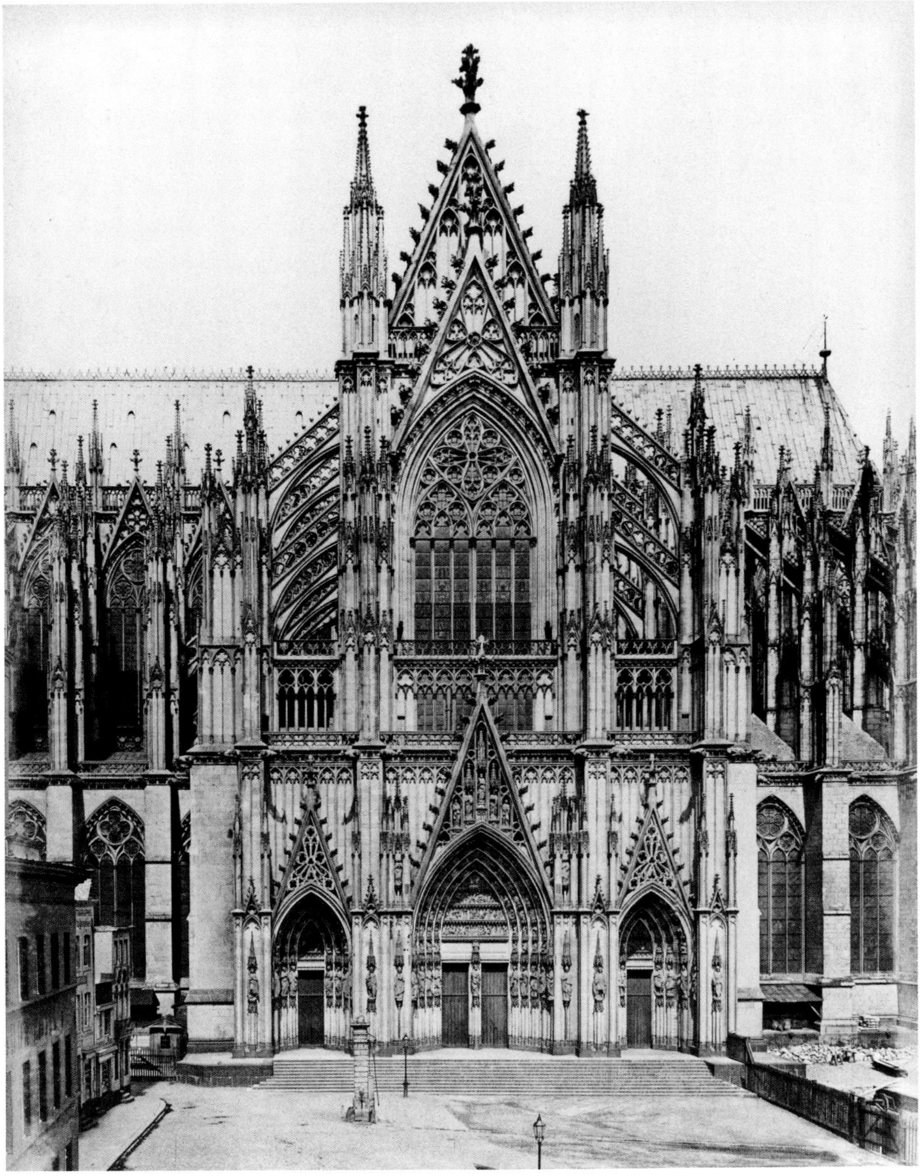

top left

WILLIAM NOTMAN (1826–1891)

Parliament Buildings, Ottawa, 1870s

Albumen print

Architects: Stent & Laver

Some of the best photographs of Canadian architecture during the nineteenth century were taken by the large generalist firm established by the Scottish-born William Notman, who settled in Montreal in 1856. Notman's firm was noted for its portraits, but buildings and city scenes also constitutec an important part of its extensive work. It became the most successful photographic enterprise in Canada, with studios across the country and in New England.

bottom left

PHOTOGRAPHER UNKNOWN

Cologne Cathedral, 1870s

Albumen print

After a gap of nearly three hundred years, building work resumed on the unfinished Cologne Cathedral in 1842. As a symbol of emergent German national unity, the cathedral's progress was recorded by many different photographers, from the Bruges-born Jan Frans Michiels (1823–1887), who moved to Cologne in 1852 and published several albums of views of the cathedral, to indigenous lensmen such as Anselm Schmitz (1831–1903) and Theodore Creifelds Jr (1839–1902), some of whose prints of the cathedral were exhibited at the 1867 Paris Universal Exposition.

opposite

HERMANN RÜCKWARDT (1845–1919)

Bank Building for Mendelssohn & Co., Berlin, c. 1874

Albumen print

Architect: Martin Gropius

Following his predecessor Ahrendts, Rückwardt established a Berlin photographic art and publishing business in 1869, which exploited the growing market for architectural photography. His photographs, employing a wide range of processes from albumen prints to collotype, reveal a greater understanding of the subject than those of his main Berlin rival, Ferdinand Albert Schwartz. Also distinctive was his publication of series of photographic portfolios devoted to specific buildings or themes, such as *Berliner Neubauten* (1890) and *Innen-Architektur und -Dekoration des XVIII. Jahrhunderts* (1884). Though geographically limited, this remarkable publishing venture can be considered a forerunner of the series publications issued by Yukio Futagawa since 1970.

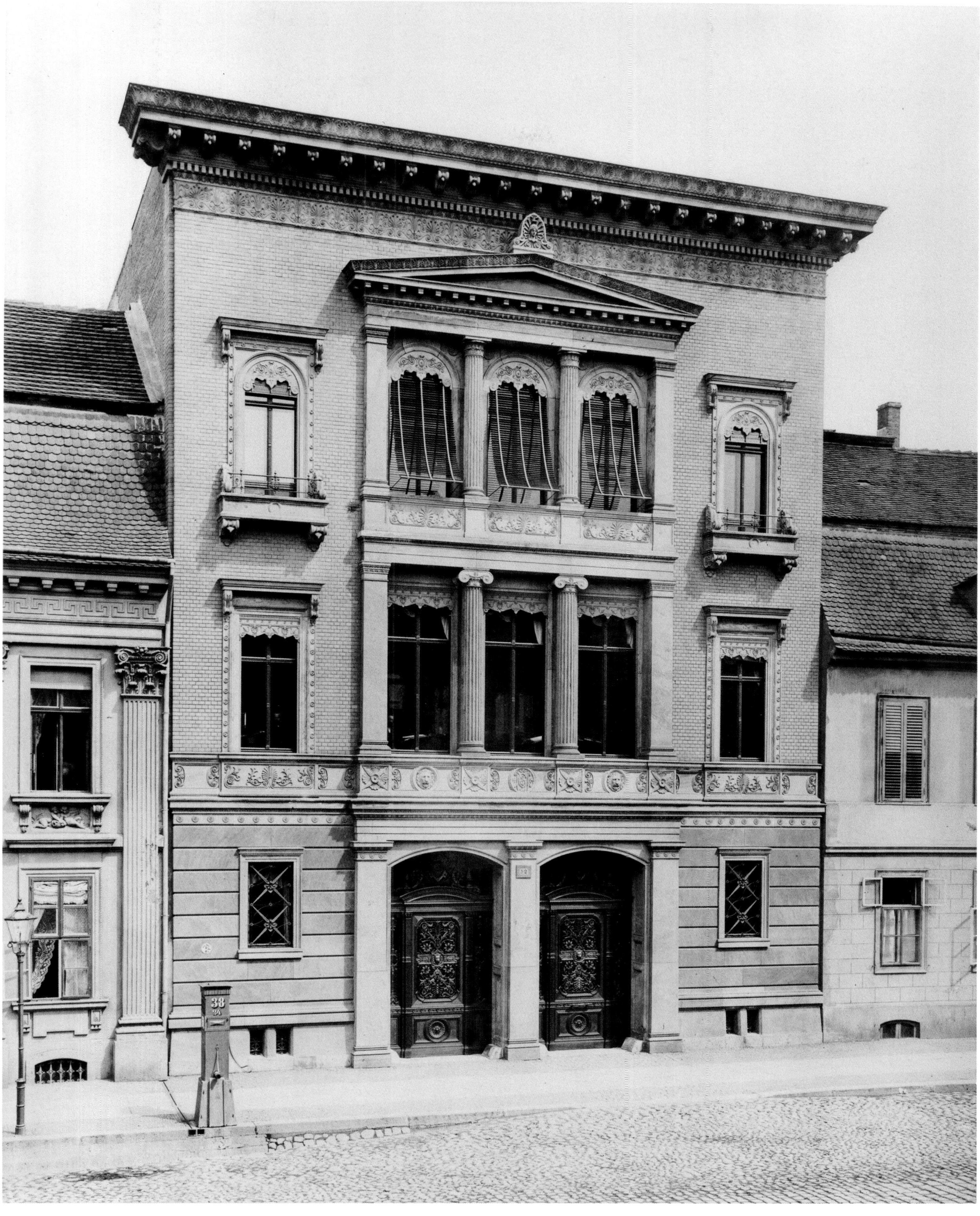

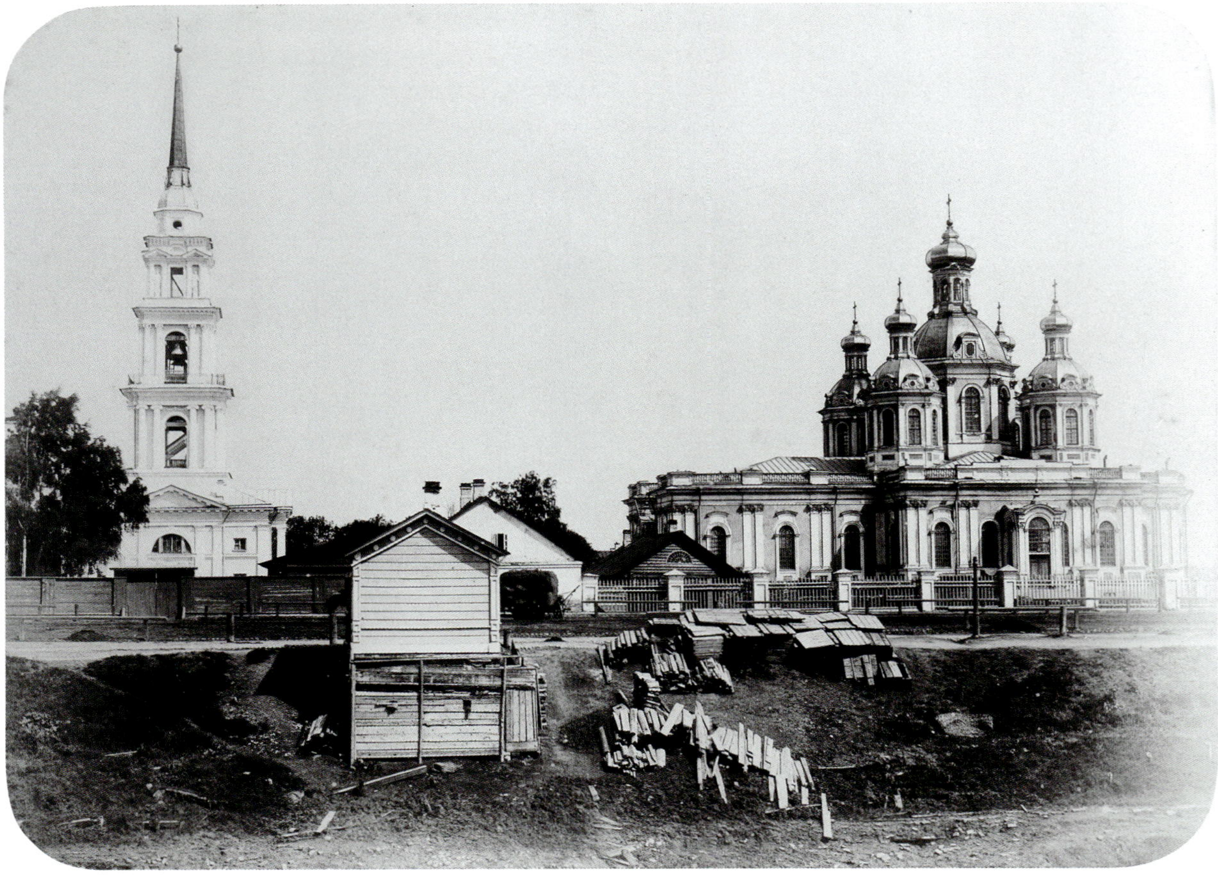

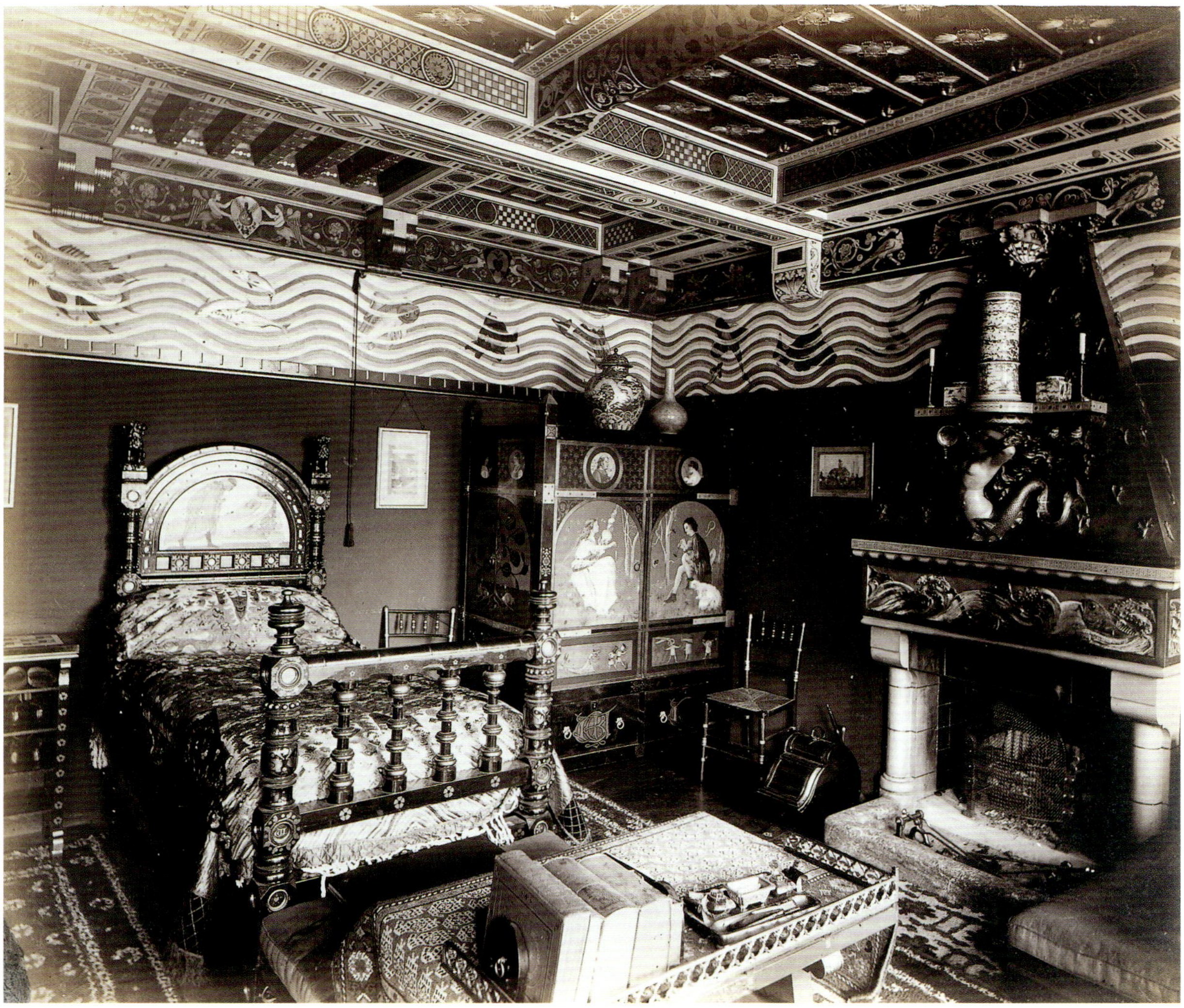

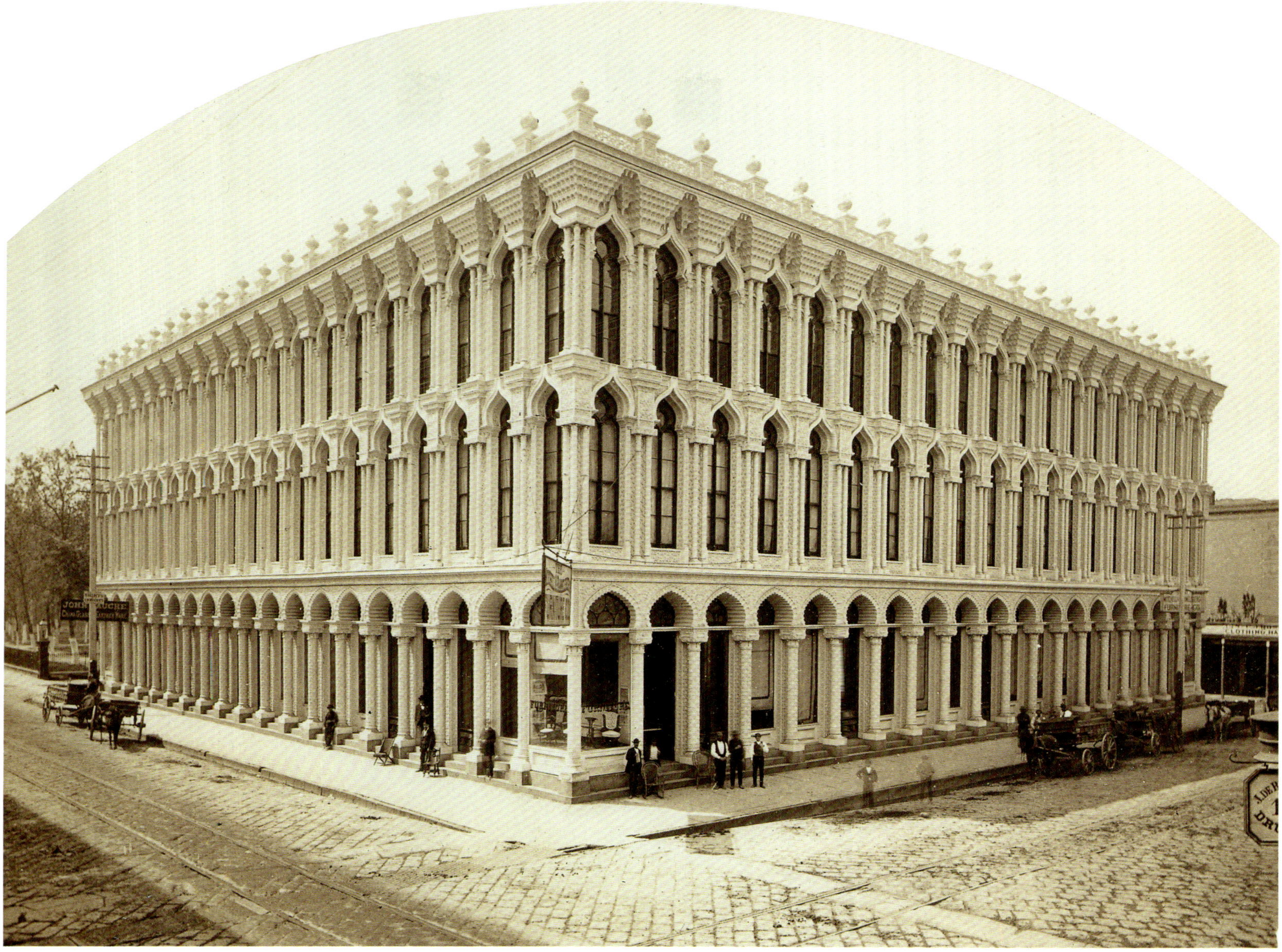

opposite top

PHOTOGRAPHER UNKNOWN

Unidentified Russian Church, 1870s

Albumen print

The development of photography in Russia broadly paralleled that in the West, with perhaps a greater emphasis on portraiture and ethnological studies. An important aspect of Russian architectural photography was the concentration on engineering and construction works, a theme that climaxed during the Soviet reconstruction programme of the 1920s and 1930s. An early instance was Roger Fenton's recording of Charles Vignoles's bridge over the Dnieper (1852), and other significant nineteenth-century examples were Josif Mygurski's documentation of the construction of Odessa Port (1869) and A.S. Murenko's views of the Simbirsk Dam (1867).

opposite bottom

PHOTOGRAPHER UNKNOWN

Mr Burges's Own Bedroom, Tower House, London, c. 1883–85

Albumen print from R.P. Pullan (ed.), *The House of William Burges*, London 1885

Architect: William Burges

Burges was a medieval fantasist deeply suspicious of the mechanistic process of photography, which he regarded as far inferior to measured drawing. By contrast his brother-in-law, Richard Popplewell Pullan, was an ardent convert who had employed photography on his archaeological expeditions. From 1883 – two years after Burges's death – until 1887, he edited a series of photographic portfolios detailing different aspects of Burges's work, such as his furniture designs and, above all, the riotous Gothic excesses of his Tower House. These portfolios, therefore, represent an early attempt to secure an architect's posthumous reputation through photography.

above

PHOTOGRAPHER UNKNOWN

Moresque Building, Camp Street, New Orleans, late 1860s

Albumen print

Architect: James Freret

Whereas, with the advent of Modernism, photography was to be condemned for its visual advocacy of that particular movement, during the nineteenth century it was widely criticized for precisely the opposite, namely fuelling the eclecticism of which Freret's Moorish building, one of the most ornate in New Orleans, was a striking example. Building 'portraits' such as these were instrumental in fabricating and promulgating an illusion of civilized urban existence in which 'how the other half lives' was conveniently ignored.

top right

CHARLES DUDLEY ARNOLD (1844–1927)

Agricultural Building, World's Columbian Exposition, Chicago, 1893

Platinum print

Architects: McKim Mead & White

Hired initially by the exposition's architect-in-chief, Daniel Burnham, to take construction views, the Canadian-born Arnold was later appointed the fair's official photographer because of his experience in photographing architecture in Buffalo (New York State) and Europe, where he had made exemplar photographs for American architects. Arnold's official views, taken on mammoth plate cameras and printed in delicately toned platinum, perfectly paralleled the orderly grandiloquence of the fair's architecture. More importantly, as examples of photography used unashamedly for public relations and seen by millions not in original print form but in reproduction, they presaged the future of architectural photography.

bottom right

GEORG KOPPMANN & CO.

View of 'Bei den Mühren' from St Catherine's Church, Hamburg, 1884

Albumen print

Georg Koppmann (1842–1909?) was a leading topographical and architectural photographer who opened a studio in Hamburg in about 1865 and photographed throughout northern and central Germany. From 1872 he was commissioned by Hamburg's Municipal Housing Committee to survey those areas that were to be demolished to create the new Free Port and a modernized city centre. Comprising over 10,000 photographs, including some, as here, in which the inhabitants stare inquisitively at the camera, Koppmann's was the most thoroughgoing and exhaustive of such nineteenth-century municipal photographic surveys.

opposite

CHARLES MARVILLE (1816–1878/79)

Carrefour des rues de la Petite et de la Grande Truanderie, Paris, c. 1865

Albumen print

If the decontextualization of buildings by photographers such as Baldus and Bisson Frères could be said to reflect Haussmann's policy of 'dégagement'[27] – that is, stripping away the clutter around architectural monuments to reveal them as focal points – Marville represents the other aspect of Haussmannization, the notion of streetscape. Using low vantage points to heighten the sense of claustrophobia, Marville's photographs of Paris's old streets expose the ravages of time through an acute feeling for texture, while his concentration on myriad details, such as shop signs and posters, asserts that, though populated only by spectral figures, these are very much living landscapes.

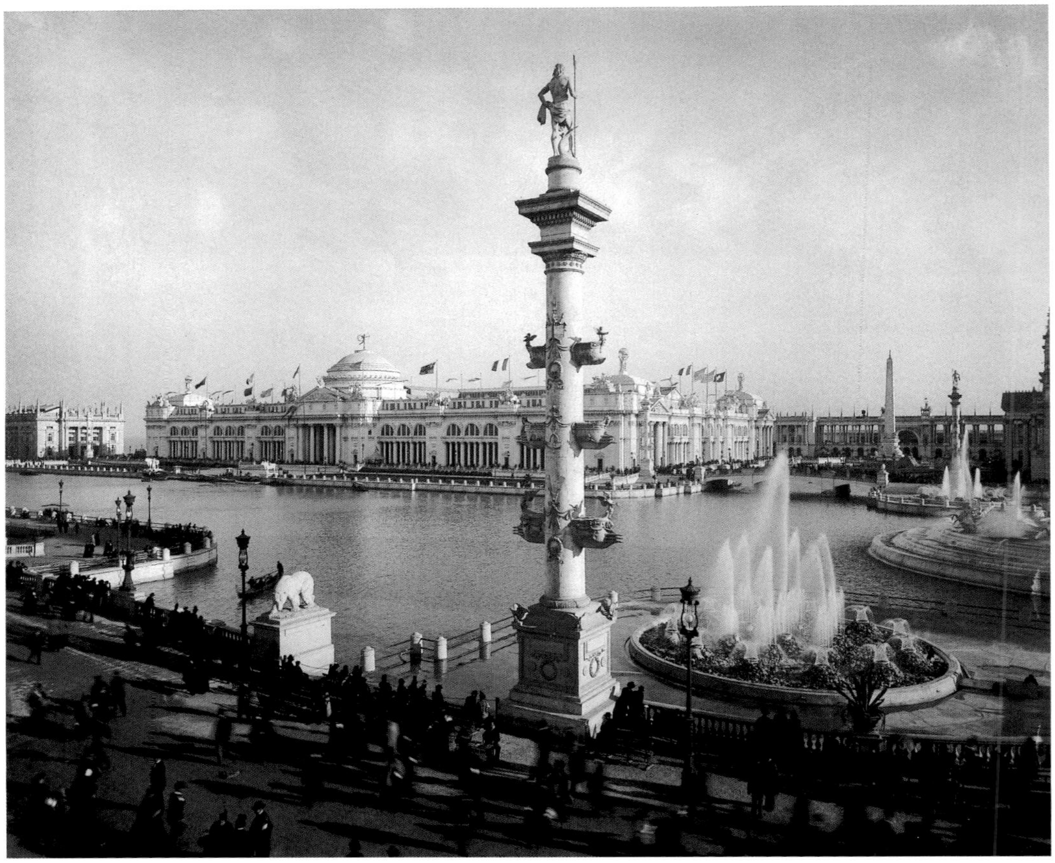

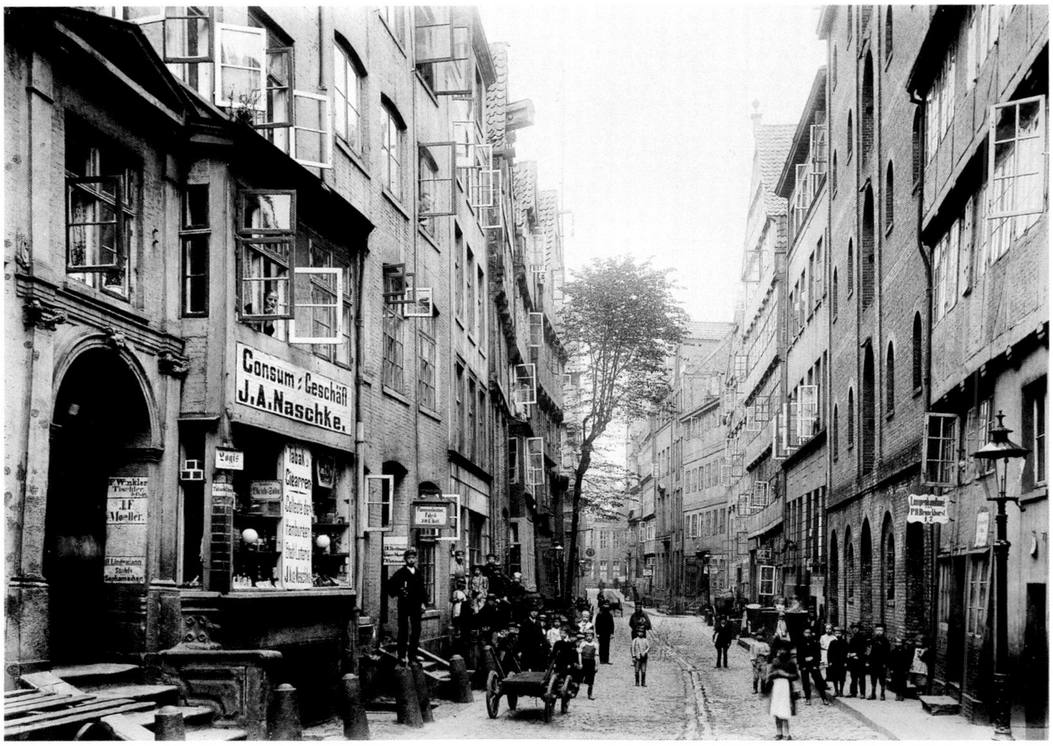

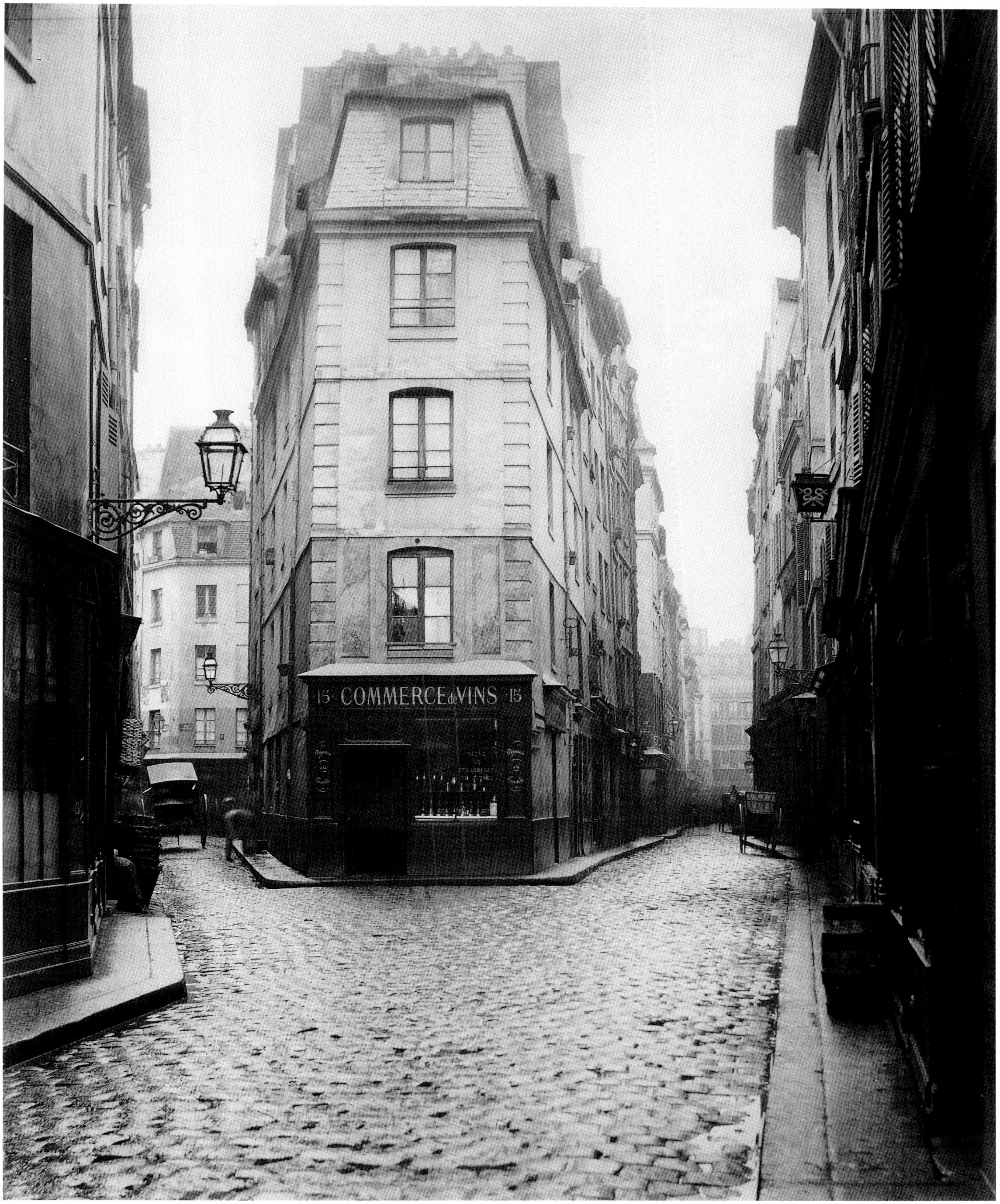
15 COMMERCE de VINS 15

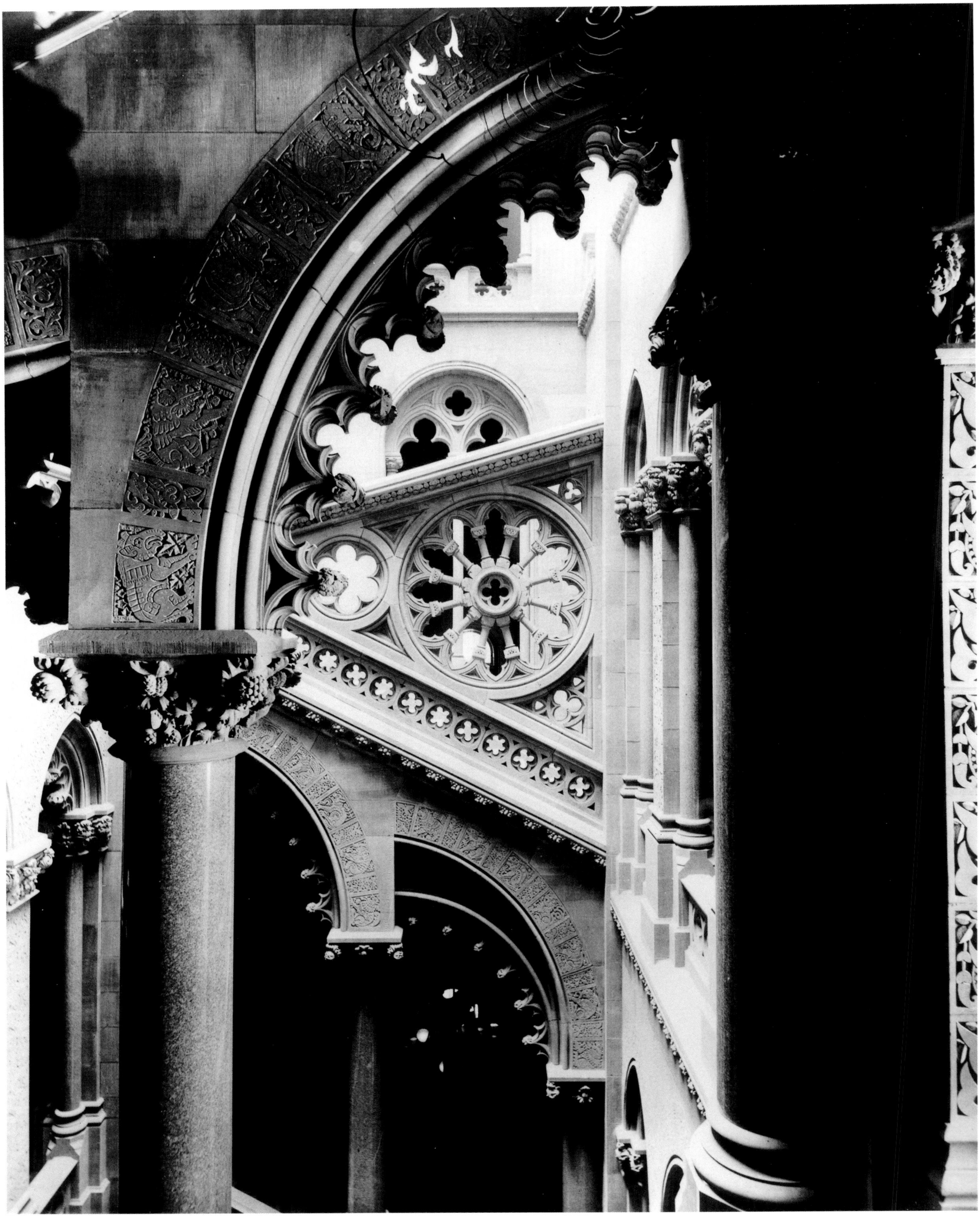

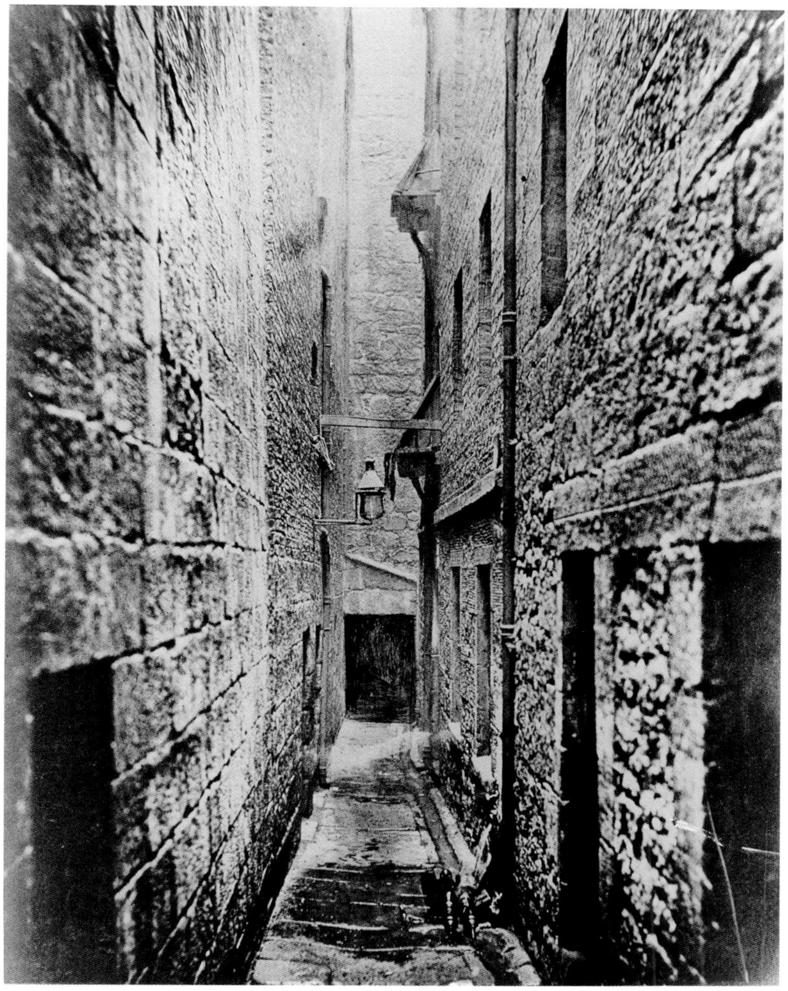

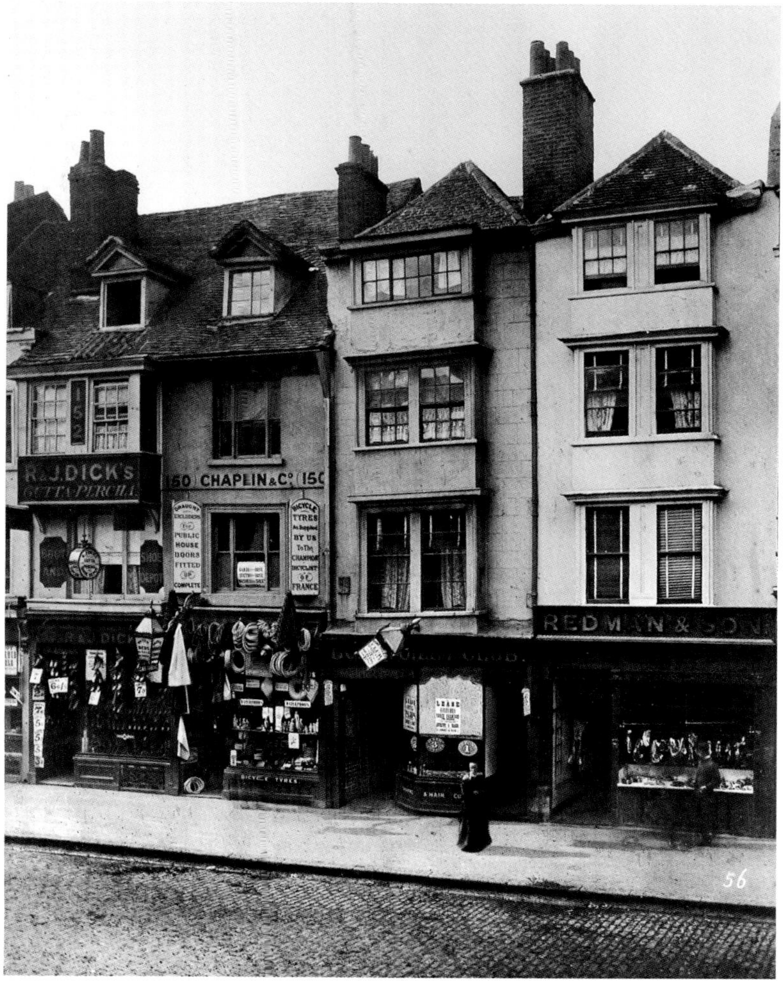

opposite

PHOTOGRAPHER UNKNOWN

Senate Staircase in New York State Capitol, Albany, 1885

Albumen print

Architect: Leopold Eidlitz

Photography during the nineteenth century was a voyage of discovery, not just geographically but also into a new world of architectural details that previously could be appreciated only by close inspection up a ladder, through the laborious process of cast-making or through frequently unreliable engravings. The camera, therefore, contributed to the proliferation of ornamental detail in late nineteenth- and early twentieth-century architecture. Eidlitz himself was a keen collector of photographs.

above left

THOMAS ANNAN (1829–1887)

Close, No. 61 Saltmarket, Glasgow, c. 1868

Albumen print

Although already a noted architectural photographer, Annan was here forced by the novel nature of his subject-matter to abandon traditional strategies and adopt new solutions. The rigid geometry of the composition accentuates the cavernous walls; the unrelenting harshness of the stone and the ever-present damp are presented so forcefully as to be almost tangible. The distribution of Annan's photographs included a limited edition of one hundred copies entitled *Photographs of Old Closes, Streets, etc Taken 1868–1877* (1878), printed not in albumen, as originally, but in carbon, a process Annan helped to pioneer.

above right

HENRY DIXON (1820–1893) & **T.J. DIXON**

for the Society for Photographing Relics of Old London

Old Houses in Borough High Street, Southwark, London, 1881

Carbon print

Between 1875 and 1886 the Society for Photographing Relics of Old London (SPROL) issued 120 photographs: six a year between 1875 and 1879, and twelve a year thereafter. Until 1881 the photographs, all carbon prints to allay fears of fading, appeared without text but were subsequently accompanied by descriptive letterpress written by SPROL's secretary, Alfred Marks, with the assistance of such experts as G.H. Birch, director of Sir John Soane's Museum. Although old houses and shops predominated, where possible each year the Society attempted to pursue a carefully worked out theme – 1885, for example, was devoted to the Inns of Court.

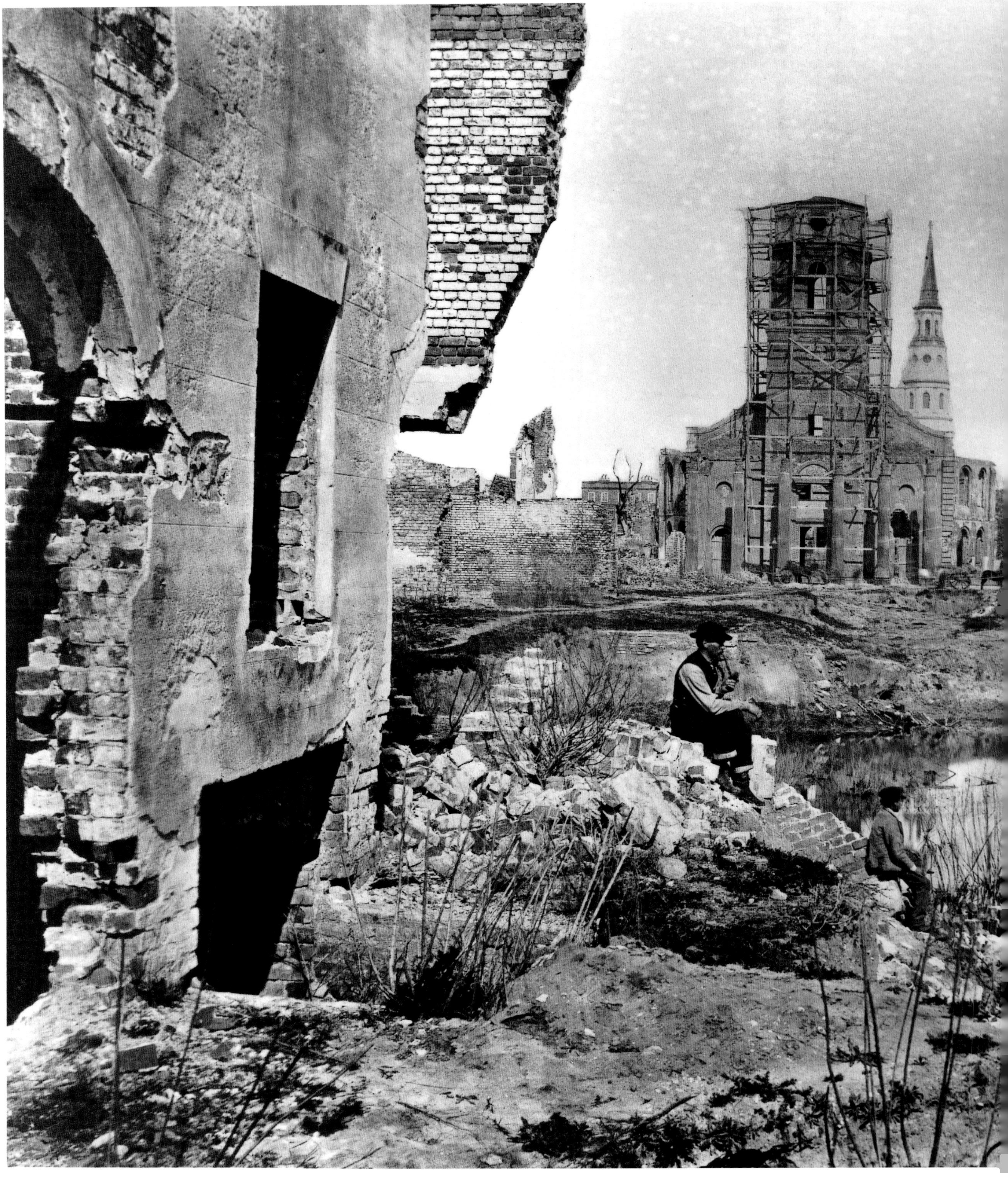

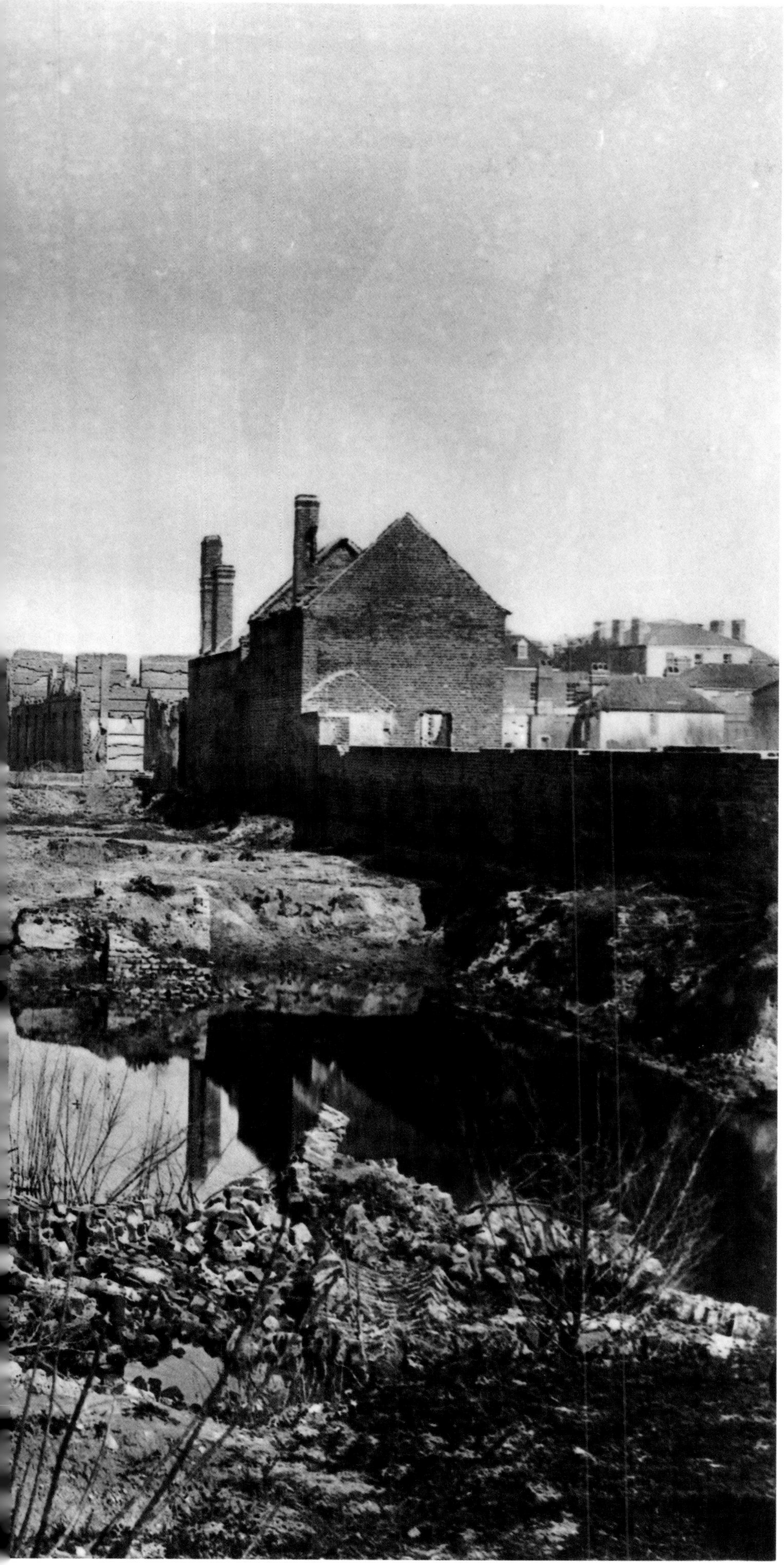

GEORGE N. BARNARD (1819–1902)

Ruins of Charleston

Albumen print from *Photographic Views of Sherman's Campaign*, New York (Wynkoop & Hallenbeck) 1866

The photography of war-ravaged buildings has provided the medium with some of its most haunting images. Two of the nineteenth century's notable examples are J.L. Andrieu's *Désastres de la guerre* (1872), a record of the aftermath of the Paris Commune, and Barnard's photographs of sites devastated during General Sherman's infamous American Civil War march to the sea, which the photographer retraced in 1866. Published in a portfolio of sixty-one views, these latter chillingly prefigure scenes in Dresden or Nagasaki and were shot by Barnard, an army employee, in a deadpan manner that further enhanced their power.

top right

ALBRECHT MEYDENBAUER (1834–1921)

Cathedral, Naumburg, 1891

Albumen print

A fall while surveying a building at close quarters prompted Meydenbauer to consider how photography could be used to measure structures instead. These investigations gave rise to photogrammetry and Meydenbauer's foundation of the Köningliche Messbildanstalt in Berlin, which he headed from 1885 to 1909. Meydenbauer's method involved the precise recording of as much of the building as possible on 40 cm (16 in.) square negatives – the metric image (*Messbild*) – from which measured drawings could be made. His archive of largely German historic architecture proved invaluable to Berlin's post-war reconstruction and underlined the practical nature of nineteenth-century architectural photography.

bottom right

DR WILLIAM HENRY PIGOU (1818–1858)

Great Gateway of a Temple, Beejanuggur, 1856

Albumen print from Philip Meadows Taylor and James Fergusson, *Architecture in Dharwar and Mysore*, London (John Murray) 1866

Between 1835 and 1842 Fergusson amassed a fortune in his Calcutta indigo factory before retiring to London and devoting much of his time to the study of Indian architecture. His concern to provide accurate illustrations saw him employ first the *camera lucida* and then, from the late 1850s, photography. By 1876, when his *History of Indian and Eastern Architecture* appeared, Fergusson possessed over three thousand photographs of Indian buildings, "with which constant use has made me as familiar as with any other object that is perpetually before my eyes".[28]

opposite

PHOTOGRAPHER UNKNOWN

Rijksmuseum, Amsterdam, 1885

Albumen print

Architect: P.J.H. Cuypers

Cuypers's career was not unlike that of Viollet-le-Duc and, like Viollet, Cuypers was heavily indebted to photography. Besides building two major landmarks in the Rijksmuseum (1877–85) and Amsterdam Central Station (1881–89), Cuypers's main work lay in restoration and a series of Gothic Revival churches. Photographs played an important part in his restoration of De Haar Castle, and his churches drew heavily on his close study of French medieval precedents, a process aided by the photographs he extensively collected, which included images by Le Secq of Rheims Cathedral.

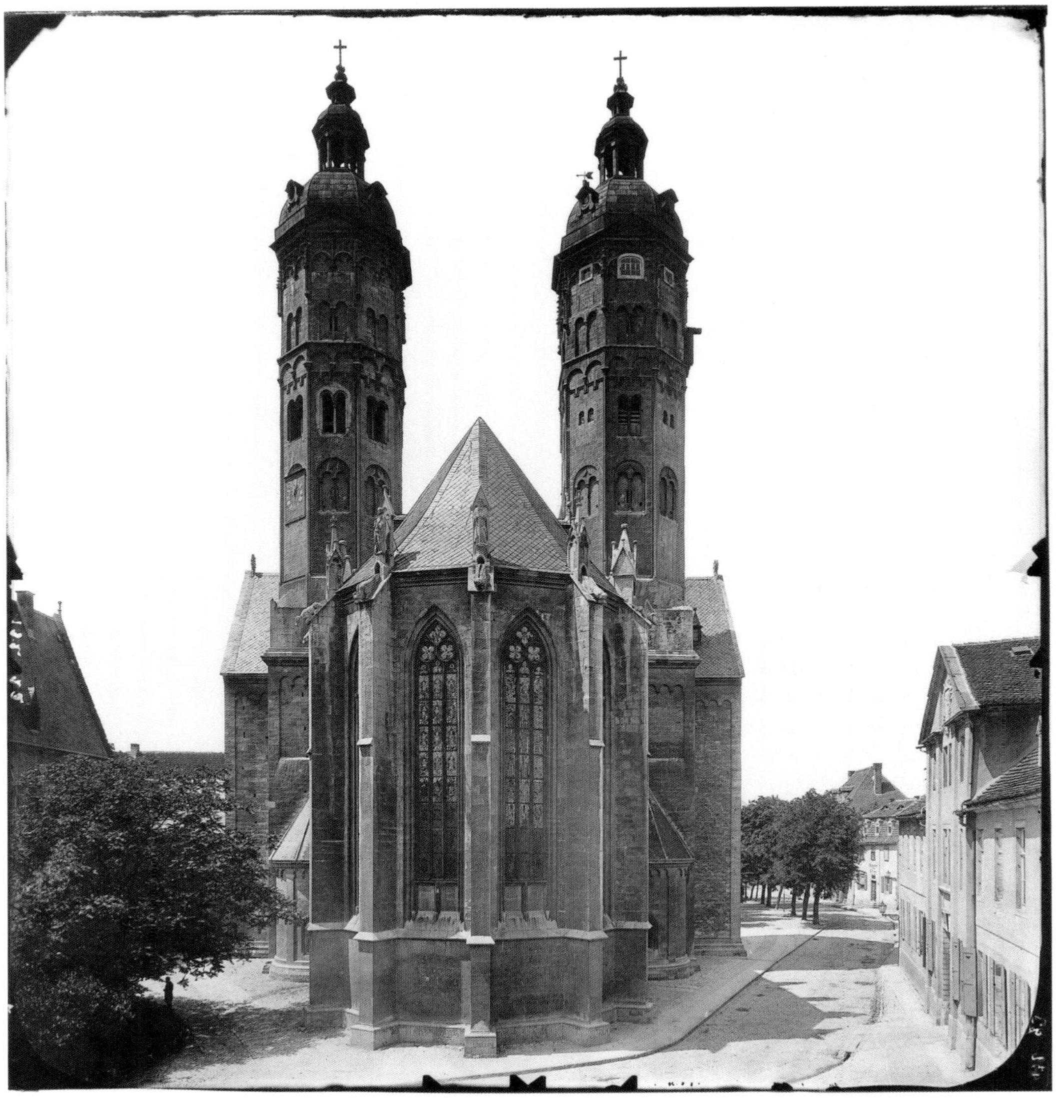

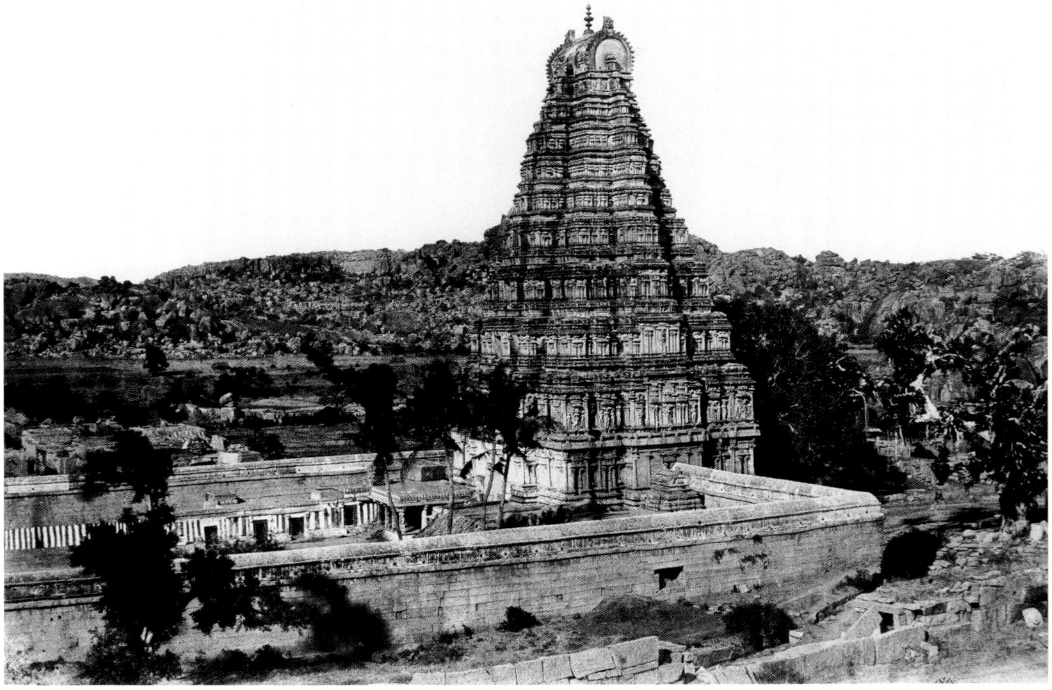

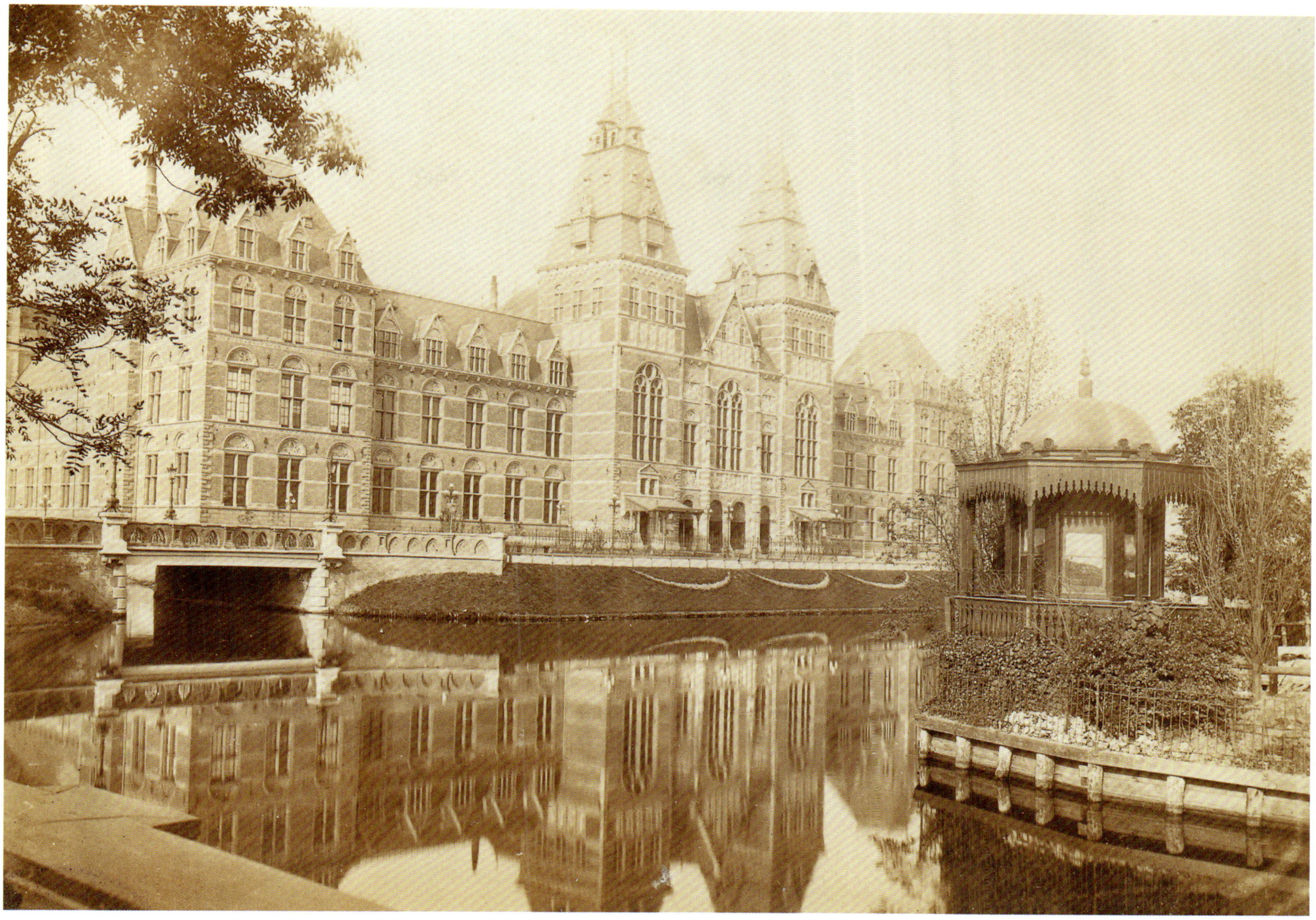

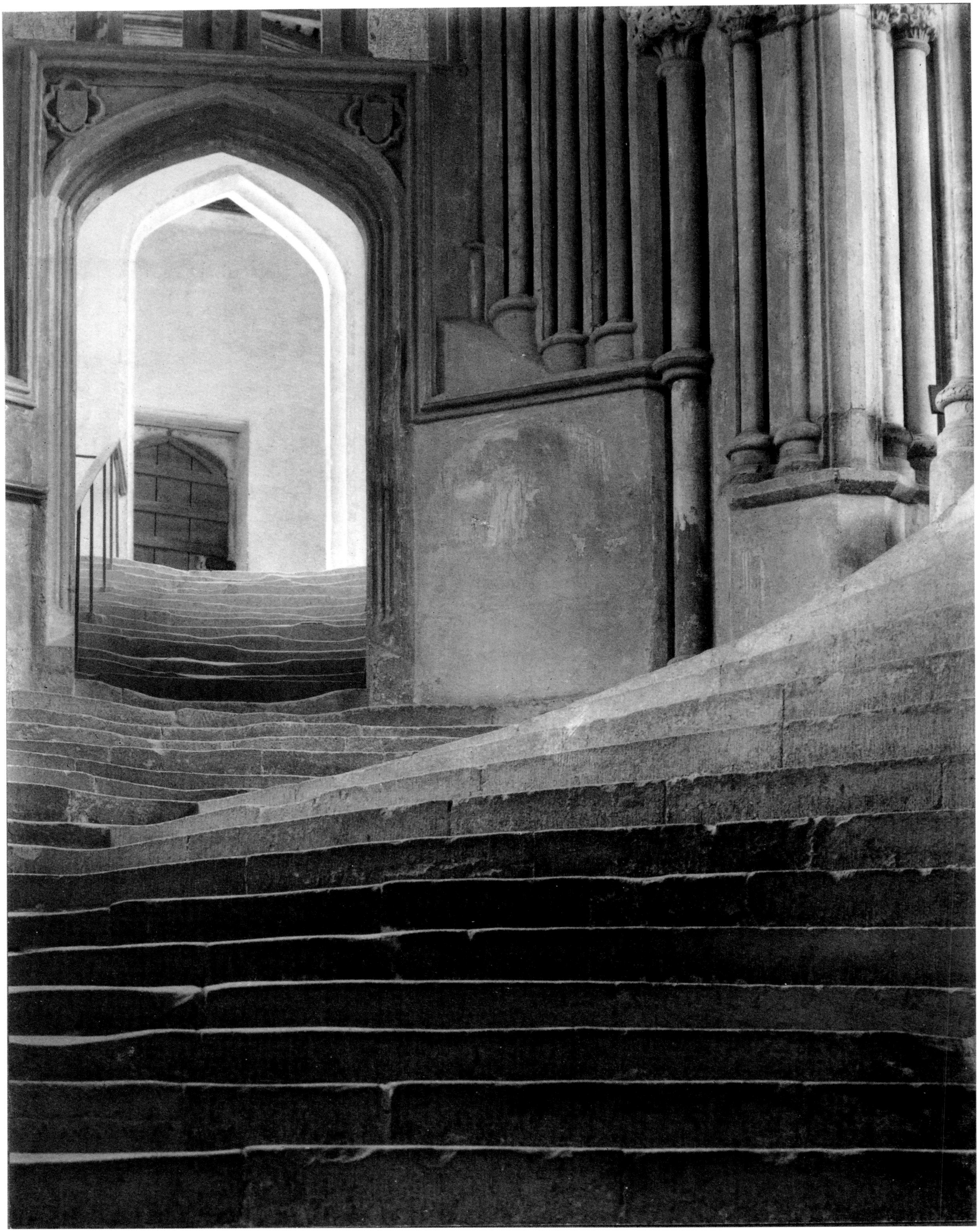

Chapter 3 **Printer's Ink and Pictorialism 1880–1925**

page 84

FREDERICK HENRY EVANS (1853–1943)

A Sea of Steps, Wells Cathedral, 1903

Platinum print

It is one of the great ironies of architectural photography that the medium was invented just as, with the establishment of magazines such as the *Revue générale de l'architecture* (1840) and *The Builder* (1843), architectural publishing was undergoing a revolution to which photography, because of its incompatibility with type, could not directly contribute. The photograph's capacity to become the pre-eminent means by which buildings were illustrated and discussed was thus severely limited. Motivated partly by fears about its impermanence, but more especially by the belief, common among photographers, that the photographic print represented merely an interim stage towards the final goal of rendering it into a surface capable of being set with type, strenuous efforts were made to overcome this problem. As already noted, copying photographs into traditional printed media or simply pasting them into books were among the expedients first adopted.

The latter practice was perhaps more widely employed in architecture, in which accurate illustrations were of paramount importance, than in other subjects. It was particularly popular in Britain, where some of the best examples were produced by the publisher Alfred W. Bennett. Among these were the handsome *Normandy, Its Gothic Architecture and History* (1865), containing twenty-five small but exquisite photographs by Cundall & Downes and a text by the Pre-Raphaelite artist and critic Frederic G. Stephens, and William and Mary Howitt's *Ruined Abbeys and Castles of Great Britain*, the first series of which appeared in 1862 and a second two years later (below left). Including photographs by Fenton, Wilson and others, *Ruined Abbeys* was hailed as a "triumph of the graphic arts".[1] Such books did not, however, bring about the hoped-for wider distribution of photographs, as most were perforce issued in expensive, limited editions resulting from their slow rate of production and the fact that there was no reduction in the unit cost of each photograph as the number required increased. These problems were compounded by the tendency of the tipped-in photographs to fade or be discoloured by the adhesives used. More importantly, although the *Revue générale* featured a pasted-in photograph by François Alphonse Fortier of the staircase at Blois in its 1856 volume, the technique was far too laborious for periodicals, which had to be produced at speed.

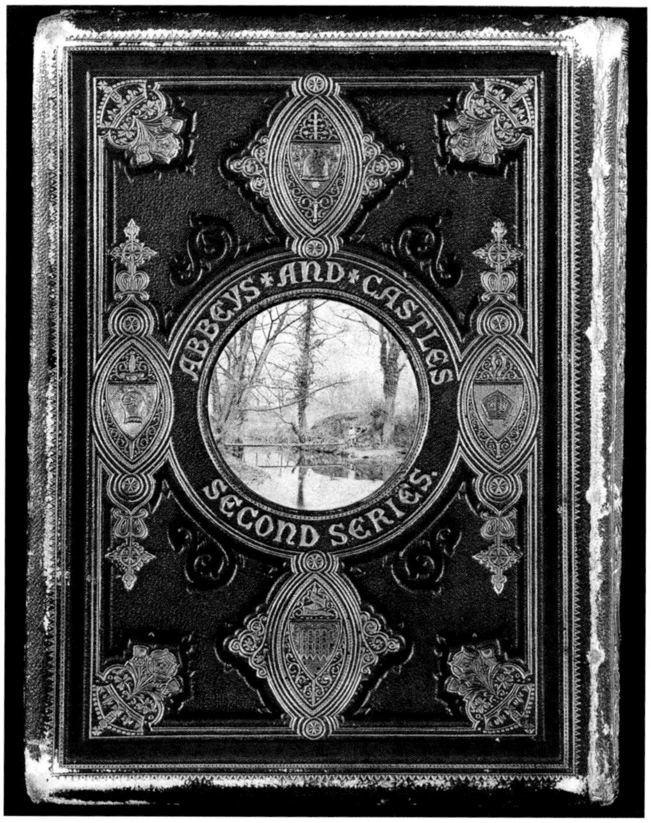

William and Mary Howitt, *Ruined Abbeys and Castles of Great Britain*, 2nd series, 1864
Back cover with inserted albumen print

Publishers therefore experimented vigorously with a plethora of photomechanical processes, perhaps the most successful of which was the ink photo developed by the London firm of Sprague & Co. and utilized to best effect in *The Architect* in the 1880s. Although often of poor quality, ink photos in their various forms were quick and cheap to produce, and, by permitting tonal reproduction, they enabled photographs to reach journal subscribers for the first time (see page 94). In essence they were an unsophisticated form of collotype, which proved to be one of the most delicate and faithful means of reproducing photographs in printer's ink. Introduced by Josef Albert in Bavaria in 1868 and shortly afterwards by Ernest Edwards in London, collotype, which was known under a variety of names – Albertype, heliotype, *lichtdruck*, *phototypie* – was a skilled, painstaking and costly process in which the printing surface was formed by gelatine film.

The film's inherent fragility permitted only short print runs, but this disadvantage was more than offset by collotype's capacity to reproduce fine detail, which saw it enjoy a brief florescence in architectural publishing around the turn of the century. Pre-eminent here was the Berlin publishing house of Ernst Wasmuth (see page 95), which issued a steady stream of sumptuous publications, including Hugo Licht's *Architektur Deutschlands übersicht der hervorragendsten Bauausführungen der Neuzeit* (1882) and Constantin Uhde's *Baudenkmäler in Grossbritannien* (1894), the fine plates for many of which were prepared by Römmler & Jonas, a Dresden firm who were leading experts in collotype printing. Wasmuth himself visited the London premises of the publishers B.T. Batsford on several occasions, and his books, particularly the series *Palast-Architektur von Ober-Italien und Toscana von XV. bis XVII. Jahrhundert*, begun in 1886, were the models for Batsford's own collotype publications. Starting with J.W. Gotch's *Architecture of the Renaissance in England* (1891–94), these sought to emulate through photography the great architectural folios of the eighteenth century.

Unusually, as it was common to credit only the printers, Batsford gave due acknowledgement to the original photographers of its collotype plates. Most were supplied by Charles Latham, whose association with the firm and with *Country Life* was to make him one of the most influential British architectural photographers of the period. His best work for Batsford came in 1896 with the publication of George H. Birch's *London Churches of the XVIIth and XVIIIth Centuries* (right). The most lavish and monumental of all collotype works, however, was produced not in Germany or England but in Italy by the Venetian publisher Ferdinando Ongania, the final volume of whose *La Basilica di San Marco* appeared in 1888 (see page 97). Over ten years in the making and heavily influenced by the precepts of Ruskin and Boito, *La Basilica* exhaustively documented St Mark's through engravings, chromolithographs and particularly "the new Heliotype permanent process", which aimed to "transmit to posterity a faithful record of this splendid monument, in the state of preservation in which it is found at the present time".[2]

These collotype publications were important, not just because of their high quality of reproduction but also because they lent architectural photography a new prestige and status, a trend given added impetus by the use of heliotypes to illustrate American architectural magazines, such as the Chicago-based *Inland Architect* and especially its Boston rival, the *American Architect and Building News*

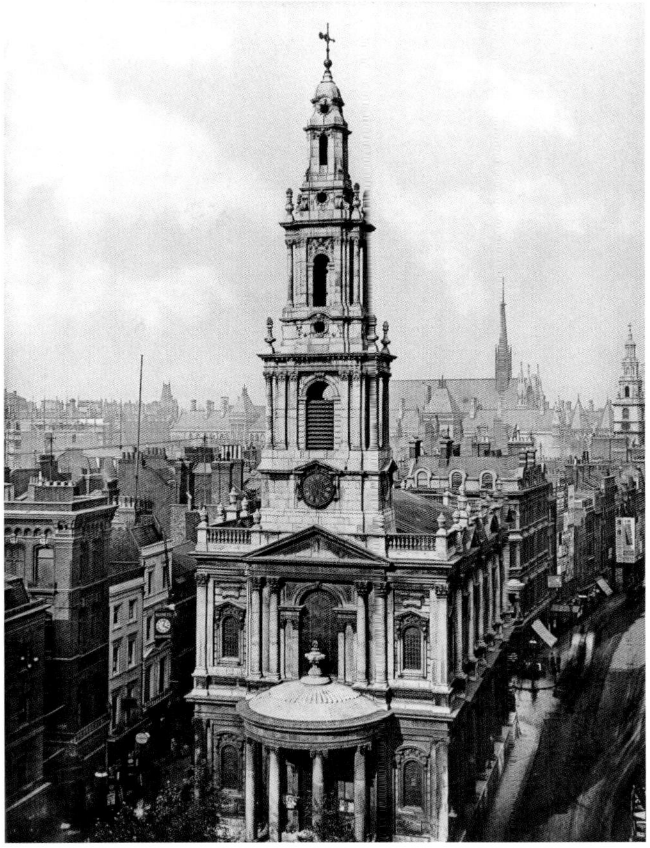

CHARLES LATHAM

St Mary-le-Strand, London

Collotype from George H. Birch, *London Churches of the XVIIth and XVIIIth Centuries*, London (B.T. Batsford) 1896

(see page 96). The latter's owner, James Osgood, who had brought Ernest Edwards to Boston in 1872 to manage his Heliotype Corporation of Massachusetts, considered heliotype too expensive to use in a weekly periodical. Significantly, however, he was forced to change his mind by reader demand and to issue different editions of the magazine, with subscribers paying more for a greater number of heliotype illustrations. In another striking testimony to the quality of the process and its role in formulating architectural opinion, Henry Hobson Richardson insisted that his buildings were illustrated only by photographs reproduced in heliotype rather than by drawings and agreed to pay part of the production costs himself. Richardson's astute use of the press, and in particular photographic reproductions, was an early instance of a practice that was to gather momentum with the introduction of half-tone printing.

None of these photomechanical processes, collotype included, could be printed with type. It was only with the invention of the half-tone block in the late 1880s and its general adoption in the following decade that it finally became possible to print photographs and type together in one operation on the same page, thus allowing photographs to be reproduced economically and in unlimited numbers in books and journals. Although the changes it set in motion were gradual, the introduction of half-tone printing transformed architectural photography, paving the way for the camera to become the supreme mediator of architectural endeavour. Its immediate result was the creation of a number of magazines, principally *Architectural Record* (1891), *Architectural Review* (1896) and *Country Life* (1897), which were specifically geared to exploit the revolutionary new technology to the full. With photographic illustrations integral to their design and marketability, such magazines would henceforth be the driving force behind developments in architectural photography, patronizing the leading practitioners, giving them access to a vast new audience and, by greatly extending the market for their imagery, encouraging more photographers to specialize in architectural subjects. For their part, photographers entered into a new relationship with an audience that would increasingly see their images not in the form of original prints but as screened reproductions, juxtaposed with one another and the text they illustrated as well as filtered through the dictates of editorial policy and the exigencies of page layouts over which they had no control. Furthermore, although of course still commissioned by architects as well, photographers were increasingly required to tailor their production methods to magazine publishing. The British photographer Edwin Dockree, a frequent contributor to *Architectural Review*, advised in 1904 that the block maker "likes a good plucky blue-black print full of 'vim' and contrast; it yields a block far superior to any other class of print".[3]

Changes were wrought, too, in the way buildings were photographed and presented. During the nineteenth century it was the norm for buildings to be illustrated in a single view, frequently set apart from the text by the need to print the picture on a heavier, coated paper. This had the effect of imbuing both the illustrations and the buildings they

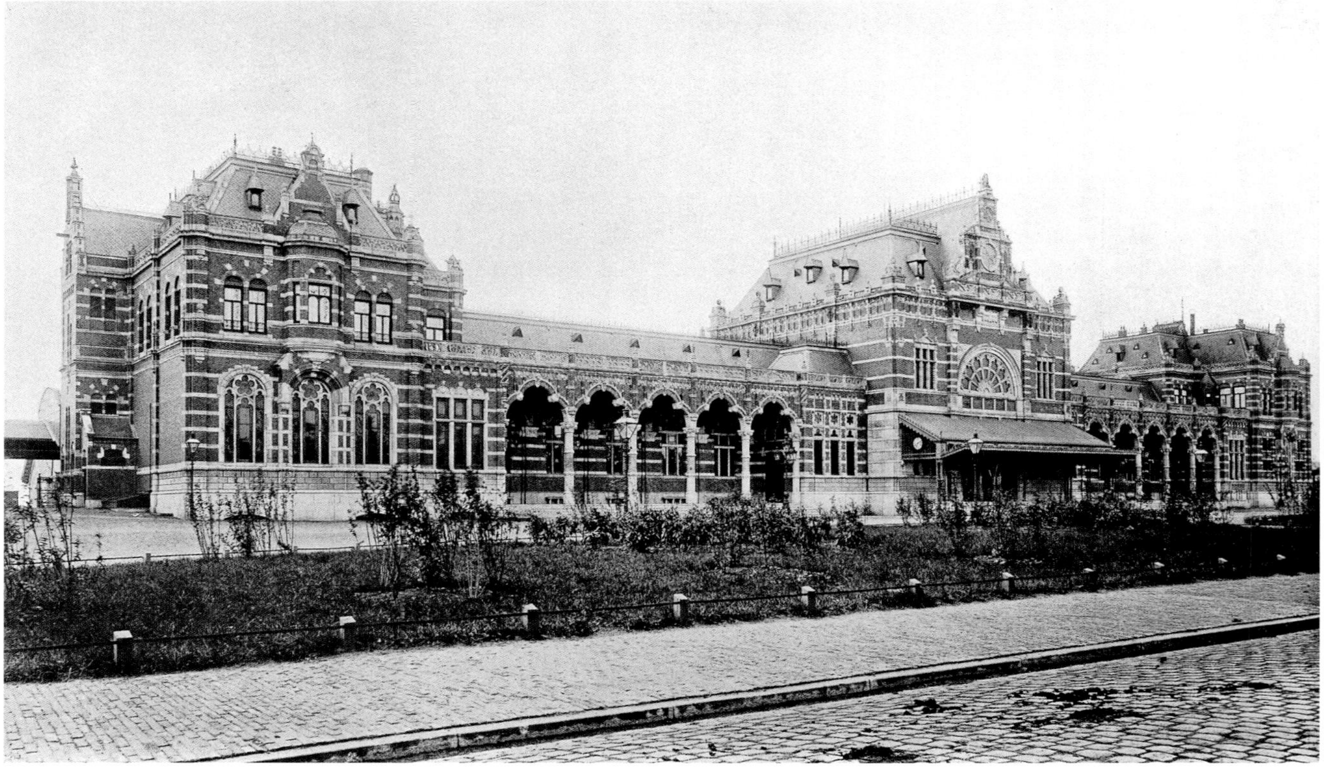

Page spread from *Bouwkundig tijdschrift*, vol. 17, 1899, showing *Railway Station, Groningen*
Architect: J. Gosschalk

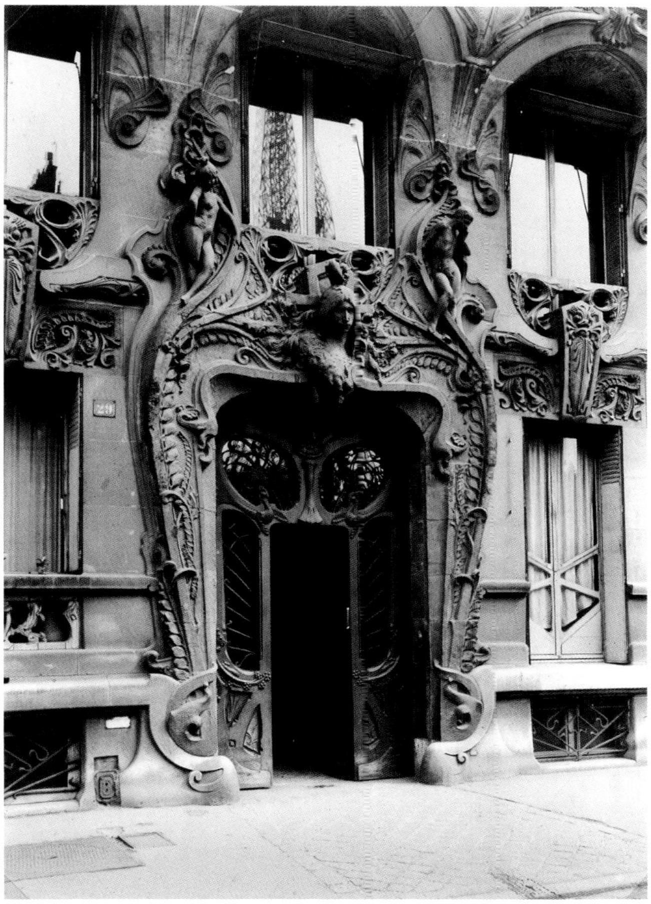

PHOTOGRAPHER UNKNOWN

29 avenue Rapp, Paris, early 1920s
Gelatine silver print
Architect: Jules Lavirotte

portrayed with a special significance. With the introduction of half-tones and the integration of text and illustrations, not only was a wider range of buildings, especially contemporary ones, featured but individual buildings were afforded more extensive pictorial coverage. For the photographer this meant a shift in emphasis away from the all-embracing single view – even though architects such as Frank Lloyd Wright continued to insist on it – to more comprehensive studies involving a greater variety of viewpoints and increased treatment of details. In 1897, for example, J.W. Taylor took no less than one hundred views of Adler & Sullivan's Auditorium Building in Chicago. For the reader, illustrations lost their mystique, becoming diluted into routine pictorial matter that was as likely to be subliminally imbibed as carefully scrutinized. At the same time, however, the abundance of photographic reproductions allowed readers, superficially at least, to form their own judgements and widened architectural discourse beyond the confines of a narrow coterie of critics. This in turn served to broaden the debate on architectural photography from the constricted nineteenth-century preoccupation with its role *vis-à-vis* sketching to a more critical examination of the way buildings were photographed and the influence of photographs on architectural taste and production.

By the end of the twentieth century's first decade, most architectural magazines were illustrated primarily by half-tone reproduction of photographs, although the quality varied enormously from the muddied, coarse-grained views in the French magazine *L'Architecture* to the more lavish plates on glossy paper contained in the Dutch *Bouwkundig tijdschrift* (opposite) and the British *Architectural Review*. Although there was a greater concentration on details, and half-tone was better able to convey the quality of light in photographs than photomechanical processes such as collotype, the style of mainstream architectural photography did not effectively change, despite the availability of faster lenses, such as the Zeiss Tessar, and the introduction of the telephoto lens in 1891, tirelessly promoted by Ernest Marriage. As Dockree maintained, "the supreme claim of the architectural photograph [was] its impersonality",[4] a claim strengthened by the anonymous presentation of published photographs without credits to individual photographers. The architectural photograph was seen simply as a purveyor of information (as in the example above), a sentiment that induced a number of British architects to argue vociferously for the inclusion of photographs in the prestigious Royal Academy annual exhibition as a factually reliable antidote to the mendacious ostentation of perspective drawing. It is indicative of the growing influence of photography, and the increasingly sophisticated audience reaction to a medium made more familiar through publication, that a mere three decades later the very criticisms levelled against perspective drawing were to be used in condemnation of the photograph.

Despite this anonymity, it is possible to identify the work of some of the period's most notable architectural photographers. In France, Chevojon Frères was a major firm recording the work of leading architects such as Auguste Perret and Henri Sauvage (see page 99). In Italy firms like Alinari still reigned supreme but were joined by such

FRANK LLOYD WRIGHT
(1867–1959)

Perspective of Tomek House, Riverside, from *Ausgeführte Bauten und Entwürfe von Frank Lloyd Wright*, Berlin (Ernst Wasmuth) 1910

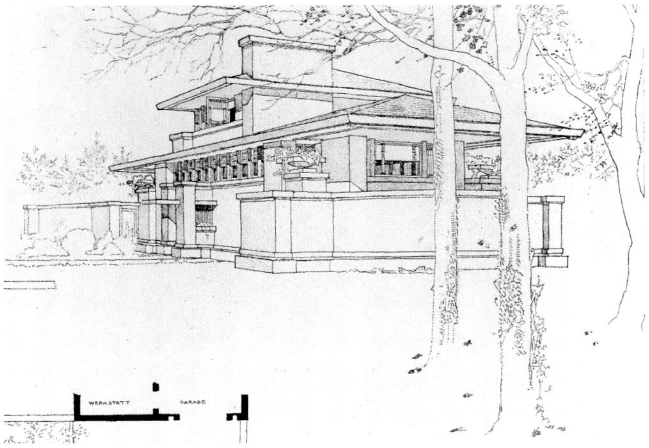

newcomers as Ferdinando Barsotti of Florence. In Germany, Hugo Schmölz and Arthur Köster were starting out on notable careers, and in Austria, Martin Gerlach turned his camera on Viennese social housing (see pages 102–03). In America, Henry Fuermann of Chicago was described as "the most famous photographer in the country",[5] while his son, Clarence, photographed work by Frank Lloyd Wright including the Larkin Building, Buffalo (1904), and the Avery Coonley House, Riverside (1908; see page 100). In England the German diplomat and art historian Hermann Muthesius, impervious to the merits of Dockree and Lemere, declared that there were only two men who could photograph architecture well – Latham and Thomas Lewis – and that Lewis was the better. While Lewis supplied some of the photographs for the collotype plates in Muthesius's *Die Englische Baukunst der Gegenwart* and *Das Englische Haus* (1904–05), Latham made the bigger impact. His softly lit photographs of country houses helped to define *Country Life*'s photographic style and influenced trends in interior design (see page 101). In South Africa the Pretoria-based Alan Yates emerged as a photographer of distinction (see page 104), while towards the end of the period Bernard Eilers established himself as the doyen of Dutch architectural photographers, aided by his friendship with H.T. Wijdeveld, a fellow member of the influential Architectura et Amitia group, and editor of its mouthpiece, *Wendigen* (see pages 104–05). Through *Wendigen*, Eilers's photographs, though somewhat poorly reproduced, helped to proselytize the work of the Amsterdam School of architects.

As some architects were quick to realize, the growth in photographically illustrated magazines afforded new opportunities for promotion. Sir Edwin Lutyens's career was significantly advanced by his friendship with *Country Life*'s owner, Sir Edward Hudson, and the frequent appearance of his work in its pages (see page 107). Hidden away in small mid-western towns, Louis Sullivan's banks, as the critic Montgomery Schuyler conceded, owed their reputation not a little to the photographs of Henry Fuermann and others, despite the fact that they were unable to reproduce Sullivan's vivid colours (see page 107). Similarly, Frank Lloyd Wright's stature was boosted by the publication in 1910 of Wasmuth's celebrated portfolio *Ausgeführte Bauten und Entwürfe von Frank Lloyd Wright*, which, although illustrated entirely with drawings, was still indebted to photography. Several of Wright's renderings, including that of the Tomek House, Riverside, Illinois (above left), represented cannily cleaned-up versions of photographs, particularly the street-level views of which he was especially fond.[6] On the other hand, a few architects rejected photography entirely. Adolf Loos, for example, revelled in the unphotogenic nature of his work, which saved it from the crass commodification he regarded as the inevitable consequence of publication. In addition it could be argued, as Wright did, that photography was ill-suited to the depiction of certain elements important to architecture of the period: "the truth concerning the elusive depth dimension involved in organic architecture defies the camera."[7]

The recognition of photography's promotional potential was accompanied by a dawning realization among architects that, far from being the mechanical act photographers liked to pretend, photography could be a creative force, playing a major role in how an architect's work was perceived. As a result, some architects began to intervene more directly in the photographic process. When the Hanover photographer Edmund Lill was commissioned to photograph Walter Gropius and Adolf Meyer's Fagus factory in 1922, Meyer travelled to Alfeld an der Leine to supervise Lill's work and ensure that he got the shots he wanted. This new recognition among architects of the camera's creativity was partly the outcome of it having become an increasingly common architectural accessory. Encouraged especially by the availability of presensitized plates, more architects now used the camera themselves (see page 109) and were aware of both its shortcomings and the benefits that it could bestow in the hands of a skilled operator. Wright, for example, used his own photographs, not as exemplars as his nineteenth-century predecessors would have done but to explore ideas of architectural space. As a result, he had pronounced views throughout his career on how his buildings should be photographed. A youthful Charles-Edouard Jeanneret (later Le Corbusier) was another convert to photography. He first used a Kodak camera, which, not surprisingly, he found unsuitable for architectural work, and then a larger format Cupido 80, which he acquired in 1911 at the outset of his formative *voyage d'orient* to the Balkans and Turkey (right). Although he effectively abandoned photography soon after, denouncing it as "a tool for idlers",[8] the first-hand experience he gained nurtured his understanding of the way buildings could be presented and explicated photographically – a lesson he later applied by closely controlling the professional photographs taken and published of his own work. The proliferation of architectural camera clubs and the increased interest shown by architects in the medium bore fruit during the inter-war years and afterwards, when architect amateurs were instrumental in extending the scope of architectural photography. These developments also presaged the rise of a new post-Second World War generation of architectural photographers, whose backgrounds lay in architecture rather than in photography.

The less formal but often more experiential images of architect amateurs offered an alternative vision to mainstream architectural photography, as did the photographs of old Paris taken speculatively from 1898 onwards by Eugène Atget, which he sold mostly to museums, libraries and other institutions concerned to preserve visual records of a city threatened afresh by the construction of the Métro (see page 111). While Atget was equipped with the usual accoutrements of the conventional architectural photographer, including a large stand camera and wide-angle lenses, his bold handling of light and shadow, together with his frequently idiosyncratic choice of viewpoints, set him apart from mainstream practice. Whereas Marville had recorded entire streets, Atget worked on a smaller scale, demonstrating his fascination with the minutiae of everyday existence, as revealed in architectural features such as

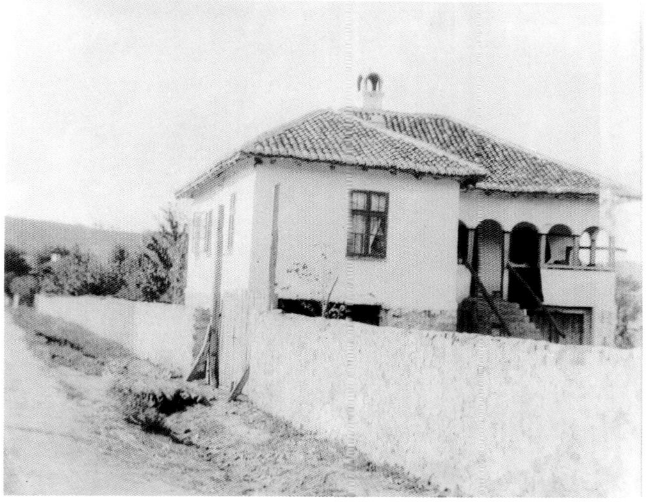

CHARLES-EDOUARD JEANNERET, 'LE CORBUSIER' (1887–1965)

Farmhouse with Loggia and Internal Courtyard, Serbia, 1911

Gelatine silver print

shop front details, door knockers and decorative ironwork (see page 112). Marville had disclosed the axial network of Haussmann's boulevards, but Atget ignored them entirely, revelling in the city's visual complexities and incongruities. If Marville's vision was that of the city planner and his drawing-board coherence, Atget's view was the fragmented, quizzical insight of the observant inhabitant. Atget's images, which he himself described as "documents, nothing but documents",[9] remained little known for most of his life until their discovery by Man Ray and the Surrealists in the mid-1920s and their subsequent championing by Man Ray's former assistant, Berenice Abbott. At her instigation, a selection of Atget's photographs was posthumously published in 1930 and greatly influenced Walker Evans and Edwin Smith, whose work perhaps came closest in subject-matter and poetic evocation of place to Atget's. More recently, Atget's obsessional interest in the intermediate, uncertain territory between town and country, epitomized in his day by the Parisian *zone militaire*, which was home to the city's social outcasts, has been echoed in the work of cityscape photographers such as Gabriele Basilico.

The biggest challenge to architectural photographic orthodoxy, however, was posed by Pictorialism, which by 1900 had become a well-developed international movement. As early as 1893 one of Pictorialism's chief protagonists, Alfred Stieglitz, in his position as editor of *American Amateur Photographer*, had launched a scathing attack on Arnold's attempt to monopolize photography at the World's Columbian

Exposition and the sterility of his monumental style of architectural image-making. Pictorialism arose principally as a reaction to the standardization of photography and its mass commercialization, which stemmed from the introduction of roll film and simple-to-use push-button cameras, such as the Kodak, which first appeared in 1888. Its adherents, mostly well-off amateurs, deliberately adopted practices well beyond the capabilities of the average snapshooter to demonstrate the artistic credentials of their work. In particular, they employed printing processes such as carbon, bromoil, platinum and gum bichromate that controversially allowed considerable scope for hand manipulation and control. These processes resulted in images that, like those produced by British amateurs of the 1840s and 1850s, more often resembled products of the pencil or brush than of the camera.

The painterly ethos of Pictorialism represented nothing less than a wholesale repudiation of the basic tenets of architectural photography. It rejected the positivist, empirical nature of photography, arguing that it should be concerned with the universal, not the specific, with emotions and ideas, not with facts. *The Builder* missed the point entirely when attacking the Pictorialist tendency to exhibit architectural subjects "under some semi-poetic title, which is irritating when the building possesses any features of interest, and we are not able to identify it".[10] Pictorialism's emphasis on soft-focus, impressionistic views more concerned with light, mood and atmosphere than the specifics of a particular locale – Alfred Stieglitz's *Flatiron Building* (1903; see page 113) exemplifies the style – was diametrically opposed to the overall sharpness aimed at by architectural photographers, whom the Pictorialist George Davison doubtless had in mind when he contemptuously dismissed the "f.64 school", who used small stops to ensure that every detail was clearly rendered. Davison's comments also underlined Pictorialism's hostility to the growing mechanical perfection of the medium. "Fuzzygraphs", as George Bernard Shaw termed hazy Pictorialist images, were becoming popular just as the introduction of high-quality anastigmatic lenses allowed the architectural photographer even finer resolution of detail.[11] Finally, Pictorialism's insistence that photography should be a means of personal expression clashed with the notion of architectural photography as anonymous and transparent.

Not surprisingly, many Pictorialists concluded that architecture was an unsuitable subject for photographic treatment, preferring to concentrate instead on landscapes, genre studies and portraits. The major exception to this trend was Frederick Evans, whose luminous meditations on English and French cathedral interiors moved Stieglitz to laud him as "the greatest exponent of architectural photography" (see page 114).[12]

On account of its given subject-matter and its limited latitude for treatment, Evans believed that architecture constituted the photographer's most daunting challenge. At the same time he was dismissive of most professional architectural photography, which he considered "devoid ... of every trace of artistic feeling"[13] and over-reliant on the use of the wide-angle lens, which produced unacceptably exaggerated perspectival effects. For Evans the golden rule was always to use the longest lens possible. His most famous and widely imitated photograph, *A Sea of Steps, Wells Cathedral* (1903; see page 84), for instance, was taken with his favourite 19 inch (48.3 cm) lens. Evans's advice to aspiring architectural photographers summed up his philosophy:

> Try for a record of an emotion rather than a piece of topography. Wait till the building makes you feel intensely, in some special part of it or other; then try and analyse what gives you that feeling, see if it is due to the isolation of some particular aspect or effect, and then see what your camera can do towards reproducing that effect, that subject.[14]

Inspired by the early architectural watercolours of J.M.W. Turner, Evans's photography is distinguished above all by its masterful rendition of light, which permeates his cathedral interiors, illuminating detail, suggesting space and depth, and charging his scenes with spiritual and emotional intensity. The appropriately entitled *'Height and Light' – Bourges Cathedral* (1904) is a particularly fine example, which was hailed by fellow photographer J. Dudley Johnston as "one of the most memorable records of architecture ever made" (see page 115).[15] Evans accomplished these effects without recourse to manipulation and by printing on platinum paper, which had a very long tonal scale.

In 1905, to the dismay of fellow Pictorialists, who were critical of half-tone reproduction, Evans accepted a roving commission from *Country Life*, ironically a strong supporter of Pictorialism, for whom he photographed French châteaux, English parish churches and, in 1911, Westminster Abbey. The hostility with which these photographs were received in Pictorialist circles, where they were denounced as arid topography, reveals the depth of feeling against architecture as a Pictorialist subject – a situation mirrored in The Netherlands, where Eilers was careful to maintain a clear division between his personal Pictorialist work and his more documentary, commissioned architectural photography. Evans's photographs also failed to find favour either with an architectural profession wedded to the concept of the photograph as record or with professional photographers who could not afford the luxury of Evans's time-consuming working methods. Nevertheless, in Evans's work we can trace Pictorialism's three-fold legacy to architectural photography: it re-emphasized the importance of the imaginative use of light; it demonstrated that photography could often say more about architecture through suggestive fragmentary views than through the all-inclusive statement; and it reasserted the need for an interpretative treatment of architecture – all themes that also run throughout Atget's work. Although achieved in very different ways and used to attain different ends, these elements were evident in Modernist photography too. This factor may help to explain the seeming incongruity of some former Pictorialists laying the ground for the establishment of Modernism and why some photographers were able to migrate between the two movements with apparent ease. It is interesting to note that Mark Oliver Dell and Herbert Felton, two of the leading photographers of British Modernist architecture in the 1930s, both emerged from amateur Pictorialist backgrounds and, indeed, after the Second World War reverted to that kind of image-making, Felton photographing cathedrals in a manner inspired by his friend and mentor Evans. A similar process of transition can also be seen in the work of the Dutch photographer Evert van Ojen and the British photographer F.R. Yerbury, whose early style was characterized by one reviewer "as rather the outlook of a painter".[16]

Already by 1910 a shift in emphasis in the work of some Pictorialist photographers away from a concern with atmospheric effects towards a fascination with form is clearly discernible. In particular, American photographers such as Alvin Langdon Coburn and Stieglitz were weary of an impressionistic style that was ill-suited to the urban themes they wished to explore, particularly the rise of the skyscraper. In 1900 Coburn had produced a series of London views in a Whistlerian vein, but his 1908 image of a fairground ride, entitled *Flip-Flap*, was criticized by a horrified Evans for its severe geometry. In 1913, while Evans was displaying one of his favourite photographs, *Across the Transepts, Westminster Abbey* (1911), Coburn was exhibiting his series *New York from its Pinnacles*, made a year earlier, which included *The House of a Thousand Windows*, a study of the then tallest skyscraper in the world, the Woolworth Building, which Coburn described as "almost as fantastic in its perspective as a Cubist fantasy" (see page 115).[17] Here were contemporary subjects being explored in radically novel ways that challenged the conservative vision of photographers such as Evans. These images, alongside others by Paul Strand – such as *The White Fence, Port Kent, New York* (1916) – and Charles Sheeler (see pages 116–17), were early intimations of a Modernist photography that was to place architectural form, for the first time since the 1850s, at the heart of the medium's agenda.

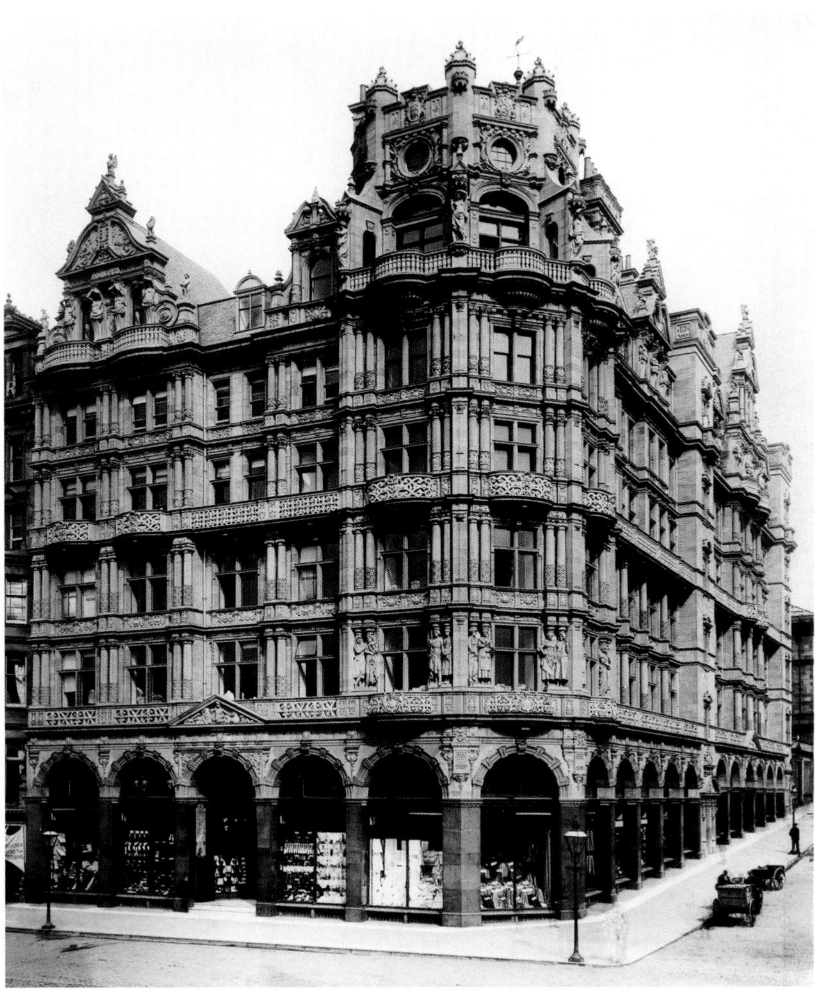

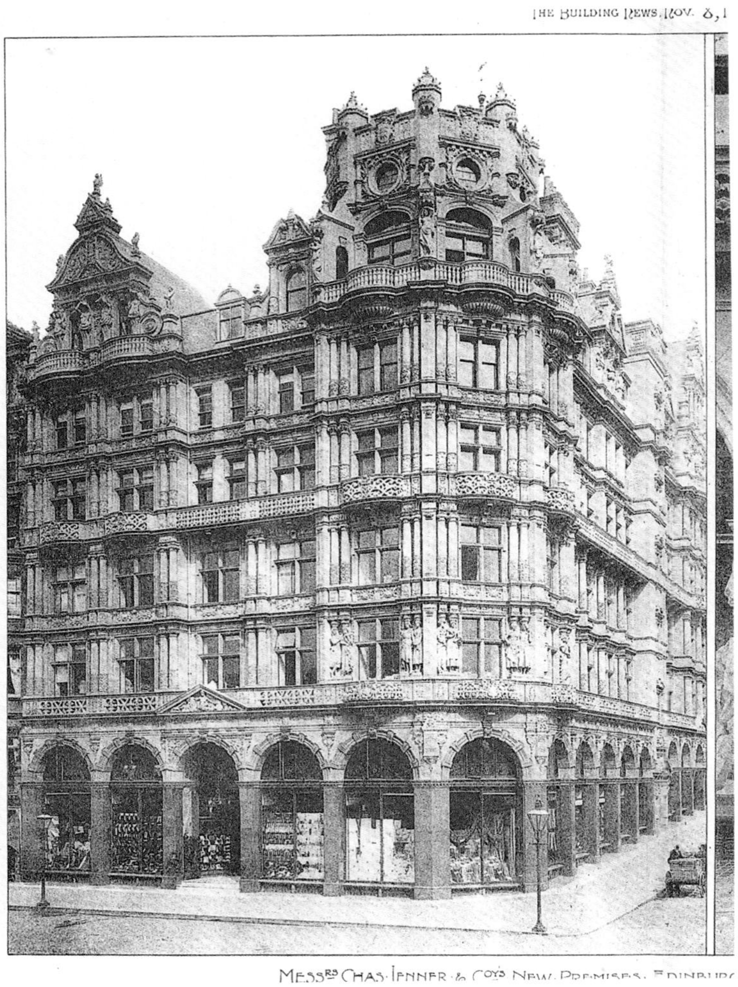
THE BUILDING NEWS, NOV. 8, 1

MESSRS CHAS. JENNER & CO'S NEW PREMISES, EDINBURG

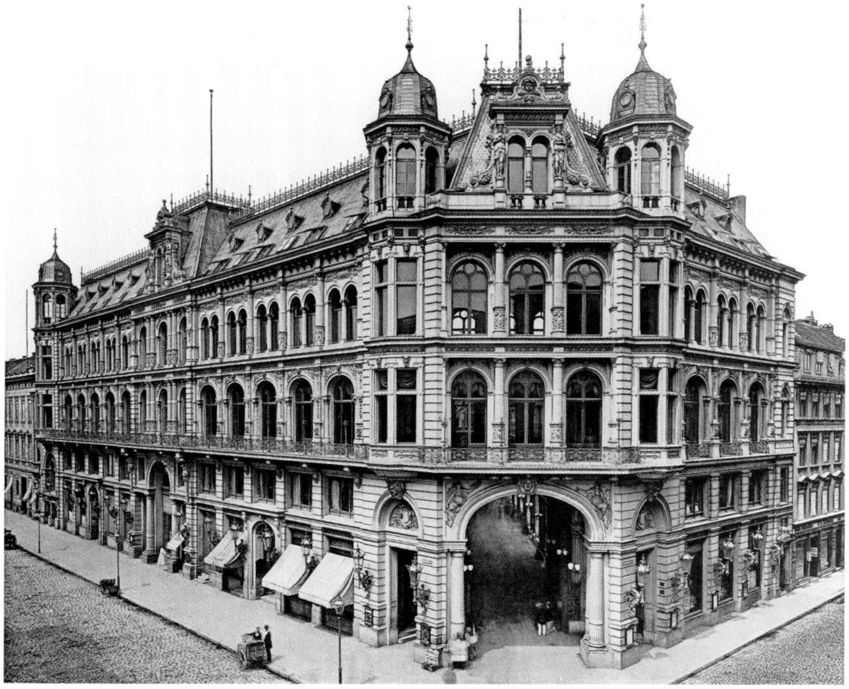

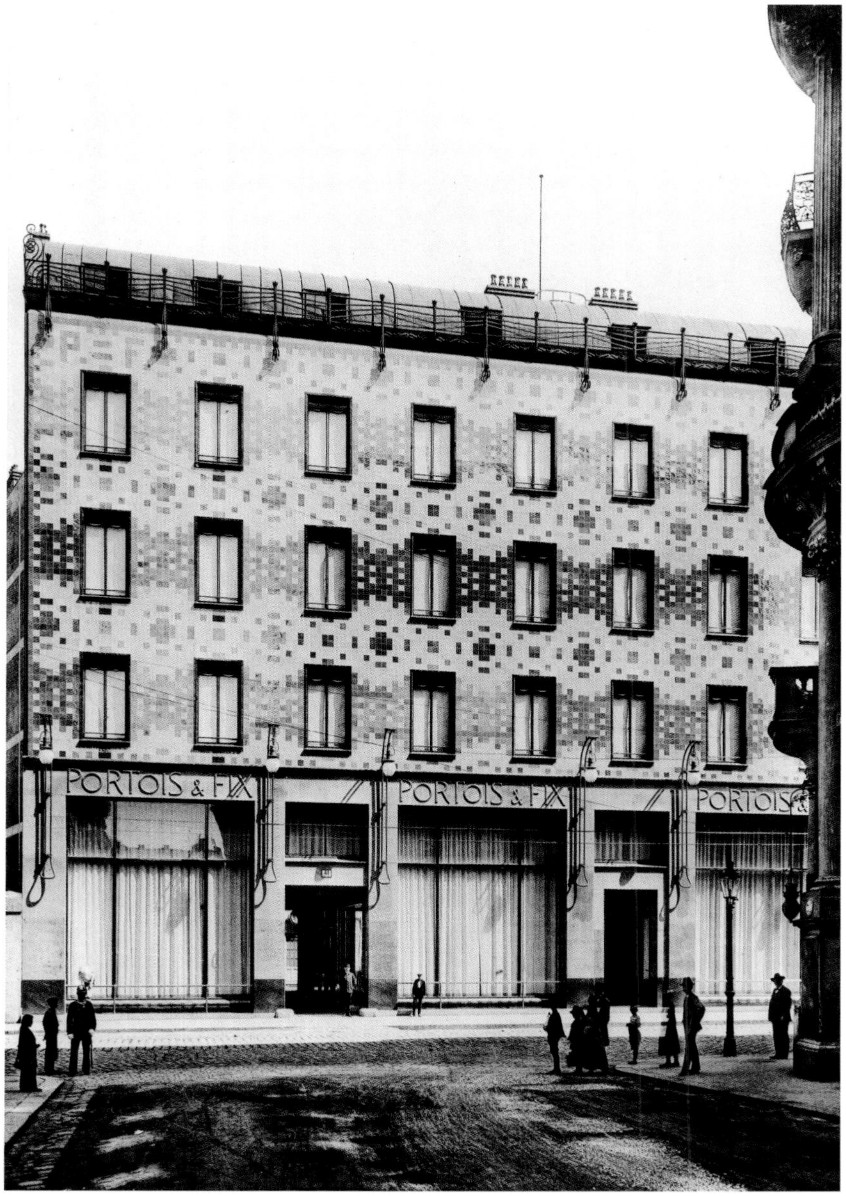

opposite

BEDFORD LEMERE & CO.

Charles Jenner & Co., Edinburgh, 1895
Gelatine silver print and 'Photo-Tint' reproduction from the *Building News*, vol. 69, 5 November 1895
Architects: George Beattie & Son

From the mid-1870s photographs reproduced by various ink photo processes appeared regularly in British architectural journals, though the results were frequently muddied and indistinct. Improved in the 1880s by Sprague & Co., and given respectability through its use by the Architectural Illustration Society to publish its images in *The Architect*, the ink photo, though soon superseded by the half-tone, was an important first step towards photography's eventual domination of the architectural press. This example of the Photo-Tint process developed by James Akerman clearly shows the ink photo's main drawback – its incapacity to render fine detail.

top left

PHOTOGRAPHER UNKNOWN

Arcade, Behrenstrasse, Berlin
Collotype by Römmler & Jonas from Hugo Licht, *Architektur Berlins*, Berlin (Ernst Wasmuth) 1882
Architects: Kyllmann & Heyden

From the early 1880s the collotype (*lichtdruck*) process flourished in Germany, especially in publications by Ernst Wasmuth. This plate illustrates well the merits and limitations of the process. It is extraordinarily detailed – a tendency that sometimes became too exaggerated, causing image distortion akin to a modern over-sharpened digital scan – but also appears flat and devoid of drama, an effect intensified by the typical absence of any sky. Although Römmler & Jonas have been described as photographers, it appears that they were mainly printers, since several of the photographs in the volume can be definitely attributed to the Berlin photographer Hermann Rückwardt.

bottom left

PHOTOGRAPHER UNKNOWN

Portois & Fix, Ungargasse 51 & 53, Vienna
Collotype from *Architektur des XX. Jahrhunderts*, III, 1903
Architect: Max Fabiani

Of all Wasmuth's collotype publications, *Architektur des XX. Jahrhunderts* issued in quarterly parts from 1901 until 1914 and containing 1400 plates, was one of the most remarkable. Although distinctly biased towards Germany and Art Nouveau, it nevertheless genuinely attempted to portray what it considered good examples of modern architecture in Europe and America, as distinct from the historicism endemic in the previous century. This it did in folio plates very much in the nineteenth-century magisterial style of architectural photography, with each building accorded its own imposing and unfettered presence.

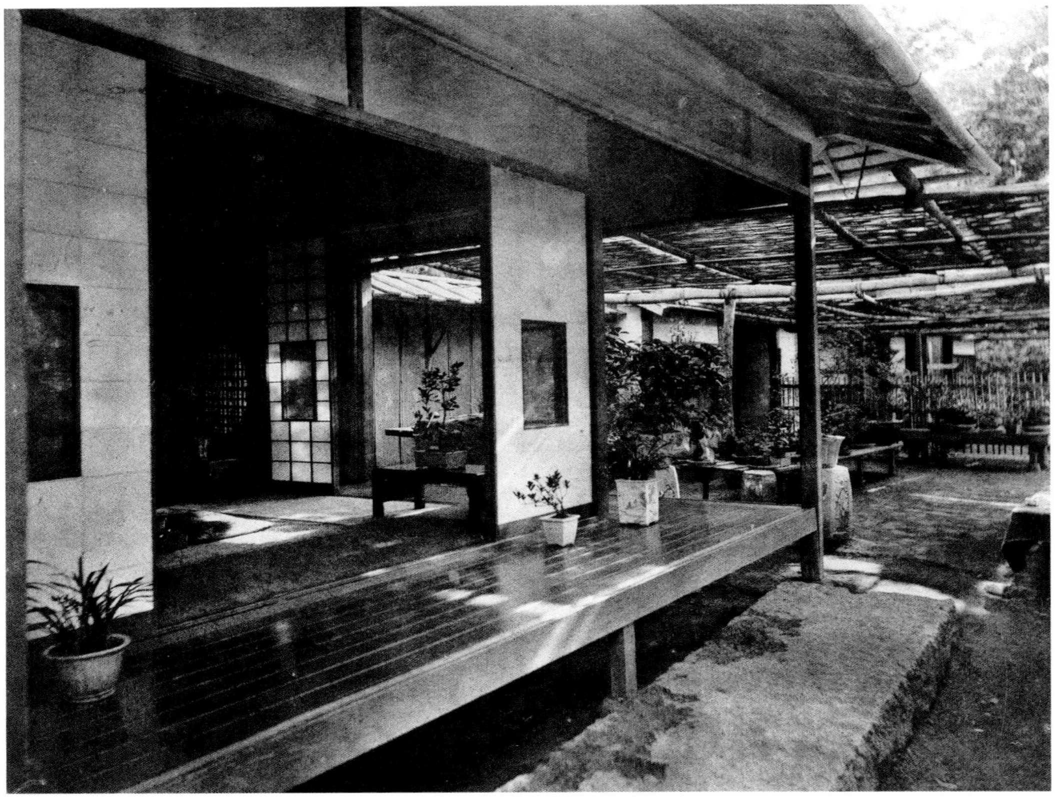

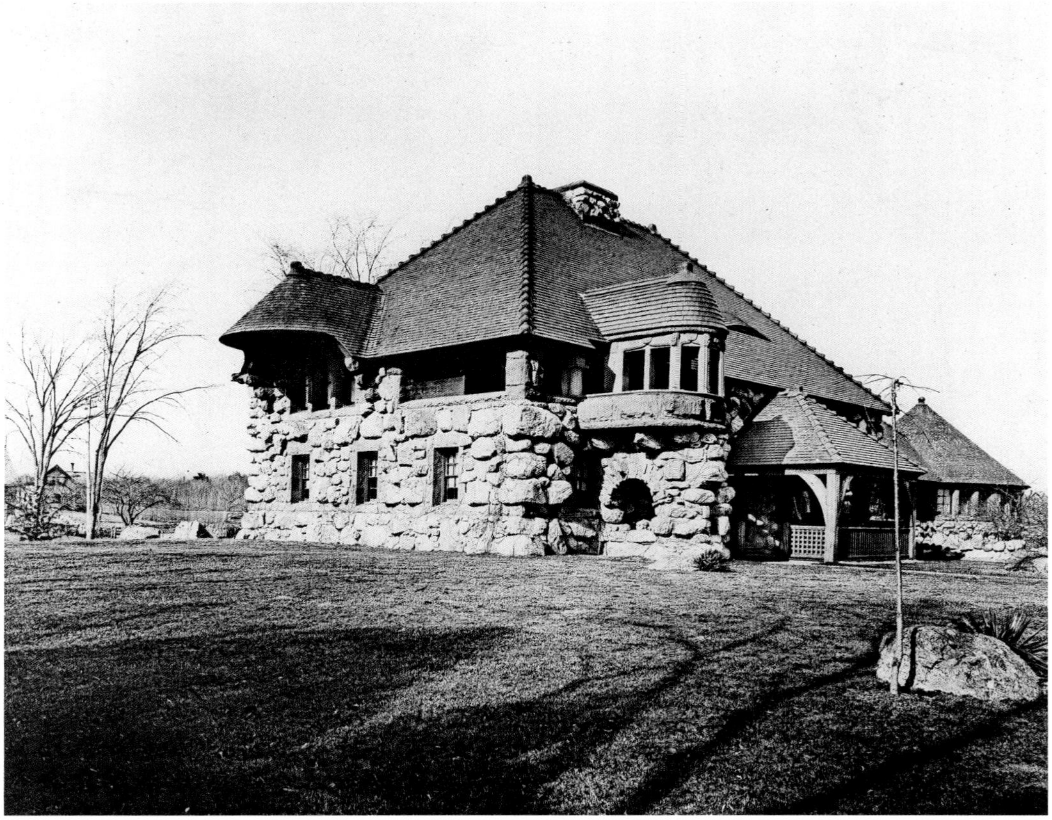

top left

EMMA LOUISE LASENBY LIBERTY

A Gardener's House, Shiba, 1883–89

Photogravure from *Japan: A Pictorial Record by Mrs Lasenby Liberty*, London (Adam & Charles Black) 1910

Emma Lasenby Liberty and her husband, Arthur, had opened their famous store in Regent Street, London, in 1875 and quickly became the leading purveyors of Japanese goods and key promoters of the cult of *japonisme*. This volume, containing fifty photographs from more than a thousand taken by Mrs Liberty on their Far Eastern tour in 1888–89, is a testament to her passion for Japanese crafts and architecture. Though the work of an amateur, the photographs show an assured compositional sense, and the manner of their 1910 publication – limited edition, photogravure reproduction, interleaving with rice paper – reflects the prevailing Pictorialist sensibility.

bottom left

PHOTOGRAPHER UNKNOWN

F.L. Ames Gate Lodge, North Easton, Massachusetts, 1885

Heliotype

Architect: Henry Hobson Richardson

The *American Architect and Building News* was distinguished by its fine-quality heliotype reproductions of photographs, which its editors argued made architecture more comprehensible to the public. By underwriting production costs, Richardson helped ensure that his work was regularly illustrated in this way, the photographic reproductions better conveying the rugged monumentality of his work than more fussy perspective drawings could do. Such illustrations fostered the Richardsonian cult that swept America and elsewhere, especially England. The magazine reckoned that "every issue of ours with one of his designs was studied in a thousand offices and imitated in hundreds".[18]

opposite

ORESTE BERTANI or **CARLO JACOBI**

Altar, Basilica of St Mark's, Venice, 1881

Heliotype from *La Basilica di San Marco a Venezia*, portfolio no. V (*Dettagli di altari, monumenti, scultura ecc.*), IV, Venice (Ferdinando Ongania Edit.) 1877–88

Ongania's immense work, printed in a limited run of 500 copies with additional French and English editions (the latter was dedicated to Ruskin, who had tirelessly campaigned for St Mark's preservation), was one of the nineteenth century's most remarkable publications. It also demonstrated a mature use of photography, in which photographs and drawings were seen not as alternative but as complementary ways of analysing a building. As one commentator wrote, "it all was ransacked, assaulted by the eye of the artist and the lens of the camera, even the most jealously guarded secrets, with a will that was a passion".[19]

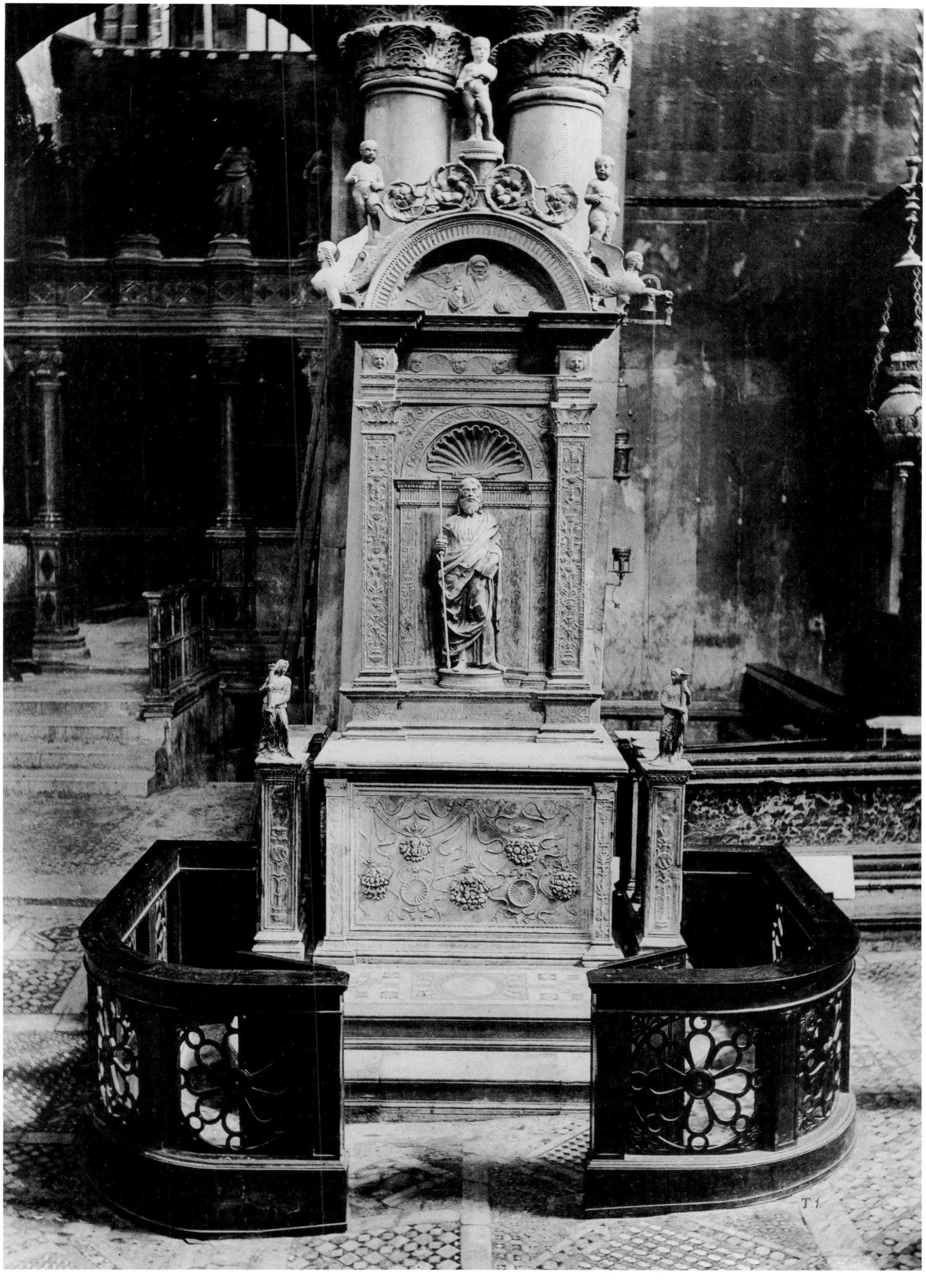

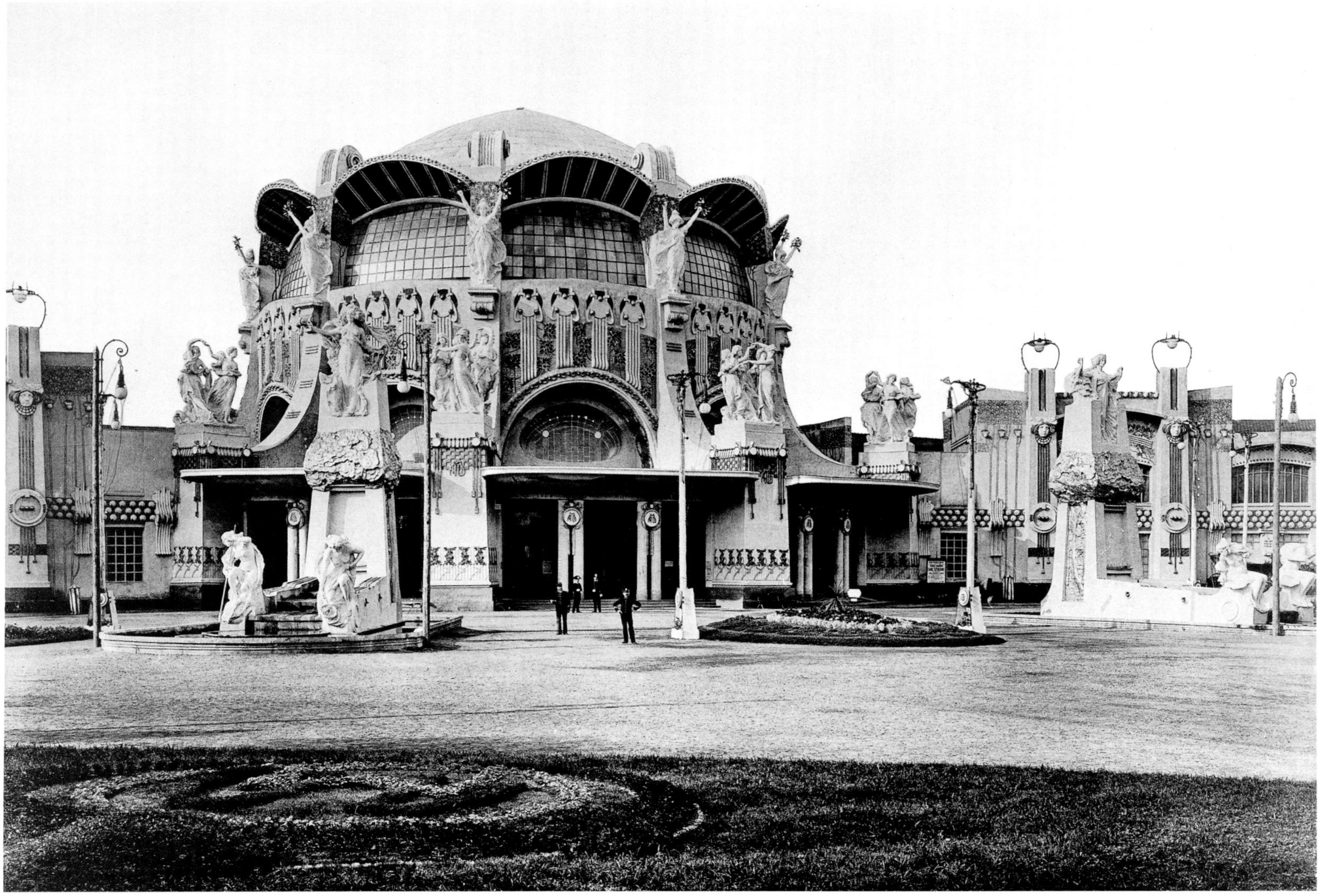

above

PHOTOGRAPHER UNKNOWN

The Rotunda, International Exhibition of Decorative Art, Turin

Collotype from *Architektur des XX. Jahrhunderts*, II, 1902

Architect: Raimondo d'Aronco

As most were designed to be short-lived, exhibition buildings have been especially dependent on photographic reproductions to secure their lasting reputations. Two prime examples are the Galerie des Machines (1889) and, before its subsequent re-erection, Mies van der Rohe's Barcelona Pavilion (1929). The Turin exhibition was regarded as an important opportunity to flaunt the artistic credentials of the young Italian state, and d'Aronco's pavilions, including one devoted to Fotografia Artistica, and their projection through photography therefore assumed an even greater significance.

opposite top

HENRY GREENWOOD PEABODY (1855–1951)

House of the Conde de Heras, Mexico City, 1899

Gelatine silver print from Sylvester Baxter, *Spanish Colonial Architecture in Mexico*, Boston (J.B. Millet) 1901

Forming the core of Baxter's pioneering study, Peabody's two hundred original boxed photographs sought to highlight the artistic merit of Mexico's neglected Spanish colonial architecture and preserve a record of it at a time of great threat. The images played an important role in the rise of Spanish colonial architecture in the United States, one of its chief exponents being Bertram Grosvenor Goodhue, who drew the book's plans. Interestingly, one of the volume's dedicatees was the artist Frederic Church, whose painting was informed by his large photographic collection, which included views of Mexican colonial architecture by Alfred Briquet.

opposite bottom

CHEVOJON FRÈRES

Esders Clothing Factory, Paris, 1919

Gelatine silver print

Architect: Auguste Perret

Chevojon Frères, the successor firm to Delmaet & Durandelle, was responsible for the images of Perret's buildings, including the Garage Ponthieu, Paris (1905), the Théâtre des Champs Elysées, Paris (1913), and Nôtre-Dame, Le Raincy (1923), that continue to feature regularly in textbooks today. These were shot in a straightforward documentary style that had a certain affinity with Perret's rationalism.

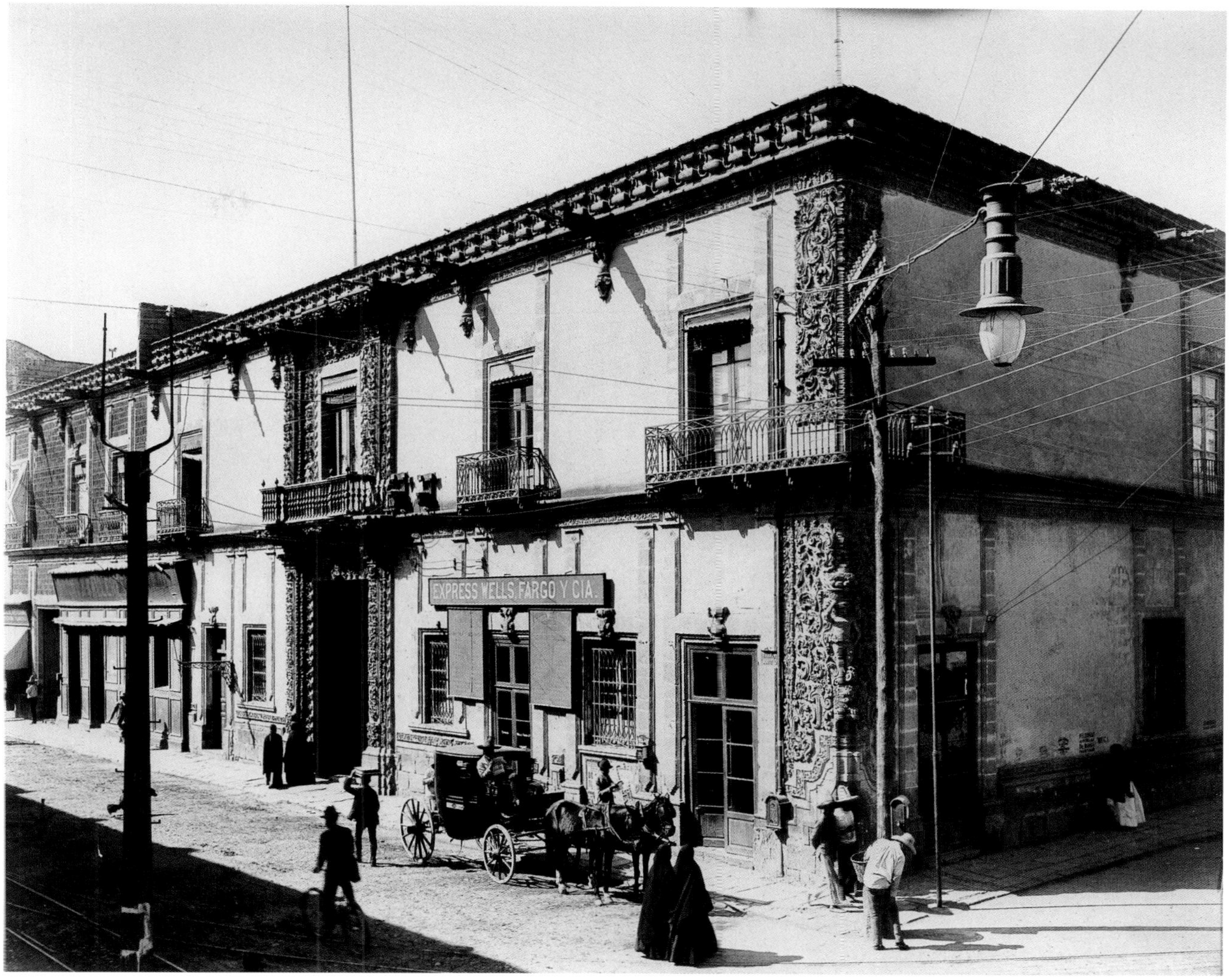
EXPRESS WELLS FARGO Y CIA.

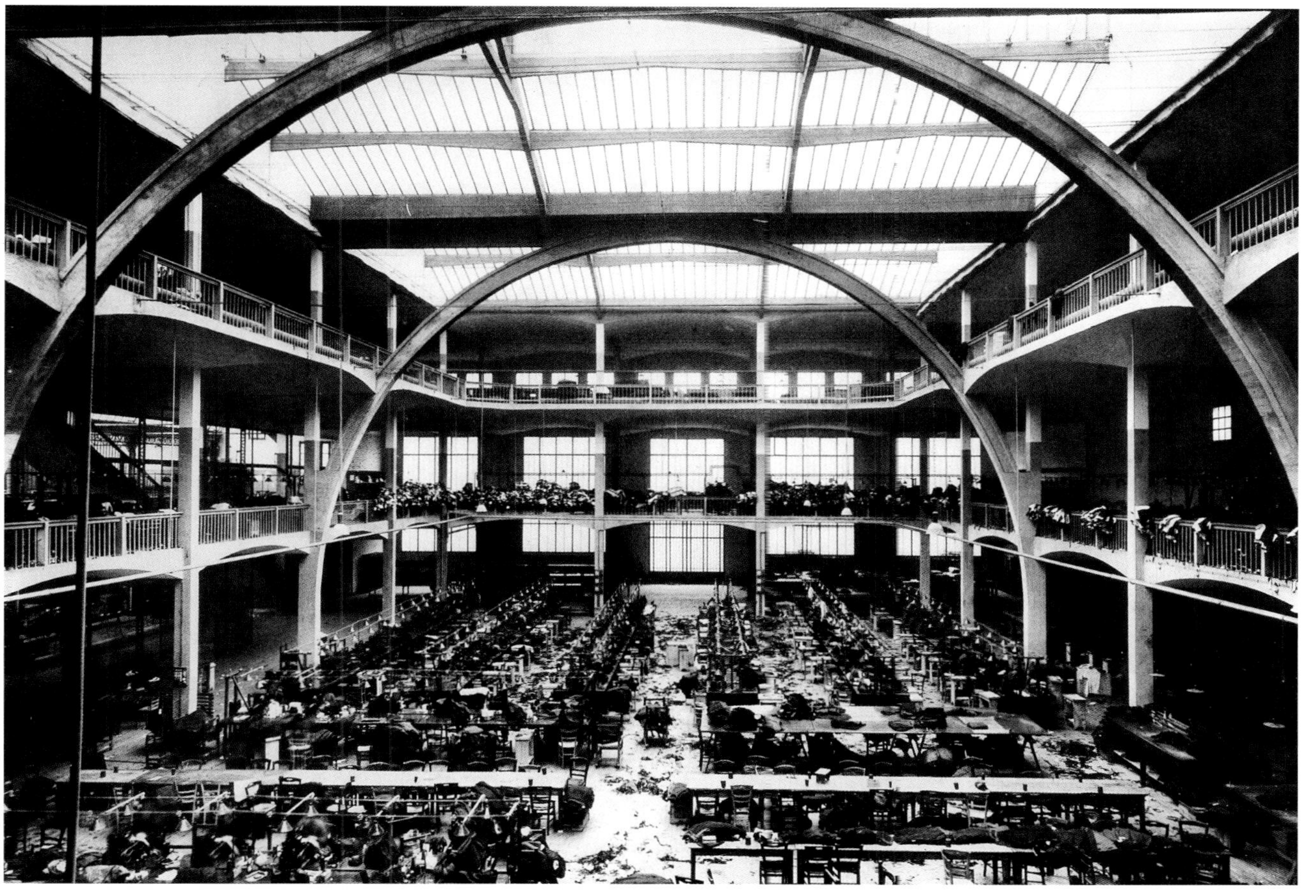

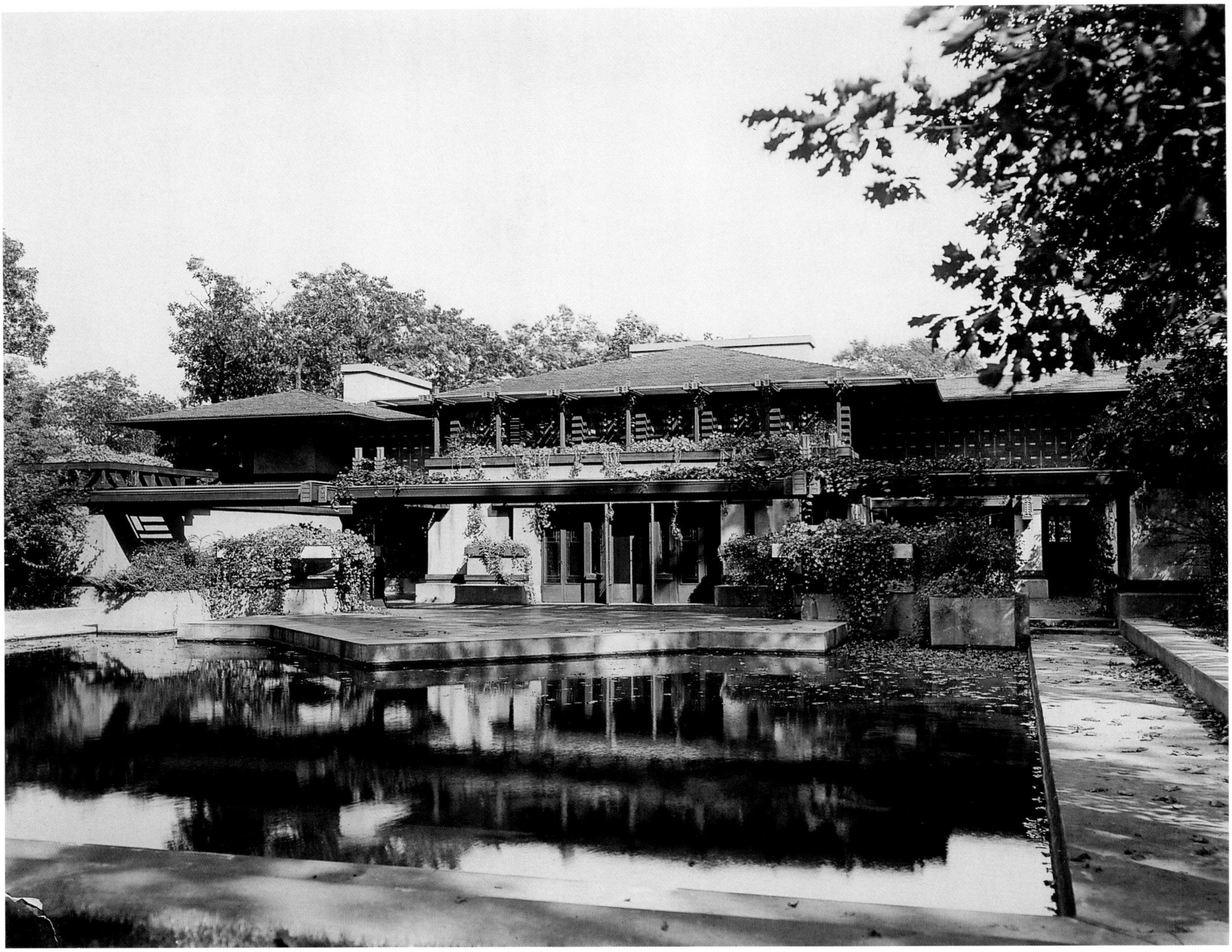

above

HENRY FUERMANN & COMPANY

Avery Coonley House, Riverside, Illinois, c. 1915

Gelatine silver print

Architect: Frank Lloyd Wright

The Chicago-based Henry Fuermann & Company was one of America's most important firms of architectural photographers at the beginning of the twentieth century, photographing the work of both Louis Sullivan and Frank Lloyd Wright. Many of the photographs of Wright's buildings, including his early Prairie houses and his studio at Oak Park, Illinois, were probably taken for the company by Henry's son, Clarence, several of them appearing in the special issues on Wright in *Wendigen* (1925–26). In 1942 some of the company's stock was purchased by the Chicago Architectural Photographing Company.

opposite

CHARLES LATHAM

East Bridge, Ightham Mote, Kent, 1907

Modern print from original glass plate negative

Already a distinguished architectural photographer, Latham was employed by *Country Life* from 1898 to 1908 and established the magazine's highly successful pictorial formula. His work combined both evenly lit, faithful records and, as here, more romantic views that perfectly evoked the *genius loci*, summoning up a vision of an idyllically tranquil, unchanging world calculated to appeal strongly to the magazine's subscribers. Such views were influenced by the Pictorialist tendencies evident elsewhere in the magazine, such as its commissioning of Frederick Evans and its publication of regular features on the photographic salons by Alfred Horsley Hinton, a noted Pictorialist landscape photographer.

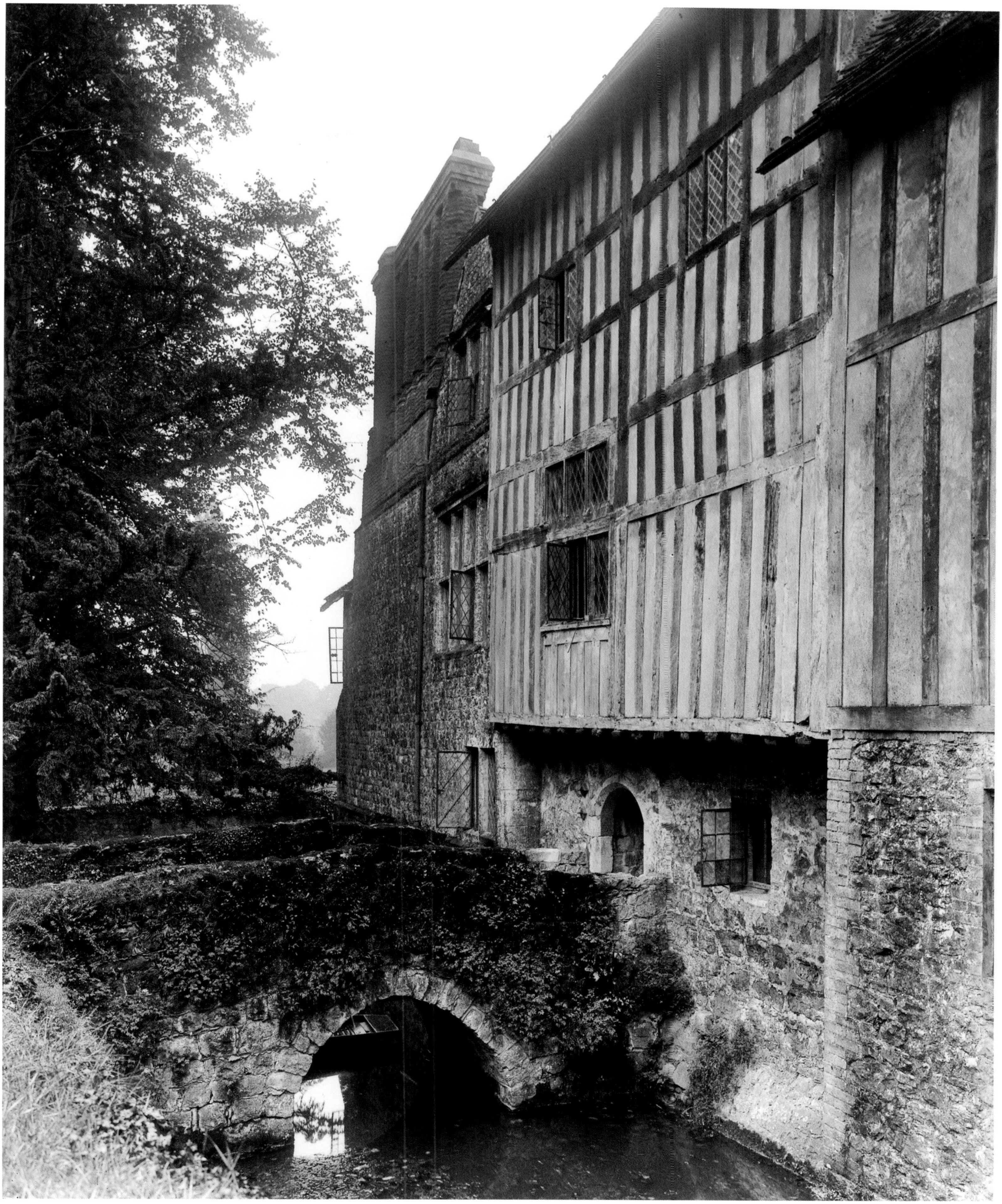

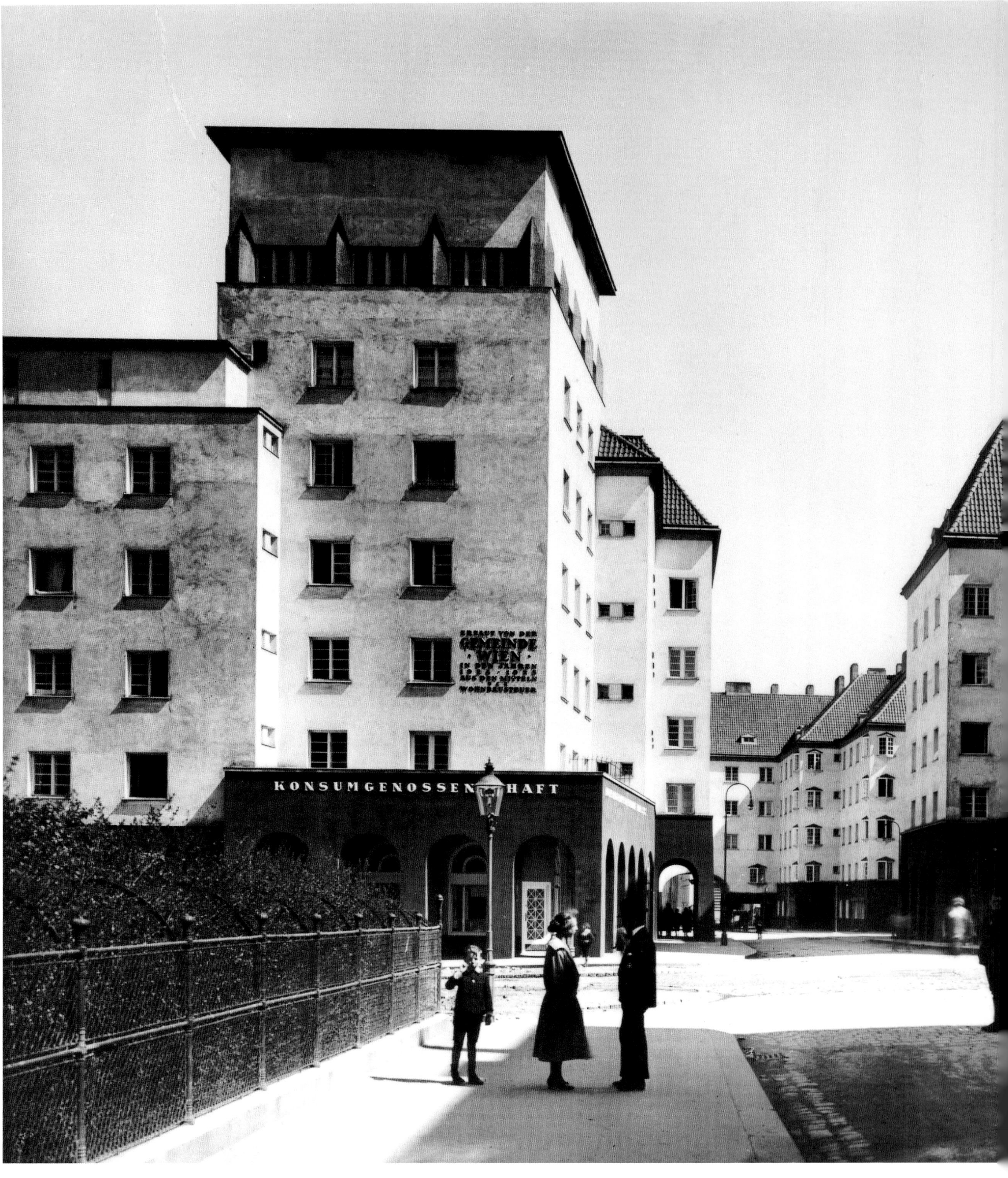
GEMEINDE
WIEN
KONSUMGENOSSEN HAFT

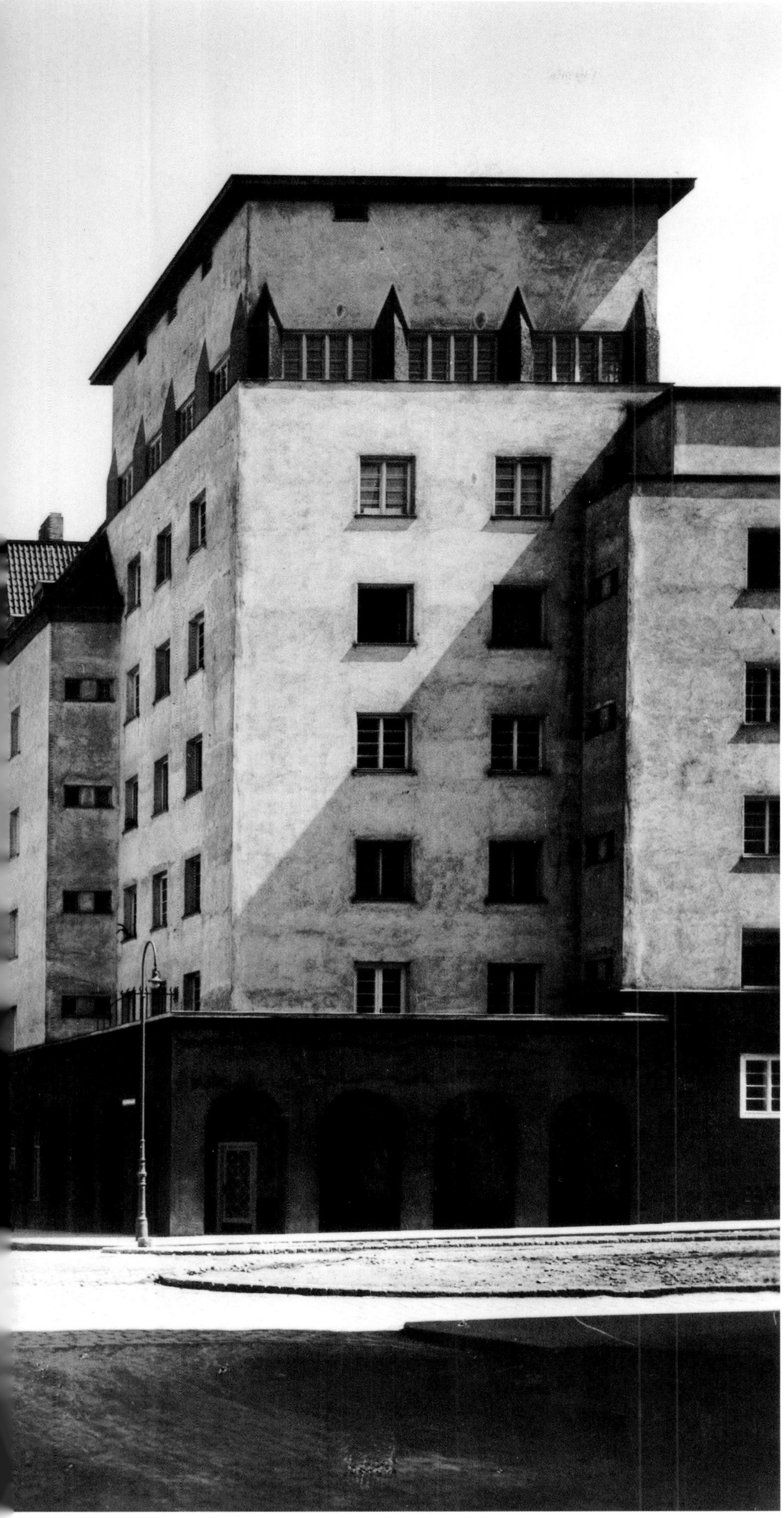

MARTIN GERLACH (1879–1944)

Fuchsenfeldhof, Vienna, 1925

Gelatine silver print

Architects: Heinrich Schmidt and Hermann Aichinger

Although virtually unknown today, Gerlach, whose father, another Martin, was also an architectural photographer, was responsible for some of the most often reproduced images of Viennese architecture, notably Loos's Steiner House and the city's social housing programme. An important aspect of this programme was the explanation of its aims and methods to potential occupants, and accordingly the flats, and particularly those communal facilities that distinguished them from their forebears, were extensively photographed. The resultant images were then used alongside models, drawings and a specially devised picture language – the Vienna method – in lectures, exhibitions and even a museum created in 1925.

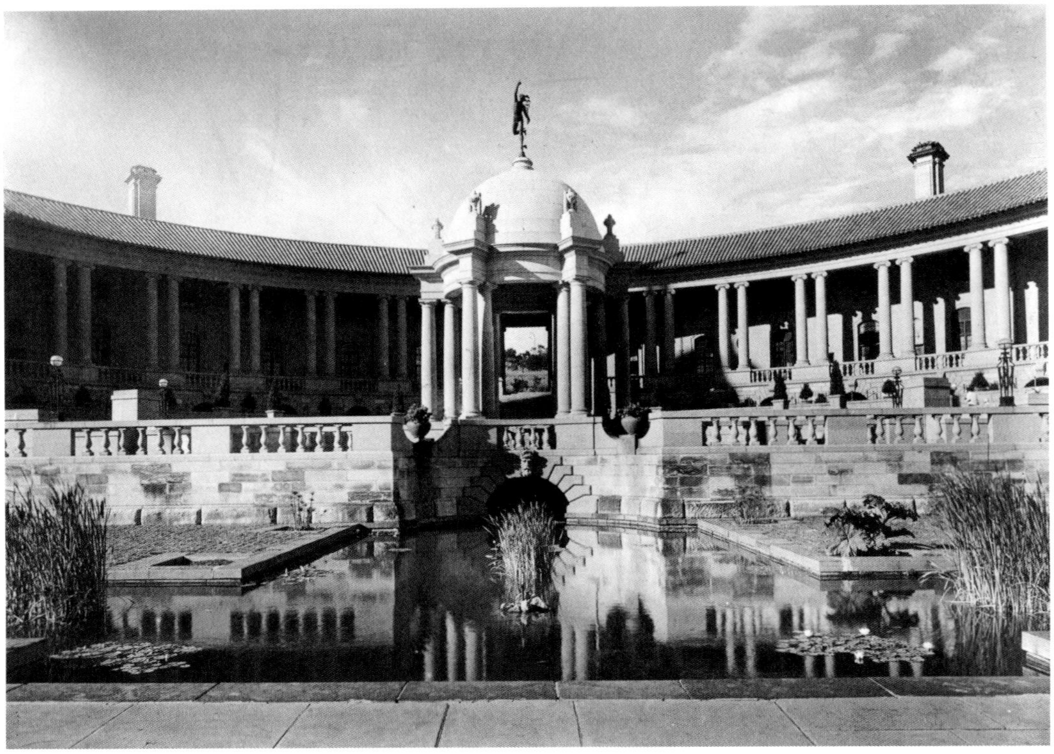

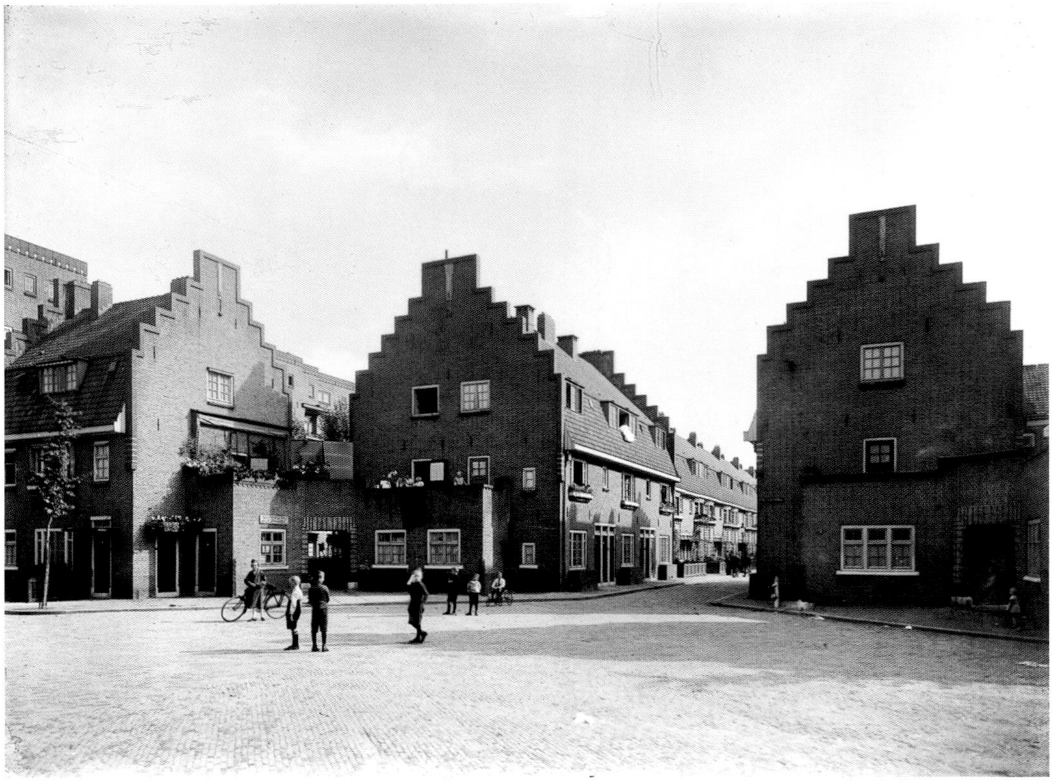

top left

ALAN YATES

Union Buildings, Pretoria, 1913

Gelatine silver print

Architects: Sir Herbert Baker with F.L.H. Fleming

Yates was a leading commercial photographer, who specialized in views of architecture both colonial and indigenous. His clients included such architects as Sir Herbert Baker, Gordon Leith, and Kallenbach Kennedy & Furner.

bottom left

BERNARD EILERS (1878–1951)

Transvaalbuurt Housing, Amsterdam, c. 1920

Gelatine silver print

Architect: Jan Gratama

For a short period, from the early years of the twentieth century to the mid-1920s, Eilers was the most prolific and important Dutch architectural photographer, his work betraying the tension between his desire to make an artistically pleasing print and the "sharpness and realism" demanded by his architect clients.[9] While his private work, therefore, shows the influence of Pictorialism in soft-focus, twilight or snow-laden scenes of his native Amsterdam (opposite), his images of work by the Amsterdam School are more matter-of-fact.

opposite

BERNARD EILERS (1878–1951)

South Church, Amsterdam, c. 1910

Oil print

Architect: Hendrick de Keyser

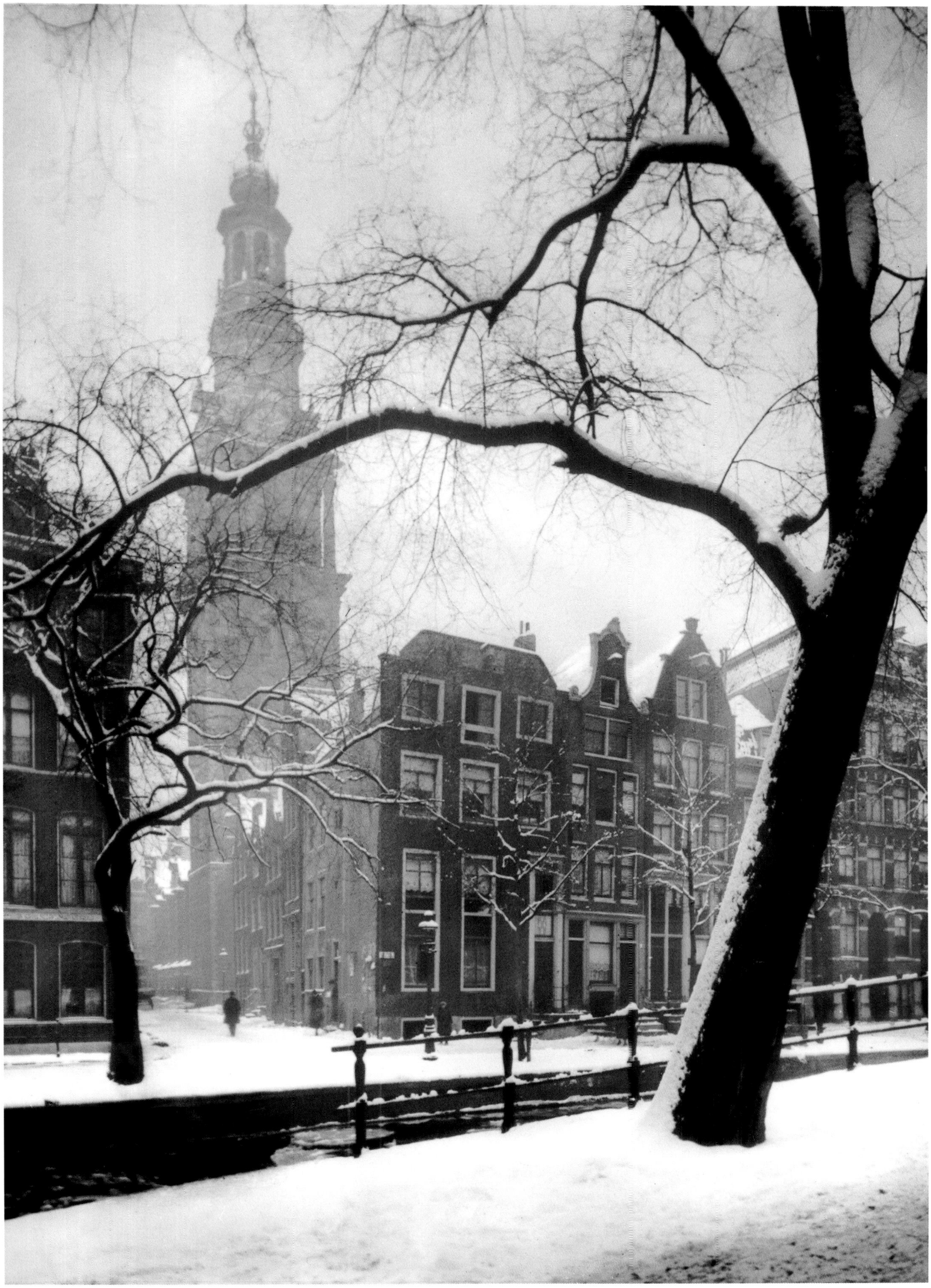

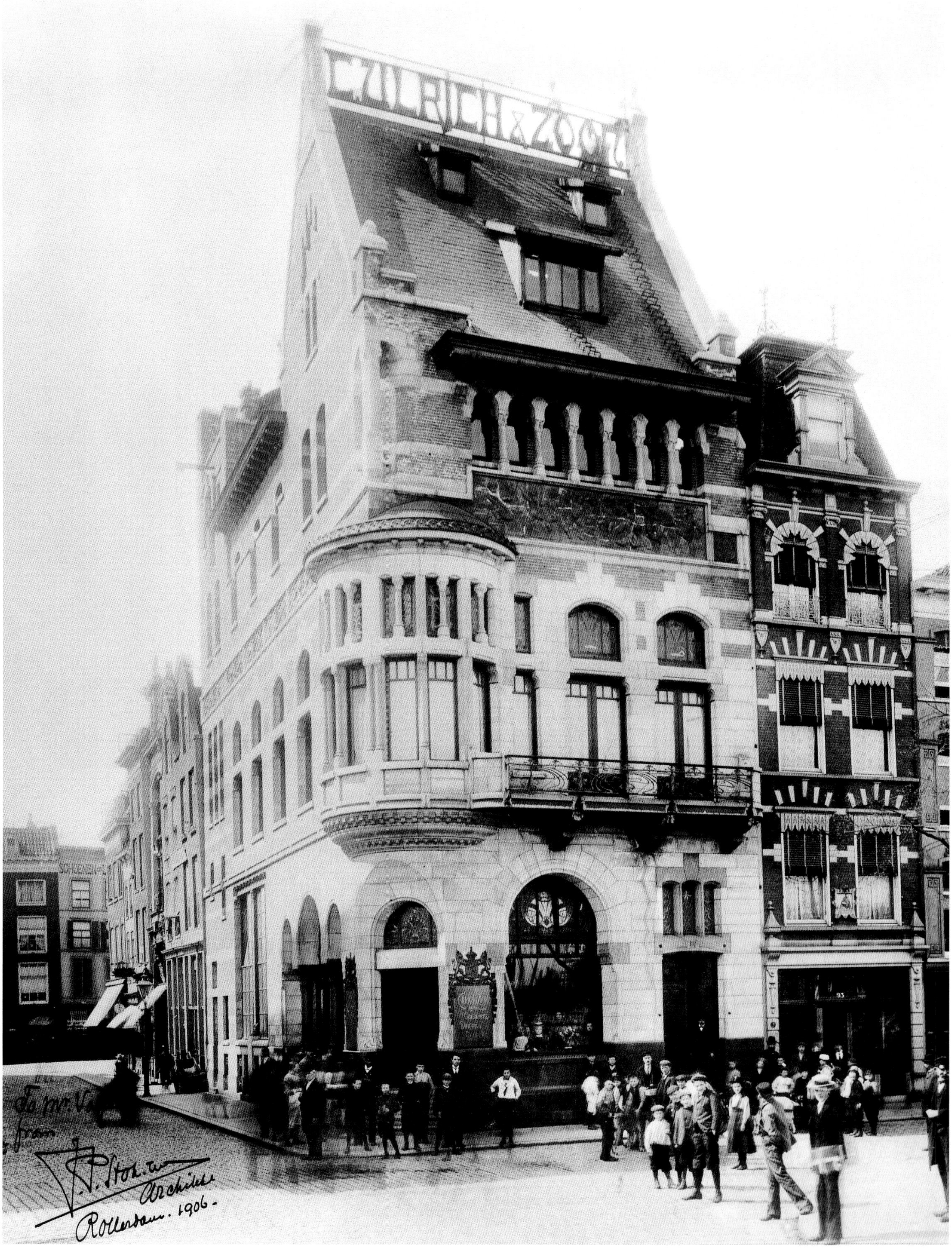
C.J.ULRICH & ZOON
SCHOENEN
Rotterdam. 1906.

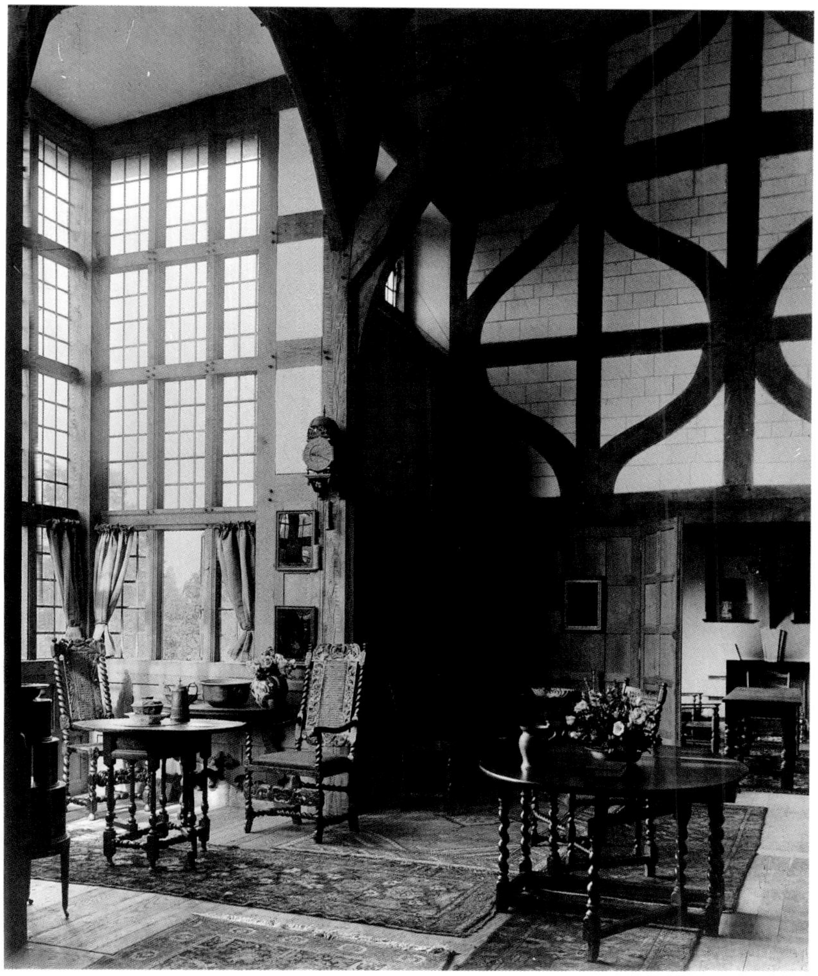

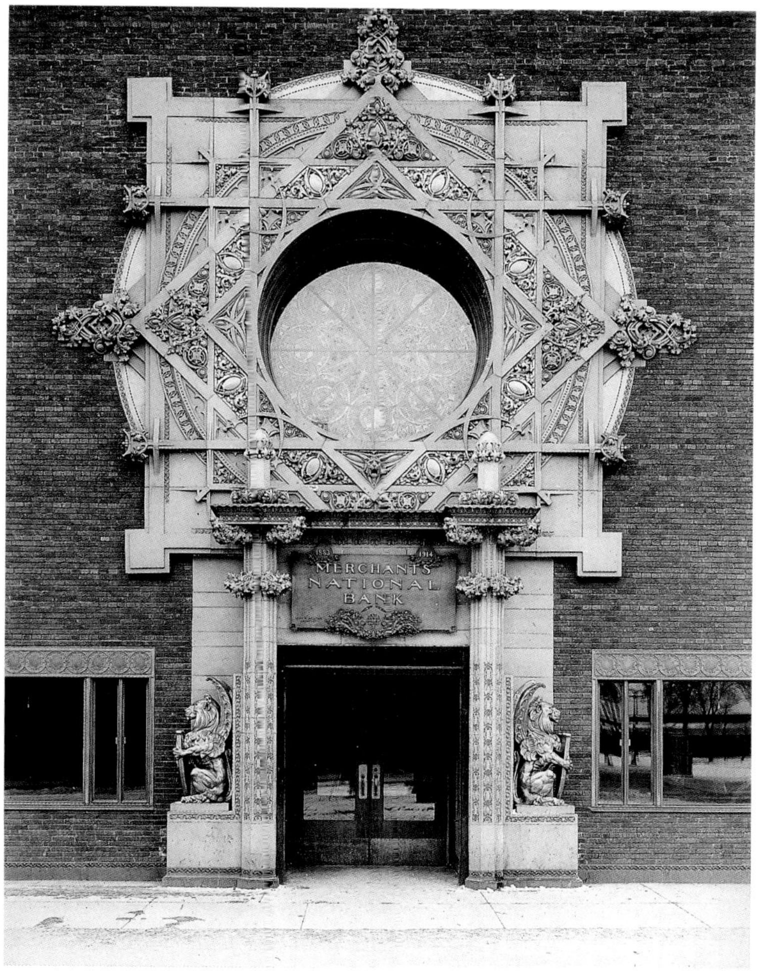

opposite

PHOTOGRAPHER UNKNOWN

C. Ulrich & Zoon Restaurant, Rotterdam, c. 1900

Gelatine silver print

Architect: J.P. Stok Wzn

This image comes from an album of photographs chronicling contemporary architecture in The Netherlands, which was presented by the Dutch architect P.A. Weeldenburg to the British architect Charles Voysey in 1906. It is indicative of the widespread informal trade in photographs that existed within the architectural profession and that helped to foster awareness of colleagues' work.

above left

CHARLES LATHAM

Deanery Garden, Sonning, Berkshire, 1903

Modern print from original glass plate negative

Architect: Edwin Lutyens

Country Life's championing of Lutyens's work from 1900 onwards, when it featured his house, Crooksbury Lodge, was remarkable for its longevity and the quality of photographic reproductions made by staff photographers such as Charles Latham, Alfred Edward Henson and Arthur Gill. This house, laid out with gardens by the famous landscape gardener Gertrude Jekyll (who herself took photographs to illustrate her garden designs), was photographed by Latham. His interior imagery was later hailed by Christopher Hussey, Lutyens's biographer and the editor of *Country Life*, as "marking a revolution in the presentation of interiors by its concentration on the spatial factor".[21]

above right

HENRY FUERMANN & COMPANY

Merchants' National Bank, Grinnell, Iowa, 1914

Gelatine silver print

Architect: Louis Sullivan

Like Richardson, Sullivan was acutely conscious of the value of good photography, without which his banks, such as that at Grinnell, Iowa, would have been far less well known. According to Schuyler, Fuermann's photographs of the bank at Owatonna, Minnesota, when published in the *Architectural Record*, resulted in it being "presently acclaimed by architects the country over as a signal success, the acclamation being produced, naturally, by an inspection of the photographs. Owatonna suddenly found itself famous, and became the Mecca of architectural pilgrimages."[22] Schuyler's use of "naturally" is itself indicative of the acknowledged pervasive power of half-tone photographic reproduction by this time.

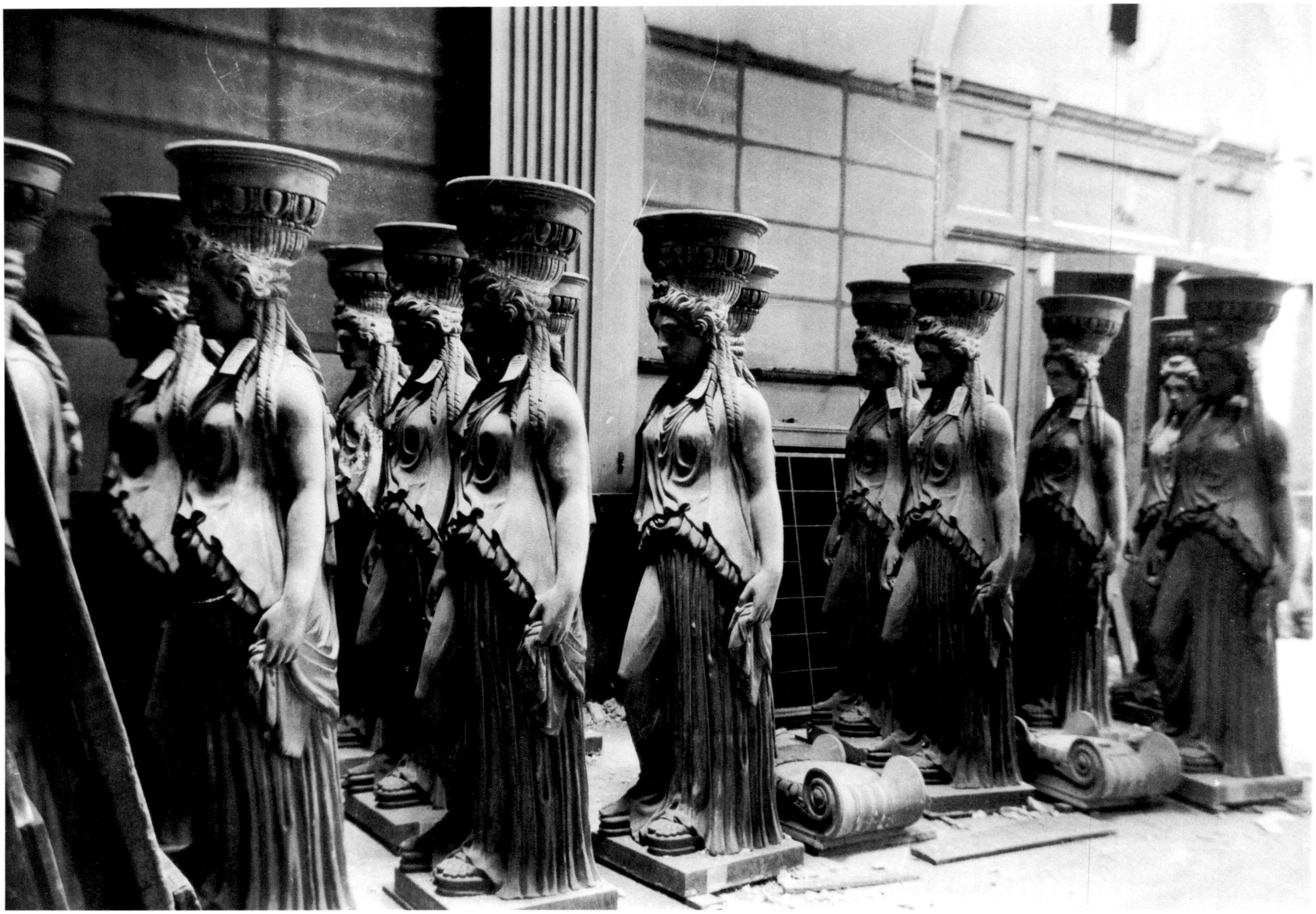

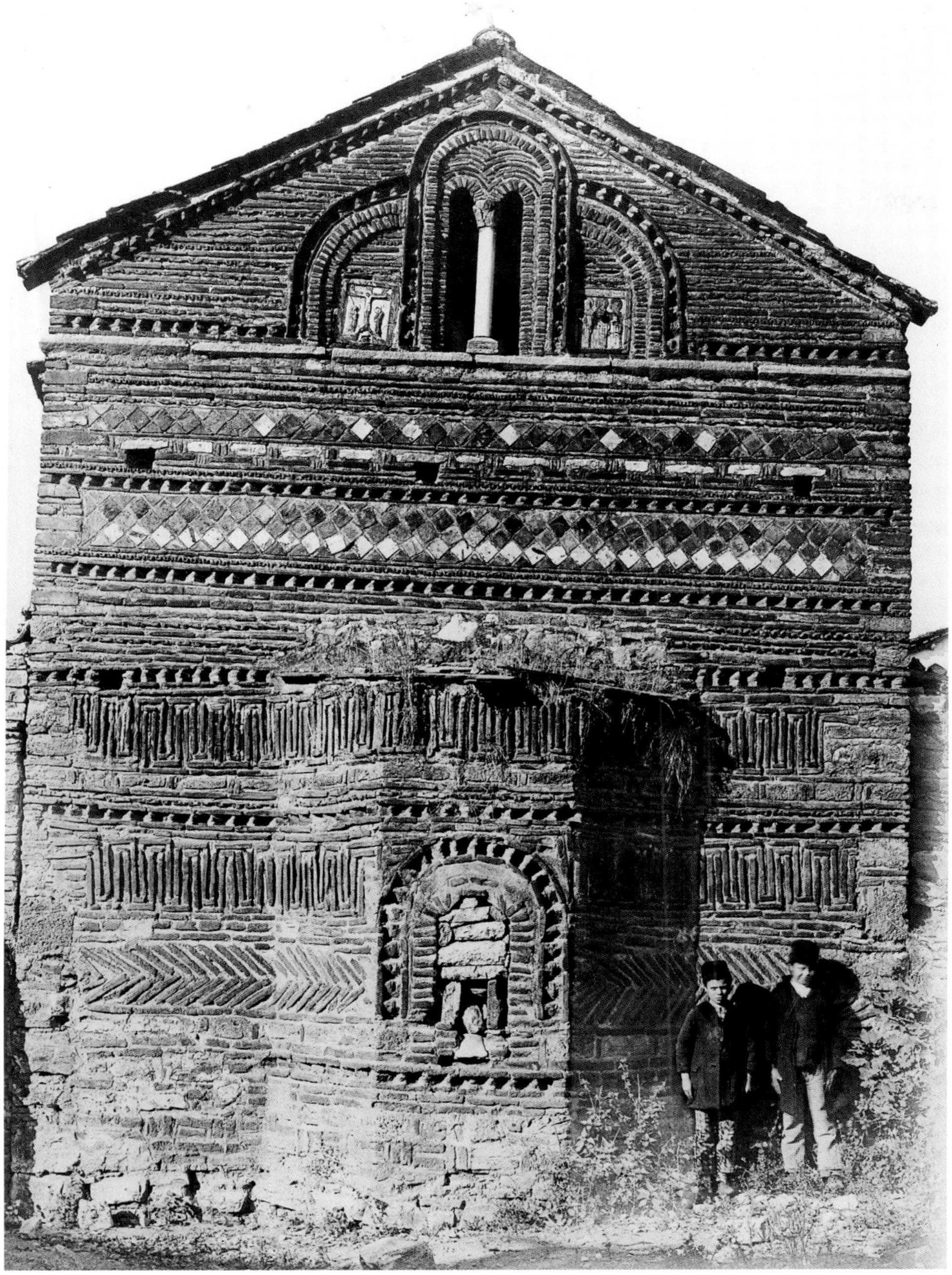

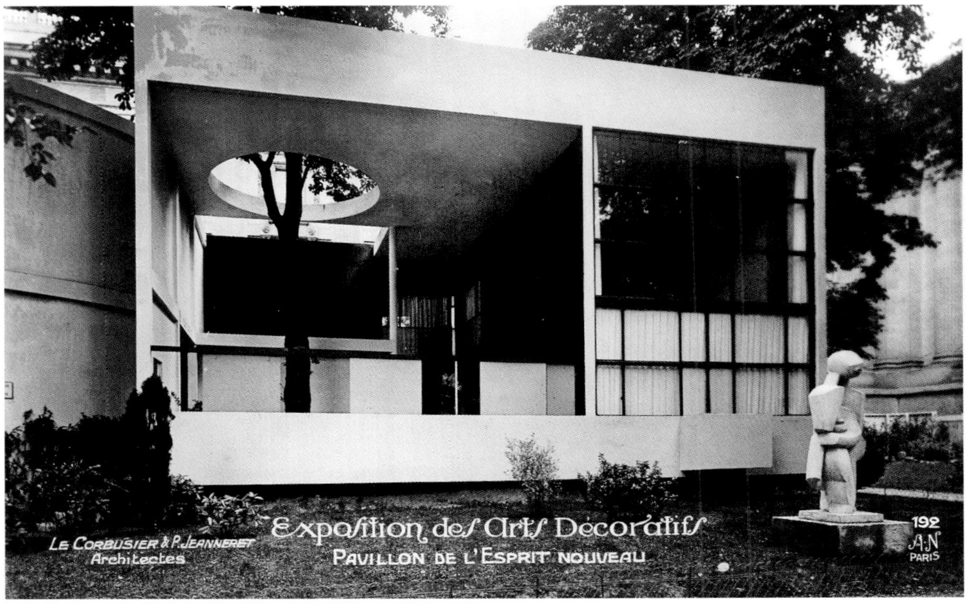

opposite

FRANCIS ROWLAND YERBURY (1885–1970)

Bank of England, London, 1925

Gelatine silver print

Architect: Sir John Soane

Although today the demolition photograph has become fashionable, when Yerbury recorded Sir John Soane's bank, not only before but also during demolition, such documentation was less usual. Perhaps the photographs were influenced by Joseph Michael Gandy's magisterial 1830 watercolour, which depicted the bank both under construction and in ruins. The pre-demolition photographs were reproduced in H. Rooksby Steele's *The Old Bank of England* (1930), and these sadly valedictory images looked back to the tradition of rescue photography advanced by SPROL and forward to the official recording of threatened buildings instituted by the creation of the National Buildings Record in 1941.

top left

ROBERT WEIR SCHULTZ (1860–1951)

Panagia Parigoritissa, Arta, Greece, c. 1889

Albumen print

During the last years of the nineteenth century and the early years of the twentieth, an increasing number of architects, among them Le Corbusier and Sigurd Lewerentz, who toured Italy in about 1909, added the camera to the drawing equipment they took on tour. Schultz, who toured Greece and the Near East in 1888–89, is a typical example. He supplemented the photographs he purchased from commercial suppliers with his own photographic studies of building methods and use of materials, which subsequently informed his contribution to the British turn-of-the-century Byzantine Revival.

bottom left

PHOTOGRAPHER UNKNOWN

Pavillon de l'Esprit Nouveau, Exposition des Arts Décoratifs, Paris, 1925

Postcard

Architects: Le Corbusier and Pierre Jeanneret

Enthusiastically collected by architects such as Le Corbusier, since their introduction at the end of the nineteenth century mass-circulation postcards have been an important conduit for the dissemination of architectural imagery and information, particularly to a wider public. The cards were issued in the form of either actual photographic prints or gravure or half-tone reproductions. Those produced at the World's Fairs were especially popular, providing cheap pictorial mementos of buildings that soon disappeared. Le Corbusier's own pavilion at Paris (1925), for example, gained some of its public notoriety through postcard reproduction.

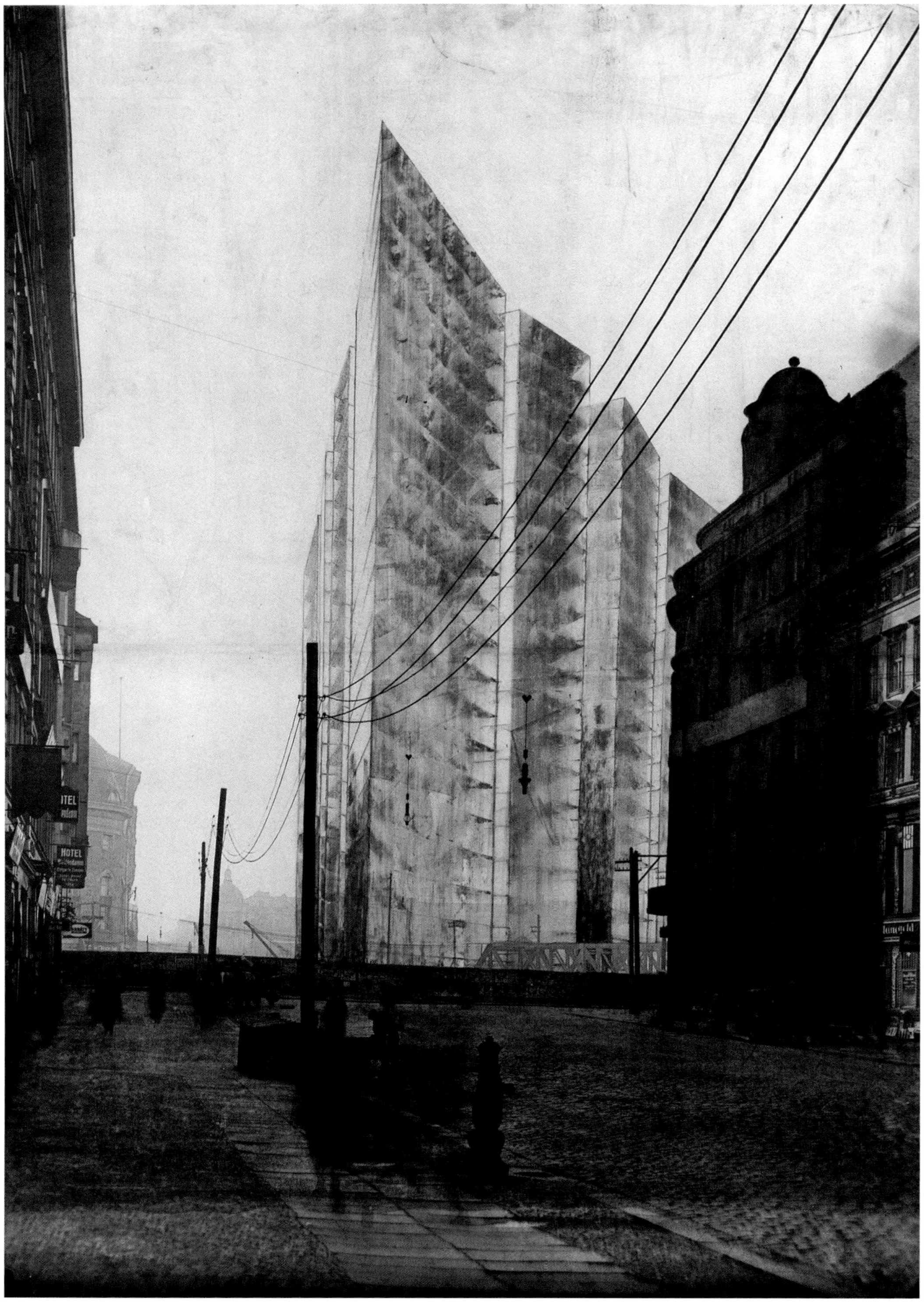

left

LUDWIG MIES VAN DER ROHE (1886–1969)

Intermediate Version of Competition Entry for Skyscraper on Bahnhof Friedrichstrasse, Berlin, 1921

Gelatine silver print and mixed med a mounted on cardboard

Photomontage – adding drawings of proposed projects to photographs of their intended sites – has become a common technique of architectural presentation. Although he did not pioneer its application, Mies was one of the first architects to make extensive and creative use of the medium. His series of photomontages of the Friedrichstrasse skyscraper are among the most enduring images of twentieth-century architecture. These demonstrate how Mies employed the technique not to fabricate an illusion of reality, as most architects would do, but to manufacture dramatic images, each version becoming progressively more expressionistic – aided here by crayoning to darken photographic details.

opposite

EUGÈNE ATGET (1847–1927)

Maison où mourut Voltaire en 1778, 1 rue de Beaune, Paris, 1909

Albumen print

Atget's vision of Paris was highly selective, concentrating largely on seventeenth- and eighteenth-century architecture, and idiosyncratic, in that he captured examples and details ignored by more tourist-oriented firms such as Neurdein Frères. Atget's world is always slightly askew. Most architectural photographers would have photographed this entrance head-on, but Atget has moved slightly to one side, adding a layer of metaphysical meaning to the architectural information imparted through his favourite device of allowing a tantalizing glimpse into the secretive world beyond the open door. Atget thus invites us to reflect not merely on the house's structure but also on its history.

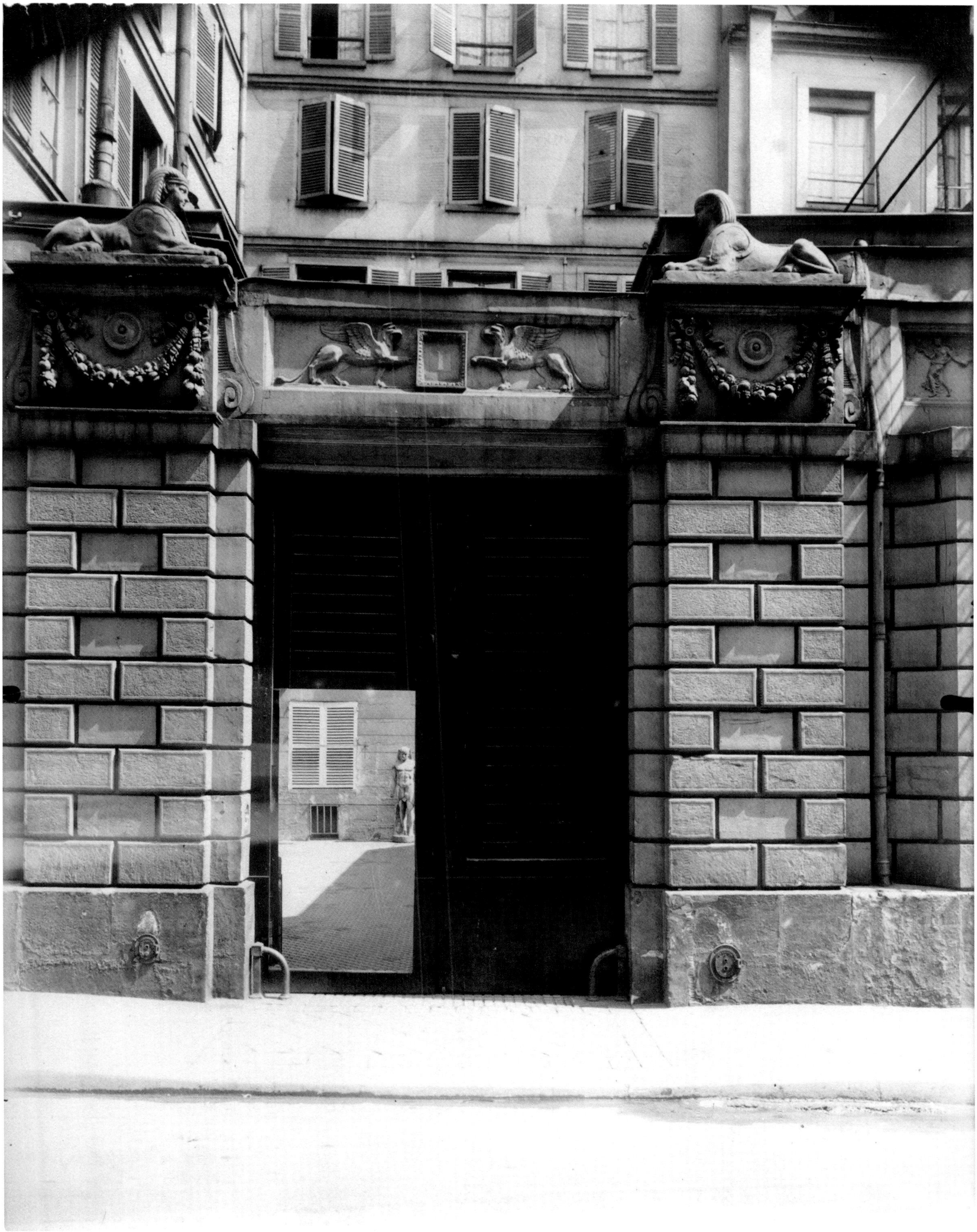

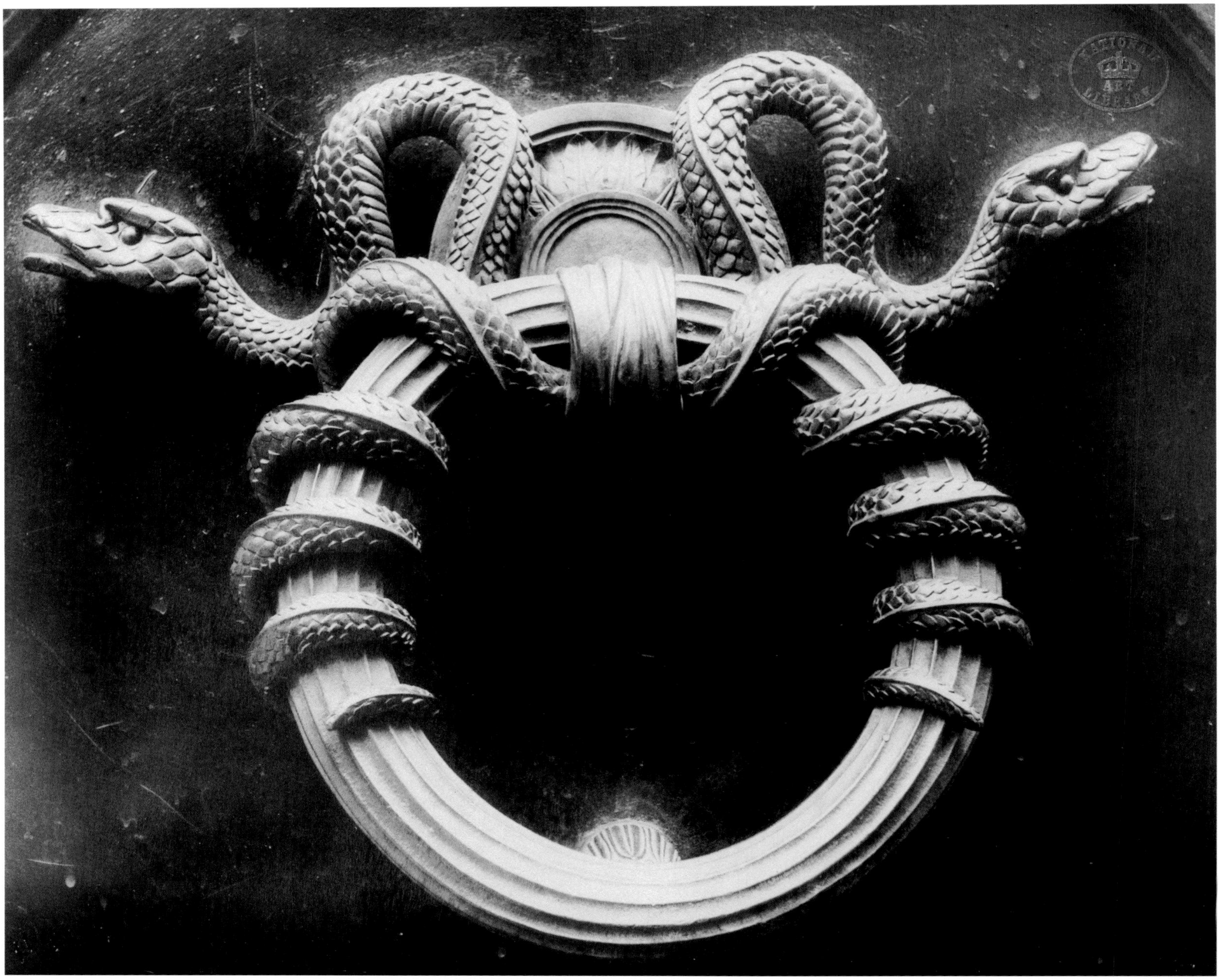

opposite

EUGÈNE ATGET (1847–1927)

Door Knocker, 5 rue Bonaparte, Paris, c. 1900

Albumen print

Ruskin's exhortation to Pre-Raphaelite artists "to descend to the lowest details"[23] found a resonant echo in Atget's photography, which, while sometimes achieving a lyrical intensity, was nevertheless practically based and essentially documentary in nature. Atget worked methodically, dividing his photographs for administrative and commercial convenience into series. A significant proportion of the ten thousand 18 x 24 cm (7 x 9½ in.) glass plates he exposed concentrated on architectural details – fireplaces, mantelpieces, staircases, door knockers. They were sold not only to public institutions but also to craftsmen and architects for use as practical exemplars. The architect W.A. Destailleur, for example, owned 450 of Atget's prints.

right

ALFRED STIEGLITZ (1864–1946)

The Flatiron Building, New York, 1903

Plate I from *Camera Work*, no. 4, October 1903

Gravure on vellum

Architect: Daniel H. Burnham

Stieglitz's ethereal view of the Flatiron, taken with a hand-held camera, typifies the Pictorialist approach to architecture. Uninterested in the building's mechanics – the determination of its shape by the difficult, triangular site, or its surface articulation – Stieglitz dissolved its corporeality into Symbolist metaphor, writing, "With the trees of Madison Square covered with fresh snow, the Flat Iron impressed me as never before. It appeared to be moving toward one like the bow of a monster ocean steamer – a picture of new America still in the making ... . The Flat Iron is to the United States what the Parthenon was to Greece."[24]

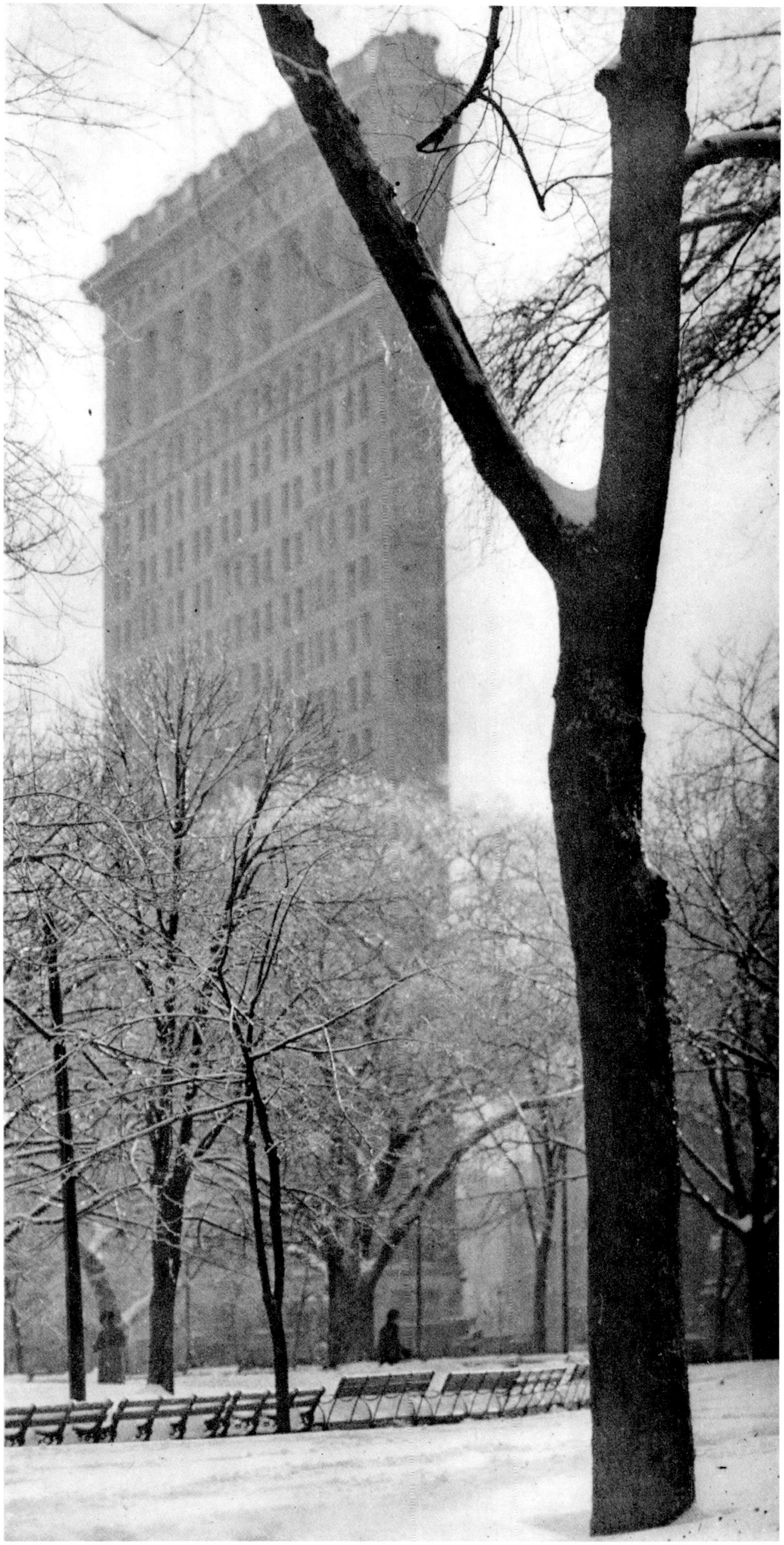

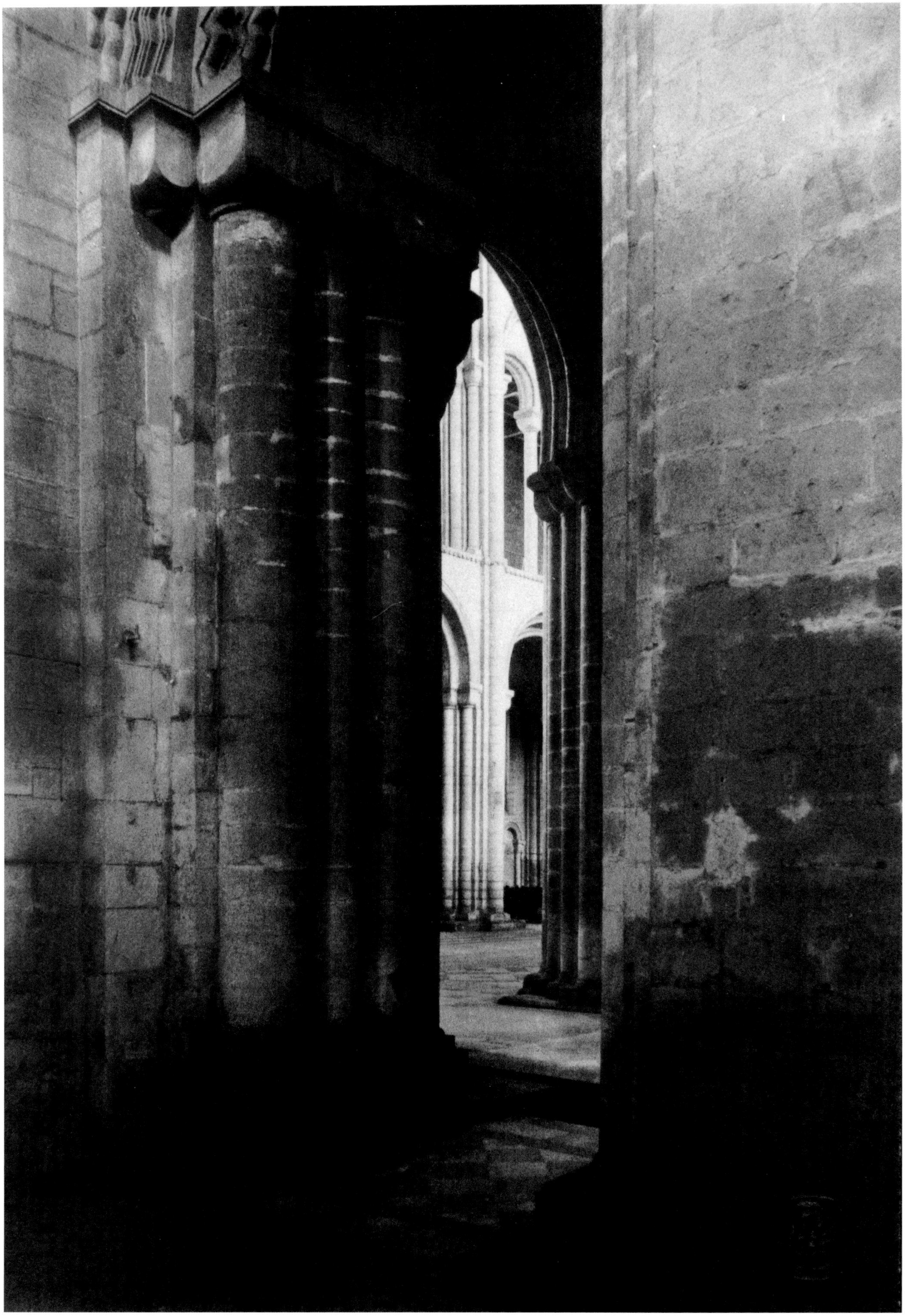

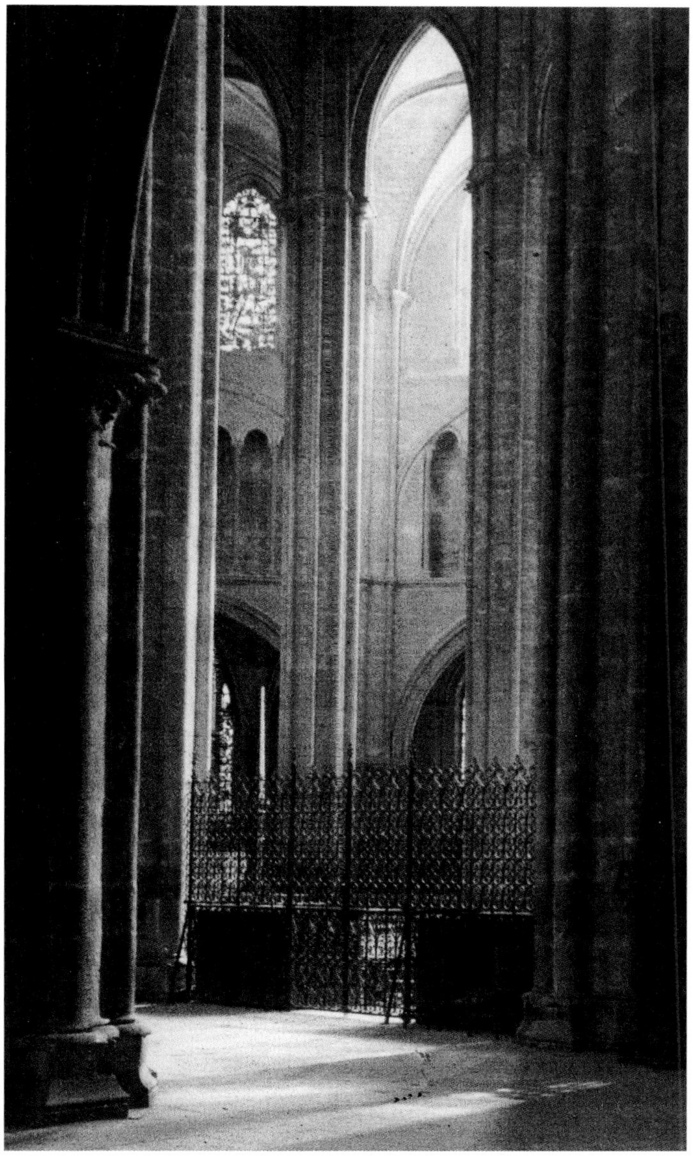

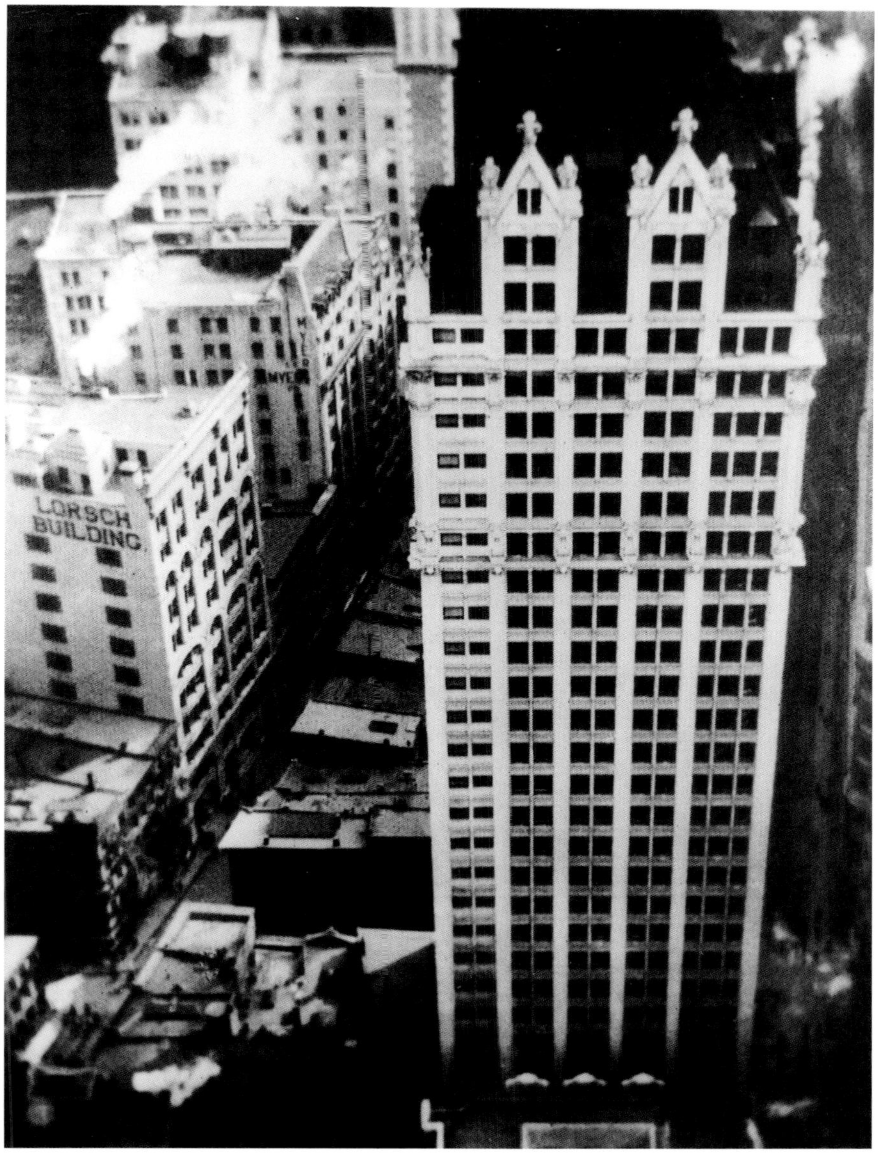

opposite

FREDERICK HENRY EVANS (1853–1943)

'A Memory of the Normans' – Ely Cathedral: Southwest Transept to Nave, 1899

Platinum print

Rather like Peter Henry Emerson's attitude to the Norfolk Fens, Evans valued the cathedral for its aloofness from the contemporary. This is a typical composition, peering between columns and remarkable for its tonal scale, in which the foreground shadows are full of soft details that tactilely suggest the texture of the stonework. Evans wrote: "Realism in the sense of true atmosphere, a feeling of space, truth of lighting, solidity and perfection of perspective (in the eye's habit of seeing it) have been my ambitious aim."[25]

above left

FREDERICK HENRY EVANS (1853–1943)

'Height and Light' – Bourges Cathedral, 1904

Platinum print

Although his subject-matter was narrow and conservative, thereby limiting his influence, Evans exploited the latest photographic techniques, such as Zeiss anastigmatic lenses. Those he used varied in focal length from 7 inches to 19 inches (17.8 to 48.3 cm), which allowed him to fill completely the ground glass with the desired image. Unusually, he also used Cristoid double film, consisting of two unsupported layers of sensitized gelatine emulsion, which Coburn described as like "developing a jellyfish"[26] but which allowed both rich detail in the shadows and modulation in the highlights. When his favoured platinum paper became scarce after the First World War, Evans abandoned photography.

above right

ALVIN LANGDON COBURN (1882–1966)

'The House of a Thousand Windows' – the Woolworth Building, New York, 1912

Gelatine silver print

Architect: Cass Gilbert

From about 1910 Coburn became increasingly preoccupied with form at the expense of mood and atmosphere. This is shown especially in *New York from its Pinnacles*, a series of bird's-eye views inspired by his 1911 photographs of the Grand Canyon, which laid bare the abstract shapes of Manhattan's streets and buildings. Here the extreme wide-angle view obtained by using a pinhole instead of a lens added to the dizzying sense of disorientation. These bird's-eye views anticipated the work of Modernist photographers, who regarded such viewpoints as central to their 'new vision' as seen, for example, in Mendelsohn's *Amerika*.

CHARLES SHEELER (1883–1965)

Bucks County Barn, Pennsylvania, 1916

Gelatine silver print

In 1914 the painter Charles Sheeler began taking photographs of Pennsylvania's vernacular architecture in a technically precise manner that highlighted form and texture. Not only did these almost abstract images assert photography's status as an autonomous medium, but they also sparked a new interest in such subject-matter, which was viewed as a paradigm of indigenous, untainted creative expression and, in its harmonious proportions and functional clarity, as a harbinger of modern design. Among those following Sheeler's example were Ralph Steiner, in his 1930s studies of rural architecture, and Walker Evans.

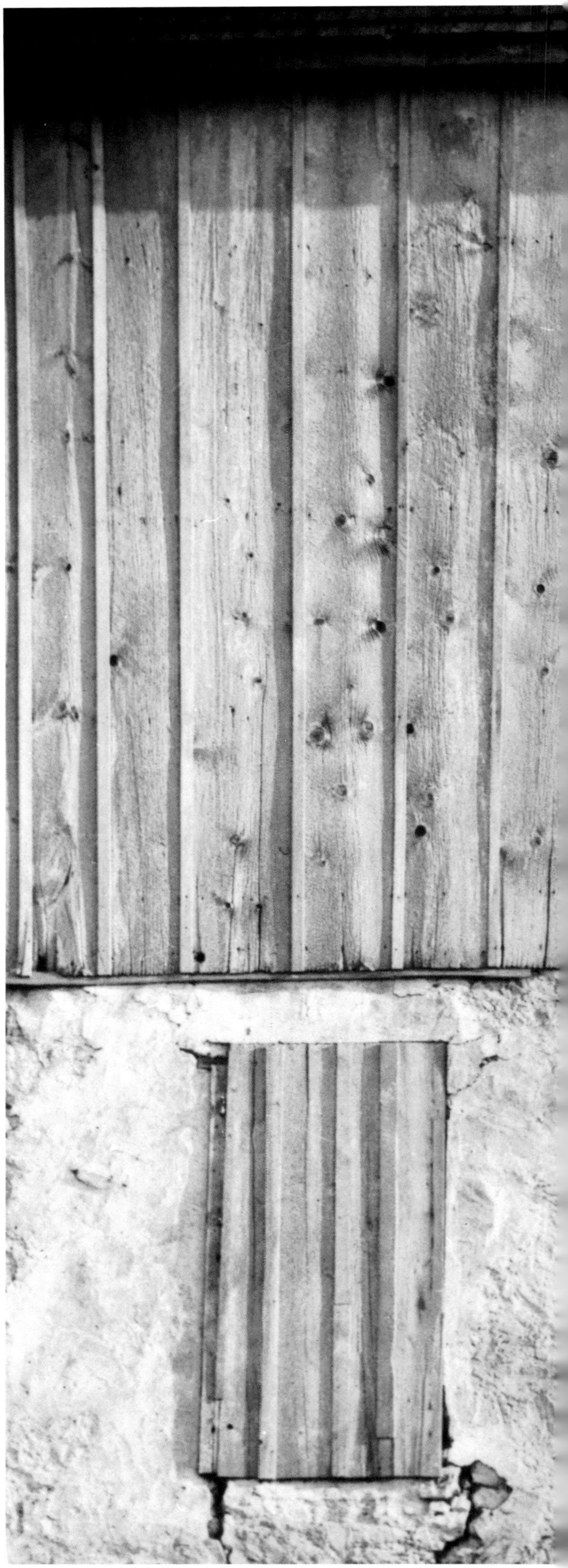

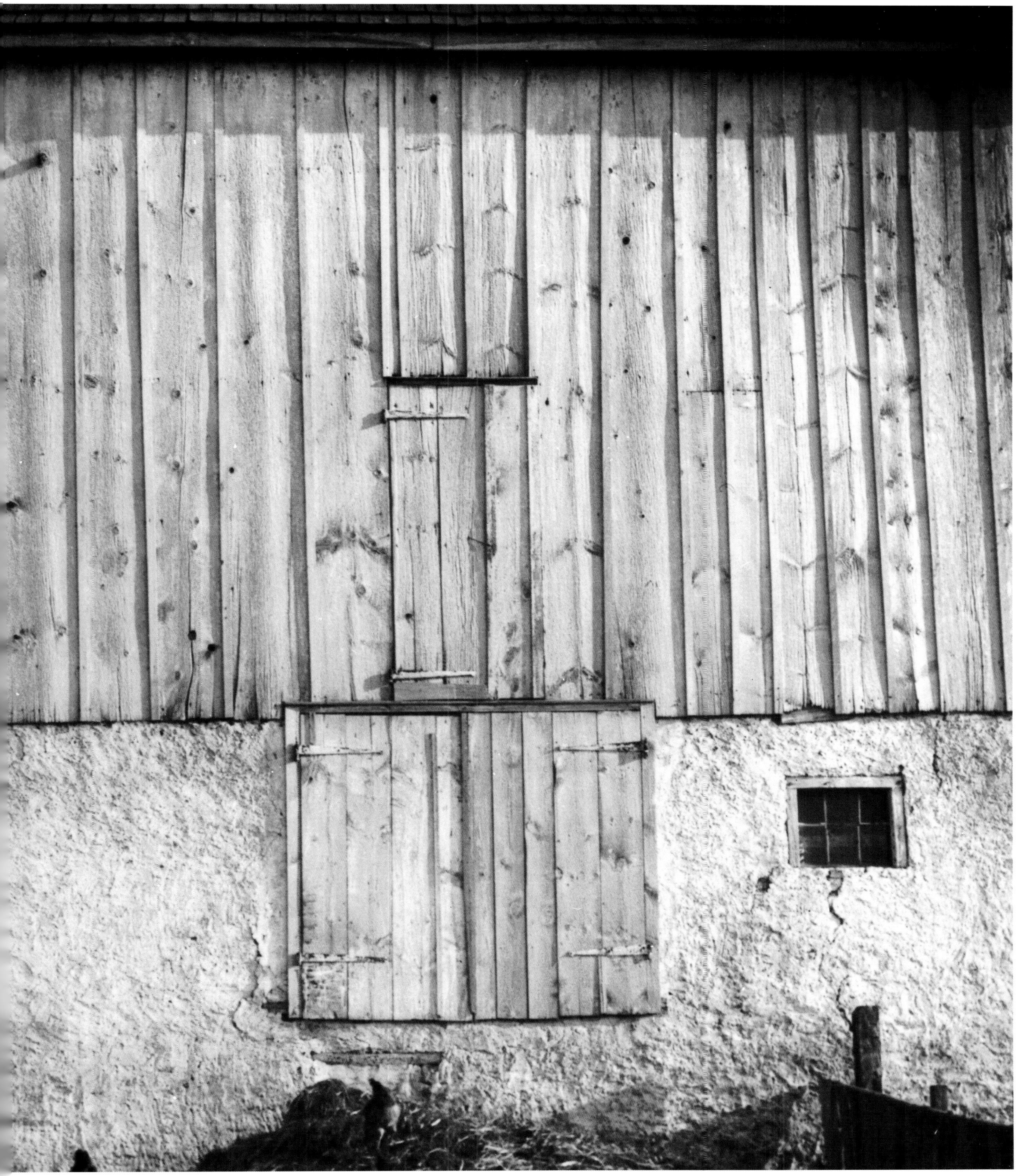

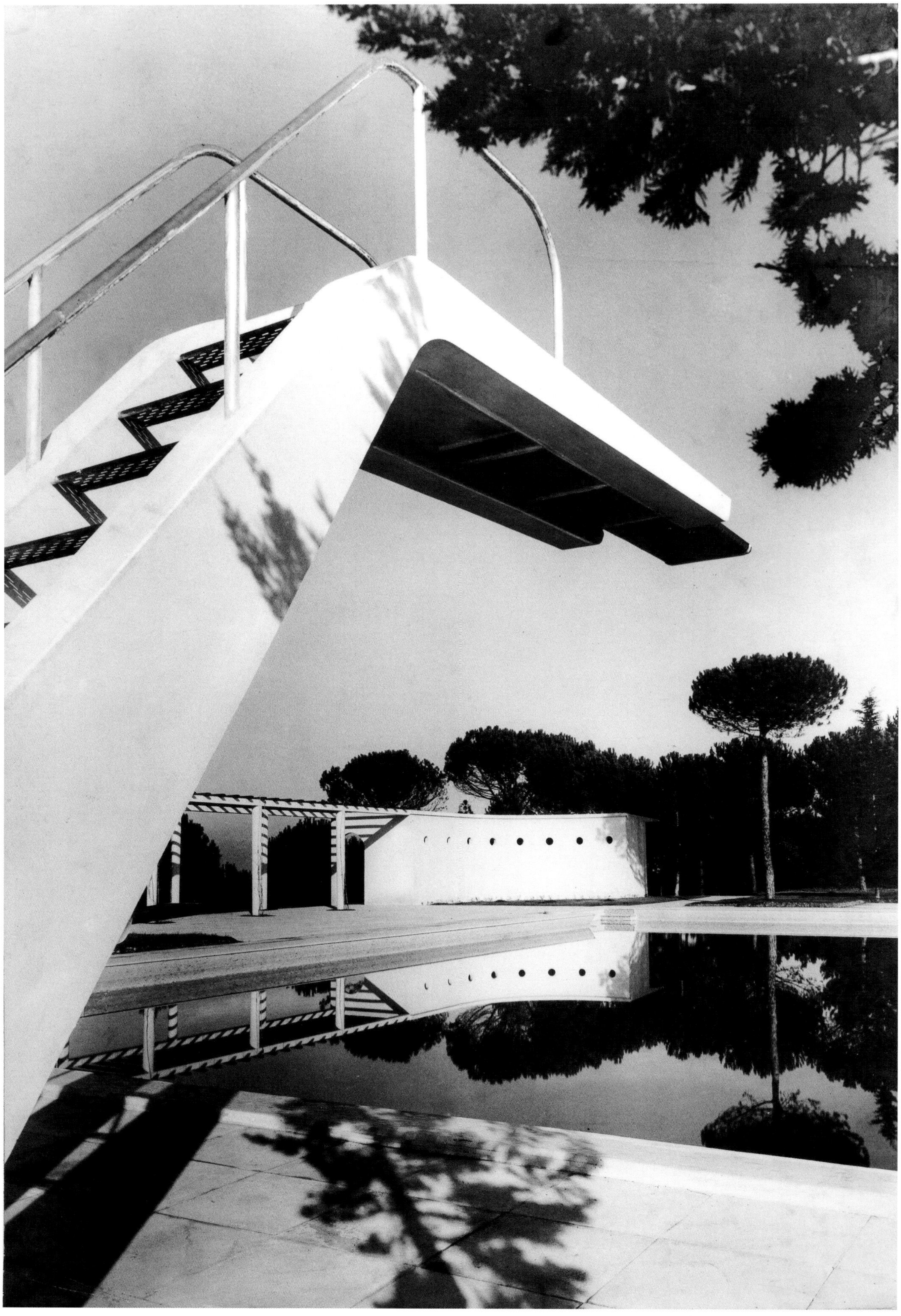

Chapter 4 **The New Vision 1925–1945**

page 118

FERDINANDO BARSOTTI

Golf Club, Ugolino, Florence, 1934
Gelatine silver print
Architect: Gherardo Bosio

ALBERT RENGER-PATZSCH (1897–1966)

Blast Furnaces, Herrenwick, 1927
Gelatine silver print

During the inter-war years the emergence of a Modernist sensibility that emphasized man-made rather than natural forms and, in particular, machine products revitalized architectural photography. Not only were photography and the greedy consumer of its imagery, the printing press, hailed as the supreme art forms of the new machine age but, as the established hierarchy of subjects deemed fit for the camera's lens fractured, images of architecture and engineering emerged from the shadows to become icons of a brave new technocratic world that was to be forged by industry, revealed in a machine-inspired architecture and evangelized by the camera's appropriately 'new vision'. Facilitated by improvements in optics and camera design, fuelled by the growing demands of advertisers and a burgeoning illustrated press, influenced by contemporary developments in cinema and painting, especially Cubism and Constructivism, and proselytized by theorists such as László Moholy-Nagy, the 'new vision' encouraged experimentation with unconventional types of photographic imagery, such as photograms and photomontages, and with unusual viewpoints, daring cropping and high tonal contrasts. While few of these techniques were new, the reverential importance attached to them was, and it resulted in a fresh and more dynamic appraisal of architectural form, the abstract qualities of which emerged as a favoured subject for many of the New Photography's most influential proponents.

Shorn of their moral imperative and theoretical buttressing, characteristic elements of the New Photography – close-ups, bird's- and worm's-eye views – filtered down from the photographic avant garde to become key ingredients of mainstream architectural photography. Furthermore, the New Photography's overthrow of the Pictorialist attempt to imitate painting, and its determination instead to exploit those qualities unique to the photographic medium, allied to its concern to distil the essence of the subjects it focused upon, were analogous to Modernist architecture's insistence on the frank expression of materials and its desire to return to fundamentals. In its images of industry, cars, ships and planes, photography also provided the visual prototypes for the new architecture. This visual and philosophical kinship saw photography and architecture move into a relationship that was closer than at any stage previously. As a result, the number of photographers investigating architectural subjects increased, and photography began to invade spheres of architectural debate from which it had previously been excluded. Echoing Moholy-Nagy's famous statement that "the ignoramuses of the future will be ... those ignorant of photography",[1] the *Architects' Journal* opined, "To no profession is a proper understanding of the whole creative and revelational scope of modern photography more important than our own. The architect of the near future will neglect it at his peril."[2]

The New Photography was not a monolithic but a broad church with several differing doctrines. Its spiritual heartland was Germany, where in the 1920s, in reaction to Pictorialism's concentration on mood and atmosphere, a group of photographers, Albert Renger-Patzsch pre-eminent among them, developed a dispassionate, sharply precise style (below). The result was images that not only were frequently compared to engineering drawings or blueprints, but that also seemed well suited to the representation of the uncompromising surfaces – glass, concrete, steel – and abstract compositions of modern architecture. This New Objectivity photography paralleled the contemporaneous *Neue Sachlichkeit* movement in art and architecture, and had its origins in the Deutsche Werkbund's turn-of-the-century

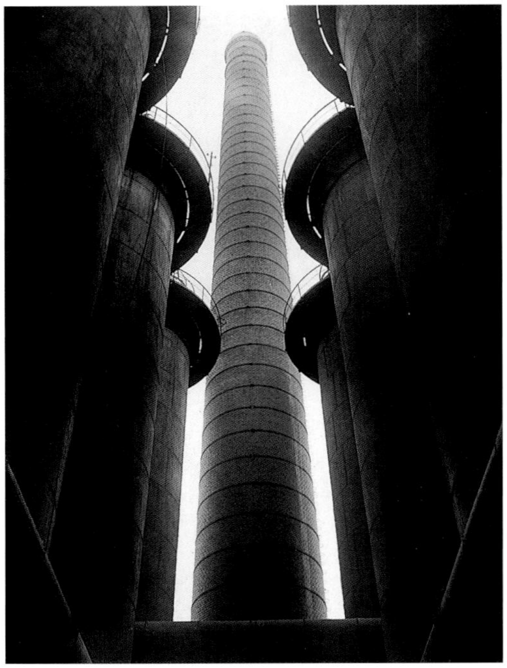

espousal of *Sachlichkeit*, the chief characteristics of which were defined by Hermann Muthesius as "restraint, sobriety and objectivity in conformity with the purpose of the object".[3] The Werkbund's magazine, *Die Form*, helped to promote New Objectivity photography, the coldly analytical tenor of which may have owed something to the precision of Meydenbauer's photogrammetric studies, as well as in some respects representing the culmination of much of architectural photography's Gradgrindian preoccupation with the presentation of facts.

In Renger-Patzsch's images of factories and industrial products, as well as of historical architecture, such as the church of St Katharine, Brandenburg (*c.* 1930; see page 130), the emphasis was, however, entirely different. It was concentrated on the clear articulation of surfaces and the depiction of formal elements isolated from their contexts to force consideration of these commonly disregarded details. The latter was especially important in leading to a wider acknowledgement among architectural photographers that more could often be revealed about a building through the judicious highlighting of a significant fragment or motif than through a general view. The British critic Philip Morton Shand's reference to "that arbitrary isolation of casual components which reveals the part as greater than the whole"[4] echoed his Soviet counterpart Viktor Shklovsky's doctrine of "estrangement" and recalled Le Gray's earlier espousal of the "theory of sacrifices". To paraphrase Mies van der Rohe's famous dictum, photographers had discovered that less could mean more.

Renger-Patzsch's influence on architectural photography was profound, ranging from the work of Jaap d'Oliveira, who, after a period in Renger-Patzsch's studio in 1930, returned to The Netherlands to become one of that country's most accomplished New Objectivity exponents (see page 131), to the post-war typological investigations of Bernd and Hilla Becher. In addition Renger-Patzsch's exploration of the architectonic forms to be found in everyday objects and nature inspired later photographers such as Eric de Maré to extend the boundaries of what constituted architectural photography. The New Objectivity movement in architectural photography was, however, best exemplified in the clinically detached, mostly elevational views of *Neues Bauen* architecture by the Cologne-based photographer Werner Mantz, who began specializing in architectural subjects following a commission from the architect Wilhelm Riphahn to photograph one of his housing estates (below; page 131).

The other major strand of the New Photography as articulated independently by Moholy-Nagy and Alexander Rodchenko was more expressive. Rejecting traditional notions of perspectival representation, or what Rodchenko derisively termed "shooting from the navel", both used worm's- and bird's-eye views to present "new experiences of space ... . With their help, and that of the new school of architects", Moholy-Nagy declared, "we have an enlargement and sublimation of our appreciation of space, the comprehension of a new spatial culture" (see page 133).[5] Moholy-Nagy's statement pointed to a new priority for architectural photographers – the rendition of space and transparency as opposed to the delineation of mass and ornament with which they had been predominantly concerned during the nineteenth century. Although both photographers helped to popularize them, the use of distorted perspectival views predated their appropriation by Moholy-Nagy and Rodchenko and arose partly as a result of the birth of the skyscraper, which not only provided a vantage point from which, as Coburn had demonstrated, the city could be viewed afresh but also afforded the photographer wishing to record it often little choice other than simply to point the camera skyward and accept the resultant converging verticals.

During the 1920s, however, a number of factors encouraged the proliferation of worm's- and bird's-eye

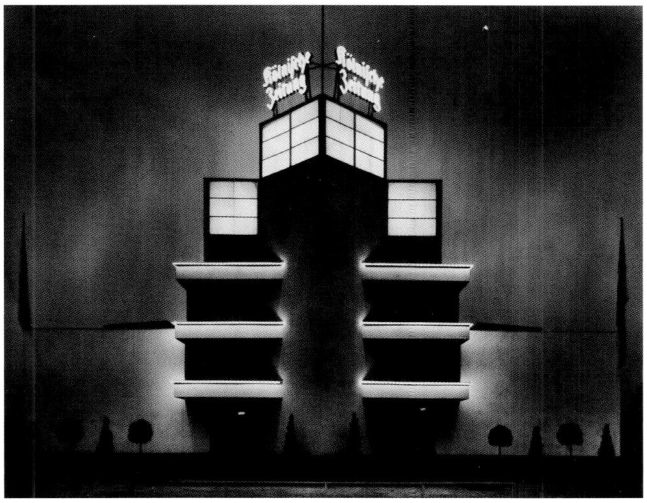

WERNER MANTZ
(1902–1983)
Kölnische Zeitung, Cologne, 1928
Gelatine silver print
Architect: Wilhelm Riphahn

views, seen, for example, in Eric Mendelsohn's *Amerika* (1926), in which the radically shifting viewpoints well conveyed the breathless excitement the architect first felt on walking through the streets of New York, Chicago and Detroit (see page 132). These factors included the introduction of more versatile, lightweight cameras, such as the Leica, used by Mendelsohn, which enabled the photographer to simulate the darting glimpse of the human eye; the influence of the movie camera, the closeness of the two media being underlined by the *Film und Foto* exhibition held in Stuttgart in 1929; and advances in aviation and aerial reconnaissance that led Le Corbusier to claim in his book *Aircraft* (1935), "By means of the airplane, we now have proof, recorded on the photographic plate, of the rightness of our desire to alter methods of architecture and town-planning" (see page 132, top).[6]

As *Modern Photography*, an annual publication issued by *The Studio*, reported in 1932, the New Photography opened up fresh horizons to the architectural photographer:

> The possibilities of views looking down, of views looking up, of extreme perspectives, of space dramatically conceived, the turning of the tables in scale by which a small object, suitably lighted, becomes dignified and impressive, and a large one, rendered small, takes on a new relation to its surroundings, all these things have been formed into a technical repertoire unknown to the photographer in the days before the war.[7]

To these must be added a number of further devices that again, though not new, acquired added significance at this time. The growing interest in photocollage, together with theories of cinematic montage, helped to raise awareness among architectural photographers of the importance of the juxtaposition of elements within the photographic frame in order to make telling points, either by contrast or comparison. Again drawing on the example of cinema, photographs were increasingly intended to be read not as complete statements in themselves but as part of a carefully choreographed and unfolding narrative sequence. Finally, enhanced by new means of illumination such as neon, night photography added a thrilling new dimension to the genre.

By the first half of the 1930s, most architectural photographers in Europe and the United States had to a greater or lesser extent appropriated these stratagems (see, for example, page 118), even though they continued to use traditional large-format cameras on tripods to create worm's- and bird's-eye views, rather than hand-held alternatives, which most considered too small for professional work. In Sweden, where Pictorialism continued to dominate throughout the 1920s, in the following decade the work of Carl Gustav Rosenberg proved to be the most imbued with the new Modernist spirit (see page 134). Besides d'Oliveira, the staunchest practitioners of the New Photography in The Netherlands were d'Oliveira's former partner, Hans Spies, who had worked for a short time for Hugo Schmölz in Cologne and who, like d'Oliveira, was drawn to the austere clarity of New Objectivity photography (see page 135); and, perhaps above all, Jan Kamman, who contributed to the *Film und Foto* exhibition and whose photographs graced the pages of the progressive architectural journal *de 8 en opbouw* (see page 137).

In France, where the photographic avant garde was seduced by Surrealism, the New Photography received a more muted response. This was reflected in the work of its main architectural photographers, although the imagery of Albin Salaün and Marius Gravot, both of whom were commissioned by Le Corbusier, betrayed its influence. By contrast, in Czechoslovakia it was eagerly embraced by such photographers as Jaromír Funke, who worked for Bohuslav Fuchs and other Functionalist architects, while a similar situation pertained in Hungary, where Zoltán Seidner photographed in a Modernist vein (opposite). That the New Photography was not tied to the representation of contemporary buildings in the modern idiom alone is demonstrated by the work of German photographers of the late 1930s, who employed its techniques, particularly cross lighting, bold highlights and deep shadows, in a manner similar to that in the films of Leni Riefenstahl to depict Nazi Neo-classical architecture. The most thoroughgoing application of the New Photography was, however, to be found in Britain and America, where Modernist architecture was generally viewed as an alien import and consequently needed to be sold more strenuously to a sceptical profession and public. In this campaign photography was the chief weapon.

The most influential British architectural photographer of the 1920s was the prolific F.R. Yerbury, Secretary to the

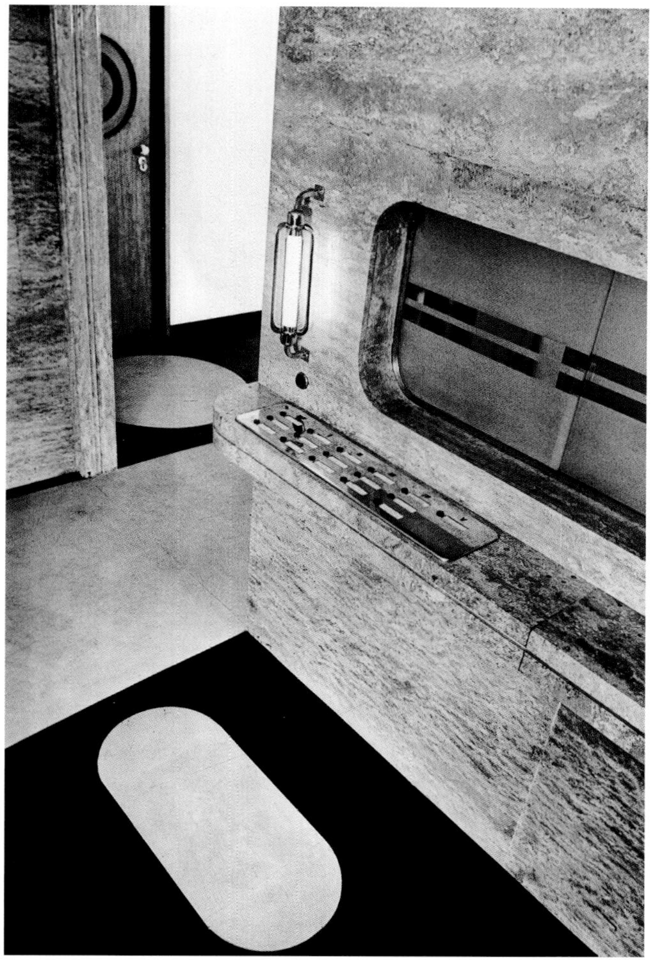

ZOLTÁN SEIDNER

Block of Flats, Budapest, 1938
Gelatine silver print
Architects: Andrew Farkas & George Farkas

Architectural Association from 1912 to 1937, whose catholic confection of images afforded many British architects their first sight of the new architectural developments that were taking shape abroad (see page 142). Reproduced in the *Architect and Building News* to illustrate articles by the architect and critic Howard Robertson, and in a series of books, Yerbury's photographs gained wide currency. The architect John Brandon-Jones recalled, "everybody used his books on continental architecture as cribs".[8] While Yerbury's choice of subject-matter was innovative, his photographic method was essentially conservative. His preference for the softer, and what he regarded as the more humane, forms of Modernism to be found in the brick architecture of northern Germany or in the Swedes' sensitive use of traditional materials was reflected in his prints, which remained unfailingly mellow in tone. This set his work at odds with the growing predilection for high gloss, "glass hard" prints that gave the impression of being machine artefacts.

The marriage of modern architecture to an appropriately modern style of photography was consummated not by Yerbury but by the partnership of Dell & Wainwright (see page 144), whose work first appeared in the *Architectural Review* in 1929 with a ground-breaking and stunning sequence of photographs of Finella, a house near Cambridge. Its architect, Raymond McGrath, wrote appreciatively of the duo, "All day they pursued shadows over the floors and furniture, all night they made moons rise and created other elusive phenomena with their arc lamps ... . It was better than Pyramus and Thisbe."[9] Appointed official photographers to the *Architectural Review* a year later – a post they held until 1946 – Dell & Wainwright transformed British architectural photography and at the same time compellingly demonstrated the power and influence the camera could exert. Their photographs were central to the magazine's fervent mission to promote the cause of modern architecture. This crusade engendered a radically new style of architectural photography in which Dell & Wainwright exploited to the full all the components of the New Photography. These included tipped views with strong diagonals; bold cast shadows; the oblique-angle shot that enabled them to emphasize the repetitive rhythms of modern architecture, whether seen in the serried ranks of protruding concrete fins at Owen Williams's Empire Pool, Wembley (1934), or in a chillingly menacing view of a row of shower units at the same architect's Pioneer Health Centre, Peckham, London (1935); and the cinematic walk-through, shown in their coverage of the new Royal Institute of British Architects headquarters, London (1934), which was replete with reverse-angle treatments and alternative close-ups and distance shots. As Sir John Betjeman recalled, "They could make anything look wonderful by putting bright lights on it and giving it shadows."[10]

It was, however, above all with their images of Modern Movement houses, the refulgent, virginal white forms of which were bathed in sunlight and contrasted with the dramatic cloud-flecked skies above, that Dell & Wainwright's photography was at its most irresistibly seductive (see pages 143, 150). In their photographs, these houses stand resolutely

JOHN HAVINDEN
(1908–1987)

Penguin Pool, London Zoo, 1934
Gelatine silver print
Architects: Lubetkin & Tecton

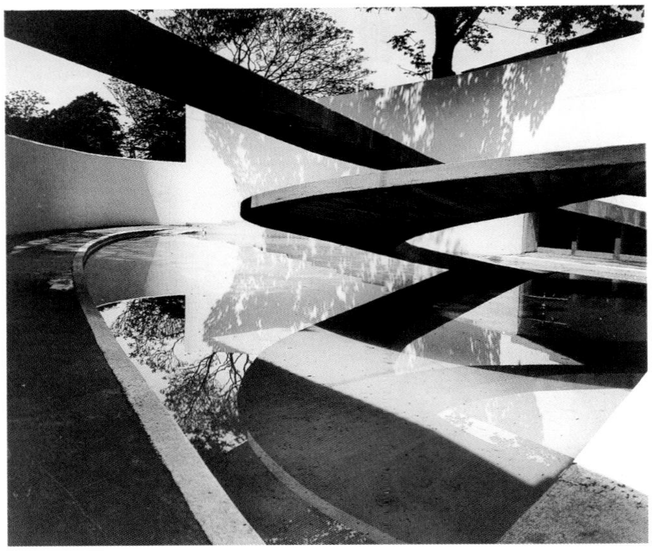

aloof from the landscape, defying picturesque conventions and visualizing the landscape architect Geoffrey Jellicoe's lament that "the modern architect will see the house as a white bird descended from the sky and parked upon the green fields."[11] Never mind that, as time passed, the gap became ever wider between the utopian dream immutably fixed in their imagery and the reality of structural faults and staining of materials to which these houses were so prone. As the *Architects' Journal* maintained, their photographs

> when reproduced on the glossy pages of the *Review* came near to the ideal their designers had in their imaginations. They were the brave new world itself, not the disappointing approximations to it that other people saw when the sun failed to shine, when awkward viewpoints emphasized the uncompromising nature of their geometry or when harsh lighting showed up angles and wall surfaces as not quite immaculately clean and white ... they played a large part in popularizing modern architecture; by bringing out its glamour and charm they made it easier for those who judge solely by appearances to accept it while its practical principles were being established.[12]

Although only John Havinden (above; page 145), whose output was not solely architectural, and to a lesser extent, John Maltby (opposite; page 144) on occasion matched the expressive flair of Dell & Wainwright, the respectable body of work assembled by such photographers as Herbert Felton, Sydney Newbery and Stuart Bale was indicative of the vigour and strength in depth of British architectural photography in the 1930s.

In America during the 1920s, Ralph Steiner's vertiginous worm's-eye views of New York skyscrapers (1926), which aped, though in a more carefully composed manner, the snapshots in Mendelsohn's *Amerika*, and Sheeler's photographs of the Ford Motor Plant at River Rouge, Detroit (1927), which transformed the factory into a labyrinthine network of interweaving conveyors and smokestacks, became frequently reproduced icons of the period. While Steiner's expressionism mirrored the imagery of European Modernist photographers such as Moholy-Nagy, whose influence could also be seen in Walker Evans's early Leica studies of New York (1930) as well as in Berenice Abbott's first photographs of the city (1929), the example of Sheeler's precise, abstract renderings proved to be the more enduring among America's photographic vanguard during the 1930s. The reason for this lay in the fact that they were more firmly rooted in the American photographic tradition, drawing as they did on the indigenous, abstract compositions of photographers such as Paul Strand and on Renger-Patzsch's advocacy of objective recording, which found a ready response in a country where the notion of documentary photography was particularly well-established.

For commercial photographers, however, both approaches seemed equally valid and were adopted with relish by the most adventurous professional architectural documenters of the period, the underrated Fay Sturtevant Lincoln and the Chicago firm of Hedrich Blessing. Lincoln, who went into partnership with Peter Nyholm in 1929 before setting up on his own, was based in New York and photographed throughout the eastern seaboard as well as in England and France. Unusually, his work combined the recording of both contemporary and historical architecture, such as Colonial Williamsburg, although he was undoubtedly at his most effective photographing the Depression-defying Art Deco extravaganzas of his many corporate clients or the more spartan creations of the International Style (see page 147). At their most daring, his photographs possess an unnerving, surreal quality that sets them at a far remove from the competent but less exciting compositions of his chief New York rivals, the Wurts Brothers and Samuel Gottscho with his son-in-law partner, William H. Schleisner.

Also founded in 1929, the firm of Hedrich Blessing established itself as a major new force in architectural photography, thanks largely to the patronage of John Wellborn Root Jr and its stylish documentation of the *Century of Progress* exhibition, Chicago (1933), which put into the shade the more conventional offerings of the Fair's official photographers, Kaufmann Fabry. The brothers Ken and Bill Hedrich were the firm's principal photographers, and the latter's 1936 shot of Frank Lloyd Wright's Fallingwater in Bear Run, Pennsylvania, has a claim to be the most reproduced architectural photograph (see pages 148–49). It is, however, atypical of the firm's work, which generally eschewed unconventional viewpoints for more traditional two-point perspectives, with an emphasis on the strongly graphic use of light and shadow and exceptional definition (see page 146). Appointed official photographers to the *Architectural Forum*, and especially skilled in night photography, Hedrich Blessing not only produced some of the most resonant images of the 1930s but, still in existence today, went on to become one of the most influential firms in the history of architectural photography, counting among its clients many of the most significant twentieth-century architects, including Mies van der Rohe and Skidmore Owings & Merrill.

As Philip Morton Shand justifiably argued, "without modern photography modern architecture could never have been 'put across'."[13] In a perceptive article published in the *Architectural Review* in 1934, entitled 'New Eyes for Old', Shand praised the pioneering work of Moholy-Nagy and stressed the unique relationship between modern architecture and the New Photography:

> The two fields in which the spirit of our age has achieved its most definite manifestations are photography and architecture. Did modern photography beget modern architecture or the converse? It is an interesting point. But since their logical development was simultaneous, and their interaction considerable, it hardly matters which. What does matter is that it was the same sort of mind and power of vision which has produced both; and that both are based on abstract form ... . In the early 1920s architectural photography was as unimaginatively true to 'life' and conventional perspective as any other sort of photography. Men with the cultural equipment of beach photographers walked round buildings at a respectful distance like policemen on their beat flashing lanterns on the impeccably obvious. But the new sort of architects had their buildings taken by the new sort of photographers. A revolution in the technique of architectural photography resulted, which has revolutionized architectural criticism.[14]

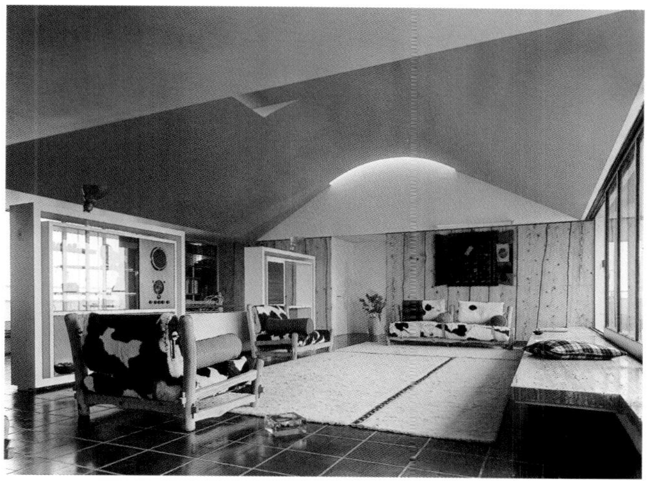

JOHN MALTBY (1910–1980)

Penthouse Flat, Highpoint II, London,
1938
Gelatine silver print
Architects: Lubetkin & Tecton

Shand's revolution was quickened by the opening up of new outlets for photographs in exhibitions and advertising, and by the increasingly inventive ways in which magazine art editors laid out photographic imagery on the page, thereby enhancing its persuasive power. Strange as it may seem, architectural exhibitions in which photographs predominated were still a cause for comment well into the 1930s. Mindful of the success of the *20 Years of British Architecture* exhibition, organized by the Architecture Club in 1923, which was recognized as being "momentous in attracting for the first time a large public to an architectural exhibition, and furthermore in consisting almost entirely of photographs",[15] the Royal Academy had been forced to admit photographs. Similarly, the New York Museum of Modern Art's landmark exhibition *The International Style* (1932), despite its curators' frequent references to it as an exhibition of models, was significant for being composed largely of blow-ups of photographs supplied by, among

Page spread from Le Corbusier, *Vers une architecture*, Paris (G. Crès & Cie.) 1924

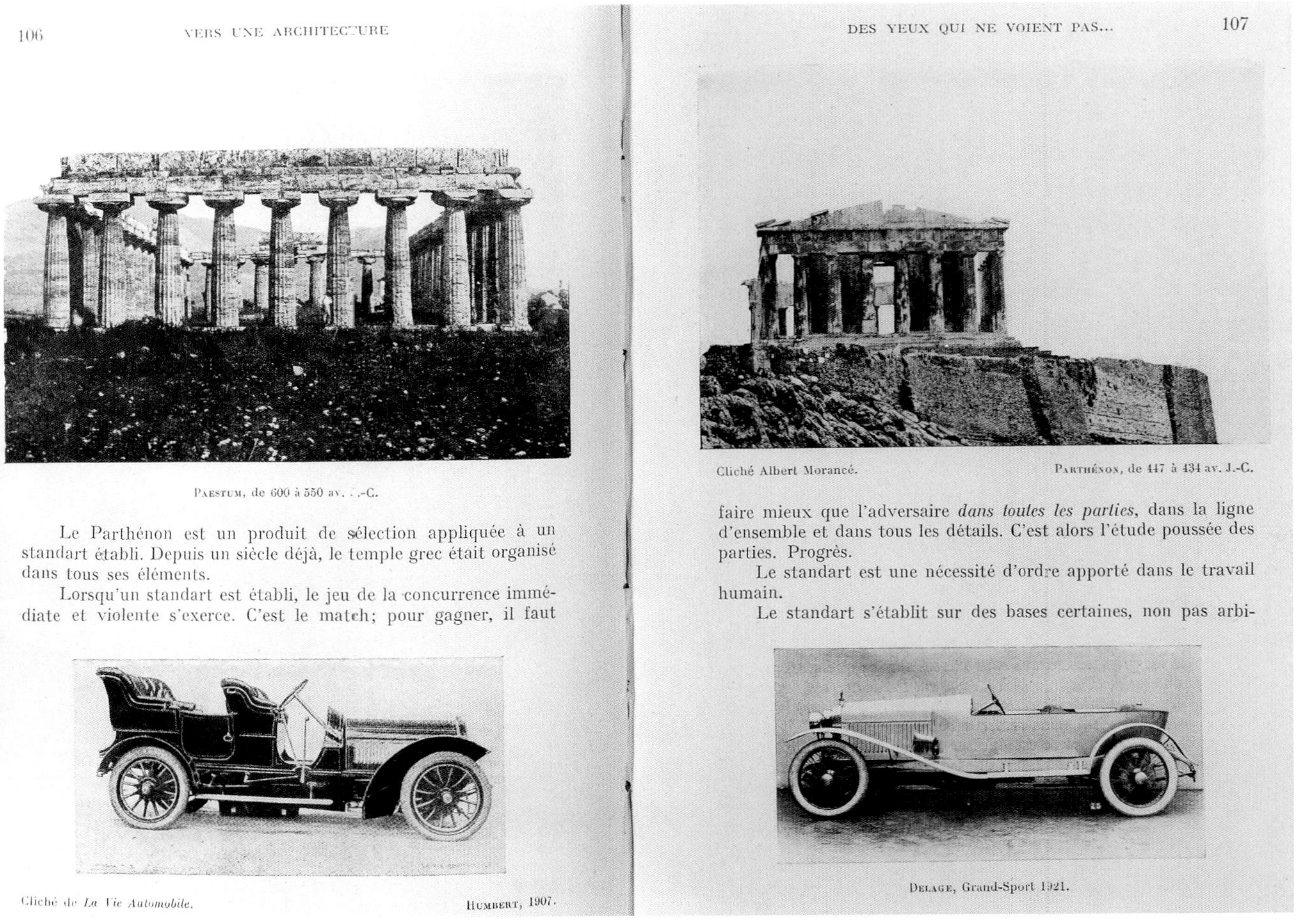
106 VERS UNE ARCHITECTURE

PAESTUM, de 600 à 550 av. J.-C.

Le Parthénon est un produit de sélection appliquée à un standart établi. Depuis un siècle déjà, le temple grec était organisé dans tous ses éléments.

Lorsqu'un standart est établi, le jeu de la concurrence immédiate et violente s'exerce. C'est le match; pour gagner, il faut

Cliché de *La Vie Automobile*. HUMBERT, 1907.

DES YEUX QUI NE VOIENT PAS... 107

Cliché Albert Morancé. PARTHÉNON, de 447 à 434 av. J.-C.

faire mieux que l'adversaire *dans toutes les parties*, dans la ligne d'ensemble et dans tous les détails. C'est alors l'étude poussée des parties. Progrès.

Le standart est une nécessité d'ordre apporté dans le travail humain.

Le standart s'établit sur des bases certaines, non pas arbi-

DELAGE, Grand-Sport 1921.

others, Van Ojen, Kamman and the Chicago Architectural Photographing Company.

Like many other photographers, Kamman, whose best-known pictures of the Van Nelle factory, Rotterdam (1931), were taken for the firm's director, benefited from the broadening of patronage provided by companies seeking advertising material. Thus Renger-Patzsch counted among his clients Siemens Elektrowärme and Jaener Glaswerke Schott; d'Oliveira, Phillips; and Maltby, the Odeon cinema chain. The demands of these companies placed a premium on eye-catching imagery, as did those of the growing number of architectural journals. The journals' editors realized that, in an increasingly competitive market, striking photographs could be crucial to the maintenance of circulation figures. Goodhart-Rendel's observation that the photograph was "not only illustration but news"[16] both underlined the new importance attached to the medium and highlighted the beginning of a trend, which was to become prevalent after the war, in which journals competed to be the first to cover new buildings, with the inevitable result that many were photographed while still incomplete. Perhaps most importantly, photographs rather than arcane drawings were seen as the best way to interpret architecture to a wider public.

These considerations prompted journals to move away from the treatment of photographs as illustrated appendages to the text, set out in an uninspiringly rigid 'window' format, to their presentation as focal points of the page and statements in their own right. This transformation was heavily indebted to the rise of a popular pictorial press, especially in Germany, where illustrated magazines such as the *Berliner Illustrirte Zeitung* and the *Münchner Illustrierte Presse* pioneered photojournalism. Architectural magazines also took advantage of a typographical revolution that encouraged the use of text and illustrations as mutually reinforcing, integrated entities. Leading the field was the *Architectural Review* (see page 151), which, in line with its principle that each page should contain a surprise, printed photographs in different coloured inks, experimented with colour printing, bled images to the edge of the page or even beyond in specially folded sheets and in July 1936 published a special issue on 'Leisure at the Seaside' imaginatively designed by Moholy-Nagy. What El Lissitzky termed "the architecture of the book" was similarly transformed, a prime example being Le Corbusier's *Vers une architecture* (1923). Adopting advertising techniques, Le Corbusier recomposed 'found' images, wrenching them from their accustomed contexts, contrasting and comparing them with pictures of his own work, and juxtaposing them with text to press his argument with the greatest force (opposite). While few books matched Le Corbusier's invention, the boom in monographs on architects, such as the Geneva series *Masters of Architecture*, provided another profitable outlet for architectural photographers.

Photography's relationship with modern architecture extended beyond its promotion to encompass its inspiration, justification and even execution. Photographic images acted as visual stimuli for Modernist architects, none more so than those depicting the primeval power and simple unadorned forms of American, Canadian and South American grain silos that Gropius first published in *Jahrbuch des Deutschen Werkbundes* in 1913. These quickly entered the visual lore of Modernism, being recycled on numerous occasions, most tellingly by Le Corbusier in *Vers une architecture*, in which examples from Argentina were labelled as Canadian and the undulating roofscape of one Buenos Aires elevator was removed by airbrushing to preserve its crisp, functional lines. Mendelsohn was also seduced by what he termed his "silo dreams" during his 1924 visit to Buffalo, where he "took photographs like mad".[17] Illustrated by the Modernist historian Sigfried Giedion on the cover of his *Bauen in Frankreich, Bauen in Eisen, Bauen in Eisenbeton* (1928), designed by Moholy-Nagy, Ferdinand Arnodin's 1905 Transporter Bridge at Marseilles achieved similar iconic status, being photographed by a veritable who's who of modern photography, including Moholy-Nagy himself, Germaine Krull and Herbert Bayer. Modern architecture was to be related visually not only to contemporary images of industry, engineering and transport, but also to rediscovered 'functional' structures from the past. Sheeler thus photographed the buttresses of Chartres Cathedral, framing them into a complex geometric web that mirrored his treatment of the conveyors at River Rouge; Renger-Patzsch cast his clinical eye over the Alsatian abbey of Murbach; and Dell & Wainwright rephotographed the Crystal Palace, London, their raking side perspective trumpeting its modernity.

This photographic reappropriation of the past should be seen in the context of attempts by historians such as Nikolaus Pevsner, Shand, Giedion and Hitchcock to establish an ancestry for Modernist architecture. With the aid of Abbott's photographs, displayed in the exhibition *The Urban Vernacular of the Thirties, Forties and Fifties: American Cities before the Civil War* at the Weslyan University, Middletown, in 1934, Hitchcock argued that the roots of American Modernism lay in *ante bellum* vernacular architecture. Two years later, again using photographs by Abbott, Hitchcock sought to establish H.H. Richardson's credentials as a key precursor of Modernism in a pioneering book and exhibition at New York's Museum of Modern Art. New life was also breathed into old photographs. Albert Chevojon's powerful image of the huge roof trusses of the Galerie des Machines found a new incarnation in Lissitzky's photomontage for the jacket of Roger Ginsburger's *Frankreich: Die Entwicklung der neuen Ideen nach Konstruktion und Form* (1930), part of the influential Austrian *Neues Bauen in der Welt* series, and reappeared in a host of Modernist writings. In the wake of the Crystal Palace's destruction by fire in 1936, a relieved *Architectural Review* announced the rediscovery of 1851 photographs of the palace, which had languished largely unknown but which subsequently enjoyed a new existence as visual testimonies to its functionalist aesthetic. Finally, photography and architecture coalesced in a novel art form made possible by enhanced means of enlarging photographs – the photomural, as employed by Lissitzky and by Le Corbusier in his Pavillon Suisse, Cité Universitaire, Paris (1931).

Despite Moholy-Nagy's contention that the New Photography provided "an impartial approach, such as our eyes, tied as they are to the laws of association, do not give",[18] the use of unusual viewpoints and other techniques to dramatize even the most banal piece of architecture had the

Page spread from the *Architectural Review*, vol. 83, January 1938, showing John Piper's photographs illustrating his article 'The Nautical Style'

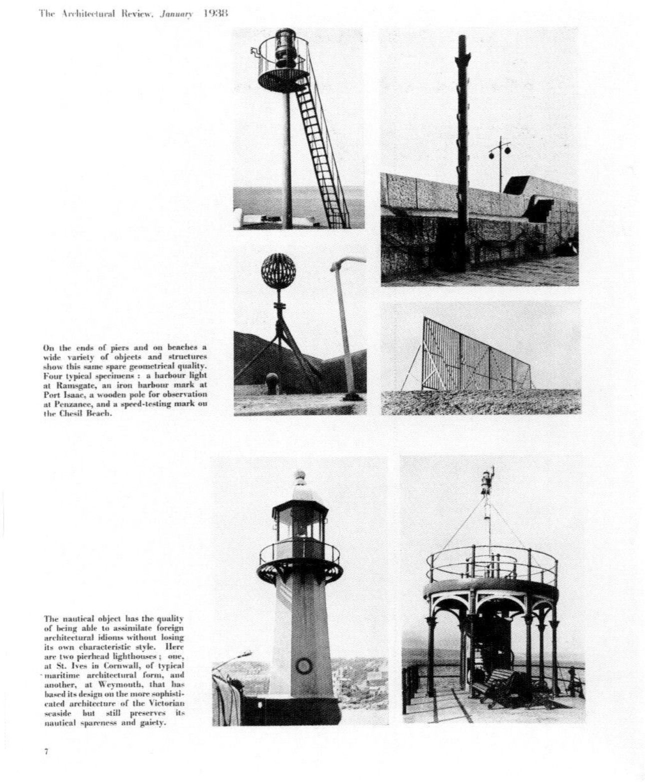

The Architectural Review, *January* 1938

On the ends of piers and on beaches a wide variety of objects and structures show this same spare geometrical quality. Four typical specimens: a harbour light at Ramsgate, an iron harbour mark at Port Isaac, a wooden pole for observation at Penzance, and a speed-testing mark on the Chesil Beach.

The nautical object has the quality of being able to assimilate foreign architectural idioms without losing its own characteristic style. Here are two pierhead lighthouses; one, at St. Ives in Cornwall, of typical maritime architectural form, and another, at Weymouth, that has based its design on the more sophisticated architecture of the Victorian seaside but still preserves its nautical spareness and gaiety.

7

effect of calling attention to the photographer himself. The increasing use of by-lines further emphasized that the photograph was not a transparent slice of reality but an artificial construct shaped by a series of choices. As more architects became aware of the latitude open to photographers, and that the camera could not only record but also interpret, flatter or even deceive, so they wanted to help determine those choices to ensure that their buildings were presented to best effect. As a result, a growing number of relationships were formed between architects and photographers sympathetic to their work – Riphahn with Mantz; Le Corbusier with Gravot; Oud with Van Ojen; Gerrit Rietveld with d'Oliveira; and Berthold Lubetkin with Maltby, to name but a few. One of the most enduring and fruitful of such collaborations began in 1936, when Richard Neutra, a friend of the photographer Edward Weston, whose images he had included in his *Amerika* (1929), purchased photographs of his Kun House from the unknown Julius Shulman, thus launching Shulman on a glittering career as an architectural photographer. At their best such relationships became creative partnerships that led to a deeper understanding of the architecture portrayed; at their worst they smacked of censorial control that raised fundamental questions about the role and independence of the photographer that became more pressing as the century progressed.

While it could be argued that close co-operation between architect and photographer simply mirrored the earlier cosy association between architect and favoured renderer (and it would, of course, be wrong to suggest that the architectural photographer in the nineteenth century had a free hand), the inter-war years nevertheless witnessed a significant increase in the degree of control exercised by some clients – not only architects but also advertisers, contractors and building owners – over how their products were visually represented. This was also true of the photographs commissioned by the architectural press. Dell & Wainwright, for example, worked under close instruction from the *Architectural Review*'s editorial staff, who frequently accompanied the photographers on reconnaissance trips to assess the best viewpoints and optimum light conditions, even if the photographers did assert their independence by usually refusing, despite requests to the contrary, to include people in their pictures. Such control could also extend to managing the supply of photographs. Thus Gropius sought to ensure that Renger-Patzsch's 1928 series of photographs of his Fagus factory at Alfeld an der Leine, begun in 1911, were the only ones reproduced. By successfully playing down the building's solidity, stressed by Gropius at the time, and highlighting instead its transparency and seeming weightlessness – both new-found concerns of the architect in the late 1920s – these images allowed Gropius to present his work as a logical continuum, in which the factory could be repositioned as a pioneering example of glass curtain-walling (see page 151).[19] Photography had become too important to be left to the photographer alone. It had entered the domain of publicity and persuasion.

Although architectural photographers were liable to a greater degree of control, at the same time the range of subjects deemed worthy of architectural image-making was expanded by the activities of British critics and journalists, and by photographers such as Walker Evans. Running alongside glossy portrayals of the latest triumphant achievement of architectural Modernism in the *Architectural Review* were unprepossessing amateur snapshots taken by members of its editorial staff or journalist contributors. These were used polemically to highlight such themes as the despoliation of the countryside by unsightly advertising hoardings, or to draw attention to previously neglected aspects of the country's architectural heritage, such as lighthouses and nonconformist churches, the simple propriety of which was held to contain important lessons for modern architects. The subject-matter of these refreshingly unselfconscious photographs, some of them taken by the artist John Piper (opposite), was to be greatly extended and put on a professional footing after the Second World War by such photographers as Eric de Maré.

In America, Evans turned his lens on comparable topics, foregrounding the kind of humble abodes that had formed the backdrop to thousands of American daguerreotypes. Thus he sought the telling image in unfamiliar locations and commonplace structures, be it the torqued outline of a Maine water pump sheltering beneath a gingerbread canopy (1933), the rudimentary corrugated façade of an Alabama contractor's shed (1936), or the unpretentious but moving forms of a South Carolina negro church (1936; see page 153). Commissioned by private individuals and the Farm Security Administration, Evans's images were shot in an impersonal but carefully composed manner, with an Atgetesque eye for contextual juxtaposition. Like those of Evans, the federally funded photographs of New York by Berenice Abbott, a selection of which was published in *Changing New York* (1939), were influenced by Atget, eschewed sentimentality and, as the book's title suggested, maintained a dialogue between past and present (see page 152). Another theme common to both photographers was their alertness to the symbolic potential of signage. In 1841 Talbot had remarked:

> it frequently happens, moreover – and this is one of the charms of photography – that the operator himself discovers on examination, perhaps long afterwards, that he had depicted many things he had no notion of at the time. Sometimes inscriptions and dates are found upon the buildings, or printed placards most irrelevant, are discovered upon their walls.[20]

In the work of Evans and Abbott, Talbot's incidentals became a central photographic preoccupation.

By the end of the 1930s the camera had emerged as the pre-eminent mediator of architectural endeavour not just to a professional audience but also to a wider public as symbolized by the choice of a Margaret Bourke-White photograph of Fort Peck Dam, Montana, for the cover of *Time*'s inaugural issue in 1936. In 1937 Goodhart-Rendel observed:

> Whatever value to the architect we put upon the change, the public appears to prefer the architectural evidence of the camera to that of the pen, pencil or paintbrush. A photograph proves that a building exists or has existed; a drawing proves only that it has been proposed. A photograph portrays in a medium so familiar to us that we ignore its occasional falsity, a drawing arouses our suspicion by its obvious power of tricking us with less familiar conventions.[21]

As Goodhart-Rendel's rueful tone betrayed, this change provoked strong misgivings in some quarters. In 1933, illustrated by spectacular Dell & Wainwright photographs, *Country Life* voted Oliver Hill's Joldwynds in Holmbury St Mary, Surrey, its 'House of the Year', while beyond the gaze of publicity its enraged owners, dismayed by the house's structural defects, wrote acidly to the architect, "Your job does not come to an end as you seem to think when you have got something that looks nice in a photograph",[22] and, "It would all photograph nicely, including the bookcases when filled, as at your suggestion, with books that no one could read, but which had good bindings. Unfortunately Joldwynds was meant for a house to live in, not a lovely film set."[23] As the supremacy of the architectural photograph was consolidated in the latter half of the century, so the criticisms of the gap between photographic illusion and reality, so starkly demonstrated by the Joldwynds saga, became ever more strident, helping to foster alternative means of photographing buildings.

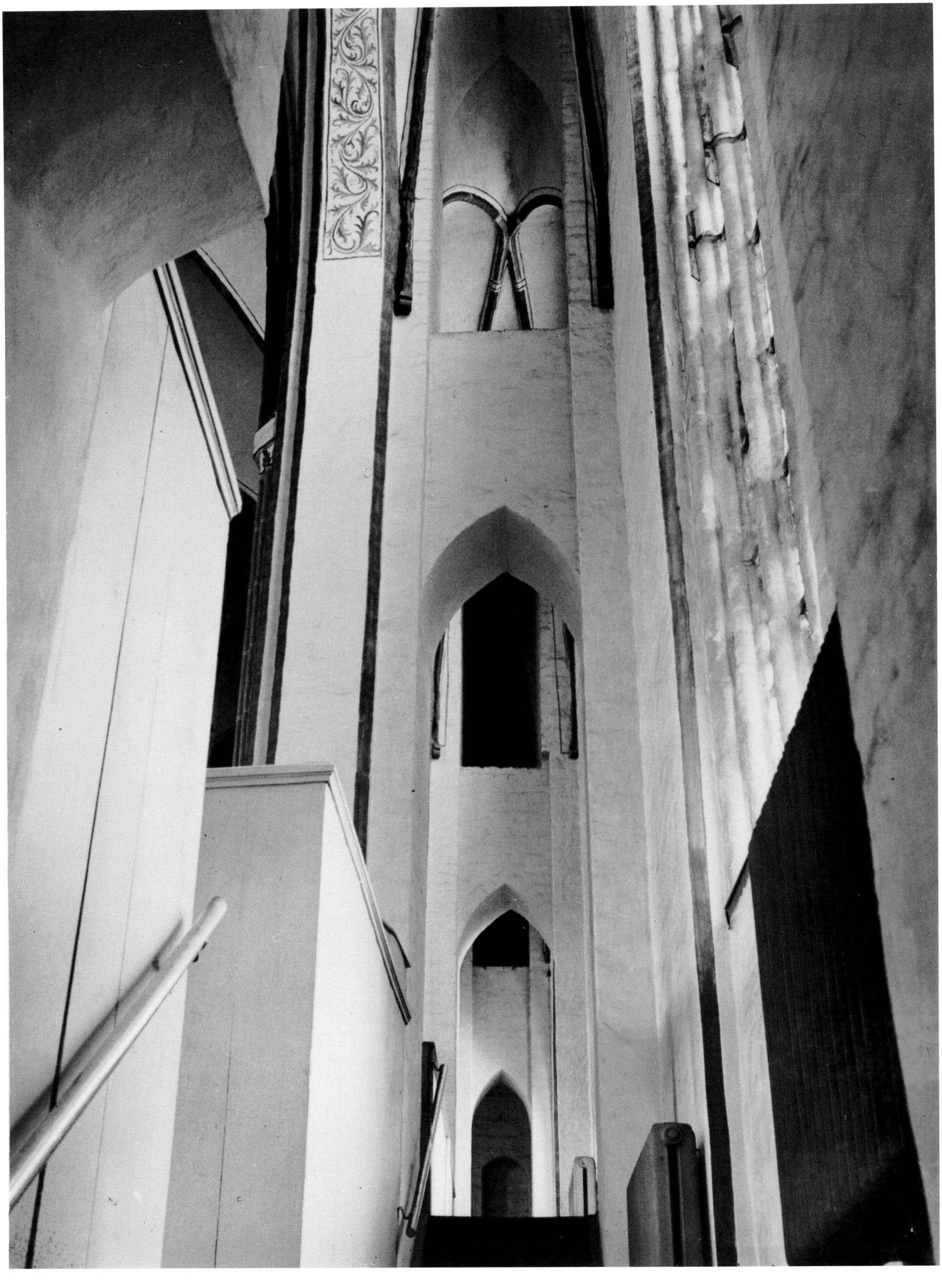

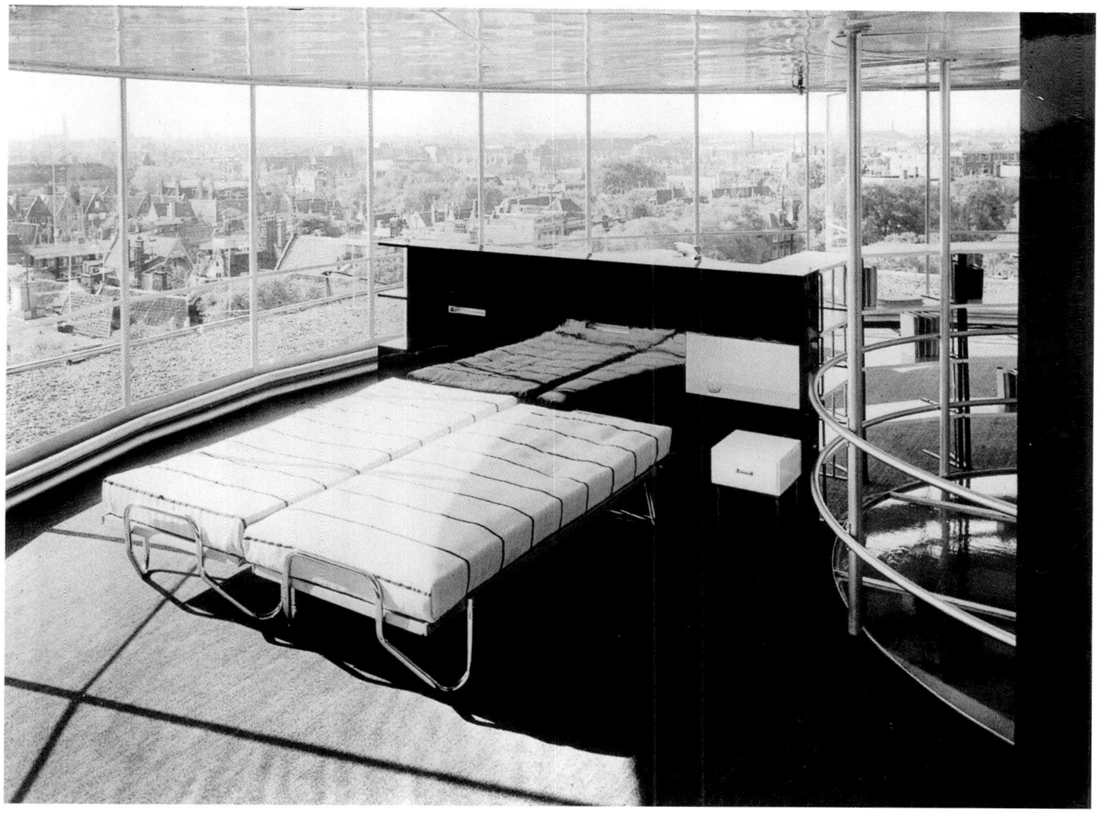

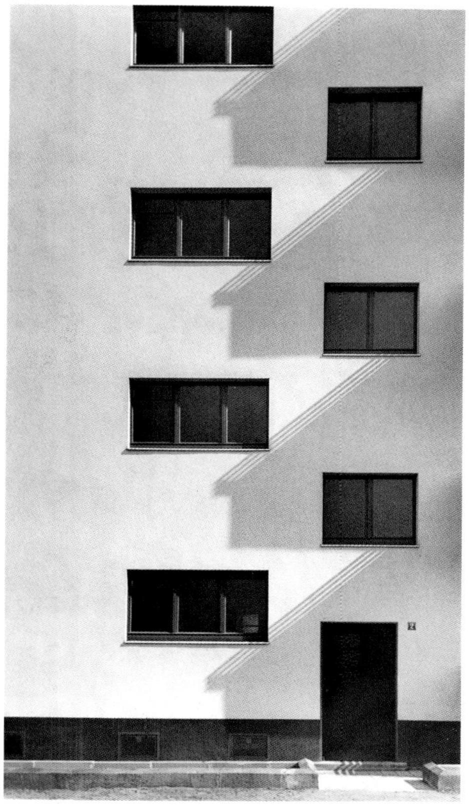

opposite

ALBERT RENGER-PATZSCH (1897–1966)

Church of St Katharine, Brandenburg, c. 1930

Gelatine silver print

With its tightly framed converging verticals, this photograph is structurally similar to Renger-Patzsch's study of the Herrenwick blast furnaces (see page 120), illustrating how he applied the same compositional stratagems to architectonic forms old and new. In contrast to Frederick Evans, Renger-Patzsch has eliminated all atmosphere and maintained an even light to concentrate on the clarity of line and form. This rigorously intellectual approach was praised by the novelist Thomas Mann, for whom Renger-Patzsch's images were "exact statements drawn from the whole … . The detail, the objective, is removed from the world of appearances, isolated, sharpened, made meaningful, animated."[24]

above left

JAAP D'OLIVEIRA (1908–1978)

Daybed in the 'Op het Dak' Furniture Exhibition Celebrating the Completion of the Cupola of Metz & Co., Amsterdam, 1933

Gelatine silver print

Architect & furniture designer: Gerrit Rietveld

After short spells in the studios of Renger-Patzsch and Hugo Schmölz, d'Oliveira was in partnership with Hans Spies from 1932 to 1934 before striking out on his own. His work concentrated almost exclusively on architecture and interior design, and his clients, who included Gerrit Rietveld and J.F. Staal, were largely drawn from the Nieuwe Bouwen movement. This image provides a reminder of the close relationship between product advertising and the New Photography.

above right

WERNER MANTZ (1902–1983)

Housing, Kalkerfeld, Cologne, 1928

Gelatine silver print

Architect: Wilhelm Riphahn

Having studied photography in Munich and worked in portraiture and advertising, Mantz took up architectural photography after being discovered by Riphahn. Commissions to record much of Cologne's new housing followed, and his empathetic treatment of Modernism's geometrical forms soon attracted further assignments from other architects, such as Bruno Paul and Mendelsohn. Here Mantz has used raking sunlight to form a strikingly abstract composition of light and dark, in which the geometry of the shadows complements that of the architecture and the shadowed presence of adjacent balconies suggests the multiplication of the housing blocks beyond the photographer's frame.

top right

PHOTOGRAPHER UNKNOWN

Karl Marx School, Villejuif, France, 1933

Gelatine silver print

Architect: André Lurçat

The First World War highlighted the importance of aerial photography and was immediately followed by a plethora of articles discussing its significance for architecture and town planning; by the creation of specialist firms such as British Aerofilms Ltd (1919) and the American Fairchild Aerial Camera Corporation (1920); and by the adoption of the aerial view as a central tenet of the 'new vision'. If architectural photography had been concerned to ape elevation and perspective drawings, it could now replicate the plan. This photograph of Villejuif emphasizes the school's radical layout and its relationship to the local community.

bottom right

ERIC MENDELSOHN (1887–1953)

Equitable Trust Building, New York

Photogravure from *Amerika: Bilderbuch eines Architekten*, Berlin (Moisse) 1926

Architect: Ernest R. Graham

Mendelsohn's book popularized distorted perspectival views. Lissitzky wrote: "Leafing through the pages for the first time grips us like a dramatic film. Completely strange pictures unwind before your eyes. You have to hold the book over your head and twist it around to understand some of the photographs. The architect shows us America, not from the distance, but from the inside; he leads us through the canyons of its streets."[25] The second edition of 1928 contained additional photographs supplied by the Danish architect Knud Lönberg-Holm; Mendelsohn's head architect, Erich Karweik; and the film director of *Metropolis* (1926), Fritz Lang.

opposite

LÁSZLÓ MOHOLY-NAGY (1895–1946)

Bauhaus Balconies, Dessau, 1926

Gelatine silver print

Architect: Walter Gropius

While at the Bauhaus, Moholy-Nagy made a number of photographs of its buildings, which, unlike the documentary views his wife, Lucia, took for Gropius, explored notions of space and form through oblique viewpoints. This worm's-eye view, reproduced in *Malerei Fotografie Film* (1927) under the title 'The optical truth of the perspectival construction', has a strong diagonal thrust reminiscent of the counter-compositions of the Bauhaus artist Theo van Doesburg. As the balcony became a visual leitmotif of Modernist architecture, Moholy's image spawned a host of imitators, among them Dell & Wainwright in their view of Highpoint II, London (1938).

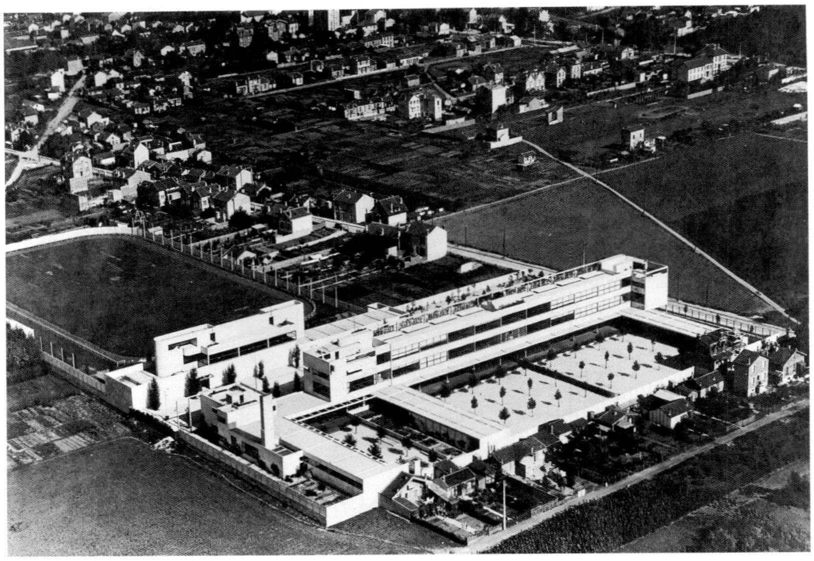

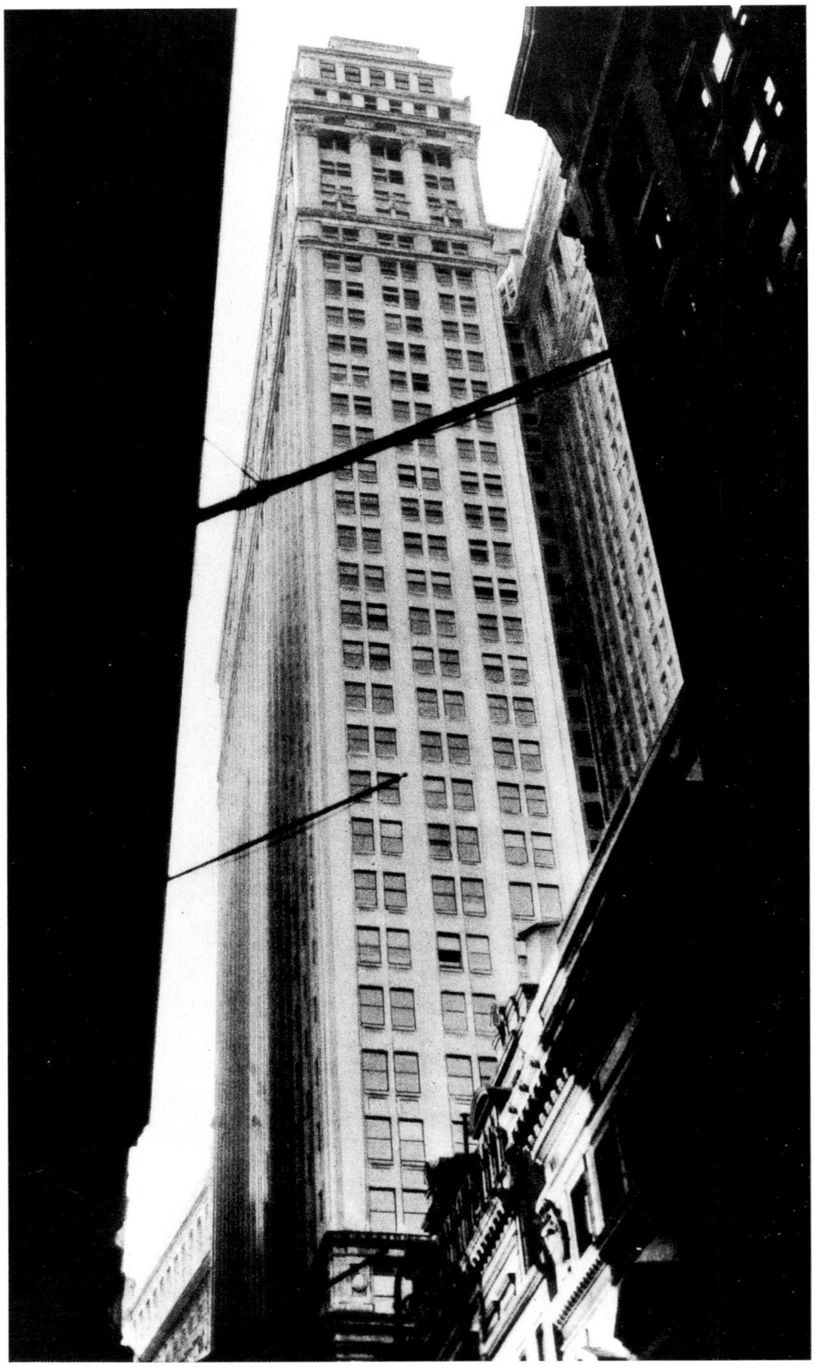

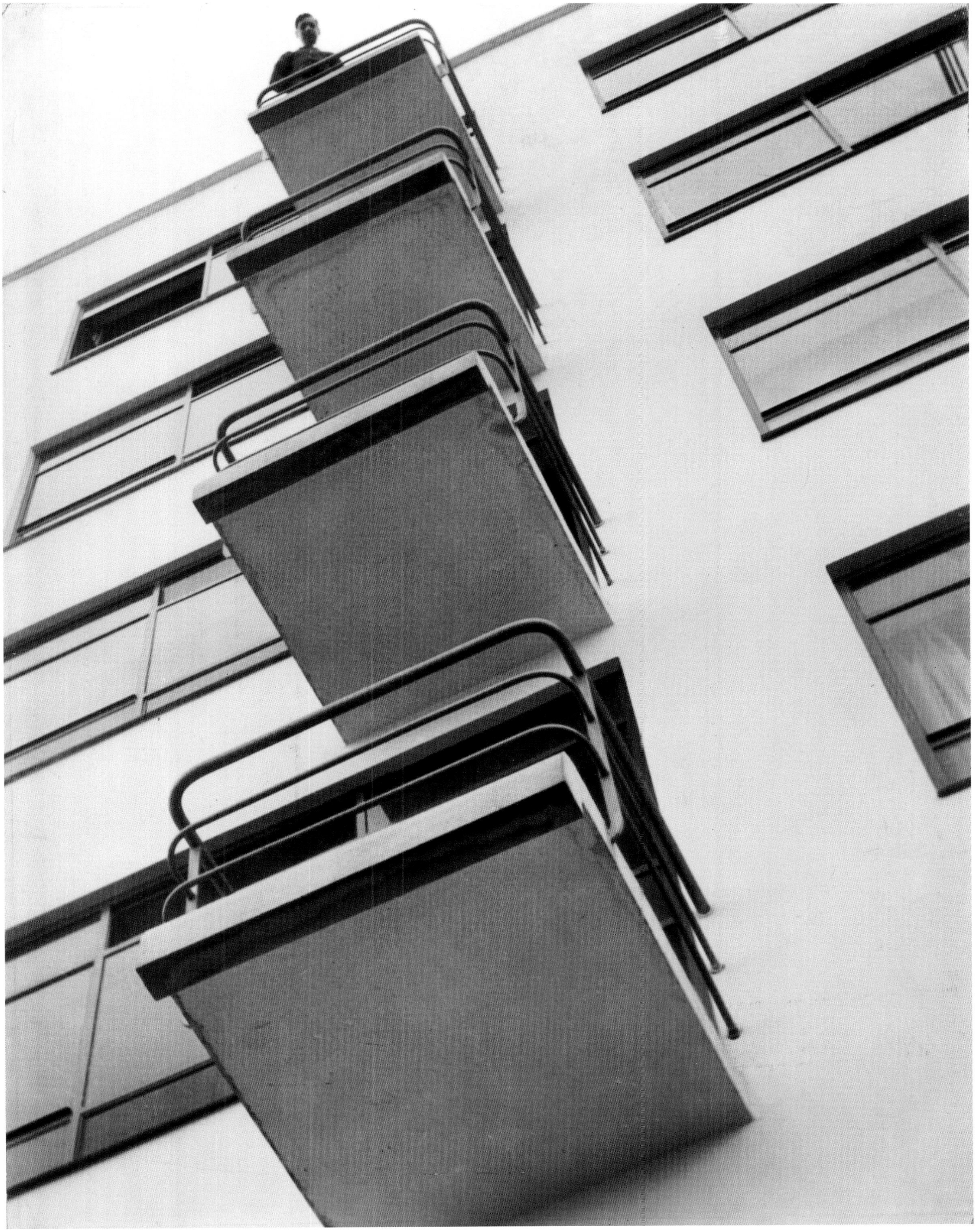

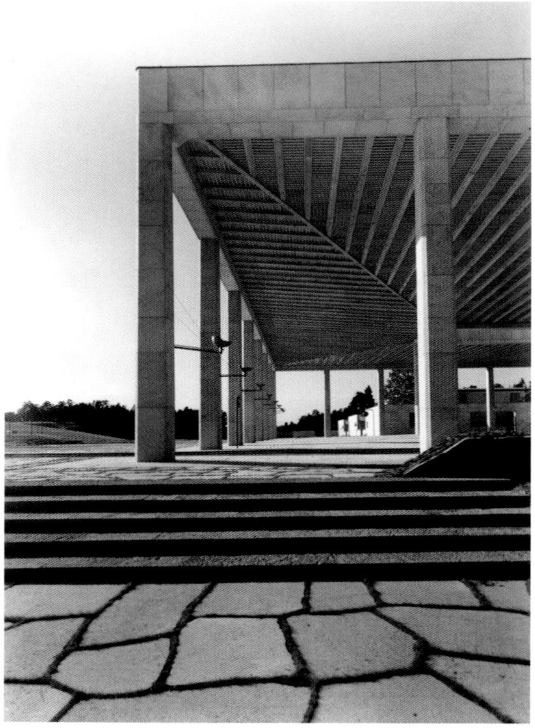

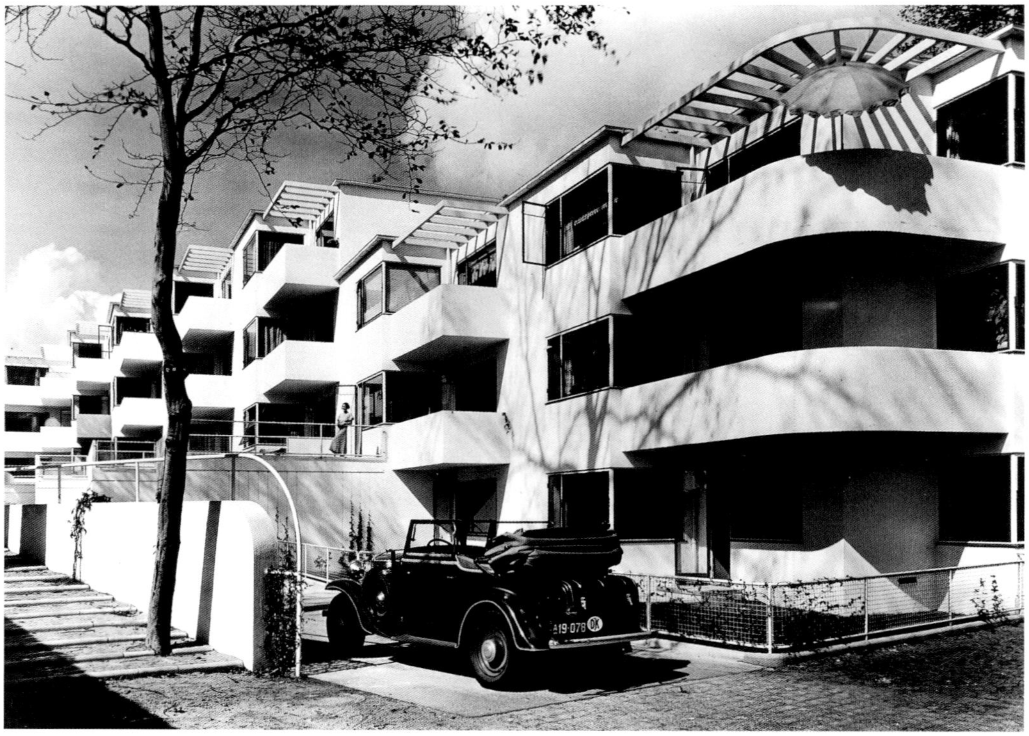

above left

CARL GUSTAV ROSENBERG (1883–1957)

Great Loggia, Woodland Crematorium, Stockholm, *c.* 1939

Gelatine silver print

Architects: Erik Gunnar Asplund and Sigurd Lewerentz

In Sweden, Pictorialism remained the dominant force in photography until the gradual dawning of a Modernist outlook in the 1930s, which was heavily influenced by developments in Germany. Key figures in this transition were the architect and amateur photographer Ture Sellman and Carl Gustav Rosenberg, the son of the painter Edward Rosenberg, who established himself as Sweden's foremost Modernist architectural photographer. As is evident in Rosenberg's imagery, Swedish Modernist photography paralleled its architectural counterpart by imbuing Modernism with a strongly humanistic aspect and placing heavier emphasis on the importance of the building's relationship to its site.

above right

PHOTOGRAPHER UNKNOWN

Bellavista Housing, Strandvej, Klampenborg, Denmark, *c.* 1935

Gelatine silver print

Architect: Arne Jacobsen

By the time this photograph was taken, the analogy between the utility and beauty of automobiles and modern architecture had become commonplace. Although not the first to suggest it, Le Corbusier had strongly promoted the relationship, both in *Vers une architecture* and in photographs of his own work, which regularly featured automobiles. The car was used to sell modern architecture and vice versa. Mercedes-Benz, for example, featured Mies van der Rohe's Weissenhof apartments, Stuttgart, in advertising photographs. Here the strategically parked car with its top down and the open parasol together suggest the progressive sunlit world of Modernism.

opposite

HANS SPIES (1905–1973)

Royal Yacht Piet Hein, 1937

Gelatine silver print

Architect: Sybold van Ravesteyn

Spies moved to The Netherlands from Germany, the country of his birth, in 1931. His work was more broadly based than that of his partner from 1932 to 1934, d'Oliveira, embracing studio photography and other commercial work as well as architecture. He did, however, count among his clients numerous architects, including, in addition to Van Ravesteyn, Jan Wils and Hein Salomonson. His interiors are especially striking.

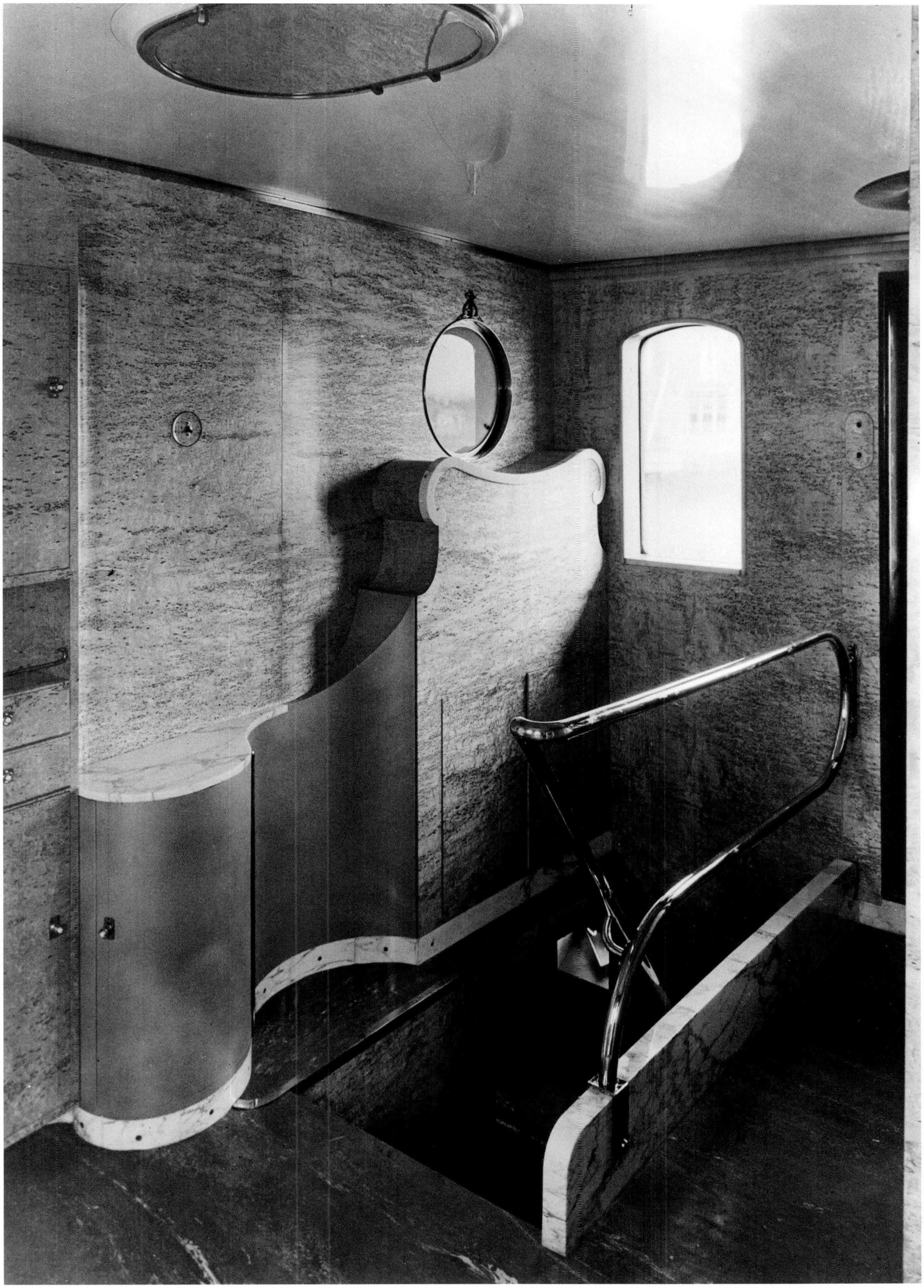

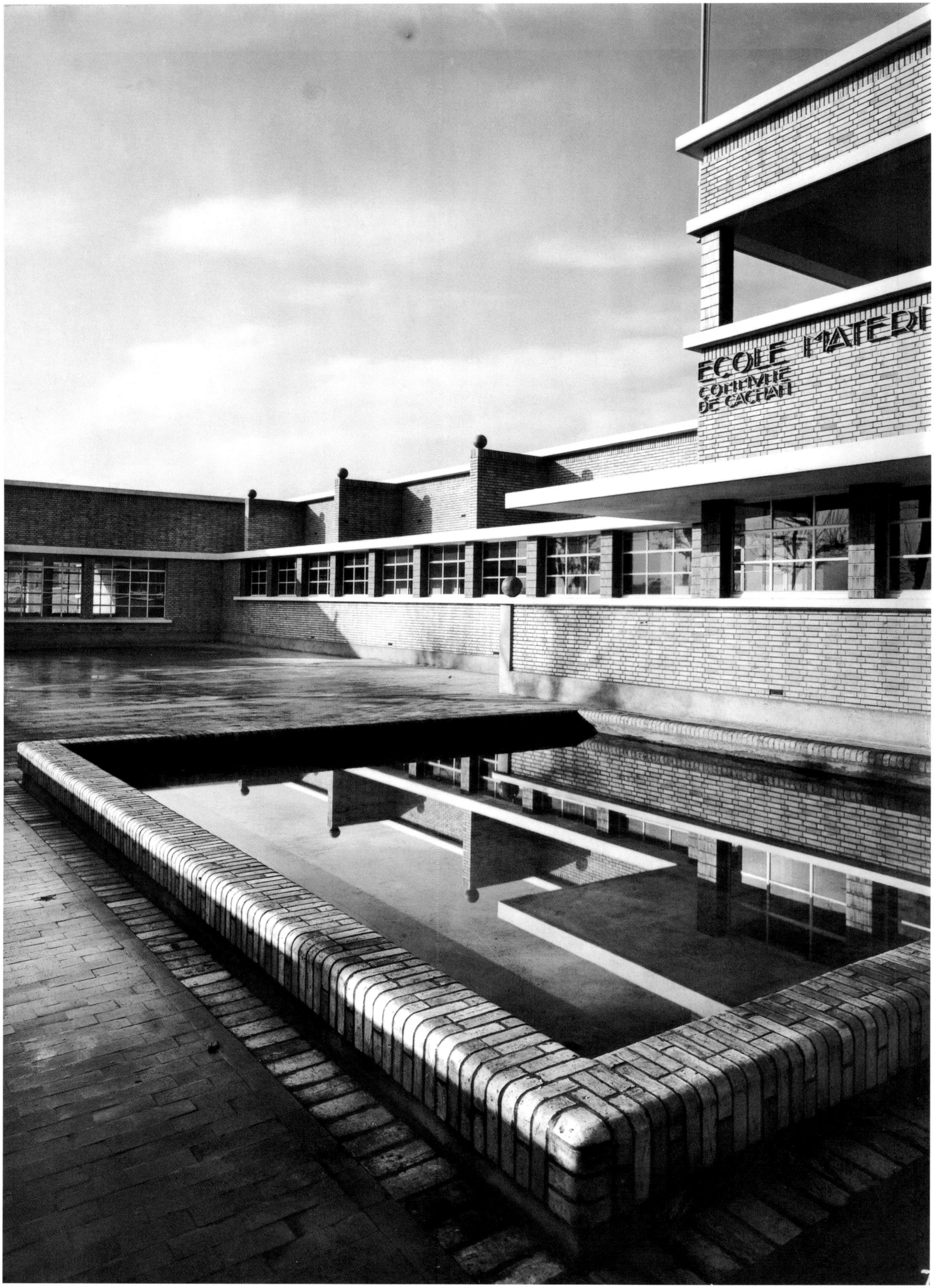
ECOLE MATER
COMMVNE
DE CACHAN

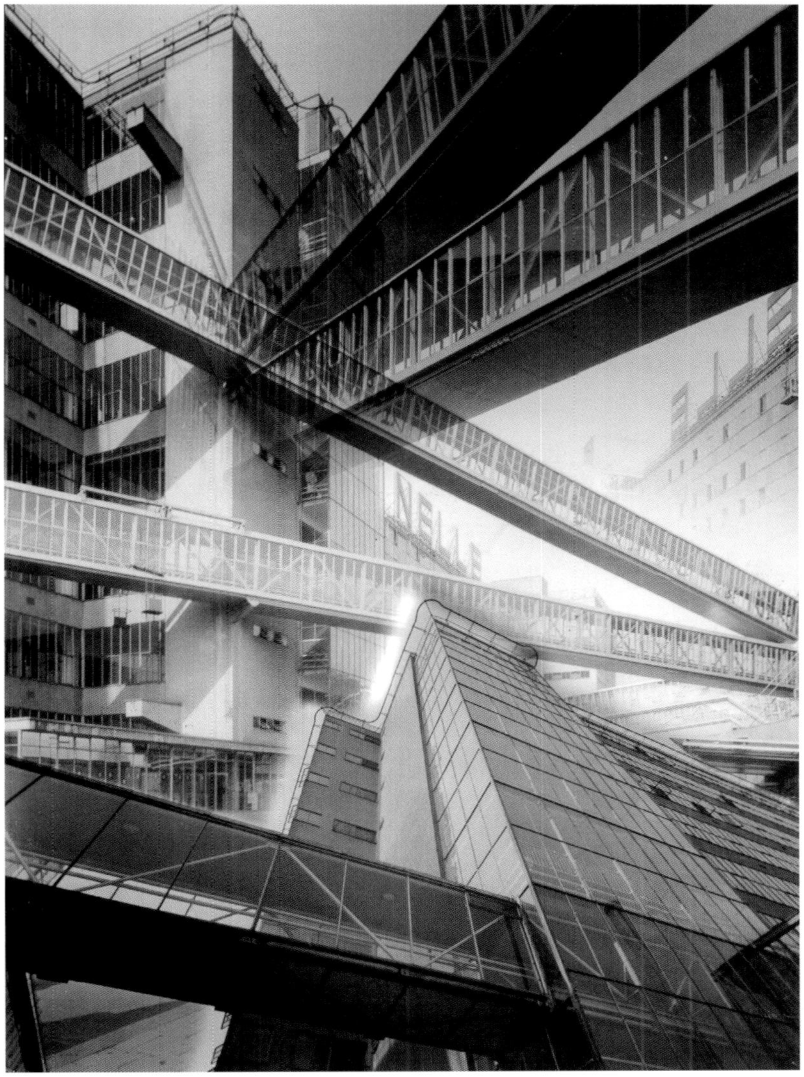

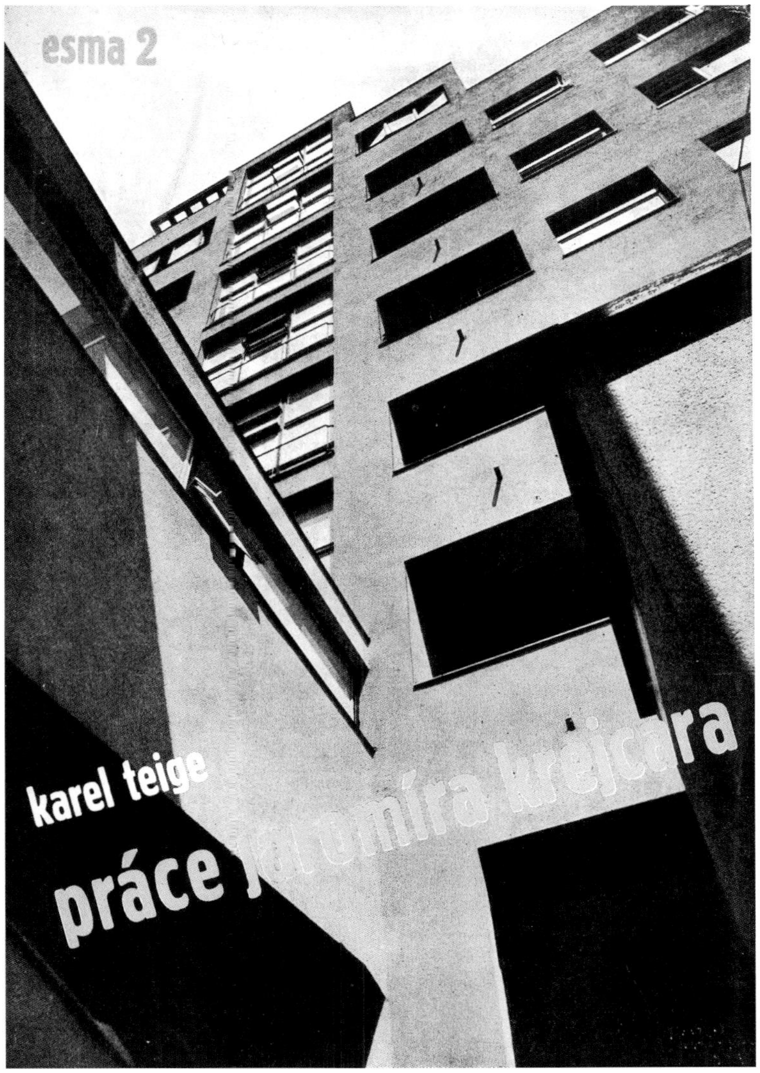

opposite

ALBIN SALAÜN

Ecole maternelle, Cachan, Brittany, 1930s

Gelatine silver print

Architects: Chollet & Mathon

With the advent of Modernism and its greater use of shiny materials such as steel and glass, reflections assumed a greater significance in architectural photography, allowing photographers to emphasize the Modernist repetition of standard elements and to enliven otherwise dull scenes. Water features were a particular boon, being employed here in a way similar to photographers' use of the pool at Hilversum Town Hall in The Netherlands by W.M. Dudok (1931). Another favoured technique, borrowed from architectural drawing and draughtsmen such as Cyril Farey, was the 'wet look', in which the floor or other surfaces were watered to provide the necessary reflective qualities.

above left

JAN KAMMAN (1898–1983)

Van Nelle Factory, Rotterdam, 1931

Gelatine silver print

Architects: Brinkman & Van der Vlugt

Based in Schiedam, Kamman was one of The Netherlands' main exponents of Modernist photography. From 1926 to 1928 he collaborated with Paul Schuitema, a pioneer of New Typography, and then with many leading avant-garde architects. Although characteristic of the New Photography, multiple exposures were not greatly used in architectural imagery. Here they have been employed to heighten the illusion of modern architecture's non-materiality and the factory's weightlessness through concentration on its transparent linking bridges and continuous fenestration. Kamman's treatment of this Modernist landmark thus differed markedly from that of such photographers as Van Ojen, who photographed it in a more straightforward documentary vein.

above right

Book cover of Karel Teige's *Práce Jaromíra Krejcara* (Prague: Nakladatel Václav Petr, 1933) illustrating the Jednota Building, Prague, 1927 (detail)

Architect: Jaromír Krejcar

As elsewhere, the introduction of the New Photography into Czechoslovakia was closely allied to the expansion of advertising and to innovations in typography. Although not a photographer but a theorist, graphic designer and editor, Teige was a key figure in this process. A leading member of the Devětsil movement, he became a talented exponent of typophoto – the combination of typography and photography propounded by Moholy-Nagy – as shown in his many publications. These became increasingly architectural in character from the late 1920s, with such works as *The Minimum Dwelling* (1932) and this monograph on one of Czechoslovakia's most prominent Functionalist architects.

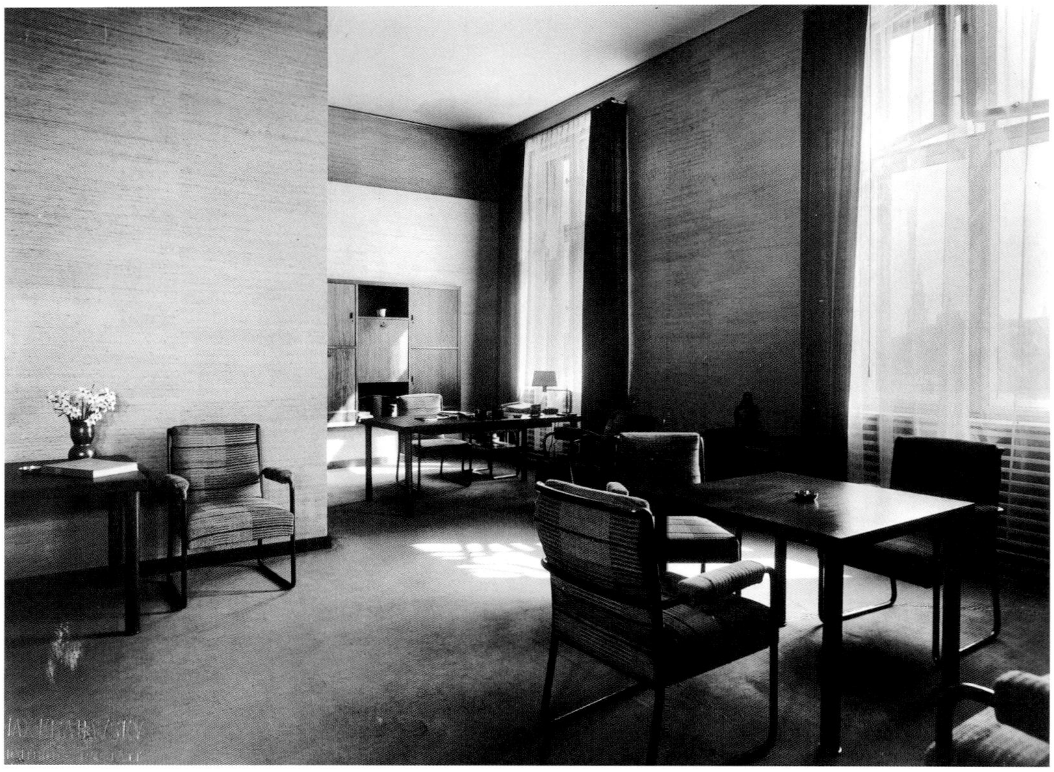

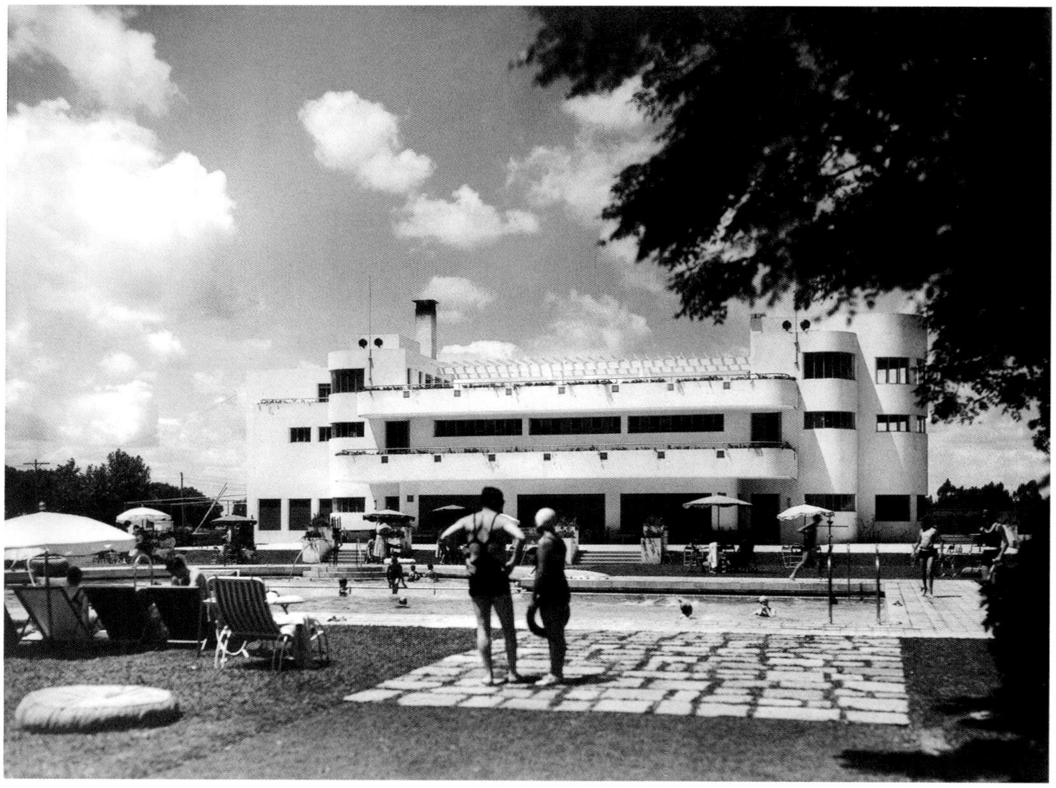

top left

MAX KRAJEWSKY (1892–1972)

Ginsberg Director's Office, Berlin, 1930

Gelatine silver print

Architect: Ernst Freud

Alongside Hugo Schmölz and Arthur Köster, Krajewsky was one of the most successful German inter-war architectural photographers. His work was heavily indebted to the art critic and founder of the Marburg archive Richard Hamann, for whom he photographed endangered artworks during the First World War. Krajewsky swam with the tide, photographing the buildings of *Neues Bauen* architects such as Mendelsohn and Bruno Taut, and later, in an unchanged photographic style, major Nazi projects, including those by Albert Speer. The destruction of his archive through bombing and by Krajewsky himself has rendered his photographs relatively scarce and consequently under-appreciated.

bottom left

FOTO GOMEZ

Jockey Club de Rosario, Rosario, Argentina, 1938

Gelatine silver print

Architects: Sanchez Lagos & De La Torre

Photography played a key role in spreading the Modern Movement. In Argentina this was accomplished through the journal *Nuestra Arquitectura*, which illustrated the work of leading European and American Modernists. As elsewhere this reliance on illustrations was seen by some critics as leading to an architecture in which image triumphed over content and surface allure was deemed more important than underlying principles. Accordingly, the Jockey Club, which, with its jaunty, nautical air, paid visual homage to the Californian architecture of Richard Neutra, was denounced for diluting Modernism into Art Deco ostentation.

opposite

EVERT MARINUS VAN OJEN (1866–1964)

Housing, Hook of Holland, c. 1927

Gelatine silver print

Architect: J.J.P. Oud

Van Ojen's output was diverse, but by the end of the 1920s his lyrical romanticism had given way to a more hard-edged treatment that was instrumental in promoting the reputations of several leading Dutch Modernist architects. In particular, his widely reproduced photographs of Oud's work brought the architect international recognition, being featured in the seminal exhibition *The International Style*, held at the Museum of Modern Art in New York (1932). Its co-curator Philip Johnson wrote to Oud, "The pictures you have provided are quite excellent and represent the best material we have received so far from any European architect."[26]

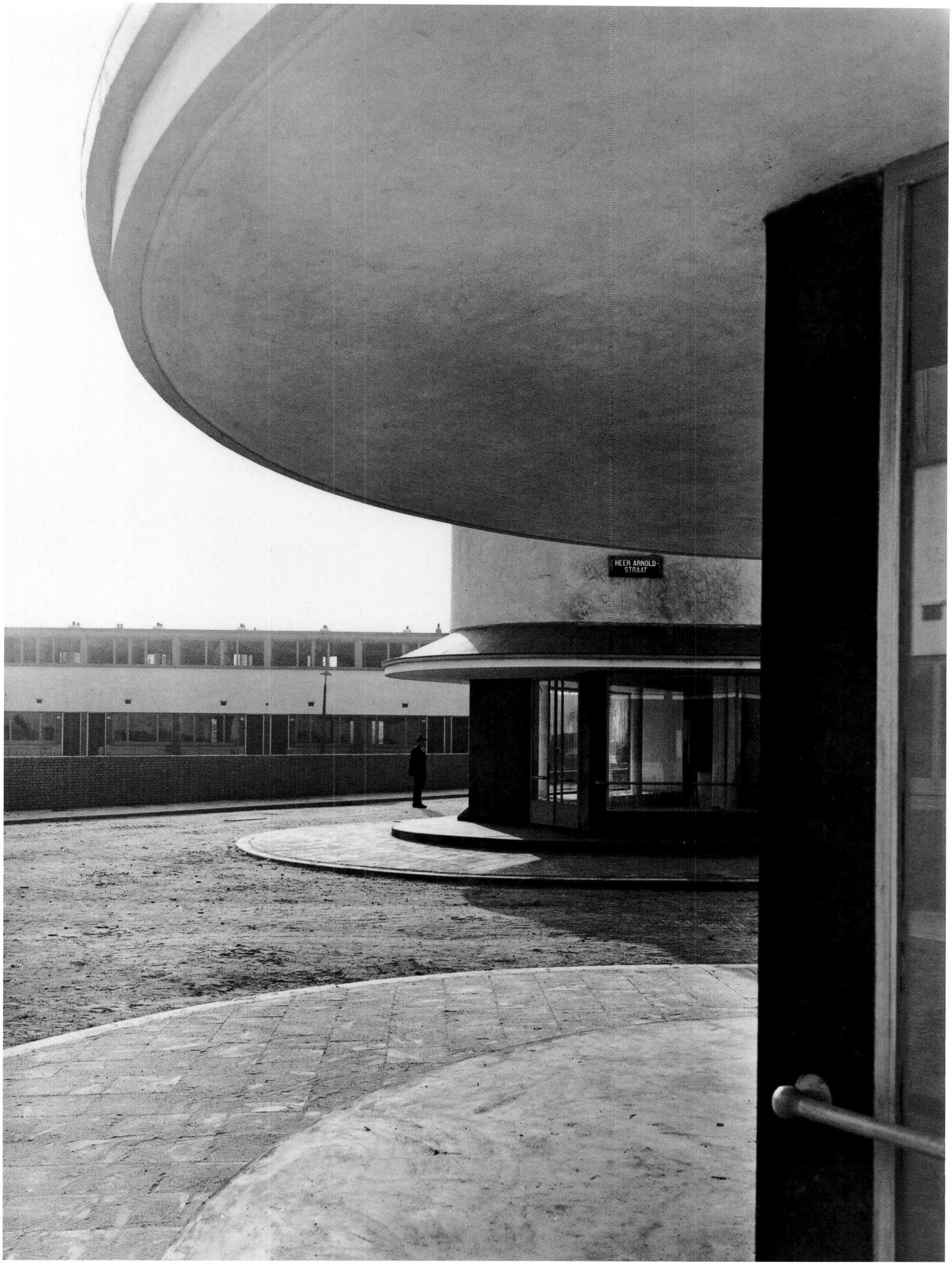
HEER ARNOLD-
STRAAT

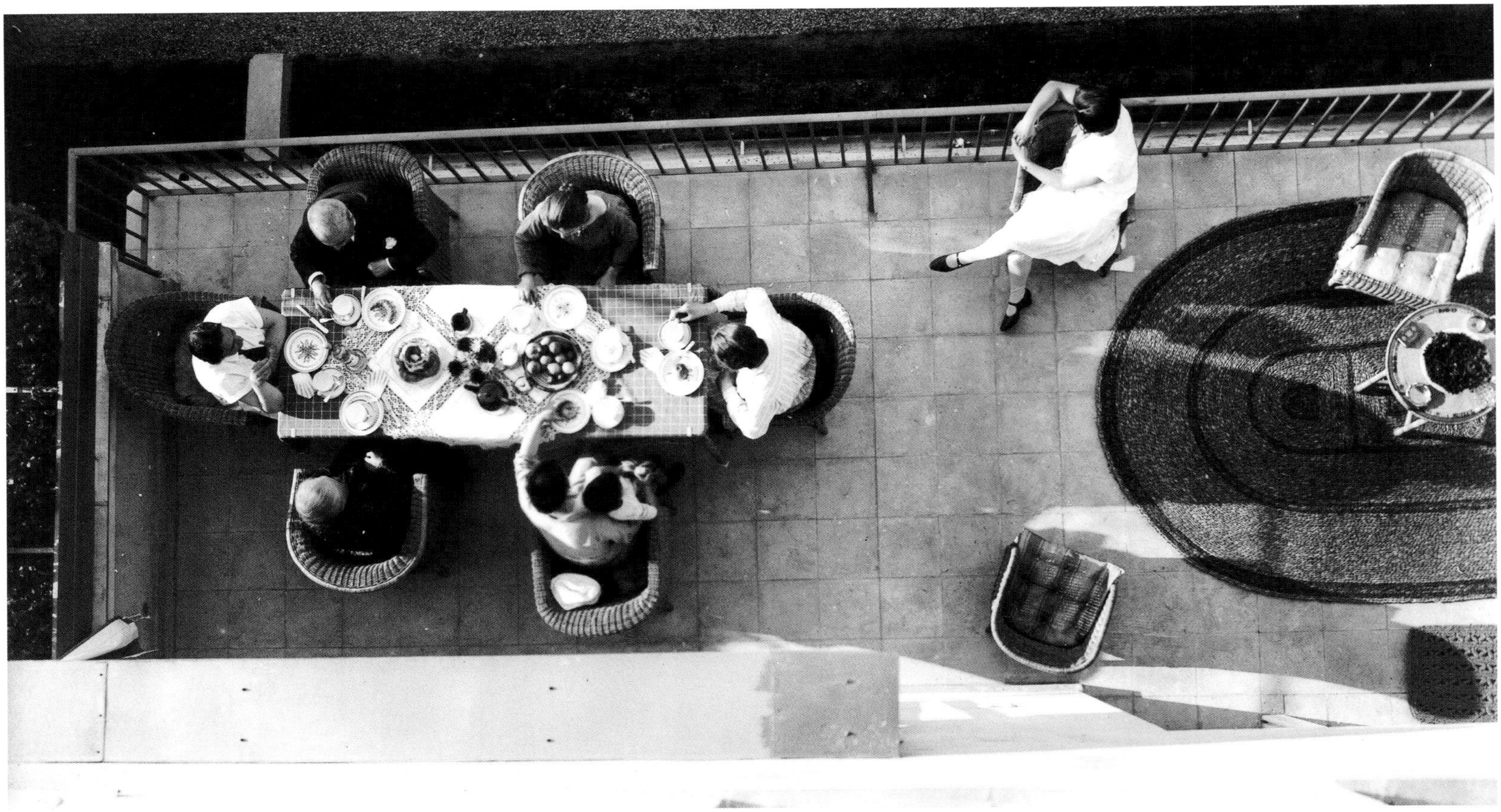

above

S. FRANK

House Overlooking the Schwielowsee, near Potsdam, 1931

Gelatine silver print

Architect: F.L. Marcus

Inhabitants rarely feature in the photography of Modernist buildings, but this image illustrates how techniques introduced by avant-garde photographers and even photojournalists could be appropriated for architectural ends. Its bird's-eye perspective recalls Moholy-Nagy's celebrated views of the hotel terrace at Belle-Ile-en-Mer (1925), hailed by Giedion as "a completely new beginning",[27] and the Bauhaus terraces at Dessau (1926–28). The inclusion of the naturalistically depicted diners brings to mind Paul Wolff's Leica studies of Ernst May's Frankfurt housing estates and their occupants.

opposite left

HUGO SCHMÖLZ (1879–1938)

Doctor's House, Remscheid, Germany, 1929

Gelatine silver print

Architect: Ludwig Lemmer

This photograph by the distinguished Cologne architectural photographer Hugo Schmölz, who worked for many of the period's leading architects, such as Dominikus Böhm and Adolf Abel, is a rudimentary example of what Julius Shulman later termed 'dressing the scene'. Although not unknown before, such staging acquired new importance during the inter-war years, encouraged by photographs of Le Corbusier's houses in which the architect's hat and spectacles were placed strategically in view. Later the stratagem was to reach new heights with Shulman and Stoller, for example, employing a wide range of props, even including portable landscaping.

opposite right

WALTER HEGE (1893–1955)

Caryatid Detail, the Erechtheion, Athens, *c.* 1929

Gelatine silver print

Hege was one of Germany's most fêted photographers. From 1925 until his death, he illustrated a stream of publications for Deutscher Kunstverlag of Berlin that concentrated overwhelmingly on historical architecture, such as the cathedrals of his native Naumburg (1925) and of Bamberg (1927) as well as German Baroque. This photograph appeared in *Die Akropolis* (1930), in which Hege interpreted the Greek monuments in a pristine, heroic fashion that accorded with the Nazi leadership's burgeoning taste for the Antique (Hitler declared the Parthenon, which he had never visited, his favourite building). Hege later photographed Nazi Neo-classical architecture in a similar laudatory manner.

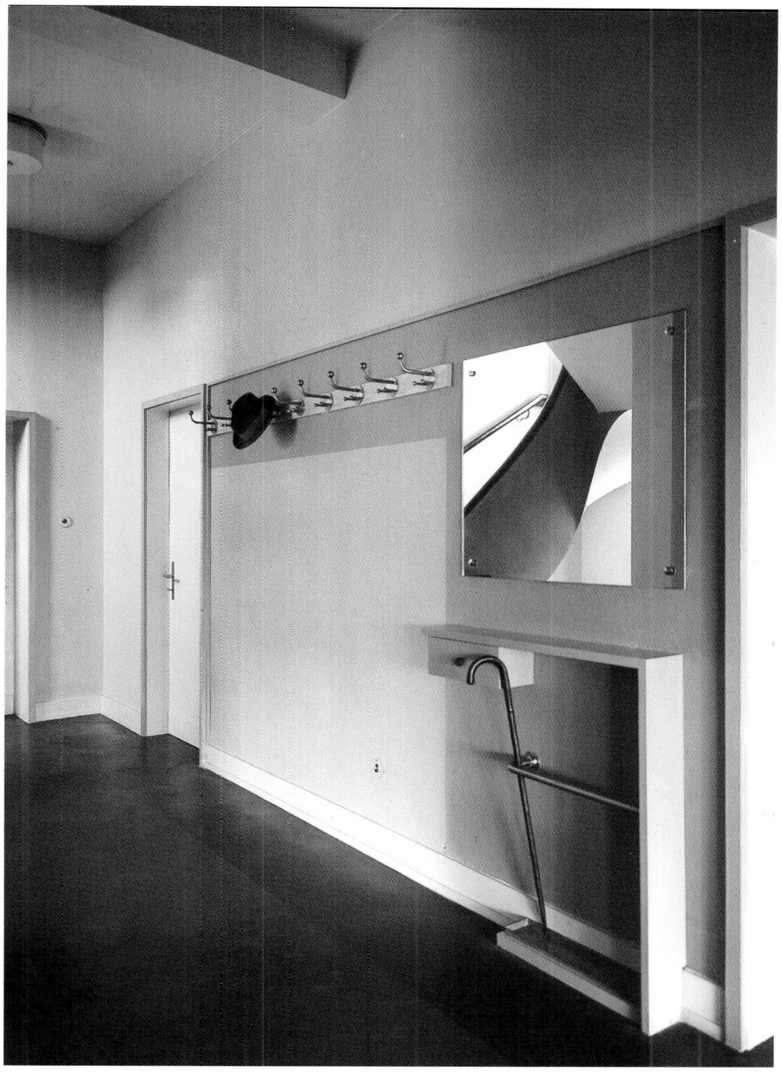

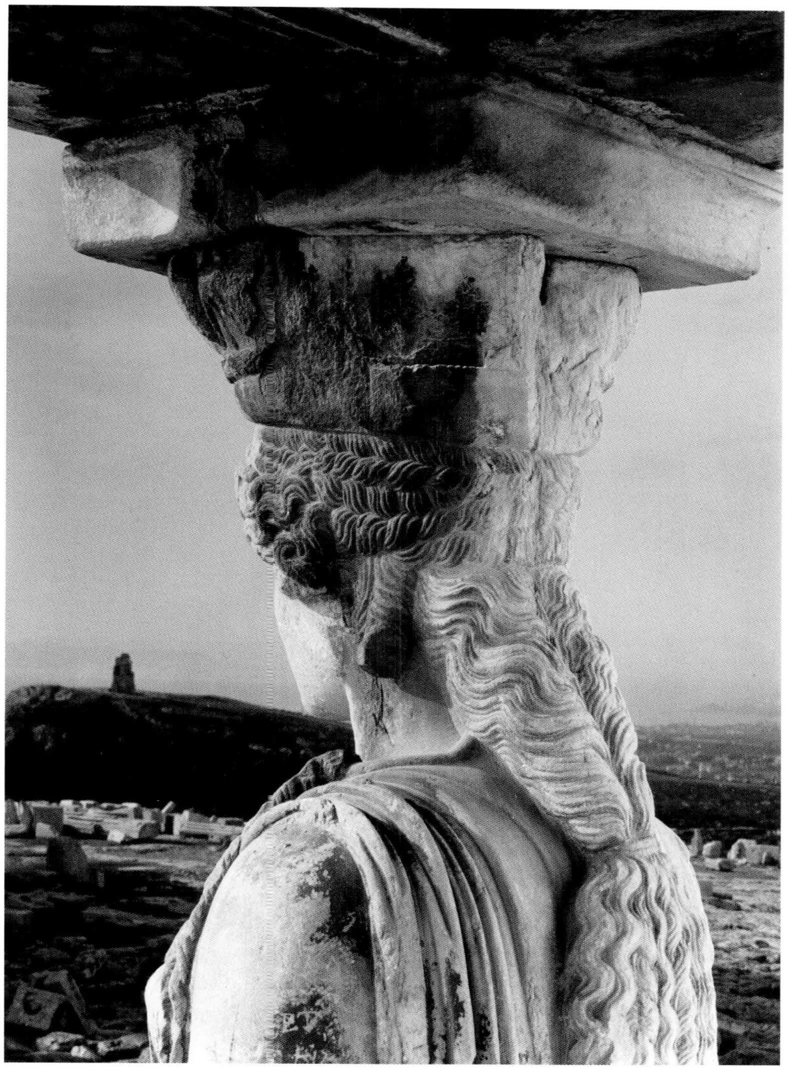

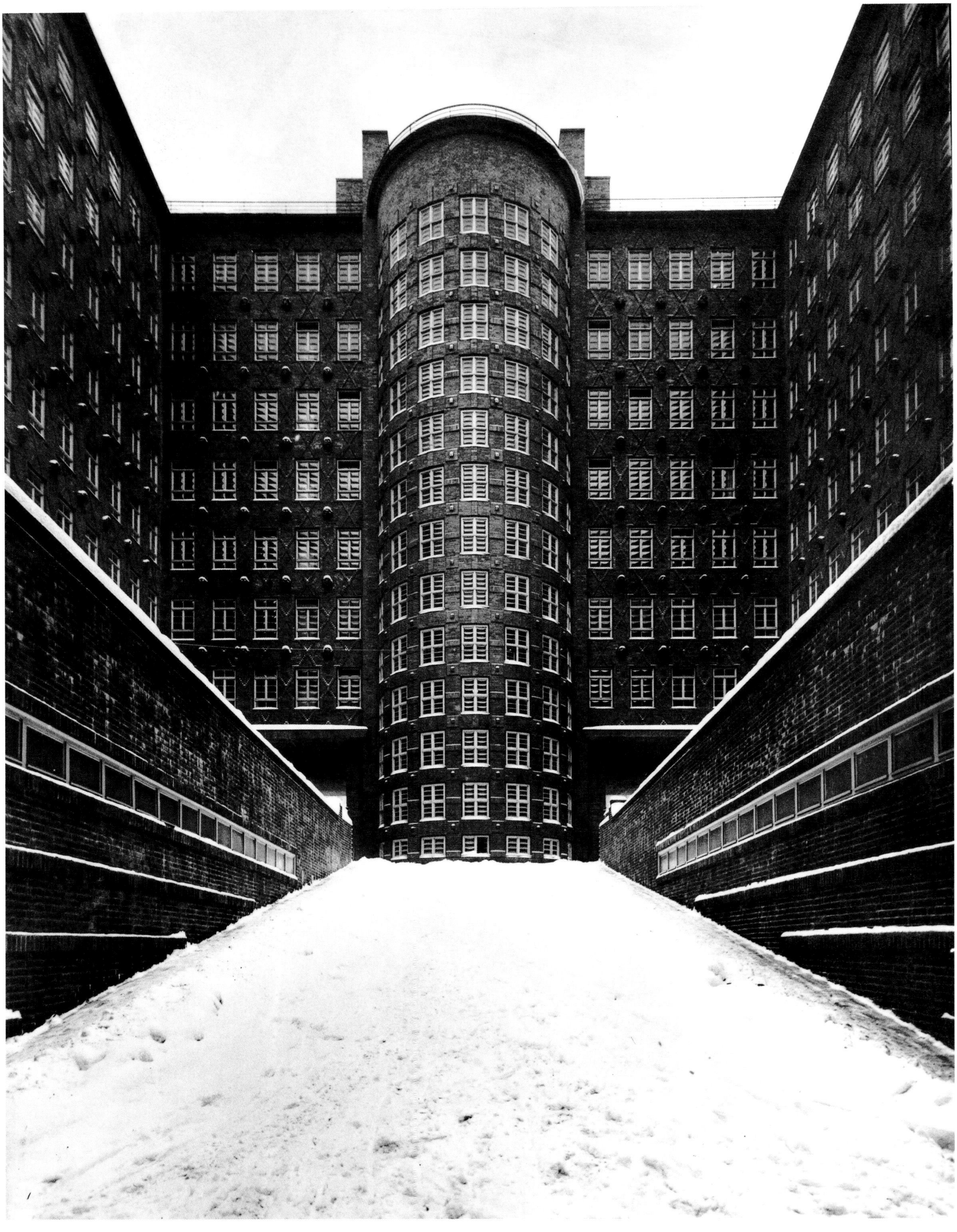

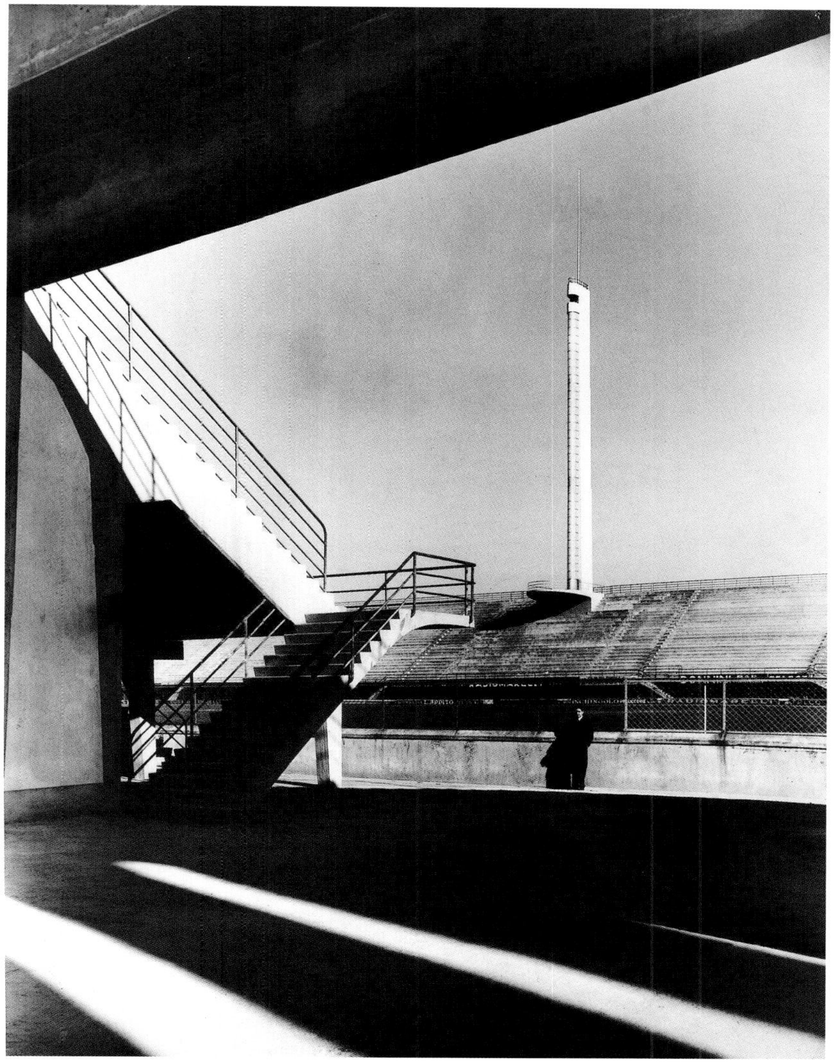

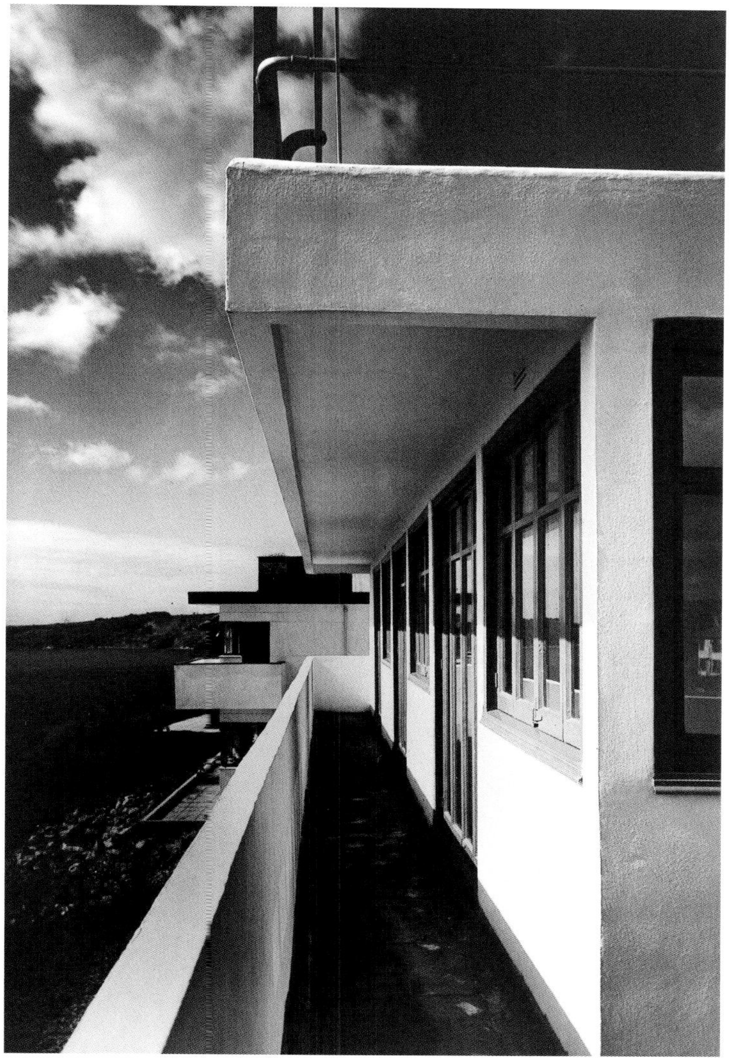

opposite

FRANCIS ROWLAND YERBURY (1885–1970)

Sprinkenhof, Hamburg, 1929

Gelatine silver print

Architects: Fritz Höger with Hans & Oskar Gerson

Yerbury's photographic interests were kindled by the excursions made by the Architectural Association's Camera and Cycling Club, and his images – principally of European Modernism – became highly influential through their regular reproduction in the *Architect and Building News* between 1925 and 1933. His eclectic portfolio, which, besides contemporary work, embraced traditional architecture, looked back to those of nineteenth-century architects who collected exemplar photographs on their foreign trips and forward to that of the American travel and architectural photographer George Kidder Smith.

above left

FERDINANDO BARSOTTI

Stadio Comunale Giovanni Berta, Florence, 1932

Gelatine silver print

Architect: Pier Luigi Nervi

The Florentine Ferdinando Barsotti, who was succeeded by his son Gino, was an architectural specialist who built up an impressive client list that included such architects as Raffaello Fagnoni and Nello Baroni. His work was particularly appreciated by two architects who were themselves accomplished amateur photographers – Giovanni Michelucci, who commissioned him to photograph his buildings, and Giuseppe Pagano, editor of *Casabella* during the 1930s, who frequently featured his images in the magazine.

above right

DELL & WAINWRIGHT

(Mark Oliver Dell [1883–1959] and H.L. Wainwright)

Gull Rock, Carlyon Bay, Cornwall, 1936

Gelatine silver print

Architect: Marshall Sisson

One of Dell & Wainwright's prime attributes was their ability to cast Modernist houses in a heroic light. In reality Sisson's Gull Rock, one of a group of houses he designed at Carlyon Bay in Cornwall, was small-scale, but here its size has been exaggerated by use of the close-up and deep perspective. Featured in F.R.S. Yorke's *The Modern House in England* (1937), it was photographs such as these that caused Hugh Casson in reviewing the book to write: "Architecture has become the handmaid of photography ... . A lot of those houses were images of houses."[28]

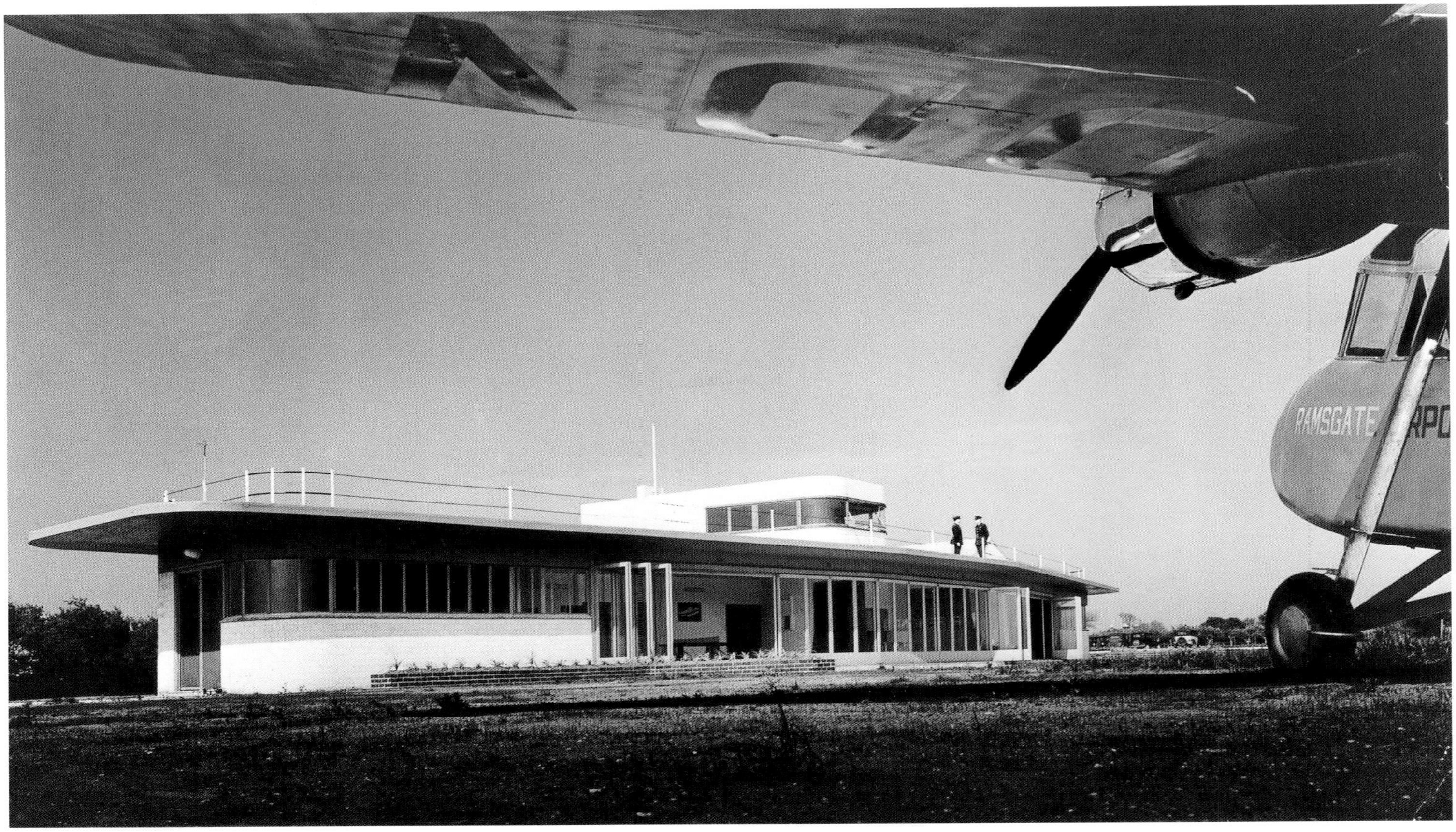
RAMSGATE

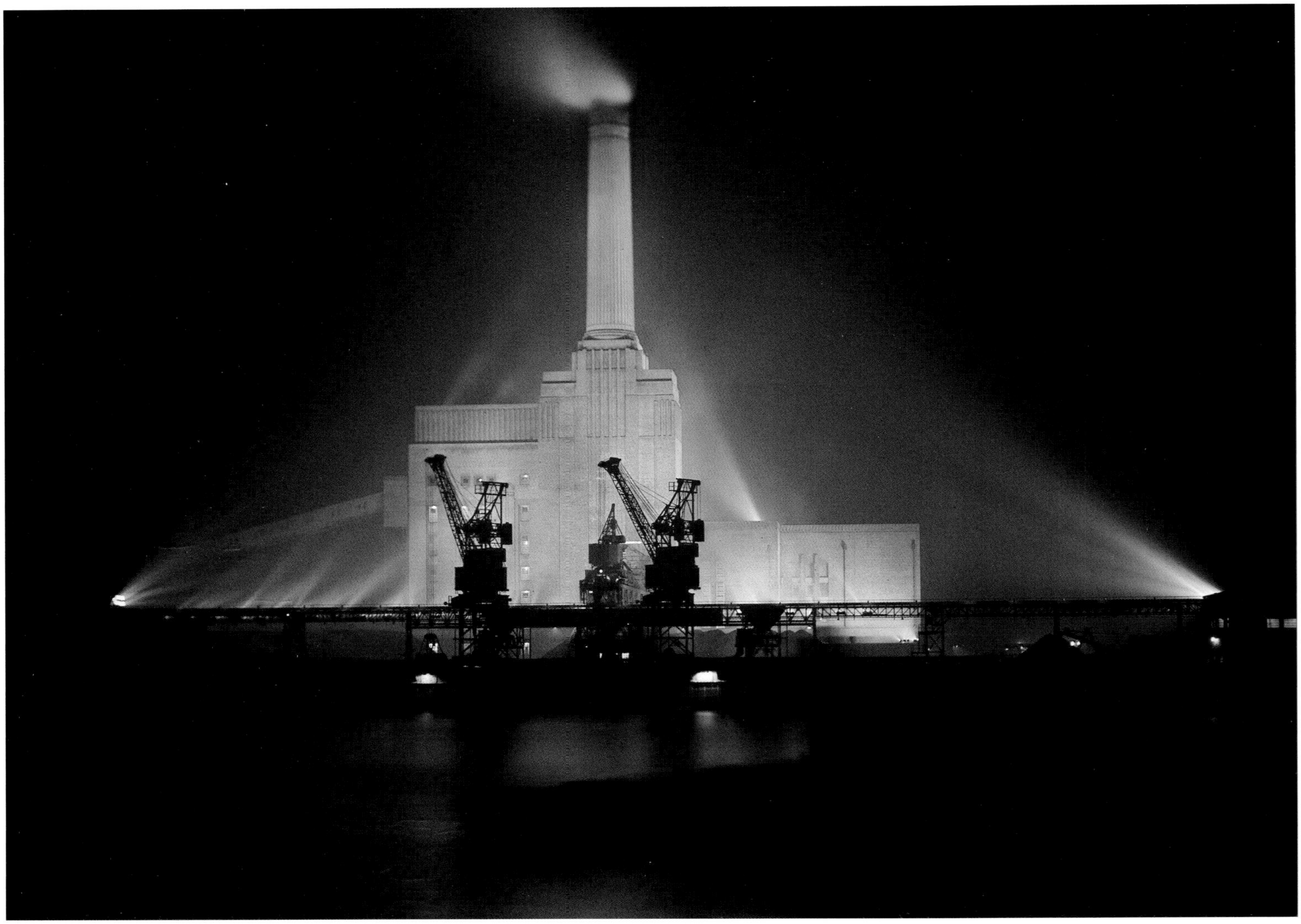

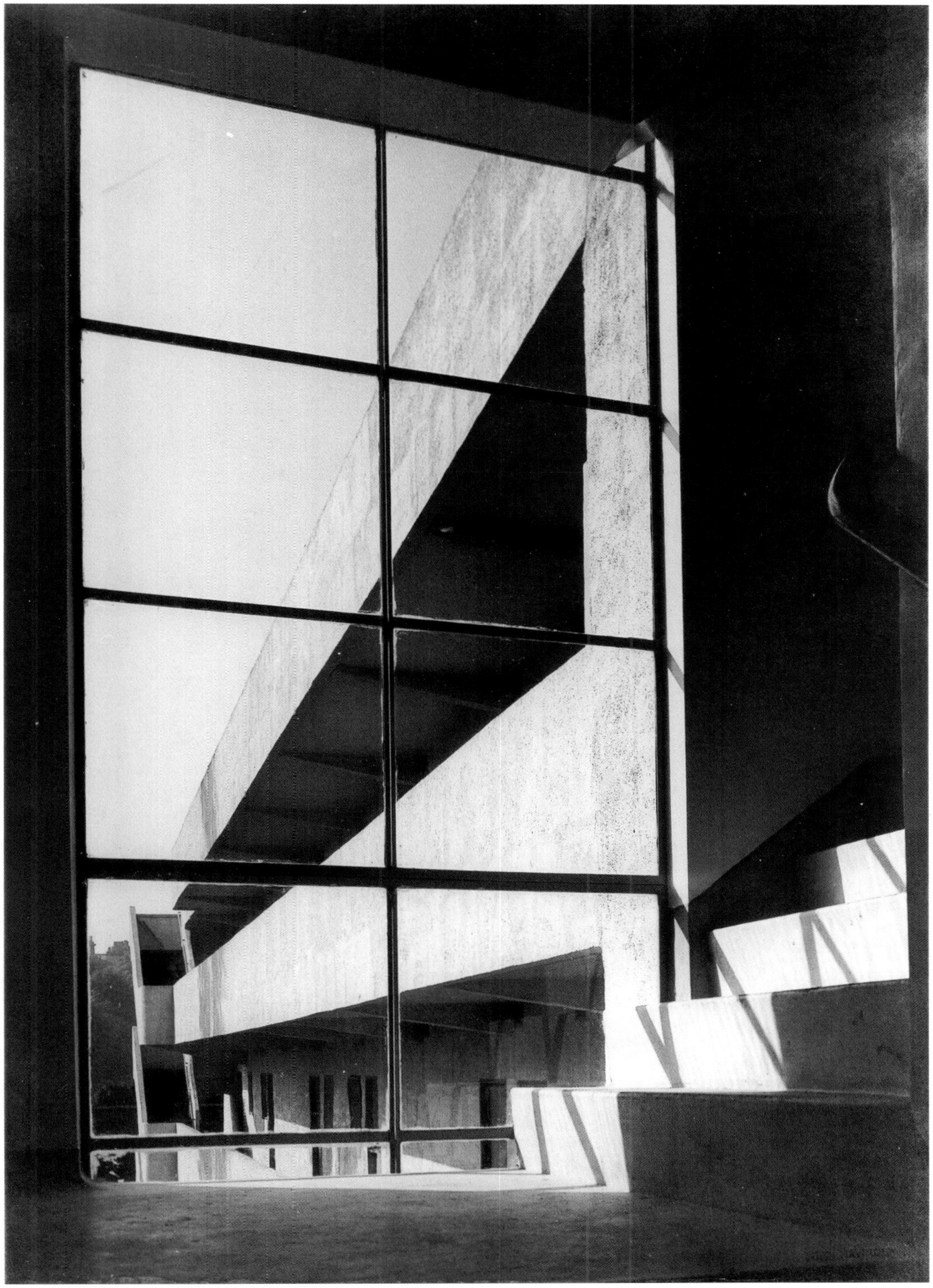

opposite top

DELL & WAINWRIGHT

(Mark Oliver Dell [1883–1959] and H.L. Wainwright)

Ramsgate Municipal Airport, Kent, 1937

Gelatine silver print

Architect: David Pleydell-Bouverie

During the inter-war years images of flight became increasingly prevalent – ranging from the helmeted airman in W.H. Auden's poetry to Le Corbusier's *Aircraft* – and were closely associated with Modernist architecture and Moholy-Nagy's 'new vision'. Here, Dell & Wainwright's photograph perfectly matches the terminal building with the fuselage of the plane in the foreground to emphasize the machine aesthetic of Modernist architecture. This juxtaposition, later to become commonplace in photographs of airport terminals, was perhaps inspired by Rosenberg's similar view of Stockholm's Bromma Airport by Paul Hedquist, made a year earlier.

opposite bottom

JOHN MALTBY (1910–1980)

Battersea Power Station, London, 1935

Gelatine silver print

Designers: Sir Giles Gilbert Scott and James Theodore Halliday

Maltby was one of the leading lights of a new generation of architectural photographers that rose to prominence in the 1930s. His career was launched by a commission in 1935 from the Odeon cinema chain to take four views of every cinema it built. He subsequently developed a close relationship with Britain's leading Modernist architect, Berthold Lubetkin. This iconic view illustrates the period's faith in progress through technology and the dawning appreciation of the drama inherent in night architecture that saw illumination become an integral element in design.

left

JOHN HAVINDEN (1908–1987)

Lawn Road Flats, London, 1934

Gelatine silver print

Architect: Wells Coates

Havinden's strikingly graphic image typifies two inter-war trends. First, it was an advertising shot, being commissioned by Crittall, the metal window manufacturers, who helped promote Modernism. Secondly, it employs the stratagem, common since photography's earliest days but more prevalent during the 1930s, of using the window as a frame within a frame to accentuate important elements – not only the window itself but also the raking access galleries. Havinden, who received many such advertising commissions – partly through his brother, Ashley, who was a director of Crawfords Advertising Agency – was one of the leading British practitioners of the New Photography.

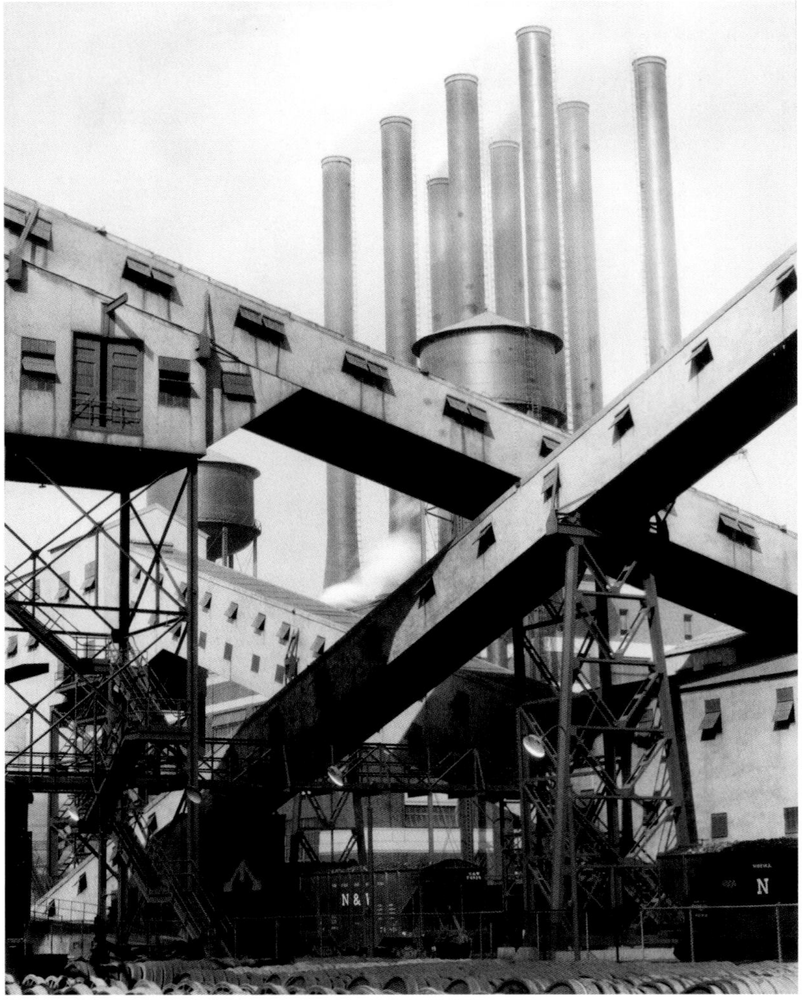

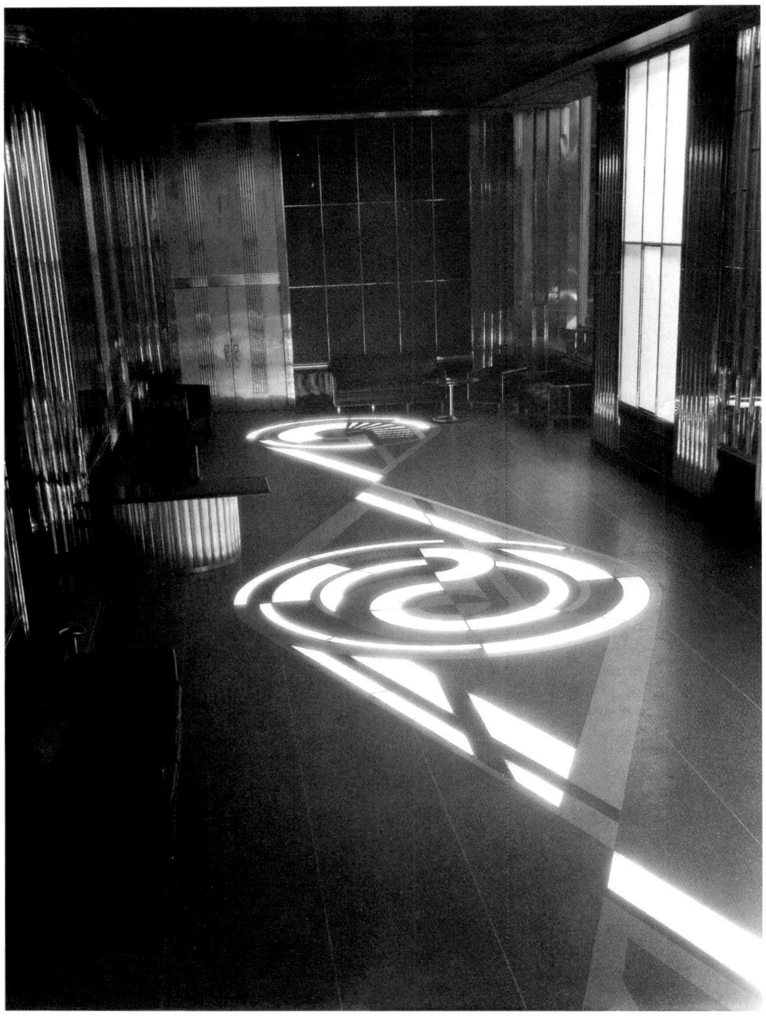

above left

CHARLES SHEELER (1883–1965)

Criss-crossed, Conveyors, Ford Plant, River Rouge, Detroit, 1927

Gelatine silver print

Architect: Albert Kahn

Sheeler took thirty-two official photographs at River Rouge for the advertising agency N.W. Ayer & Son, which was in charge of Ford's promotional campaign for the new plant. As well as spreading knowledge of Kahn's work – he was invited to open an office in Moscow in 1929 – Sheeler's photographs, especially this one, which through a taut geometric arrangement dramatically extolled the majestic sublimity of the factory, became potent symbols of America's new machine age.

above right

KEN HEDRICH (1908–1972)

A.O. Smith Building, Milwaukee, 1930

Gelatine silver print

Architects: Holabird & Root

Cleverly accentuating the indirect lighting from the glass panels in the terrazzo floor with the photographer's own, this image is an early instance of the dramatic use of lighting that characterized Hedrich Blessing's work during the 1930s. As Joseph Molitor wrote in his manual *Architectural Photography*, Ken Hedrich "challenged the documentary way of photographing a building. His photographs had new and dramatic viewpoints and much bolder techniques."[29] The firm's influence was not just stylistic but organizational, as reflected in its introduction of more businesslike methods that helped to professionalize the practice of architectural photography.

opposite

NYHOLM & LINCOLN

(Peter Nyholm and Fay Sturtevant Lincoln [1894–1975])

Chrysler Building, New York, 1930

Gelatine silver print

Architect: William van Alen

Lincoln studied chemical engineering and then, after the First World War, biology at the Massachusetts Institute of Technology. In 1929 he took up photography professionally, being especially skilled in dramatically lit interiors. Undeservedly overshadowed by the work of larger American firms, his oeuvre was among the most distinctive of the period, appearing in the architectural press and more general magazines, such as *House and Garden* and *Time*. The device of the surrogate viewer within the frame, who sees as the photographer does, has a long history. It was used particularly in early topographical photography to reinforce the camera's claim to truthful recording.

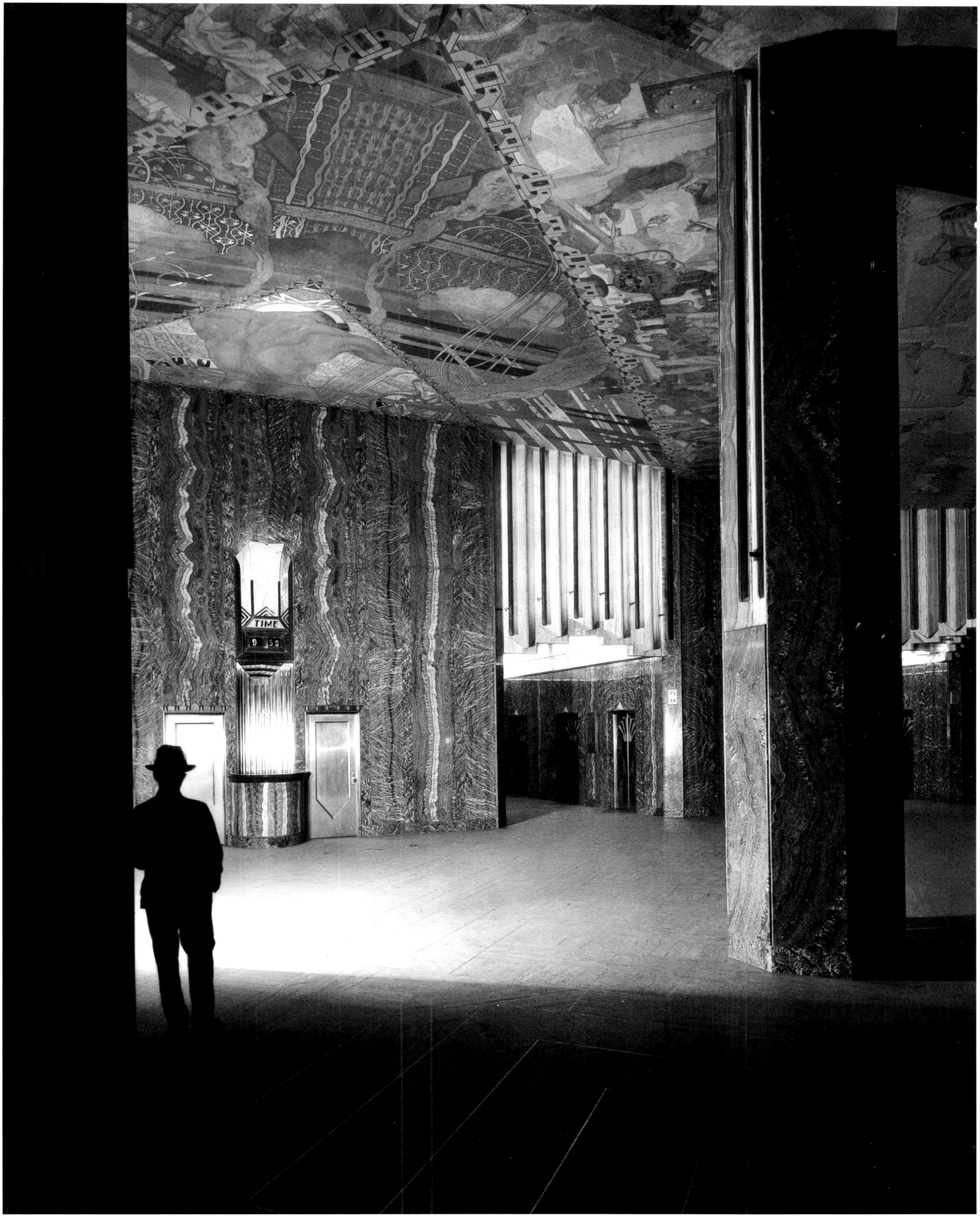
TIME

BILL HEDRICH (born 1912)

Fallingwater, Bear Run, Pennsylvania, 1937

Gelatine silver print

Architect: Frank Lloyd Wright

One of the most celebrated architectural photographs ever taken, this picture was initially dismissed by Wright as "acrobatic" but later became one of his favourite views of Edgar Kaufmann's house. Its supreme merit lies in the way it portrays the building as rising almost organically from the landscape, while the low viewpoint emphasizes both the structural daring of Wright's cantilevered balconies and their rhythmic repetition of the rock formations below. Contrast this with photographs of European Modernist houses in which, even if the architects regarded landscaping as important, photographers tended to keep house and landscape rigidly separate.

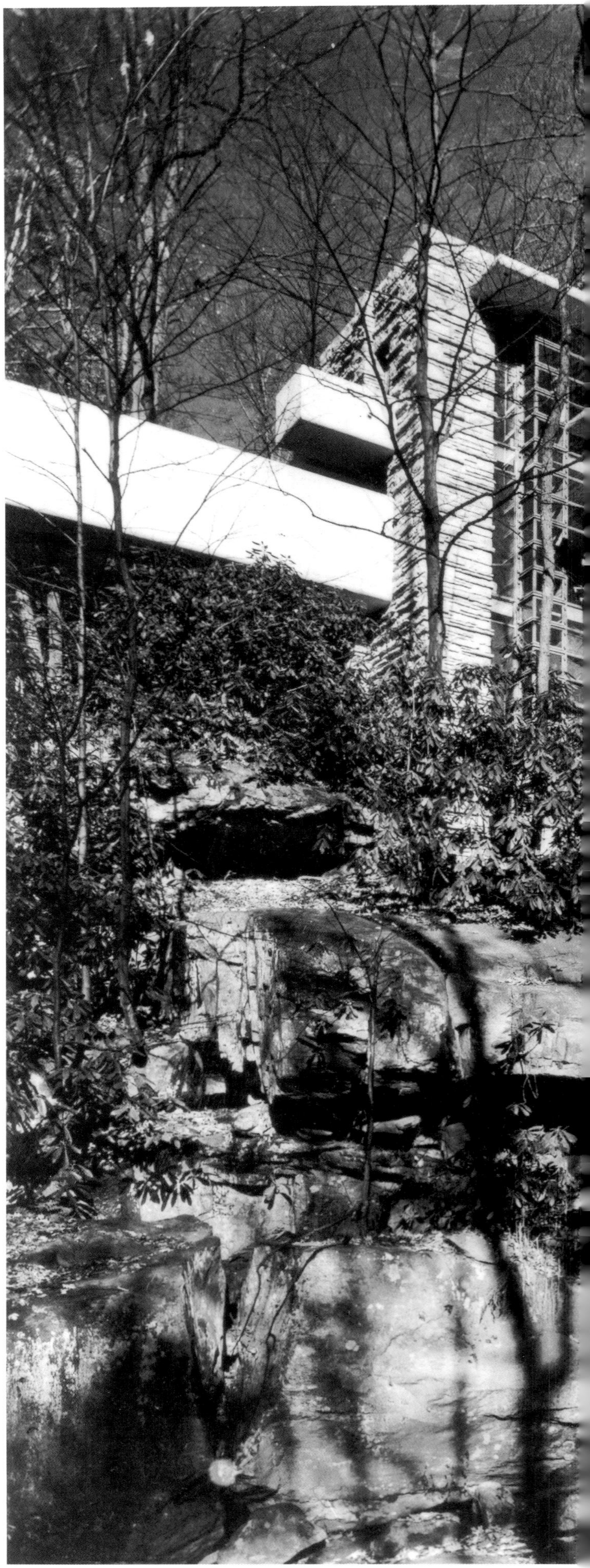

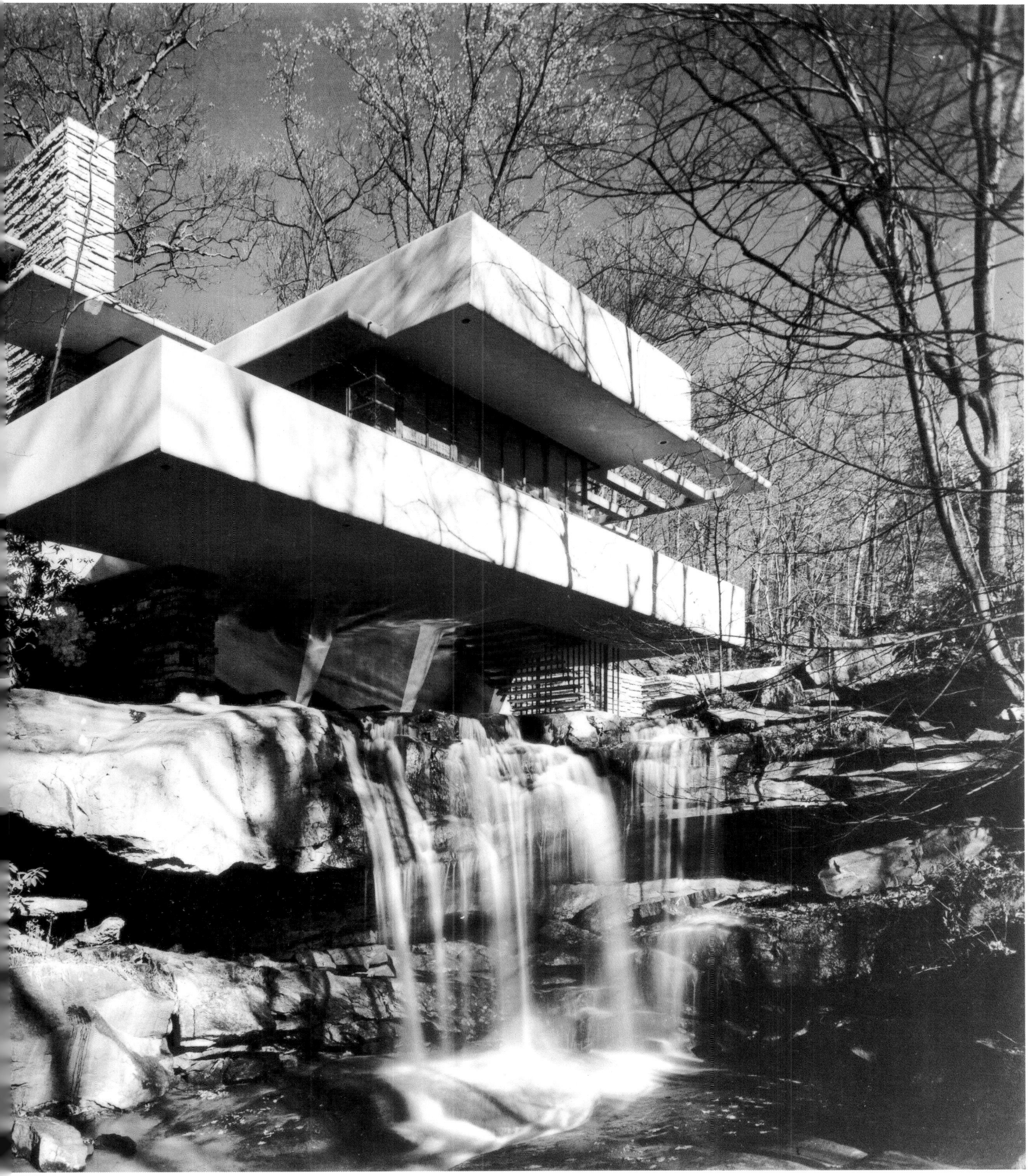

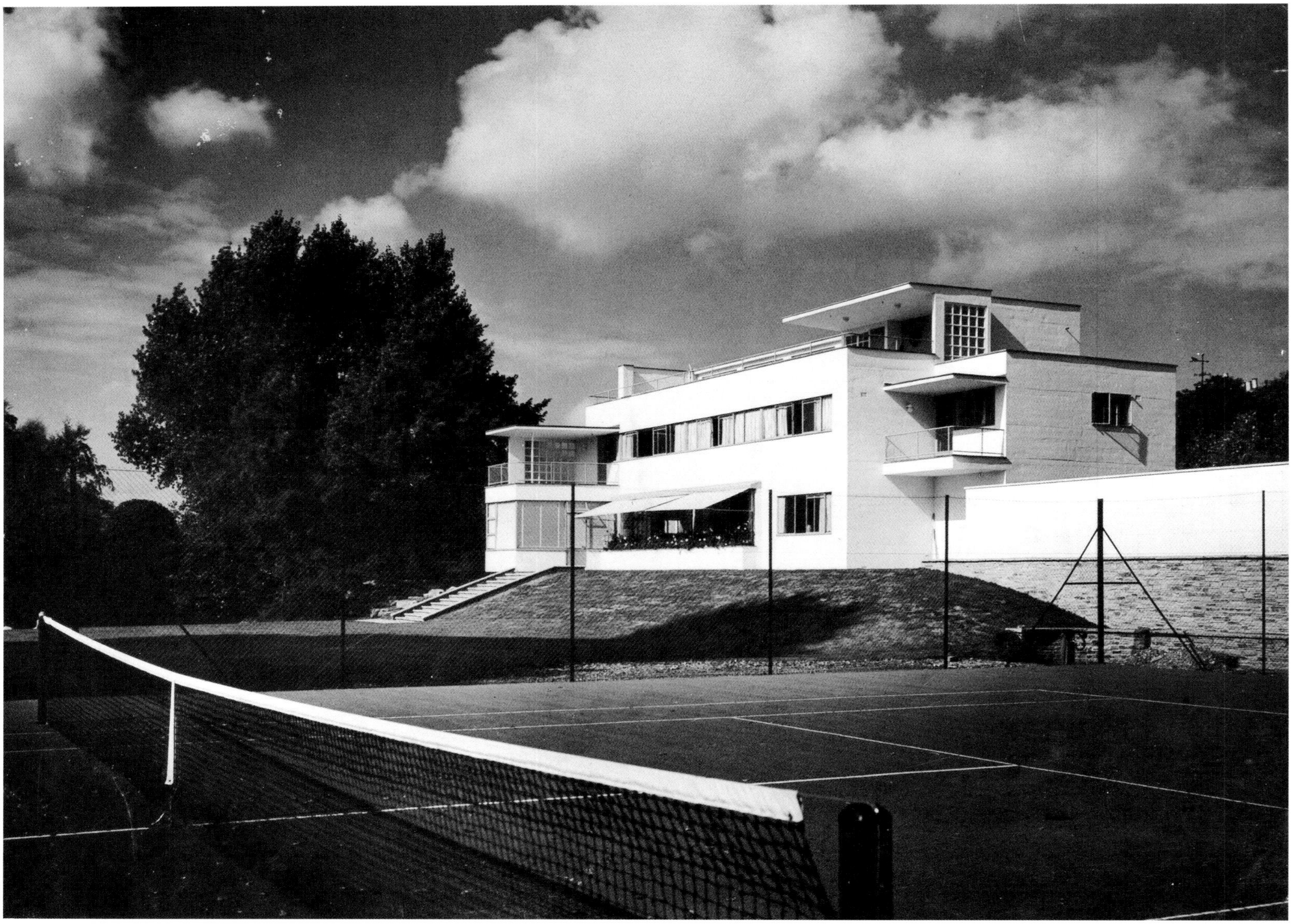

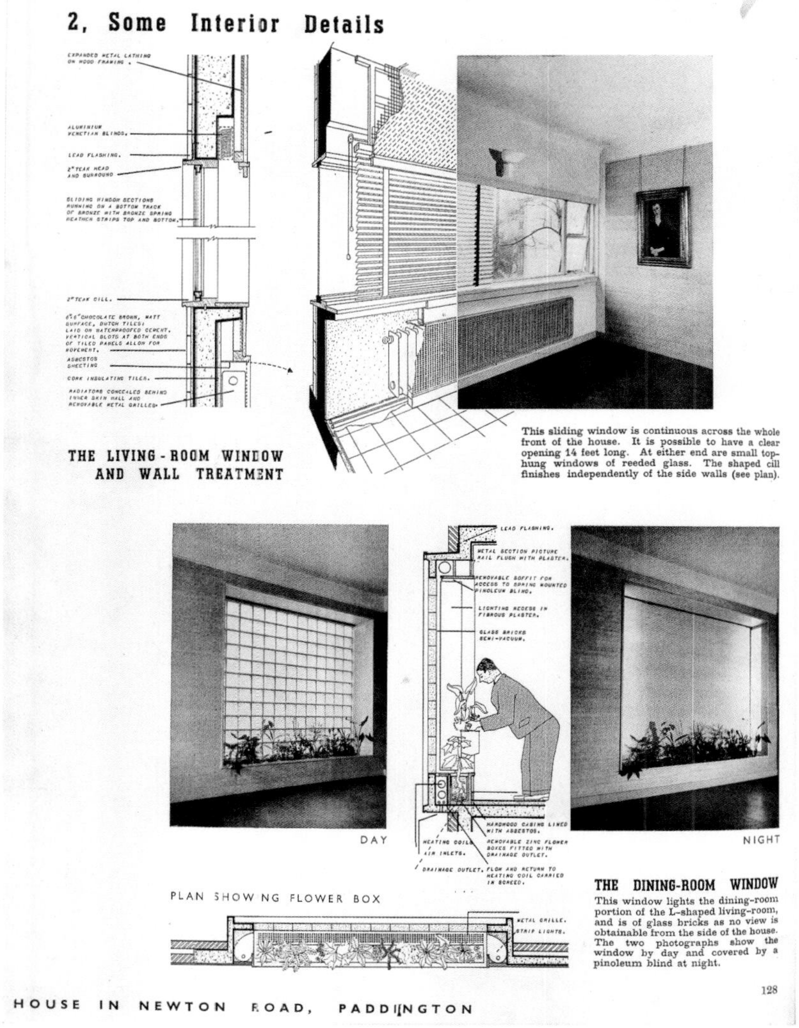
2, Some Interior Details

THE LIVING-ROOM WINDOW AND WALL TREATMENT

This sliding window is continuous across the whole front of the house. It is possible to have a clear opening 14 feet long. At either end are small top-hung windows of reeded glass. The shaped cill finishes independently of the side walls (see plan).

DAY

NIGHT

PLAN SHOWING FLOWER BOX

THE DINING-ROOM WINDOW

This window lights the dining-room portion of the L-shaped living-room, and is of glass bricks as no view is obtainable from the side of the house. The two photographs show the window by day and covered by a pinoleum blind at night.

128

HOUSE IN NEWTON ROAD, PADDINGTON

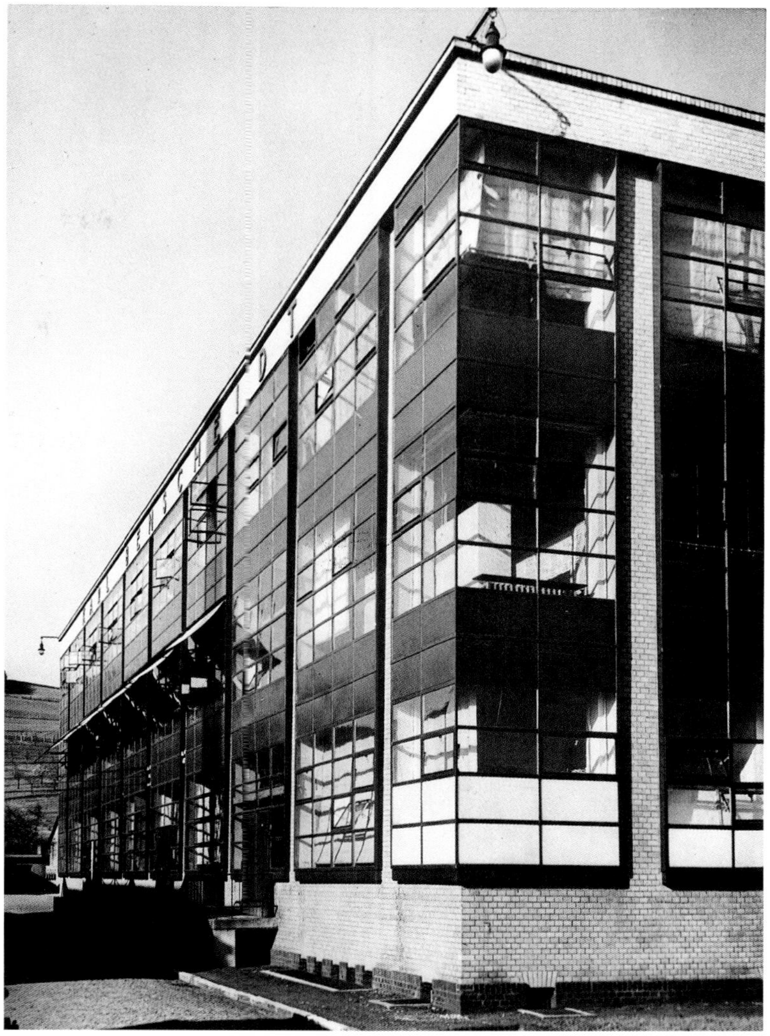

opposite

DELL & WAINWRIGHT

(Mark Oliver Dell [1883–1959] and H.L. Wainwright)

Miramonte, Coombe, Surrey, 1937

Gelatine silver print

Architect: Edwin Maxwell Fry

The inter-war period saw an increasingly effective compositional use of skies, which had previously been restricted by the over-sensitivity of plates to blue, rendering prints characteristically 'bald-headed'. As even panchromatic plates introduced in 1904 retained a blue bias, these new effects were often obtained by using colour filters, particularly contrast types like orange or red. By darkening blue skies and intensifying clouds, these enabled them to be presented as dramatic and irregular foils to the rigid geometry of white-box Modernism. Separate, specially taken sky negatives could also be combination printed with negatives in which the sky was vapid.

above left

Page spread from *Architectural Review*, vol. 85, March 1939, showing *House in Newton Road, London*, with photographs by Alfred Cracknell

Architect: Denys Lasdun

During the 1930s the *Architectural Review* was without peer among its competitors in its creative use of photography. Blow-ups, pointed juxtapositions, photomontages all contributed to its eye-catching page layouts, while, married to text and drawings, photographs formed part of indivisible analytical sequences. Freed from their traditional white borders, photographs became fully integrated elements of the magazine, rather than mere illustrative ancillaries. Photographs were also routinely cropped and, less often, retouched. Favourite practices included airbrushing of undesirable features; the application of whitener to façades; and drawing around the building's outline to make it stand proud of its surroundings.

above right

ALBERT RENGER-PATZSCH (1897–1966)

Fagus Factory, Alfeld an der Leine, Germany, 1928

Gelatine silver print

Architects: Walter Gropius and Adolf Meyer

Renger-Patzsch's series of photographs of the Fagus factory encompassed studies of the machinery and products and portraits of its owners, as well as pictures of the buildings. Some were published in his controversial *Die Welt ist schön* (1928), the key text of New Objectivity photography. Although Renger-Patzsch was not commissioned by the architects, and indeed rejected collaboration with architects as an erosion of his independence, this close view, emphasizing the fenestration at the expense of the brick piers, became Gropius's favourite. Regularly reproduced, it was instrumental in establishing the building's reputation as one of international Modernism's formative works.

top right

BRYAN and **NORMAN WESTWOOD**
(Bryan Westwood [1909–1990] and Norman Westwood [born 1912])

Black & White Milk Bar, Gray's Inn Road, London, c. 1937
Gelatine silver print
Architects: Sir John Brown & A.E. Henson

The brothers Bryan and Norman Westwood used photography in a semi-professional capacity to supplement their income from architectural practice. Both studied at the Architectural Association in London and were heavily influenced by the image-making of F.R. Yerbury. Much of their architectural output concentrated on shop design, and many of their photographs reproduced in the *Architectural Review*, *Smaller Retail Shops* (1937) and *The Modern Shop* (1952) campaigned for improvements in the quality of commercial architecture and such details as lettering.

bottom right

BERENICE ABBOTT (1898–1991)

Columbus Circle: Broadway, Central Park West and West 59th Street, New York, 1936
Gelatine silver print

Inspired by Atget's example, Abbott conceived the idea of photographing New York in 1929 but was unable to realize her ambition until she received funding from the Works Progress Administration's Federal Art Project in 1935. Her photographs reveal a fusion of European Modernism, an Atgetesque dalliance with the idiosyncratic, and an adherence to the artless primitivism of the American documentary tradition she admired in the work of such photographers as the Civil War chronicler Mathew Brady. Here advertising is presented as a new form of urban iconography, supplanting traditional civic statuary as embodied in the dwarfed 1892 representation of Christopher Columbus.

opposite

WALKER EVANS (1903–1975)

Negro Church, South Carolina, 1936
Gelatine silver print

This seemingly simple photograph, one of a number of studies of negro churches made for the Farm Security Administration, bears the characteristic hallmarks of Evans's work: his capacity to convey the nobility of the unassuming; his emphasis on meticulous description, here aided by the strong, brilliant sunlight; his classical reserve, shown by the typically head-on vantage point, which gives the building the attribute of a stage flat; his delight in imperfection, revealed in the church's bowing and split wooden columns; and his self-confessed overriding interest in "what any present time will look like as the past".[30]

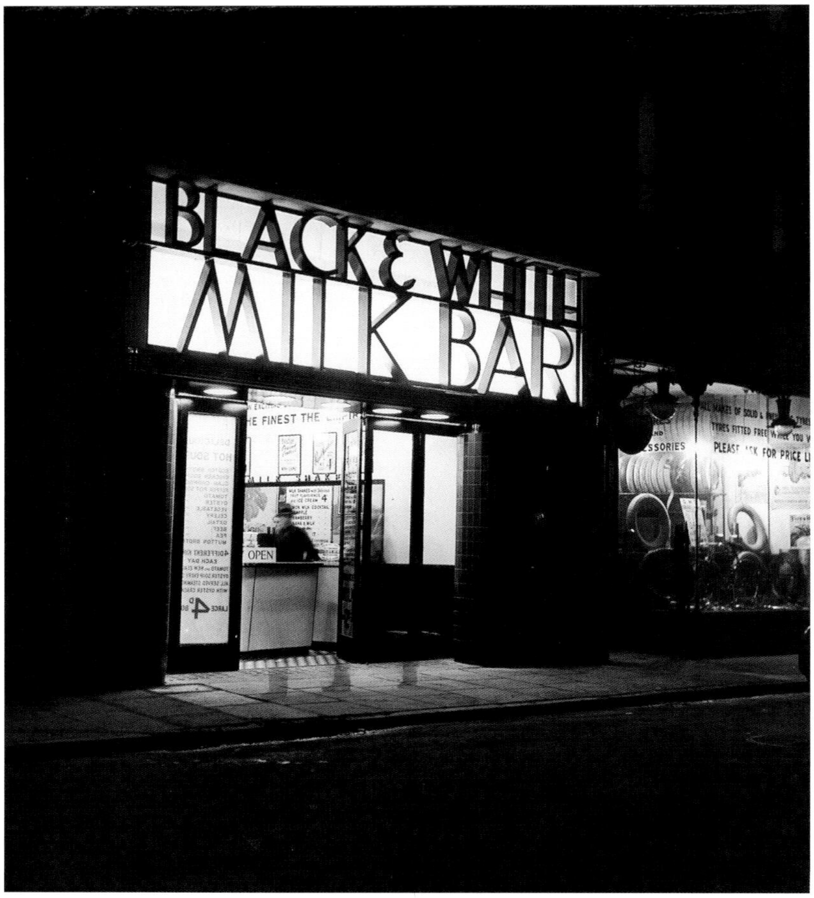

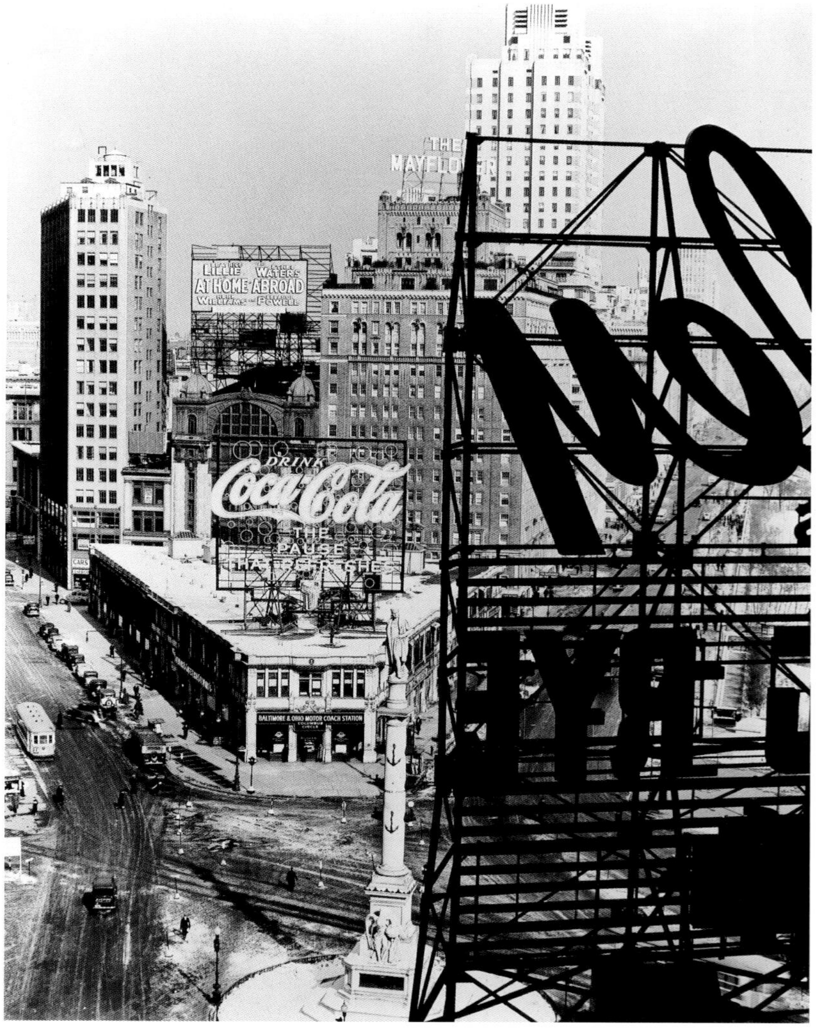

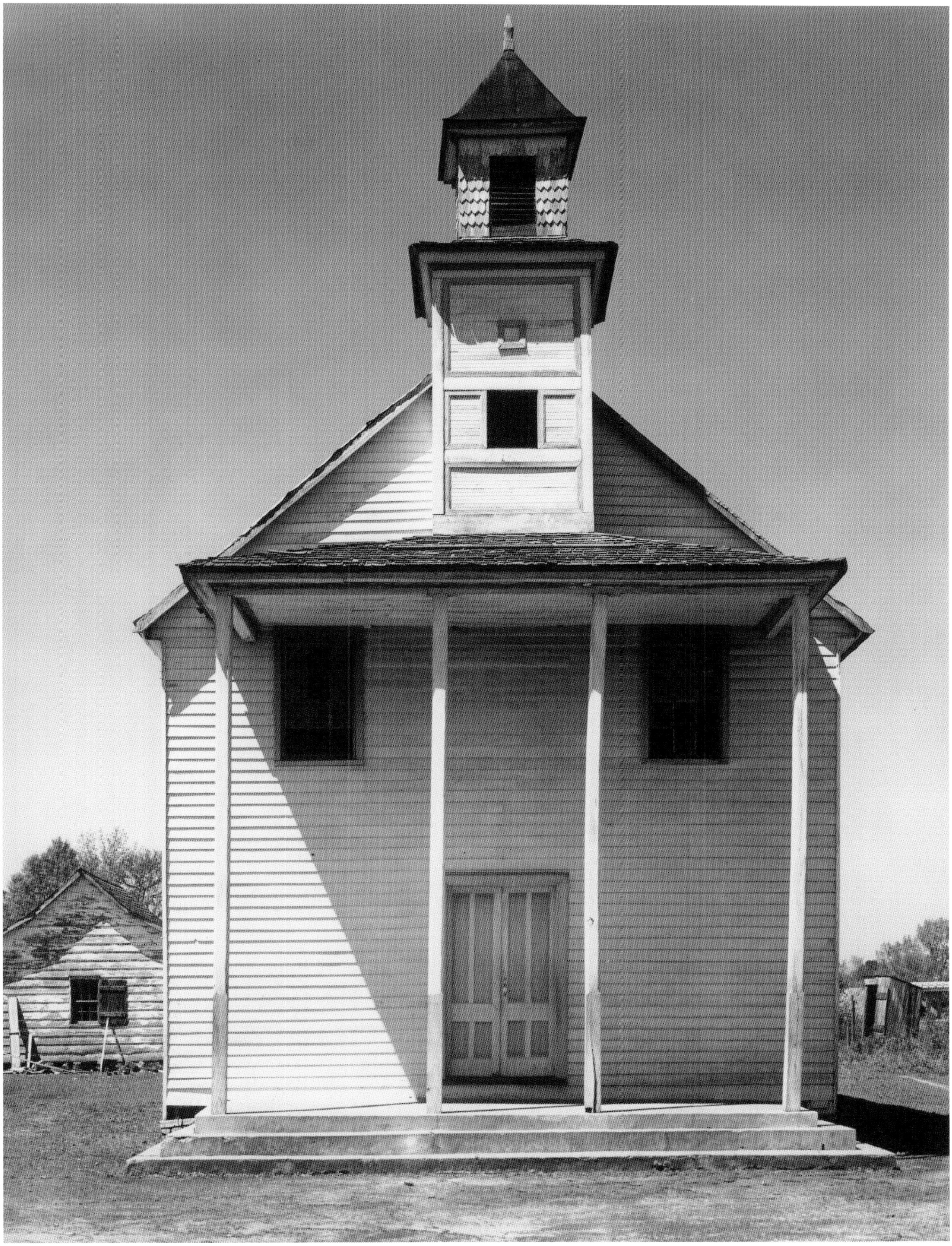

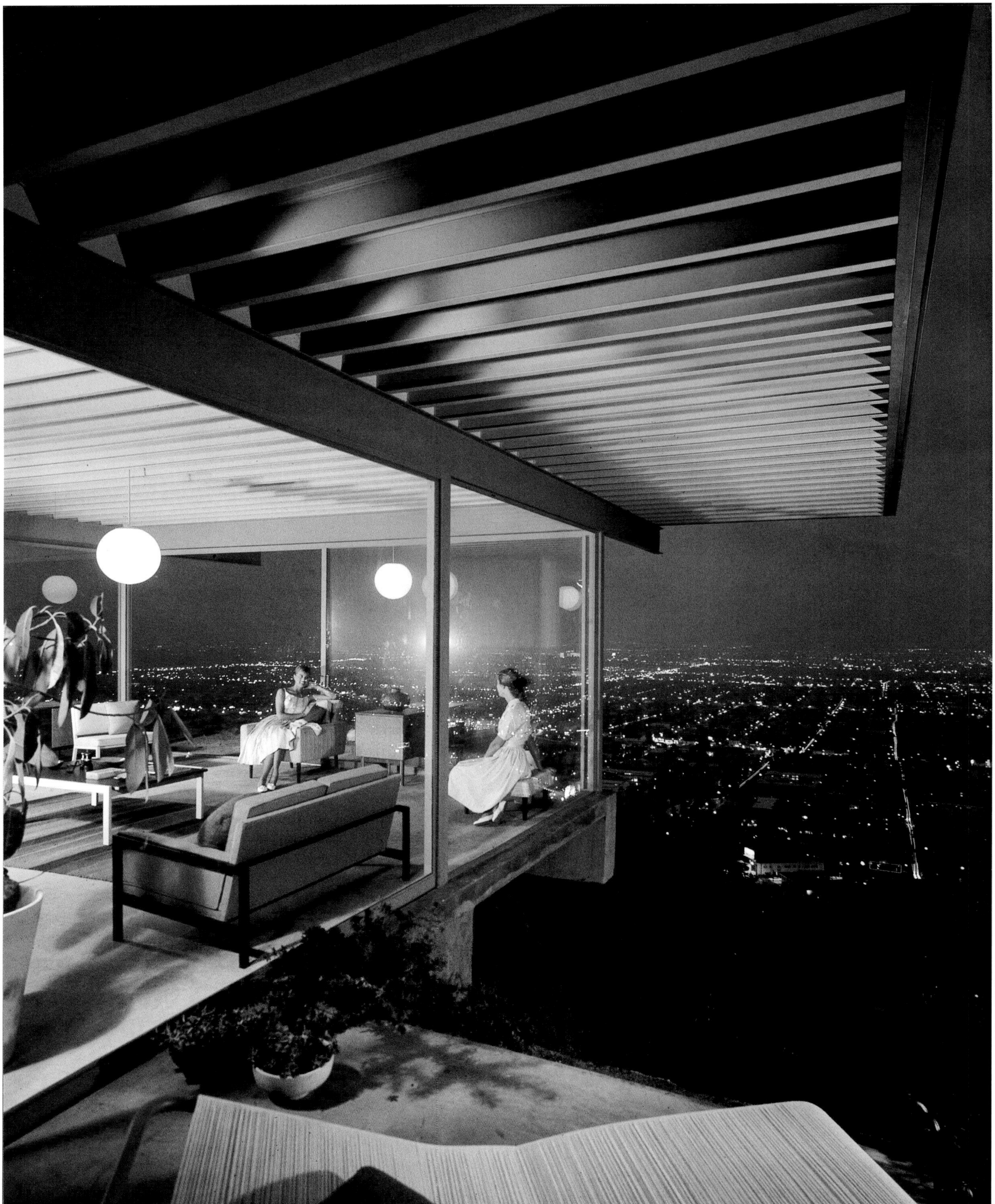

Chapter 5 **Photography Ascendant 1945–1975**

page 154

JULIUS SHULMAN
(born 1910)

Case Study House #22, Los Angeles, 1960
Gelatine silver print
Architect: Pierre Koenig

During the post-war period photography consolidated its role as the primary means of architectural communication and helped to establish Modernism as the new architectural orthodoxy. As, with some notable exceptions, few of the photographers who had dominated the architectural scene before the war enjoyed significant careers thereafter – Mark Dell retired in 1946; F.S. Lincoln's business fizzled out; Jan Kamman's archive was destroyed in a bombing raid – this was largely accomplished by a new, younger generation of architectural photographers. While much of their production in the war-ravaged areas of Europe and the Far East championed the economic and social benefits of reconstruction, architectural photography became a less cohesive, more protean genre. Whereas in the nineteenth century it had tended to meld into topography, now it was just as likely to dissolve at one extreme into lifestyle and at the other into treatment of the environment, the space between and around buildings or what in contemporary parlance was dubbed 'townscape'.

The period also witnessed a progressive blurring of the boundaries between photography and art that spurred a number of more artistically inclined photographers to seek self-expression through an examination of architectural form. At the same time, the fact that the new post-war generation of architectural photographers were often trained in architecture rather than in photography, as many of their inter-war predecessors had been, widened the rift between architectural image-makers and the photographic establishment. This new generation introduced few stylistic innovations but rather refined and extended the methodology formulated by their 1930s forebears – a fact that may account in part for the slow uptake of colour. Although colour stock became more readily available and was used to an increasing extent, especially in magazines devoted to the home and interiors, architectural photographers, sharing de Maré's opinion that colour was "less creative",[1] remained predominantly craftsmen in black and white. It was for only a brief period in the 1960s, with a sustained attempt to apply photojournalistic methods to architectural depiction, that the visual conventions established by such photographers as Dell & Wainwright and Hedrich Blessing were seriously challenged.

The war itself had a significant impact on architectural photography. With the outbreak of hostilities, movable art objects were despatched to safe hiding places, but this was obviously impossible with buildings, and photographing them was therefore considered the best option. In England, as bombing intensified, the National Buildings Record was founded in 1941 to collect and create drawings and photographs of significant monuments at risk. Herbert Felton, and, for a short time, Bill Brandt were among its early photographers. After an interval of nearly a century, England at last possessed a body analogous to the Mission Héliographique that gave official sanction to architectural photography. Similar governmental initiatives elsewhere, including that by Italy's Ministero della Pubblica Istruzione, were supplemented by individual campaigns, such as that waged by Walter Hege, who forsook his bombastic studies of Nazi architecture to photograph imperilled German castles and cathedrals. During the war photography and the use of photographs were of course strictly censored, and photographs of buildings were required to elicit from their audience the appropriate mix of moral indignation and determination to stand firm. Perhaps the most compelling instance was Herbert Mason's shrewdly constructed view of London's St Paul's Cathedral standing proud and unflinching amidst blitzed houses, which quickly became a potent symbol of national defiance (see pages 164–65).

This propaganda use of building photographs continued in the immediate aftermath of the war, which saw the release of a plethora of photographic books with emotive titles such as *The Mutilated Budapest* (n.d.) and *This Pearl Vienna: A Book of Pictures Taken from Vienna's Most Dreadful Time* (1946). Alongside these anti-Fascist rants were books that essayed a more measured, documentary appraisal of the destruction wrought. The most important of these was *Lost Treasures of Europe* (1946), a compilation with commentaries of more than four hundred photographs drawn from a wide variety of sources. In the book's introduction, its editor, Henry La Farge, recounted the difficulties involved in assembling the images, quoting from a moving letter from the director of the Hamburg Museum, "The good photographer in Lübeck lost all his plates in a bombing raid. Renger [*i.e.* Patzsch], who had made the best photographs of Hamburg, has been completely bombed out in Essen."[2] The survival of photographic collections and other archival records was to prove crucial to the reconstruction of historic buildings and city centres, such as those of Warsaw, Nuremberg and Cologne, architects in the last city relying heavily on the pre-war imagery of August Sander.

The war heightened the sense of historical consciousness, and several architectural photographers contributed to the fresh investigation of what had been fought for and preserved, and to the search for cultural identity and roots that it prompted. One photographer whose work was infused with this 'presence of the past' was the architect-trained Edwin Smith (see page 166), who began increasingly to specialize in landscape and architecture after the war, partly as a result of commissions from Thames & Hudson for two books, *English Parish Churches* (1952) and *English Cottages and Farmhouses* (1954). In the former, Smith tackled his favourite subject in imagery that, in its spiritual intensity if not its luminosity, matched the work of Frederick Evans. The latter book, as Atget's views of Paris had done, captured a traditional way of life on the cusp of change. Both volumes bear the characteristic hallmarks of Smith's work, which was to grace nearly thirty further books until his death in 1971: a pervasive sense of the human presence, even when no people were in shot; a near-tactile rendering of materials and landscape; an intuitive affinity with place; and a technique that relied whenever possible on natural lighting, that was without artifice and was almost totally self-effacing. At odds with mainstream British output during the period, Smith's photography was one of patient seduction, not visceral shock.

Smith's photography had little polemical intent, but elsewhere photographers' engagement with the past was conducted with one eye fixed firmly on the present. This was especially evident in Japan, where photography made a telling contribution to the great 'tradition' debate, which sought to determine whether indigenous or imported architectural forms were more appropriate to apply to the daunting task of rebuilding the country's shattered infrastructure. In 1953, at the suggestion of the Modernist architect Sutemi Horiguchi, with whom he had worked before the war, Yoshio Watanabe was commissioned by the Society for International Cultural Relations to make a series of photographs of the shrine at Ise (see page 167). Watanabe was the first photographer granted permission to photograph in the shrine's inner compounds, and his images, heavily influenced by the Western Modernist aesthetic, in particular the work of Mendelsohn and Renger-Patzsch, were instrumental not only in demystifying the shrine but also in stripping it of its tainted nationalistic and imperialistic associations. Instead they recast it as a pure architectural masterpiece in which intimations of Modernism could be divined.

Although some of his photographs had appeared in print before, it was with their 1962 publication, translated three years later with the significant title of *Ise: Prototype of Japanese Architecture*, that the contemporary relevance of Watanabe's documentation became apparent, emphasized as it was in a persuasive introduction by Kenzo Tange, one of the debate's most outspoken architectural participants.[3] It was Tange who had earlier collaborated with the photographer Yasuhiro Ishimoto on *Katsura: Tradition and Creation in Japanese Architecture* (1960), an intriguing photographic "dismembering", to use Tange's word, of the sixteenth-century palace into a series of "sequentially shifting textures, patterns, and spaces" (see page 168).[4] In their bold isolation of such elements as stepping stones, rock formations and bamboo screens, Ishimoto's photographs emphasized the palace's sculptural nature, while the interior spaces were photographed in such a way as to resemble a succession of Mondrian abstracts (below).

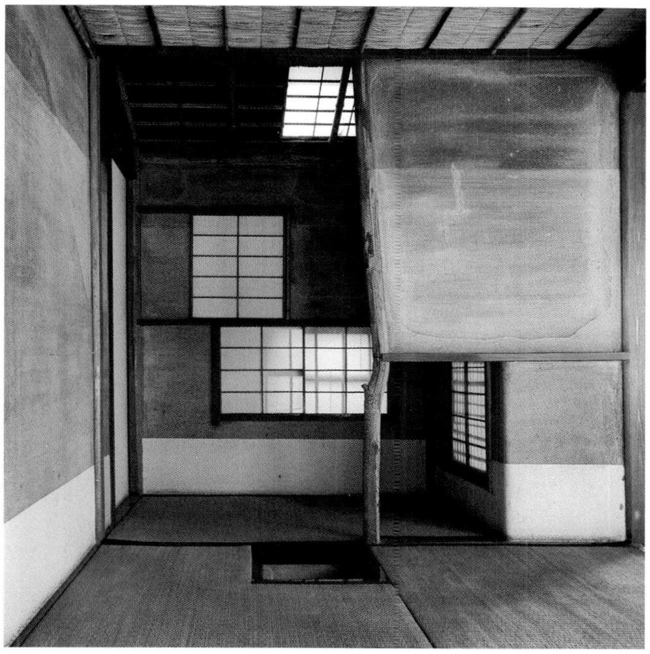

YASUHIRO ISHIMOTO
(born 1921)

Tearoom of the Shokintei Pavilion, Katsura, Kyoto, 1960
Gelatine silver print

GEORGE E. KIDDER SMITH (1913–1997)

Workers' Housing, via Marittima, Naples, *c.* 1954
Gelatine silver print
Architects: Cocchia De Luca & Della Sala

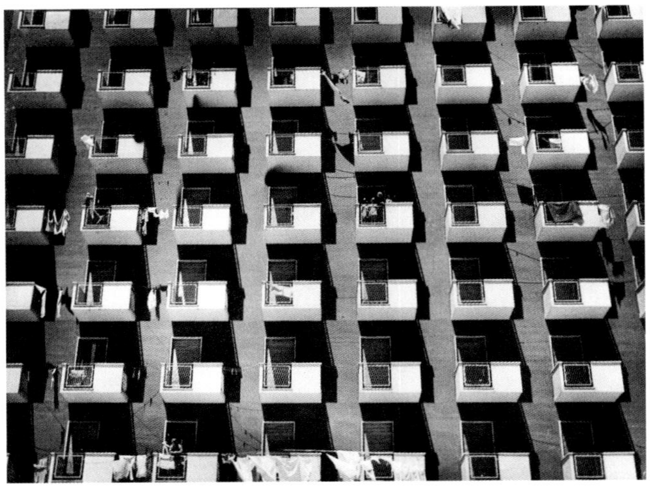

The last major contribution to this Japanese cycle suggesting the need for an accommodation between past and present came in a series of three books with texts by Teiji Itoh and photographs by Yukio Futagawa that appeared in the 1960s: *The Essential Japanese House* (1962); *The Roots of Japanese Architecture* (1962); and *The Elegant Japanese House* (1967; see page 169).[5] In contrast to those of Watanabe and the American-born and -educated Ishimoto, which used sun and shadow in Western fashion graphically to highlight details and textures, Futagawa's photographs were usually taken in even light and often with the frame cut-offs characteristic of Japanese woodblock prints. In their standardized format and photographic style, these books presaged Futagawa's highly successful *Global Architecture* series, begun under his own A.D.A. Edita imprint in 1970, and its spin-offs such as *Global Interiors* and *GA Houses*, in which speed of production was of the essence and the photography was consequently reduced to a formula that enabled the indefatigable Futagawa to achieve a high turnover of serviceable pictures of the world's architecture. If confirmation were needed of the mutual interdependence of photography and publishing, then Futagawa's remarkable career has strikingly provided it. With the worldwide distribution of Futagawa's images and the high standards achieved in the documentation of both historical and contemporary architecture – seen to magisterial effect in the photographs of Osamu Murai (see page 168) – this period represented a golden age for Japanese architectural photography that was instrumental in promoting interest in Japanese architecture in the West.

The interrelationship between the historical and contemporary implicit in these Japanese publications was made explicit in the work of the American architect and photographer George E. Kidder Smith (left). Smith was the archetypal 'photographer on the run', travelling widely, seldom taking more than fifteen minutes over a shot, never using lights and relying on local labs to process his film, yet still producing consistently impressive, richly textured prints. His *Brazil Builds: Architecture New and Old 1652–1942* (1943; see page 170), produced in association with New York's Museum of Modern Art, was followed by three similar grant-aided volumes: *Sweden Builds*, *Switzerland Builds* (both 1950) and *Italy Builds* (1955). Together these contained a mixture of past and present architecture and experimented with colour. As Jim Richards, editor of the *Architectural Review*, astutely observed, "One of the things that has made his previous books so useful has been the marrying of the local topography and architectural tradition with what modern architects are trying to do."[6] In contrast to the earlier publications, *Italy Builds* demonstrated Smith's awakened interest in the then much-discussed notion of townscape, with the changes in level, texture, scale and vista of Italy's historic *piazze* being proffered as prototypes for contemporary practitioners charged with the redevelopment of city centres (see page 171). Significantly, the end-papers of the British edition of the book were designed by the foremost apostle of townscape, Gordon Cullen. The body of historical photographs that had the most demonstrable influence on contemporary practice, however, was assembled by Cullen's close friend and associate at the Architectural Press, Eric de Maré.

From the late 1940s de Maré photographed Britain's neglected industrial heritage – anonymous, vernacular structures, such as warehouses, textile factories and canal buildings, which came to be collectively labelled the 'functional tradition' (see page 171). Published in a special issue of *Architectural Review* in July 1957, and in expanded form a year later in Jim Richards's *The Functional Tradition in Early Industrial Buildings*, de Maré's vigorous and well-composed photographs not only built on the pre-war work of Piper and Richards but also represented a typically British, scaled-down version of the fascination of the Modern

Movement's pioneers with the austere sublimity of North American grain silos. In addition, like the work of Edwin Smith they reflected the rekindled interest in Britishness as well as the growth of industrial archaeology (a term that first came into common usage in the 1950s), which bore further fruit in the Bechers' photographs. Suggesting that here was an indigenous harbinger of Modernism, a vernacular tradition evincing "the forthright, spare and logical use of materials"[7] that should serve as an inspiration to modern architects, de Maré's images heavily influenced both the work of James Stirling and, although he deplored it, the development of New Brutalism in the 1960s. By broadening the perception of where architecture was to be found, and putting on a professional footing the kind of subject-matter that had hitherto been the preserve of campaigning amateur photographers, de Maré proved a pivotal figure in British architectural photography. Furthermore, his close association with the Architectural Press and publication of over twenty books on a wide variety of subjects, including the perennially popular Penguin handbook *Photography* (1957), and the perceptive *Photography and Architecture* (1961), not only gained his photographs wide currency but also brought a new respectability to architectural photography by extending its influence beyond the narrow confines of professional discourse.

The concentration by de Maré and Edwin Smith on historical architecture, to the virtual exclusion of contemporary projects, is symptomatic of a familiar divide in architectural photography that few photographers at this time crossed, Kidder Smith and Cervin Robinson (see page 185) being two notable exceptions. For those photographers concerned to portray the post-war world, the graphic economy of inter-war photography remained the norm. As the early work of the Swedish-born de Maré (see page 172) and Kidder Smith demonstrated, Sweden, untouched by the war and with wide-ranging welfare facilities and low-cost housing, afforded a seductive role model for reconstruction in the late 1940s. This view was encouraged by the photographs of Sune Sundahl, whose first commission had been to photograph Gunnar Asplund's summer house at Sorunda in 1939 and who, in succession to Carl Gustav Rosenberg, emerged as Sweden's foremost post-war architectural photographer (see page 173). In contrast to Sundahl's more humanistic imagery, in neighbouring Denmark the opposite and more typical approach was adopted by Aage Strüwing, a frequent collaborator with Arne Jacobsen, who developed an arresting style of pared-down incisiveness (see page 175).

As the lure of Sweden waned, the *béton brut* ('raw concrete') creations of Le Corbusier came to be regarded as the new architectural talismans, their chief propagator being a Hungarian-born photographer domiciled in Paris, Lucien Hervé. Hervé's early career was in photojournalism, and it was the techniques learnt in this discipline, together with a fondness for the oblique views typical of the New Photography, that he brought to bear on his coverage of Le Corbusier's Unité d'Habitation, Marseilles. Here in 1949, on commission from *Plaisir de France*, he took a staggering 650 pictures with his Rolleiflex in a single day (see page 174). On seeing examples Hervé had sent to him, Le Corbusier declared that the photographer possessed "the soul of an architect".[8] Thus began a close collaboration and friendship that saw Hervé photograph all Le Corbusier's new works, and selected older ones, until the architect's death in 1965 (see page 174). No photographer so well captured the sculptural plasticity and expressiveness of concrete, as seen in his treatment not just of Le Corbusier's architecture but also that of Pier Luigi Nervi and, memorably, Oscar Niemeyer, although Havinden's images of Lubetkin's 1930s zoo buildings are worthy precursors (see page 124). Hervé's photographs are marked by their violent contrasts and uncompromising geometrical construction. These attributes are equally evident in the few historical structures he photographed,

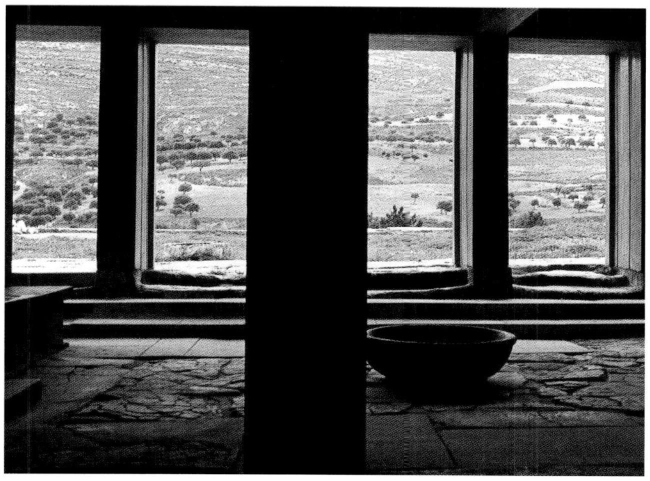

LUCIEN HERVÉ
(born 1910)

Knossos, Crete, 1956
Gelatine silver print

most notably the Jaipur Observatory and the Cistercian abbey of Le Thoronet, the latter the subject of a book illustrated by his pictures and entitled *La Plus Grande Aventure du monde* (1956). In his portrayal of both buildings Hervé deliberately emphasized their abstract qualities. An unusual view of Knossos (1956; see page 159), which looks out through the palace's rectangular openings to the plain beyond, not only betrayed the influence of Japanese traditional architecture on Hervé's compositional sense but was also replete with contemporary resonance: photographers were increasingly required to confront the problem of photographing the open house in which the division between inside and outside was no longer clearly demarcated.

Perhaps the photographer whose imagery best embodied the ideals of post-war reconstruction and the determination to build a brave new world was the Dutchman Jan Versnel, who began photographing in 1947. He shared the aspirations of the Nieuwe Bouwen architects and designers such as Gerrit Rietveld, Van den Broek & Bakema and Alexander Bodon, whose work he predominantly covered (below right). Like Hervé, Versnel was trained in graphic art, but in contrast to Hervé's pyrotechnics Versnel's pictures of social housing, public amenities and open-plan offices, guided partly by the example of his teacher, Bernard Eilers, and frequently featured in magazines such as *Forum*, were muted in tone. An important part of Versnel's practice was his photography of show homes for the Goed Wonen Foundation, published in *Goed wonen*, where he often employed an all-embracing high-angle viewpoint to reveal the way in which interiors could be economically furnished and organized (see page 177).

The austerity evident in Versnel's early photographs had by the 1960s given way to the new-found affluence revealed in Britain in the images of Henk Snoek (see pages 178, 179), hailed by the *Architects' Journal* as one of the "high priests of architectural photography",[9] and Richard Einzig (see page 178), who took up photography in 1964 after a short career as an architect. Both photographed in an ascetic idiom well-suited to the New Brutalism of the period and very much in the tradition of Dell & Wainwright. Dell & Wainwright's work was also a major influence on Ezra Stoller, who began photographing in 1939 and subsequently became, with Hedrich Blessing and Julius Shulman, one of the great triumvirate whose image-making dominated the post-war scene in the United States. Hedrich Blessing built on its pre-war success to become the quintessential well-organized business, employing a team of photographers who nevertheless maintained a distinctive house style. While Stoller shared the business outlook of Hedrich Blessing, establishing Esto Photographics in 1966 to distribute his work, he eschewed the overt drama of its photography, believing that the photographer's task was to distil the architect's idea and that this placed a premium on clarity and accuracy (see pages 180, 181).

Echoing Atget, whose work he knew and admired, Stoller referred to his photographs as "pure documents". Highly controlled and meticulously planned, Stoller's was the classical approach to architectural photography – crisp, precise, restrained, with frequent use of elevational shots – that would have been appreciated by Baldus or Bedford Lemere. The major difference was that now the emphasis was overwhelmingly on conveying spatial relationships, which Stoller maintained was better done in black and white than in colour, and by remembering that "we are not shooting at space but as a part of it, a sense which is rather subtle and easily distorted by resorting to queer angles, exaggerated composition, forced perspective and overdramatic lighting."[10] Stoller's wide-ranging clientele, which included magazines, advertisers and museums as well as architects as diverse as Frank Lloyd Wright, Skidmore Owings & Merrill and Richard Meier, saw him construct some of the period's most captivating images – the smooth-skinned monumentality of Mies van der Rohe and Philip Johnson's Seagram Building (1958) dwarfing

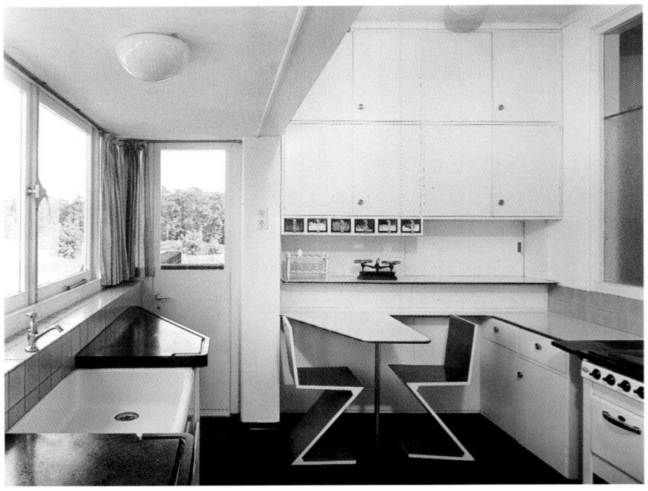

JAN VERSNEL (born 1924)
House Stoop, Velp, The Netherlands, 1951
Gelatine silver print
Architect: Gerrit Rietveld

all else on New York's Park Avenue (see page 6); or the serpentine contours of the interior of Wright's Guggenheim Museum, New York (1959; right); or the hovering presence of the roof support at Dulles International Airport, Washington, DC (1963), designed by Eero Saarinen. This was architecture seen not in a moment of revelation, as with Hervé at Marseilles, but as the formal set-piece distilled through an 8 x 10 inch (20.3 x 25.4 cm) or 5 x 4 inch (12.7 x 10.1 cm) view camera and captured with boldness and a seeming simplicity that belied Stoller's careful preparation. The coining of the term 'Stollerized image' was at once a tribute to the consistency of Stoller's vision and to the widespread influence that vision exerted.

While Stoller plied his trade on the East Coast, on the West Coast architectural photography was enjoying a revival in the work of such photographers as Roger Sturtevant, Morley Baer (see page 180) and particularly Shulman, which recalled the creative period during the 1840s and 1850s when outdoor photography flourished in California owing to its sunny climate. In contrast to Stoller, Shulman had assembled a significant body of pre-war work, but it was really after the war when his career blossomed, especially through his close association with *Arts and Architecture* and his recording of eighteen of its twenty-six pioneering Case Study houses between 1945 and 1967 (see page 182). This is the world of 'California dreamin'', with not a hint of its mean streets; of continual sunshine and luminous twilights; of unquenchable optimism; of architecture metamorphosing into lifestyle; above all, of architecture as consumer product – a process reinforced by the reproduction of Shulman's photographs in popular magazines, such as *House and Garden*, *Good Housekeeping* and *Life*, as well as in the professional press.

In this documentation the characteristic traits of Shulman's photography are readily apparent. The deep raking perspective draws the viewer's eye precisely to where he intends, and the dramatic use of light and shadow delineates form and structure. There is a compositional strategy in which, unusually, people as well as objects play a prominent role, and a concern for landscape. Shulman's photographs go beyond the simple facts of the building fabric to propose a blueprint for living. His two most iconic images, Neutra's Kaufmann House, Palm Springs (1947; see page 183), romantically bathed in a soft twilight glow and seeming to rest on the edge of infinity like a figure in a Caspar David Friedrich

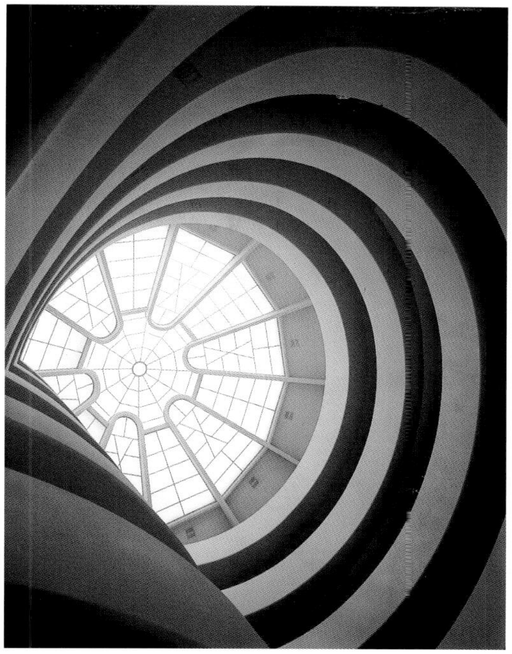

EZRA STOLLER
(born 1915)

Solomon R. Guggenheim Museum, New York, 1963
Gelatine silver print
Architect: Frank Lloyd Wright

painting, and Pierre Koenig's Case Study House #22 (1960; see page 154), hovering majestically over the shimmering lights of the Los Angeles Basin, transcend the architecture. Rather, they capture a mood – the former is suggestive of Modernism's limitless potential, the latter of a country at ease with itself. These seductive and compelling images by Shulman and Stoller, together with those of other photographers such as Balthazar Korab (see page 184), not merely enthralled a domestic audience but were also instrumental in exporting the American Modernist dream.

If Shulman's oeuvre illustrates a broadening of the appeal of architectural photography to encourage the embrace of more popular and fashionable magazines, then that of the Bechers demonstrates its growing union with the art world (see page 187). Inspired by earlier Rhineland photographers, especially Renger-Patzsch and Sander, whose portraits were informed by similar typological concerns, from the late 1950s the Bechers have documented a variety of doomed industrial structures, such as mineheads, water towers and gas-holders, in an impersonal and systematic manner that exaggerates the norms of architectural photography. The Bechers talk less about photographing their subjects, which in their first book in 1970 they revealingly referred to as "anonymous sculptures", than about collecting and categorizing them to facilitate comparative analysis. To achieve these illuminating typological studies, the Bechers devised a formula, reminiscent of Meydenbauer's photogrammetry, to which they have adhered so rigidly over the years that it is all but impossible to determine when a particular photograph was taken. Each subject, usually placed in the centre of the picture, is photographed from up to eight slightly elevated viewpoints. Perspective distortion is avoided, as are strong cast shadows, the Bechers preferring a wan sky so that no detail is lost. As important as this neutral stance is the Bechers' mode of presentation. On the gallery or museum wall this often revolves around what Hilla has called "the magic square",[11] a group of perhaps nine photographs framed together – oddly prescient of a computer screen grid of thumbnails – where the typology of the structure can be studied. As with the photographs of Lewis Baltz, we are close here to the world of Conceptual art. If the Bechers' influence has perhaps been limited architecturally, photographically it has been profound, setting in train a process by which successors such as Thomas Struth can be regarded as artists first and photographers second.

For architectural photography's growing band of critics, the Bechers' orientation towards abstract art, and what these critics regarded as the sterile perfection of much mainstream imagery, seemed symptomatic of a discipline that, in establishing its hegemony in architectural depiction and helping to consolidate the Modern Movement, had lost touch with reality. The architect Sir William Holford thus witheringly observed:

> Life is suspended while the camera is adjusted. Architecture becomes, not a background to people, but a series of studio portraits. Ordinary folk have to look at these buildings through the lens and the filter, instead of moving in and through them, and becoming conscious of them, as it were, by absorption and use. The tyranny of the drawing-board, with its emphasis on two dimensions at a time, is superseded by the tyranny of the glossy photograph with its emphasis on pose. Luminosity and tone have become more important than formal decoration and silhouette.[12]

The American architect Russell Lynes similarly decried a photography that encouraged viewers to exercise their architectural taste rather than judgement and to concentrate on style not structure.[13] In perhaps the most outspoken attack, the writer and photographer Tom Picton railed against "the craven image", a soulless piece of flattering deception ever ready to accord as much photographic reverence to the most mundane housing as to the Parthenon and foisted on an unsuspecting public by a conspiratorial, unholy trinity of architect, photographer and art editor.[14] Picton's criticisms were given added weight by a gradual shift in patronage over the period, which saw the role of the staff photographer and direct photographic commissioning by magazines decline as editors were enticed by the free pictures offered to them and commissioned by architects. Whereas the photographer working for a magazine could at least claim some degree of independence from the architect, the dangers of this growing collusion were all too obvious. The fact that photographs were frequently either jointly commissioned by, or sold on to, contractors, who used them to advertise their products, merely served to augment their consumerist aura.

While most photographers would doubtless have agreed with Shulman's defiant assertion that they were in the business of "selling architecture" to the public, some partly shared the concerns expressed and looked to the example of photojournalism to reinvigorate a genre that they felt had become too obsessed with graphic pattern-making at the expense of conveying any real sense of the architecture. The photographic roots of this movement were diverse but included the photographs of Walker Evans, the street photography of Henri Cartier-Bresson and others, and the polemical amateur snapshots that had become so prominent a feature of the *Architectural Review* in the 1930s and continued in the same vein after the war, with abrasive contributions from journalists such as Ian Nairn (opposite). Employing smaller-format cameras and the faster films then appearing on the market, in preference to the conventional 5 x 4 inch (12.7 x 10.1 cm) or larger stand cameras, the movement's adherents sought to show buildings in context and in use by people performing real tasks, as opposed to figures stiffly posed to give a sense of scale. The attempt by photographers such as Einzig or Stoller to reclaim the drawing-board innocence of the architect's original, unsullied design was replaced by a commitment to portraying architecture in the messy, real world of complexity and contradiction, where buildings and people often interacted in ways completely unforeseen. Stoller's mantra that "the name of the game from beginning to end is control"[15] was supplanted by a photography that prized the fleeting glimpse, the sudden flash of experiential revelation. The daily ritual of a handful of painstakingly choreographed pictures bowed to what John Donat termed "trigger diarrhoea".[16] Images dense with detail gave way to prints that, enlarged from smaller negatives and often retaining the frame's black border, emphasized the film's grain to present an illusion of gritty reality. An early manifestation of this new mood came in 1956 with the publication of *The Idea of Louis Sullivan* (see page 188), a photographic tribute by John Szarkowski, later Curator of Photography at New York's Museum of Modern Art. In his introduction, Szarkowski maintained, "In our own day perhaps the best architectural photographs have been the casual products of the photographer-journalist, where the life that surrounds and nourishes the buildings is seen or felt. If to such an approach were added an understanding of architectural form, photography might become a powerful critical medium, rather than a superficially descriptive one."[17]

In The Netherlands the impetus for change came from architects such as Aldo van Eyck and Herman Hertzberger, who, in seeking to emphasize the human aspect of architectural design, demanded that their buildings be photographed in a less static, more naturalistic manner (see page 189), and from magazines such as *Forum* and *Wonen–TA/BK*, which became increasingly socially committed and highly critical of much contemporary architectural practice. The results can be seen in the photographs of, among others, Willem Diepraam and Violette Cornelius, who collaborated with Van Eyck. The high point of photojournalism applied to architectural photography, however, came in Britain, where an indigenous inspiration was Roger Mayne's photographs of North Kensington's streets and his coverage of Sheffield's Park Hill housing estate (1961). The latter was a particular influence on John Donat, whose work perhaps best exemplifies the movement (see page 190). Donat was an eloquent champion of its principles, not least in a lecture delivered to the Royal Institute of British Architects in 1967, provocatively entitled 'The Camera Always Lies', in which he castigated an architectural photography in which "reality and experience disappear – ART prevails".[18] Drawing on the example of Cartier-Bresson, in whose pictures he admiringly considered "life came first and architecture second and yet was essentially part of it",[19] Donat tried to convey what he termed "an experience of a slice of time in the life of a building",[20] even if this meant on occasion sacrificing technical perfection to realize a 'live' picture.

Donat's outlook was shared by 'shooting-star' Tim Street-Porter, who had similarly studied architecture and was a prominent contributor to the most thoroughgoing application of photojournalistic methods to architectural depiction, the *Architectural Review*'s notorious 'Manplan' series. Published in eight issues between September 1969 and 1970, the series delivered a damning verdict on the state of the nation in architecture and town planning (see page 191). These issues were illustrated not by the customary raft of professional architectural photographers or crusading amateurs but by specially commissioned photojournalists, including, in addition to Street-Porter, Peter Baistow, Patrick Ward and Tony Ray-Jones (see page 191), whose hard-hitting images brutally exposed the dystopia architects and planners had created. Unused to having their work questioned in so forthright a manner, many architects were outraged and cancelled their subscriptions. Although the movement continued in the work of Donat and others, 'Manplan' was a watershed. If bitter truths were unpalatable, the beguiling blandishments of colour photography were at hand.

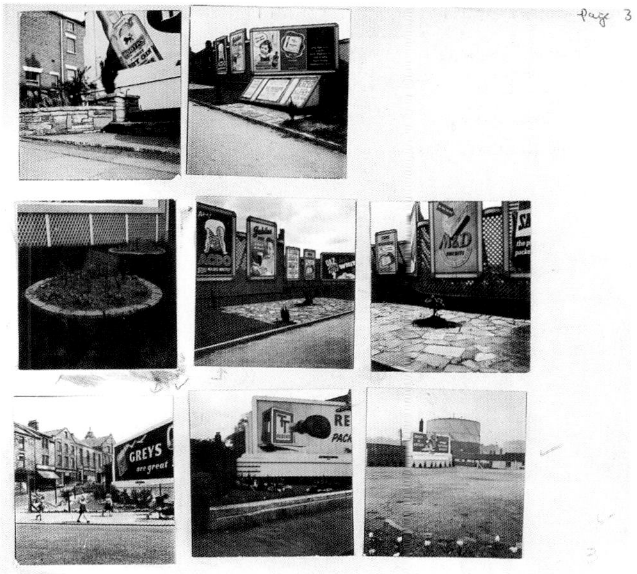

IAN NAIRN (1930–1983)

'Advertising Stations' – Pasted-up Snapshots for Use in 'Architectural Review', 1955

Gelatine silver prints

HERBERT MASON (1903–1964)

Saint Paul's, London, in the Blitz, 29 December 1940

Gelatine silver print

St Paul's Cathedral was a favourite photographic subject, not only for its architectural merit but also as a tourist souvenir and metaphor. The last category included Walter Benington's 1903 Pictorialist picture *The Church of England*, depicting the cathedral as a haven of spirituality in a benighted world. Published in the *Daily Mail* in 1940, Mason's image, the most celebrated of all, was heavily doctored. Large portions, including the blazing buildings in the foreground, were enhanced by the application of paint. Ironically, this symbol of national resolve was pirated and published in *Berliner Illustrirte Zeitung* to illustrate precisely the opposite – that London was burning.

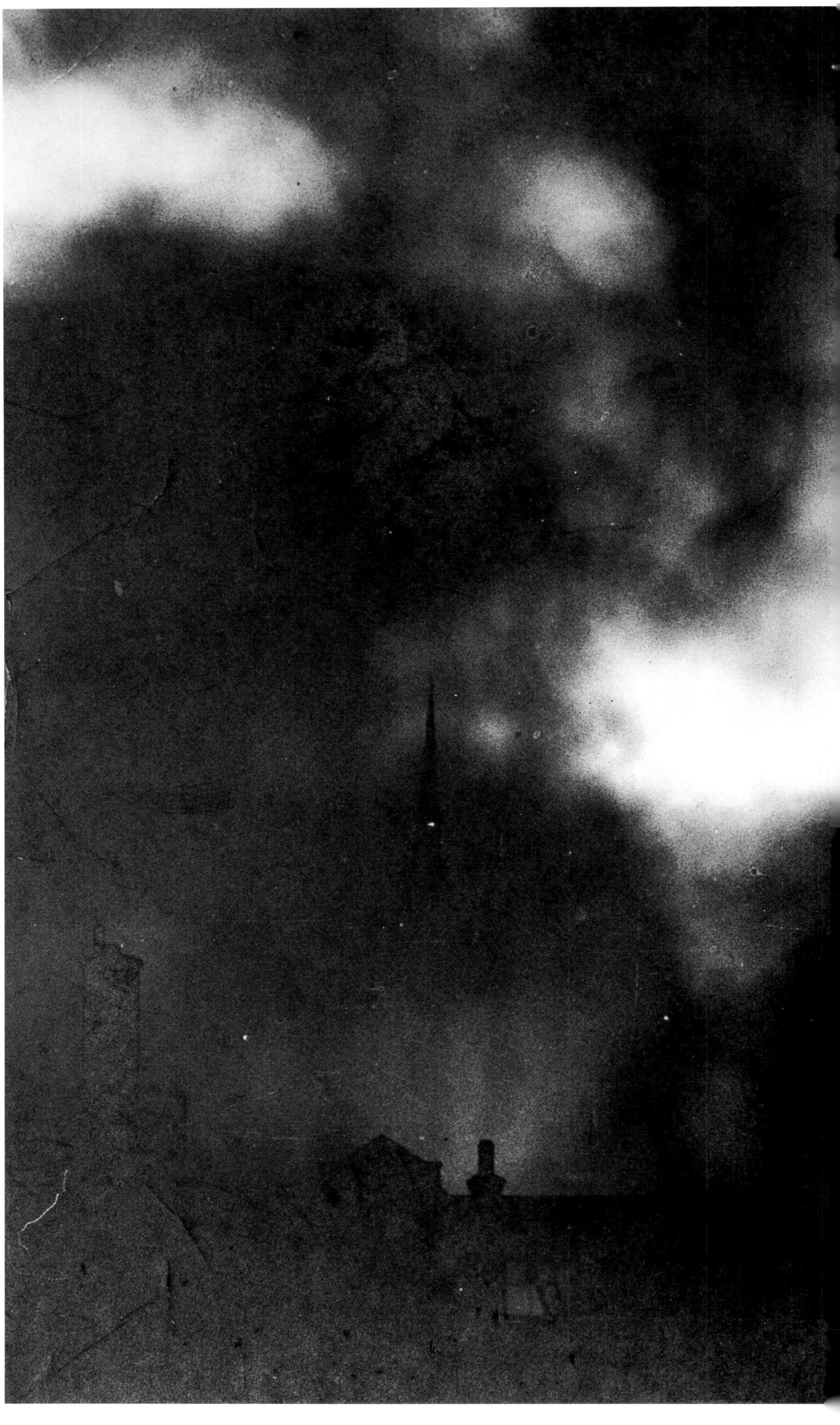

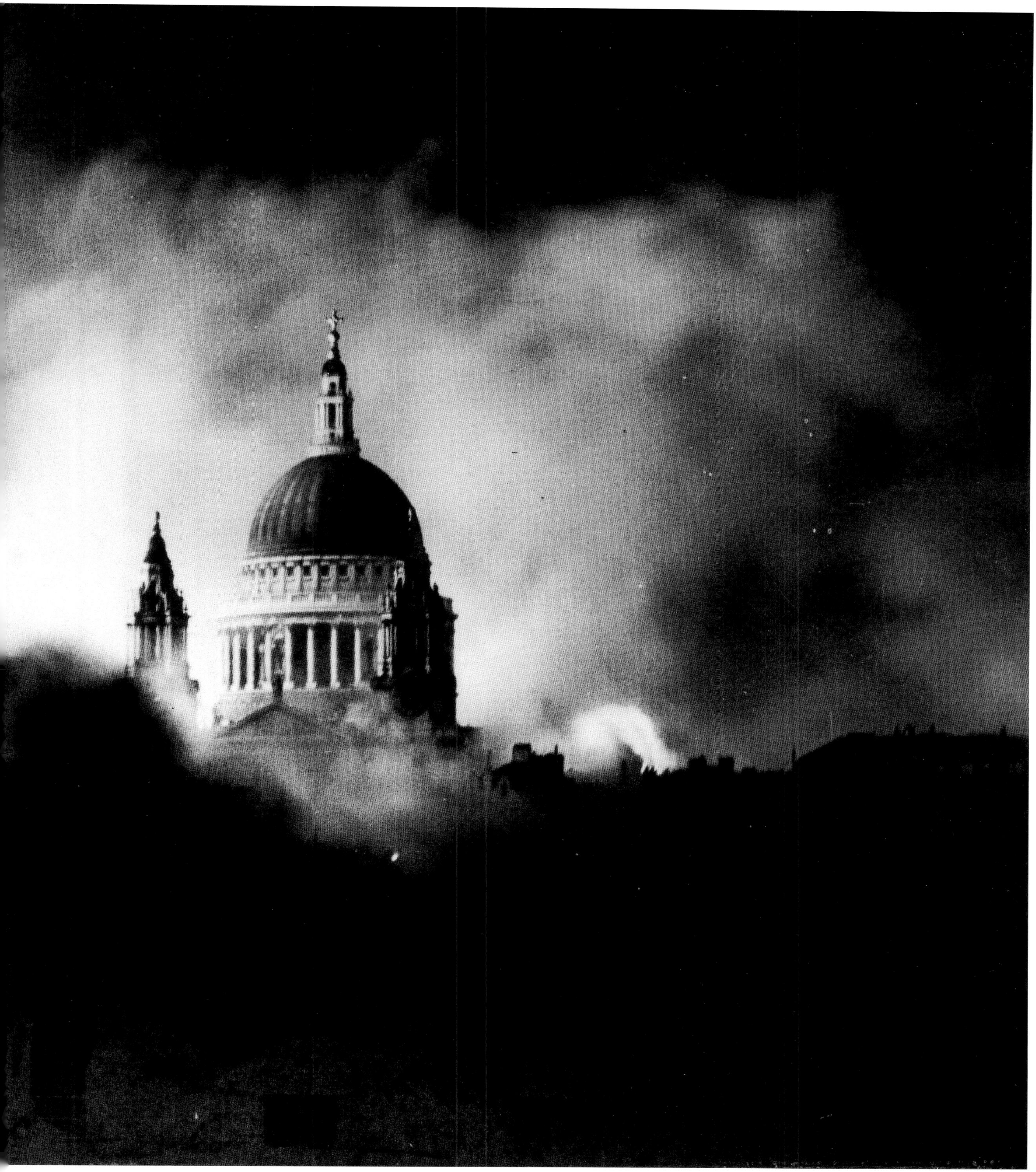

right

EDWIN SMITH (1912–1971)

Parish Church, Westhall, Suffolk, 1959

Gelatine silver print

Acclaimed by John Betjeman as "a genius at photography",[21] Smith photographed throughout Europe, his images reaching a non-professional audience through a succession of popular books. Highlighting its unassuming nature, Smith described his photography as "co-operating with the inevitable".[22] Compassionate and humanistic, it was marked above all by Smith's intuitive ability to impart a sense of place, whether of a French château, Italian Renaissance garden or English parish church. This is especially evident in his photographs revealing an empathy with local materials, crafts and traditions. These are often elegiac in tone with an understated but nevertheless intense lyricism.

opposite

YOSHIO WATANABE (1907–2000)

Main Sanctuary, Shrine at Ise, 1953

Gelatine silver print

Watanabe was among the photographers instrumental in the 1930s in introducing the New Photography into Japan. This influence is apparent in his Ise photographs, especially in their dissection of the shrine into its discrete elements, an approach accentuated by the cropping and layout adopted for their publication in *Ise: Prototype of Japanese Architecture* (1965). That a similar proclivity is evident in Ishimoto's and Futagawa's contemporaneous work additionally suggests a specifically Japanese inspiration analogous to that infusing the emergent Metabolism movement – as articulated by two of the book's contributors, Kenzo Tange and the critic Noboru Kawazoe – which viewed architecture as a living organism with individual parts that could be added or subtracted.

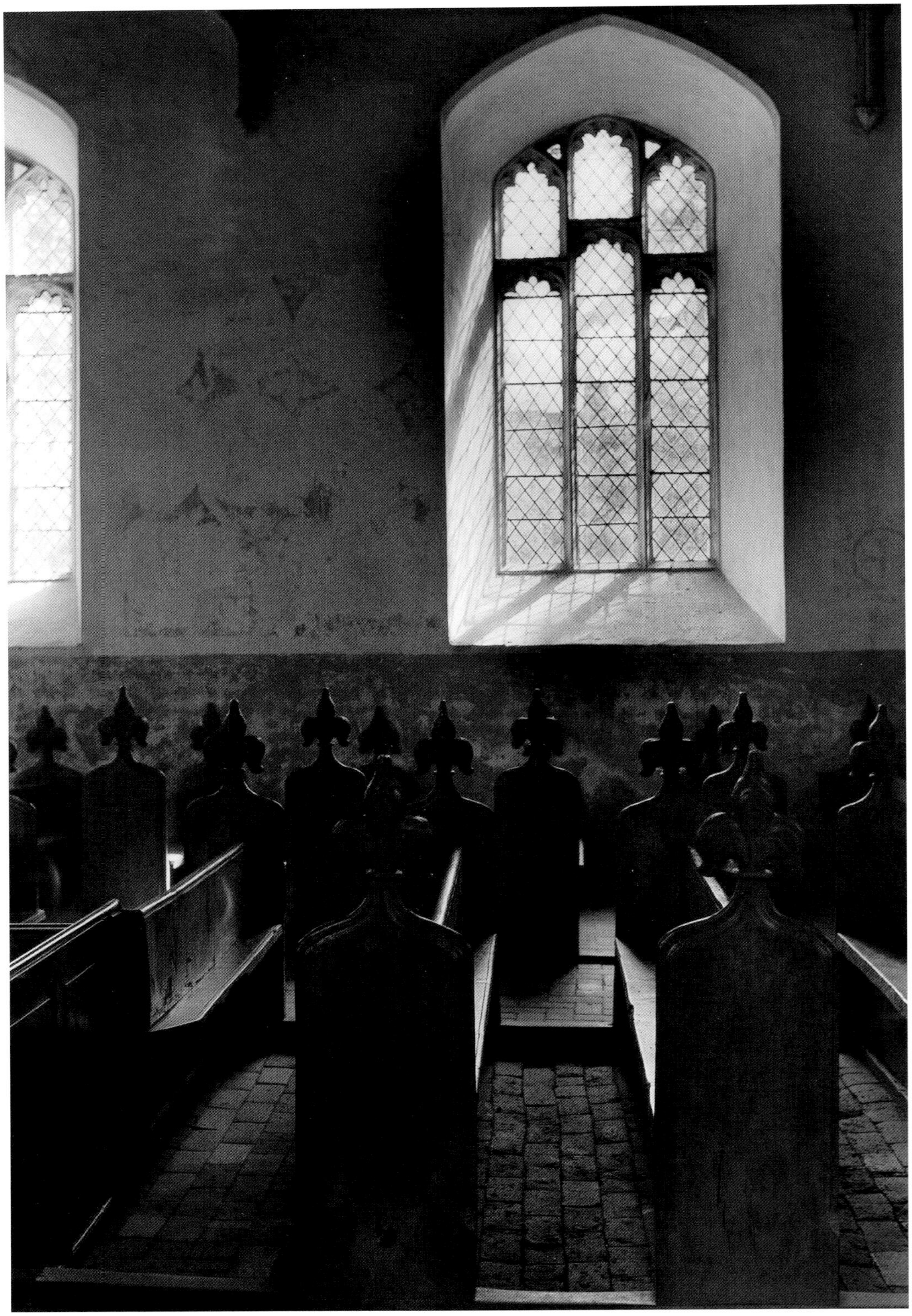

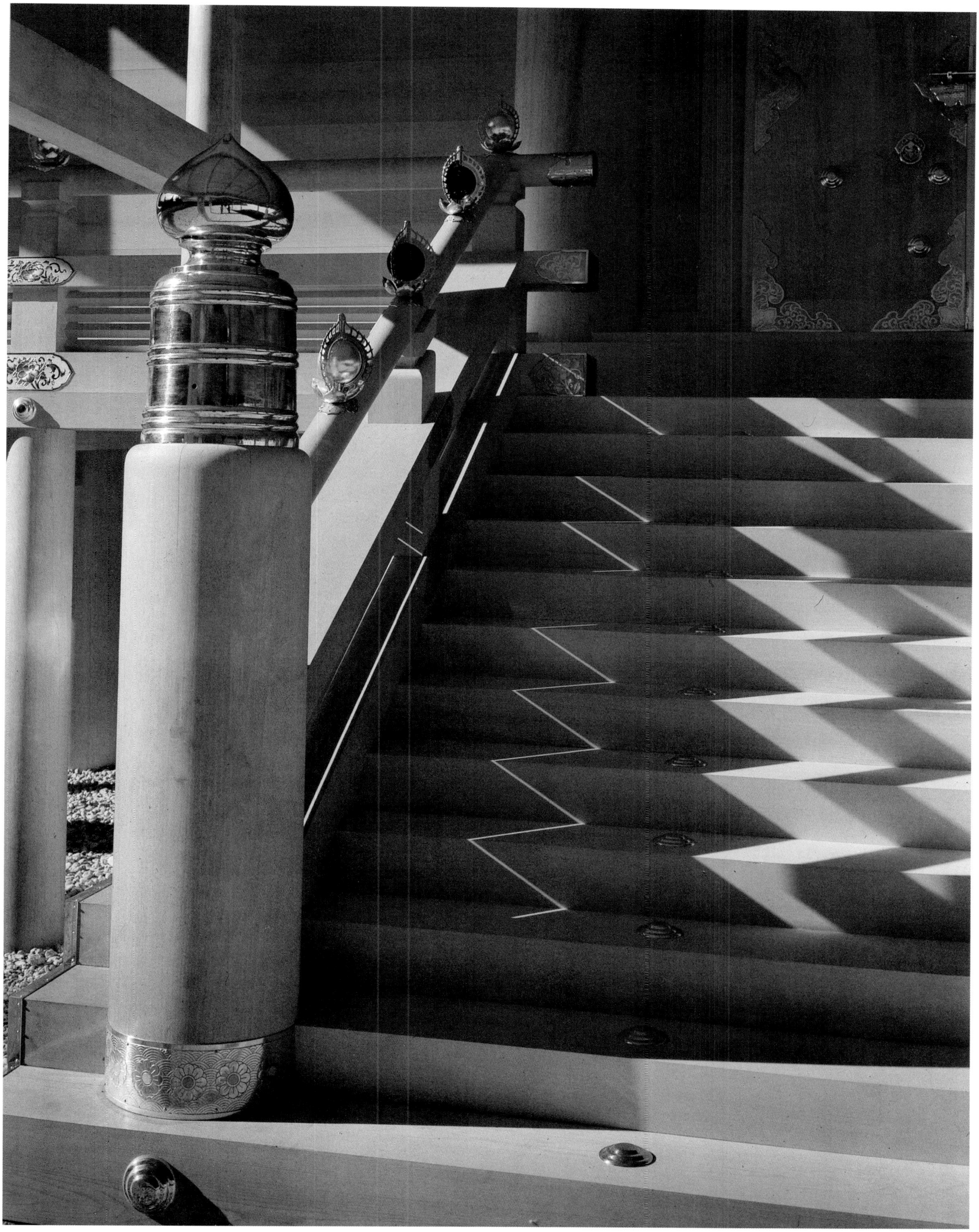

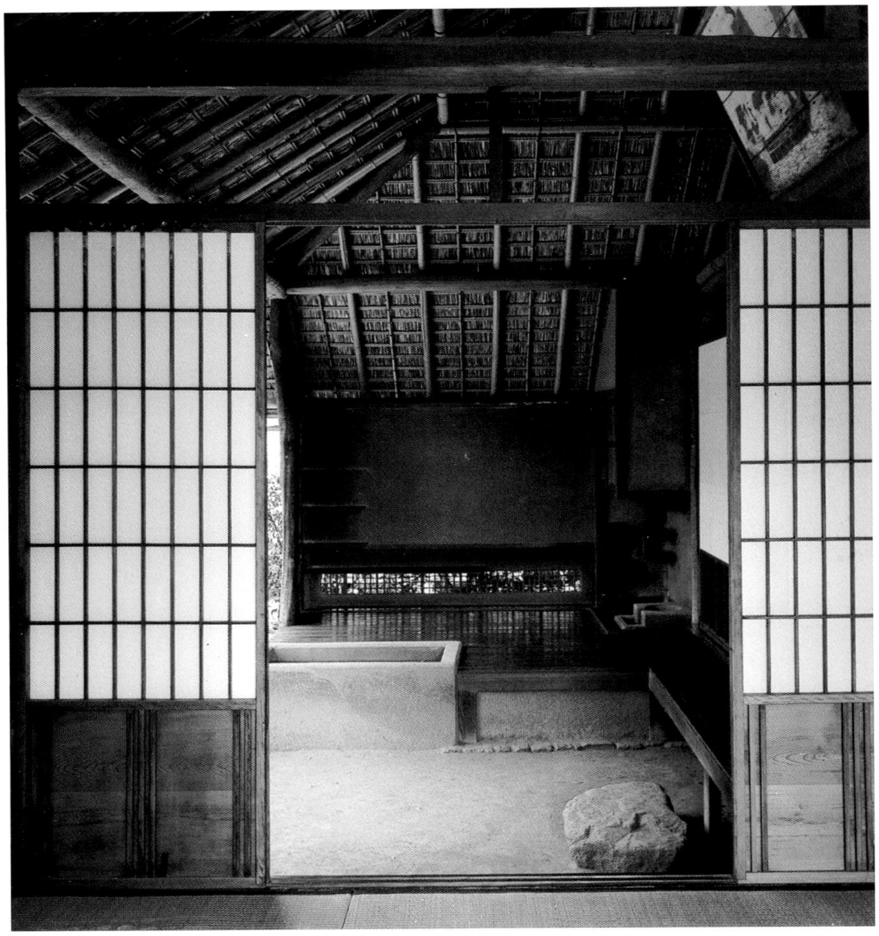

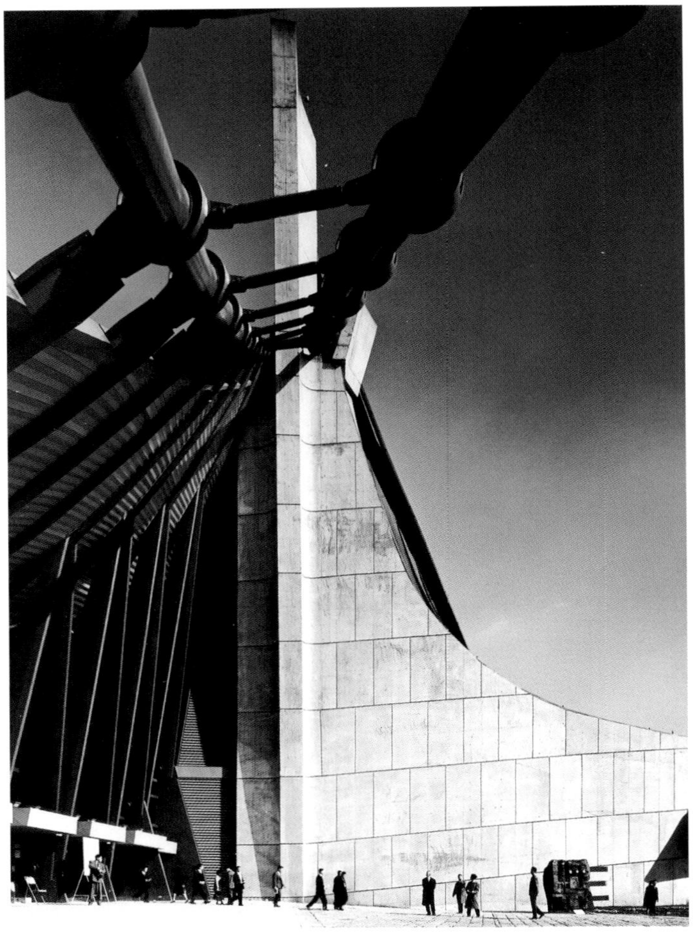

above left

YASUHIRO ISHIMOTO (born 1921)

Scullery of the Gepparo Pavilion, Katsura, Kyoto, 1960

Gelatine silver print

With an essay by Walter Gropius, design by Herbert Bayer and photographs by the Chicago Institute of Design-trained Ishimoto, *Katsura: Tradition and Creation in Japanese Architecture*, which featured this image, had strong Bauhaus as well as Japanese influences. In his foreword, Tange described the photographic strategy: "Our attention has been trained largely on details. We have looked at forms and spaces – sometimes at time as well. Our angle of vision has been narrow, because we are interested in the small segments which make up the whole and because our medium, the photograph, is most effective when focused on small areas."[23]

above right

OSAMU MURAI (born 1928)

National Gymnasia, Tokyo, 1964

Gelatine silver print

Architect: Kenzo Tange

With the Tokyo Olympics of 1964, the Osaka Expo of 1970 and the exciting, new space-age forms generated by its Metabolist architects, Japanese architecture was propelled on to the world stage. This process was abetted by photographers such as Murai, one of Japan's most outstanding post-war lensmen, whose image of Tange's structure conveys both its monumentality (note the dwarfed figures) and its dynamic energy.

opposite

YUKIO FUTAGAWA (born 1932)

Fushin-an Teahouse, Omotesenke School of Tea, Kyoto, c. 1967

Gelatine silver print

Futagawa's career has been one of the most remarkable architectural and publishing phenomena of the last thirty years. His *Global Architecture* series, featuring mostly twentieth-century architectural classics in an easily digestible format of photographs, minimal text and a few drawings, has proved immensely popular, especially with students. Earlier in his career, however, his photography concentrated largely on historical architecture, demonstrating a typically Japanese sensitivity to different textures and materials and to architecture's relationship with nature. According to the sculptor Isamu Noguchi, the latter was presented with an "extremely three dimensional quality ... that focuses attention upon the sculptural aspect of this ... relationship".[24]

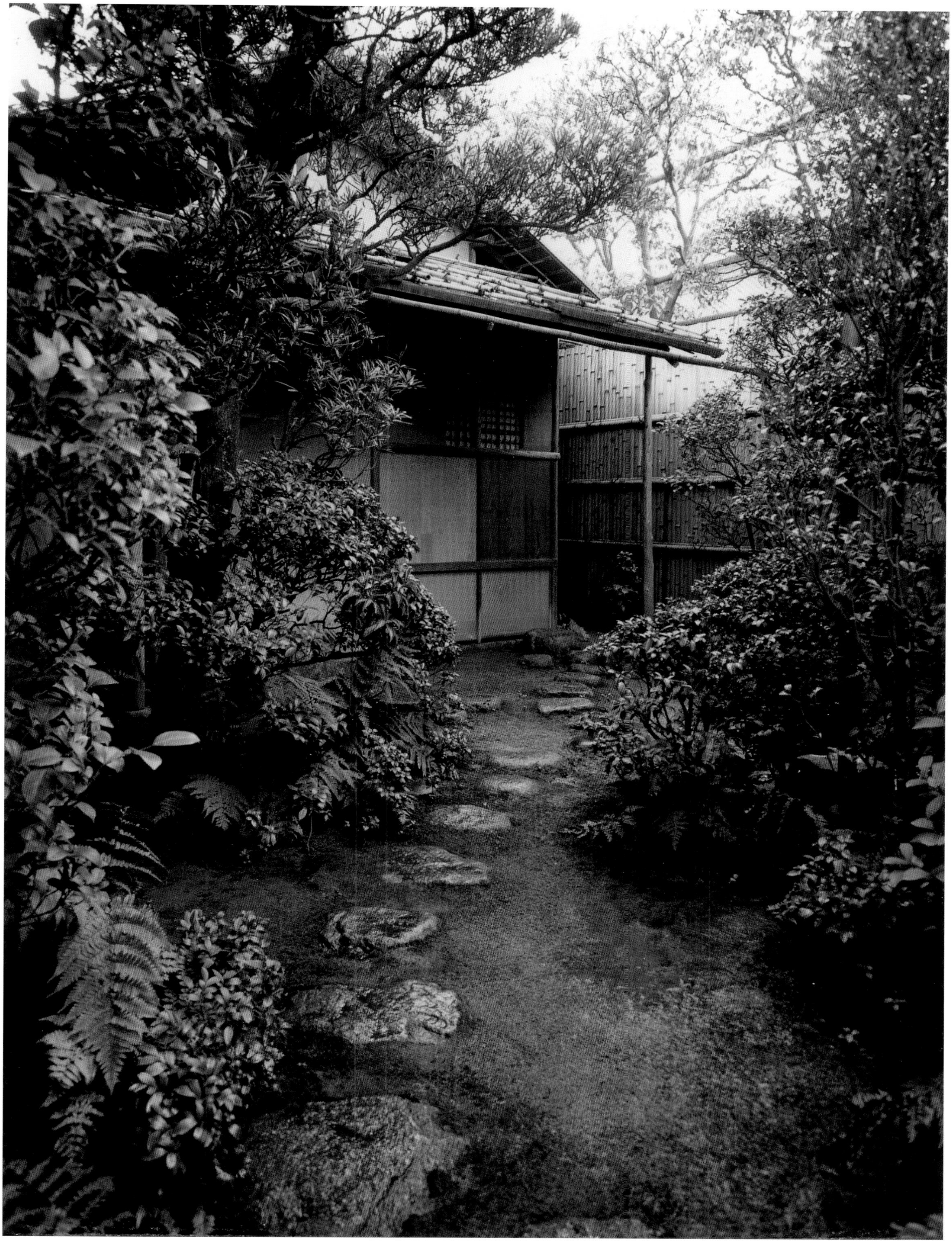

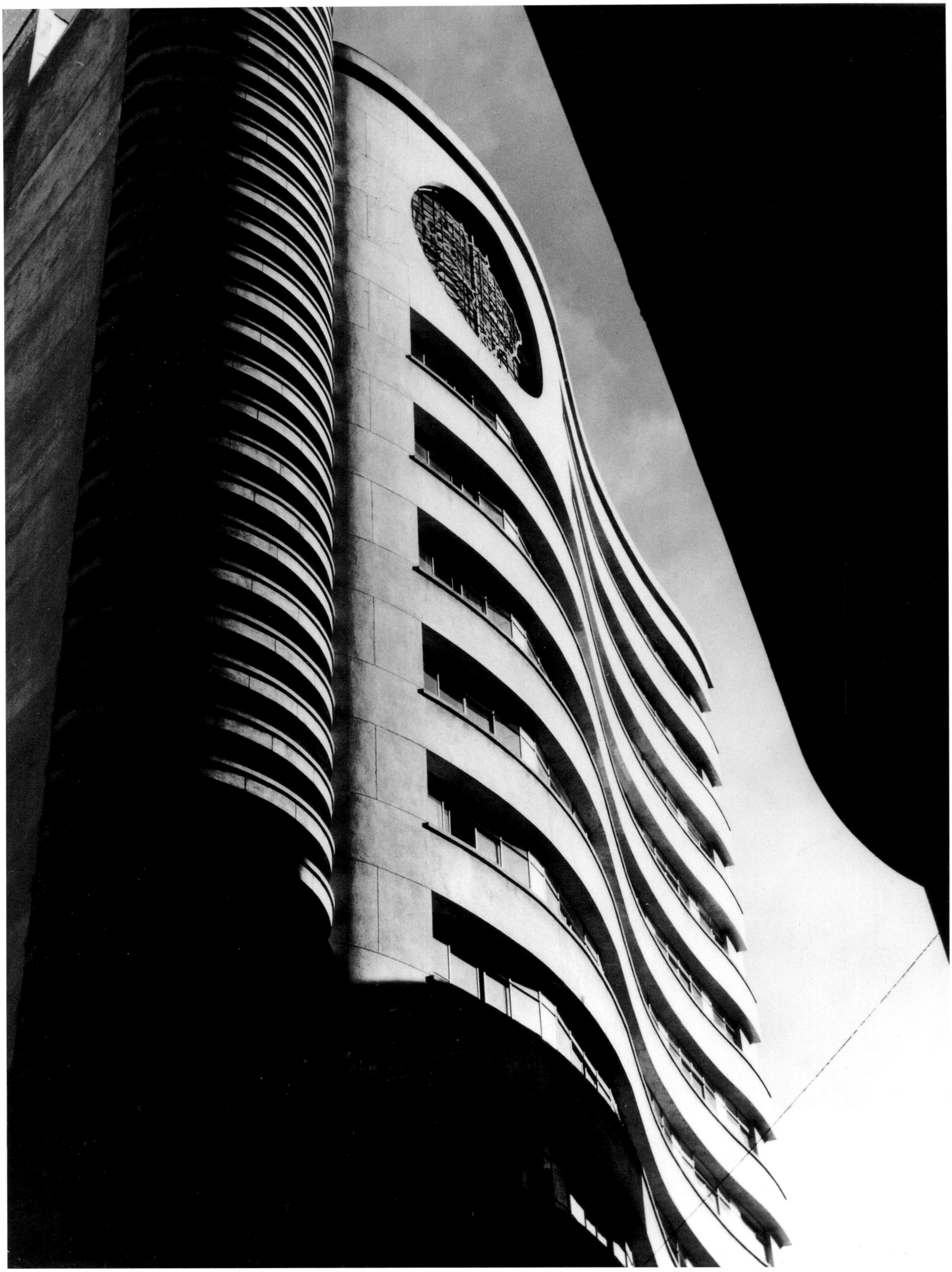

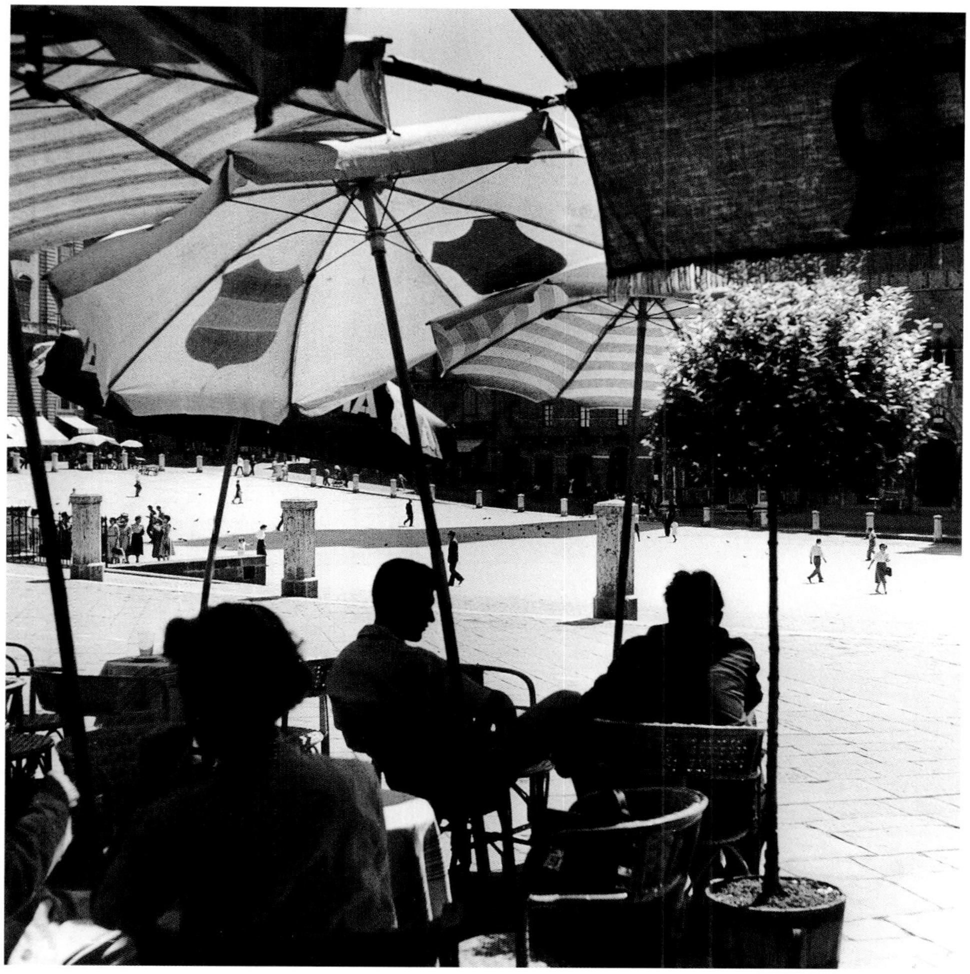

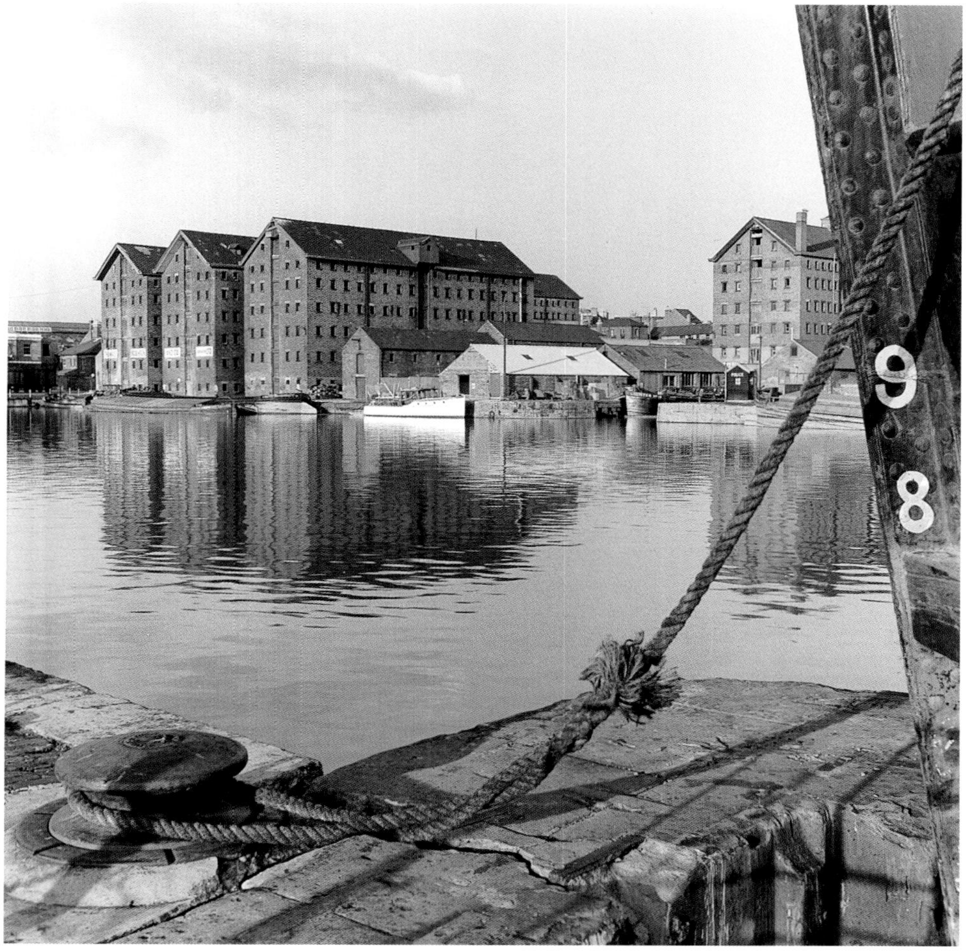

opposite

GEORGE E. KIDDER SMITH (1913–1997)

Office Building, São Paulo, 1942

Gelatine silver print

Architect: Ramos de Azevedo

In a manner reminiscent of F.R. Yerbury, Smith travelled widely, photographing both historical and contemporary architecture over a fifty-year period from the late 1930s. As shown by this photograph from *Brazil Builds* (1943), the hallmark of Smith's photography was his keen compositional sense, stressed in his injunction to fellow photographers to "seek a picture *in* the subject, not *of* it. If one seeks a good composition, the building generally will take care of itself."[25]

top left

GEORGE E. KIDDER SMITH (1913–1997)

Piazza del Campo, Siena, *c.* 1954

Gelatine silver print

An architect as well as a photographer and an author, Smith was acutely conscious of contemporary architectural issues. His *Italy Builds*, in which this photograph appeared, suggested that, by studying Italy's squares, "we can make finer suburban shopping centres, more agreeable urban cores, and develop a keener understanding of the psychological and physical factors which go into making the space solutions we call architecture and town planning".[26] The book's monochrome images were taken on smaller cameras than those used by most professionals – a 9 x 12 cm (3½ x 4½ in.) Zeiss Juwel, or in crowded spaces an inconspicuous, more 'candid', Rolleiflex.

bottom left

ERIC DE MARÉ (1910–2002)

Gloucester Docks, 1956

Gelatine silver print

De Maré's involvement with the 'functional tradition' both predated and succeeded his 1958 book encompassing studies of canals, bridges and, finally, seaside architecture. Although he used smaller formats, de Maré's photographs were not casual but carefully composed. "A picture will not tell its story half so effectively", he wrote, "if it is not held together by a firm, simple, structural composition which makes a whole."[27] In this image from *The Functional Tradition* he has employed one of his favourite devices, including in the foreground objects close to the camera to enhance the picture's depth.

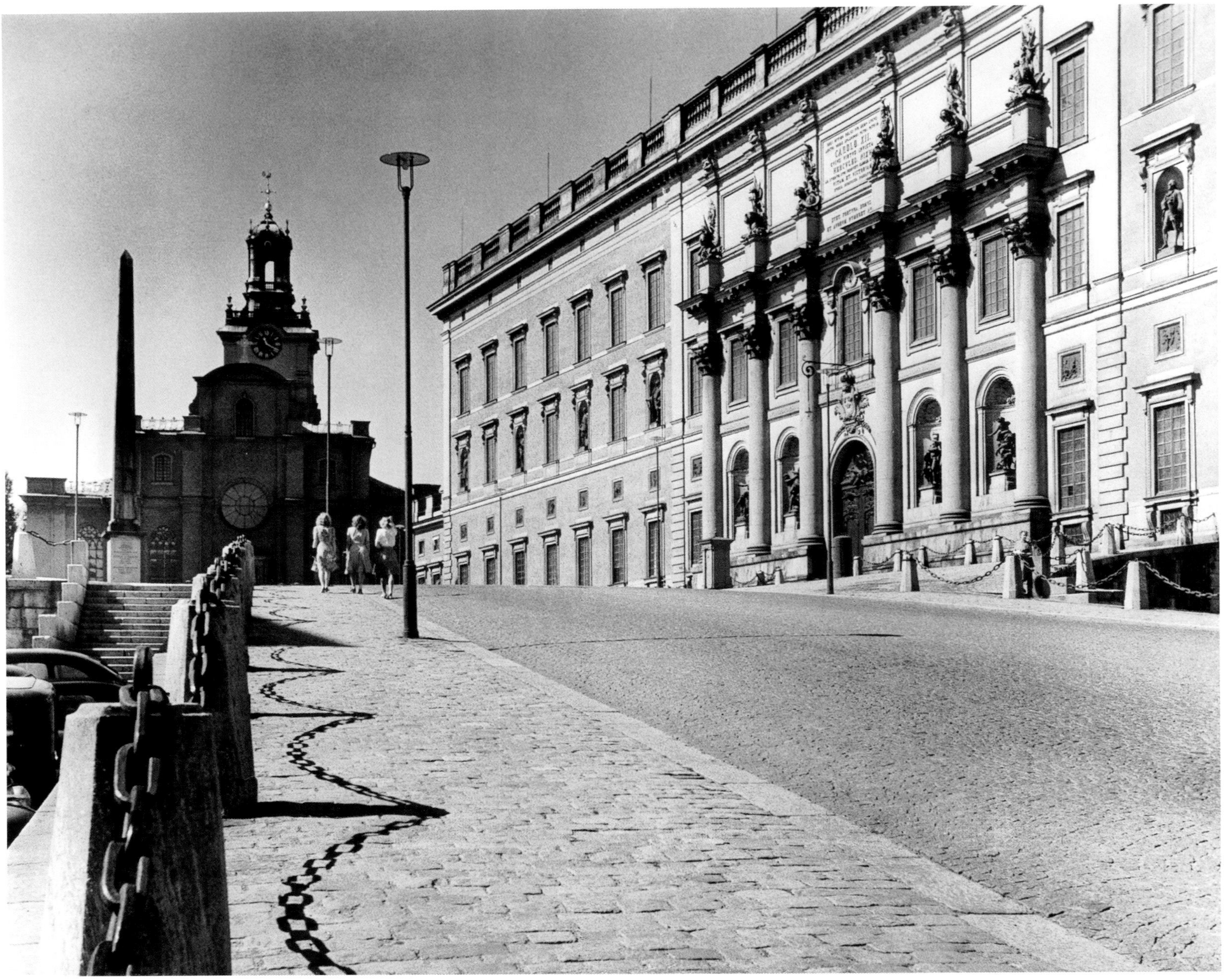

opposite

ERIC DE MARÉ (1910–2002)

Royal Palace with the Storkyrkan, the Great Church, Stockholm, 1952

Gelatine silver print

Architects: Nicodemus Tessin the Younger/C.W. Carlberg

This image illustrates both de Maré's enthusiasm for the architecture, old and new, of his native Sweden and his concern to bring visual coherence to the norm of urban clutter by highlighting historic examples of sensitive civic design. The low viewpoint emphasizes the change in street level and vista, while the shadows accentuate the rhythms of the street furniture. The photograph, made relatively early in de Maré's career, was taken with a twin-lens Rolleicord (a cheaper version of the Rolleiflex), which, being held at waist level, tended to give undue stress to what de Maré termed "floorscape".

top right

SUNE SUNDAHL (born 1921)

Office Building for Svenska Dagbladet, Stockholm, 1962

Gelatine silver print

Architect: Tengboms Arkitektkontor

Wherever possible, Sundahl, together with Lennart Olson, the key documenter of Swedish post-war architecture, attempted to humanize his pictures. He recalled, "Architects of the older generation wanted clean, precise pictures. Sometimes they went and took away bicycles in front of a building and posted people to make sure that no one walked through the doors and disturbed the picture. I reacted against these demands to remove all signs of life."[28]

bottom right

HEIKKI HAVAS (born 1926)

Kärjensiuu Terrace House, Helsinki, 1955

Gelatine silver print

Architect: Viljo Revell

Particularly in Scandinavia and Finland during the post-war years, the prevalent graphic severity of architectural photography was leavened by a renaissance of national romanticism and by the frequent inclusion of children, the implication of the latter being that architects were building a better tomorrow for the next generation. Although architectural photography as a distinctive genre was scarcely recognized in Finnish photographic circles in the 1950s, the needs of the architectural profession and journals such as *Arkkitehti* were serviced by numerous highly competent photographers, including Otso Pietinen, Eino Mäkinen, a frequent collaborator with Alvar Aalto, and the architect-photographer Heikki Havas.

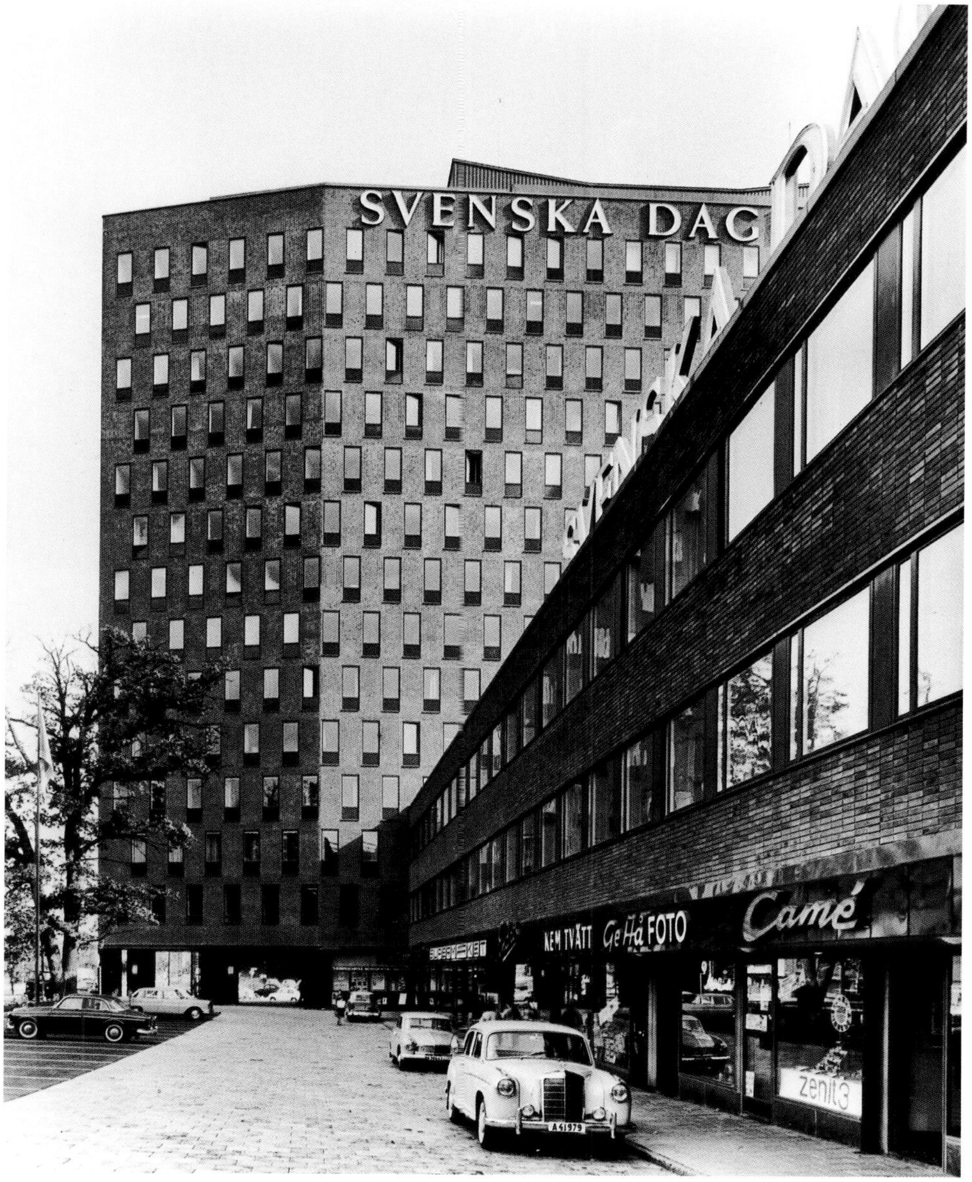

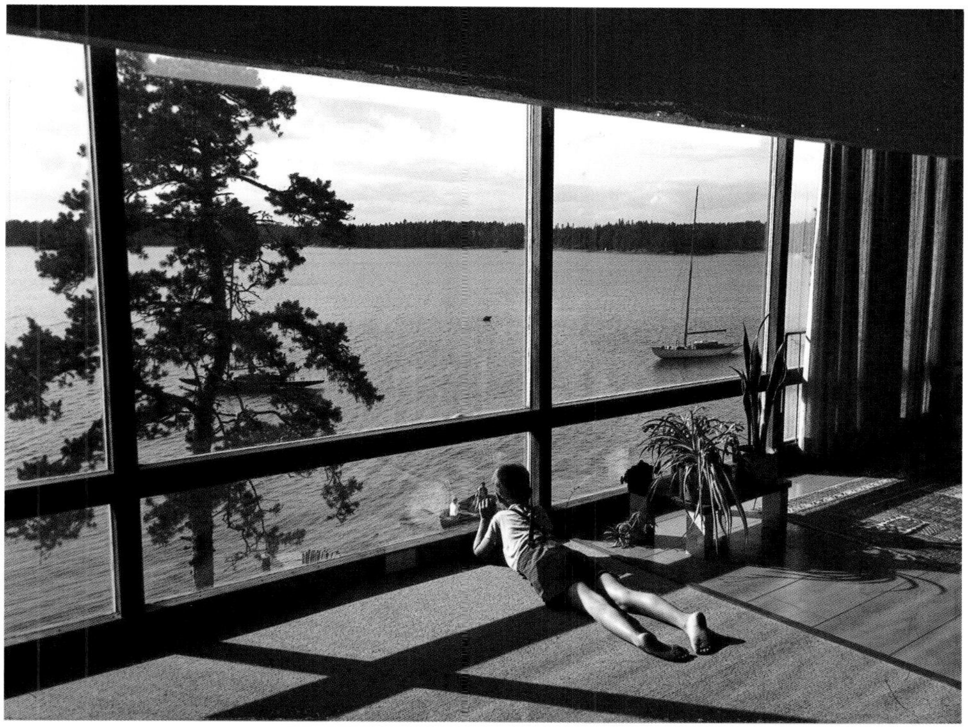

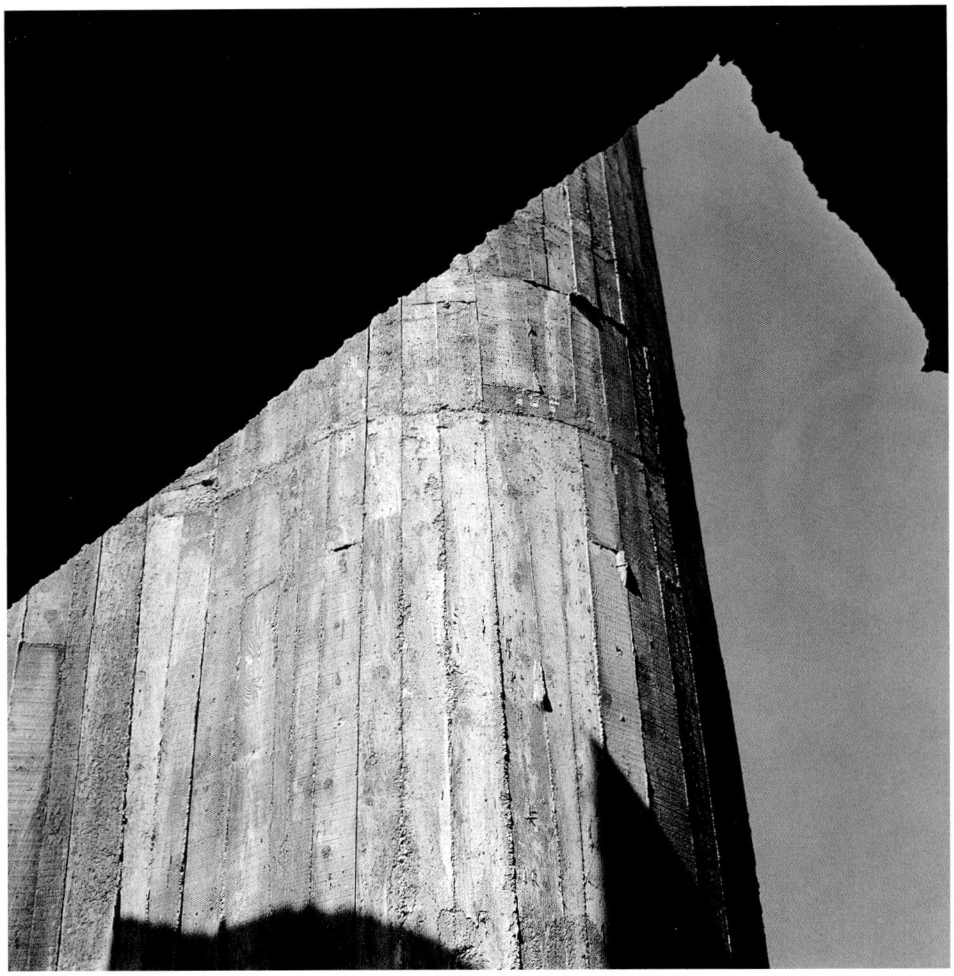

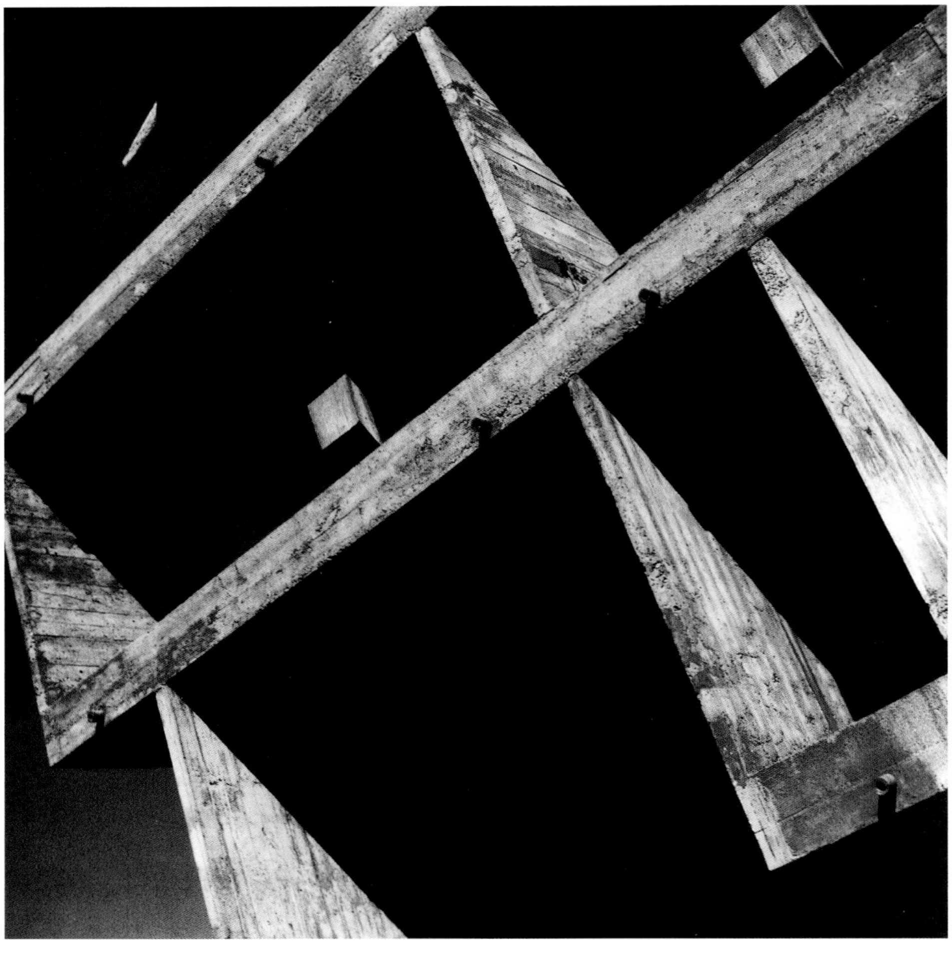

top left

LUCIEN HERVÉ (born 1910)

Unité d'Habitation, Marseilles, 1949

Gelatine silver print

Architect: Le Corbusier

Hervé acknowledged that, for both himself and Le Corbusier, "it is not the theme that is important, it is not the subject, but essentially the plastic expression".[29] His pictures are not, therefore, literal transcriptions of buildings or places but abstract compositions forged out of his obsession with closely observed details. This approach failed to find favour with the commissioning magazine of the Marseilles pictures, *Plaisir de France*, but has been adopted by other photographers of architecture, most notably Judith Turner in her images of the work of the New York Five and, more recently, Hélène Binet.

bottom left

LUCIEN HERVÉ (born 1910)

Villa Shodan, Ahmedabad, 1955

Gelatine silver print

Architect: Le Corbusier

Hervé's photographs taken at Ahmedabad in India are among his finest. As this image forcibly demonstrates, his photography is one of contrasts – light versus dark; rough versus smooth; dynamic versus static; void versus corporeality – that together enable him to achieve an astonishing illusion of three-dimensionality. The whites, and particularly the blacks, were often intensified in printing, reflecting Hervé's admiration for the tenebrous qualities of Rembrandt's paintings. "I look at everything that I see", Hervé declared, "with enormous intensity and *dramatize* the picture."[30]

opposite

AAGE STRÜWING

City Hall, Rødovre, Denmark, 1956

Gelatine silver print

Architect: Arne Jacobsen

Strüwing was probably Denmark's pre-eminent twentieth-century architectural photographer. At Rødovre his pared-down photographic style was well attuned to the rigorous asceticism of Jacobsen's city hall, making it appear both externally and internally as a piece of abstract sculpture.

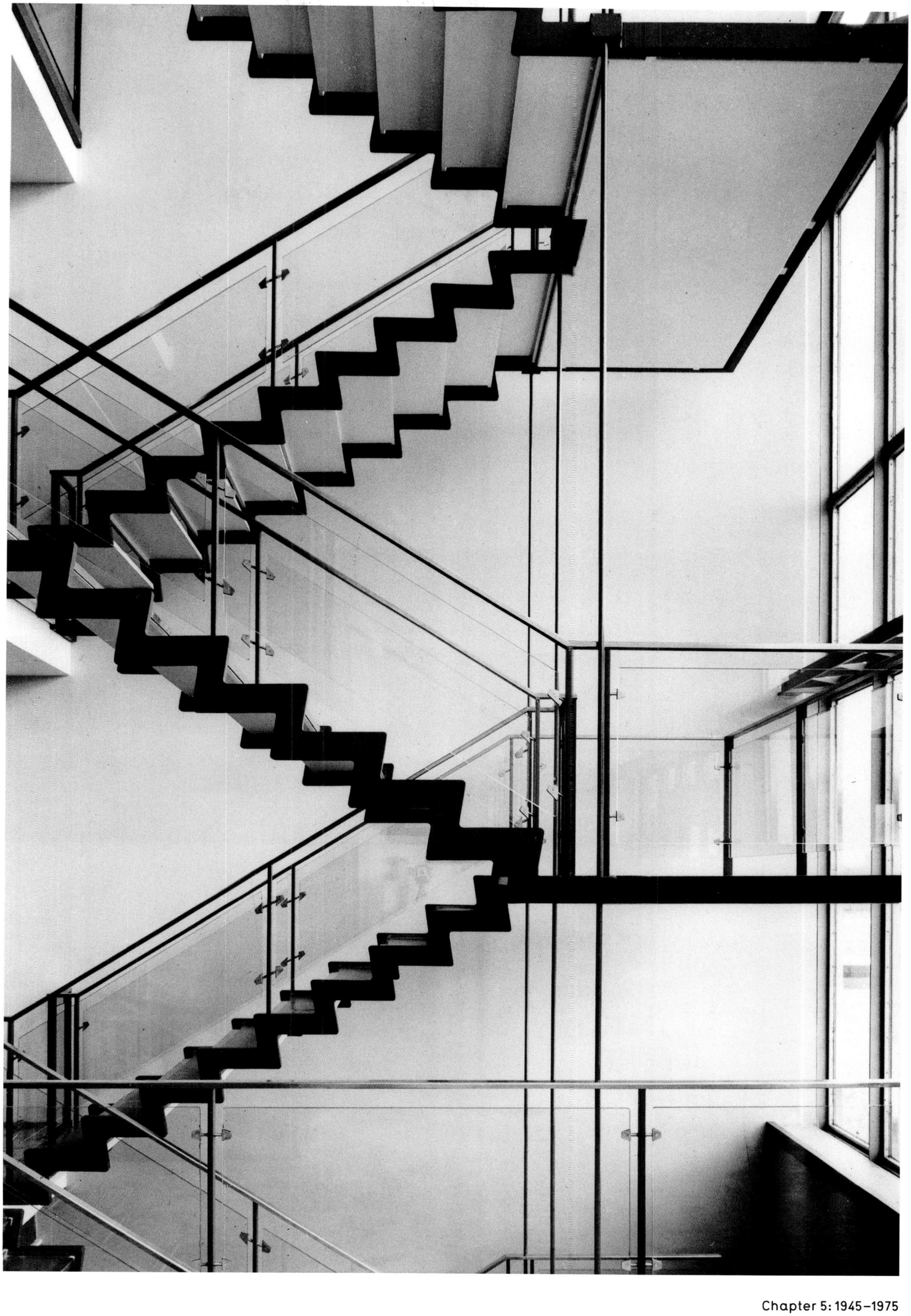

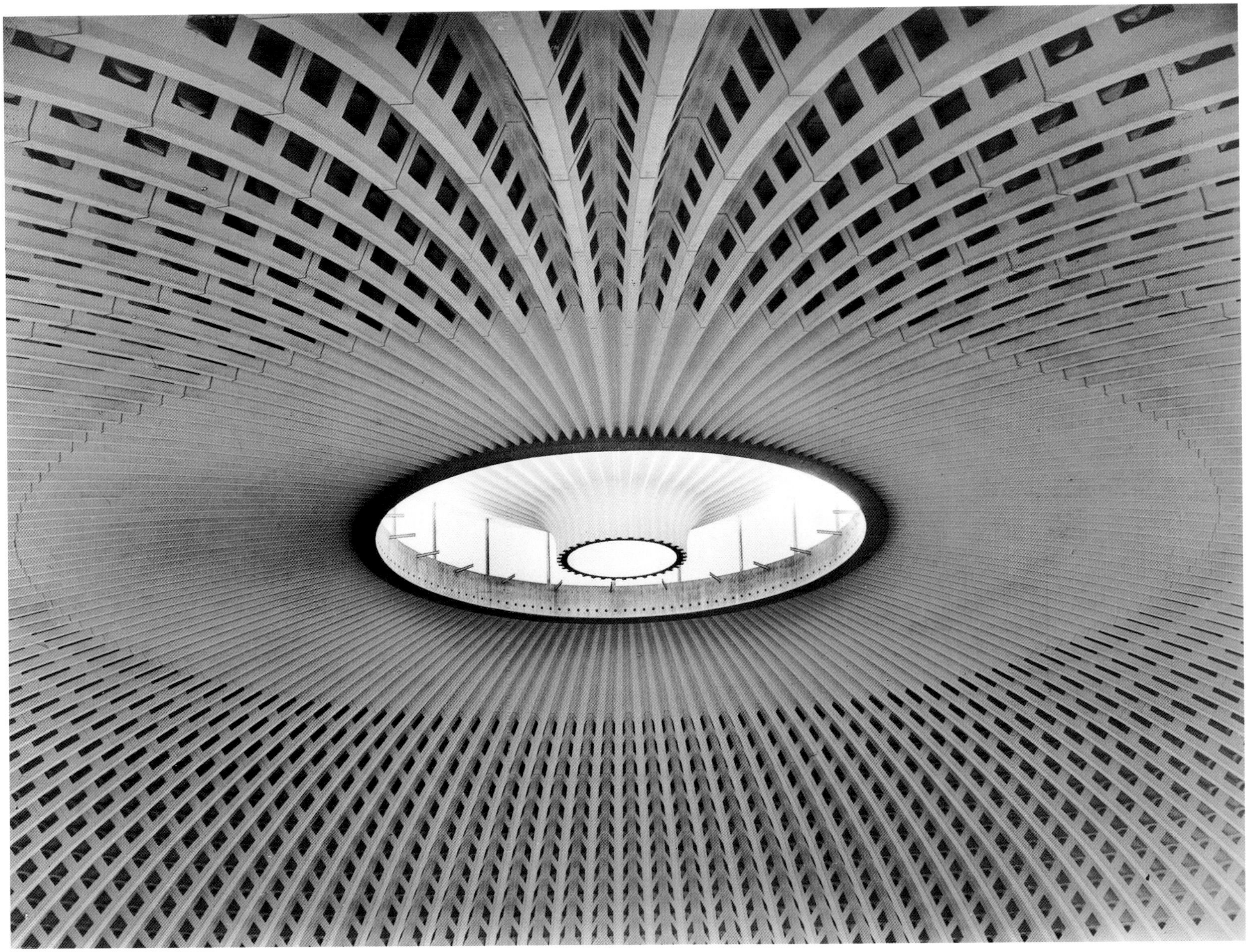

opposite

OSCAR SAVIO

Palazzo dello Sport, Rome, 1960

Gelatine silver print

Architect: Pier Luigi Nervi

No single architectural photographer established a dominant position in post-war Italy, although a number of fine photographers were active. These included the Milanese Giorgio Casali, who photographed contemporary buildings for *Domus*, and Oscar Savio, a Roman photographer of art and architecture, principally of a historic nature. His photographs of the Palazzo dello Sport and its dramatic domed ribbed vault are in a long line of arresting images of Nervi's work. Besides those of Borsotti, one thinks, for example, of Foto Vasari's views of the aircraft hangars at Orbetello and Orvieto (1939–41) and Lucien Hervé's of the UNESCO Building, Paris (1953–56).

top right

FRANCESC CATALÀ-ROCA (1922–1998)

Thau School, Carretera d'Esplugues, Barcelona, 1975

Gelatine silver print

Architects: Martorell Bohigas Mackay

At his peak during the 1950s and 1960s, Català-Roca, who also worked in other genres, was for three generations one of Spain's leading photographers of architecture. After his introduction to the documentation of modern Catalan architecture by Antoni de Moragas, who admired the photographs Català-Roca had taken of Gaudí's Sagrada Familia, Català-Roca included among his clients José Antonio Coderch (himself a fine photographer), Josep Lluís Sert and Martorell Bohigas Mackay. Català-Roca maintained that he belonged to an achromatic generation who saw only in black and white, although he occasionally took colour pictures.

bottom right

JAN VERSNEL (born 1924)

Model House for Goed Wonen, 1960

Gelatine silver print

Designer: Kho Liang Ie

Together with such photographers as J.A. Vrijhof and Hans Sibbelee, as well as survivors from the pre-war era such as d'Oliveira and Spies, Versnel was one of the leading chroniclers of post-war Dutch architecture. Having served an apprenticeship with the photographer Nico Jesse, who introduced him to Gerrit and Jan Rietveld, Versnel established his own business in 1947 and continued working until the 1990s, almost exclusively for Modernist architects. His heyday, however, was during the 1950s and 1960s, when his diligently crafted and adroitly lit photographs perfectly captured the optimism, drive and social commitment of the architecture of reconstruction.

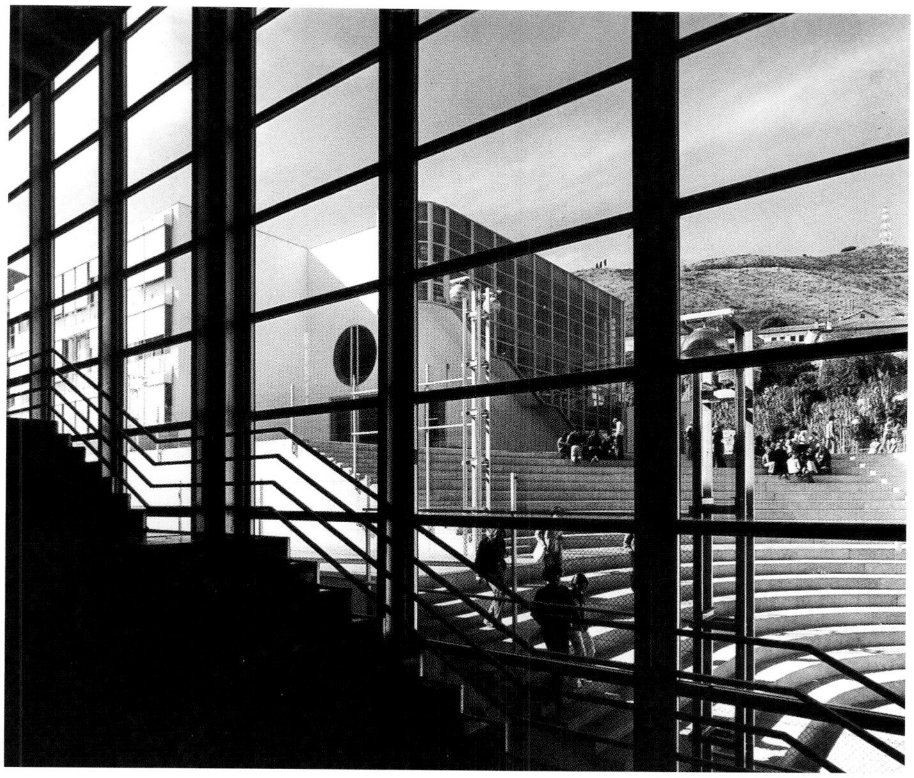

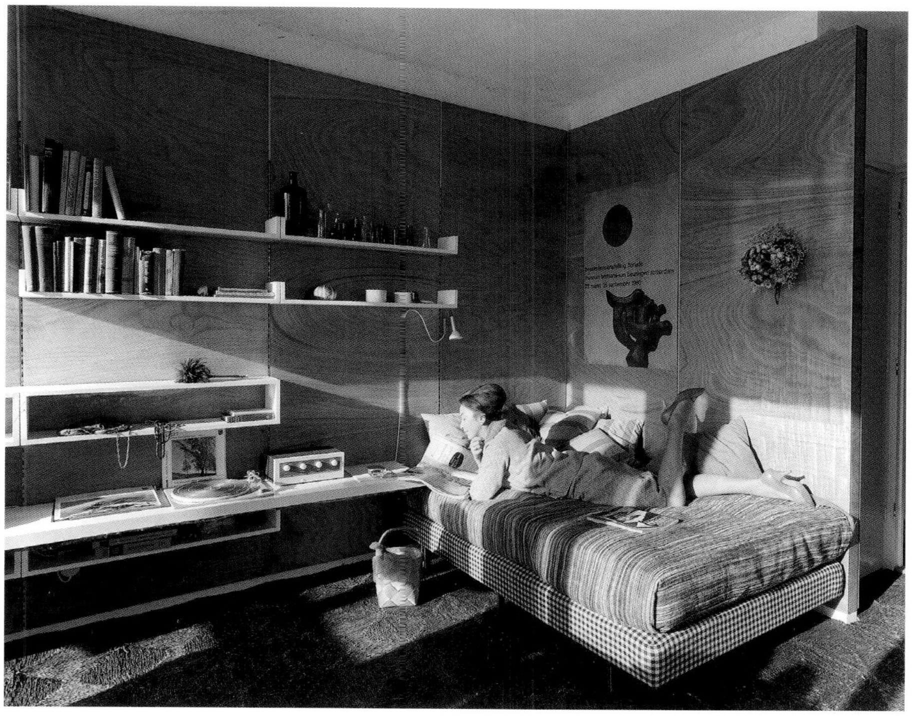

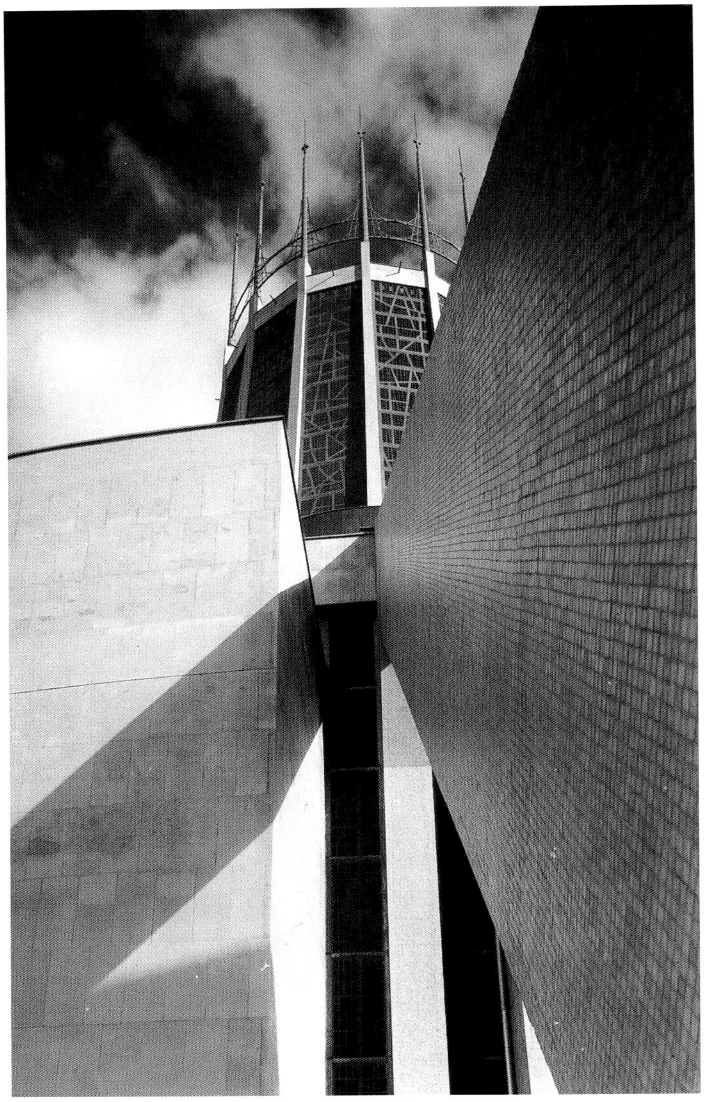

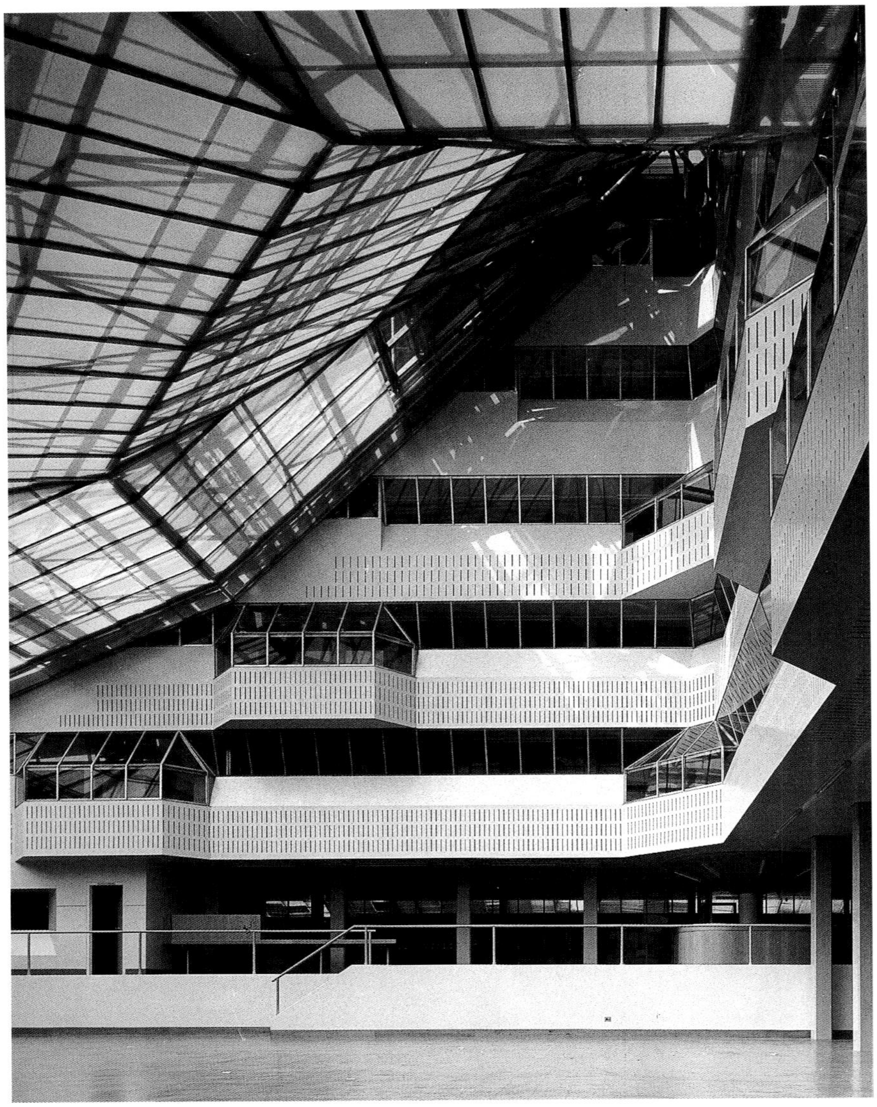

above left

HENK SNOEK (1915–1980)

Cathedral of Christ the King, Liverpool, 1967

Gelatine silver print

Architects: Frederick Gibberd & Partners

Snoek was one of Britain's leading architectural photographers of the 1960s and 1970s. Born in The Netherlands, he studied photography, typography and commercial design at The Hague School of Art, the Bauhaus principles of which, together with his fondness for the abstract compositions of his fellow countryman Mondrian, can be readily discerned in his work. His photographs, well-suited to the New Brutalism of the period, are characterized by their strong sense of drama, simple forceful lines and high contrasts – effects he often enhanced by using a red filter to counteract the drabness of the British weather.

above right

RICHARD EINZIG (1932–1980)

History Faculty Building, Cambridge University, 1968

Gelatine silver print

Architect: James Stirling

Einzig began photographing while still studying architecture in the late 1950s, but his earliest professional commissions came later and included a house by Peter Aldington and Stirling & Gowan's Engineering Building at Leicester University, photographed in 1964. Among his clients were many of the younger cutting-edge architects of the day, such as Norman Foster and Richard Rogers. Like Stoller, Einzig strove to represent the essence of the building as the architect first conceived it, without recourse to photographic gimmickry. "I am an architect's photographer, not a photographer's photographer", he declared.[31] This frequently resulted in head-on elevational images of great rigour.

opposite

HENK SNOEK (1915–1980)

University of Sussex, Brighton, 1962

Gelatine silver print

Architect: Sir Basil Spence

In its initial stages Snoek's career owed much to the patronage of Basil Spence, for whom he photographed a succession of projects, above all Coventry Cathedral. Forty-six of his photographs of the cathedral were published with commentaries by Spence in *Out of the Ashes: A Progress through Coventry Cathedral* (1963). Here he has effectively depicted the forms of Spence's Sussex University – inspired by Le Corbusier's houses for André Jaoul – in a typical, graphically taut composition. Snoek's optimistic vision of contemporary architecture should be contrasted with Tony Ray-Jones's dystopian revelations of a few years later.

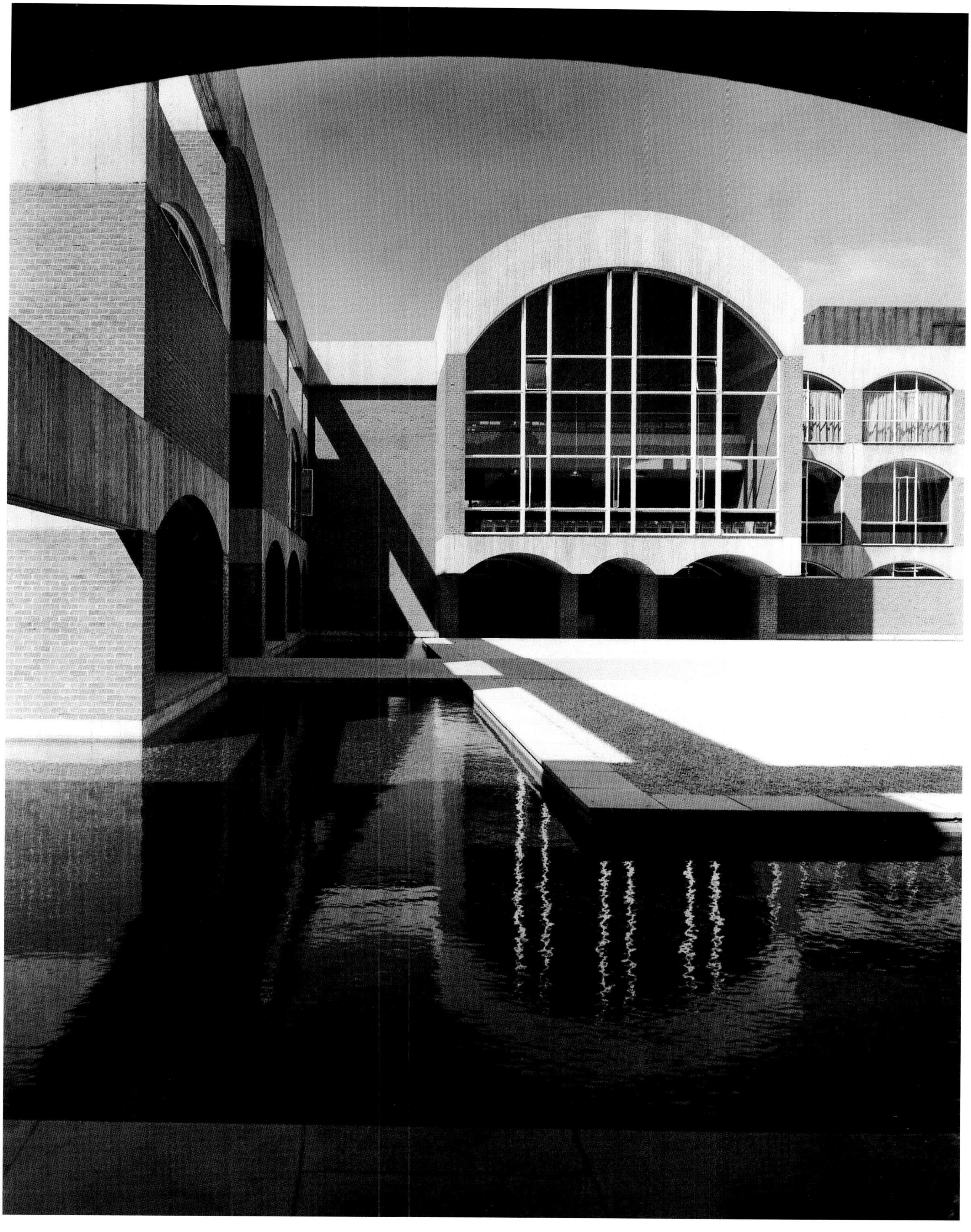

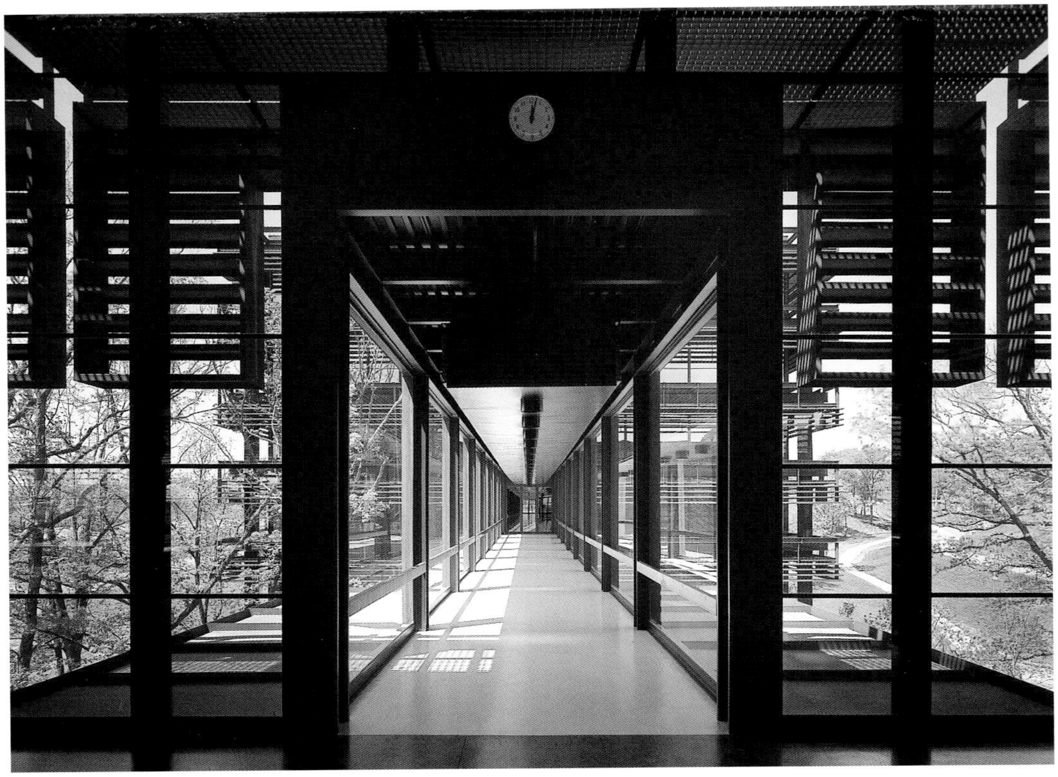

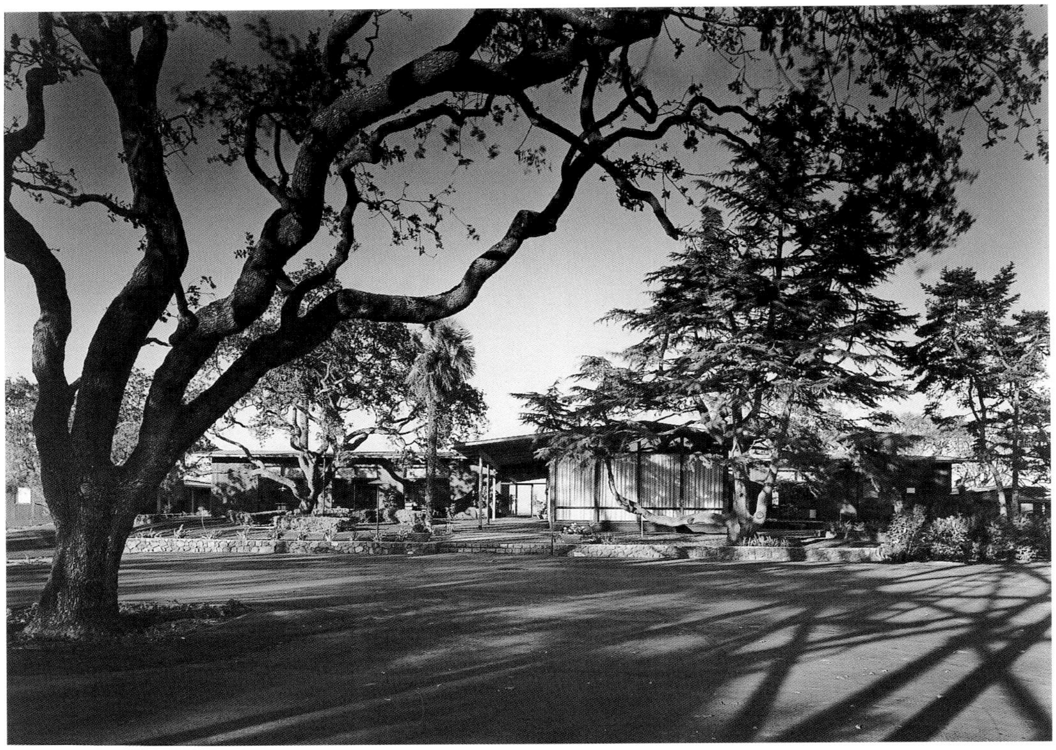

top left

EZRA STOLLER (born 1915)

John Deere and Company Administration Center, Moline, Illinois, 1963

Gelatine silver print

Architect: Eero Saarinen

Stoller's love of architecture was kindled during his studies at New York University, from where he graduated with a degree in industrial design in 1938. His major photographic influences were Atget; Strand, with whom he briefly worked; and Dell & Wainwright, whose *Architectural Review* photographs he studied closely. Some of his best photographs were taken for Saarinen. This example contains the classic ingredients of a Stoller picture: an elevational viewpoint; a strongly symmetrical composition; the use of one-point perspective to increase dramatically the sense of depth; and sharp focus over the entire image area.

bottom left

MORLEY BAER (1916–1995)

Center for Advanced Study in the Behavioral Sciences, Palo Alto, California, 1955

Gelatine silver print

Architects: Wurster Bernardi & Emmons

Inspired by the example of Edward Weston and his stress on "simplicity, simplicity, simplicity", Baer with his 8 x 10 inch (20.3 x 25.4 cm) large-view camera and smaller 2¼ inch (5.7 cm) Hasselblad produced pictures of the utmost professionalism of largely modern architecture in California and to a lesser extent elsewhere. A characteristic of Baer's photography was his frequent use of lenses of short focal length, which he felt gave "more drawing power to dominant lines ... especially when they run to or from the camera".[32] This can be seen here particularly in the shadows, which enliven an otherwise dull foreground.

opposite

EZRA STOLLER (born 1915)

S.C. Johnson Administration Building and Research Tower, Racine, Wisconsin, 1944

Gelatine silver print

Architect: Frank Lloyd Wright

Normally one of the first undertakings of any architectural photographic assignment is to determine the building's orientation and when each of its façades will best be illuminated by the sun. Here Stoller has done the reverse and used backlighting. As he recalled, "Wright made the point that the building was to be seen as a tree with its floors like branches, cantilevered from the central trunk ... it occurred to me that working with the sun behind the building might be the way to use the transparency of the building to reveal its structure."[33]

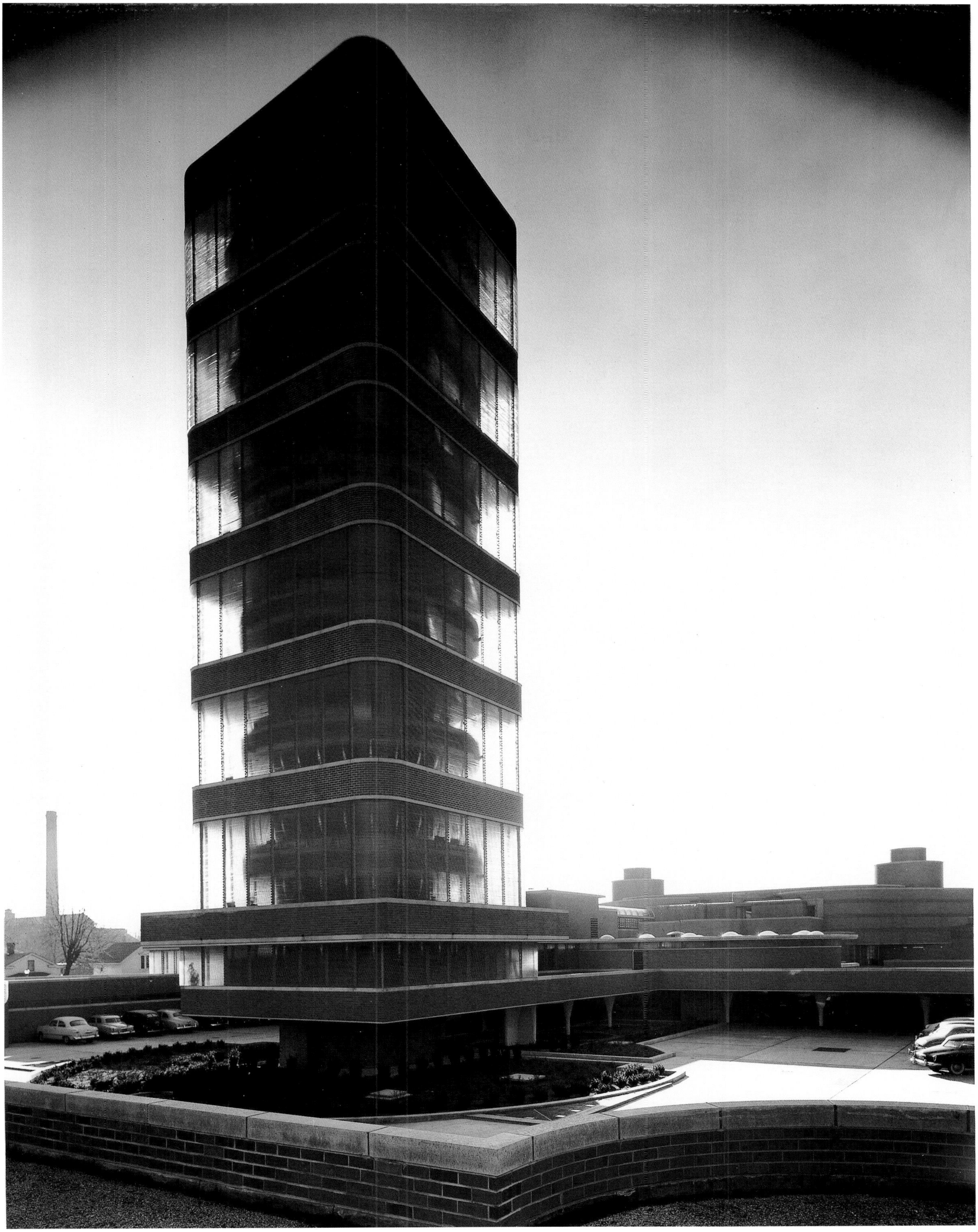

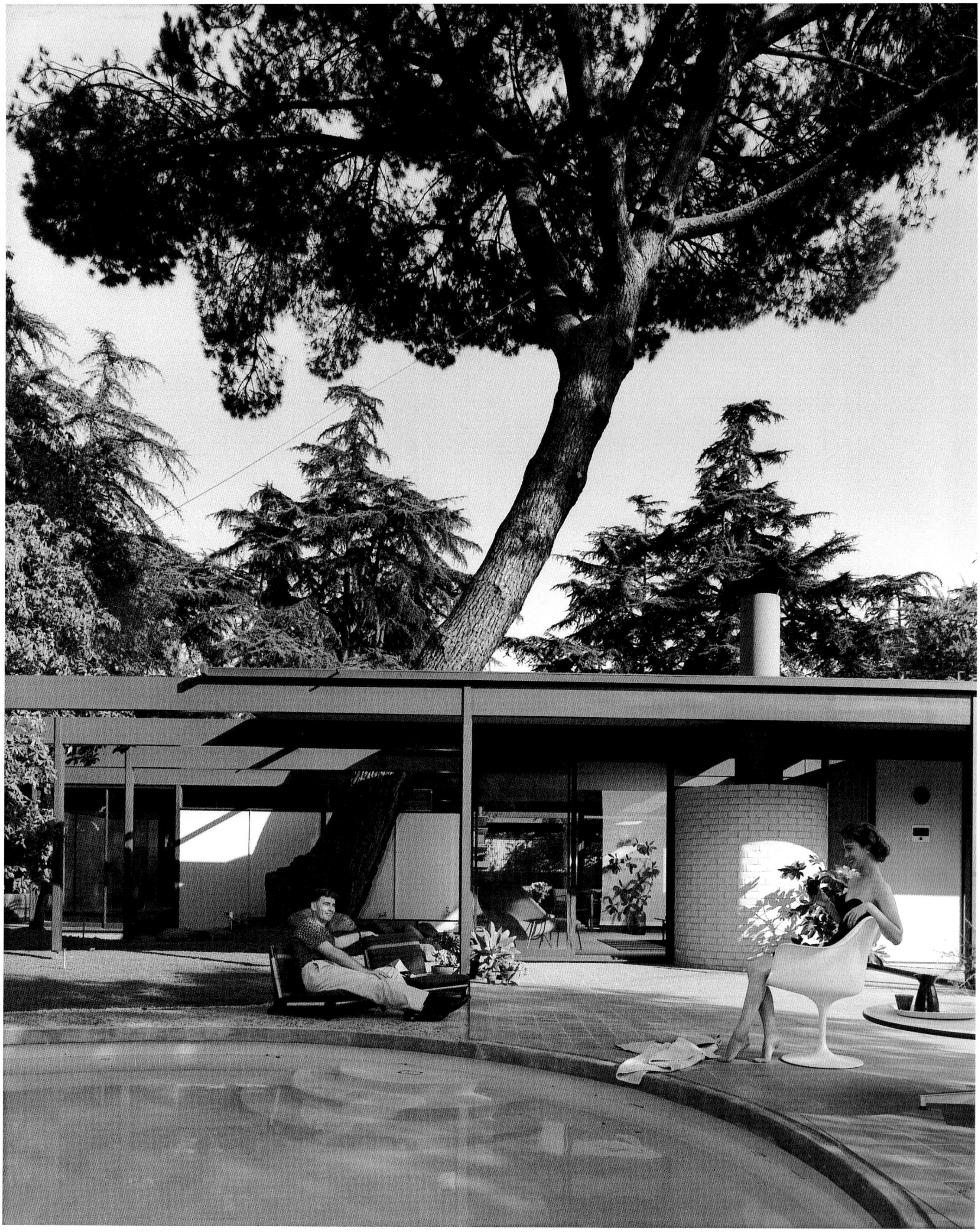

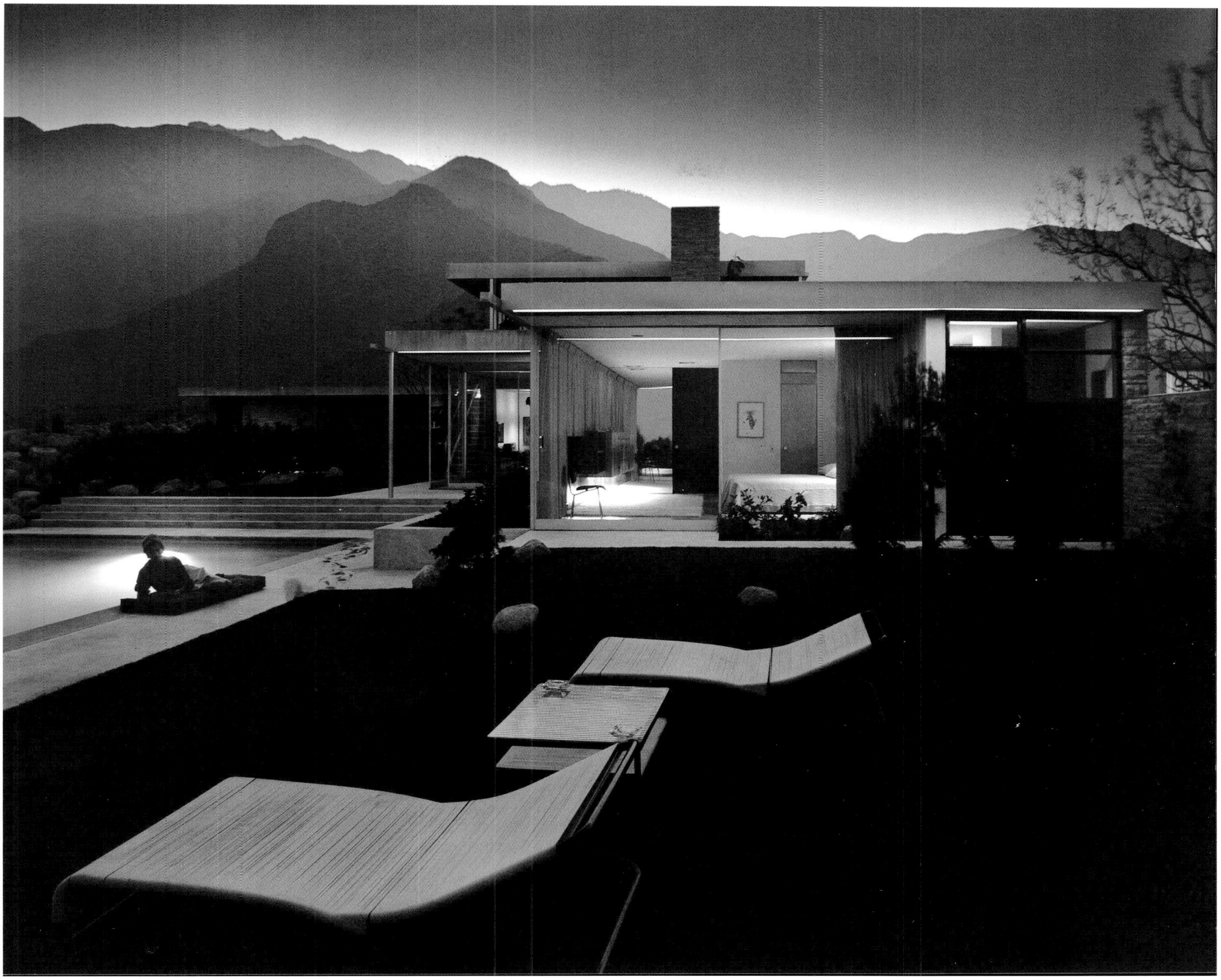

opposite

JULIUS SHULMAN (born 1910)

Case Study House #20 (Bass House), Altadena, California, 1958

Gelatine silver print

Architects: Buff Straub & Hensman

A notable feature of Shulman's photography is his inclusion of people, suggesting that Modernist architecture, despite its rigour, is desirable and accessible. The viewer is encouraged to imagine him/herself in that setting, enjoying a similarly hedonistic lifestyle. Whereas in the 1930s modern buildings had often provided the backdrop to fashion shoots, now the architecture itself has almost become the fashion accessory. Another Shulman trait is the importance attached to landscape and the fluid transition between interior and exterior, with the sliding patio door becoming as emblematic of Californian Modernism as the balcony had been of its European precursor.

above

JULIUS SHULMAN (born 1910)

Kaufmann House, Palm Springs, California, 1947

Architect: Richard Neutra

Following his conviction that the "photographer must be able to stage a scene",[34] Shulman's pictures are nearly always carefully choreographed. Here he had to work quickly as the light faded, the image being composed of three separate exposures totalling forty-five minutes, with Mrs Kaufmann posed during the final one to block glare from the swimming pool light. The sky was later burnt in. Featured in *Life* in 1949, the photograph, like Stieglitz's *Flatiron Building*, reveals little of the building's structure but is poetically allusive, symbolizing the ability of human ingenuity to transform even the desert into habitable terrain.

page 184

BALTHAZAR KORAB (born 1926)

TWA Terminal, John F. Kennedy Airport, New York, 1959

Gelatine silver print

Architect: Eero Saarinen

The Hungarian-born and architect-trained Korab worked in Saarinen's office from 1955 to 1958. Here, in the days before computer simulation, he pioneered the use of model photography as both a design aid and a marketing tool – a process later refined by architects Roche & Dinkeloo. After abandoning architecture for photography, Korab produced highly influential pictures, chiefly of American Modernist architecture – including twenty-four projects by Saarinen. Like those of Stoller, who also photographed several Saarinen buildings, his images are optimistic in tenor but marked by a greater expressiveness and spontaneity, sometimes achieved by using a 35 mm camera.

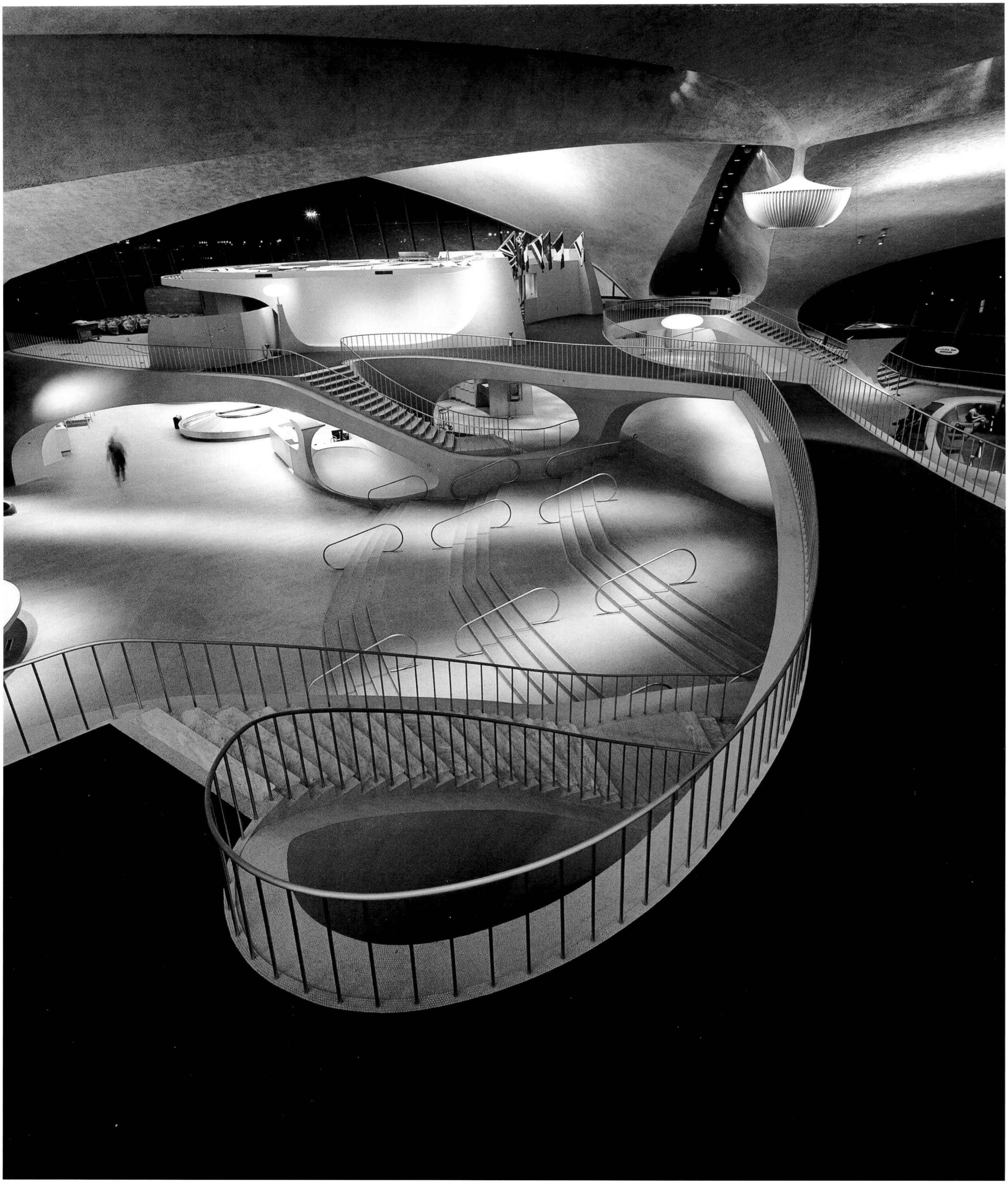

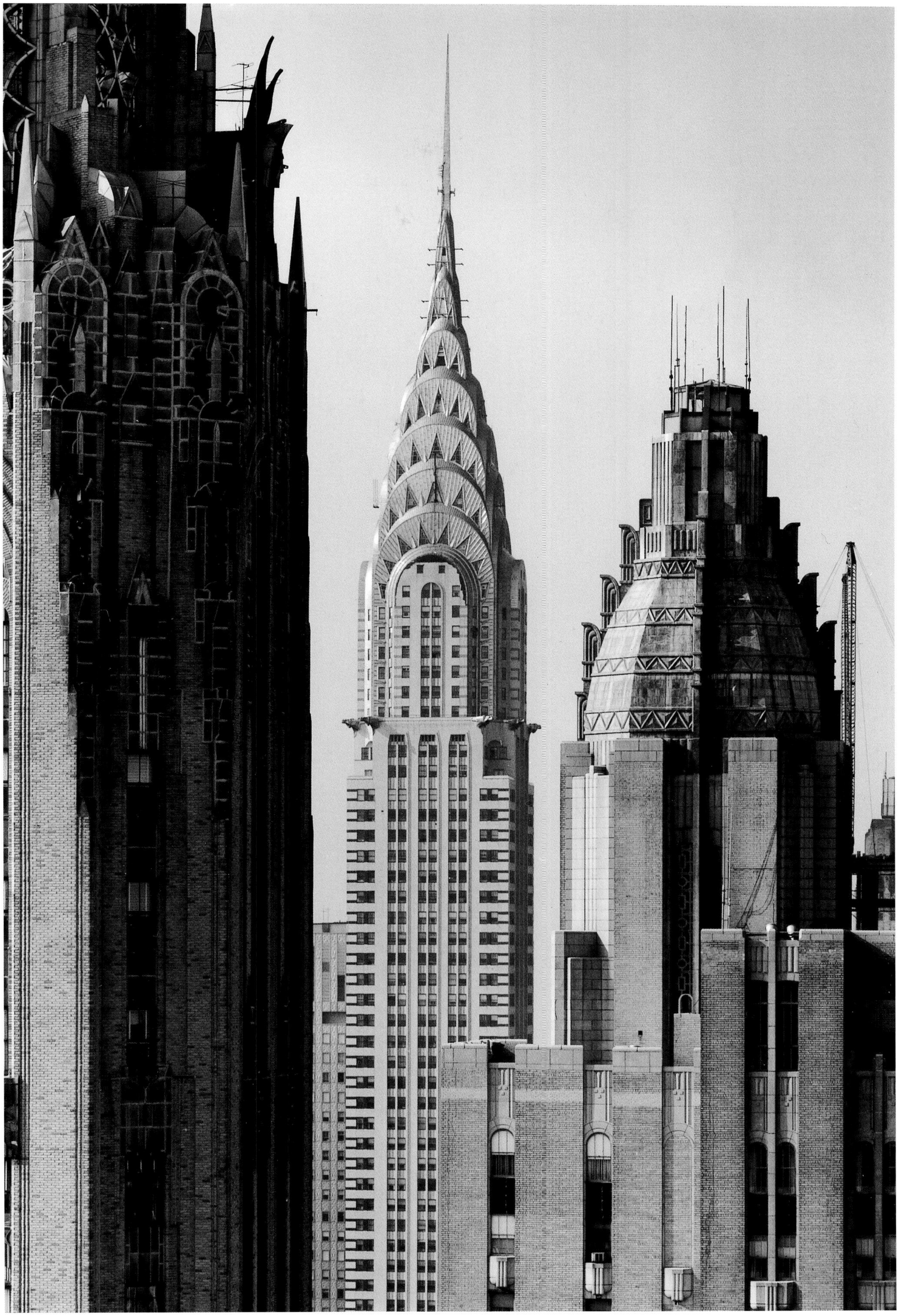

page 185

CERVIN ROBINSON (born 1928)

Chrysler Building with RCA Victor Building and Waldorf-Astoria Hotel, New York, 1966

Gelatine silver print

Architects: William van Alen/ Cross & Cross/ Schultze & Weaver

Concern with context and intelligent juxtaposition lie at the heart of Robinson's photography. Here the Chrysler Building has been shot with a long lens from an upper storey of the Seagram Building. This approach has compressed the space and rendered the image rather flat, in a manner reminiscent of Walker Evans, to whom Robinson was assistant from 1953 until 1957. However, it also tellingly allows Robinson to contrast and compare the Chrysler with its Art Deco 'neighbours' – the RCA Victor Building and Waldorf-Astoria Hotel – which are in reality several blocks away.

right

DAVID MOORE (1927–2003)

Central Sydney, 1963

Gelatine silver print

The famed Australian photographer David Moore worked in several genres, but after 1960 architecture held a special fascination for him. He treated it in several different ways: formally, while working in the studio of Max Dupain; as a stimulus to preservation, demonstrated in his book *The Australian Functional Tradition*, which was published in 1988 with a text by the architect Philip Cox and which represented an antipodean version of de Maré and Richards's earlier volume; and finally, photojournalistically, as seen in this view of Sydney's busy shopping district.

opposite

BERND and **HILLA BECHER**

(Bernd Becher [born 1931] and Hilla Becher [born 1934])

Water Tower, Railway Station, Weil am Rhein, Germany, 1963

Gelatine silver print

The pale sky, neutral background and deadpan view are all consistent features of the Bechers' photography, examples of which were included in the seminal *New Topographics* exhibition at the International Museum of Photography at George Eastman House in Rochester, New York (1975), alongside Lewis Baltz's photographs of desolate cityscapes. For artist Carl Andre, the Bechers' work echoed his Minimalist sculptures. For architecture critic Reyner Banham, their photographs, though deliberately alienating and paradigmatic of a Post-modern world in which the once heroically treated Functionalist precursors of the Modern Movement had been sanitized, nevertheless underscored the human inventiveness revealed by even the most modest industrial structures.

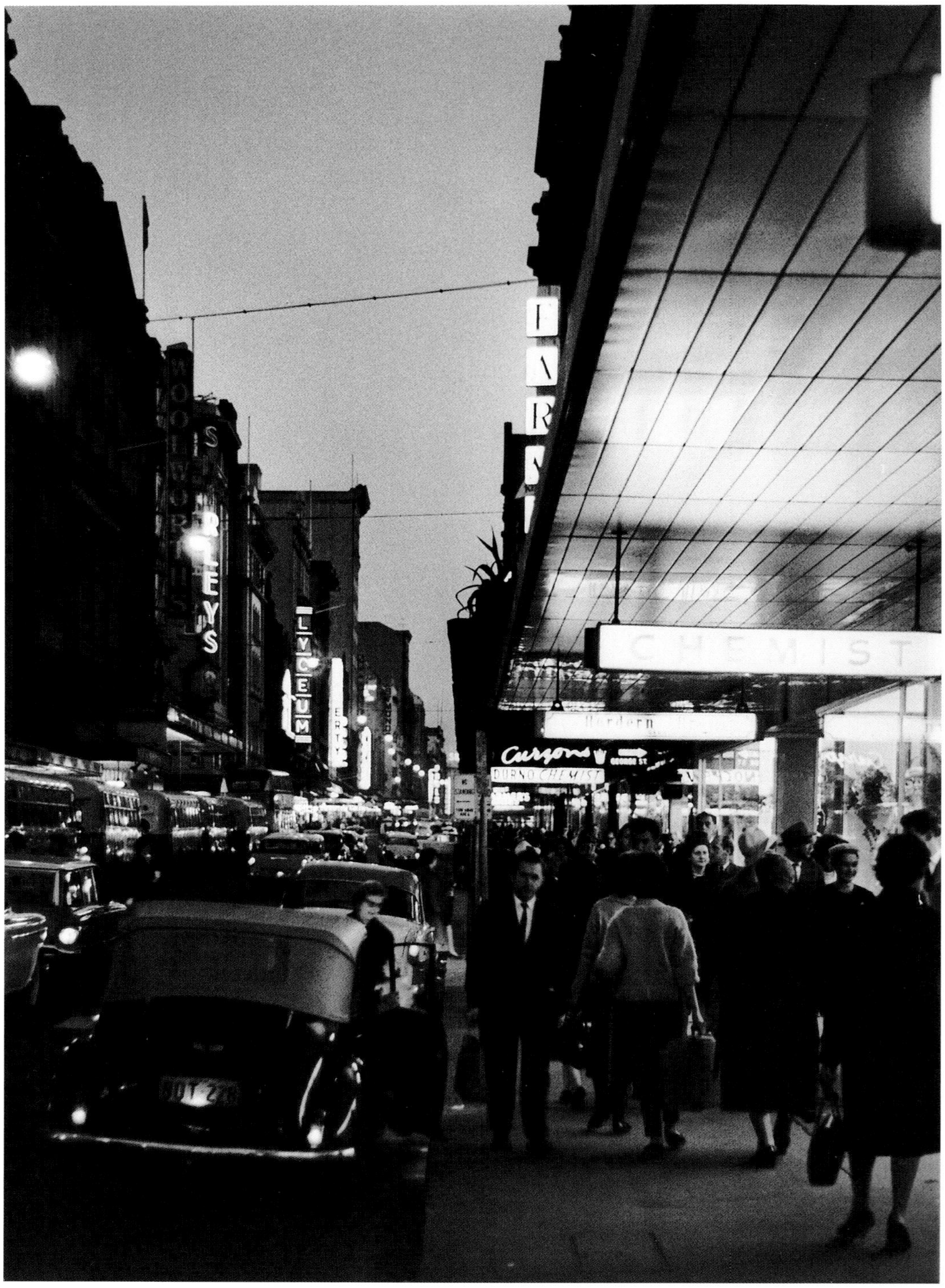

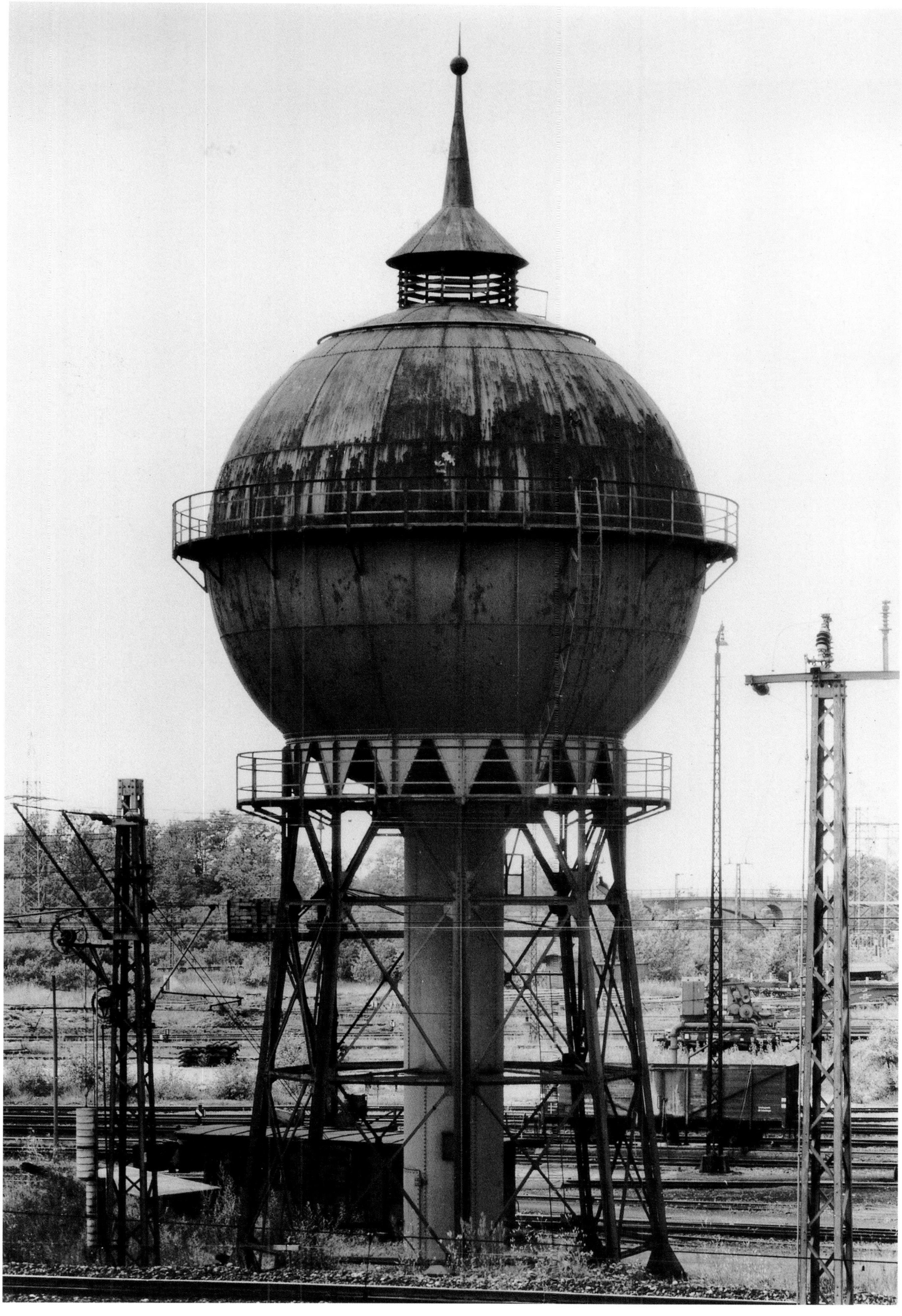

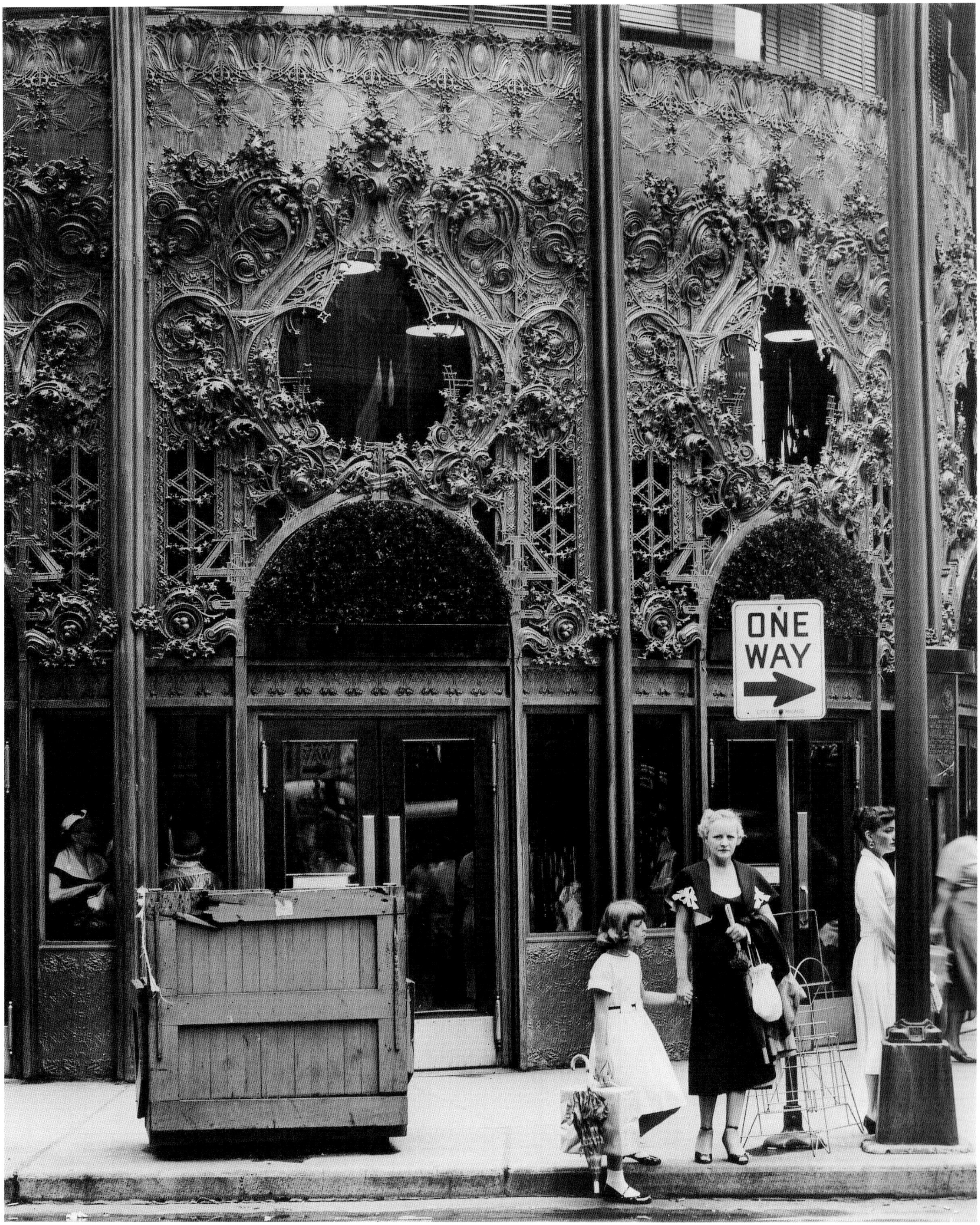
ONE
WAY

opposite

JOHN SZARKOWSKI (born 1925)

Carson Pirie Scott Building, Chicago, c. 1954

Gelatine silver print

Architect: Louis Sullivan

Szarkowski's photographs were no *in memoriam* lament for the decay of Sullivan's architecture but a celebration of its continuing vital relationship with the everyday rituals of city life. Taken either on a 5 x 4 inch (12.7 x 10.1 cm) Graphic view camera or, less often, with an automatic Rolleiflex, they combine conventional architectural shots with photojournalistic images in which no attempt has been made to exclude the thronging crowds or the usual urban trappings of telephone wires and signage. Whereas other photographers emphasized the plain outlines of Sullivan's store to establish its proto-Modernist credentials, Szarkowski undermined this argument by highlighting its exuberant ornament.

right

JOHAN VAN DER KEUKEN (1938–2001)

Centraal Beheer Office Building, Apeldoorn, The Netherlands, c. 1974

Gelatine silver print

Architect: Herman Hertzberger

Hertzberger has criticized conventional architectural photography for being "cut off from life and unpeopled" and representing more of "a portrait of the architect himself and his client" than a living building.[35] Instead, he has pleaded for photography to concentrate on the "habitable space between things" that "represents a shift in attention from the official level to the informal, to where ordinary day-to-day lives are led, and that means in the margins between the established meanings of explicit function".[36] This new sensibility was well seen in the images of the film editor and photographer Johan van der Keuken.

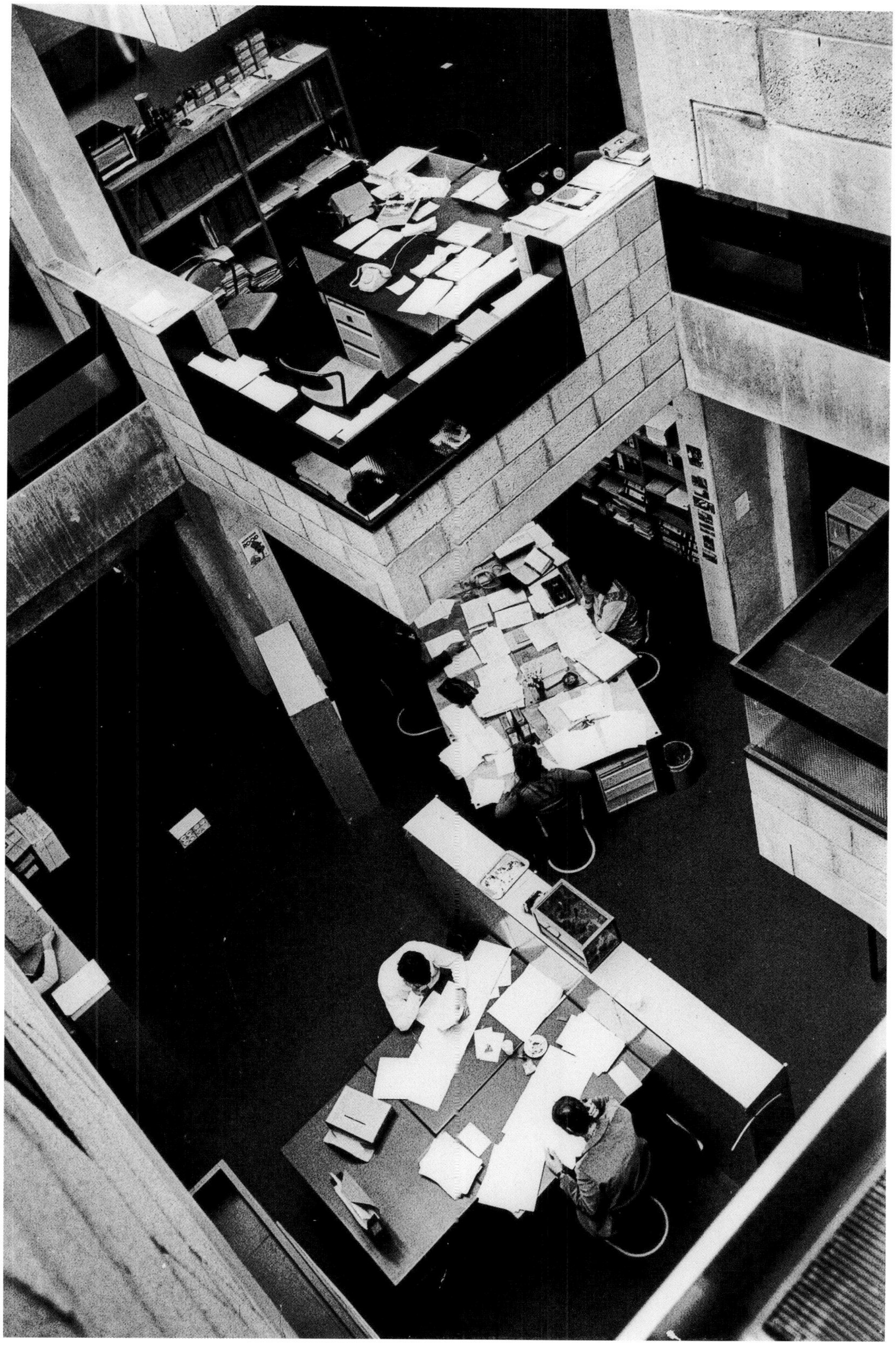

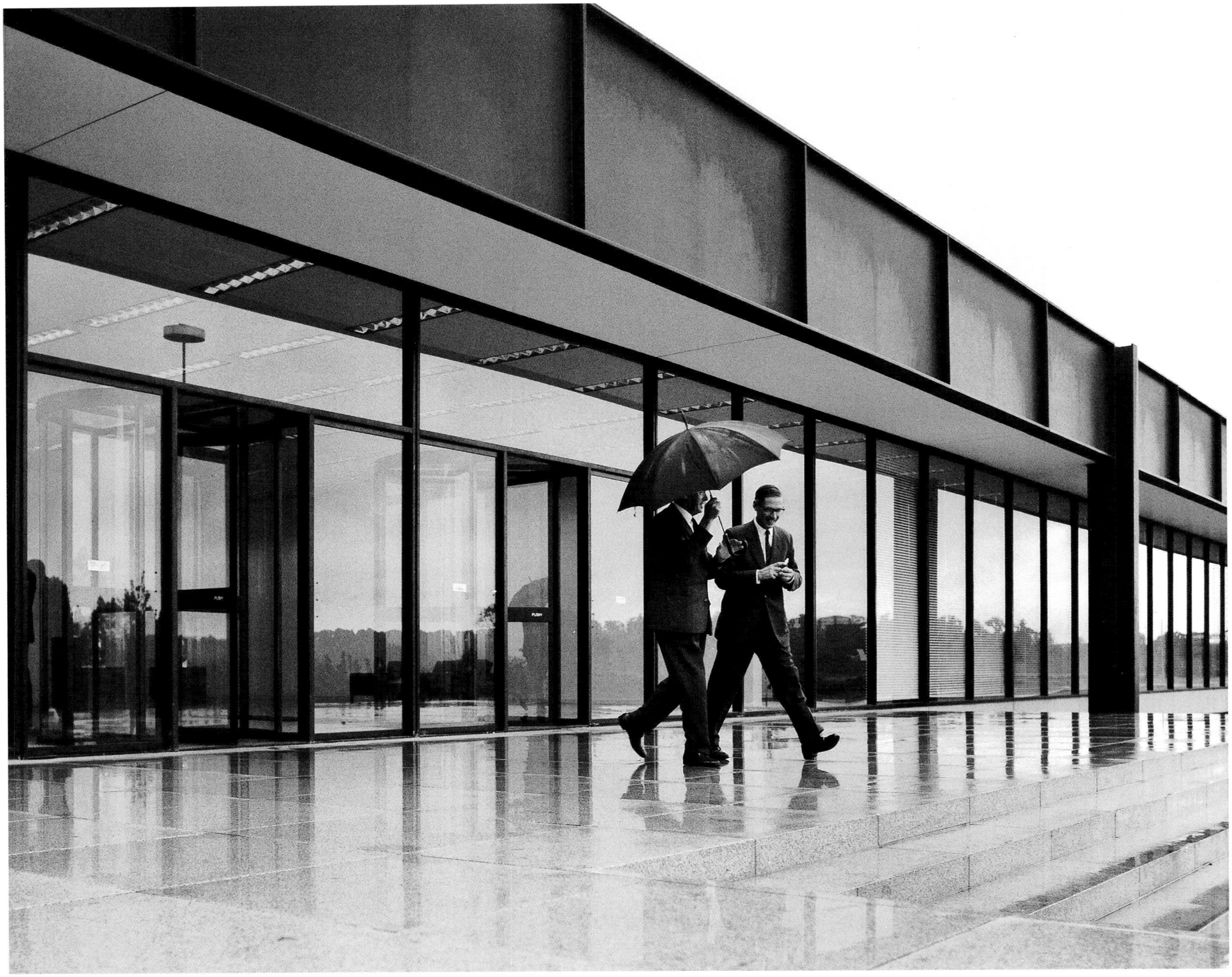

above

JOHN DONAT (born 1933)

Boots, Nottingham, 1968

Gelatine silver print

Architects: Skidmore Owings & Merrill with Yorke Rosenberg & Mardall

After briefly practising architecture, Donat took up photography professionally in the early 1960s. Lambasting the "ponderous predictability" of conventional architectural photography, he exclusively used small cameras – a 35 mm Nikon and 2¼ inch (5.7 cm) square Hasselblad – to depict buildings in use and context. His work reflects his belief that "because architectural photographs are a substitute for the experience of buildings for most of us, it is far more important for a photographer to recreate that experience through the lens than to take a few perfect and beautiful photographs".[37] This could even entail forsaking the usual obsession with sunshine to photograph in the rain.

opposite top

PATRICK WARD (born 1937)

The Richness of East End Life Is Replaced by Monotony and Inhumanity

Page spread from 'Manplan 1: Frustration', *Architectural Review*, vol. 146, September 1969

The controversial 'Manplan' series was the high-water mark of photojournalism applied to architectural image-making. Following polemical special numbers such as 'Outrage' (June 1955), the entire magazine was given over to those campaigning subjects that had customarily formed parentheses to its coverage of significant buildings. Each of the eight 'Manplan' issues was devoted to a guest photographer's interpretation of a specific theme. Magnum's Ian Berry, for example, covered society, health and welfare in 'Manplans' 2 and 6. This image is typical in its use of an extreme wide-angle lens to thrust the viewer into the frame.

opposite bottom

TONY RAY-JONES (1941–1972)

Pepys Estate, Deptford, London, 1970

Gelatine silver print

Architects: Greater London Council, Department of Architecture and Civic Design

Generally acknowledged to have been among Britain's finest social documentary photographers, Tony Ray-Jones owed much to the work of Robert Frank and Bill Brandt, as well as to the street photography of Lee Friedlander and Garry Winogrand, which he encountered while studying and working in America. He brought these social concerns to bear on the less well-known architectural subjects to which, at the end of his life, he briefly turned, partly as a result of a commission from *Architectural Review* for its 'Manplan' series. The naturalism of this 35 mm shot is far removed from Snoek and Einzig's more formal imagery.

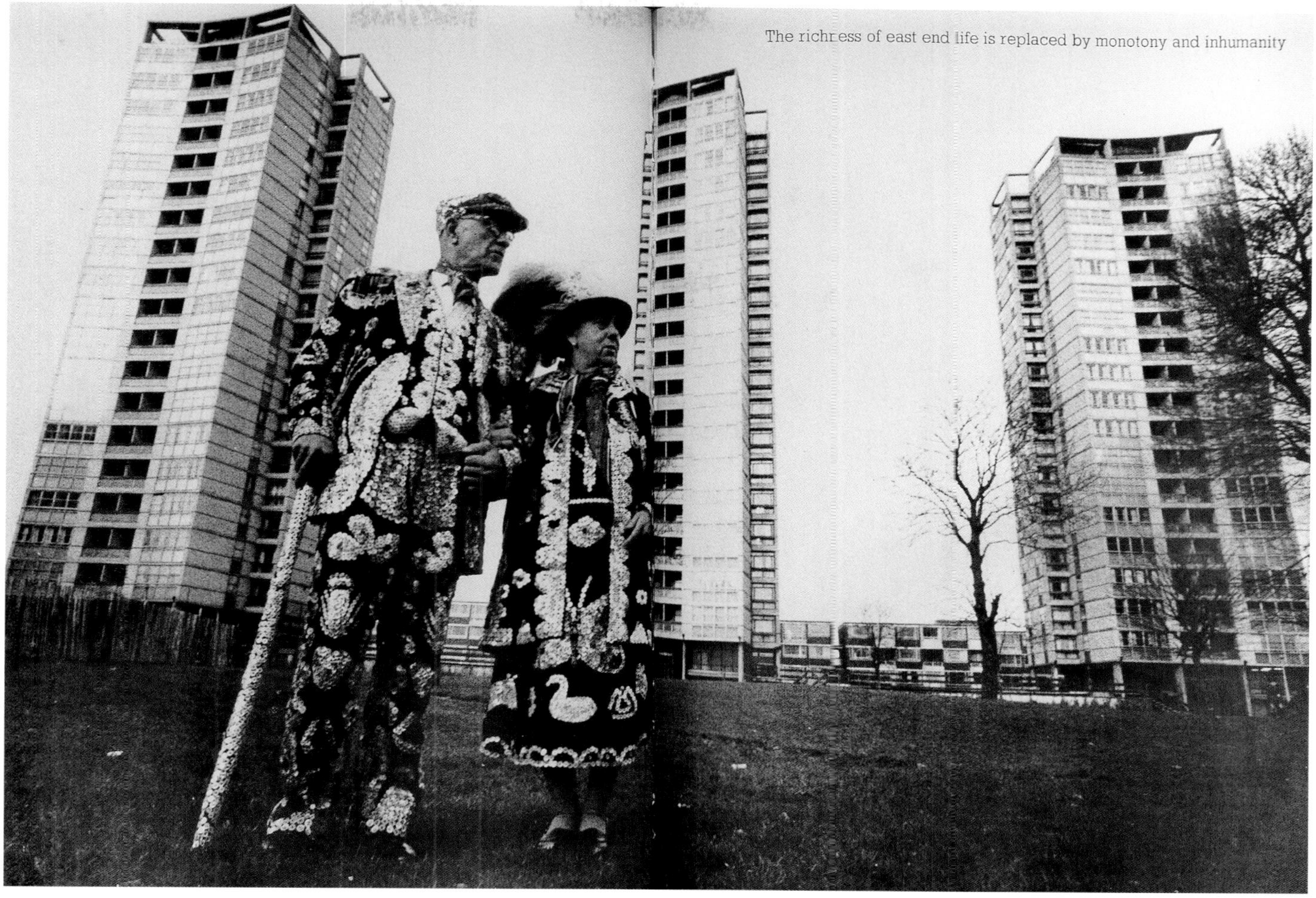
The richness of east end life is replaced by monotony and inhumanity

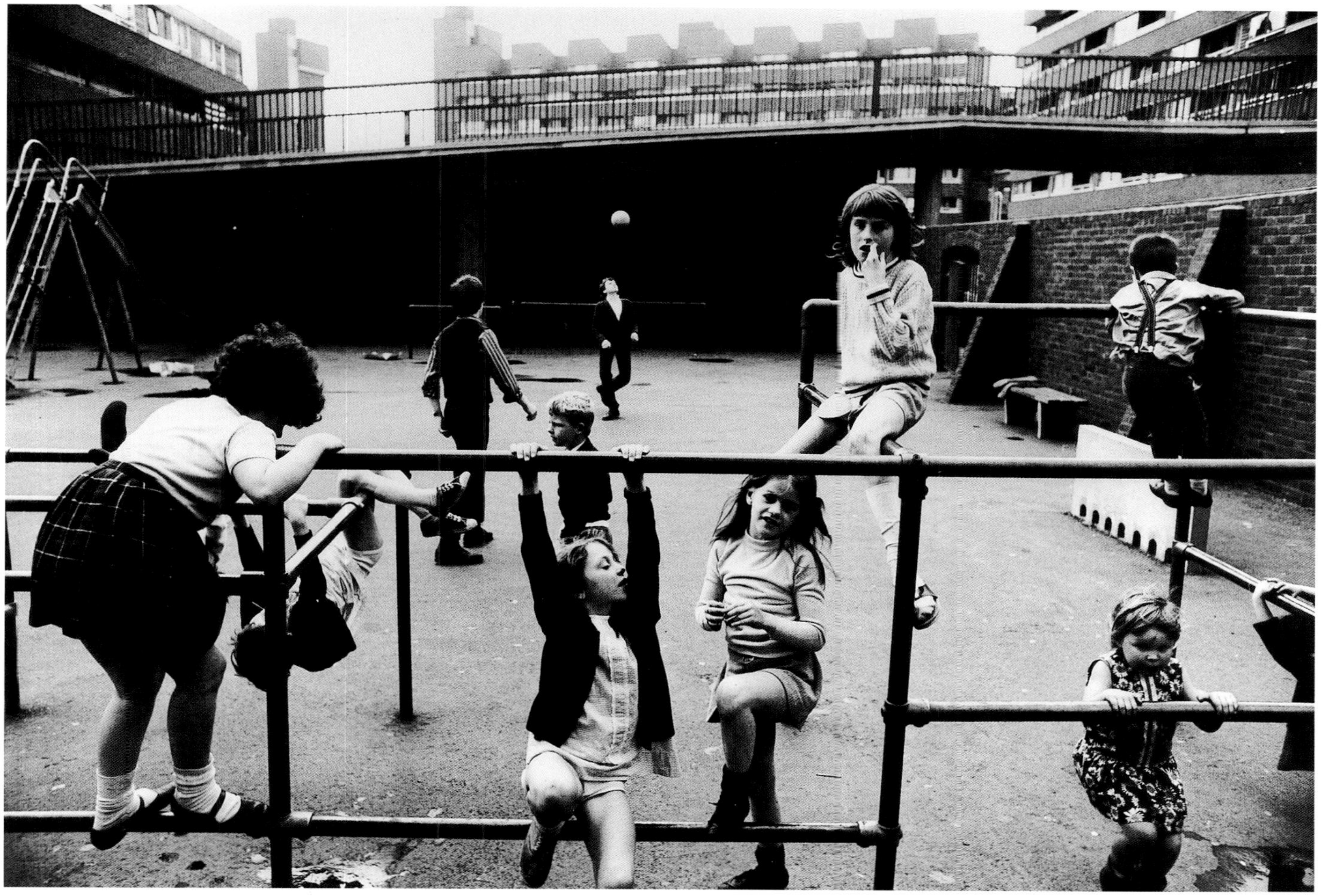

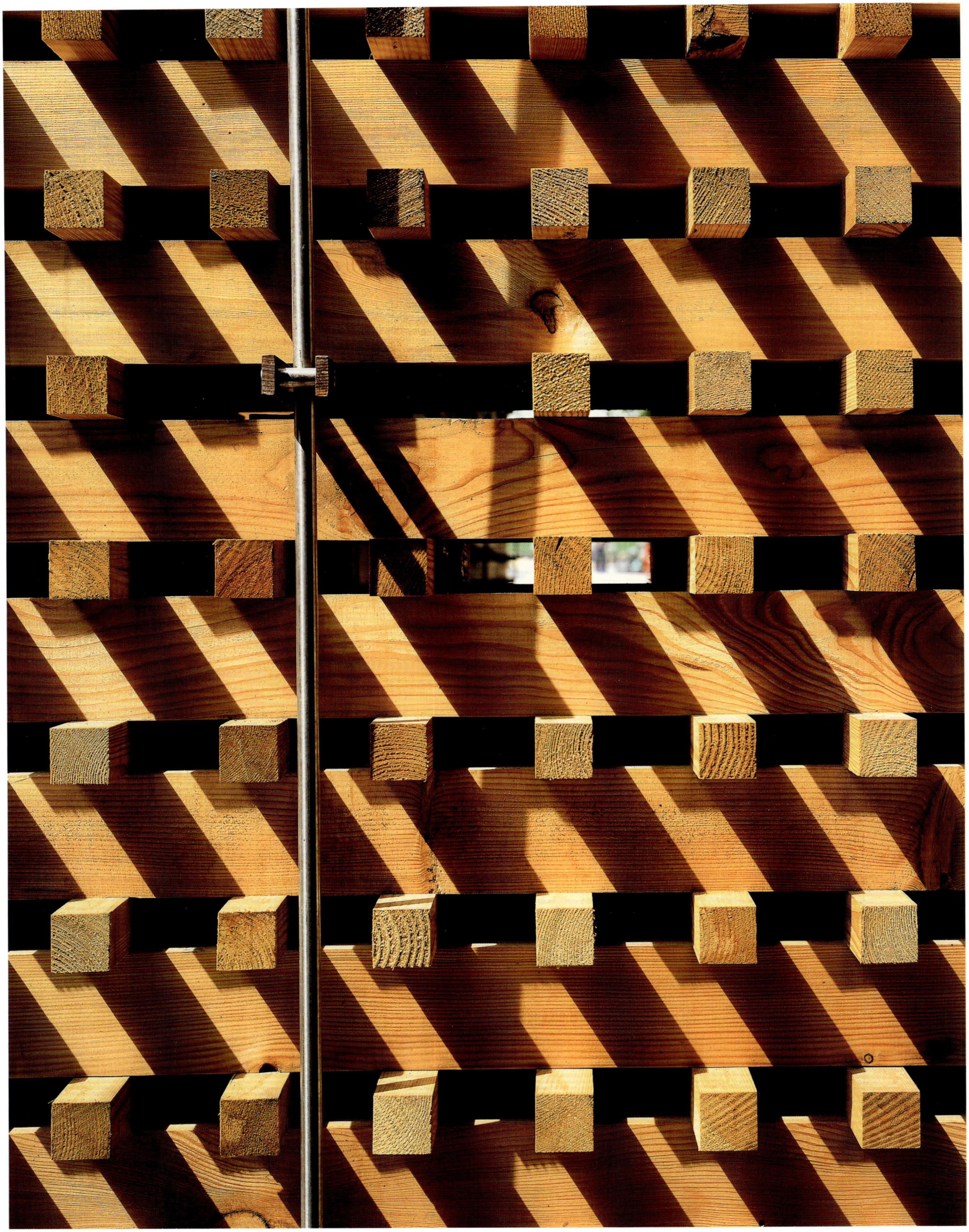

Chapter 6 **Colour and Computers 1975–Present**

page 192

ROLAND HALBE
(born 1963)

Swiss Pavilion, Expo 2000, Hanover, Germany, 2000
Colour transparency
Architect: Peter Zumthor

In 1977 the architectural critic Charles Jencks, in his book *The Language of Post-modern Architecture*, announced the death of Modernism with a dramatic monochrome still of the dynamiting of Minoru Yamasaki's Pruitt-Igoe housing complex in St Louis five years earlier. Black-and-white photography, which could be considered the midwife of Modernism, was here cast in the role of its undertaker. Not surprisingly, several architectural photographers whose work had empathetically promoted the Modernist cause found the changed architectural landscape uncongenial. Shulman quit in disgust at what he perceived as the trivialities of Post-modernism, and Stoller retired from the scene after one last hurrah in a fertile collaboration with Richard Meier. These withdrawals, combined with the deaths of photographers such as Einzig and Snoek in 1980, left architectural photography largely in the hands of a new crop of practitioners, whose work was to become increasingly global and less restricted to a single locale. In addition to this infusion of new blood, the development of architectural photography during the last thirty years has been governed by three major factors: the predominance for the first time of colour; an upsurge in interest in the genre from museums, galleries and collectors; and, more recently, the introduction of digital technology.

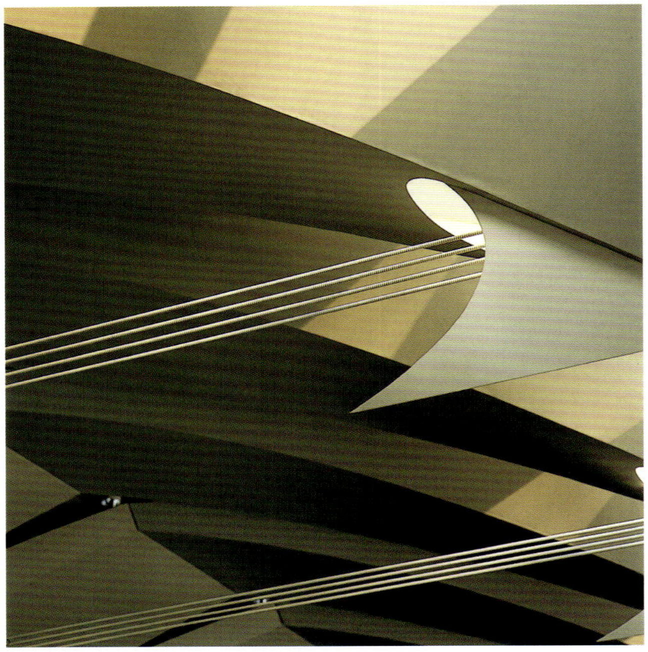

PAOLO ROSSELLI
(born 1952)

Bärematte Community Centre, Suhr, Switzerland, 1986
Colour transparency
Architect: Santiago Calatrava

Although attempts to develop colour photography originated with the invention of the medium itself, and during the nineteenth century prints were often toned and occasionally hand-coloured, it was only with the introduction of Kodachrome transparency film in 1935, followed by Kodacolor negative stock in 1942, that the first significant steps forward were taken. Accordingly, during the 1930s Maltby experimented with colour; the *Architectural Review* essayed its first major attempt at colour printing in its feature on the new British Broadcasting Corporation building in 1932 (opposite); and, at the end of the decade, one of Stoller's first assignments resulted in colour pictures of the New York World's Fair, which were published in *Architectural Forum* in 1939. In the ensuing decades, when obliged to by the requirements of lifestyle magazines in particular, photographers such as Shulman often covered jobs in colour as well as black and white. For the professional press, however, colour remained too expensive an option, and most photographers continued to regard it with suspicion. Edwin Smith resented the loss of creative control that stemmed from the fact that few photographers had the facilities to process their own colour material. Versnel felt that colour was a distraction from the photographer's primary task of delineating space. Stoller shared the widespread belief that the fairly crude colour stock then available was gaudily 'inauthentic', and even Shulman saw colour as no more than a veneer that could never match the form-giving qualities or dramatic force of black and white. This point is borne out by a comparison of his iconic monochrome shot of Koenig's Case Study House #22 (see page 154) with its contemporaneous colour equivalent, in which the sense of the house's breathtaking suspension in space and the remarkable depth of field achieved in the former are lost in the earthbound, flat appearance of the latter.

To these misgivings could be added well-grounded fears about the stability of colour dyes and a certain *hauteur* that saw colour shunned for its perceived association with amateur photography. The contrary argument that black-and-white imagery was spawning an "architecture deficient in chromatic values"[1] but which appeared enticing when published in the monochrome pages of the architectural press went unheeded, despite its perceptive expression by the artist Michael Rothenstein

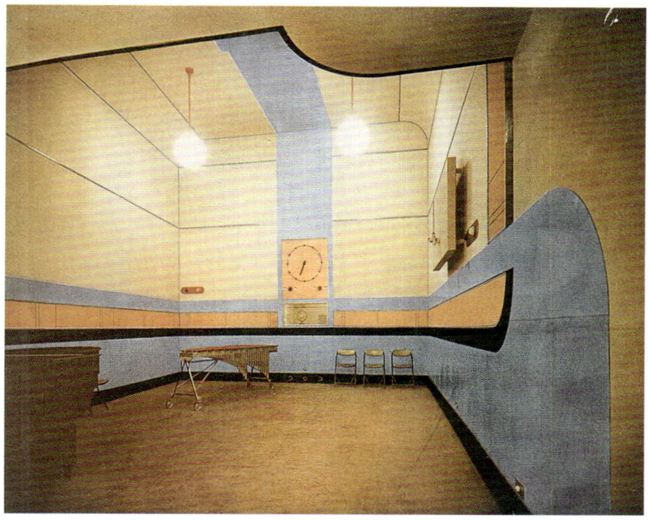

PHOTOGRAPHER UNKNOWN

Dance Band Studio BB, Broadcasting House, London, 1932
Colour half-tone reproduction from *Architectural Review*, vol. 72, August 1932
Architect: Raymond McGrath

in an article entitled 'Colour and Modern Architecture or the Photographic Eye':

> The modern architect imitates the photographer; he builds with lights and shadows, with black and white. The infinitely varied polychromatic possibilities of his medium are neglected. The great majority of modern buildings are conceived in an uninteresting chiaroscuro, an empty scheme of lights and half-tones which rely upon the window-openings to afford relief.[2]

Against this backdrop, the explosion of colour photography in the late 1970s and early 1980s, which saw the amount of black-and-white work undertaken by a leading professional such as Steve Rosenthal (see page 202) subsequently shrink from 90% to 10% of his output between 1974 and 1989, appears all the more remarkable. There were, however, pressing reasons for the transformation. The insistent demands of advertisers enthralled by colour's irresistibly seductive appeal played a major role, one further enhanced by architecture's increasing confluence with the worlds of fashion and advertising, in which the merits of colour photography and its commercial benefits had long been extolled. Additionally, not only had the quality of colour film greatly improved but new printing techniques made colour reproduction in the professional press economically viable for the first time. Editors, too, embraced the change, having become frustrated by a pictorial medium that inadequately expressed the increasingly polychromatic nature of contemporary architecture, while for their travelling readership the discovery that Modernist landmarks such as the Unité d'Habitation in Marseilles afforded not merely a Hervéesque monochromatic dance of light and shadow but a rhythmic suite of bold colour came as a revelation. Finally, the work of photographers such as Stephen Shore, and more especially Joel Meyerowitz, in such publications as *Cape Light* (1978) – a book much admired by Stoller – and *St Louis and the Arch* (1980), endowed colour with a new photographic respectability. The crisply detailed black-and-white print ceded its authority to a new photographic deity – the 5 x 4 inch (12.7 x 10.1 cm) colour transparency shimmering into lustrous life on the indispensable lightbox.

The effects of this colour revolution on the practice of architectural photography have been pronounced. The technical difficulties of working with colour – the frequent recourse to bracketing exposures, the need to make multiple exposures for some interiors and the relatively slow speed of large-format colour emulsions – conspired to undermine the reportage movement in architectural photography, once again banishing people from the frame and encouraging a return to the formal abstraction associated with photographers such as Dell & Wainwright and Stoller. This tendency is readily apparent in the imagery of many contemporary architectural photographers – in the compact compositions of Roland Halbe, for instance (see pages 192, 203) – but is perhaps best seen in the photography of Richard Bryant, one of the leading professionals at work today with a worldwide clientele (see page 204). Bryant, who describes himself as "a very 'tight' photographer, very into composition ... a certain combination of angles, planes and materials seems to please me",[3] began photographing in 1975 and has himself acknowledged that his work has become progressively more spare, based on his observation that "in terms of line or texture, the less you show, the more you communicate."[4] His photography is, therefore, marked as much by its concentration on beautifully observed and lit details as it is by general overall shots (see page 196). While before the lens of a skilled exponent such as Bryant the telling detail can provide true architectural insight, it has also to be admitted that the unthinking use of architectural

RICHARD BRYANT
(born 1947)
John Young Penthouse, London, 1991
Colour transparency
Architect: John Young

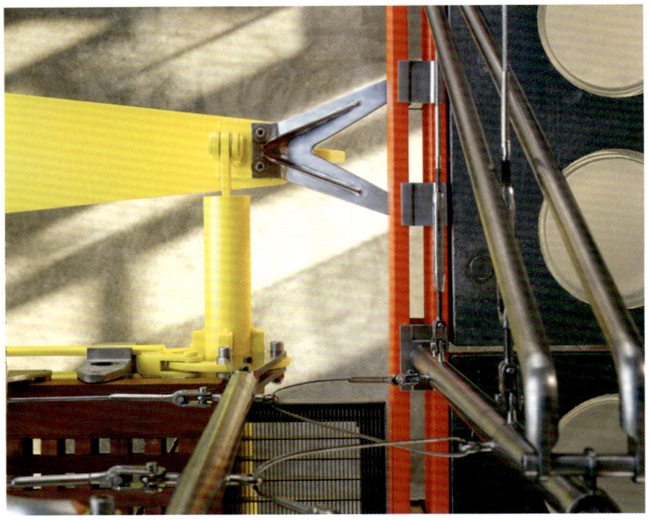

TIMOTHY HURSLEY
(born 1955)
Renaissance Center, Detroit, 1978
Colour transparency
Architect: John Portman

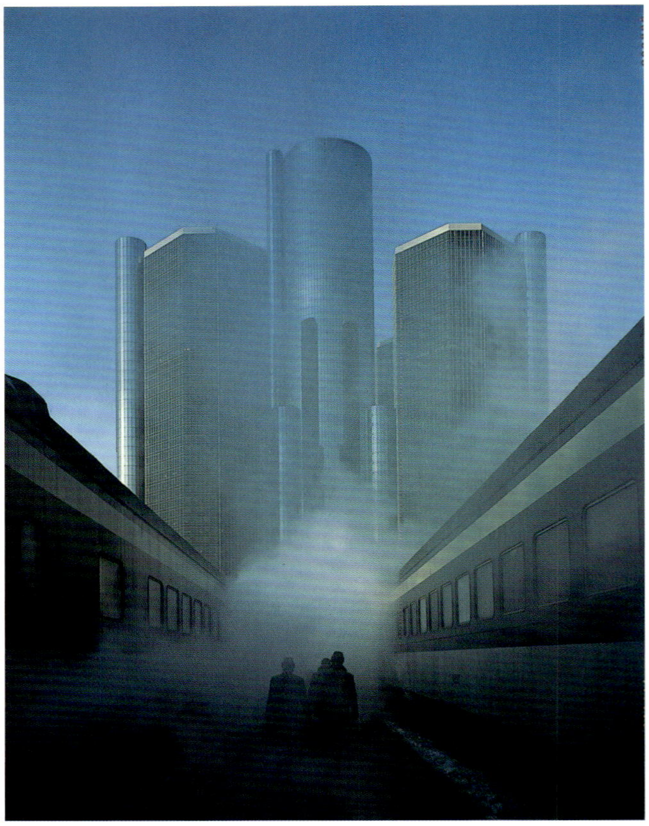

details as the raw material for abstract photographic compositions has become one of the most deadening clichés of today's photography of architecture.

Fostered by the growing amount of conversion work undertaken by architects and the continuing popularity of voyeuristic peeps into the lifestyles of the rich and famous, the increased attention lavished on interiors, to which it can do full, alluring justice, has been another effect of the transition to colour. Indeed, interior photography has become a major subgenre in its own right, commanding an extensive literature and boasting a phalanx of specialists. Among them is Jaime Ardiles-Arce, whose theatrically lit pictures are predominantly designed to showcase the furnishings and goods displayed, rather than to explore notions of space. Nevertheless, the dividing line between this type of interior design photography, seen for example in *Architectural Digest* and *House and Garden*, and architectural photography *per se* is not always easily drawn. An illustration of the increased importance of interiors to the architectural photographer's portfolio and the problems they present can be found in Norman McGrath's manual *Photographing Buildings Inside and Out* (1987), in which the major portion of the book is devoted to the inside. These problems principally relate to the greater difficulty of lighting interiors for colour than for black-and-white. They include the use of supplementary lights to counteract the fact that colour film has a lower contrast range than that of the human eye, and the reconciliation of incompatible light sources, such as fluorescent, tungsten, incandescent and daylight, through filtering or the laborious process of making separate exposures. The complex and time-consuming set-ups required have not only rendered photography more formal and expensive (the American photographer Peter Aaron reckons his maximum daily rate of interior shots to be five as opposed to between fifteen and twenty exterior shots) but have also placed exaggerated emphasis on the need for each shot to justify itself by being 'special', no matter how unremarkable the interior.

Colour, too, has had a major impact on the economics and patronage of architectural photography, accelerating the trend noted earlier, whereby magazines have trimmed production costs by relying on pictures commissioned and paid for by the architects. In a deregulated world in which restrictions on advertising by architects have been lifted, the architectural photographer is more than ever, as Einzig recognized previously, "in the public relations business".[5] His or her images are as likely to illustrate the architect's glossy practice brochure and award submissions or the contractors' advertising as the pages of a professional journal.

For Cervin Robinson, an articulate and knowledgeable writer on architectural photography as well as a practising photographer, the influence of colour has been wholly baleful, creating a situation whereby technical expertise is exaggerated at the expense of artistic vision, photographs have been made duller by the exclusion of people, and photographers themselves reduced from "expressive individuals" to "anonymous renderers".[6] While Robinson's strictures contain a degree of truth, they are overstated. As we have seen, photographers have long worked directly for architects, and magazines do still commission some of their own photography. In addition, evidence of individual expression is provided by the variety of responses to the subject that encompass not only the hard-edged imagery of Bryant but also the ethereal creations of Timothy Hursley (opposite; page 210); the filmic compositions of Peter Aaron (see pages 208–09); the contemplative unravelling of buildings by Duccio Malagamba (see page 214); the geometrical abstractions of Kim Zwarts (see page 213); and the contextual revelations of Paolo Rosselli (see page 212). If people remain excluded from architectual photographs, this is now less to do with the technical limitations of colour and more to do with deeply embedded attitudes on the part of photographers, architects and editors.

The close relationship between black-and-white photography and the Modern Movement poses the question of whether a similar association can be posited between colour photography and Modernism's successors. Certainly, there can be little doubt that the rise of colour photography has coincided with a greater use of colour in contemporary architecture. While Stoller was enjoying his swansong photographing the buildings of Richard Meier (above right) – significantly an architect whose work is best conveyed in black-and-white – Norman McGrath was producing his vibrantly colourful depiction of Charles Moore's Piazza d'Italia, New Orleans (1979; see page 215), one of the iconic buildings of Post-modernism and a polychromatic phantasmagoria unrenderable in black-and-white. Just as photography fuelled nineteenth-century eclecticism, Post-modernism's emphasis on the importance of – to borrow a phrase from Banham *à propos* New Brutalism – "memorability of image" and frequent use of historical references could be said to have resulted from the world's architecture having been made more superficially assimilable through photographic imagery, not least through that ubiquitous teaching aid, the colour slide. William Feaver is not the only critic to have insinuated that Post-modernism is what happens "when style-swapping breaks out in the slide library".[7]

In this respect, the fascination of the Italian architect Aldo Rossi – one of the prime movers of Post-modernism – with Polaroid images, which offer an instant, fragmented, collaged view of the world, seems all the more apposite. Whereas in the 1930s it had been photographers and artists who had made collages from the imagery of other photographers, during the 1980s this task was performed by Post-modernist architects, whose works could be described as a collage of built images, a tectonic cluster of historical motifs recollected through their capture on film. Similarly, just as Henry Russell Hitchcock suggested that the nineteenth-century British architect William Butterfield had developed a style of strong tonal contrasts that could be effectively reproduced in *The Builder*'s woodcuts, so James Stirling and others have been accused of designing buildings with the photographer's lens and with colour reproduction in mind. For Peter Rice, the strong, comprehensible façade images of Post-modernism can be ascribed to their architects' realization that they were more likely to be seen and judged through photographs than in actuality. From a

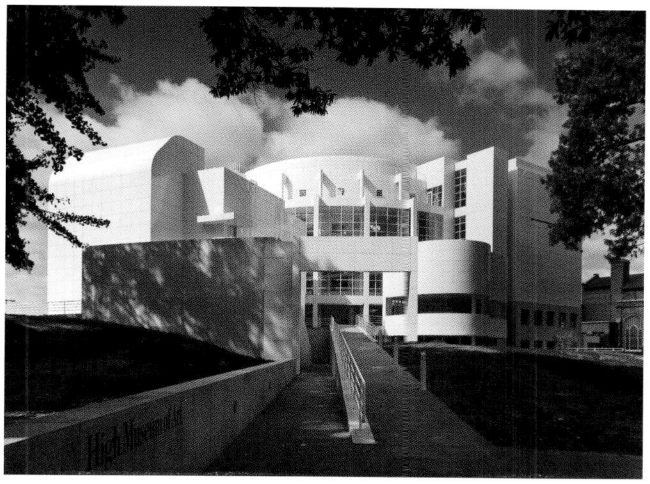

EZRA STOLLER (born 1915)
High Museum of Art, Atlanta, Georgia, 1983
Gelatine silver print
Architect: Richard Meier

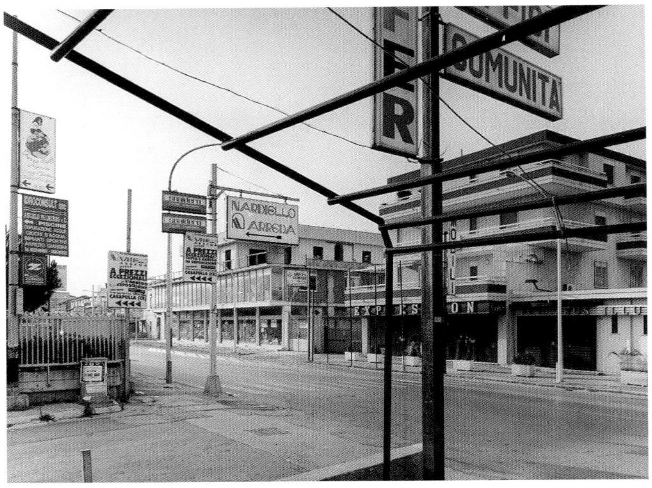

GABRIELE BASILICO
(born 1944)

Campania, Italy, 1996
Gelatine silver print

photographer's perspective Aaron has complemented this view with his assertion that Post-modernist architecture is "great for photography".[8]

It could also be argued that colour photography has had a similar transformative effect on the reputations of a number of architects. Although it had been known previously chiefly through black-and-white publication in *Arts and Architecture*, interest in the work of the Mexican architect Luis Barragán mushroomed after the 1976 retrospective at New York's Museum of Modern Art, where the accompanying catalogue's colour reproductions of the stunning images of Barragán's long-time photographic collaborator Armando Salas Portugal (see page 218) conveyed the bold polychromy of Barragán's architecture to a wide audience for the first time. In addition, the revival of interest in Art Nouveau architects such as Gaudí and Victor Horta, though occasioned partly by the more pluralist outlook of Post-modernist critics and historians, has also been aided by colour photography, which is better able to render the fecund prolixity of their decoration than black-and-white. It is surely no accident that of all the major iconic images of monochrome photography, none features Art Nouveau architecture.

The dominance of colour has not only confirmed the status of black-and-white as the medium of documentary authenticity but also paradoxically as the primary vehicle for artistic expression. The latter tendency is well illustrated by the photography of the American Judith Turner and the Swiss-born Hélène Binet (see page 219). Both of them, in their differing ways, have been significantly influenced by the precepts of the architect and teacher John Hejduk, particularly his observation that "it is impossible to see architecture in its full complexity at once. Architecture *is* made up of details, fragments, fabrications. And the very idea behind it can be captured in a fragment, in a detail."[9] This reductive sentiment informs the work of both photographers – Turner in her predominantly black-and-white studies of the New York Five, including Hejduk (1980), and Israeli Modern Movement buildings in *White City – International Style Architecture in Israel* (1984), where architecture is stripped down to its elemental forms and rendered as a series of abstract flat planes; and Binet in her numinous, microscopic examinations of the creations of leading-edge architects such as Daniel Libeskind, Peter Zumthor and Zaha Hadid.

Despite these similarities, however, there are significant differences between the two. While Turner's photographs deal in ambiguity and are muted symphonies in grey, Binet's, with their intense blacks reminiscent of those of Hervé, reveal an almost obsessional concern with the vigorous interplay of light and shadow. Both photographers candidly admit that their modes of treatment require a special affinity with the type of architecture they portray, Turner recognizing that the surface detailing of Post-modernism and Binet that High Tech's lack of "hierarchy of detail or form"[10] would not suit their respective approaches. These admissions underline the fact that their work is not predominantly intended for the professional press. Rather, both have exploited an outlet for architectural photography that has developed apace over the last two decades, namely the book filled with images by a single photographer, exploring a particular architect's work, place or theme. Binet's photographs have, for example, been reproduced in a series of publications such as *The Inns of Court* (1996) and *Architecture of Zaha Hadid* (2000), in which the photographer has collaborated closely with the designers to ensure the images achieve maximum impact by being floated free of text and arranged in a coherent sequence that allows adjacent pictures to enjoy a meaningful dialogue. Other photographers for whom book publication is similarly important include Philip Trager, with his sensitive renditions of architecture and place, and Richard Pare, whose *Tadao Ando: The Colours of Light* (1996) is a sympathetic analysis of the spatial complexities of Ando's architecture (see page 220).

The continued vitality of black-and-white documentary photography is perhaps best seen in its deepening engagement with urbanism, most especially in the work of the Italian architect-photographer, as he likes to term himself, Gabriele Basilico (opposite). Together with compatriots such as Mimmo Jodice (see page 223), Vincenzo Castella and Guido Guidi, Basilico has been striving to comprehend the changed nature of the urban experience in an age that has seen the city dissolve from a recognizable entity with a defined centre and periphery into a loose patchwork of semi-autonomous developments anarchically stretching ever further into the countryside (see page 222). Basilico's desolate, monochrome cityscapes represent a kind of 'neutron bomb' photography, in which all structures remain intact but the inhabitants have chillingly vanished. Beneath the surface repose lurks an edgy disquietude that recalls the films of Michelangelo Antonioni. Usually empty foregrounds, devoid of photographic devices for drawing the viewer's eye into the picture, intensify the mood of alienation, while the normal concentration by architectural photographers on significant buildings yields to an analysis of urban space in which all structures are deemed equal, whatever their architectural pedigree.

Basilico's methodological approach to his subject, which remains the same whether he is photographing in Italy or in cities further afield, such as Barcelona or Berlin, has a similar levelling tendency on regional differences and allows Becheresque typological comparisons to be made. As such, his imagery represents a major contribution to the way we perceive our cities, abjuring the optimism implicit in the photography of Giorgio Casali and Oscar Savio, and instead revealing how the post-war dream has been soured by years of untrammelled development and civic corruption. In addition it rejects the notion advanced by nineteenth-century photographers that the city is a product of controlled growth and presents a close-up rebuttal of conventional urbanistic theories based on the distant eye of aerial photography. Similarly, Guidi's bleached colour photography of the decaying industrial remains of Marghera, which seem to belong to the post-apocalyptic world of Andrei Tarkovsky's *Stalker*, rebuke Renger-Patzsch's heroic industrial vision. In the imagery of Jodice and others, reproduced in the ironically entitled *Gibellina: Utopia Concreta* (1990), the material visually celebrated by Hervé has been transformed into an implacable symbol of landscape desecration.

Photographers such as Basilico, Turner and Binet have benefited from the increased attention paid to the photography of architecture by museums, galleries and collectors. This trend has been accelerated by a further blurring of the boundaries between photography and art. There is also a widening gulf between those, often from architectural backgrounds, such as Bryant, Rosenthal and Basilico, who engage directly with the subject, and those, usually trained in photography or art, who view it primarily as a signifier of larger social, political or cultural concerns. The latter category includes the Japanese photographers Ryuji Miyamoto (see pages 224–25) and Hiroshi Sugimoto (see page 226), and above all the new wave of German photographers, among them Thomas Ruff, Thomas Struth (see page 227), Andreas Gursky and Candida Höfer, all of whom studied under the Bechers and whose work is eagerly coveted by museums and galleries devoted to modern art. While, for all their self-conscious artistry, Turner and Binet's photographs remain committed to architectural interpretation, an image such as Gursky's dispassionate, hyper-realistic rendering of Norman Foster's Hong Kong and Shanghai Bank (see page 200) foregoes formal architectural analysis, emphasizing instead the robotic, soulless nature of modern life as part of his wider investigation into the behavioural patterns of people congregated into large crowds. Although there are significant differences between these artist-photographers, certain common themes emerge. Aping painting, their images are frequently very large; the images are often produced in limited runs; the mimetic representational nature of conventional architectural photography is undermined by a stress on artifice, be it the nebulous ambiguity of Sugimoto's shadow images, digital manipulation or the staged fabrications of Thomas Demand; and, not only are canonical buildings reinterpreted, but, as with Basilico, architecture is demonumentalized by a readiness to photograph humdrum buildings, such as the bland 1960s housing blocks that occupy Struth's pictures.

As far as architectural photography *per se* is concerned, the most interesting body of work has been produced by Ruff, whose found and manipulated photographic material

ANDREAS GURSKY
(born 1955)

Hong Kong & Shanghai Bank, Hong Kong, 1994
Mixed media
Architects: Foster Associates

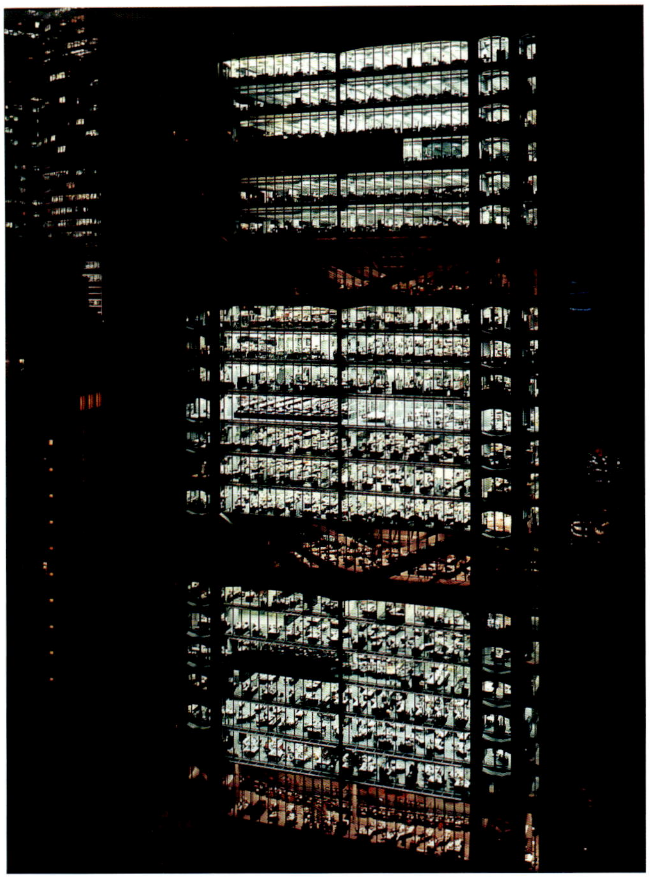

applied to the façades of Herzog & de Meuron's Ricola building, Mulhouse, France (1994), and the library at Eberswalde University in Germany (1999) represents a notable instance of the growing creative collaboration between architects and photographers. More recently, Ruff was commissioned by the Museum of Modern Art in New York to extend his series on the buildings of Mies van der Rohe for its *Mies in Berlin* exhibition (2001; see page 228). This major reassessment of Mies's career graphically demonstrated how the architect sought to manipulate the way in which he wished his oeuvre to be viewed by critics and historians. In this process, black-and-white photographs, often carefully cropped and enhanced for publication, played a key role. It is a tribute to their enduring iconic force that Ruff found it necessary to reinterpret not only the buildings themselves but also their monochrome visual surrogates through digital manipulation and colorization.

Although some may question how much such artist-photographers have contributed to our understanding of architecture, the patronage of museums and galleries has at least enabled a small body of photographers to examine architecture from a standpoint independent of the architectural profession. Against this it could be argued that museums' and galleries' policy of acquiring and promoting the work of a limited number of current artist-photographers has, when applied to their retrospective acquisitions, skewed the history of architectural photography towards a kind of photographic equivalent of the Leavisite literary "Great Tradition", in which the artistic torch is handed on from one 'significant' photographer to another to illumine an otherwise benighted genre. From this history firms such as Bedford Lemere & Co., among the most important in the nineteenth century, are totally expunged.

As the major use of digital technology by these artist-photographers demonstrates, we are in the midst of a digital revolution that represents the most far-reaching development since photography's invention and that is beginning radically to transform image production and dissemination. Already the new technology has had a profound effect on mainstream architectural photography, not so much on location, where, although perhaps used for visual note-taking, digital cameras and camera backs have yet to match the quality of film, but in the studio and in image distribution. Photographers have always worked on their imagery in the darkroom – Baldus, for instance, excised whole buildings, while Bedford liberally applied lampblack to his negatives to suppress unwanted details – but Photoshop has greatly extended the possibilities of creative as well as ethically dubious image manipulation, not just for the photographer but for art editors and end users. How these new powers will be exercised is one of the most crucial questions facing the medium. From the users' standpoint, as more images are received via ISDN or scanned to a disk, provided quality is maintained, the format of the original will become increasingly irrelevant. Already this has begun to liberate the photographer from the stranglehold of the 5 x 4 inch (12.7 x 10.1 cm) transparency, encouraging experimentation with a wider range of more portable, smaller formats as well as colour negatives. On the minus side, the likelihood that users will view and buy imagery on the Internet may place an even greater premium on the single dazzling image that can stand out in a screen full of thumbnails, thereby lessening the opportunities for photographers to take a more considered approach to building documentation and ensuring the same limited number of images are reproduced *ad nauseam*.

Despite the new opportunities afforded by digital technology and photography's unrivalled success in conveying architecture to the profession and wider public, architectural photography today is under closer critical scrutiny than ever before. Its dominant position is assailed by new media such as video and computer-imagery and older media such as film and television, which have become increasingly interested in, and adept at, architectural interpretation. A rising chorus of disapprobation has denounced architectural photography for its perceived degeneration into a series of 'fashion shoots', in which the daguerreotype's 'warts and all' inclusivity, condemned by Merimée, has been transformed into an edited world of sanitized perfection. Buildings glow in the effervescence of eternal youth; appearance and style are lauded to the neglect of structure, spatial planning and use; graphic drama and visual excitement are prized above exegesis; and the overriding consideration is to appease the ravenous god of marketing, not to stimulate a deeper understanding of architectural creativity. While it is to be expected that photographers' first loyalty is to their clients, the fact that many of these clients are architects, whose background and outlook the photographers often share, has perhaps engendered an undue, if understandable, emphasis on what many photographers avow as their prime motivation, namely "to get back to the original moment of inspiration where the architects started the creative process".[11] This is an ironic echo of Talbot's conception of photography as the "royal road to drawing".[12]

Yet, just as the photographer's task does not end with the push of a button, the architect's responsibility is not confined to the computer screen or drawing board. Architecture is a public art, and its depiction must embrace not only the unblemished innocence of the design but its social dimension as well. We need, and currently lack, an architectural photography that communicates the experience of the building not just as the architect hoped it might be but as it is perceived in reality by the user. If architects need to be freed from the tyranny of the compulsion to design photogenic buildings, photography similarly requires liberation from the straitjacket of marketing and from a publishing environment in which buildings are treated as news and rushed to publication. Together these factors conspire to restrict the photographer to the narrowest window of opportunity between the building's photographically presentable completion and its anticipated spoliation through use. In such a context, the more measured assessment of a building's worth, once the landscaping has taken shape and the users have moved in, is totally precluded. We have the architectural photographer as celebrant and as artist, but what about the role as envisaged by Eric de Maré – "the photographer is perhaps the best architectural critic, for by felicitous framing and selection he can communicate direct and powerful comments both in praise and protest"?[13] Amid all the undeniably good and exciting work that is being done, a little more protest might not come amiss.

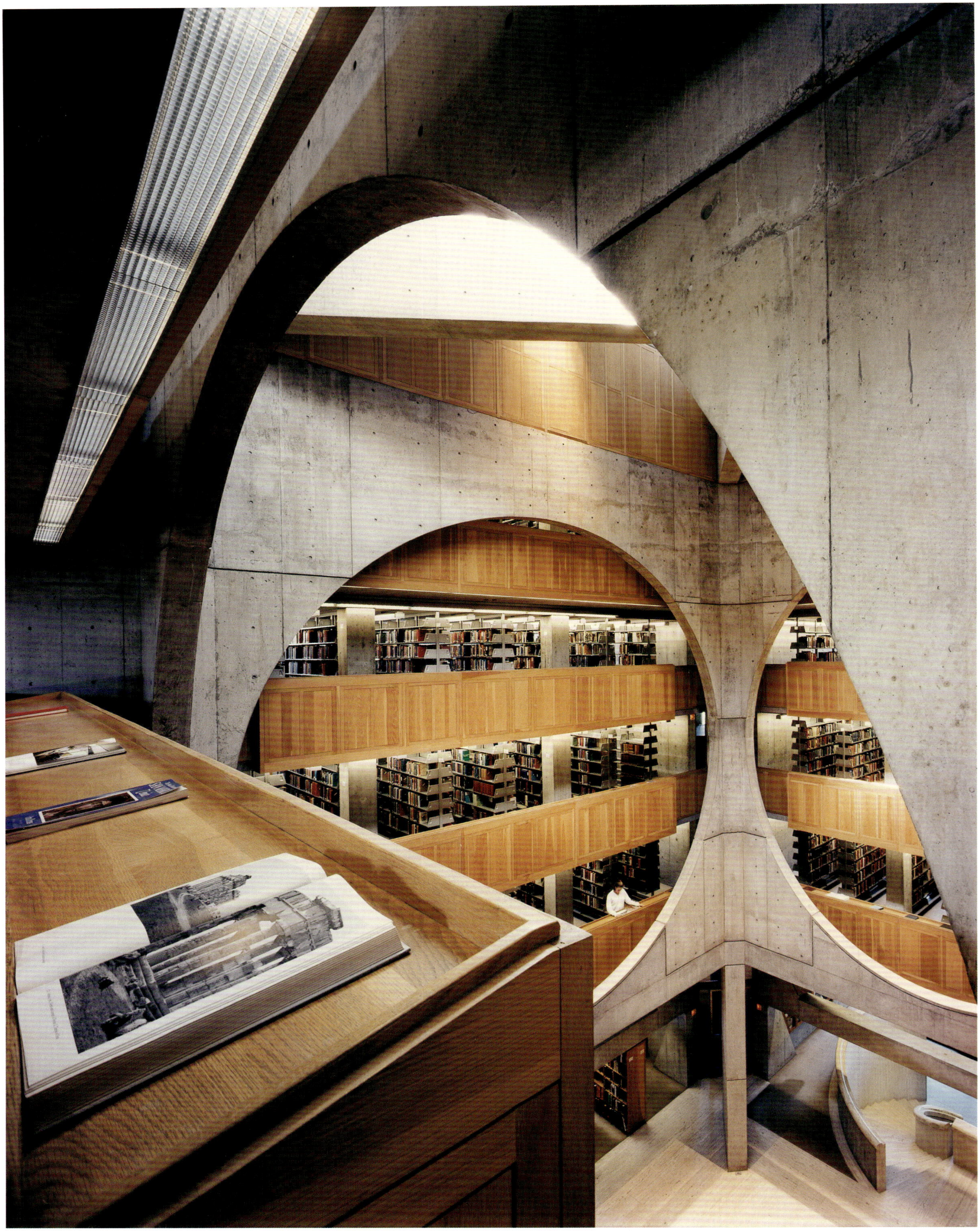

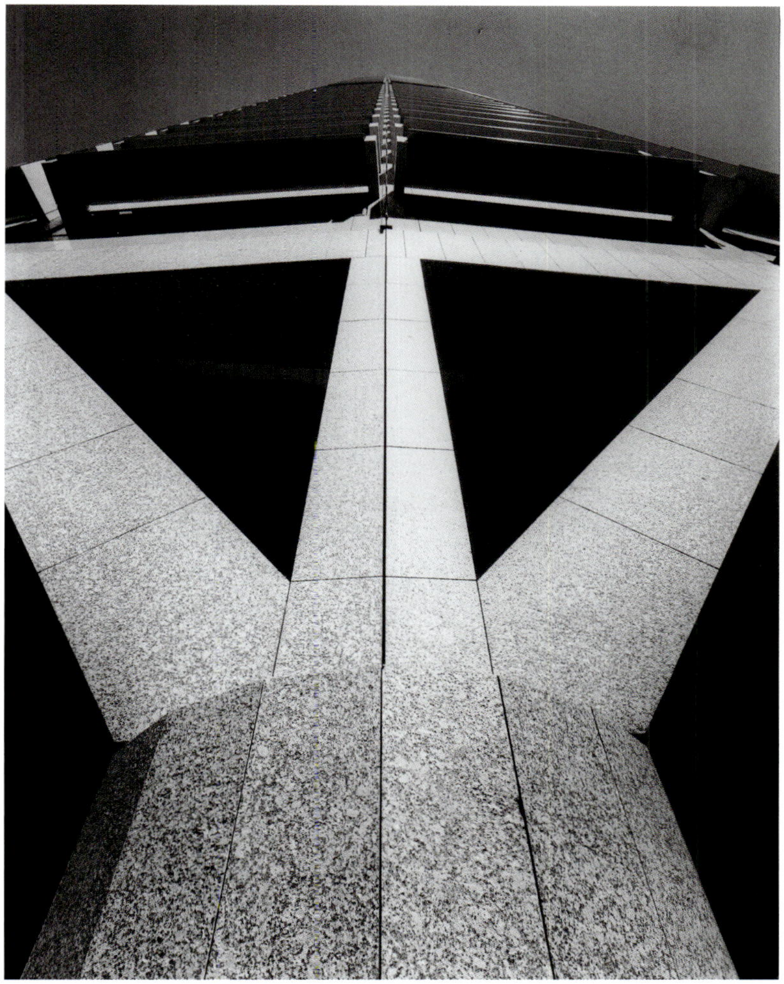

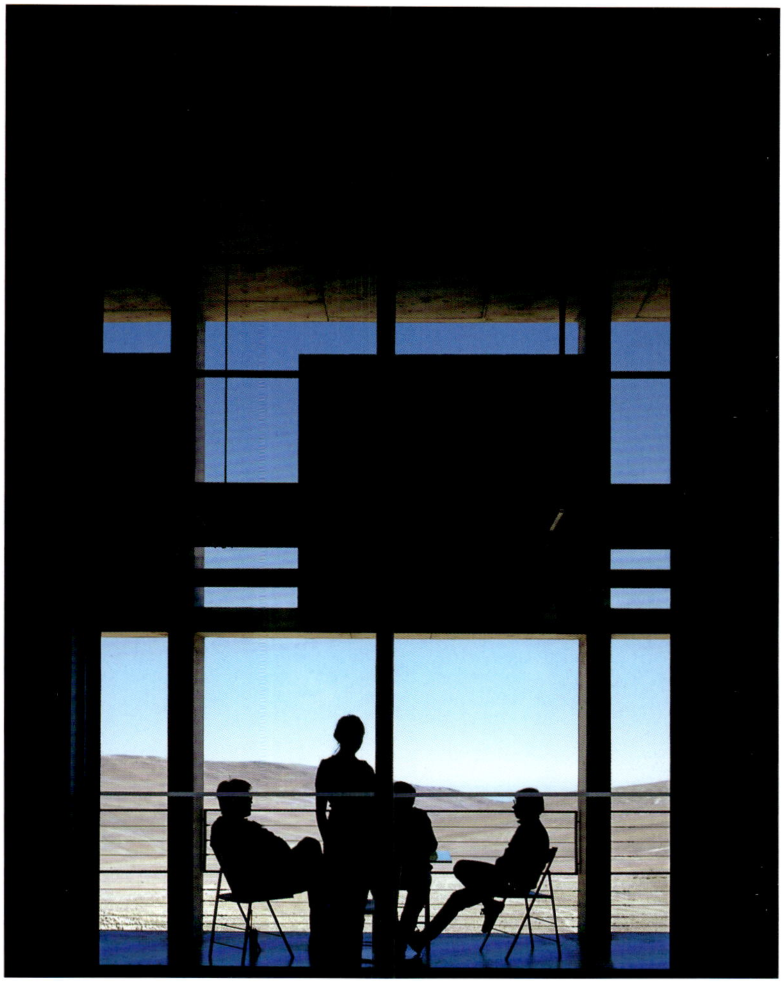

opposite

STEVE ROSENTHAL (born 1940)

Class of 1958 Library, Phillips Exeter Academy, Exeter, New Hampshire, 1971

Colour print

Architect: Louis I. Kahn

Having studied and practised architecture, Rosenthal began photographing in 1971, his mentors being Baer, Shulman and, above all, Stoller. A strong believer in setting buildings in their context, Rosenthal in his interior work avoids strobes and the overdramatic lighting characteristic of much interior design photography. Instead, he seeks a clear articulation of volumetric space and a naturalistic appearance, with supplementary lighting employed only to compensate for film's deficiencies compared to the human eye. This image was shot on colour negative, which has greater tonal subtlety than the more contrasty transparency and is accordingly favoured by several American photographers.

above left

MAX DUPAIN (1911–1992)

Grosvenor Place, George Street, Sydney, 1988

Gelatine silver print

Architects: Harry Seidler & Associates

Dupain established his first photographic studio in Sydney in 1934. Although a photographer of other subjects, such as portraits and advertising, the architectural photography that formed an increasingly large part of his post-war business was of the first rank. Characterized by its deceptive simplicity and strong lines, Dupain's imagery was instrumental in achieving international recognition for such architects as Glen Murcutt, Philip Cox and Harry Seidler, who hailed Dupain as "an incomparable master of his art".[14] Dupain's atelier also served as a training ground for other distinguished photographers, such as David Moore and Eric Sierins.

above right

ROLAND HALBE (born 1963)

Paranal Residencia, European Southern Observatory, Cerro Paranal, Chile, 2002

Colour transparency

Architects: Auer & Weber & Architekten

Halbe is one of a growing number of significant German architectural photographers whose ranks include Christian Richters, Jörg Hempel and Dieter Leistner. Here Halbe has shown how shooting into the sun and framing architecture against a lighter background to produce a silhouette effect can be a compelling means of lending visual force to the abstract patterning of Modernism.

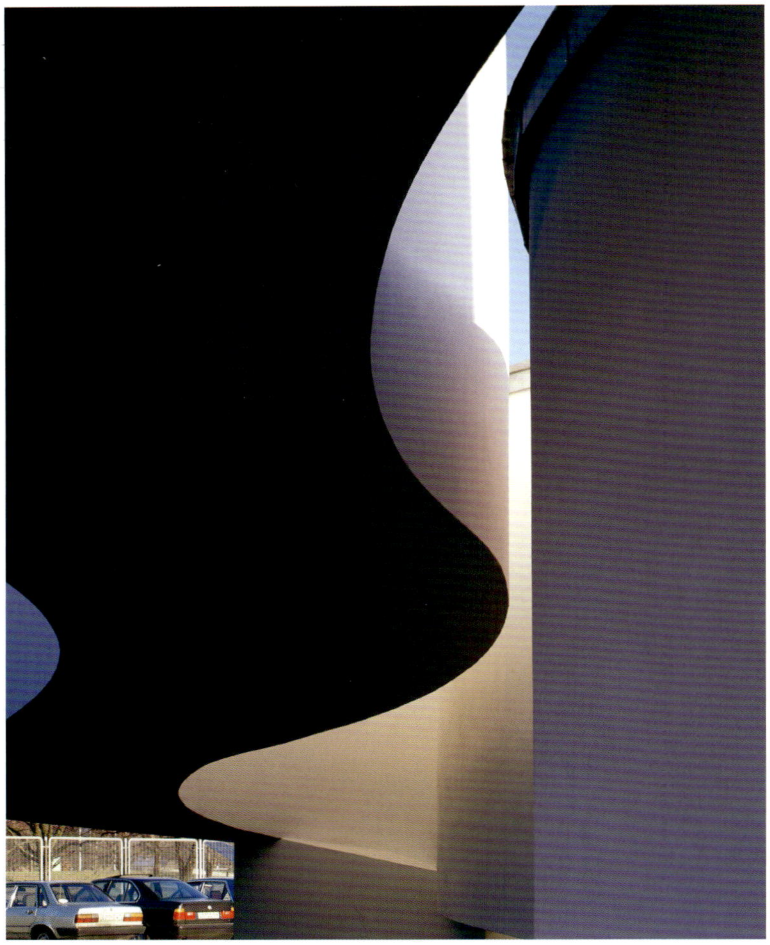

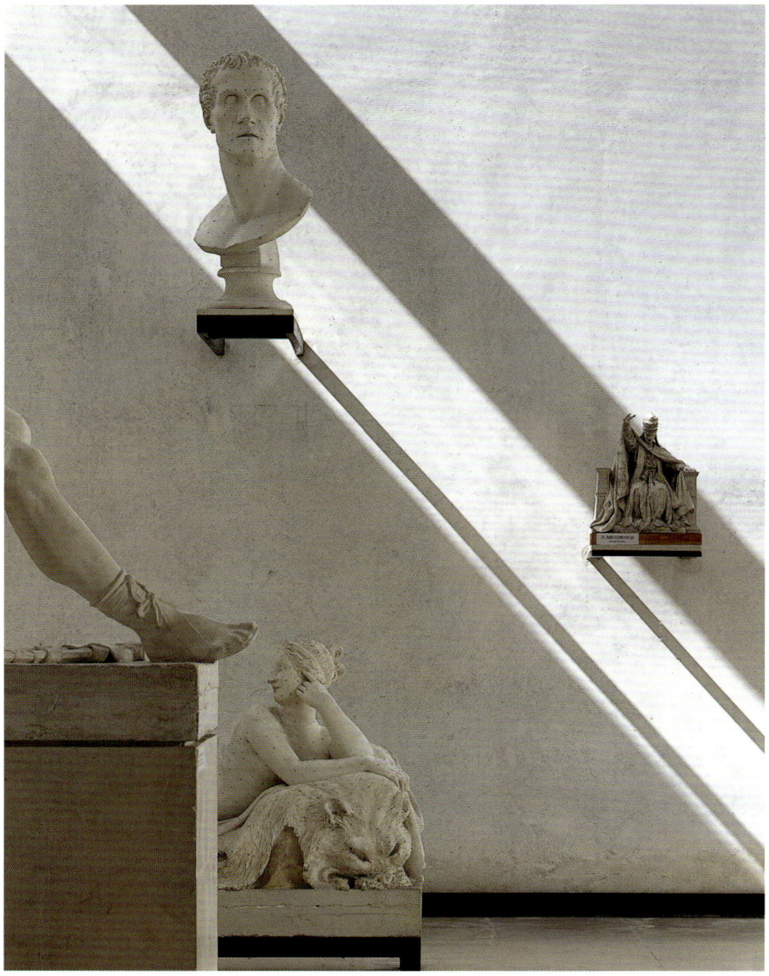

top left

RICHARD BRYANT (born 1947)

Vitra Museum, Weil am Rhein, Germany, 1990

Colour transparency

Architects: Frank O. Gehry & Associates

Carefully considered and meticulously crafted, Bryant's photography leaves nothing to chance. Above all, it is notable for its precision, intense colour saturation and crisply rendered details captured through long lenses. Black-and-white Polaroids are crucial to his painstaking working method, being used to assess composition and tonal values before the final shot is taken on his 5 x 4 inch (12.7 x 10.1 cm) or 6 x 7 cm (2¼ x 2¾ in.) Linhof Technikardan. The end result is a thought-provokingly distinctive style, highly regarded by both fellow photographers and architects.

bottom left

RICHARD BRYANT (born 1947)

Gipsoteca Museo Canoviano, Possagno, Italy, 1996

Colour transparency

Architect of remodelling: Carlo Scarpa

Bryant's Canova Museum photographs were not commissioned but resulted from his admiration for Scarpa's sympathetic 1957 restoration and extension. "In the life of a photographer", Bryant observed, "the idyllic project comes rarely. This was an occasion when all the pleasurable parts – light, aesthetic qualities of the subject, and place – were in perfect harmony."[15] Above all, the series eloquently testifies to Bryant's confessed source of inspiration in the paintings of Vermeer and de Hooch – "Wonderful glimpses from one room through to another with wonderful light. Very spatial. In a way, they're what I'm trying to do."[16]

opposite

LUIGI GHIRRI (1943–1992)

The Ossuary in Winter, Cemetery of San Cataldo, Modena, Italy, 1986

Colour transparency

Architect: Aldo Rossi

Ghirri's photographs of the unfinished cemetery at his native Modena, Italy, marked the beginning of a personal odyssey into Rossi's architecture for this evocative chronicler of the Po Valley's landscapes and customs. These images were made independently of the architect – the two rarely met – and represent a deeply personal response to Rossi's work, in which a fascination with its sharply defined geometric forms and their chameleon nature under the Po Valley's changing and fugitive light is most keenly felt. On Ghirri's death, Rossi remarked of his photographs, "I see in them something I was looking for but never found."[17]

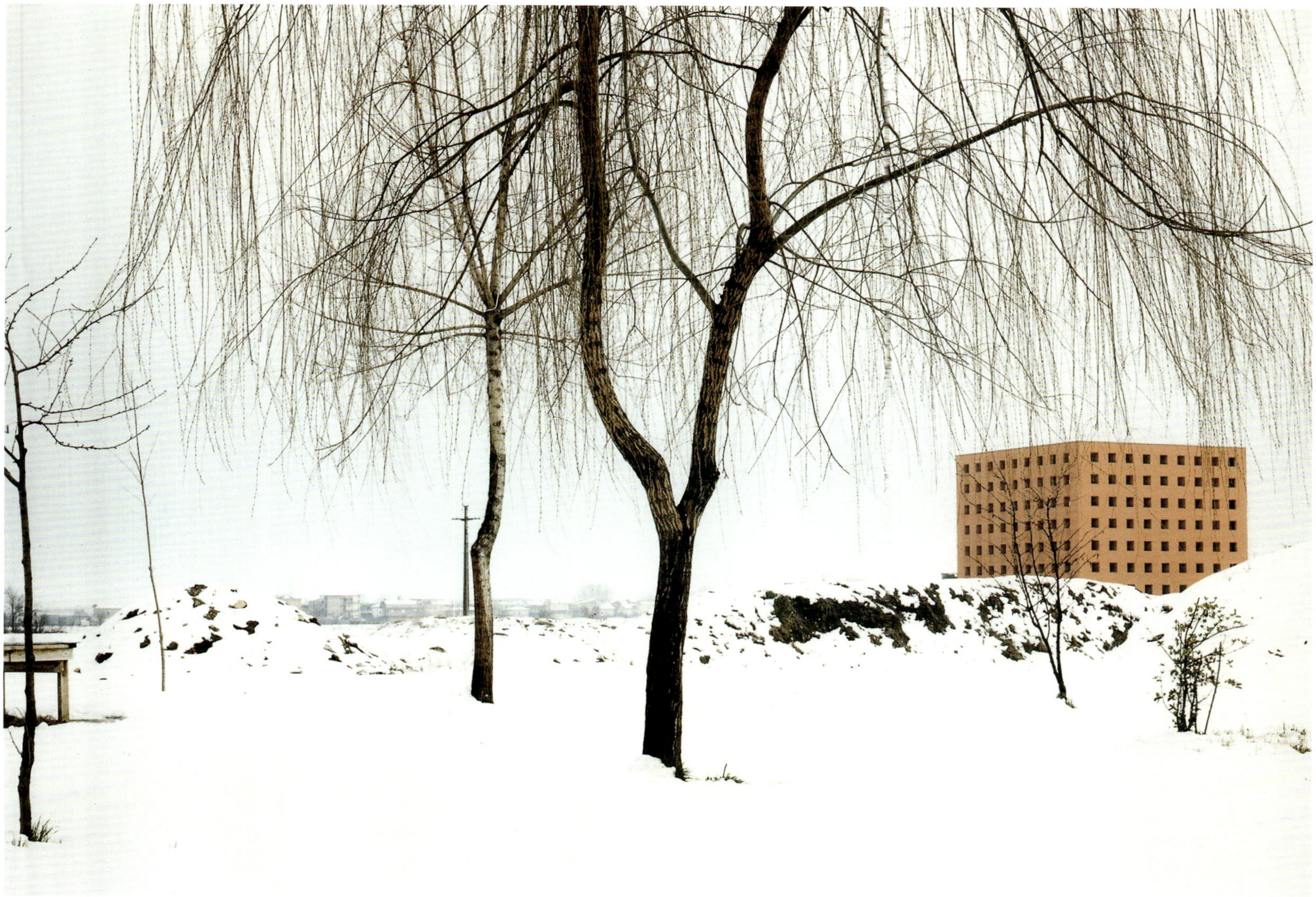

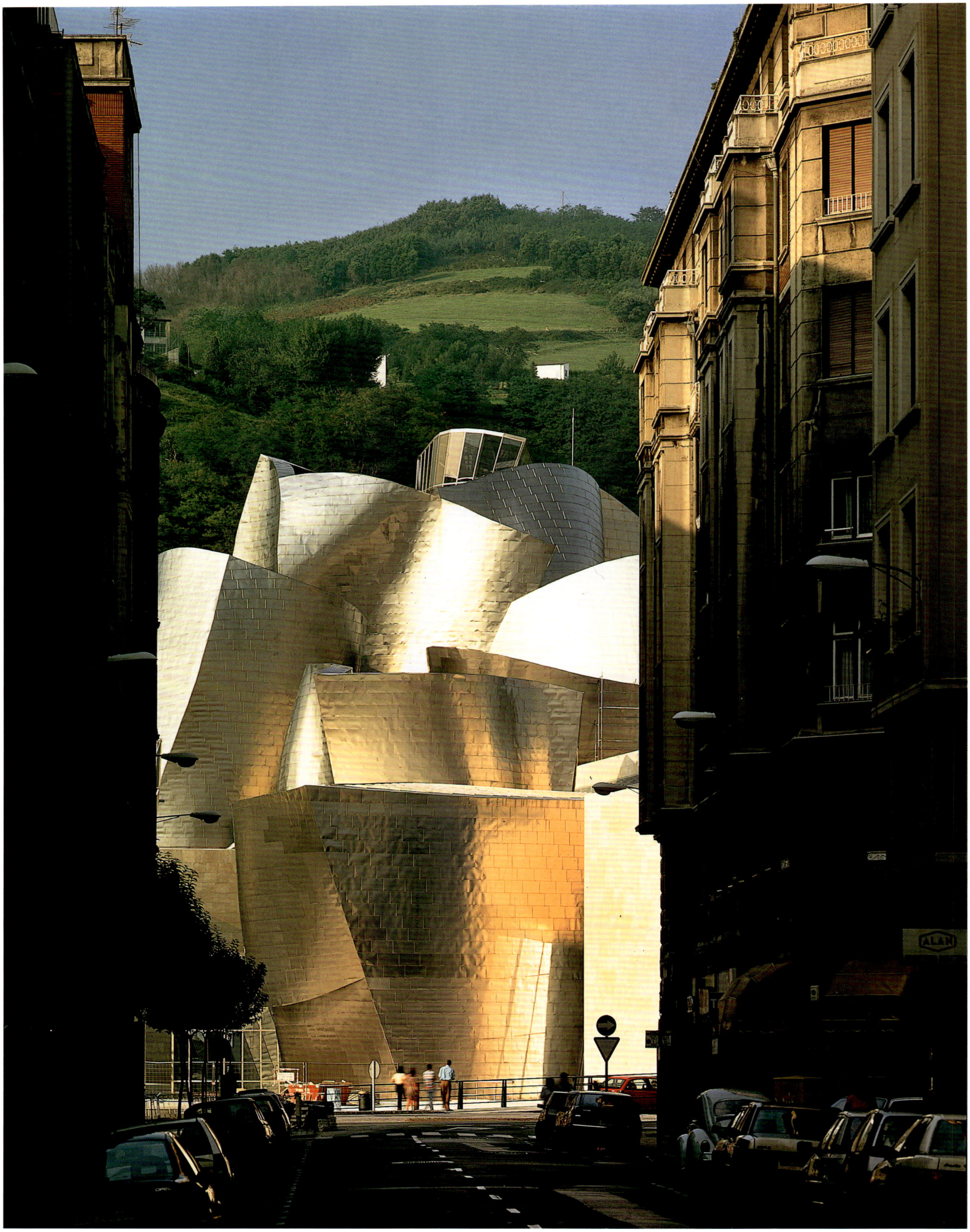
ALAN

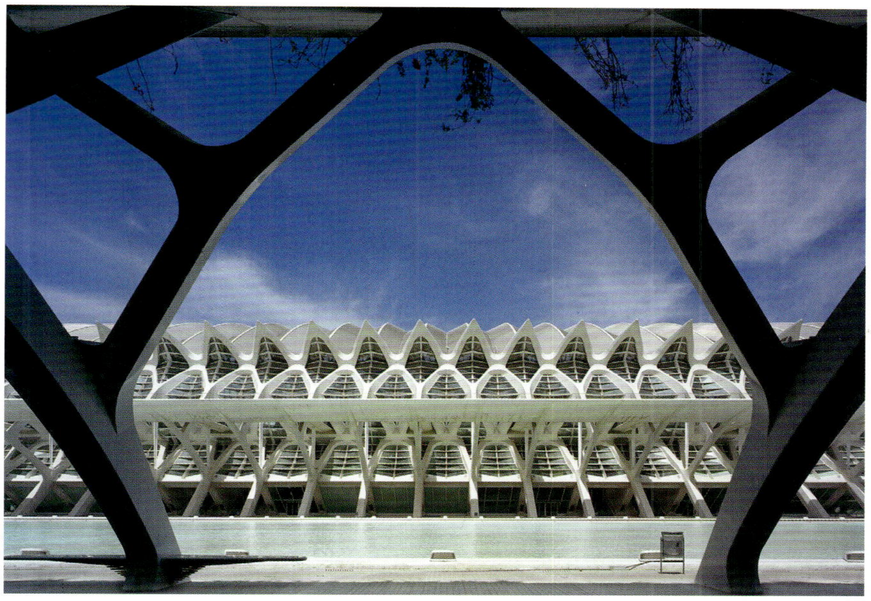

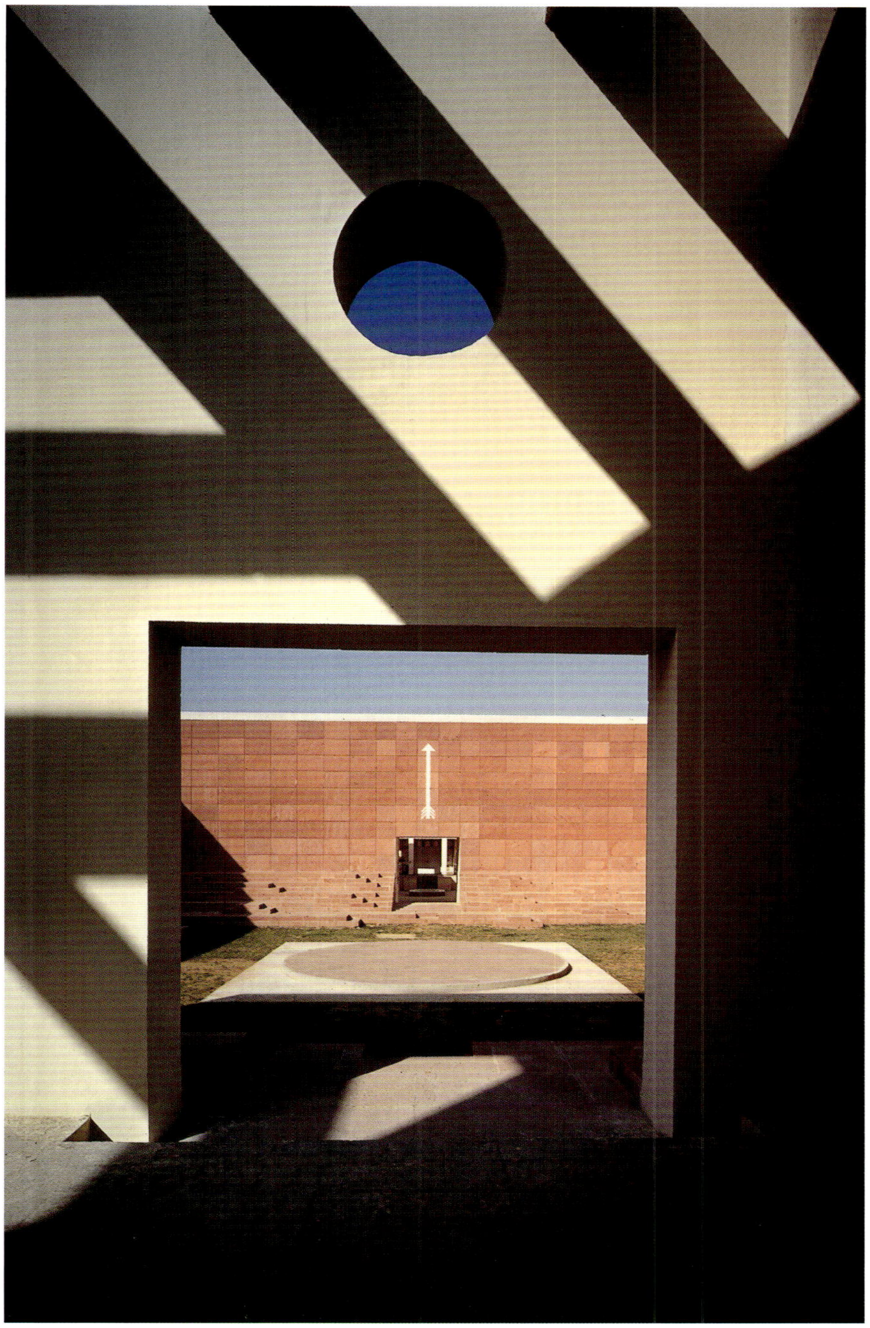

opposite

JEFF GOLDBERG (born 1961)

Guggenheim Museum, Bilbao, 1997

Colour transparency

Architects: Frank O. Gehry & Associates

Although there is a tendency for some photographers, such as Gabriele Basilico, to subvert the usual architectural hierarchies by treating all buildings, however important or humble, in the same matter-of-fact fashion, the significance of the landmark building promulgated by the camera cannot be denied. It is a commonplace that the Guggenheim has put Bilbao on the map, but, although the museum has become a place of architectural pilgrimage, the 'Guggenheim effect' – its potency as an urban signifier – could more rightly be ascribed to the ubiquitous dissemination of the building's memorable image through photographs such as top American photographer Jeff Goldberg's award-winning series.

top left

GER VAN DER VLUGT (born 1942)

Museu de les Ciències Príncipe Felipe, Ciutat de les Artes i de les Ciències, Valencia, 2002

Colour transparency

Architect: Santiago Calatrava

Ger van der Vlugt is one of The Netherlands' top architectural photographers, having been drawn to this specialization in 1980 by an emerging new wave of Dutch architecture, particularly in social housing and office buildings. After being employed by the Stichting Wonen, the foundation that published the leading Dutch magazine *Archis*, he began working for himself in 1988 and now counts among his clients Claus & Kaan and Mecanoo. He has a special interest in Spanish architecture and, like many other photographers, has been seduced by the photogenic qualities of Calatrava's structures.

bottom left

RAM RAHMAN (born 1955)

Jawahar Kala Kendra, Jaipur, 1992

Colour transparency

Architect: Charles M. Correa

Educated at the Massachusetts Institute of Technology and Yale University, Rahman has photographed for a clutch of India's most prestigious architects, among them Balkrishna Doshi, Raj Rewal and Charles Correa, whose work has come increasingly to public prominence in the last twenty years. His photographs betray his family background in architecture – his father was an architect – as well as his keen interest in graphic design.

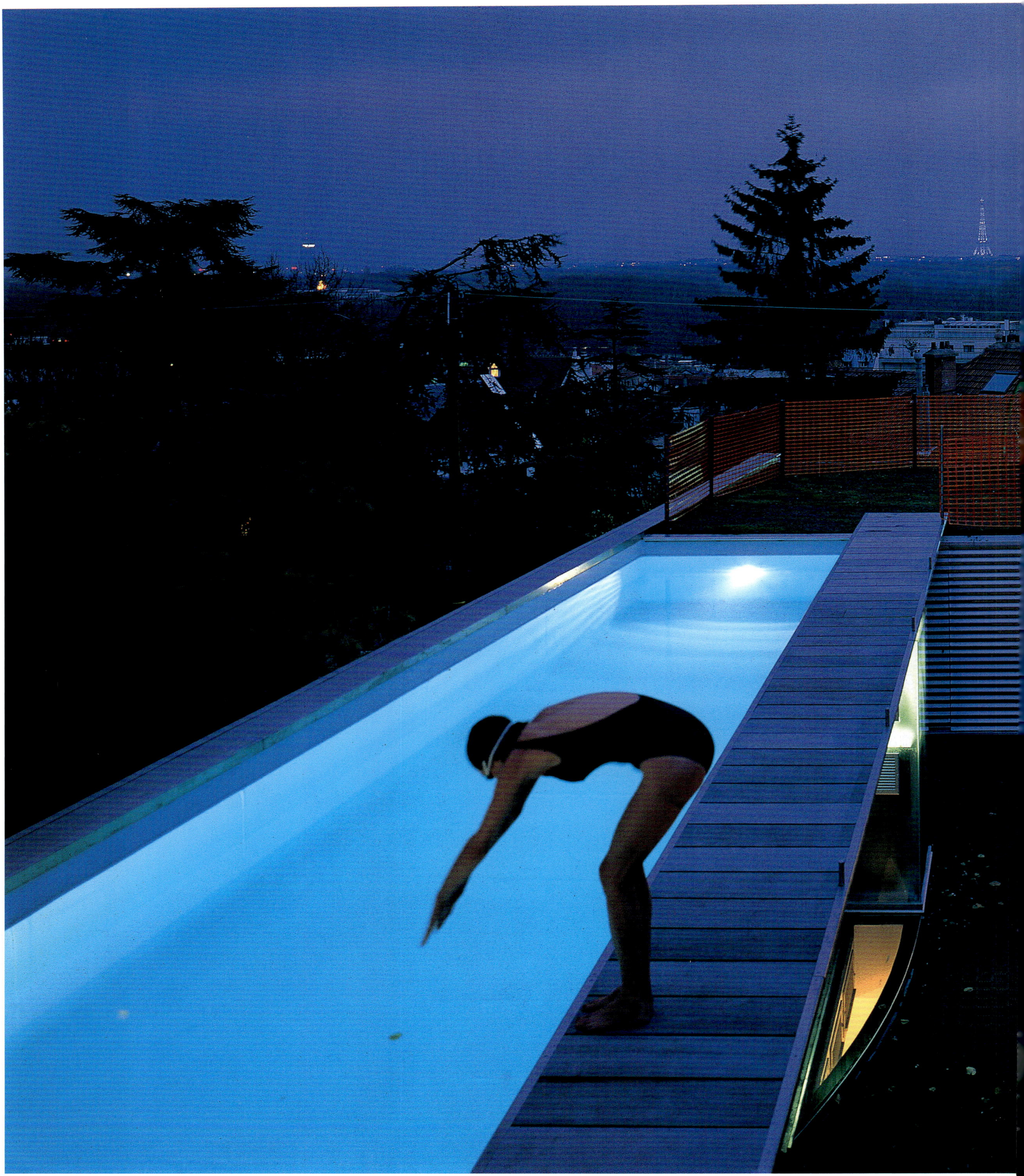

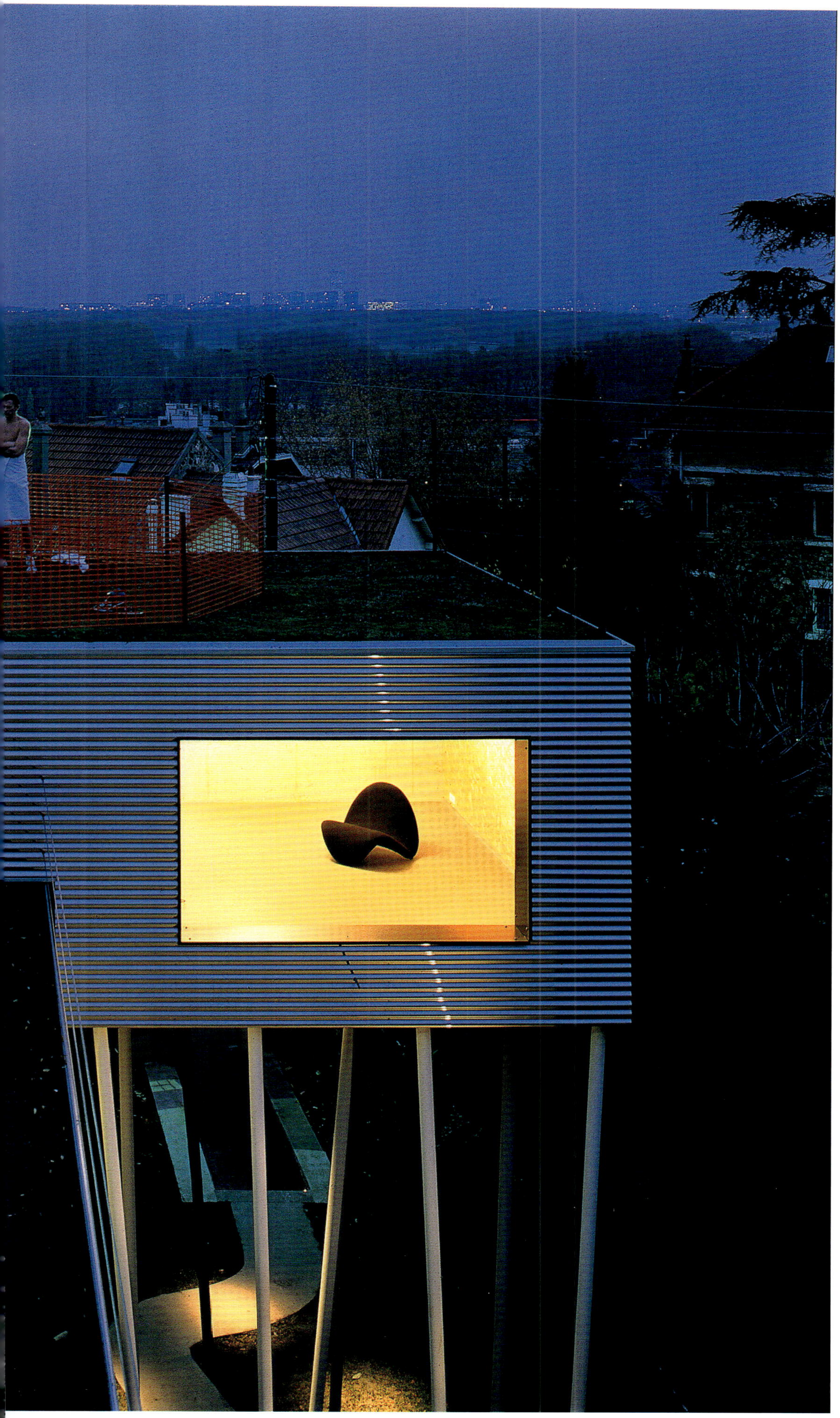

PETER AARON (born 1946)

Villa dall'Ava, St Cloud, Paris, 1991

Colour transparency

Architects: Rem Koolhaas of Office for Metropolitan Architecture

Aaron worked with Ezra Stoller for two years, but it is his background as a film cameraman that most informs his photography, which is marked by a cinematic compositional sense and his pioneering use of moody movie lighting with focusable spots that illuminate key features. In this striking instance of the twilight shot, which has become increasingly fashionable in architectural photography, the swimmer, whose arrested motion recalls a still from Man Ray's film about Robert Mallet-Stevens's Cubist villa, *Les Mystères du Château du Dé* (1928), anchors the composition by providing an intriguing 'sculptural' counterpoint to the chair illuminated in the window.

top right

TIMOTHY HURSLEY (born 1955)

Mariott Apartment, Chicago, 1985

Colour transparency

Architects: Krueck & Olsen

The apprenticeship system has been crucial to the development of architectural photography. From 1971 to 1980 Hursley worked for Balthazar Korab in his Detroit office before setting up his own studio in Little Rock, Arkansas, in 1982. His career well illustrates how architectural photographers need to be skilled all-rounders, from the challenging task of lighting interiors – here to romantically atmospheric effect – to the more gritty response required for his documentation of Mockbee's architecture of recycled materials in his book with Andrea Oppenheimer Dean entitled *Rural Studio: Samuel Mockbee and an Architecture of Decency* (2001).

bottom right

REID & PECK
(Jo Reid [born 1944] and John Peck [born 1943])

International Terminal, Waterloo Railway Station, London, 1993

Colour transparency

Architects: Nicholas Grimshaw & Partners

From 1973 to 1995 Jo Reid, who had formerly worked for Henk Snoek, and John Peck formed a partnership that produced some of the best and most distinctive photographs of contemporary British architecture. Shooting the same views on colour transparencies and colour and black-and-white negatives, Reid & Peck built up an impressive client base that included Terry Farrell, Nicholas Grimshaw and Piers Gough, as well as such firms as Hunt Thompson and Levitt Bernstein.

opposite

JAN DERWIG (born 1937)

Pietermaaiweg 4–4a, Willemstad, Curaçao, 1990

Colour print

A former architect, Jan Derwig is one of a number of photographers, including those featured and others such as Piet Rook and Jannes Linders, who are continuing The Netherlands' reputation for fine architectural photography. His portfolio includes coverage not only of contemporary buildings but also of traditional architecture in The Netherlands and further afield. As this image, featured in a publication on Curaçao, indicates, the photographic book exploring previously largely neglected architectural subjects has become increasingly popular in recent years.

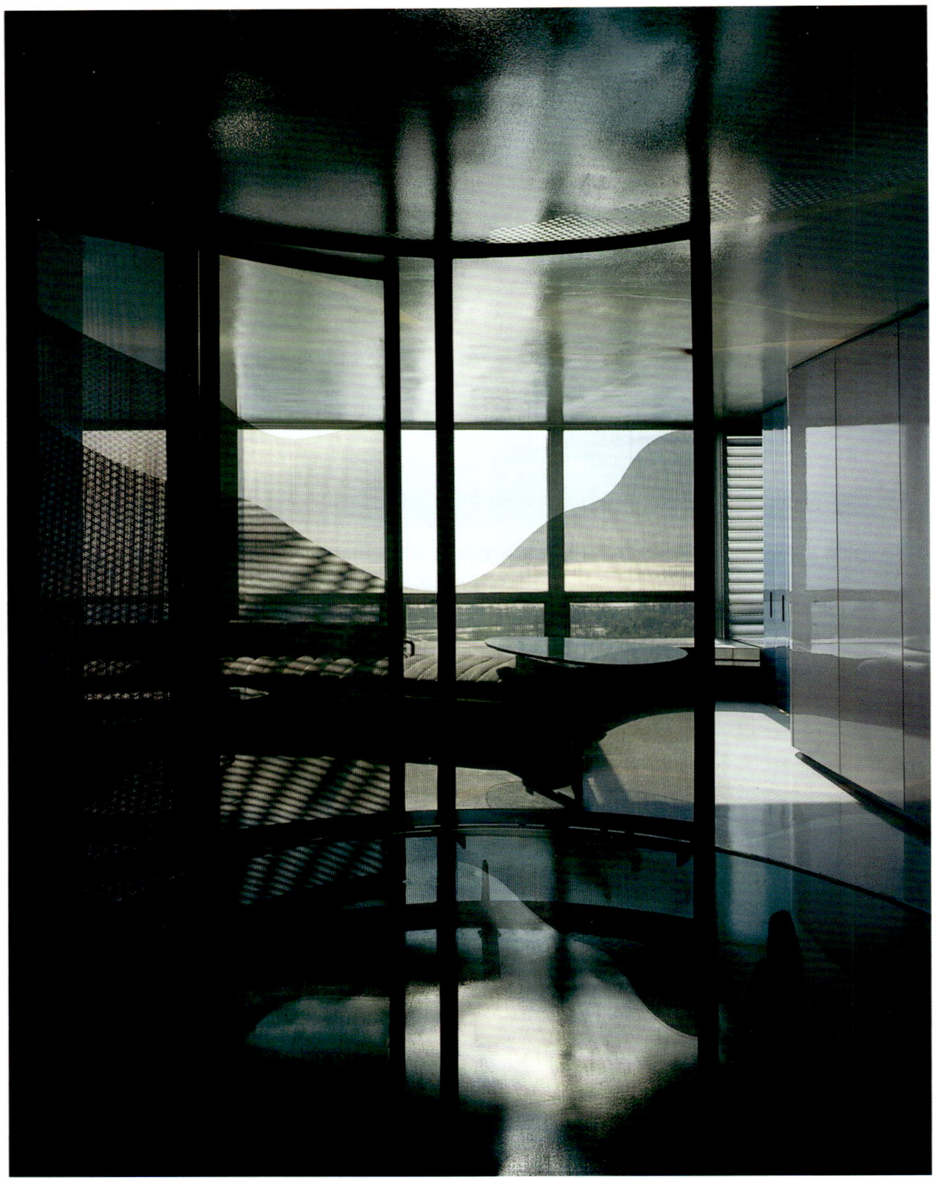

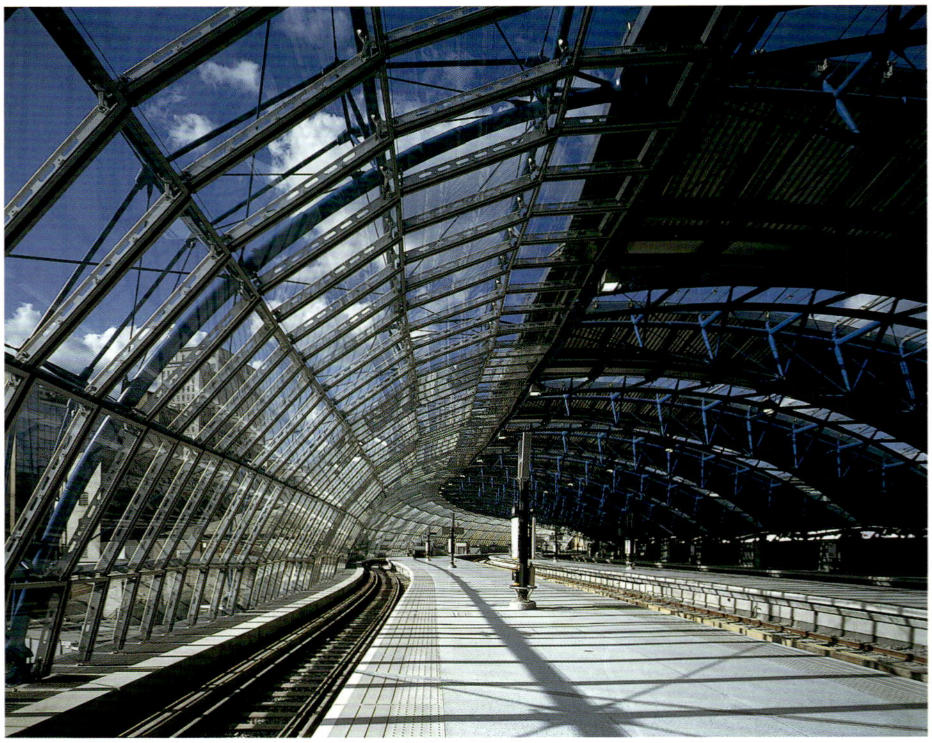

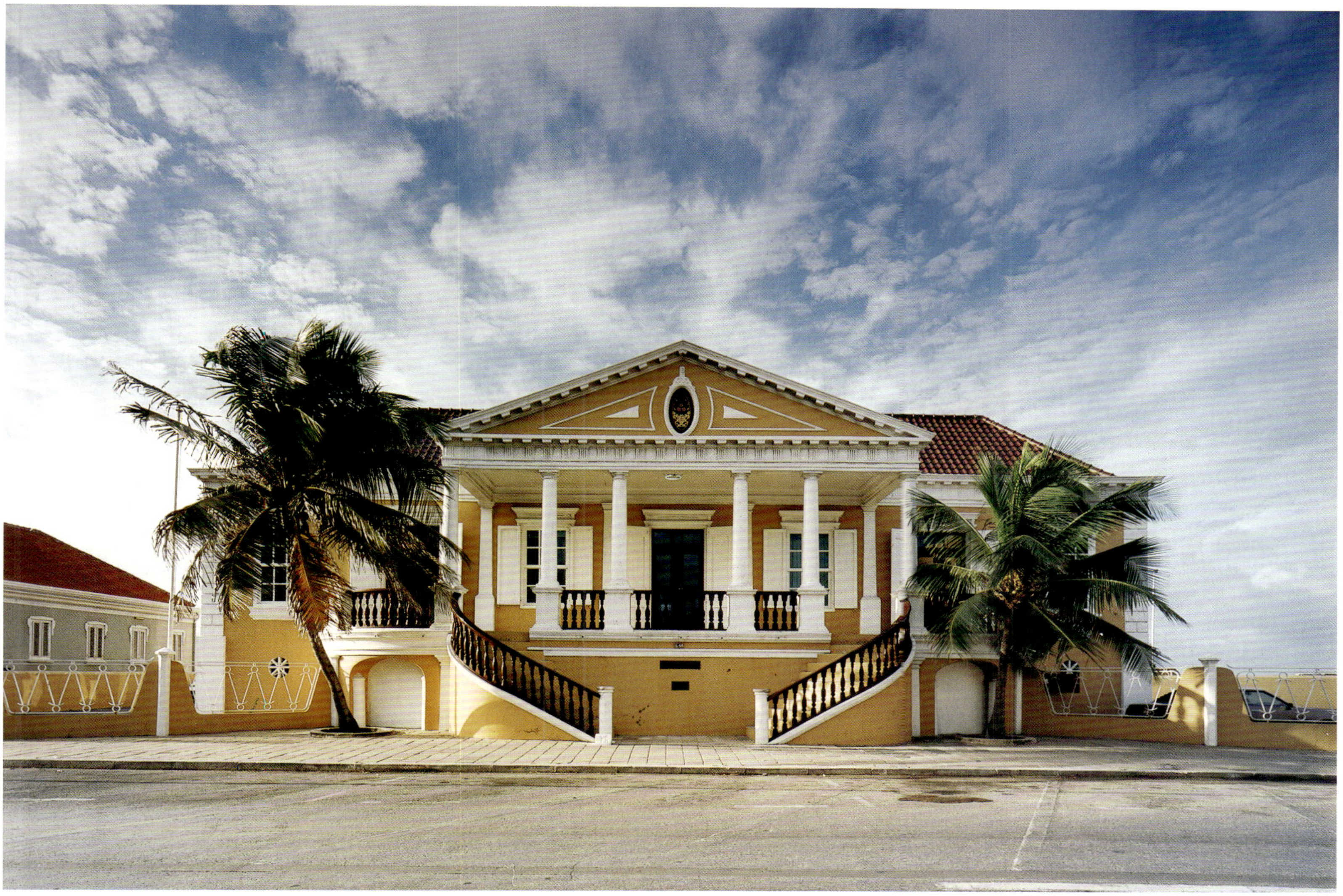

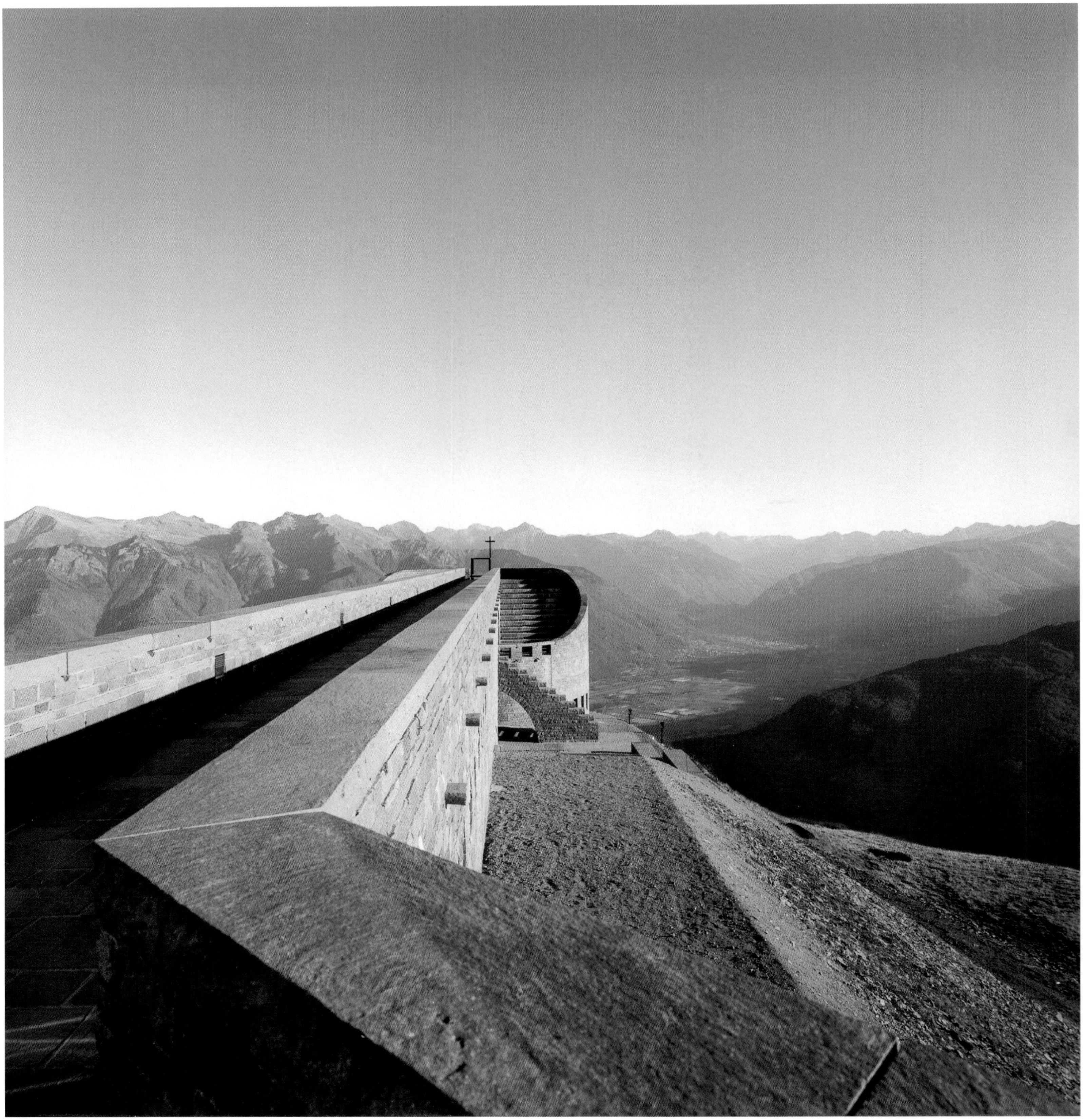

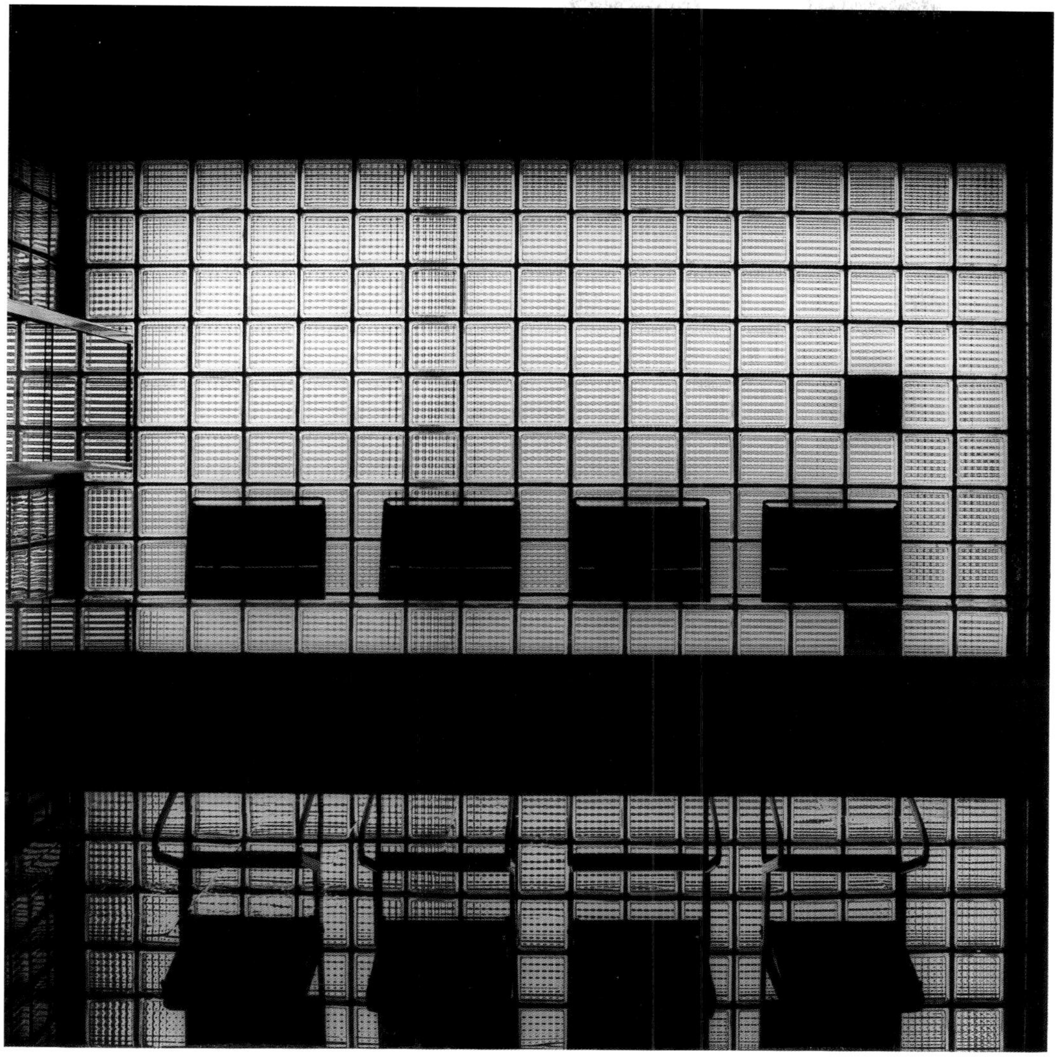

opposite

PAOLO ROSSELLI (born 1952)

Santa Maria degli Angeli, Monte Tamaro, Switzerland, 1996

Gelatine silver print

Architect: Mario Botta

Trained as an architect, and an admirer of Atget, Walker Evans and Friedlander, Rosselli began independent photography in 1981. His imagery – taken both to commission and for his own pleasure – is especially notable for its investigation of buildings in their context, whether man-made or natural. The architecture is 'stretched', both laterally (through the use of wide-angle lenses) and in terms of spatial depth through a deliberate distancing that not only challenges Renaissance perspectival notions but also reveals the building's relationship to the far horizon.

left

KIM ZWARTS (born 1955)

Albert & Bergsma Medical Centre, Weert, The Netherlands, 1987

Gelatine silver print

Architect: Wiel Arets

The strong lucid geometry of Dutchman Zwarts's imagery, combined with its studied neutrality and lack of highlights, not only accords well with the work of the architects he photographs, such as Wim Quist and Wiel Arets, but also represents a continuance of the tradition of the New Objectivity photography of the 1930s, as articulated especially by Werner Mantz, who moved to The Netherlands from Germany in 1932. It is fitting, therefore, that Zwarts should have won the Werner Mantz Prize for Photography in 1997.

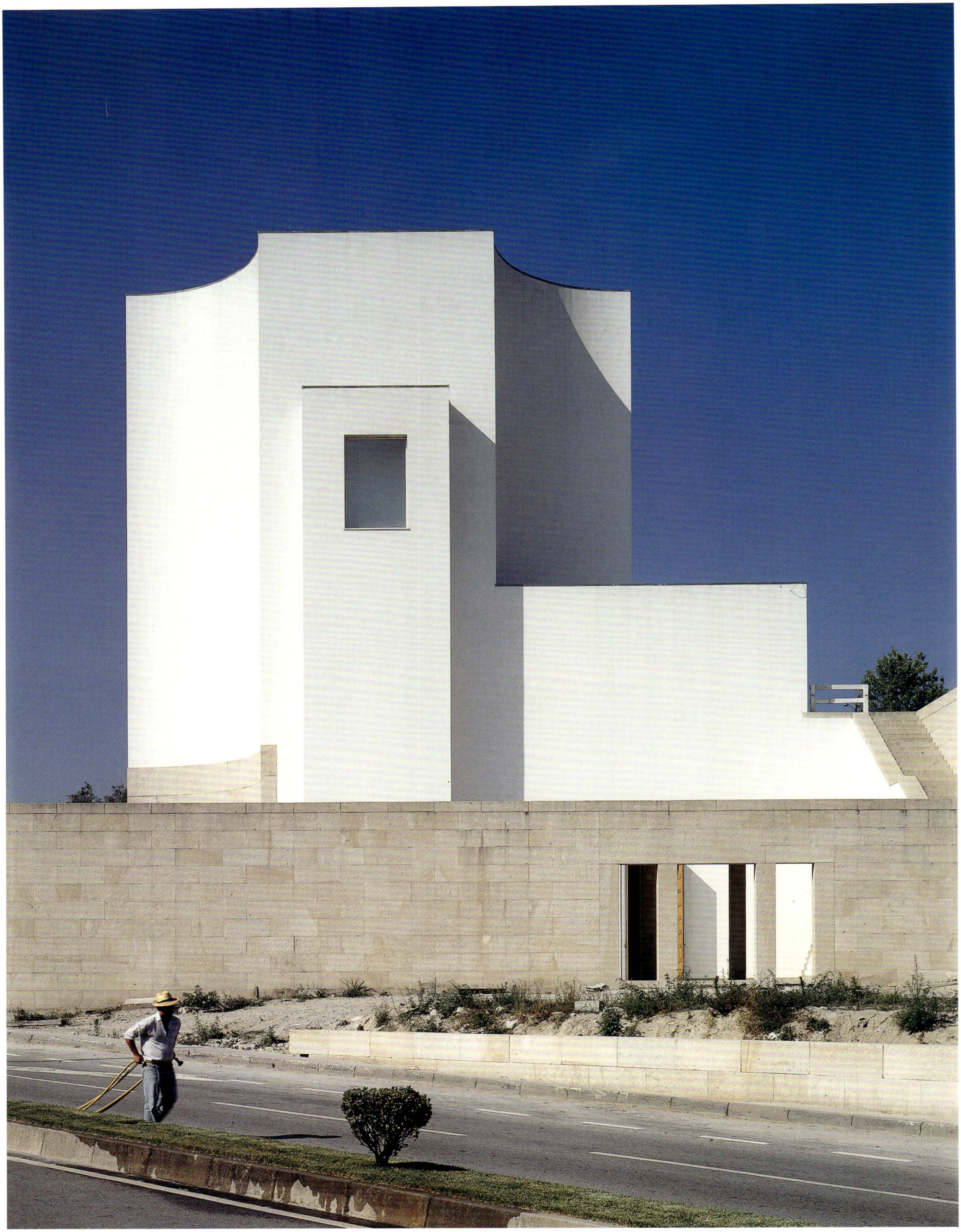

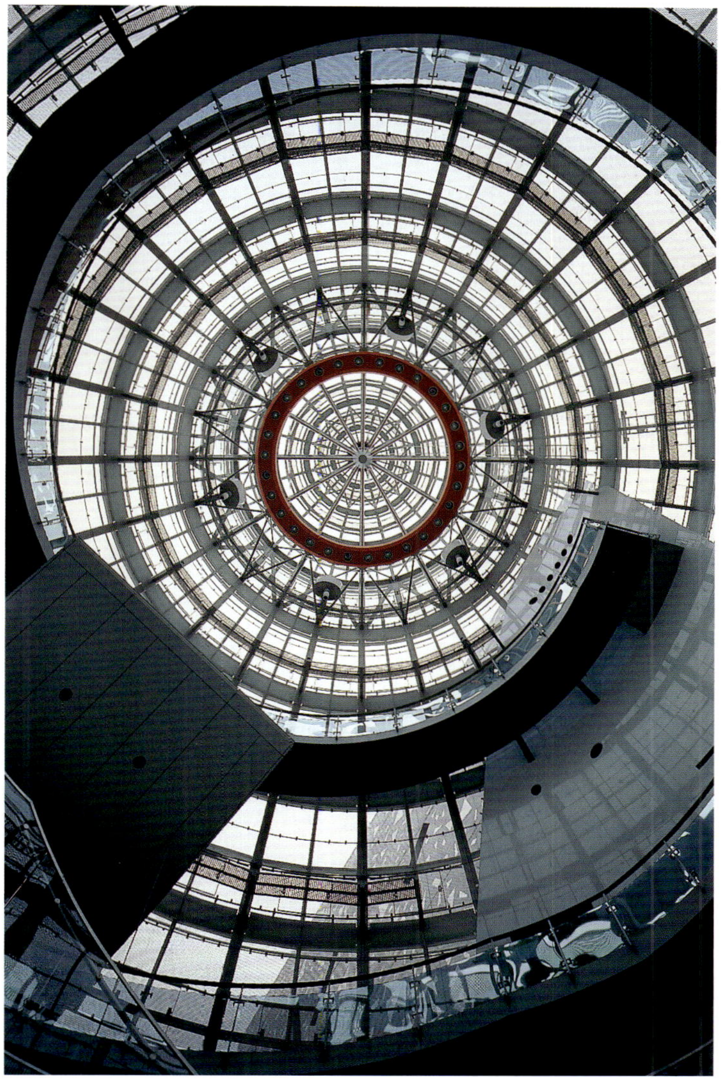

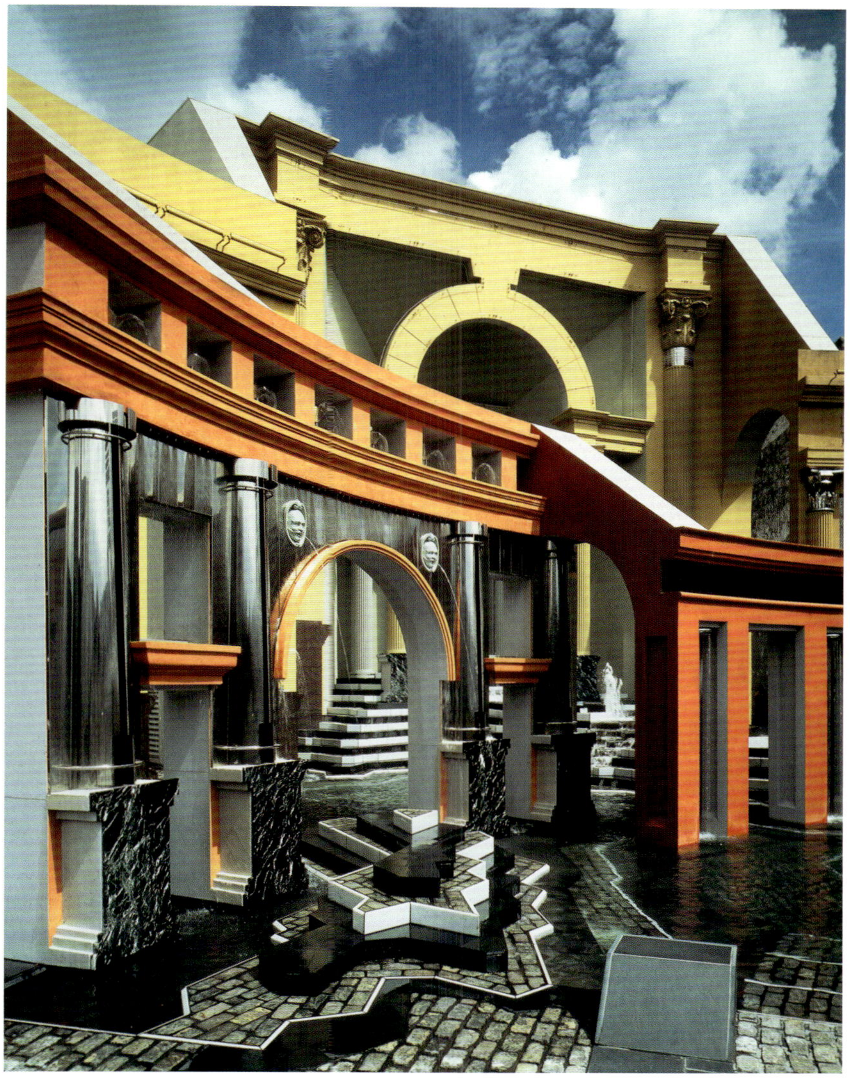

opposite

DUCCIO MALAGAMBA (born 1960)

Church of Santa Maria, Marco de Canavezes, Portugal, 1997

Colour transparency

Architect: Alvaro Siza

Born in Italy, Malagamba studied architecture and then moved to Barcelona to work in the office of Mortorell Bohigas Mackay before turning full-time to architectural photography in 1991. He is now one of Spain's top architectural photographers and his work features in journals worldwide. Malagamba's manner is one of studied concentration, working slowly and in series, as he himself has underlined, to "transmit a complex range of emotions and experiences" rather than "taking portraits of buildings".[18]

above left

TOMIO OHASHI (born 1932)

Ehime Prefectural Science Museum, Niihama, 1998

Colour transparency

Architects: Kisho Kurokawa Architect & Associates

With its strong grounding in camera and film manufacture, many of the best architectural photographers since the 1960s have emanated from Japan, among them Masao Arai, Mitsuo Matsuoka and Tomio Ohashi. Ohashi turned freelance in 1961 and began photographing for major architectural magazines such as *Kenchiku Bunka*. After a period in medical photography from 1968 to 1988, he returned to architectural subjects, driven by his strong interest in "architecture, cities and clusters that have powers to dramatically change and establish human mental states".[19]

above right

NORMAN McGRATH (born 1931)

Piazza d'Italia, New Orleans, 1978

Colour transparency

Architect: Charles Moore

Norman McGrath (son of Raymond McGrath, the noted Irish Modern Movement architect) worked first as a structural engineer before switching to professional architectural photography in the early 1960s. During the course of this career transition, he assembled a highly atmospheric collection of photographs of the dismantling of New York's Pennsylvania Station and thereafter established himself as one of America's foremost architectural photographers. His view of the Piazza d'Italia, an eclectic set-piece that could be said to resemble a photographically inspired collage of Classical references, has become one of the iconic images of Post-modernism.

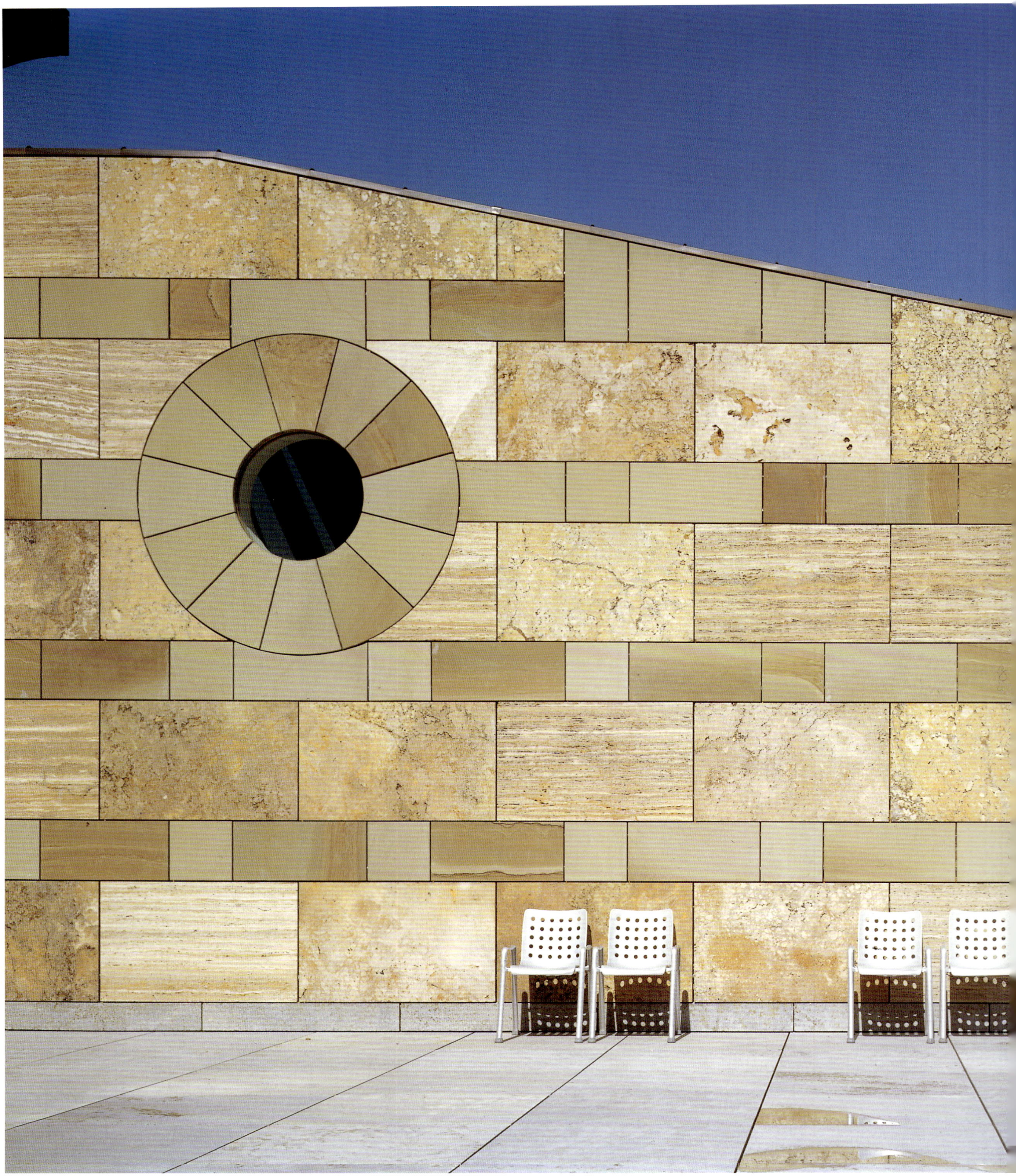

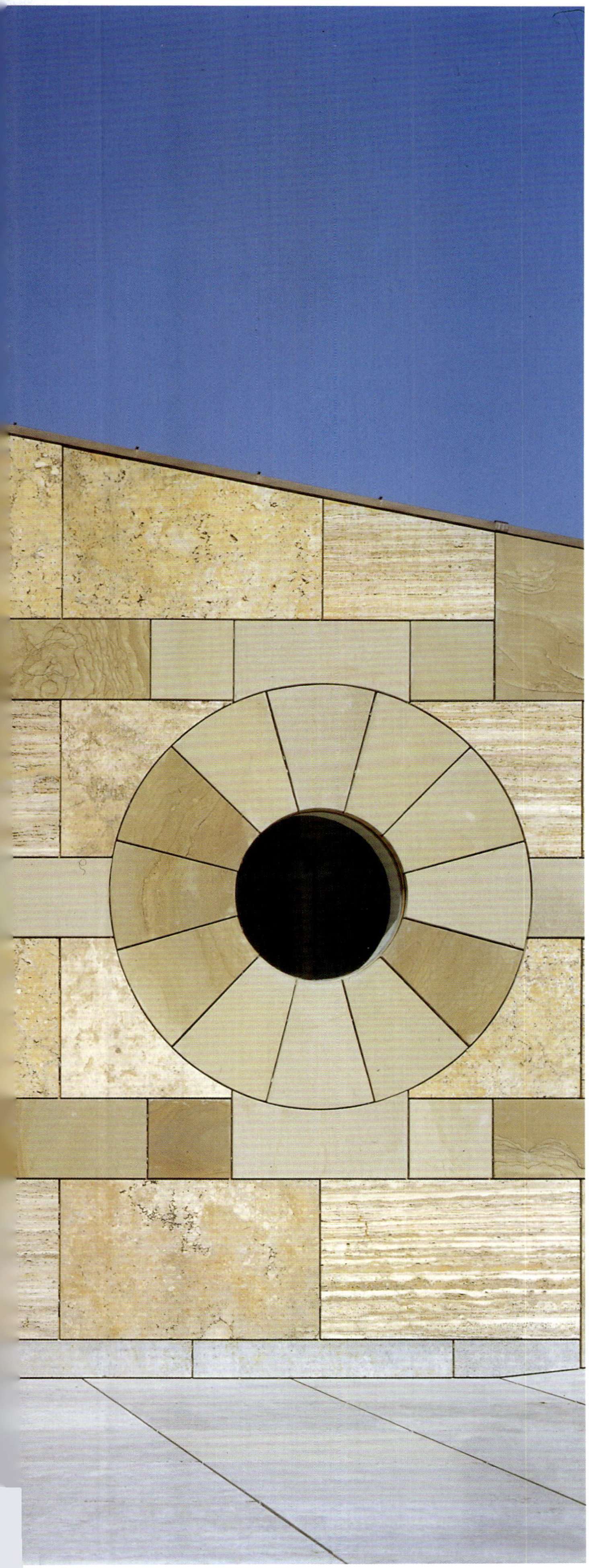

ALASTAIR HUNTER (1938–1991)

Staatsgalerie Extension, Stuttgart, 1983

Colour transparency

Architects: James Stirling Michael Wilford & Associates

Hunter began photographing in Edinburgh in 1960 and subsequently became Scotland's prime architectural photographer, his clients including Basil Spence and, later, Foster, Rogers and Stirling. His output in the late 1970s and 1980s reflected contemporary trends in architectural photography, in particular the great outburst of colour. Hunter was responsible for some of Stirling's favourite views of the Staatsgalerie, and the building's image has become even better known through popular advertising campaigns.

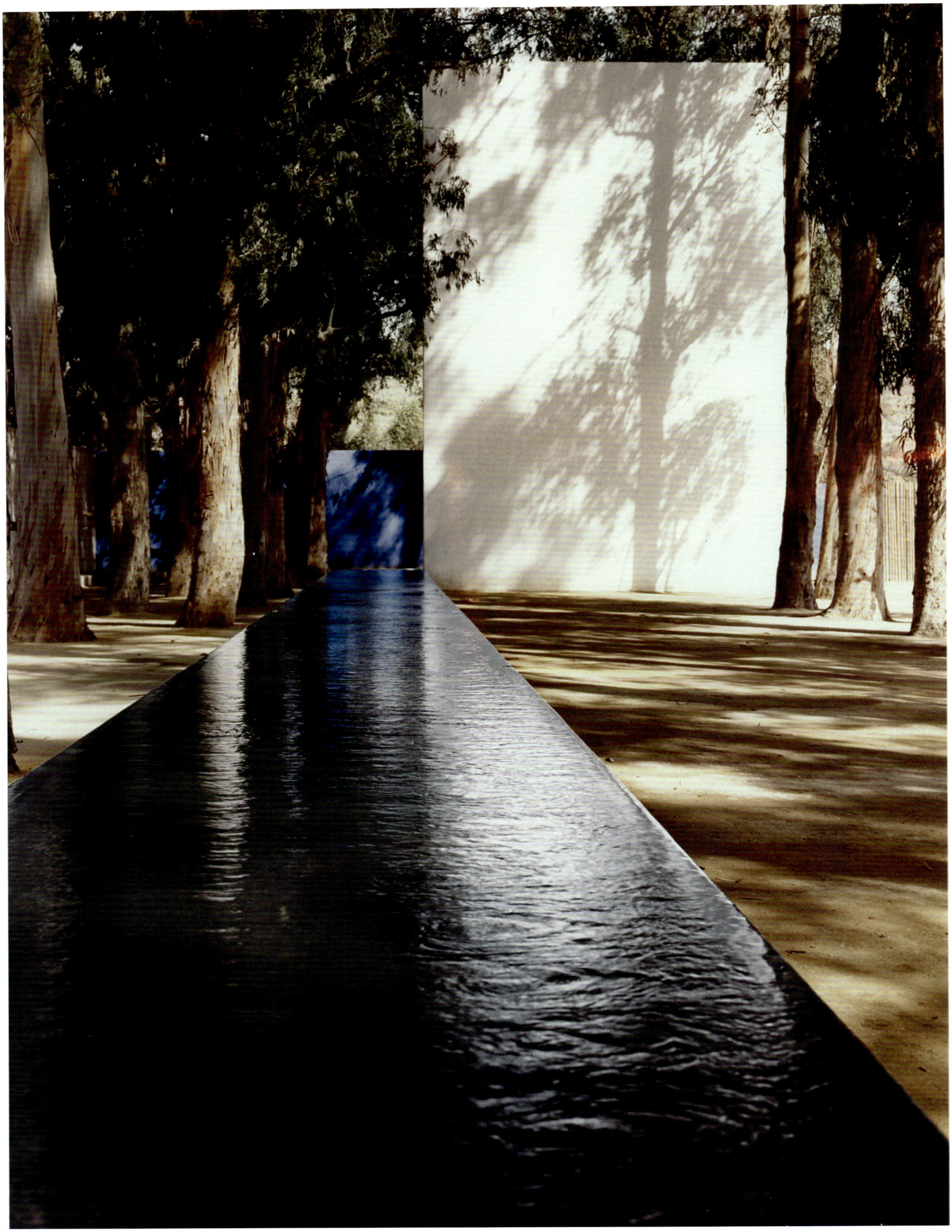

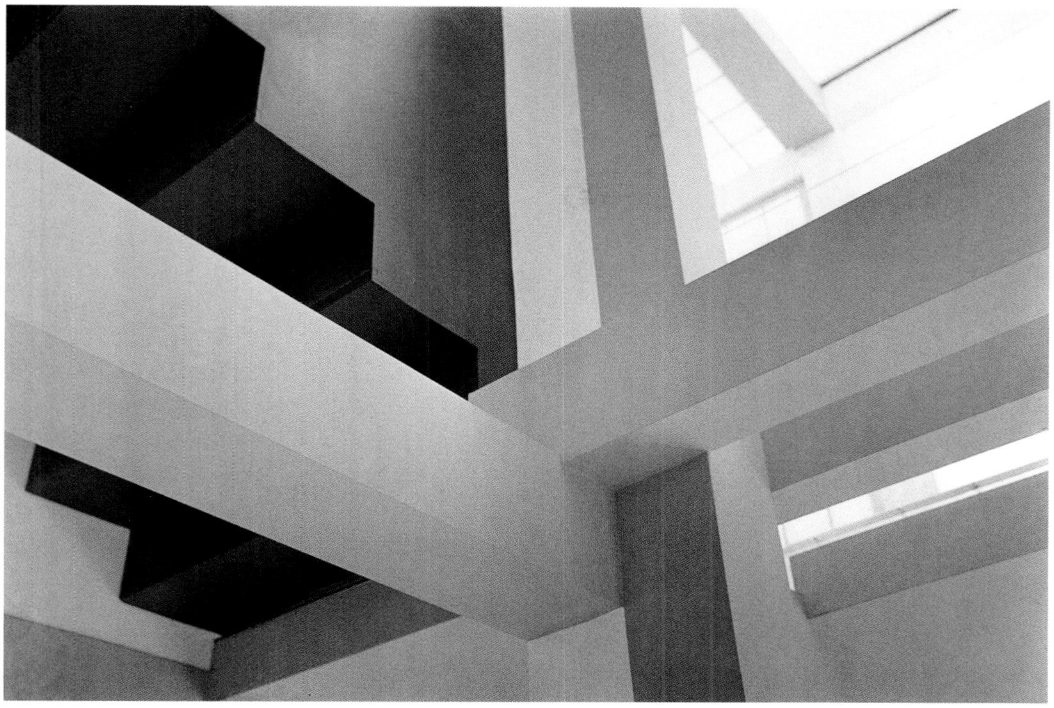

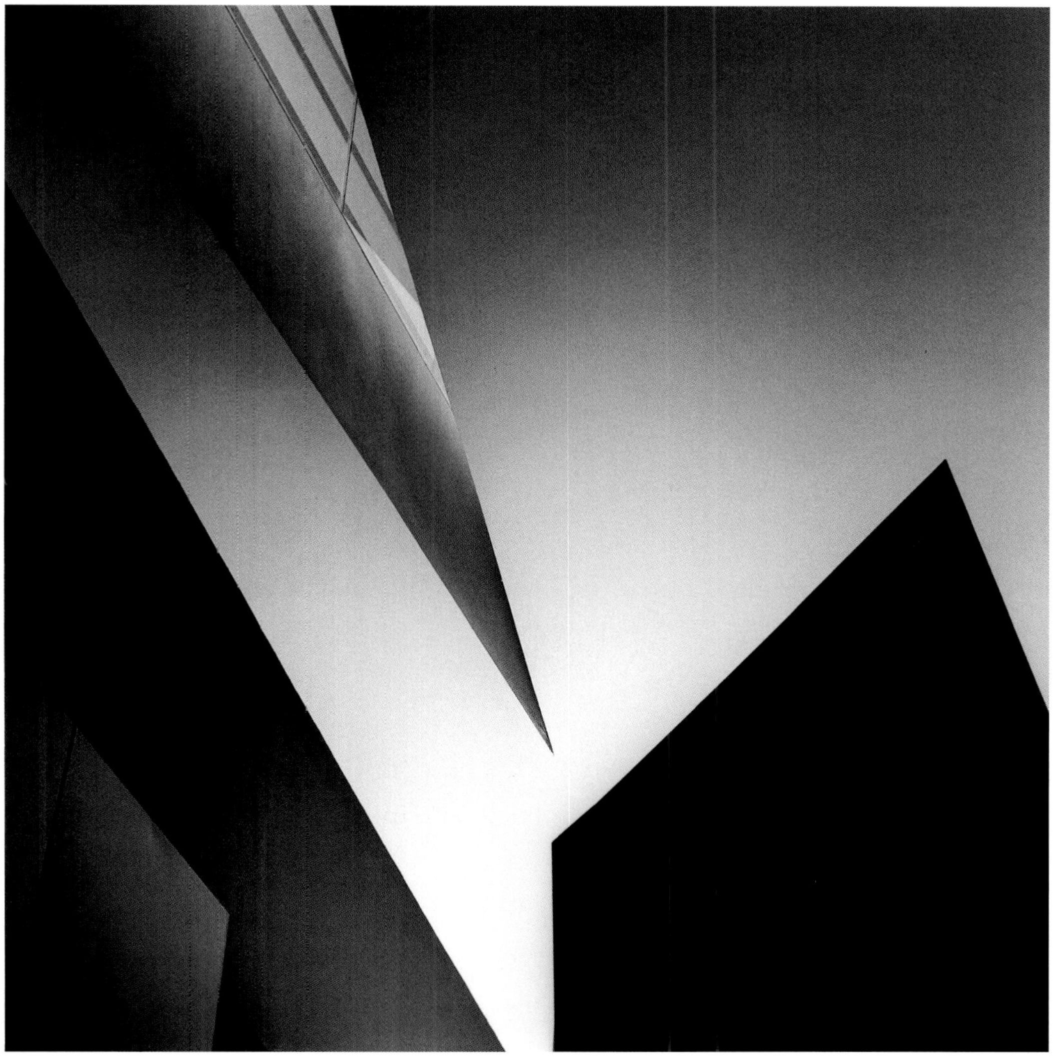

opposite

ARMANDO SALAS PORTUGAL (1916–1996)

El Bebedero Fountain, Las Arboledas, Mexico City, 1960s

Colour transparency

Architect: Luis Barragán

Barragán used photographs both to promote his own work, painstakingly selecting and annotating images for publication, and as part of his creative process. His remarkable collaboration with Salas Portugal, one of Mexico's most sensitive portrayers of its architecture and landscape, lasted from 1944 until his death in 1988. Becoming progressively less literal and more fragmentary, Salas Portugal's photographs of Barragán's work before and after completion, first in black-and-white and later in colour, suggested to the architect how designs could be improved, and at the same time conveyed his photogenic architecture, with its bold colours and textured surfaces, to a wider audience.

top left

JUDITH TURNER (born 1939)

Frank Residence, Cornwall, Connecticut, 1976

Gelatine silver print

Architect: Peter Eisenman

Turner began photographing in 1972, drawn especially to architectural Modernism by her interest in graphic design and fascination with abstract form. These pursuits have remained critical to her photography, an early example being *Judith Turner Photographs Five Architects* (1980), a study of the New York Five in which this image appeared. Turner deconstructs architecture into a succession of often ambiguous fragments that, while confounding viewer expectations through their distortions of scale and perspective, and the way voids are rendered corporeal and solidity is dissolved, seek both to reflect the architect's intent and create Turner's own "divergent dream worlds of architecture".[20]

bottom left

HÉLÈNE BINET (born 1959)

Vitra Fire Station, Weil am Rhein, Germany, 1983

Gelatine silver print

Architect: Zaha Hadid

Having studied art history and trained as a photographer in Italy, Binet moved to London in the early 1980s and began specializing in architectural photography. Her photographs of Hadid's work, inspired by a close study of the architect's drawings and exemplifying her belief that the photographer cannot relate architecture's complex totality but must instead communicate "one very strong but smaller experience",[21] are powerfully dynamic, an animated interaction of jagged angles and intersecting lines. For Libeskind, her photography "reveals architecture's inner intensity by materialising the phenomenon of light, texture and density, all within a composition that is wholly conceptual".[22]

top right

PHILIP TRAGER (born 1935)

Villa Barbaro, Maser, Italy, 1984

Gelatine silver print

Architect: Andrea Palladio

Although not a full-time photographer, Trager has published several books on architectural topics, including *Philip Trager Photographs of Architecture* (1977) and *The Villas of Andrea Palladio* (1986), and examples of his work can be found in leading American museums. His photographs, which, like those of Edwin Smith, are imbued with an innate humanism and an obvious affection for his subjects, exude an air of diffidence. They beguile by gentle persuasion rather than arrest with dramatic force.

bottom right

RICHARD PARE (born 1948)

Church on the Water, Tomamu, Hokkaido, 1992

Colour print

Architect: Tadao Ando

Ando's work is considered by many photographers to be extremely photogenic, but few have matched Pare's sensitivity to the changing forms and colours of Ando's architecture under different light conditions. This shows to particularly mesmeric effect in his photographs of the Church on the Water. Pare, a former curator of photographs at the Canadian Centre for Architecture and author of a major book on photography and architecture, photographed Ando's buildings between 1985 and 1996, guided by his realization that it was "this sense of dissolving mass in the constantly changing light that is a distinguishing characteristic of Ando's architecture".[23]

opposite

MARTIN CHARLES (born 1940)

Ducrow Mausoleum, Kensal Green Cemetery, London, 2001

Gelatine silver print

From the early 1970s Charles emerged as one of Britain's pre-eminent architectural photographers, covering both modern and historic architecture but with an increasing bias towards the latter, as evidenced by his work for the 'Masters of Building' series in the *Architects' Journal*. An admirer of Frederick Evans, Eric de Maré and Edwin Smith, Charles is an ardent proponent of their alternative tradition of architectural photography, which emphasizes place and the human dimension rather than architecture *per se*. "You don't actually have to have people in the shot," he maintains, "but you do need to have the signs, the evidence of people's work."[24]

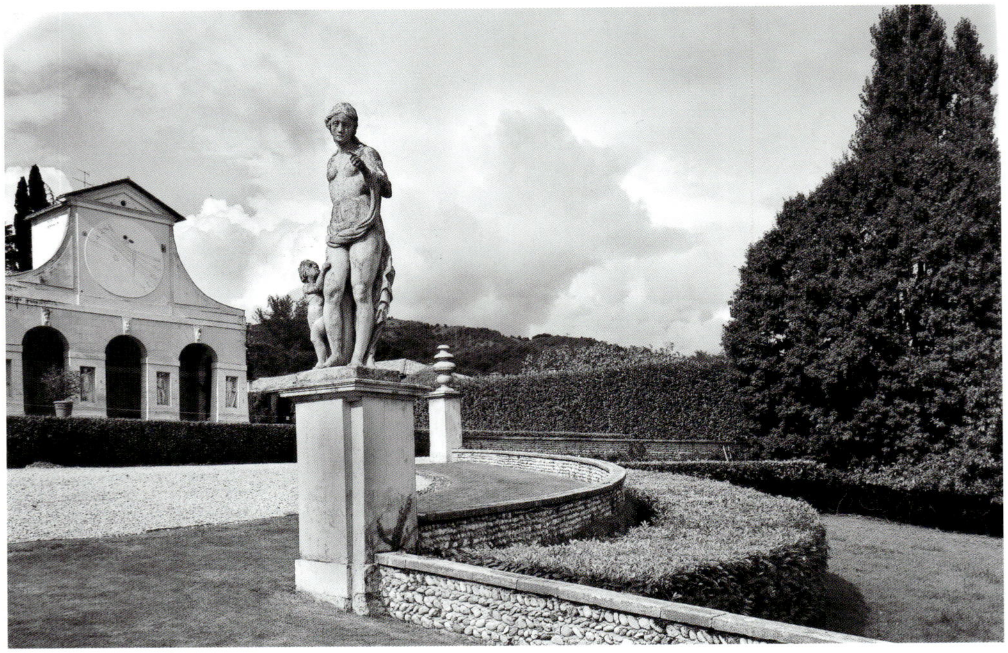

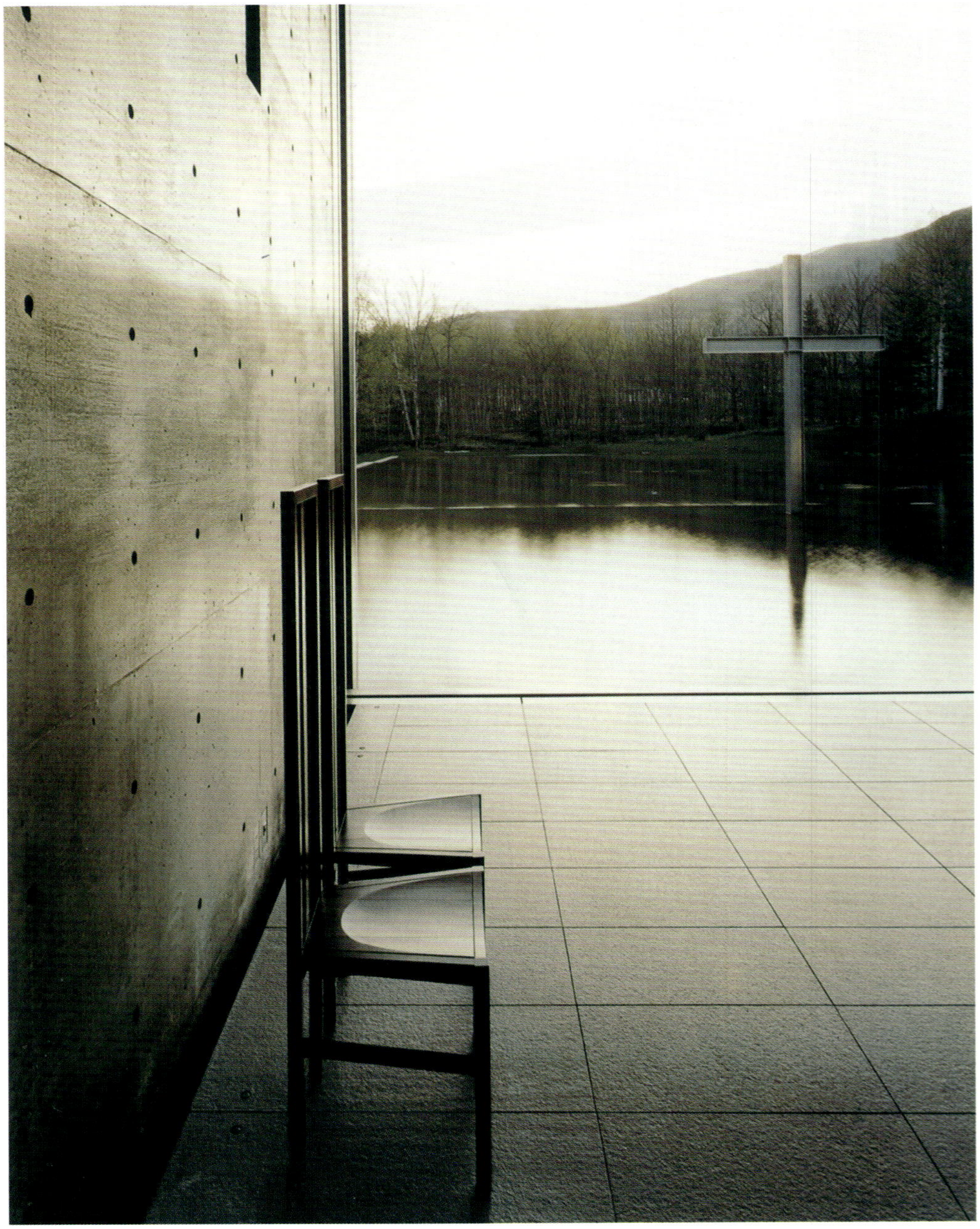

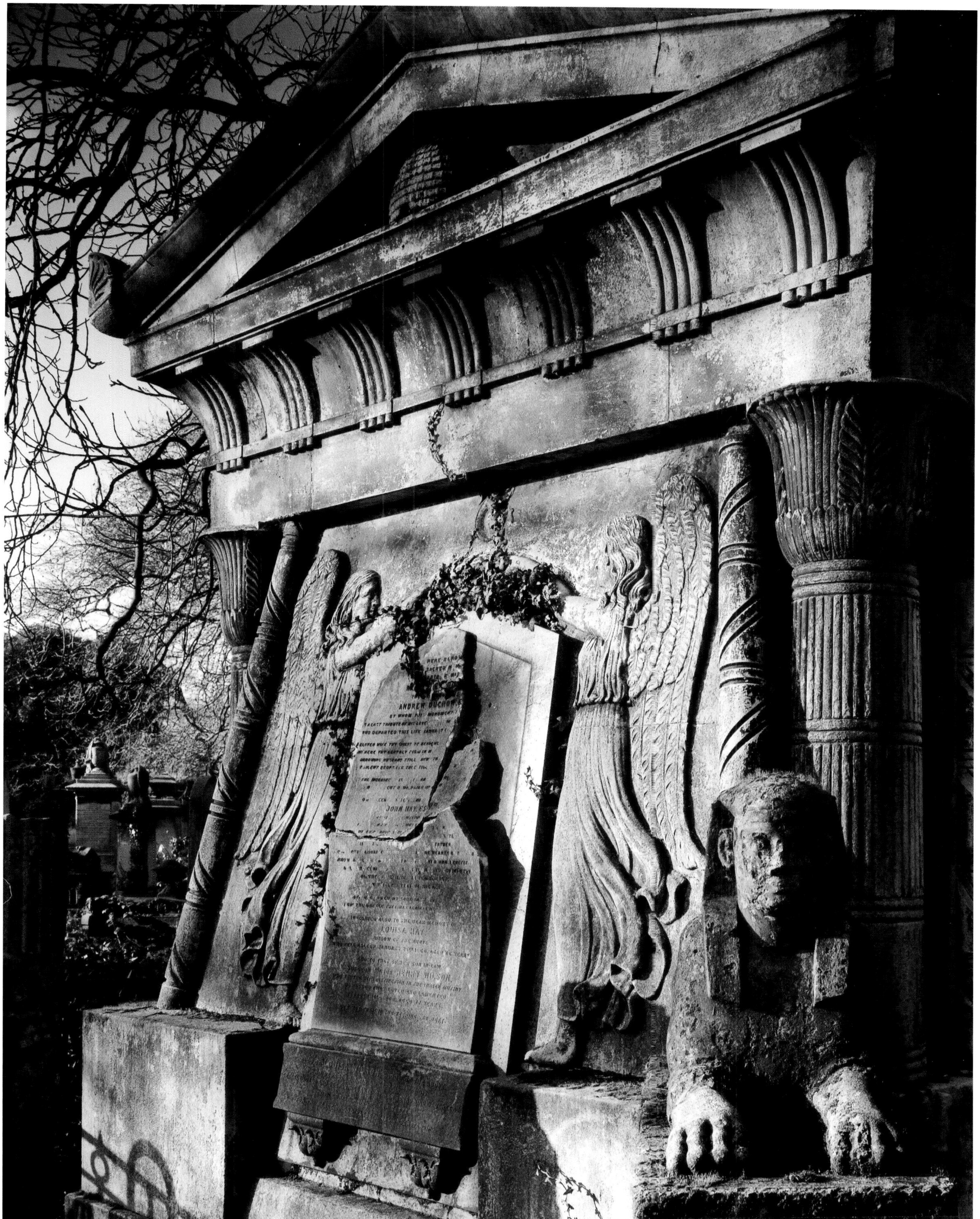

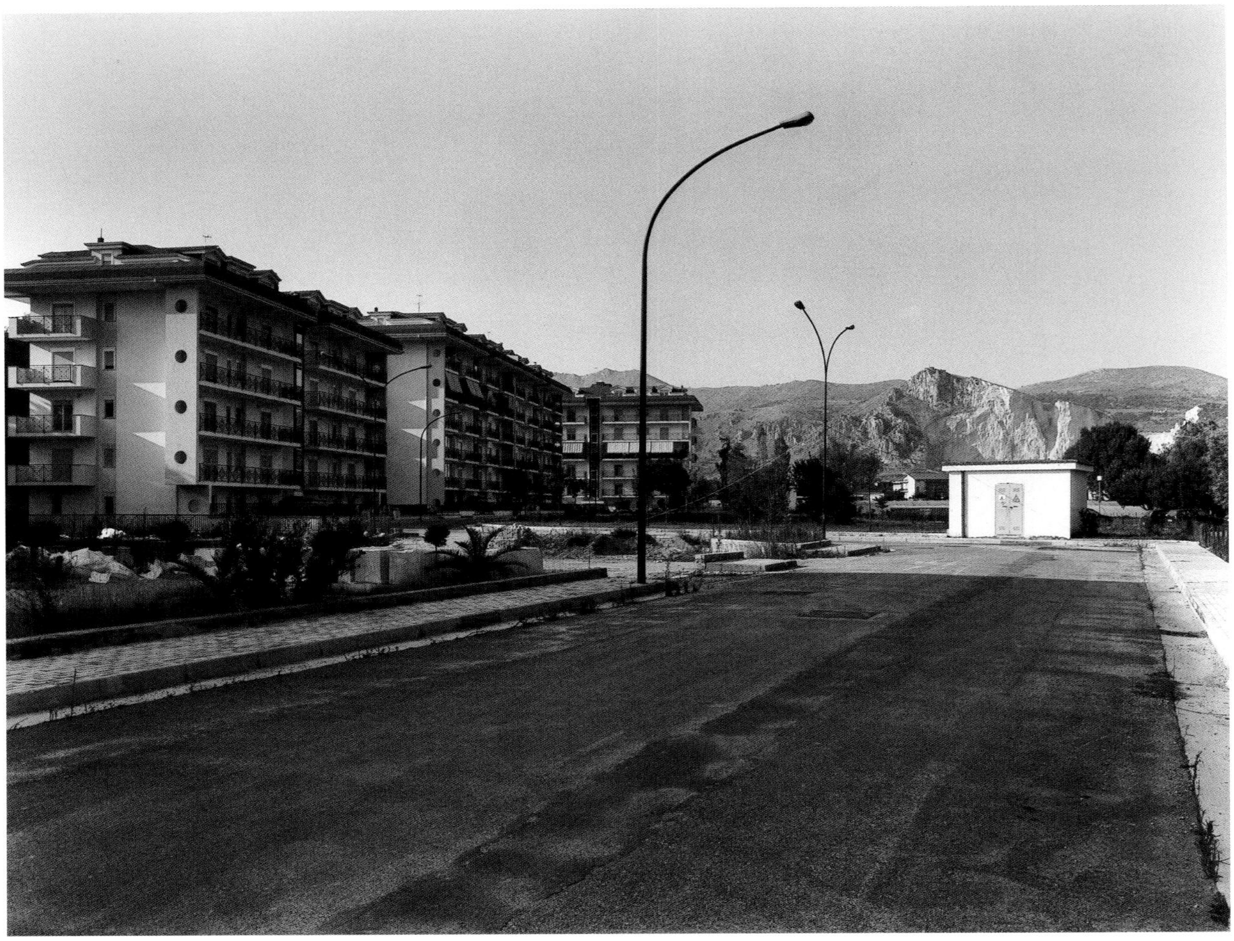

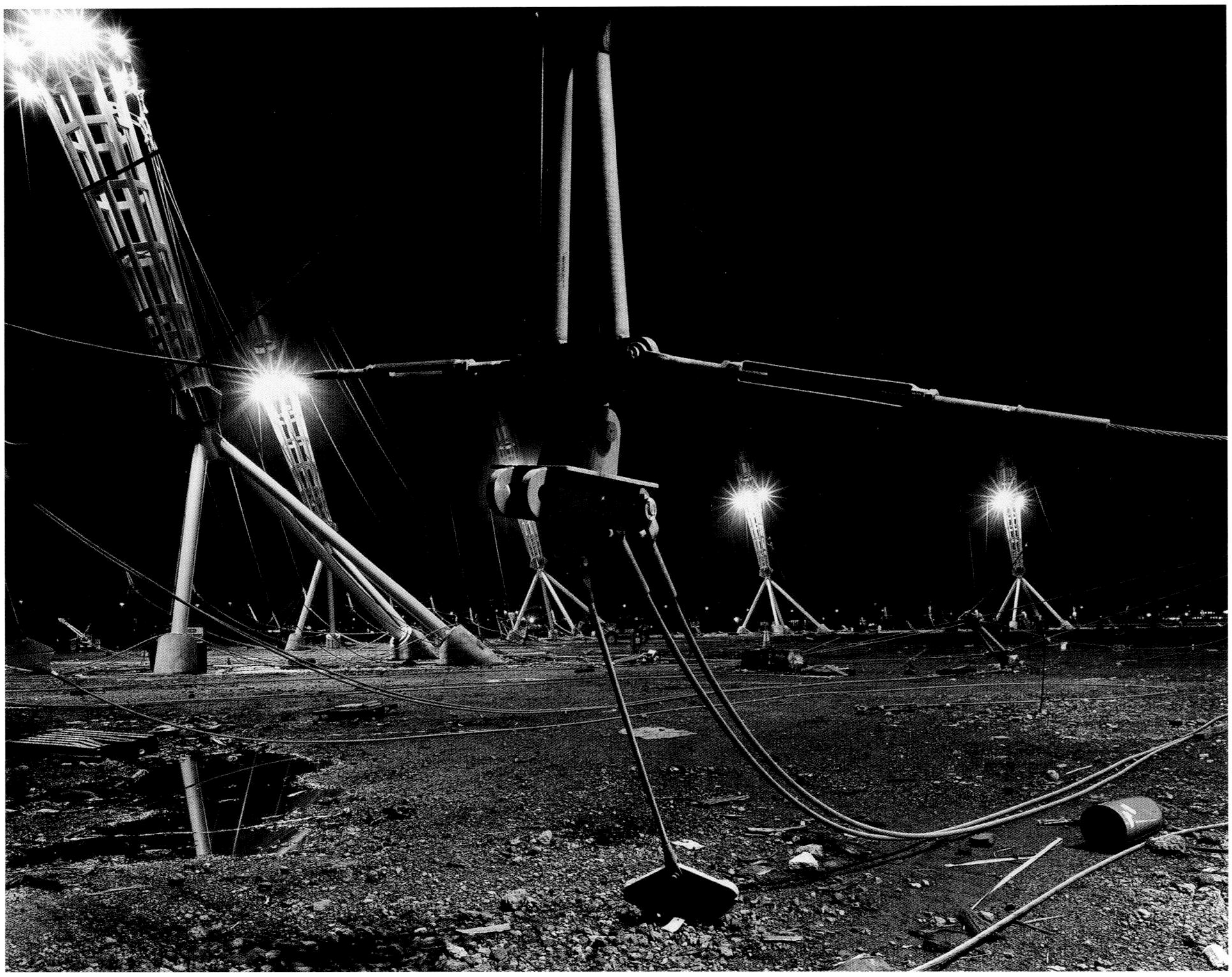

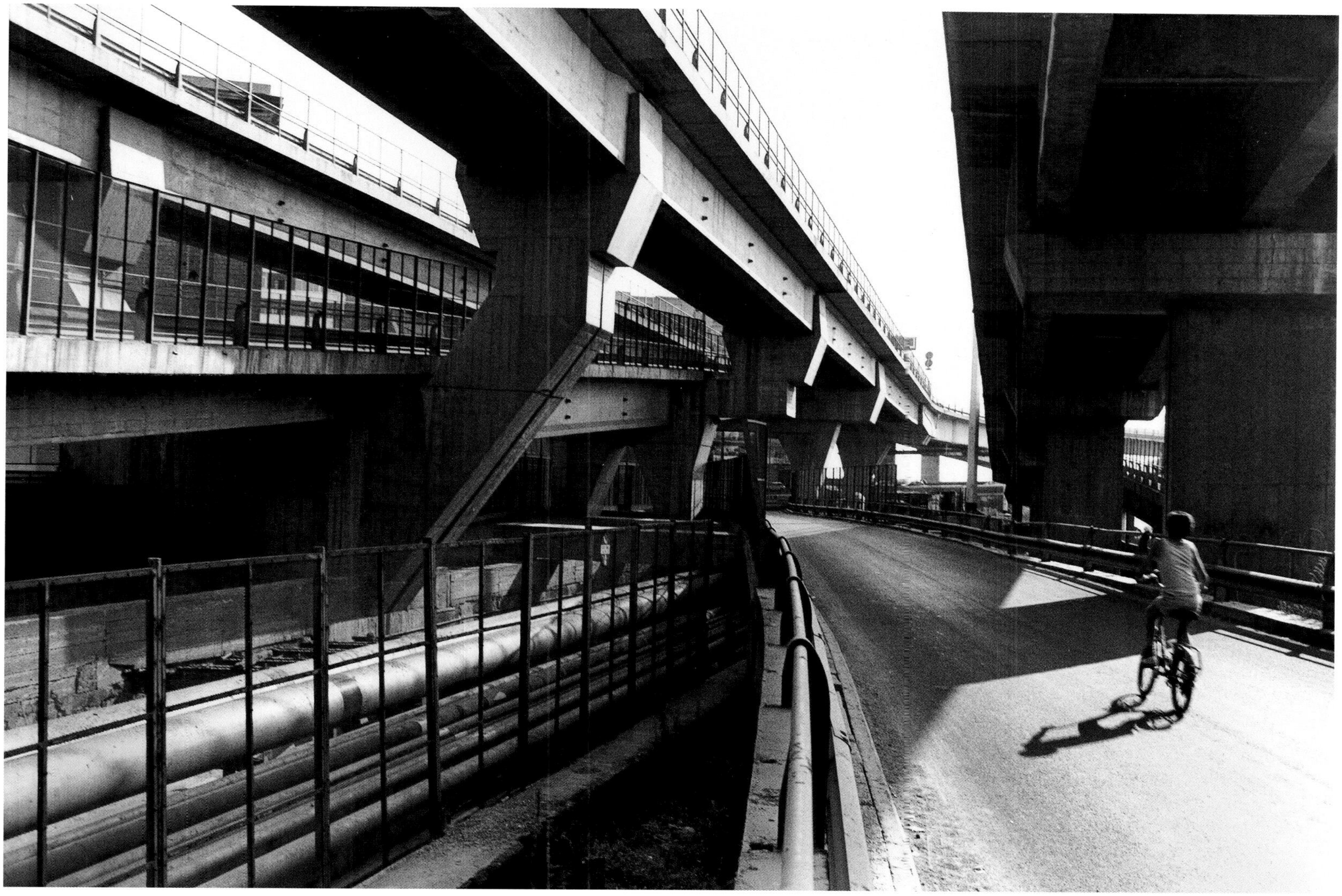

opposite top

GABRIELE BASILICO (born 1944)

Napoli-Caserta, Italy, 1996

Gelatine silver print

Basilico is the visual chronicler *par excellence* of the modern city. Although utilizing similar classical compositions, his photographs, at once desolate and provocative, undermine the traditional notion of the Italian city as advanced by such firms as Fratelli Alinari. This image is part of a series presented at the 1996 Venice Biennale in concert with the architect Stefano Boeri, which analysed urban development in six geographically distinct but analogous territorial corridors. It exemplifies Basilico's disquiet at "the unrestrained cementing over of the country"[25] – another inchoate blot on the landscape awaiting further development, as the stacked building materials ominously signify.

opposite bottom

MARK POWER (born 1959)

Erecting Tension Cables, Millennium Dome Under Construction, Greenwich, London, 15 December 1997

Gelatine silver print

Architects: Richard Rogers Partnership

Power's chronicling of the Dome, from site preparation to completion, stands in a long tradition of series that document major construction projects. Beginning with Delamotte's images of the Crystal Palace and continuing with those of the Louvre, the Paris Opéra, and the Empire State Building by Lewis Hine (1930–31), the tradition subsequently fell somewhat into abeyance until its recent revival. Whereas the Opéra photographs acted as *aides-mémoires* to architect and contractor, thus prefiguring modern progress photography, Power's images serve no practical purpose. Instead, they display an aesthetic sensibility alive to the construction site's drama, its messy race against time, and its human foibles and absurdities.

above

MIMMO JODICE (born 1934)

Naples, 1978

Gelatine silver print

Focusing on the contrasts and ambiguities of his native Naples – its beauty and repose set against its poverty, insensitive developments and grinding traffic – Jodice has significantly contributed to the re-evaluation of urbanism that has been such a feature of recent Italian photography. In this photograph, the motorway flyover has become not the harbinger of civilization, as envisaged by the theorists of the Modern Movement, but a symbol of chaotic development, devouring ever larger areas of recreational space and countryside. Where are – this accusatory image seems to ask – the *soleil, espace, verdure* that such elevated roads were supposed to liberate?

RYUJI MIYAMOTO (born 1947)

Grosses Schauspielhaus, Berlin, 1985

Gelatine silver print

Architect: Hans Poelzig

Reflecting the contemporary Japanese obsession with *haikyo* (the cult of the modern ruin), Miyamoto has taken as his terrain scenes of devastation, be it the twisted remains of Kobe after the 1995 earthquake or buildings such as the Grosses Schauspielhaus that have fallen prey to the wrecker's ball. Haunting meditations on the fragility of the built environment, Miyamoto's photographs proffer a comforting reassurance that, contrary to the myth propagated by mainstream architectural photographers, where all is youthful vigour, buildings do decay and die. This message is rendered more poignant here by the organic symbolism of Poelzig's crumbling columns, which resemble Karl Blossfeldt's plant photographs of the 1920s.

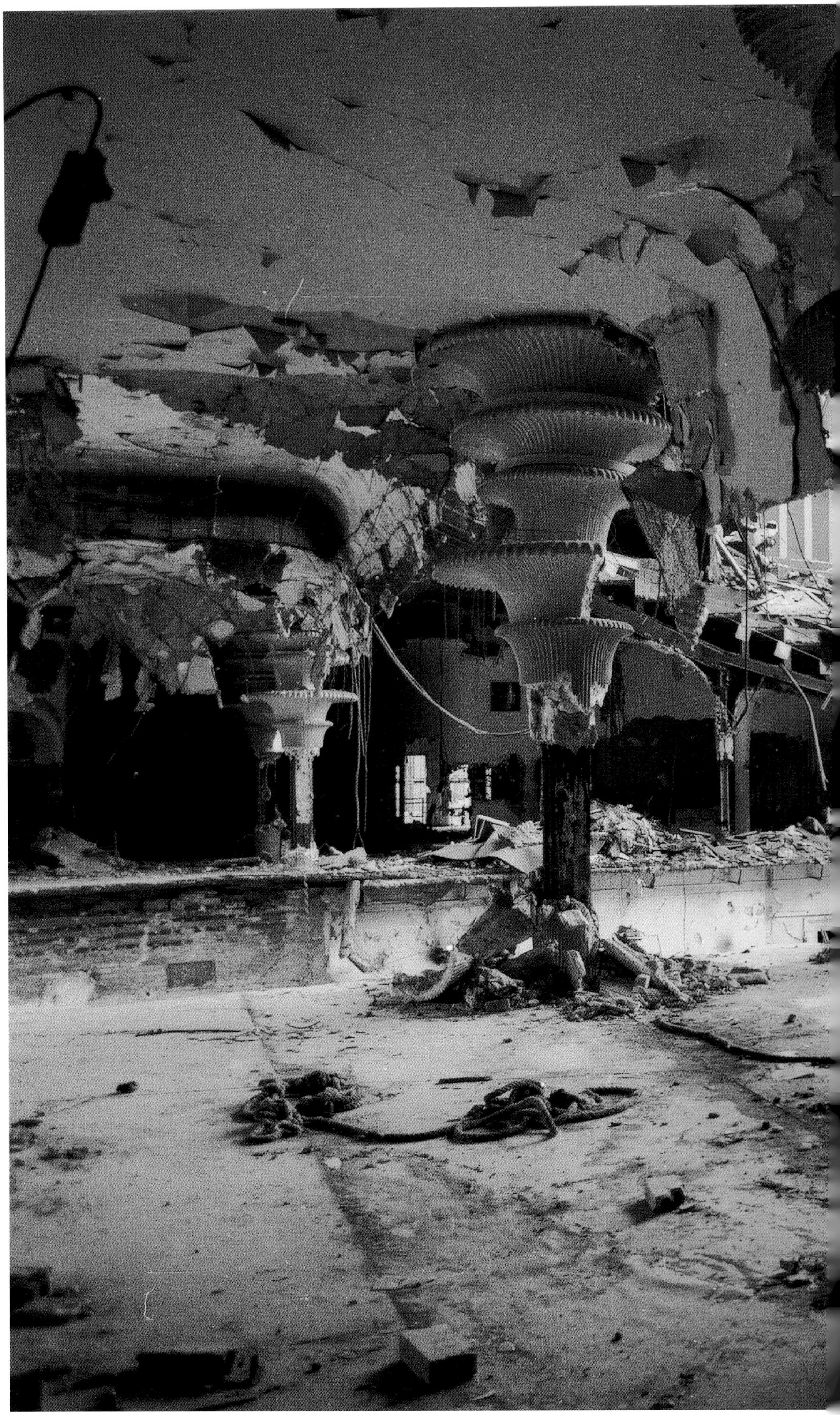

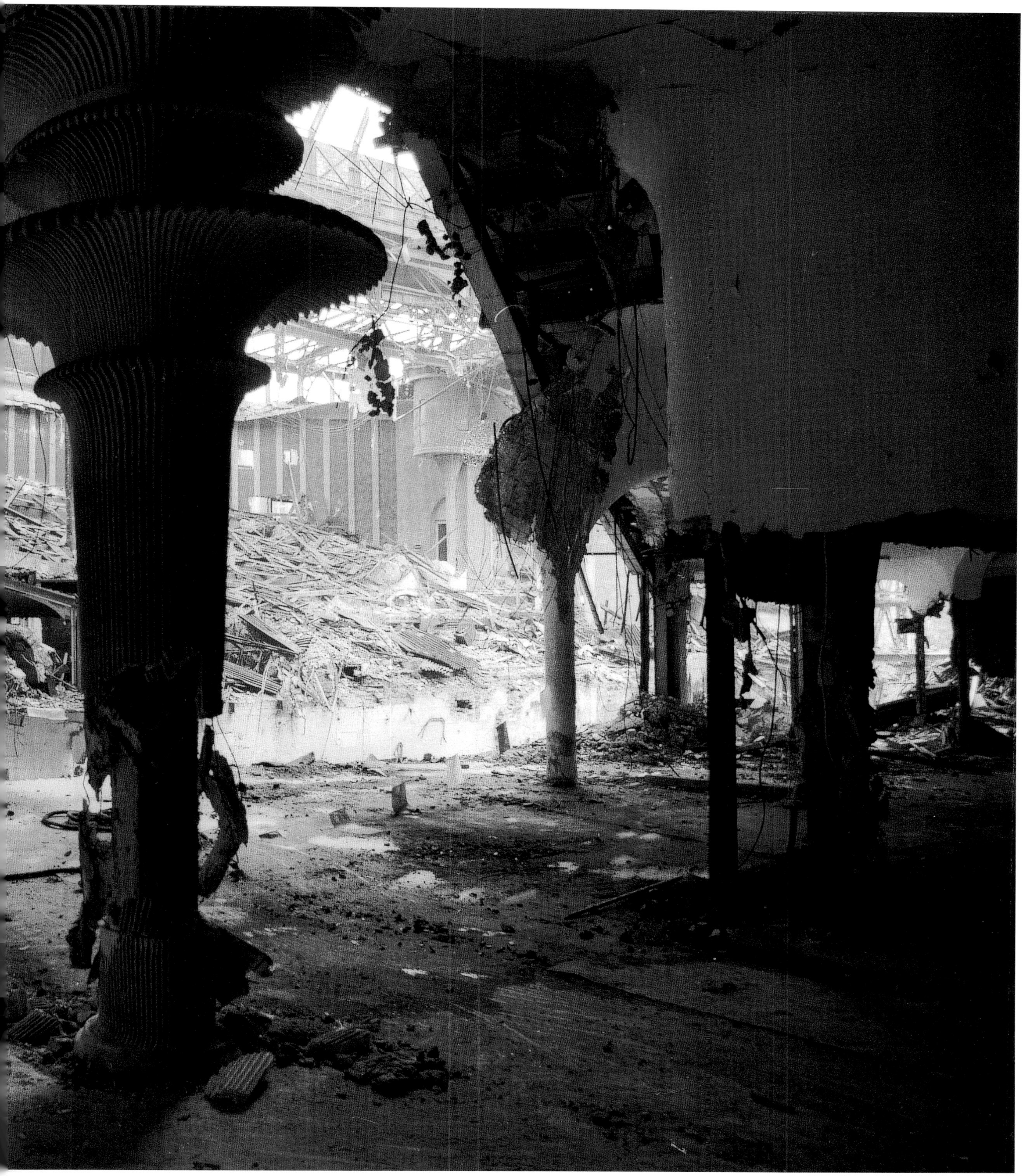

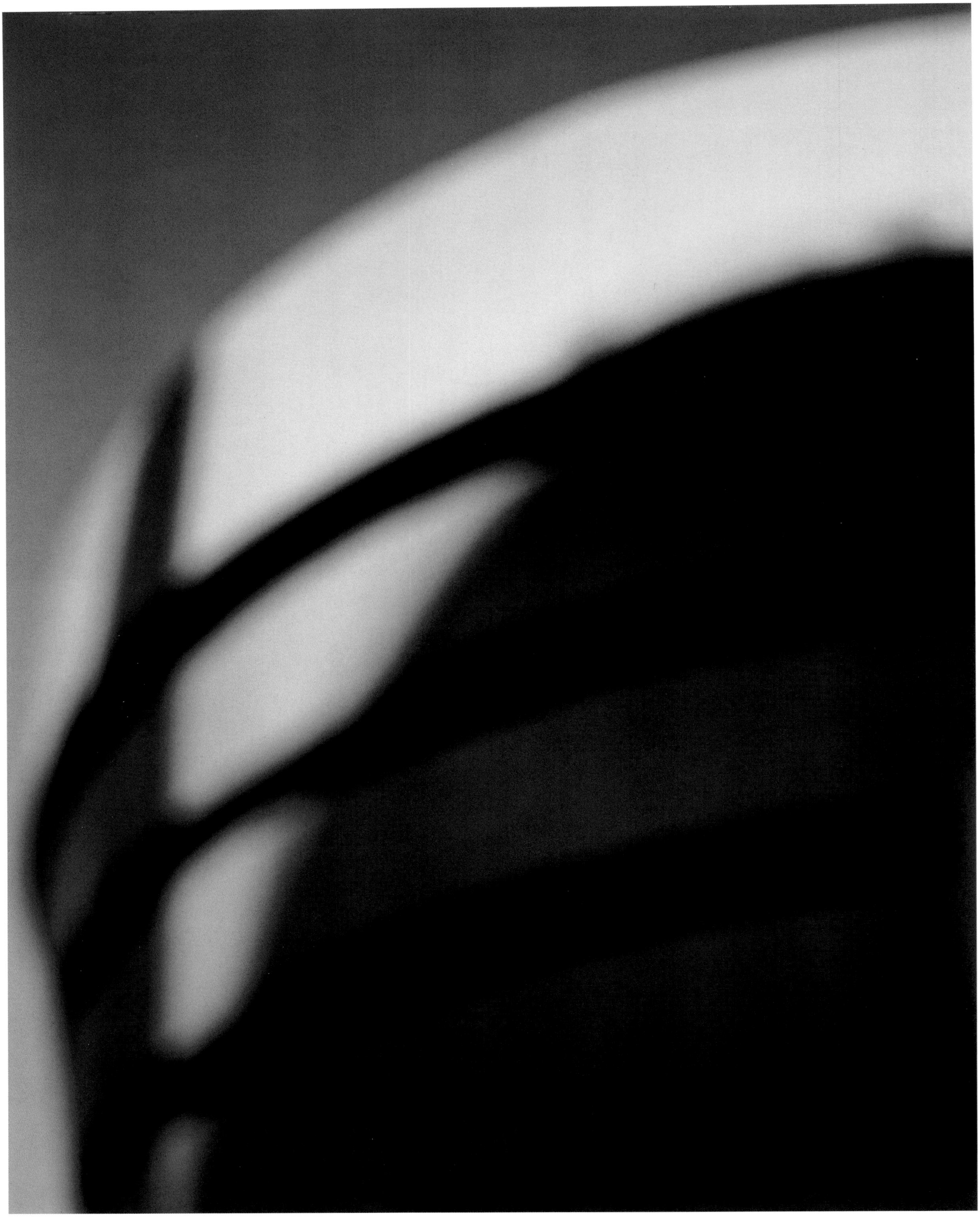

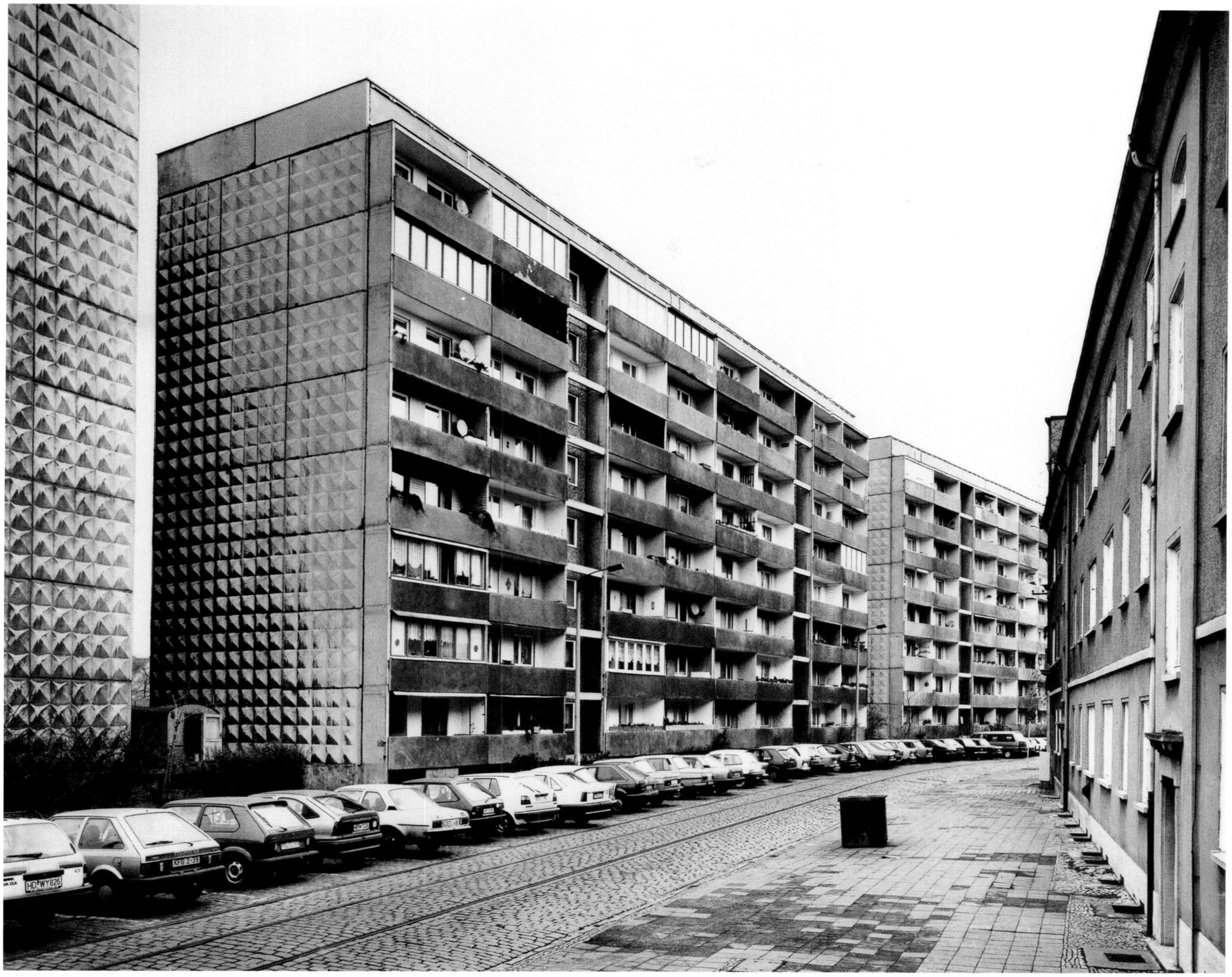

opposite

HIROSHI SUGIMOTO (born 1948)

Solomon R. Guggenheim Museum, New York, 1997

Gelatine silver print

Architect: Frank Lloyd Wright

Whereas Miyamoto discourses on the mortality of buildings by photographing ruins, Sugimoto has taken some of the key works of twentieth-century architecture – Mendelsohn's Potsdam Tower, the Seagram Building, Wright and Gehry's Guggenheims – and stressed their inherent fragility by dissolving the certainties of their concrete and glass forms into an eerie shadow-world. In both their long exposures – up to three hours – and their quivering monochrome forms, these photographs recall the tenebrous, unearthly qualities of the first photographic experiments.

above

THOMAS STRUTH (born 1954)

Ferdinand-von-Schill-Strasse, Dessau, 1991

Gelatine silver print

Struth's wide-ranging subject-matter includes an important series of urban studies in Japan, America and the former East Germany – the latter begun in 1991 – to which he brought a rigorous visual methodology akin to that of his mentors, the Bechers. Although Struth's photographs reflect the nineteenth-century street vista tradition, unlike it they focus not on major arteries but ordinary thoroughfares and unremarkable buildings. These are usually viewed from street level in one-point perspective, under the neutral sky favoured by the Bechers, with significant amounts of empty space rendering the images melancholic and alienating.

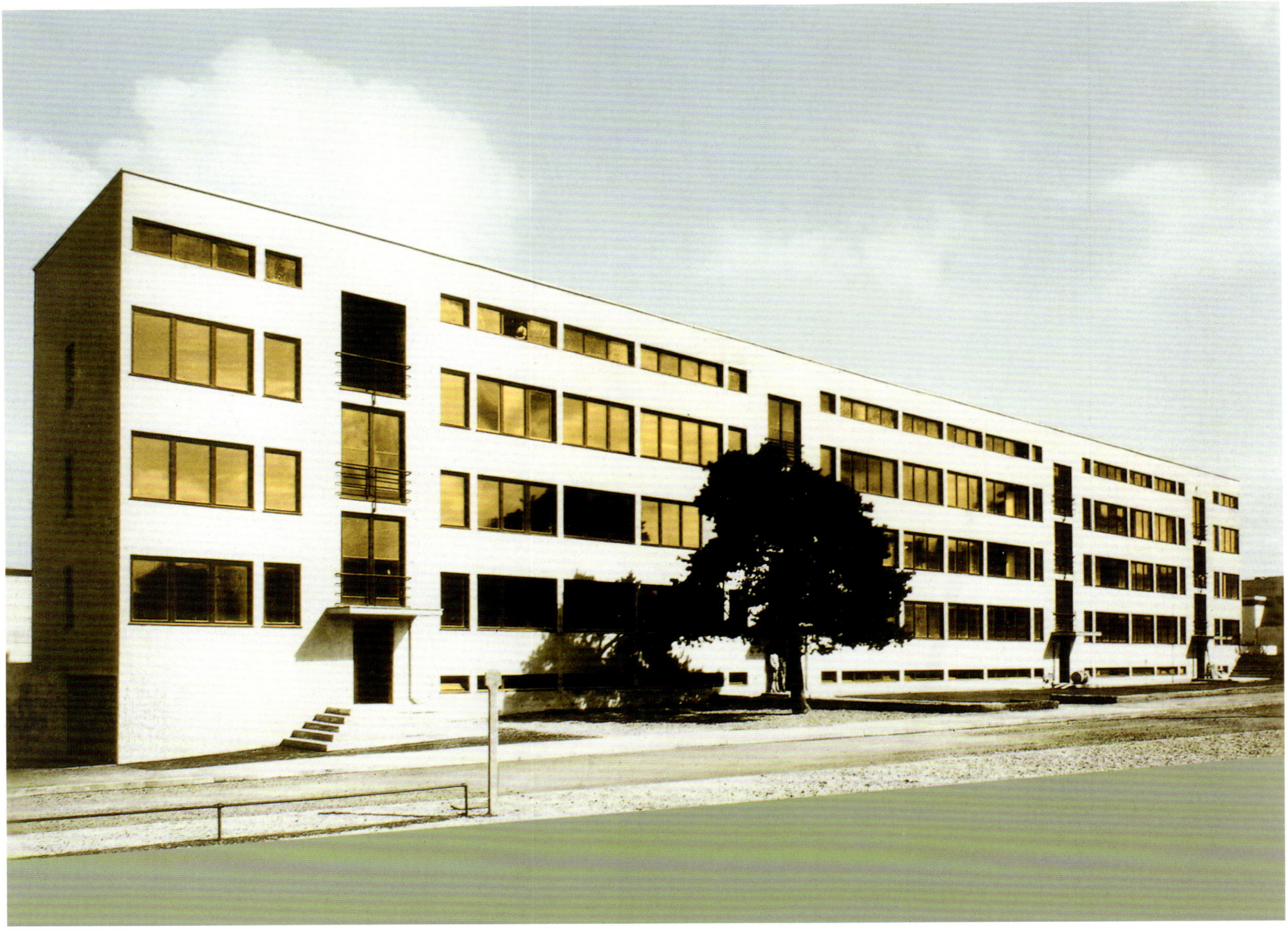

above

THOMAS RUFF (born 1958)

w.h.s.01 – Weissenhof Apartment House, 'Die Wohnung' Exhibition, Stuttgart, 2000

Chromogenic colour print

Architect: Ludwig Mies van der Rohe

Ruff's series on Mies combines new images – the Barcelona Pavilion seen in a blur as from a passing car – with, as here, the 'heretical' digital manipulation and colorization of historic monochrome shots. These challenge the literally 'fixed' vision of Mies's architecture that such shots, often astutely selected and edited by Mies himself and repeatedly reproduced, have engendered. The deliberately synthetic nature of Ruff's imagery and its lurid colour emphasize that these photographs are not slices of reality but are commentaries as much on the way we perceive buildings through photography as on the buildings themselves.

opposite

KENT LARSON (born 1953)

Hurva Synagogue, First Proposal, Jerusalem. View from Pylon on Second Level Toward Inner Sanctuary, 2000

Computer-generated image

Architect: Louis I. Kahn

Through computer animation, Larson has created 'photorealistic' renditions of several of Kahn's unbuilt projects. Computer-aided design (CAD) models are constructed from Kahn's drawings; to these are then added textures and light sources. The final image is produced by computer graphics software, mimicking the 'virtual camera', and views are made "that might have resulted if a flesh-and-blood architectural photographer had carried a view camera to the realized buildings".[26] The fact that even unexecuted drawings now require visualization in this way is surely the ultimate tribute to the perceived power of photography in architectural representation.

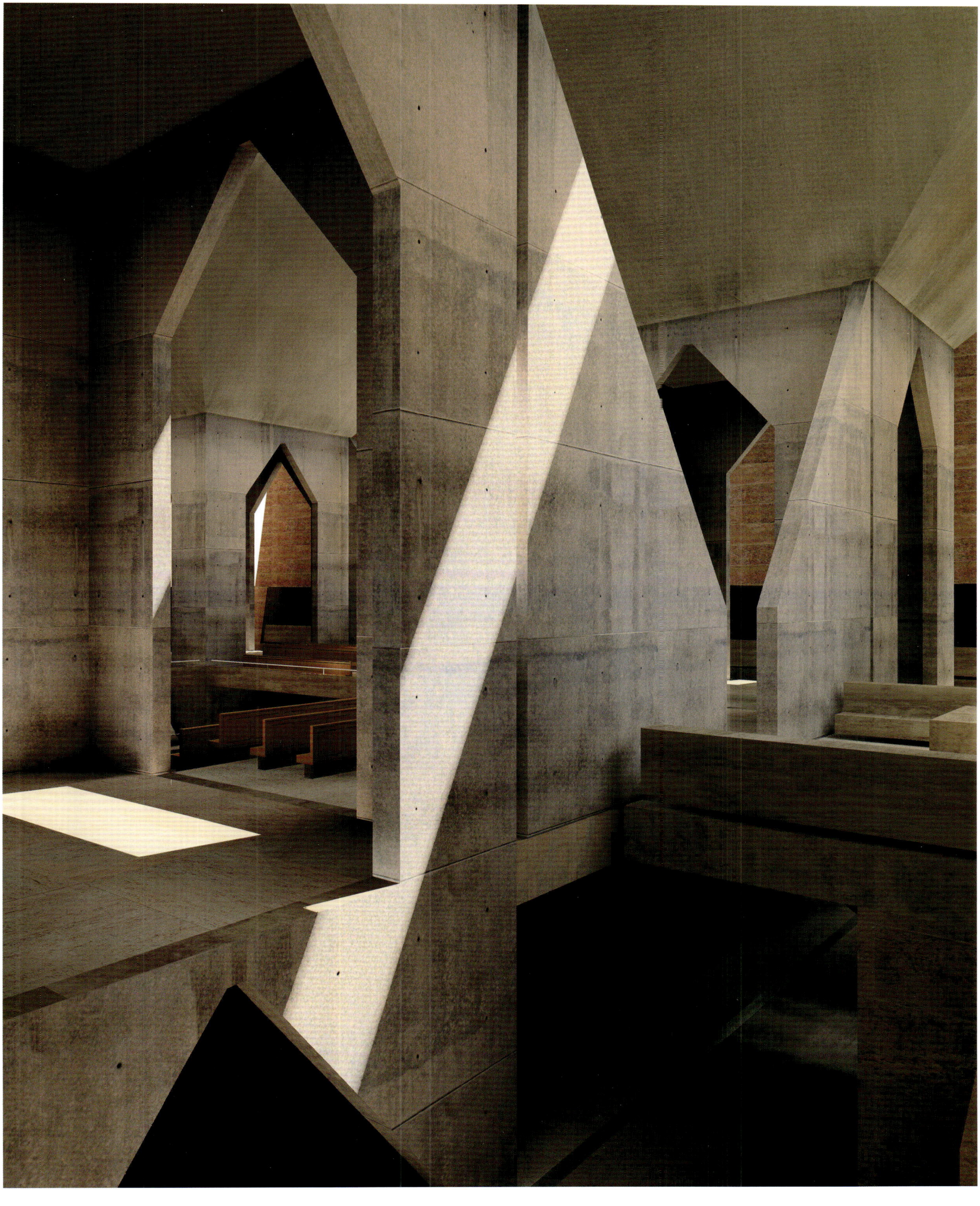

Notes

Introduction

1 Le Corbusier, *Towards a New Architecture*, trans. Frederick Etchells, London (John Rodker) 1927, p. 29.
2 Eric de Maré, *Photography*, 6th edn, Harmondsworth (Penguin Books) 1977, p. 57.
3 *RIBA Journal*, vol. 90, February 1983, p. 41.
4 Peter Rice, *An Engineer Imagines*, London (Artemis) 1994, p. 131.
5 Quoted in '"Bliss Was It in That Dawn to Be Alive": An Interview with John Brandon-Jones', *Architectural Design*, vol. 49, nos. 10–11, 1979, p. 98.

Chapter 1

1 Sir John Robison, 'Notes on Daguerre's Photography', *Edinburgh New Philosophical Journal*, July 1839, pp. 155–57.
2 *Gazette de France*, 6 January 1839, quoted in Helmut and Alison Gernsheim, *L.J.M. Daguerre: The History of the Diorama and the Daguerreotype*, London (Secker & Warburg) 1956, p. 82.
3 *Civil Engineer and Architect's Journal*, vol. 2, October 1839, p. 366.
4 As translated in Charles Wethered, *On Restoration by E. Viollet-le-Duc and a Notice of his Works in Connection with the Historical Monuments of France*, London (Sampson Low, Marston, Low & Searle) 1875, p. 68.
5 *Building News*, vol. 3, 26 June 1857, p. 657.
6 Letter from Horace Vernet to Monsieur Fabreguettes, French consul at Malta, 23 November 1839, quoted in Beaumont Newhall, *The History of Photography from 1838 to the Present*, London (Secker & Warburg) 1982, p. 27.
7 *Building News*, vol. 7, 22 March 1861, p. 252.
8 Notice by the publishers Longman, Brown, Green & Longmans issued June 1844, announcing the imminent publication of *The Pencil of Nature*, Fox Talbot Collection, Science Museum, London.
9 *Building News*, vol. 7, 22 March 1861, pp. 251–52.
10 Ludwig Pfau, *Kunst und Gewerbe*, part I, Stuttgart 1877, pp. 115–17, quoted in Helmut Gernsheim, *The Origins of Photography*, London (Thames & Hudson) 1982, p. 45.
11 *Industry of All Nations Exhibition. London, 1851. Reports by the Juries*, London (Spicer Brothers and W. Clowes & Son) 1852, II, p. 601.
12 Quoted in André Jammes and Eugenia Parry Janis, *The Art of French Calotype*, Princeton NJ (Princeton University Press) 1983, p. 53.
13 William Gilpin, *Three Essays*, London (R. Blamire) 1792, p. 46.
14 *Journal of the Photographic Society*, vol. 2, 21 October 1854, pp. 53–54.
15 There were very few professional photographers at this time, and most were engaged in portraiture. Whereas the daguerreotype was made freely available in France, in England it was patent protected, as was Talbot's rival calotype. The expense of buying the appropriate licences meant that fewer people took up photography as a business, and as a result the photographic profession took longer to evolve.
16 Gustave Le Gray, *Photographie: traité nouveau theorique et pratique des procédés et manipulations*, Paris (Lerebours et Secretan) 1854, p. 2, quoted in Jammes and Janis, *The Art of French Calotype*, p. 62.
17 Charles Nègre, *Midi de la France* (manuscript, 1852?), quoted in James Borcoman, *Charles Nègre 1820–1880*, Ottawa (National Gallery of Canada) 1976, pp. 6–7.
18 *Building News*, vol. 4, 10 December 1858, p. 1218.
19 In the wet collodion-on-glass process, the negative was formed by coating a glass plate with collodion, a sticky, syrupy substance that bound light-sensitive silver iodide to the plate. The negatives thus produced were most commonly printed in the form of albumen prints, where the coating of the paper with egg white produced a shiny, smooth surface better able to render fine detail than its more coarse-grained salt print predecessors.
20 *Photographic News*, vol. 3, 10 February 1860, p. 266.
21 *The Builder*, vol. 15, 2 May 1857, p. 249.
22 *Photographic News*, vol. 3, 9 March 1860, p. 320.
23 *Building News*, vol. 4, 29 January 1858, p. 97.
24 Elizabeth Anne McCauley, *Industrial Madness: Commercial Photography in Paris 1848–1871*, New Haven CT and London (Yale University Press) 1994, p. 97.
25 *Photographic News*, vol. 13, 15 October 1869, p. 495.
26 India and Bengal Despatch, no. 22, 7 February 1855, India Office Records, British Library.
27 Letter from Tripe to Murray, 22 July 1856, Fort Saint George Public Consultations, no. 12, 30 September 1856, India Office Records.
28 Fort Saint George Public Consultations, 15 April 1859, India Office Records, IOR/P/249/69.
29 *Photographic News*, vol. 1, 24 December 1858, p. 185.
30 *United States Journal*, 29 January 1846, p. 2.
31 *The Works of John Ruskin*, ed. E.T. Cook and A. Wedderburn, III, London (George Allen) 1903–12, p. 210.
32 *Ibid.*
33 Quoted in H. Gernsheim, *The Origins of Photography*, London (Thames & Hudson) 1982, p. 54.
34 *Royal Society of Arts: Transactions*, vol. 55, 1845, p. 108.
35 Quoted in Eugenia Parry Janis, *The Photography of Gustave Le Gray*, Chicago (Art Institute of Chicago and University of Chicago Press) 1987, p. 35.
36 See Ernest Lacan, 'Exposition photographique, 2e article', *Le Moniteur de la photographie*, 15 June 1861, p. 49.
37 Baldus was one of a number of early photographers who experimented with photogravure – or, as he termed it, héliogravure – a photomechanical process in which the photographic image was chemically rather than manually etched on to a copper plate and then printed in ink on paper. The process was perfected by the Czech Karl Klíč in 1879 and, on account of its expressive qualities, found favour with many Pictorialist photographers, including Alfred Stieglitz.
38 Letter in *The Builder*, vol. 17, 1 January 1859, p. 6.
39 *Photographic Journal*, vol. 6, 16 February 1860, p. 152.
40 *Photographic Journal*, 15 September 1863, p. 361.
41 Letter to "Mr. Rogier, Ministre de l'Interieur", 1860, quoted in *Camera Gothica: Gotische kerkelijke architectuur in de 19de-eeuwse Europese fotografie*, Antwerp (Provincie Antwerpen) 1993, p. 95.
42 Letter from Tripe to Chief Secretary, Madras Government, 1 September 1856, Board's Collections, India Office Records, IOR/F/4/2725, no. 198065.
43 Letter from Tripe to the Private Secretary to the Governor of Madras, 22 July 1856, Board's Collections, India Office Records, IOR/F/4/2725, no. 198065, p. 9.
44 *Handbook of Rome and Its Environs*, 7th edn, London (John Murray) 1864, p. xxii.
45 *Deutsches Kunstblatt*, vol. 7, 1856, p. 34, quoted in Sigrid Schulze, '"Sent by the Princess Frederick William": A Portfolio of Photographs of Berlin by Leopold Ahrendts', *History of Photography*, vol. 26, Winter 2002, p. 340.

Chapter 2

1 *Building News*, vol. 4, 15 January 1858, p. 59.
2 William and Mary Howitt, 'Preface', *Ruined Abbeys and Castles of Great Britain*, London (A.W. Bennett) 1862.
3 C. Jabez Hughes, 'On Art Photography', *American Journal of Photography*, vol. 3 (new series), 1861, p. 107.
4 Autotype was another name for the carbon print, a process invented by Alphonse Poitevin in 1855 but which only came into its own after improvements by Joseph Swan in 1864. Printed in a permanent pigment, carbon prints had the great advantage of not fading and were often used in book illustration.
5 A stimulating account of American urban photography can be found in Peter B. Hales, *Silver Cities: The Photography of American Urbanization, 1839–1915*, Philadelphia (Temple University Press) 1984.
6 Thomas Annan, 'Introduction', *The Old Country Houses of the Old Glasgow Gentry*, Glasgow (James MacLehose) 1870, p. xi.
7 Quoted in Barry Bergdoll, 'A Matter of Time: Architects and Photographers in Second Empire France', in Malcolm Daniel, *The Photographs of Edouard Baldus*, New York (Metropolitan Museum of Art) 1994, p. 105.
8 Wethered, *On Restoration by E. Viollet-le-Duc*, pp. 68–69.
9 Sir George Gilbert Scott, *Personal and Professional Recollections*, London (Sampson Low, Marston, Searle & Rivington) 1879, p. 309.
10 *The Architect*, vol. 8, 28 September 1872, p. 167.
11 *American Architect and Building News*, vol. 16, 27 December 1884, p. 304.
12 Henry-Russell Hitchcock, *The Architecture of H.H. Richardson and His Times*, Hamden CT (Archon Books) 1961, p. 248.
13 *Journal of the Royal Institute of British Architects*, vol. 3, 1896, p. 231.
14 Emerson, speech of 3 March 1904, *Journal of the Queen Victoria Memorial Fund*, no. 2, March 1904, p. 13.
15 T.R. Smith, 'The Practice of an Architect', *British Quarterly*, 1880, p. 426.
16 *Architectural Record*, vol. 3, January–March 1894, p. 292.
17 Hippolyte Jean Blanc, 'Photography as an Aid to the Architect', *British Journal of Photography*, vol. 44, 7 May 1897, p. 296.
18 *Civil Engineer and Architect's Journal*, vol. 21, 1858, p. 63.
19 See Lauren M. O'Connell, 'Viollet-le-Duc on Drawing, Photography, and the "Space Outside the Frame"', *History of Photography*, vol. 22, Summer 1998, pp. 139–46.
20 Ruskin, *Works*, XIX, p. 89.
21 Quoted in J. Mordaunt Crook, *William Burges and the High Victorian Dream*, London (J. Murray) 1981, p. 105.
22 *The Builder*, vol. 50, 16 January 1886, p. 113.
23 *The Builder*, vol. 16, 16 October 1858, p. 688.
24 William James Stillman, *The Acropolis of Athens*, London (F.S. Ellis) 1870, p. 3.
25 Quoted in Christopher Curtis Mead, *Charles Garnier's Paris Opéra: Architectural Empathy and the Renaissance of French Classicism*, New York and Cambridge MA (Architectural History Foundation and MIT Press) 1991, p. 139.
26 *British Journal of Photography*, vol. 91, 6 October 1944, p. 358.
27 For this intriguing argument see Bergdoll, 'A Matter of Time', pp. 108–111.
28 James Fergusson, *History of Indian and Eastern Architecture*, 2nd edn, London (John Murray) 1910, p. ix.

Chapter 3

1 Advertisement in Frederic G. Stephens, *Flemish Relics, Architectural, Legendary, and Pictorial, as Connected with Public Buildings in Belgium*, London (A.W. Bennett) 1866.
2 Quoted in Paolo Costantini, 'Ferdinando Ongania and

the Golden Basilica: A Documentation Programme in 19th-Century Venice', *History of Photography*, vol. 8, October–December 1984, p. 326.
3 *Builders' Journal and Architectural Record*, vol. 20, 19 October 1904, p. 206.
4 *Ibid*., p. 203.
5 *Owatonna Journal-Chronicle*, 13 July 1908, p. 1.
6 See Allen Brooks, 'Frank Lloyd Wright and the Wasmuth Drawings', *Art Bulletin*, vol. 48, June 1966, pp. 193–202.
7 Quoted in Crombie Taylor and Jeffrey Plank, *The Early Louis Sullivan Building Photographs*, San Francisco (William Stout Publishers) 2001, p. 14.
8 Le Corbusier, *Creation Is a Patient Search*, New York (Frederick Praeger) 1960, p. 203.
9 Quoted in *Atget's Paris*, ed. Hans Christian Adam, Cologne (Taschen) 2001, p. 28.
10 *The Builder*, vol. 103, 20 September 1912, p. 323.
11 Early lenses had a relatively narrow angle of view and suffered from a number of aberrations, including astigmatism, which resulted in a lack of sharpness particularly at the periphery of the image. These defects were largely eliminated with the development of barium crown glass and the subsequent introduction of a series of anastigmatic lenses by such German firms as Carl Zeiss and Goerz from 1890 onwards. These lenses allowed much sharper definition over the entire image area.
12 *Camera Work*, no. 4, 1903, p. 25.
13 Frederick H. Evans, 'Camera Work in Cathedral Architecture', *Camera Work*, no. 4, 1903, p. 18.
14 *Amateur Photographer*, vol. 39, 12 May 1904, p. 372.
15 *Photographic Journal*, vol. 84, November 1944, p. 328.
16 *RIBA Journal*, vol. 29 (3rd series), 1922, p. 507.
17 Quoted in Newhall, *History*, p. 199.
18 *American Architect and Building News*, 11 January 1890, p. 18.
19 Quoted in Costantini, 'Ferdinando Ongania and the Golden Basilica', p. 326.
20 Quoted in Anouk de Wit and Loes van Harrevelt, 'Architectural Photography in the Collections of the Netherlands Architecture Institute (NAI) and the Netherlands Photo Archives (nfa)', *Architectuur Fotografie: Architectuuragenda 2000* (*Architectural Photography: Architecture Diary 2000*), Rotterdam (NAI Uitgevers) 1999, pp. 4–5.
21 *Country Life*, vol. 141, 12 January 1967, p. 54.
22 *Architectural Record*, vol. 31, January 1912, p. 46.
23 Ruskin, *Works*, III, p. 33 (preface to the 2nd edition of *Modern Painters*).
24 Quoted in Dorothy Norman, *Alfred Stieglitz: An American Seer*, New York (Random House) 1973, p. 45.
25 Quoted in J.R.H. Weaver, 'The Man and his Work', *Photographic Journal*, vol. 85, February 1945, p. 38.
26 Alvin Langdon Coburn, 'Frederick H. Evans', *Photographic Journal*, vol. 85, February 1945, p. 35.

Chapter 4

1 Quoted in Helmut Gernsheim, *Creative Photography: Aesthetic Trends 1839–1960*, London (Faber & Faber) 1962, p. 117.
2 *Architects' Journal*, vol. 78, 28 September 1933, p. 375.
3 Quoted in Marcel Franciscano, *Walter Gropius and the Creation of the Bauhaus in Weimar*, Urbana IL (University of Illinois Press) 1971, p. 28, note 37.
4 *Architectural Review*, vol. 75, January 1934, p. 12.
5 László Moholy-Nagy, 'A New Instrument of Vision', *Telehor*, vol. 1, February 1936, p. 36.
6 Le Corbusier, *Aircraft*, London (The Studio) 1935, p. 11.
7 Studio Annual, *Modern Photography*, ed. C.G. Holme, London (The Studio) 1932, p. 7.
8 '"Bliss Was It in That Dawn to Be Alive"', p. 97.
9 Finella Collection, Caius College Archives, Cambridge. Quoted in Alan Powers, 'Simple Intime – the Work of Raymond McGrath', *Thirties Society Journal*, no. 3, 1982, p. 5.
10 Quoted in an anonymous manuscript history of the Architectural Press.
11 Geoffrey Jellicoe, *Garden Decoration and Ornament for Smaller Houses*, London (Country Life Ltd) 1936, p. 5.
12 *Architects' Journal*, vol. 103, 13 June 1946, p. 445.
13 *Architectural Review*, vol. 75, January 1934, p. 12.
14 *Ibid*.
15 *Architect and Building News*, vol. 150, 9 April 1937, p. 33.
16 *Ibid*.
17 *Eric Mendelsohn: Letters of an Architect*, ed. Oskar Beyer, London (Abelard-Schuman) 1967, p. 69.
18 László Moholy-Nagy, *Painting, Photography, Film*, London (Lund Humphries) 1969, p. 7.
19 For a good analysis see Annemarie Jaeggi, *Fagus: Industrial Culture from Werkbund to Bauhaus*, New York (Princeton Architectural Press) 2000.
20 William Henry Fox Talbot, *The Pencil of Nature*, London (Longman Brown Green & Longmans) 1844–46, unpaginated text opposite plate XIII.
21 *Architect and Building News*, vol. 150, 9 April 1937, p. 33.
22 Letter from Wilfred Greene to Oliver Hill, 26 November 1934 [HiO/16/1], *Oliver Hill Collection*, RIBA Library Manuscripts Collection.
23 Letter from Nancy Greene to Oliver Hill, 21 June 1934 [HiO/16/1], *Oliver Hill Collection*, RIBA Library Manuscripts Collection.
24 Quoted in Newhall, *History*, p. 192.
25 Quoted in Newhall, *History*, p. 201.
26 Quoted in Anouk de Wit and Loes van Harrevelt, 'Architectural Photography', p. 5.
27 Quoted in Andreas Haus, *Moholy-Nagy: Photographs and Photograms*, London (Thames & Hudson) 1980, p. 64.
28 *Architectural Review*, vol. 83, February 1938, p. 90.
29 Joseph Molitor, *Architectural Photography*, New York (Wiley) 1976, p. 148.
30 Quoted in Luc Sante, *Walker Evans*, London (Phaidon Press) 2001, p. 9.

Chapter 5

1 Eric de Maré, *Photography and Architecture*, London (Architectural Press) 1961, p. 21.
2 Quoted in Henry La Farge (ed.), *Lost Treasures of Europe*, London (B.T. Batsford) 1946, p. 10.
3 For an excellent analysis, see Jonathan M. Reynolds, 'Ise Shrine and a Modernist Construction of Japanese Tradition', *Art Bulletin*, vol. 83, June 2001, pp. 316–41.
4 Kenzo Tange, 'Foreword', *Katsura: Tradition and Creation in Japanese Architecture*, New Haven CT (Yale University Press) 1960, p. v.
5 Unless otherwise indicated, the publication dates given for these Japanese books relate to their original editions. The titles are those of their later English translations.
6 *Journal of the Royal Institute of British Architects*, vol. 59, May 1952, p. 239.
7 Eric de Maré, *The Canals of England*, London (Architectural Press) 1950, p. 95.
8 Letter from Le Corbusier to Lucien Hervé, 15 December 1949.
9 *Architects' Journal*, vol. 170, 1 August 1979, p. 230.
10 Akiko Busch, *The Photography of Architecture: Twelve Views*, New York (Van Nostrand Reinhold Company) 1987, p. 15.
11 *Building Design*, no. 904, 30 September 1988, p. 23.
12 Quoted in de Maré, *Photography and Architecture*, p. 18.
13 Russell Lynes, 'Introduction' in Wayne Andrews, *Architecture in America: A Photographic History from the Colonial Period to the Present*, London (Thames & Hudson) 1960, pp. i–ii.
14 See *Architects' Journal*, vol. 170, 25 July 1979, pp. 175–90.
15 Busch, *Photography of Architecture*, p. 15.
16 *RIBA Journal*, vol. 75, February 1968, p. 63.
17 John Szarkowski, *The Idea of Louis Sullivan*, Minneapolis (University of Minnesota Press) 1956, p. i.
18 *RIBA Journal*, vol. 75, February 1968, p. 62.
19 Quoted in Neil Parkyn, 'Photography: Amateur or Pro?', *RIBA Journal*, vol. 90, February 1983, p. 39.
20 John Donat, *Architecture Through the Lens*, audio cassette/slide publication, London (Pidgeon Audio Visual) 1980.
21 Sir John Betjeman, review of Olive Cook, *English Cottages and Farmhouses* in *The Daily Telegraph*, 1954.
22 Quoted in Olive Cook, 'Introduction', *Edwin Smith: Photographs 1935–1971*, London (Thames & Hudson) 1984, p. 11.
23 Kenzo Tange, 'Foreword', *Katsura*, p. v.
24 Isamu Noguchi, 'Foreword', *The Roots of Japanese Architecture: A Photographic Quest by Yukio Futagawa*, New York and London (Harper & Row) 1963, p. 7.
25 G.E. Kidder Smith, *Looking at Architecture*, New York (Harry N. Abrams) 1990, p. 7.
26 G.E. Kidder Smith, *Italy Builds: Its Modern Architecture and Native Inheritance*, London (Architectural Press) 1955, p. 44.
27 Eric de Maré, *Photography and Architecture*, p. 13.
28 *Arkitektur: The Swedish Review of Architecture*, vol. 80, December 1980, p. 35.
29 *Parametro*, vol. 26, January–February 1995, p. 77.
30 *Ibid*., p. 83.
31 *Building Design*, no. 320, 22 October 1976, p. 10.
32 Morley Baer, *Adobes in the Sun: Portraits of a Tranquil Era*, San Francisco (Chronicle Books) 1972, p. 144.
33 William S. Saunders, *Modern Architecture: Photographs by Ezra Stoller*, New York (Harry N. Abrams) 1990, p. 77.
34 *Spazio e società*, vol. 19, October–December 1997, p. 21.
35 *Herman Hertzberger: Articulations*, London (Prestel) 2002, p. 51.
36 *Ibid*.
37 *RIBA Journal*, vol. 75, February 1968, p. 62.

Chapter 6

1 *Architectural Review*, vol. 99, June 1946, p. 159.
2 *Ibid*., p. 160.
3 Janet Abrams, 'Out of the Darkroom', *Blueprint*, no. 73, December–January 1990–91, p. 18.
4 *Ibid*.
5 *Architects' Journal*, vol. 172, 13 August 1980, p. 295.
6 *The American Architectural Photographer: Profiles of the Top Talent in Architectural Photography*, Rockport MA and Natick MA (Rockport Publishers and Resource World Publications) 1994, p. 144.
7 William Feaver, 'Light Fantastic Meters', *Observer*, 1 September 1991.
8 *The American Architectural Photographer*, p. 95.
9 *Judith Turner Photographs Five Architects*, London (Academy Editions) 1980, p. 11.
10 *Architects' Journal*, vol. 216, 5–12 December 2002, p. 17.
11 *Ibid*.
12 Notice by the publishers Longman, Brown, Green & Longmans issued June 1844, announcing the imminent publication of *The Pencil of Nature*; Fox Talbot Collection, Science Museum, London.

13 Eric de Maré, 'Eric de Maré', *Art Without Boundaries 1950–1970*, ed. Gerald Woods *et al.*, London (Thames & Hudson) 1972, p. 100.
14 *Harry Seidler: Selected and Current Works*, Mulgrave (Images Publishing Group) 1997, p. 252.
15 *Architectural Record*, vol. 185, April 1997, p. 130.
16 *Blueprint*, no. 73, December–January 1990–91, p. 20.
17 Quoted in Paolo Costantini, *Luigi Ghirri – Aldo Rossi: Things Which Are Only Themselves*, Milan (Electa) 1996, p. 11.
18 In correspondence with the author.
19 In correspondence with the author.
20 Judith Turner, 'Out of Context', *Between Spaces: Smith-Miller + Hawkinson Architecture, Judith Turner Photography*, New York (Princeton Architectural Press) 2000, p. 21.
21 *Architects' Journal*, vol. 216, 5–12 December 2002, p. 16.
22 Quoted in Jonathan Glancey, 'The Dream Life of Buildings', *The Guardian*, 15 April 2002, p. 12.
23 Richard Pare, 'Afterword', *Tadao Ando: The Colours of Light*, London (Phaidon) 1996, p. 204.
24 *British Journal of Photography*, vol. 134, 29 May 1987, p. 626.
25 Gabriele Basilico, *Berlin*, London (Thames & Hudson) 2002, p. 11.
26 Kent Larson, *Louis I. Kahn: Unbuilt Masterworks*, New York (Monacelli Press) 2000, p. 228.

Select Bibliography

Contemporary journals – too many to be listed here – have been an invaluable source of information, and references to some of these will be found in the footnotes. Otherwise, I have found the sources listed below the most useful.

The American Architectural Photographer: Profiles of the Top Talent in Architectural Photography, Rockport MA and Natick MA (Rockport Publishers and Resource World Publications) 1994

Thomas Annan, *Photographs of the Old Closes and Streets of Glasgow 1868–1877, with a Supplement of 15 Related Views*, New York (Dover Publications) 1977

Architectural Photography and the Growth of Cities 1850–1914, Stuttgart (Institut für Auslandsbeziehungen) 1980

Architettura e fotografia: La scuola fiorentina, Florence (Fratelli Alinari) 2000

Peter Barr, 'Berenice Abbott's *Changing New York* and Urban Planning Debates in the 1930s', *The Built Surface*, ed. Karen Koehler, II: *Architecture and the Pictorial Arts from Romanticism to the Twenty-First Century*, Aldershot (Ashgate) 2002, pp. 257–82

Gabriele Basilico and Stefano Boeri, *Italy – Cross Sections of a Country*, Zurich, Berlin and New York (Scalo) 1998

Gabriele Basilico, *Berlin*, London (Thames & Hudson) 2002

Bernd and Hilla Becher, *Water Towers*, Cambridge MA and London (MIT Press) 1988

Angelika Beckmann and Bodo von Dewitz, *Dom, Tempel, Skulptur: Architekturphotographien von Walter Hege*, Cologne (Agfa Foto-Historama) 1993

Olivier Beer, *Lucien Hervé: L'homme construit*, Paris (Seuil) 2001

Barry Bergdoll, 'Félix Duban: Early Photography, Architecture, and the Circulation of Images', *The Built Surface*, ed. Karen Koehler, II: *Architecture and the Pictorial Arts from Romanticism to the Twenty-First Century*, Aldershot (Ashgate) 2002, pp. 12–30

Berlin zwischen Residenz und Metropole: Photographien von Hermann Rückwardt 1871–1916, Berlin (Nicolaische Verlagsbuchhandlung) 1994

Eve Blau and Edward Kaufman (eds.), *Architecture and Its Image: Four Centuries of Architectural Representation*, Montreal (Canadian Centre for Architecture) 1989

James Borcoman, *Charles Nègre 1820–1880*, Ottawa (National Gallery of Canada) 1976

De Bouwkunst vereeuwigd: Fotografie voor monumentenzorg (*Architecture Immortalized: Photography for Conservation*), Zwolle (Waanders Uitgevers) 2000

Building Images: Seventy Years of Photography at Hedrich Blessing, San Francisco (Chronicle Books) 2000

Akiko Busch, *The Photography of Architecture: Twelve Views*, New York (Van Nostrand Reinhold Company) 1987

Graham Bush, *Old London*, London (Academy Editions) 1975

Camera Gothica: Gotische kerkelijke architectuur in de 19de-eeuwse Europese fotografie, Antwerp (Provincie Antwerpen) 1993

Cervin Robinson: Photographs, 1958–1983, Wellesley MA (Wellesley College) 1983

Beatriz Colomina (ed.), *Architecturproduction*, New York (Princeton Architectural Press) 1988

Beatriz Colomina, *Privacy and Publicity: Modern Architecture as Mass Media*, Cambridge MA and London (MIT Press) 1994

Fani Constantinou and Fani-Maria Tsigakou, *Photographs by James Robertson: 'Athens and Grecian Antiquities', 1853–1854 from the Photographic Archive of the Benaki Museum*, Athens (Benaki Museum) 1998

John Cornforth, *The Search for a Style: 'Country Life' and Architecture 1897–1935*, London (André Deutsch) 1988

Paolo Costantini, *Luigi Ghirri – Aldo Rossi: Things Which Are Only Themselves*, Milan (Electa) 1996

Paolo Costantini and Italo Zannier (eds.), *I dagherrotipi della collezione Ruskin*, Venice (Arsenale Editrice) 1986

Malcolm Daniel, *The Photographs of Edouard Baldus*, New York (Metropolitan Museum of Art) 1994

Eric de Maré, *Photography and Architecture*, London (Architectural Press) 1961

Janet Dewan, 'Delineating Antiquities and Remarkable Tribes: Photography for the Bombay and Madras Governments 1855–70', *History of Photography*, vol. 16, Winter 1992, pp. 302–17

Edwin Smith: Photographs 1935–1971, introduction by Olive Cook, London (Thames & Hudson) 1984

David Elliott (ed.), *Photography in Russia 1840–1940*, London (Thames & Hudson) 1992

Robert Elwall, '"The Foe-to-Graphic Art": The Rise and Fall of the Architectural Photographic Association', *Photographic Collector*, vol. 5, no. 2 (1985), pp. 142–63

Robert Elwall, 'James Fergusson (1808–1886) – A Pioneering Architectural Historian', *RSA Journal*, vol. 139, May 1991, pp. 393–404

Robert Elwall, *Photography Takes Command: The Camera and British Architecture 1890–1939*, London (RIBA Heinz Gallery) 1994

Robert Elwall, *Eric de Maré* (*Architecture in Camera* series), London (RIBA Publications) 2000

Robert Elwall, *John Maltby* (*Architecture in Camera* series), London (RIBA Publications) 2000

Pille Epner and Liina Jänes, *Kahemõõtmelised majad: Arhitektuurifoto Eestis 1860. aastatest tänapäevani*, Tallinn (Eesti Arhitektuurimuuseum) 2002

Eric de Maré: Photographer Builder with Light, London (Architectural Association) 1990

John Falconer, *India: Pioneering Photographers 1850–1900*, London (British Library) 2001

Thomas Fisher, 'Image Building', *Progressive Architecture*, vol. 71, August 1990, pp. 88–97

Fotografi a Pompei nell'800 dalle collezioni del Museo Alinari, Florence (Fratelli Alinari) 1990

Frank Yerbury: Itinerant Cameraman: Architectural Photographs 1920–35, London (Architectural Association) 1987

Helmut Gernsheim, *Focus on Architecture and Sculpture: An Original Approach to the Photography of Architecture and Sculpture*, London (Fountain Press) 1949

Giuliano Gresleri, *Le Corbusier, Viaggio in Oriente: gli inediti di Charles Edouard Jeanneret, fotografo e scrittore*, Venice and Paris (Marsilio Editori and Fondation Le Corbusier) 1984

Maija Häivä, 'Arkkitehtuurivalokuvauksesta – asiakuva vai kaunokuva' ('Architectural Photography – Record or Art'), *Sankaruus ja arki – Suomen 50-luvun miljöö* (*Heroism and the Everyday – Building Finland in the 1950s*), Helsinki (Museum of Finnish Architecture) 1994, pp. 195–99, 254–55

Peter B. Hales, *Silver Cities: The Photography of American Urbanization, 1839–1915*, Philadelphia (Temple University Press) 1984

Peter B. Hales, *Constructing the Fair: Platinum Photographs by C.D. Arnold of the World's Columbian Exposition*, Chicago (Art Institute of Chicago) 1993

Anne Hammond, *Frederick H. Evans: Selected Texts and Bibliography*, Oxford (Clio Press) 1992

David Harris with Eric Sandweiss, *Eadweard Muybridge and the Photographic Panorama of San Francisco*,

1850–1880, Montreal (Canadian Centre for Architecture) 1993
Andreas Haus, *Moholy-Nagy: Photographs and Photograms*, London (Thames & Hudson) 1980
Eleanor M. Hight, *Picturing Modernism: Moholy-Nagy and Photography in Weimar Germany*, Cambridge MA and London (MIT Press) 1995
Kathryn Horste, 'The Neurdein Frères and the Photography of Medieval Architecture', *History of Photography*, vol. 26, Winter 2002, pp. 276–95
Annemarie Jaeggi, *Fagus: Industrial Culture from Werkbund to Bauhaus*, New York (Princeton Architectural Press) 2000
André Jammes and Eugenia Parry Janis, *The Art of French Calotype*, Princeton NJ (Princeton University Press) 1983
Jan Versnel (Monographs of Dutch Photographers 6), Amsterdam (Focus Publishing) 1997
Eugenia Parry Janis, *The Photography of Gustave Le Gray*, Chicago (Art Institute of Chicago and University of Chicago Press) 1987
Steven F. Joseph and Tristan Schwilden, *A l'aube de la photographie en Belgique: Guillaume Claine (1811–1869) et son cercle*, Charleroi (Crédit Communal) 1991
Judith Turner: Near Sitings. Photographs 1975–1995, Oklahoma City (City Arts Center) 1995
Alexander Lavrentiev, *Alexander Rodchenko: Photography 1924–1954*, Cologne (Könemann) 1995
Andres Lepik, 'Mies and Photomontage, 1910–38', in Terence Riley and Barry Bergdoll, *Mies in Berlin*, New York (Museum of Modern Art) 2001, pp. 324–29
Elizabeth Anne McCauley, *Industrial Madness: Commercial Photography in Paris 1848–1871*, New Haven CT and London (Yale University Press) 1994
Norman McGrath, *Photographing Buildings Inside and Out*, London (Architectural Press) 1987
David Mellor (ed.), *Germany: The New Photography 1927–33*, London (Arts Council of Great Britain) 1978
Rudolf Meyer (ed.), *Albrecht Meydenbauer: Baukunst in historischen Fotografien*, Leipzig (VEB Fotokinoverlag) 1985
Janine A. Mileaf, *Constructing Modernism: Berenice Abbott and Henry-Russell Hitchcock*, Middletown CT (Davison Art Center, Wesleyan University) 1993
László Moholy-Nagy, *Painting, Photography, Film*, London (Lund Humphries) 1969
Anne de Mondenard, *La Mission héliographique: Cinq photographes parcourent la France en 1851*, Paris (Monum, Editions du Patrimoine) 2002
Gilles Mora and John T. Hill, *Walker Evans: The Hungry Eye*, London (Thames & Hudson) 1993
Gabriele Morrione, *Fotografare l'architettura*, Rome (Edizioni Kappa) 1984
Gloria Moure (ed.), *Architecture without Shadow*, Barcelona (Ediciones Polígrafa) 2000
Daniel Naegele, 'Intervista a Lucien Hervé', *Parametro*, vol. 26, January–February 1995, pp. 71–83
Beaumont Newhall, *Frederick H. Evans: Photographer of the Majesty, Light and Space of the Medieval Cathedrals of England and France*, New York (Aperture) 1973
Richard Pare, *Photography and Architecture 1839–1939*, New York (Callaway Editions) 1982
Le Photographe et l'architecte: Edouard Baldus, Hector-Martin Lefuel et le chantier du Nouveau Louvre de Napoléon III, Paris (Réunion des musées nationaux) 1995
Photographier l'architecture 1851–1920: Collection du musée des monuments français, Paris (Réunion des musées nationaux) 1994
Gertrude Mae Prescott, 'Architectural Views of Old London', *Library Chronicle of the University of Texas at Austin*, new series no. 15, 1981, pp. 8–48
Reconstructing Space: Architecture in Recent German Photography, London (Architectural Association) 1999
'Representations/Misrepresentations', *Harvard Design Magazine*, Fall 1998, pp. 2–63
Shelley Rice, *Parisian Views*, Cambridge MA and London (MIT Press) 1997
Cervin Robinson and Joel Herschman, *Architecture Transformed: A History of the Photography of Buildings from 1839 to the Present*, Cambridge MA and London (MIT Press) 1987
Joseph Rosa, *A Constructed View: The Architectural Photography of Julius Shulman*, New York (Rizzoli) 1994
Joseph Rosa *et al.*, 'Photography and Architecture', *History of Photography*, vol. 22, Summer 1998, pp. 98–146
Paolo Rosselli, *Architecture in Photography*, Milan (Skira) 2001
Antonella Russo (ed.), *An Eye for the City: Italian Photography and the Image of the Contemporary City*, Albuquerque NM (University of New Mexico Art Museum) 2001
Rolf Sachsse, *Photographie als Medium der Architekturinterpretation: Studien zur Geschichte der deutschen Architekturphotographie im 20. Jahrhundert*, Munich (K.G. Saur) 1984
William S. Saunders, *Modern Architecture: Photographs by Ezra Stoller*, New York (Harry N. Abrams) 1990
Karl-Hugo Schmölz and Rolf Sachsse, *Hugo Schmölz: Fotografierte Architektur 1924–1937*, Munich (Mahnert-Lueg Verlag) 1982
Leo Schubert, 'Jeanneret, the City, and Photography', *Le Corbusier Before Le Corbusier: Applied Arts, Architecture, Painting, and Photography, 1907–1922*, ed. Stanislaus von Moos and Arthur Rüegg, New Haven CT and London (Yale University Press) 2002, pp. 54–67
Sigrid Schulze, '"Sent by the Princess Frederick William": A Portfolio of Photographs of Berlin by Leopold Ahrendts', *History of Photography*, vol. 26, Winter 2002, pp. 324–40
Julius Shulman, *Architecture and Its Photography*, Cologne and London (Taschen) 1998
Julius Shulman, *Photographing Architecture and Interiors*, Los Angeles (Balcony Press) 2000
Site Work: Architecture in Photography since Early Modernism, London (Photographers' Gallery) 1991
G.E. Kidder Smith, *Looking at Architecture*, New York (Harry N. Abrams) 1990
Robert A. Sobieszek (ed.), *The Architectural Photography of Hedrich-Blessing*, New York (Holt, Rinehart and Winston) 1984
Robert A. Sobieszek, *'This Edifice is Colossal': 19th-Century Architectural Photography*, Rochester NY (International Museum of Photography at George Eastman House) 1986
Le Studio Chevojon: Une dynastie de photographes parisiens, Paris (Créaphis) 1994
John Szarkowski, 'Photographing Architecture', *Art in America*, vol. 49, 1959, pp. 84–89
John Szarkowski and Maria Morris Hambourg, *The Work of Atget*, 4 vols., London (Gordon Fraser) 1981–85
Marie de Thézy, *Marville Paris*, Paris (Hazan) 1994
Crombie Taylor and Jeffrey Plank, *The Early Louis Sullivan Building Photographs*, San Francisco (William Stout Publishers) 2001
Anneke van Veen, *Jacob Olie Jbz 1834–1905*, Amsterdam (Focus Publishing) 2000
Robbert van Venetië and Annet Zondervan, *Geschiedenis van de Nederlandse architectuurfotografie*, Rotterdam (Uitgeverij 010) 1989
Vues d'architectures: Photographies des XIXe et XXe siècles, Grenoble (Musée de Grenoble) 2002
Werner Mantz: Architekturphotographie in Köln 1926–1932, Cologne (Verlag Locher) 1982
Anouk de Wit and Loes van Harrevelt, *Architectuur Fotografie: Architectuuragenda 2000* (*Architectural Photography: Architecture Diary 2000*), Rotterdam (NAI Uitgevers) 1999
Mary N. Woods, 'The Photograph as Tastemaker: The *American Architect* and H.H. Richardson', *History of Photography*, vol. 14, April–June 1990, pp. 155–63
Bonnie Yochelson, *Berenice Abbott: Changing New York*, New York (New Press) 1997
Federica Zanco (ed.), *Luis Barragán: The Quiet Revolution*, Milan (Skira) 2001
Italo Zannier, *Architettura e fotografia*, Rome and Bari (Editori Laterza) 1991

Acknowledgements

The publication of this book has been made possible by generous grants from the Marc Fitch Fund; the Scouloudi Foundation in association with the Institute of Historical Research, University of London; and the Kraszna-Krausz Foundation. I am deeply grateful to them all, as well as to the RIBA, whose award of the Gordon Ricketts Memorial Fund allowed me to fill vital gaps in my studies. Any book such as this, which is the outcome of many years' research, must inevitably be heavily dependent on the expertise and goodwill of too many people to be thanked individually here. If they remain unsung, let them rest assured that they do not remain unappreciated. In addition to the photographers who have generously contributed material, particular mention must, however, be made of the following, to whom I owe especial thanks: first and foremost Hugh Merrell and Julian Honer, for bravely tackling a subject that many others thought too recondite, as well as the excellent staff at Merrell, especially Sam Wythe and Michelle Draycott; Gavin Stamp and Margaret Richardson, for generously agreeing to support my grant applications; Andrew Mead and Ian Leith, who have been characteristically generous with help and advice; Richard and Lynne Bryant; Martin Charles; John Donat; Etsuko Yoshii of Kisho Kurokawa Architect & Associates; Hervé Degand; Loes van Harrevelt and her colleagues at the Nederlands Fotoarchief; Jan Derwig and Jan Versnel, for their hospitality in Amsterdam; Rolf Sachsse; Catherine Sorel; Collette Lewington; Erica Stoller of Esto (I wish doing business were always so pleasurable); Jonathan Reynolds; my good friends Julian Osley and Valeria Carullo, not least for their invaluable translations of key texts; my colleague Jonathan Makepeace for his support and encouragement; and A.C. Cooper (Colour) Limited for copy photography. Finally, the book would never have happened without the unflagging help and organizational prowess of my wife, Cathy. She is 'simply the best'.

Photographic Credits

Illustrations are referred to by page number. The dates given in the captions are those when the photographs were taken.

Apart from those listed below, all illustrations come from the RIBA Library Photographs Collection (© ARS, NY and DACS, London, 2004: 90; © FLC/ADAGP, Paris and DACS, London 2004: 109 (b); courtesy Chicago Historical Society, photograph Hedrich Blessing HB-04414-D3: 148–49; © Popperfoto: 164–65; © Osamu Murai: 168 (r); © Richard Einzig/Arcaid: 178 (l); © the Estate of Morley Baer: 180 (b); gift of Harry Siedler: 203 (l); © Mark Power: 222 (b)).

Architectural Review: 9 (© FLC/ADAGP, Paris and DACS, London 2004), 123, 158 (© G.E. Kidder Smith/CORBIS), 163, 170 (© G.E. Kidder Smith/CORBIS), 171 (t) (© G.E. Kidder Smith/CORBIS), 173 (t) (courtesy The Swedish Museum of Architecture), 177 (t), 186 (David Moore, © estate), 187 (© Bernd & Hilla Becher), 189 (© Johan van der Keuken)
Courtesy The Art Institute of Chicago: 76 (t), 100, 107 (r)
Barragán Foundation, © DACS 2004: 218
Gabriele Basilico: 198, 222 (t)
Bauhaus-Archiv: 110 (© DACS 2004), 151 (r) (© Albert Renger-Patzsch Archiv/Ann u. Jürgen Wilde, Köln/VG Bild-Kunst, Bonn and DACS 2004)
Bibliothèque de la Ville de Chaux-de-Fonds, © FLC/ADAGP, Paris and DACS, London 2004: 91
Fonds Le Secq, Bibliothèque des Arts Décoratifs, Paris: 15
Hélène Binet: 219 (b)
Brandenburgisches Landesamt für Denkmalpflege und Archäologisches Museum Messbildarchiv: 82 (t)
By permission of the British Library: 43 (t+b) [BL 101(25), BL 955/13]
Richard Bryant/Arcaid: 196 (t), 204 (t+b)
Collection Centre Canadien d'Architecture/Canadian Centre for Architecture, Montreal: 62, 76 (b), 77, 130 (© Albert Renger-Patzsch Archiv/Ann u. Jürgen Wilde, Köln/VG Bild-Kunst, Bonn and DACS 2004), 131 (r), 205 (© Archivio eredi di Luigi Ghirri)
Centraal Museum, Utrecht © DACS 2004: 131 (l)
© Centre des Monuments Nationaux, Paris: 31, 32, 33 (t)
Martin Charles: 221
Courtesy Chicago Historical Society, photograph Hedrich Blessing HB-1000-s: 146 (r)
The *Country Life* Picture Library: 101, 107 (l)
Wim Cox: 141 (l)
Jan Derwig: 211
John Donat: 190
Reproduced by permission of English Heritage. NMR: 30 (b), 33 (b), 79 (r)
Esto: © Peter Aaron: 208–09; © Jeff Goldberg: 206; © Ezra Stoller: 6, 161 (© ARS, NY and DACS, London, 2004), 180 (t), 181, 197
GA Photographers: Yukio Futagawa/courtesy Omotesenke School of Tea: 169
Galerie Kicken, Berlin: 45
Gemeentearchief Amsterdam: 71, 105
Courtesy George Eastman House, Rochester NY: 23, 80–81, 115 (r), 116–17, 133
Research Library, The Getty Research Institute, Los Angeles (2000.R.41): 174 (t+b) (©FLC/ADAGP, Paris and DACS, London 2004)
Andreas Gursky, courtesy Monika Sprüth/Philomene Magers: 200
Roland Halbe: 192, 203 (r)
Harry Ransom Humanities Research Center, The University of Texas at Austin: 13, 24
Lucien Hervé: 159
Timothy Hursley: 196 (b), 210 (t)
© 2003 Yasuhiro Ishimoto/Photo Gallery International, Tokyo: 157, 168 (l)
Courtesy of the J. Paul Getty Museum, Los Angeles: 25 (t)
Mimmo Jodice: 223
Balthazar Korab: 184
Kent Larson: 229
London Metropolitan Archives: 35
© Norman McGrath: 215 (r)
Duccio Malagamba: 214
Mitchell Library, Glasgow: 79 (l)
Ryuji Miyamoto, courtesy Taro Nasu Gallery, Tokyo: 224–25
Museum of Finnish Architecture, Helsinki: 73 (b)
© 2002 Museum of Modern Art, New York: Abbott-Levy Collection. Partial gift of Shirley C. Burden: 111; Purchase: 113; Gift of Lincoln Kirstein: 146 (l); Gift of Willard Van Dyke: 153
Museum of the City of New York: 'Federal Arts Project: Changing New York' (#70), 152 (b)
National Museum of Photography, Film & Television, Bradford/Science & Society Picture Library: 27 (b)
Netherlands Architecture Institute, Rotterdam/© The Netherlands Photo Archives, Rotterdam: 135
Bernard Eilers/The Netherlands Photo Archives, Rotterdam: 104 (b)
Courtesy of the Oakland Museum of California: 25 (b)
Tomio Ohashi: 215 (l)
Richard Pare: 220 (b)
Reproduced with the permission of the Special Collections Library, The Pennsylvania State University Libraries: 147
© Photothèque des Musées de la Ville de Paris: Choiselat & Ratel, 22
Ram Rahman: 207 (b)
Cervin Robinson: 185
Steve Rosenthal: 202
Paolo Rosselli: 194, 212
© Royal Botanic Gardens, Kew: 28–29
Royal Collections, The Hague, The Netherlands: 44 (t)
Royal Photographic Society/National Museum of Photography, Film & Television, Bradford: 84, 114, 115 (l)
Thomas Ruff © DACS 2004: 228
Ruskin Foundation (Ruskin Library, University of Lancaster): 27 (t)
Historical Center Sara Lee/Douwe Egberts: 137 (l)
Julius Shulman: 154, 182, 183
Collection Société française de photographie, Paris: 26
Courtesy of the Society of Antiquaries, London (Ashpitel Photograph Albums): 38 (t), 46
Stadsarchief Antwerpen: 41 (b)
Courtesy Hiroshi Sugimoto and Sonnabend Gallery, New York: 226
© John Szarkowski, courtesy Pace/MacGill Gallery, New York: 188
C.G. Rosenberg/The Swedish Museum of Architecture: 134 (l)
Photo © Thomas Struth, courtesy Schirmer/Mosel Publishers, Munich; copy supplied © Tate, London 2003: 227
Philip Trager: 220 (t)
Judith Turner: 219 (t)
V&A Picture Library, London: 38 (b), 39, 47, 68, 112, 121
Ger van der Vlugt: 207 (t)
Jan Versnel: 160, 177 (b)
Yoshio Watanabe, courtesy Shashin Kosha Co.: 167
© Albert Renger-Patzsch Archiv/Ann u. Jürgen Wilde, Köln/VG Bild-Kunst, Bonn and DACS 2004: 120
Zentralinstitut für Kunstgeschichte Phototek, Munich: 141 (r)
Kim Zwarts: 213

Every effort has been made to identify and contact copyright holders. Any errors or omissions should be notified to the Royal Institute of British Architects, which will ensure that the necessary corrections are made to future editions.

Page numbers in *italic* refer to illustrations